AF793382

Emancipating International Law

Emancipating International Law

Confronting the Violence of Racialized Boundaries

Edited by
MOHSEN AL ATTAR
Reader in International Law, Head of the Department of International Studies, and Associate Dean for the School of Humanities and Social Sciences, Xi'an Jiaotong-Liverpool University, China

CLAIRE SMITH
PhD Student, University of Amsterdam, Netherlands (the)

OXFORD
UNIVERSITY PRESS

OXFORD
UNIVERSITY PRESS

Great Clarendon Street, Oxford, OX2 6DP,
United Kingdom

Oxford University Press is a department of the University of Oxford.
It furthers the University's objective of excellence in research, scholarship,
and education by publishing worldwide. Oxford is a registered trade mark of
Oxford University Press in the UK and in certain other countries.

© The Several Contributors 2026

The moral rights of the authors have been asserted

This is an open access publication, available online and distributed under the
terms of a Creative Commons Attribution-Non Commercial-No Derivatives 4.0
International licence (CC BY-NC-ND 4.0), a copy of which is available at
https://creativecommons.org/licenses/by-nc-nd/4.0/.
Subject to this license, all rights are reserved.

Enquiries concerning reproduction outside the scope of this licence should be sent
to the Rights Department, Oxford University Press, at the address above.

Public sector information reproduced under Open Government Licence v3.0
(https://www.nationalarchives.gov.uk/doc/open-government-licence/)

Published in the United States of America by Oxford University Press
198 Madison Avenue, New York, NY 10016, United States of America.

British Library Cataloguing in Publication Data
Data available

Library of Congress Control Number: 2025950277

ISBN 9780198935575

DOI: 10.1093/9780198935605.001.0001

Printed and bound by
CPI Group (UK) Ltd., Croydon, CR0 4YY

MIX
Paper | Supporting
responsible forestry
FSC® C013604

The manufacturer's authorized representative in the EU for product safety is
Oxford University Press España S.A. of Parque Empresarial San Fernando de Henares,
Avenida de Castilla, 2 – 28830 Madrid (www.oup.es/en or product.safety@oup.com).
OUP España S.A. also acts as importer into Spain of products made by the manufacturer.

Acknowledgements

We are grateful to Xi'an Jiaotong-Liverpool University and the UCLA Promise Institute for their support of this project, which has made open access possible. Our sincere thanks to Ata Hindi, Rohini Sen, and Binxin Zhang for their contributions as co-editors earlier in this process. Finally, we extend our gratitude to the team at Oxford University Press for their guidance and support.

We dedicate this collection to the colleagues, comrades, and activists whose struggles against racism inspire and sustain us. Their unwavering pursuit of justice, both within and beyond the academy, shapes the antiracist praxis that underpins this work. And to S, N, J, and B—as always—everything is for you.

Contents

PART V. TAKING THE STRUGGLE(S) FORWARD

List of Figures

Acronyms and Abbreviations

AJIL	American Journal of International Law
ANC	African National Congress
AOSIS	Alliance of Small Island States
ASIL	American Society of International Law
BASIL	Blacks of the American Society of International Law
BJP	Bharatiya Janata Party
CBDR-RC	Common But Differentiated Responsibilities and Respective Capabilities
CEDAW	Convention on the Elimination of All Forms of Discrimination against Women
CERD	Committee on the Elimination of All Forms of Racial Discrimination
CESCR	UN Committee on Economic, Social and Cultural Rights
CLAS	Community Legal Assistance Society
CLASS	Critical Law and Security Studies
CLEAR	Creating Law Enforcement Accountability and Responsibility
COP	Conference of Parties
COVAX	COVID-19 Vaccines Global Access
CPP	Colombian Peace Process
CRC	Convention on the Rights of the Child
CRPD	Convention on the Rights of Persons with Disabilities
CRT	Critical Race Theory
DDPA	Durban Declaration and Programme of Action
DPAD	Decade for People of African Descent
DPO	Disabled Persons Organizations
DRT	Dahlit Radical Tradition
ECHR	European Convention of Human Rights
ECOSOC	Economic and Social Council
ECtHR	European Court of Human Rights
ESCR	Economic, Social and Cultural Rights
EU	European Union
FET	fair and equitable treatment
FTA	fair trade agreement
GC	General Comment
GR	General Recommendation
GREN	Global Racial Equality Norm
GWoT	Global War on Terror
HRC	Human Rights Committee
IACtHR	Inter-American Court of Human Rights
IBRC	International Business Research Co-operative
IBRD	International Bank of Reconstruction and Development
ICC	International Criminal Court

ICCPR	International Covenant on Civil and Political Rights
ICERD	International Convention for the Elimination of Racial Discrimination
ICESCR	International Covenant on Economic, Social, and Cultural Rights
ICJ	International Court of Justice
ICSID	International Centre for Settlement of Investment Disputes
ICTR	International Criminal Tribunal of Rwanda
IDC	International Disability Caucus
IDP	Internally Displaced Person
IEL	International Economic Law
IFHP	Interim Federal Health Program
IFI	International Financial Institutions
IHL	international humanitarian law
IHRL	international human rights law
IL	international law
ILI	International Law as Ideology (ILI)
IMF	International Monetary Fund
IPCC	Intergovernmental Panel on Climate Change
IR	international relations
Kampala Convention	African Union Convention for the Protection and Assistance of Internally Displaced Persons in Africa
LAC	Latin American and Caribbean
LDP	Liberal Democratic Party
MoU	Memorandum of Understanding
NAACP	National Association for the Advancement of Coloured People
NATO	North Atlantic Treaty Organization
NGO	non-governmental organization
NIEO	New International Economic Order
OHCHR	Office of the High Commissioner of Human Rights
OIC	Organization of Islamic Cooperation
PBF	Bolsa Familia
PCA	Permanent Court of International Arbitration
PMC	Permanent Mandates Commission
PWD	persons with disabilities
R2P	Responsibility to Protect
RSS	Rashtriya Swayamasewak Sangh
SAP	structural adjustment programmes
SGBV	sexual and gender based violence
SVS	savage-victim-saviour
TFEU	Treaty on the Functioning of the European Union
TITP	Technical Internship Trainee Programme
TNC	transnational companies
TRIPS	Trade-Related Aspects of Intellectual Property Rights
TWAIL	Third World Approaches to International Law
UAE	United Arab Emirates
UDHR	Universal Declaration of Human Rights

UK	United Kingdom
UN	United Nations
UNDRIP	United Nations Declaration on the Rights of Indigenous Peoples
UNESCO	United Nations Education, Scientific and Cultural Organization
UNFCCC	United Nations Framework Convention on Climate Change
UNGA	United Nations General Assembly
UNGPID	United Nations Guiding Principles on Internal Displacement
UNHCR	UN High Commissioner for Refugees
UNRWA	United Nations Relief and Works Agency for Palestine Refugees in the Near East
UNSC	United Nations Security Council
UNSCOP	United Nations Special Committee on Palestine
UPR	Universal Periodic Review
US	United States
VLRL	Victims' and Land Restitution Law
WBG	World Bank Group
WCAR	World Conference against Racism, Racial Discrimination, Xenophobia, and Related Intolerance
WEOG	Western Europe and Other States Group
WIM	Warsaw International Mechanism for Loss and Damage associated with Climate Change Impacts
WJC	World Jewish Congress
XUAR	Xinjiang Uyghur Autonomous Region

List of Contributors

E Tendayi Achiume is Professor of Law at Stanford University and an international legal scholar focusing on international human rights law, international refugee law, and international migration law. Her research explores the global governance of racism and xenophobia, and the legal and ethical implications of colonialism and other forms of empire for the governance of international migration.

Folúkẹ́ Ifejola Adébísí is a Professor at the Law School, University of Bristol. Dr Adébísí's scholarship focuses on decolonial thought in legal education and its intersection with a history of changing ideas of the 'human'.

Henrique Weil Afonso is a Lecturer at Universidade de Pernambuco and a Lecturer of Legal Sociology at Universidade Estadual da Paraíba. His research explores the interplay between legal history and decolonial approaches to law and society in Latin America.

Faisal al-Asaad is a teaching fellow at the School of Social and Cultural Studies, Victoria University of Wellington.

Mohsen al Attar is a Reader in International Law and Associate Dean for Learning and Teaching at the School of Humanities and Social Sciences at Xi'an Jiaotong-Liverpool University. His research explores the power dynamics inherent in international law and the potential for other universals to emerge.

Fuimaono Dylan Asafo is a Senior Lecturer of Law at the University of Auckland. His primary areas of research include race and the law, climate justice in the Pacific, constitutional and human rights law in the Pacific, and criminal justice and abolition.

Asli Ü Bâli is the Howard M Holtzmann Professor of Law at Yale Law School. Bâli's teaching and research interests include public international law—particularly human rights law and the law of the international security order—and comparative constitutional law, with a focus on the Middle East.

Jinan Bastaki is Associate Professor of Legal Studies at NYU Abu Dhabi. Dr Bastaki researches forced displacement, human rights, refugee law, and citizenship.

Sarah Riley Case is an Assistant Professor at the Faculty of Law, McGill University. Dr Riley Case's research and teaching focus on slavery and the law, Critical Race Theory, Black life, Third World Approaches to International Law, colonialisms, arts, and governing the natural world.

Ruby Dhand is a Full Professor at the Faculty of Law at Thompson Rivers University in Kamloops, British Columbia, Canada, where she researches mental health law and disability law.

Radha D'Souza is a Professor of Law, Development, and Conflict Studies at Westminster Law School as well as a writer, critic, and commentator on Third World issues and a social justice activist.

Christopher Gevers is an Associate Professor and the Director of the Centre for Applied Legal Studies at the Faculty of Commerce, Law, and Management at the University of the Witwatersrand.

Suraj Girijashanker is a residential fellow at the Institute for Global Law and Policy at Harvard Law School.

Yang Han is a DPhil candidate in international relations and Swire scholar at St Antony's College, Oxford University. Her doctoral research focuses on China's outlook on international hierarchies through its discourse on Africa.

Jason Haynes is an Associate Professor of Law at Birmingham Law School.

Paulina Jimenez Fregoso is an Advocacy Advisor on Latin America and the Caribbean, and she currently works on sexual and reproductive health and rights issues.

Dimitrios A Kourtis is a postdoctoral researcher and teaching fellow at the Faculty of Law of the Aristotle University of Thessaloniki.

Darryl Li is an Associate Professor of Anthropology and Associate Member of the Law School, University of Chicago.

Harrison Otieno Mbori is a postdoctoral fellow at the Luxembourg Center for European Law (LECL), University of Luxembourg and an adjunct lecturer at Kabarak Law School, Kenya.

Frédéric Mégret is a Professor of Law and the holder of the Hans & Tamar Oppenheimer Chair in Public International Law at McGill University.

S Priya Morley is the Director of the Racial Justice Initiative, Bernstein Institute for Human Rights, and a Project Advisor at the Global Justice Clinic, New York University School of Law.

Roxanne Mykitiuk is Professor of Law and Academic Director of the Disability Law Intensive Program at Osgoode Hall Law School, York University, Canada.

Nciko wa Nciko is an Amnesty International Climate Justice Advisor in East and Southern Africa as well as its lead advisor on human rights in Madagascar. He holds an LLM in Public International Law from the Geneva Graduate Institute.

Shahab Saqib is an Assistant Professor of Law at the University of Birmingham and a teaching fellow at the SOAS University of London. His research focuses on critical examination of antidiscrimination and equality laws with a focus on different fields such as international human rights law and Islamic law.

Karla Schröter is a doctoral researcher at Åbo Akademi University within the Institute for Human Rights and the Minority Research profile.

Tess Sheldon is an Associate Professor at the University of Windsor Faculty of Law. Dr Sheldon writes, presents, and teaches extensively on a variety of mental health, access to justice, disability, and human rights topics.

Claire Smith is an international lawyer and a PhD candidate at the University of Amsterdam.

Saul Takahashi is a Visiting Professor of Legal Studies at NYU Abu Dhabi. From March 2009 to May 2014, Saul served as Deputy Head of Office at the Office of the UN High Commissioner for Human Rights in Palestine.

Kamya Vishwanath is an international lawyer and early-career researcher based in New Delhi, India. Her interest lies in exploring the intersections between law and literature, examining their tensions in theory and in practice, and in challenging these bifurcations.

Raghavi Viswanath is a postdoctoral researcher and teaching fellow at the SOAS University of London. She is also a law and humanities fellow at the Institute of Advanced Legal Studies. She writes and teaches on issues of human rights law, international criminal justice, sensory approaches to law, epistemic injustice, and decolonization.

Adrien Katherine Wing is Associate Dean for International and Comparative Law Programs at the University of Iowa College of Law, where she has taught since 1987. She is also the Bessie Dutton Murray Distinguished Professor of Law. She received her AB degree from Princeton, MA degree from UCLA, and JD degree from Stanford.

Prologue

Adrien K Wing

It is my honour to contribute the prologue to this impressive collection, *Emancipating International Law: Confronting the Violence of Racialized Boundaries*. With a diverse array of authors from around the globe, the editors, Mohsen al Attar and Claire Smith, have curated a volume that seeks to interrogate 'intersecting themes of race, epistemology, and international law, offering pathways to critically examine the discipline's foundational and enduring complicities with the racialised violence of this world'.[1] The questions considered went beyond the basic—'is international law racist?'—to more nuanced and urgent reflections about:

> [W]hat forms of racism does international law facilitate, engender, and promote? How is international law complicit with white supremacy? What are the connections between international law's myriad forms of racialisation and racism? And, is international law's race-thinking endemic, systemic, or terminal to its framework?[2]

The volume addresses these questions across a range of topics including: situating international law's racism problem; the tools, techniques, and technologies of legalized racial inequality; a right to be free from racism; antiracism in the pluriverse; and, crucially, taking the struggle(s) forward. In this prologue, I focus on the final theme: how we advance the struggle within and beyond this volume.

In 1903, the eminent Black scholar WEB DuBois famously wrote that the problem of the twentieth century would be the problem of the colour line.[3] More than 120 years later, his words proved prescient, perhaps even on a larger scale than what DuBois might have imagined. I write this reflection at the beginning of the second Trump administration in the United States in 2025, at a time when we are witnessing renewed and intensified attacks on both the domestic and international elements of the post-Second World War status quo ideals of Western liberal democracy, a model that at least nominally upheld certain kinds of equality.

While the authors offer comprehensive and insightful analyses of the racialized structures embedded in international law, I am left grappling with a question that may be taken up by future scholars and practitioners. My mentor, the late NYU law professor Derrick Bell, founder of Critical Race Theory, thought that racism might well

[1] Mohsen al Attar and Claire Smith, 'Beyond Silence: Confronting Racial Hierarchies in International Law', in Mohsen al Attar and Claire Smith (eds), *Emancipating International Law: Confronting the Violence of Racialized Boundaries* (Oxford University Press, forthcoming) this volume, 5.

[2] ibid 5.

[3] WEB DuBois, *The Souls of Black Folk* (Yale University Press 2015).

be permanent and that racial progress was cyclical—rather than linear—in nature. In his book, *Faces at the Bottom of the Well: the Permanence of Racism*, Bell wrote, '[e]ven those herculean efforts we hail as successful will produce no more than temporary "peaks of progress", short-lived victories that slide into irrelevance as racial patterns adapt in ways that maintain white dominance'.[4] If Bell was correct and racism is permanent, continuously reconfiguring itself, then we must ask: are we drawing the right analytical tools from international law, or even domestic law, if we are to confront it effectively?

To borrow some medical analogies: if racism were like a bee sting, we might need a simple remedy. A salve would relieve the immediate discomfort and maybe even make us feel better. In this vein, press statements or perhaps quaint international declarations, so common today, can soothe the pain and perhaps make the problem go away. But if racism is more akin to a systemic disease—serious but potentially curable—the response demands a different kind of intervention. Here, international treaties, cases, and treatises, function as much more potent medicine. They offer the promise of meaningful change, even the eradication of the violence of global racism, after which the tools would become moot. Yet, as the editors caution, there may be a 'learned inability to prevent recurrences',[5] requiring special and careful attention to the shape-shifting of racialized injustices.

If, however, racism is permanent, comparable to chronic conditions like alcoholism, then the approach must be even more unique. We would need to administer ongoing treatment, closely monitoring the patient—in this instance, the international community—likely, *forever*. Whether racism is incurable or not, the response must be as adaptable as the affliction it seeks to treat. This might mean taking an intersectional approach,[6] ensuring we simultaneously bombard the disease in all its manifestations, including racism, sexism, colourism, ableism, homophobia, Islamophobia, and others.

What tools do we need in these ongoing and dynamic struggles against racism? Academic anthologies can be both sharp and blunt tools in these existential fights for racial justice. Edited collections require years to write, edit, and publish. By the time they reach readers, the material may feel out of step with the developments that could not be foreseen at the time of drafting. These books are usually expensive, limiting their accessibility to a tiny pool of libraries and fellow travellers. While the rise of open access publishing is theoretically wonderful and offers a partial remedy—one the editors have wisely pursued—many authors and their institutions cannot afford it. Too often, authors are left with only a handful of free copies, keeping the work confined to the very narrow, privileged spaces the authors are struggling against.

I am delighted that this volume has intersected with quicker methods of communication as well. For example, al Attar has done wonderful work on the *Opinio Juris* blog for some years now. This book project was mooted on the site, and a post elicited

[4] Derrick Bell, *Faces at the Bottom of the Well: The Permanence of Racism* (Basic Books 1992) 12.

[5] al Attar and Smith (n 1) 5.

[6] Paulina Jimenez Fregaso, 'De-essentializing Race: Intersectionality as a Feminist Approach in International Human Rights Law' in al Attar and Smith (n 1); Adrien K Wing (ed), *Critical Race Feminism: A Reader* (2nd edn, NYU Press 2003).

participation, ultimately including some of the contributors. I was elated to learn the editors carried out a variety of public-facing activities in the development of the volume and have planned several more leading up to and after the actual publication. There can be follow-up podcasts, online symposia, and other mechanisms used to get the word out to various audiences. Of course, these types of methods must be considered carefully, especially for junior scholars, since such content may not be respected in hiring, promotion, or tenure decisions.

Pushing out information through online journals, which have quicker turnaround times, is very useful as well. As a member of the Board of Editors of the American Journal of International Law (AJIL), I have seen the value of this model as a managing editor of AJIL Unbound symposia.[7] These are topic-specific contributions, made freely available and published more promptly than standard journal articles. *Unbound* was created in part to get around the traditional biases in organization and content that had characterized AJIL for a century. Such creation was possible as a result of major reforms resulting in the election of a very diverse editorial board, representing a wide variety of races, ethnicities, nationalities, genders, as well as institutions studied at and worked in. Many of us have embraced critical perspectives that influence us as we consider submissions.

Hybrid or solely online conferences on cutting edge topics such as race or AI could also be convened within a relatively short time, as was done with the Symposium on Race, Racism, and International Law convened by E Tendayi Achiume and James Thuo Gathii.[8] Authors can present succinct and accessible material. Such conferences may also be turned into class materials that could be distributed as a dynamic supplement to traditional textbooks. These types of engagement are faster and more responsive, and could complement the longer gestation periods needed for books like this one.

To make my own contribution to this collection, I propose something more radical: the widespread and sustained engagement of scholars in antiracist praxis, a commitment that cannot be left to a token few.[9] Coming down from the ivory tower should be obligatory for as many as possible. This requires genuinely respecting those who are not part of the legal academy or legal profession, as much as we value scholarly or professional expertise. It means that one should not think that there is an essentialized 'other' for whom we are qualified to speak. It also means appreciating the lived knowledge of people who will never earn a doctorate, but whose understanding of systemic oppression and resistance is essential to the struggle. It is wonderful that several contributors do engage with a variety of social movements in their chapters and I celebrate the contributions of Paulina Jimenez Fregoso, Nciko wa Nciko, Kamya Vishwanath, and Dylan Asafo.[10]

[7] Adrien K Wing and Catherine Powell, 'Introduction to the Symposium, Feminist Approaches to International Law Thirty Years On: Still Alienating Oscar' (2022) 116 AJIL Unbound 259; Adrien K Wing and S James Anaya, 'Introduction to the Symposium on Rabiat Akande, "An Imperial History of Race-Religion in International Law"' (2024) 118 AJIL Unbound 103.

[8] E Tendayi Achiume and James Theo Gathii, 'Introduction to the symposium on Race, Racism, and International Law' (2023) 117 AJIL Unbound 26.

[9] Asli Bâli, E Tendayi Achiume, and Priya Morley, 'Conceptualizing Race and Resisting Racism in International Law' in al Attar and Smith (n 1).

[10] In this volume see: Tess Sheldon, Ruby Dhand, and Roxanne Mykitiuk, 'Racialised Ableism and the Need for Intersectional Discourse and Action'; Arnold Nciko wa Nciko, 'Racial Capitalism and Climate Justice: A Critique of the UN Guiding Principles on Internal Displacement'; Suraj Girijashanker, 'Indian

Another tool in the fight against international racism, therefore, lies in building collaborative relationships and actions with non-academic groups such as community and non-governmental organizations. Scholars must be willing to present their works in ways that are accessible, abandoning discipline-specific jargon in exchange for modes of communication that resonate with a variety of audiences. I recall participating in a taped talk on global intersectionality and privilege for a community group in Canada. The interviewer, an experienced podcaster, worked with me to vet the questions so that I could answer in an accessible way, promoting a thoughtful exchange free of academic speak. The audience—professionals from a range of fields—was very engaged, and I left the discussion wishing that I could have brought together this audience with the scholars I was also addressing during my trip. There is immense potential for such collaborations. Joint plans of action on particular topics could emerge, whether at the international, national, and/or local policy levels, nurturing collective approaches to confront systemic racism that extend beyond a university's halls.

Additionally, we need more scholar-activists, as argued by Bâli, Achiume, and Morley in this collection.[11] They could follow in the legacy of DuBois, who modelled the role of the engaged intellectual, operating on both domestic and international levels. He was not only the first sociologist studying Black peoples in Philadelphia, but was also a founder of the National Association for the Advancement of Coloured People (NAACP), author of the *Souls of Black Folks*, and signatory to the petition to the then-new United Nations on *We Charge Genocide.*[12] His career illustrates the fusion of scholarship and activism that struggle demands.

Black male and female law professors have a long history of engaging in antiracist praxis on the international level as scholar-activists. Professor Henry Richardson, emeritus at Temple Law School, wrote *The Origin of African-American Interests in International Law*,[13] and led the battle to get the ASIL to divest its portfolio from companies doing business in South Africa during the apartheid era. He co-founded the ASIL South Africa interest group as well as the Blacks of ASIL Task Force (BASIL), creating enduring spaces for Black international lawyers within the discipline. Richardson also chaired an important ASIL task force that researched the history of racism and exclusion within ASIL over the decades. Professor Gay McDougall, Distinguished Scholar-in-Residence at the Leitner Center on International Law and Justice at Fordham Law School, was the first American elected as an independent expert for the International Convention on the Elimination of All Forms of Racial

Approaches to Racism and Related Forms of Subordination under International Law: A Question of Interest Convergence'; Kamya Vishwanath, 'Bodies of Knowledge: Re-framing Emancipation in International Law through Dalit Praxis; Paulina Jimenez Fregaso, 'De-essentializing Race: Intersectionality as a Feminist Approach in International Human Rights Law'; Dylan Asafo, 'The Slow Benevolent Violence of International Law: An Oceanian Perspective'.

[11] Bâli, Achiume, and Morley (n 9).

[12] Civil Rights Congress, *We Charge Genocide: The Historic Petition to the United Nations for Relief from a Crime of the United States Government Against the Negro People* (Civil Rights Congress 1951).

[13] Henry Richardson III, *The Origin of African-American Interests in International Law* (Carolina Academic Press 2008).

Discrimination Committee (CERD), where she served for many years, eventually winning the MacArthur Genius Fellowship as well.

Several of the scholars featured in this volume have also engaged in antiracist praxis throughout their careers. In my own work, I have always championed this approach.[14] My antiracist praxis has involved advising the founding mothers and fathers of three constitutions: post-apartheid South Africa, post-genocide Rwanda, and Oslo Accord-era Palestinian Basic Law.[15] My experiences, like those of others, confirm to me that international legal scholars must actively participate in building legal frameworks grounded in justice and the lived realities of racialized peoples, in addition to critiquing the structure of oppression they survive under.

In deciding whether global racism is a serious but curable condition, a permanent affliction, or perhaps a lethal one, we must consider the famous quote from the late African American lesbian feminist Audre Lorde. Writing about gender, but with insight that is applicable to race as well, Lorde warned: 'For the master's tools will never dismantle the master's house. They may allow us temporarily to beat him at his own game, but they will never enable us to bring about genuine change.'[16] Some of the authors in this volume, but not most, were educated in the master's house, if we define that house as the house of imperialism and neocolonialism in the Global North. Many authors were not educated in the master's house and retain strong political and intellectual ties in the Global South, a reality of difference that we must strive for.[17] Yet, no matter where educated or employed, critical scholars may be evaluated within the framework of norms rooted in Western, white, Christian, male heteropatriarchy upon which the international law house has been based.

For those of us concerned with global racism, what is the solution? Do we do the safest thing by seeking to tinker with the existing structure, renovating it by creating new laws or revising old ones, or calling for better enforcement of the few protections already in place? Can elements of the system be repurposed in ecologically and ethically progressive ways? Alternatively, do we seek to dismantle the house, to destroy some or all of it, whether figuratively, discursively, or literally? These are the difficult questions we face when imagining and enacting antiracist praxis within and beyond international law.

The plain reading of Lorde's quote might seem pessimistic. Yet, a more generative reading is possible, one that invites us to design and wield our own tools in the fight against the master. The next line in Lorde's famous quote is rarely mentioned. 'And this fact is only threatening to those women who still define the master's house as their only source of support.'[18] Thus, the perceived threat only materializes when our worldview

[14] Adrien K Wing, 'One L Redux' (2010) 78 University of Missouri-Kansas City Law Review 1119.

[15] Adrien K Wing and Mark Johnson, 'The Promise of a Post Genocide Constitution: Healing Rwandan Spirit Injuries' (2002) 7 Michigan Journal of Race & Law 247; Adrien K Wing, 'The New South African Constitution: An Example for Palestinian Consideration' (1992–1994) 7 Palestine Yearbook of International Law 105.

[16] Audre Lorde, 'The Master's Tools Will Never Dismantle the Master's House' in Audre Lorde, *Sister Outsider: Essays and Speeches* (Crossing Press 1984).

[17] For further discussion on the master's house, see Adrien K Wing, 'Poverty, Lawyering and Critical Race Feminism in the Trumpian Era' in Maria Grahn Farley (ed), *Activism: Addressing the Work of Adam Gearey* (Uppsala Press 2021).

[18] Lorde (n 16).

is so narrow that we can only see the master's house and the master's tools as our salvation. As demonstrated by this volume, the challenge—and the opportunity—is to build our own houses, using our own tools, drawing on our own epistemologies, and grounded in our lived experiences and struggles.[19]

I look forward to reading the future work of the editors and contributors to this collection as we face global challenges, whether they were created in the past, are being designed in the present, or confront us in the future. Perhaps one or more of these brilliant thinkers will be the DuBois, Richardson, or Achiume of their generation, scholars who not only analyse and critique, but lead and inspire the transformation of international law and beyond.

[19] One example would be the Tokyo Women's Tribunal organized by the Korean Council for the Women Drafted for Sexual Slavery by Japan. The Women's International War Crimes Tribunal for the Trial of Japan's Military Sexual Slavery, *The Prosecutors and the Peoples of the Asia-Pacific Region v Hirohito Emperor Showa et al* (Judgement on the Common Indictment and the Application for Restitution and Reparation) 4 December 2001.

Beyond Silence

Confronting Racial Hierarchies in International Law

Mohsen al Attar and Claire Smith

1. Introduction

Silence soothes and grates in equal measure. This is especially true in instances where we observe social injustices that we feel powerless before. Silence shields us from confrontation, protecting us against the social tension precipitated by our actions and the inevitable reactions of others. Yet, silence also traps us in complicity. It is difficult to unsee social injustice, troubling our thoughts and gnawing at our conscience. In those instances, silence morphs into an ever-present awareness of our inadequacies, or even our cowardice.

This paradox illuminates how the discipline of international law has remained silent on race, its racist origins, and the persistence of racialized hierarchies for so long.[1] Despite the mounting rage within its midst, the discipline has avoided a confrontation with its complicity.[2] For orthodox publicists the silence was expedient—a way to reap the distributive privileges of whiteness in the academy. Whether overt or tacit, accord cemented the participation of these scholars at the apex of an institutionalized racial hierarchy. Likewise, critical or anti-racist academics also found themselves in a conundrum, albeit of a different type.[3] While their eyes were wide open to the racialized violence of international law and its associated institutions, they were presented with few options: to participate in the silencing of their oppression or to speak out and risk alienation by the same white supremacist forces they opposed. As WEB Du Bois observed, the double-consciousness of negatively racialized peoples is always a curse first and a blessing only a distant second.[4]

Even today, the contours of the relationship between international law and race—just as it is between international legal scholarship and race—remain paradoxical. On one hand, the struggle against racism, both within and beyond law, has gained momentum, generating a surge of critical scholarship including articles, special issues,

[1] James Gathii, 'Studying Race in International Law Scholarship Using a Social Science Approach' (2021) 22(1) Chicago Journal of International Law 71.

[2] Henry Richardson III, 'Reflections on Race and the American Society of International Law' (2023) 117 AJIL Unbound 31.

[3] E Tendayi Achiume and Devon W Carbado, 'Critical Race Theory Meets Third World Approaches to International Law' (2021) 67 UCLA Law Review 1463.

[4] WEB Du Bois, *The Souls of Black Folk* (Yale University Press 2015); Derek Bell, *Faces at the Bottom of the Well: The Permanence of Racism* (Hachette 1992).

Mohsen al Attar and Claire Smith, *Beyond Silence* In: *Emancipating International Law*. Edited by:
Mohsen al Attar and Claire Smith, Oxford University Press. © Mohsen al Attar, and Claire Smith 2026.
DOI: 10.1093/9780198935605.003.0001

conferences, edited collections, and symposia dedicated to identifying racist practices and exploring anti-racist praxis. Some journals and scholarly societies have sought to engage with anti-racist voices, inviting them to join editorial boards or speak at annual conferences.[5] Most significantly, anti-racist scholars have exposed the silence of international law, forcing their once complacent colleagues to take notice.[6]

Yet, this modicum of progress has been met with a fervent backlash. Old wine in new bottles has resurfaced, with familiar efforts marshalled to neuter anti-racist discourse.[7] Instead of meaningful anti-racist action, those oppositional forces offer watered down alternatives, if they offer anything at all: anti-discrimination in place of anti-racism while affirmative action is substituted with diversity initiatives or, worse, the promise of inclusivity, a tactic that equates oppressors and oppressed as equals in need of a shared platform and mutual understanding. As Mohsen al Attar explains in this collection, Charles Mills captured this dynamic when warning us about white ignorance's pugilistic character: it does not go quietly, he tells us—it fights back and, ultimately, refuses to know.[8] For this text, the dynamic also raised the conundrum of the delineation between a critique of international law *and* race and a critique of international legal scholarship *about* race. This tension, one we attempted to mediate throughout the chapters, albeit with a heavy focus on developments in international legal spaces which we tacitly, sometimes overtly, link to legal scholarship. Readers can thus anticipate engagement both with the theme and the medium(s), as observed by Adrien K Wing in her prologue.

Who is allowed to *know* has always been a central question in lawmaking and in legal scholarship. In the answers proffered, we locate the identity of those who wield sufficient authority to produce 'valid' legal knowledge and, by extension, to make legitimate law.[9] Like its domestic counterparts, international law could never have existed without a distinct epistemology. Yet, international lawyers always bristled at this limitation, preferring to imagine their field as an episteme-free zone. The idea of law unmoored from cultural, historical, or epistemic roots was always a fiction, designed to legitimize fantastical claims to universality.[10] In truth, international law was shaped by a panoply of exclusionary and belligerent epistemic practices that denied the validity of non-Western ways of knowing, being, and legislating.[11] Silence rears its head once more, this time as the violence of silenc-*ing*, defining boundaries of what counts

[5] Mohsen al Attar, 'Tackling White Ignorance in International Law—"How Much Time Do You Have? It's Not Enough"' (*Opinio Juris*, 20 September 2022) <https://opiniojuris.org/2022/09/30/tackling-white-ignorance-in-international-law-how-much-time-do-you-have-its-not-enough/> accessed 30 November 2024.

[6] Zoltán I Búzás, 'Racism and Antiracism in the Liberal International Order' (2021) 75(2) International Organization 440.

[7] Mohsen al Attar and Claire Smith, 'Shades of Ignorance: A Critique of the Epistemic Whiteness of International Law' in Devon W Carbado and others (eds), *Race, Racism and International Law* (Stanford University Press 2025).

[8] Charles Mills, *Black Rights/White Wrongs* (Oxford University Press 2017).

[9] George A Martínez, 'Law, Race, and the Epistemology of Ignorance' (2020) 17(2) Hastings Race and Poverty Law Journal 507.

[10] Mohsen al Attar, 'Reframing the "Universality" of International Law in a Globalizing World' (2013) 59(1) McGill Law Journal 95.

[11] José Medina, *The Epistemology of Resistance: Gender and Racial Oppression, Epistemic Injustice and the Social Imagination* (Oxford University Press 2013).

as international legal knowledge, while denying others the possibility of contributing to its articulation.

With awareness of international law's racialized violence comes resistance, but resistance breeds fatigue and, eventually, cynicism. Indeed, the inadequacy of a meaningful response to its entrenched hierarchies has led some scholars to somberly declare that 'international law is dead'.[12] Despair is both a natural and understandable response when faced with the daunting realization that, like white ignorance, international legal hierarchies will also fight back. The obituary, however, is overstated; any reading of international law through the rubric of race reveals that both the frame and its prejudicial commitments remain ever present and, frankly, quite sturdy.[13] As Claire Smith argues in her chapter, the racialized dynamics these scholars lament *is* international law. Indeed, racial violence manifests not only in settler-colonial projects, but also in the seemingly benign spaces of the economic, diplomatic, and administrative, all of which are supported by and supportive of transnational white supremacist structures.[14] These matrices of race-thinking and making are not aberrations but the very foundation of the machinery of international law itself, inspiring the collaboration that led to this collection.

When drafting this introduction, we grappled with how to characterize the distinctly racial moment we found ourselves in without eliding the historical context that made this moment possible. We considered, foremost, how international law engaged with the racialized events that marked its history. As the contributors showcase throughout this text, such moments span a vast spectrum, eliciting critiques, justifications, and competing normativities in equal measure. Some, like the murder of George Floyd and the call for a fact-finding mission by the Human Rights Council, briefly captured global attention, only to see its effectiveness diluted by transnational white allyship.[15] Others, like the global pandemic, whose disproportionate effects on racialized populations underscored the entrenched proprietary dimensions of whiteness, manifested in—as Folúkẹ́ Adébísí examines—vaccine apartheid. The twentieth anniversary of the Durban Declaration and its programme of (in)action exposed the hollowing out of its promises, while the racial machinations of the Ukraine invasion and the immediate outpouring of assistance and of visa and refugee approvals by European states, highlighted the glaring neglect of non-white refugees as seen with Afghans, Syrians, and Palestinians (not to mention Europe's active support of what the ICJ has opined amounts to a genocide in Palestine). Indeed, international law has always demonstrated a fleeting interest in race, except when facilitating the pursuits of whiteness, and its own intra-hierarchy. Even the decolonization struggle, as meaningful as the first wave proved for Third World states and the second wave for legal scholars, is an

[12] Ata Hindi, 'International Law is Dead' (*TWAILR*, 20 November 2023) <https://twailr.c'om/international-law-is-dead/> accessed 20 November 2024.

[13] Matiangai Sirleaf, 'Rendering Whiteness Visible' (2023) 117(3) American Journal of International Law 484.

[14] Sherene Razack, *Nothing Has to Make Sense: Upholding White Supremacy through Anti-Muslim Racism* (University of Minnesota Press 2022).

[15] E Tendayi Achiume,'Transnational Racial (In)Justice in Liberal Democratic Empire' (2021) 144(7) Harvard Law Review Forum 378; E Tendayi Achiume and Gay McDougall, 'Anti-Racism at the United Nations' (2023) 117 AJIL Unbound 82.

inadequate substitute for anti-racist theorizing and action. Indeed, decolonization is not synonymous with anti-racism and, while the struggles may overlap, they are also denoted by distinct grammars and strategies. The risk when seeing these movements as interchangeable is that we flatten each struggle and, in fact, harm anti-racism most of all since decolonization has consistently been pursued through the lens of liberal racial equality—what Mills terms white liberalism—and is thus inconsistent with the struggle as well as the associated calls for epistemic justice.

In our haste to find an anchor for this introduction—to capture the flux of again visible transnational and international white supremacy—we were reminded that there is no singular racial moment. International law operates not in fleeting instances but within a persistent racial reality—a reality that may ebb and flow in visibility but which remains an orienting axis around which international law's racial predilections and predations revolve. Gradually, we came to realize that the initial question we pitched to the contributors and publisher—is international law racist?—was too narrow, failing to capture the nuanced and evolving machinations of these dynamics. Instead, we must pose compound and concentric questions: what forms of racism does international law facilitate, engender, and promote? How is international law complicit with white supremacy? What are the connections between international law's myriad forms of racialization and racism? Where do Indigenous peoples—oft-forgotten groups within international law who continue to mobilize for liberation—fit in these practices? And is international law's race-thinking endemic, systemic, or terminal to its framework? Unlike the sledgehammer question we began with, these layered ones draw attention not only to the overtly visible moments of racial injustice but also those crises that are sidelined or made invisible. Indeed, alongside those events that garnered global sympathy are many more that have not registered in the international imaginary: the handling of the Occupied Palestinian Territories prior to 7 October 2023 (some would also say since); the unregistered crises in Yemen, Tigray, Haiti, the Congo, and Sudan; the ongoing struggles faced by Indigenous peoples to exist at all; and as Nciko wa Nciko and Dylan Asafo each demonstrate, the climate crisis's devastating and disproportionate impacts on racialized and materially disadvantaged peoples. Across these instances, international law has consistently operated to uphold a racially capitalist, extractive order, its primary function being one of preservation instead of progress.

Still, despite the consistency of its depredations, critical faith in the regime persists. We were particularly perplexed by the way that, in times of crisis, international law is perceived as a potential panacea for racialized ills.[16] Even those penning obituaries petition for its application to ease suffering, our impotence before international law's past and present brutalities provoking another degree of desperation (we are guilty of this as well). Notice, for example, the celebratory climate surrounding the International Court of Justice's preliminary measures regarding plausible genocide and the International Criminal Court's arrest warrants for the Israeli Prime Minister and (former) Minister of Defence, even as Israel continues to pummel the Palestinians

[16] OHCHR, 'Gaza: ICJ ruling offers hope for protection of civilians enduring apocalyptic conditions, say UN experts' (*OHCHR*, 31 January 2024) <https://www.ohchr.org/en/press-releases/2024/01/gaza-icj-ruling-offers-hope-protection-civilians-enduring-apocalyptic> accessed 1 November 2024.

with reckless abandon.[17] Like silence, formalism, too, possesses a soothing allure, a salve against the unbearable calamities unfolding before us. But this veneer of reliance and wished-for justice obscures the discipline's role in perpetuating the very violence its interlocutors lament. We might even suggest, with delicate realism, that racialized violence is good for the business of international legal scholarship—the myriad conferences, roundtables, and speaking engagements that flow from genocide represent a perverse playground where the immoral and unintelligible are intellectualized and translated into scholarly outputs and academic promotions.

Ultimately, what many see as incomprehensible or plain vile is submerged into legal discourse, reduced to questions of correct application, false equivalency, or the limits of the law. What is lost in this abstraction are the racial projects that underpin these crises—the anti-Palestinian racism of zionism or the anti-Black racism of sovereign debt—and international law's complicity in creating and maintaining the conditions for such atrocities, not to mention its learned inability to prevent their reoccurrence.[18] Silence once again plays a dual role, sanitizing international law's facilitation of global white supremacy while obscuring the politics of disposable lives. Legal (white) ignorance—the failure to name white supremacy or the epistemic solipsism of whiteness—produces material, epistemic, and physical violence, reinscribing the racial relationalities that international law claims to challenge, all the while maintaining its innocence. As we grapple with these realities, the risks of reinscription loom large, demanding a reckoning with the violence that silence both conceals and perpetuates. This reckoning underscores the need for this collection, which seeks to dissect the intersecting themes of race, epistemology, and international law, offering pathways to critically examine the discipline's foundational and enduring complicities with the racialized violence of this world.

2. Key takeaways from this collection

Coordinating this collection has been a colossal endeavour. It has required us to be grounded within the epistemic boundaries of international law, while attempting to imagine a universe beyond them.[19] In essence, the experience was a microcosm of the challenge anti-racist scholars are up against: racial hierarchies—particularly the hegemony of whiteness—are embedded in the epistemic borders that shape both the international legal order and its ideological universe. Consequently, debates about race have been mostly contained within the putatively *humanitarian* arm of international law, where international human rights law including the International Convention on the Elimination of Racial Discrimination and the common articles of

[17] ICC, 'Statement of ICC Prosecutor Karim A.A. Khan KC: Applications for arrest warrants in the situation in the State of Palestine' (*ICC*, 20 May 2024) <https://www.icc-cpi.int/news/statement-icc-prosecutor-karim-aa-khan-kc-applications-arrest-warrants-situation-state> accessed 18 November 2024.

[18] Noura Erakat, Darryl Li, and John Reynolds, 'Race, Palestine and International Law' (2023) 117(2) AJIL Unbound 77; Maria Giannacopoulos, 'Sovereign Debts: Global Colonialism, Austerity and Neo-Liberal Assimilation'(2015) 19 Law, Text, Culture 166.

[19] Luis Eslava, Michael Fakhri, and Vasuki Nesiah, *Bandung, Global History, and International Law: Critical Pasts and Pending Futures* (Cambridge University Press 2017).

human rights treaties dominate the discourse. Consistent with white ignorance, practices of containment—such as individualization and the substitution of racism with discrimination mentioned earlier—have stripped race of its 'historic, systematic and epistemic qualities'.[20] This deliberate narrowing of focus ensures that foundational questions about white supremacy and systemic racism are never identified as harms relevant to international legal debate.

For the editors of this collection, but also for the contributors, the disciplinary boundaries of the academy ultimately worsened the silencing effect. We could gesture to race, racialization, and racism in international law, however, we were constrained in how to theorize against white supremacy from inside the discipline. Indeed, the concepts of racial violence and racial justice, so familiar in departments of Black Studies, Cultural Studies, and Post-Colonial Studies, proved elusive in mainstream international legal scholarship.[21] Excluded from the dominant framework, these ideas often linger on the periphery—occasionally experiencing moments of visibility—but are more often muted, sidelined, or transformed into something unrecognizable within the confines of orthodox debate.[22] In the end, we were confronted by the tension between critique and action, between dismantling the structures of international law and imagining what might replace them.

Throughout this project, which spanned four years, over fifty contributors (of which twenty-eight remain), and five editors (of which two remain), we found ourselves perpetually questioning what exactly it was we were doing. Were we advancing a debate about international law's complicity in the racial dynamics and racist predations that bludgeon negatively racialized peoples? Were we pushing the boundaries of international legal debate, declaring, as cyclical critical movements consistently do, that the status quo is unacceptable, intolerable, and, frankly, immoral, even if it is not always unlawful? Or perhaps our aspiration was more sociological, driven by a desire to be part of a movement that pushes international law, the academy, and ourselves to be better than we are? Ultimately, as editors and contributors, we debated whether we were charting a path for change within the discipline or merely reiterating the recurring critiques—bandwagoning if you will—that, while powerful, often leave international law fundamentally the same. The project became a space for collective reflection on how to push the boundaries of intellectual inquiry, including scholarly engagement with anti-racist praxis.[23]

Anti-racist praxis is the deliberate effort to dismantle systemic and structural racism through concrete strategies that address both overt and subtle forms of racial oppression.[24] It challenges embedded inequalities by centring the lived experiences of negatively racialized communities and confronting the assumptions and privileges

[20] al Attar (n 5). See also Shannon Sullivan and Nancy Tuana (eds), *Race and the Epistemologies of Ignorance* (State University of New York Press 2007).

[21] Vincent Llyod, *Black Dignity: The Struggle Against Domination* (Yale University Press 2022).

[22] ibid.

[23] Adelle Blackett, 'Follow the Drinking Gourd: Our Road to Teaching Critical Race Theory and Slavery and the Law, Contemplatively' (2017) 62(4) McGill Law Journal 1251.

[24] Kristine Aquino, 'Anti-Racism 'From Below': Exploring Repertoires of Everyday Anti-Racism' (2014) 39(1) Ethnic and Racial Studies 105.

of whiteness or other dominant racial groups. Key to anti-racist praxis is the transformation of existing systems into something closer to a material ideal. In the context of international law, anti-racist praxis demands a commitment to deconstructing the omnipresent legacies of colonialism, racial capitalism, and white supremacy such as the racialized origins of core doctrines like sovereignty or the vital roles played by economic exploitation and citizenship control in perpetuating transnational white supremacy. Likewise, in academia, anti-racist praxis involves upending its culture of elite knowledge production, in our case by amplifying scholarship from racialized perspectives.[25] By bridging critical thought and transformative scholarship, the type of anti-racist praxis we were hoping to engage in would confront systemic oppression in both global governance and legal academia. However, the challenges of sustaining anti-racist praxis within our discipline are formidable, as critical efforts often encounter resistance, co-optation, dilution or—most often—silencing within structures designed to preserve the status quo.

Similar to the fleeting momentum of Black Square Summer, the surge in scholarly inquiries into whether international law is racist and the broader examinations of racial oppression are already slowing, possibly coming to an end. This reflects the central challenge posed by the pervasive whiteness of international law and its persistent arc towards safeguarding white supremacy. While neoliberal academia has allowed some space for critical scholarship, this tolerance is often accompanied by efforts to sanitize its impact—satisfying diversity, equity, and inclusion quotas or framing race as a trend within scholarly debate. Such measures create the perception of progress in knowledge production while protecting orthodoxy, resulting in pious but ultimately superficial self-reflection.[26] For racialized scholars, the risks of engaging in such scholarship are borne unevenly, further impeding the potential for genuine transformation.[27]

To counter this exhausting cycle, we offer this collection. It is our hope that these chapters provide a wedge: for some, a deliberate disruption to the status quo that keeps open the window of international law's potential, if not its soul, while, for others, a provocation against and beyond international law. For both editors, this is not the simple addition of race to a research agenda. Instead, we urge academics, practitioners, and students to think about and through race differently than international law has heretofore permitted. We regard this text as a hopeful beginning, a jumping-off point, so to speak, for the continuation of a life-affirming debate about the myriad ways in which race shaped and continues to shape our present realities—material and epistemic, physical and intellectual—and to provide inspiration as we reimagine futures where the racial violence of international law is talked about with the same fervour with which it has historically been silenced.

[25] Folúkẹ́ Adébísí, *Decolonisation and Legal Knowledge: Reflections on Power and Possibility* (Bristol University Press 2023); Folúkẹ́ Adébísí, Suhraiya Jivraj, and Ntina Tzouvala (eds), *Decolonisation, Anti-Racism, and Legal Pedagogy: Strategies, Successes, and Challenges* (Routledge 2023).

[26] Jasmine K Ganni and Rebea M Khan, 'Positionality Statements as a Function of Coloniality: Reflexive Methodologies' (2024) 68(2) International Studies Quarterly 1.

[27] Brenna Bhandar, 'Theft in Broad Daylight: Racism and Neoliberal Legality' (2021) 32 Law and Critique 285.

3. Some definitions and the structure of this collection

We have organized the chapters of the text along three overarching themes: race, epistemology, and international law. We define race as a social construct—a concept that encapsulates 'wide ranging racist ideas that infiltrate and thread through societal institutions, organisations and networks'.[28] Some forms of racism tackled by our contributors occur at the micro- and meso-levels, through the ideas, attitudes, biases, narratives, and emotions of individuals and groups. These forms are integral to understanding racism at the macro-level where racism takes on systemic and epistemic qualities. By approaching racism on all three planes, we centre 'the foundational nature of oppression ... recognising the deeply connected roots of past racial oppression' while being cognizant to its evolutions and innovations.[29] Despite being a social construct, racism generates heavy social, political, and material costs including in racially hierarchical intellectual thought such as the academy. This extends to the naturalization of epistemic dominance, through which racially framed beliefs, values, and knowledge are articulated and sanctified. Race, in this sense, is a 'mode of social organization ... that categorizes with impassable boundaries ... that references the body, nature, an underlying and unchangeable essence that signals unpassable difference'.[30]

Our approach to epistemology is similarly contextual. By epistemology, we refer to the construction of knowledge in international law—how it comes to know the world and, in turn, structures its worldmaking responses.[31] Less often examined in this dialectic is the production and legitimation of international legal knowledge itself. By reflecting on the kinds of knowledge international law perpetuates and produces—particularly racemaking, racialization, and racism at an epistemological level—we can uncover the racial dynamics embedded within its foundations. An epistemic lens allows us to evaluate the weaving of race into the norms and commitments, thereby shaping international law's conceptual core.[32] When looking at law through the prism of epistemic violence, we capture the totality of the matrix of race and situate race with its relationships with the wider ecosystem.[33] We can then conceptualize race holistically, grasping the effect of racialization and racism over generations of knowledge production about international legality and, by extension, knowledge about racialized worldmaking.

We use this approach to draw connections between non-linear points and disparate lines. Racial regimes are mercurial, constantly evolving to meet the overarching demands of racial capitalism.[34] However, thinking epistemologically requires both

[28] Sean Elias and Joe Feagin, 'Systemic Racism and the White Racial Frame' in John Solomos (ed), *Routledge Handbook on Contemporary Racisms* (Routledge 2020) 15–22.

[29] ibid.

[30] Gargi Bhattacharyya, *Rethinking Racial Capitalism: Questions of Reproduction and Survival* (Rowman & Littlefield 2018).

[31] Martínez (n 9).

[32] Achiume (n 15).

[33] Andrea J Pitts, 'Decolonial Praxis and Epistemic Injustice' in Ian James Kidd, José Medina, and Gaile Polhaus, Jr (eds), *The Routledge Handbook of Epistemic Injustice* (Routledge 2017).

[34] As Robinson notes: 'Race presents all the appearance of stability. History, however, compromises this fixity. Race is mercurial – *deadly and slick*.' Cedric Robinson, *Forgeries of Memory and Meaning: Blacks and the Regimes of Race in American Theater and Film before World War II* (North Carolina University Press 2007) 4.

backwards and forward-looking enquiry—connecting elements to understand what, when, and why links exist, ultimately to disrupt present realities and imagine alternative futures. Central to this pursuit is ideation around epistemic justice: a justice that challenges prevailing orders of knowledge to achieve a state of epistemological equivalency. Indeed, without attending to the interlocking epistemes of domination such as race, these systems remain untroubled, available for reconstruction and reformation in new guises as we remain trapped within the conceptual and dialectical comfort of old debates.[35] As Radha D'Souza details, a critical outlook on race demands alternative methodologies. To imagine epistemic (in)justice is to underscore the importance of thinking about race and racism as well as the subjectivities and positionalities they impose. Once we adopt epistemology as an overarching paradigm, we are compelled to confront our own complicities—as both individual scholars and interlocutors of a discipline—in perpetuating the divisions and exclusions of white supremacy. This approach also highlights the limits of a racialized epistemology, where the validation of white epistemic authority continues to shape the questions asked, the problems identified, and the proposals for anti-racist praxis emerging from within the discipline. With these definitions in mind, we have arranged the book in five sections.

The first situates the reader within the historical context of international law's relationship with race, examining its embeddedness in colonial and racially capitalist legacies and the enduring reinscription of these structures in international law's present day. Mohsen al Attar begins by exploring the role of Charles Mills' *white ignorance* in the establishment and perpetuation of white supremacy, arguing that international law's epistemic foundations, rooted in colonial priorities and whiteness, marginalize the histories and epistemes of non-white peoples while elevating European subjectivity to a universal standard. To counter this racialized domination, al Attar advocates for epistemic resistance and the collective dismantling of white ignorance, necessary to facilitate the emergence of alternative universals that can foster an anti-racist praxis and reshape legal knowledge. Folúkẹ́ Adébísí follows with an analysis of international law's colonial logics and racial demarcations in its structuring of bodies, property, and space. Using vaccine apartheid as a case study, Adébísí delves into international law's necropolitics of life- and death-making.

Tackling similar themes but also novel ones, Jason Haynes critiques international investment law in the Latin American and Caribbean region, demonstrating how it is rooted in and perpetuates a centuries-old obsession with the extraction of precious materials. Using the Eco-Oro Award as a case study, Haynes argues that the practices of fetishism, narcissism, and primitive accumulation uphold an arbitral system that exploits and subordinates racialized peoples, treating non-European populations as valuable only for their extractable resources and labour. Advancing Haynes' argument about the racial capitalist origins of international law, Harrison Mbori critiques sovereignty doctrine, arguing that its claim of universal equality conceals its systemic and racialized inequalities. Centring European colonialism and neocolonialism in the

[35] Miranda Fricker, *Epistemic Injustice: Power and the Ethics of Knowing* (Oxford University Press 2017); Bonaventura de Sousa Santos, *Epistemologies of the South: Justice Against Epistemicide* (Routledge 2016); Nancy Dikas, 'Epistemic Justice and Injustice' in Miranda Fricker and others (eds), *The Routledge Handbook of Social Epistemology* (Routledge 2019).

doctrine, he reveals how the formal equality of sovereignty masks deeper layers of inequality, which Mbori exposes via a discussion of the racial grammar of international law when its doctrines are applied to Third and First World states respectively. Sarah Riley Case and Frédéric Mégret close this section with the politics of demarcations, excavating the racialized machinations of *jus cogens*. Rather than dismantling racial hierarchies, they reveal the paradoxical ways in which peremptory norms often reinforce and re-entrench the global colour line.

In our second part, we explore specific manifestations of racialization and racism in international law, examining the tools, techniques, and technologies that structure and sustain racial stratification across specific frameworks. Eurocentrism is central to the opening chapter by Shahab Saqib, where he argues that the legal construction of citizenship as a neutral category enabled international law to justify inequalities simply by assigning lesser value to citizenships in the Global South. In other words, under the guise of sovereignty and equality, international law cemented a racial hierarchy, with citizenship transformed into a modern and sanitized colour line. Next, Dimitrios Kourtis writes about the inclusion of racial groups as a protected category in the Genocide Convention, engaging with the definitional and interpretative challenges this poses. Similar to Saqib, Kourtis argues that racial groups, like other protected collectives, are dynamic and relational social constructs, demanding a standalone analysis to better understand manifestations of ethno-chauvinist violence. Turning to Palestine, Kourtis explores how the inclusion of racial groups in the Convention has concurrently enhanced and undermined their protection. Staying with the subtext of Kourtis' chapter, Faisal al-Assad writes about a common spark for many negatively racialized peoples: settler-colonialism. Drawing on Patrick Wolfe's theory of exception, al-Assad frames international law as a 'raced discourse', rooted in settler colonial conquest, that abstracts juridical categories from anthropological presuppositions. By assessing these dynamics through recent scholarship on international humanitarian law and the war on terror, he explores opportunities for critique and transformation of international law at the 'frontier'.

Jinan Bastaki's chapter naturally flows from al-Assad's, providing a critique of *non-citizenship* via the 1951 Refugee Convention. She argues that the Convention's origins and implementation reflect colonial and racialized conceptions of sovereignty, where states retain the power to admit or exclude based on racialized borders. Using case studies of Palestinian refugees and the contrasting treatment afforded to Syrian and Ukrainian ones, Bastaki further argues that international refugee law creates a racialized 'hierarchy of the excluded', intersecting with class, gender, and broader systems of oppression. Nciko wa Nciko closes this section with an analysis of the United Nations Guiding Principles on Internal Displacement, specifically its dismissal of climate change in its considerations, despite climate change's role as a leading cause of displacement. He argues that the historical processes behind the Guiding Principles established a racialized divide, blaming internal displacement on Global South states while celebrating the Global North's humanitarian aid efforts, even in climate-induced crises. In keeping with the theme of epistemology, Nciko concludes by proposing that African states adhere to the principles of the Kampala Convention instead, principles that can help unify Global South countries in addressing these silences.

The third part shifts the conversation towards international human rights law, showing how key frameworks sustain, rather than dismantle, racial hierarchies. The discussion begins with Raghavi Viswanath, who argues that the International Covenant on Economic, Social, and Cultural Rights (ICESCR) fails to live up to its anticolonial origins. While it emerged from Third World states' efforts to address the economic inequalities established during the colonial period, rather than promote redistributive justice, it entrenched forms of economic racism. By reflecting on the ICESCR's drafting history and contemporary interpretations, Viswanath exposes how the Covenant deflects from the global economic order's systemic economic and social exploitation of oppressed peoples. Continuing with Tess Sheldon, Ruby Dhand, and Roxane Mykitiuk, we are regaled with a critique of the Convention on the Rights of Persons with Disabilities (CRPD). Despite including the concept of 'multiple discrimination', the CRPD remains silent on the compounded vulnerabilities faced by racialized and Indigenous persons with disabilities. Using copious empirical data, Sheldon, Dhand, and Mykitiuk highlight the risks of a race-evasive approach to disability discrimination and advocate for an intersectional framework that addresses systemic racism when implementing Convention commitments. Also motivated by transformative equality, Paulina Jimenez Fregoso explores the mainstreaming of intersectionality. Focusing on cases related to race, colourism, and racial discrimination in the Inter-American system, she demonstrates how traditional single-axis approaches fail to address the harm experienced by multiply-burdened individuals. By incorporating intersectionality, adjudicative bodies can more accurately assess the complex and layered experiences of victims of racism, offering a pathway towards more comprehensive forms of racialized justice. Returning to the issue of Eurocentrism, Karla Schröter examines jurisprudence from the European Court of Human Rights and how its application of *freedoms* to different identities can quickly legitimize ontologies rooted in whiteness and masculinity. She analyses the Court's rulings on the wearing of Islamic veils—hijabs—in public spaces, developing a frame of three colonial fantasies: Muslim women as victims, objects, and savages. Schröter links these fantasies to Europe's colonial past and present, exposing the ongoing epistemic violence that instrumentalizes Muslim women and perpetuates a civilizing dynamic that bolsters the White Man's (neverending) burden.

In Part Four, we shift our gaze to the pluriverse of international law, recognizing that inclusivity alone is insufficient and that anti-racist praxis requires epistemological equivalence. Contributors explore the constructed peripheries of international law, examining how race is mediated through local articulations and its reflections—or at times refractions—within the international legal framework. We open with Suraj Girijashanker's chapter, where he explores India's historical and contemporary engagement with anti-racism in international law, arguing that its stance was paradoxically shaped by both genuine solidarity and geostrategic interests. Applying Derrick Bell's theory of interest convergence, he critiques India's double-move of invoking its anti-racist history while deflecting scrutiny of domestic subordination, including caste-based oppression and the racialization of Muslims under Hindu nationalism. Next, Saul Takahashi explores Japan's historical relationship with international law, focusing on its use as a tool to assert Japan's 'civilized' status and justify regional colonial expansion based on its own racial taxonomy. He explains how the narrative of

Japan as a *tan'itsu minzoku* (homogeneous nation) proliferated across the Japanese landscape, creating an ethno-chauvinist doctrine. In response, anti-racist scholars and NGOs have advocated for the reform of Japan's self-perception, often by latching on to elements of international law. Yet, as Takahashi underscores, Japan's international engagements are Janus-faced: showcasing itself on the world stage as equal to leading authors of international law while demonstrating inward resistance to perceived foreign influence via the same framework.

Often absent from international legal debates is the discipline of international relations.[36] Yang Han addresses this gap by examining the role of racialized power in international relations, arguing that Global North countries act as norm contesters on racial equality, while the Global South—specifically China—serve as norm entrepreneurs advocating for change. Through a case study of the collaboration between the Africa Group and China, Han demonstrates how the Global North obstructs the establishment of a global racial equality norm, seeking to sustain a racial hierarchy that privileges superficial progress over transformative change. Travelling thousands of miles, Henrique Weil Afonso concludes this section with a dash of decolonial thinking, which he deploys to uncover the power dynamics linking law and racialization in Brazilian society. He critiques the myths of miscegenation and singularity embedded in Brazilian constitutionalism, locating these fictions within Brazil's origins in colonialism and the transatlantic slave trade, key international legal themes across this collection. Afonso is especially interested in the ways both domestic and international law enforce silences ranging from deliberate amnesia to epistemic erasure of conquest. By examining Haitian constitutionalism and Quilombola resistance, Afonso highlights popular rejection of the myth of a homogeneous nation, calling into question a key pillar in international legal discourse.

Our fifth part is the most prescriptive, seeking to demarcate a future research agenda and plan of action for those troubled by international law's enduring racial violence. With a shared commitment to anti-racist praxis, the authors propose a mix of ways forward including working within, against, and beyond extant international law. Darryl Li opens this section, exploring how theorizing international law from the institution of transatlantic chattel slavery—a foundational element of capitalist modernity—can address its deficiencies in engaging with race and racialization. Calling upon Sylvia Wynter, he critiques international law's tendency to treat race as a generic and localized category, arguing instead for an understanding of racialization as a global and historically specific process rooted in anti-Black racism. Next, Kamya Vishwanath expands on the earlier discussion about caste-based discrimination, focusing on the absence of Dalits in international legal discourse and the epistemological erasure of their embodied experiences. By highlighting the absence of Dalits from international legal discourse, her chapter examines how their unique epistemology—rooted in subordination and pain—offers an alternative framework for emancipation. Vishwanath challenges international law's privileging of academic knowledge, arguing that Dalit poetry provides transformative visions of freedom beyond the limitations of existing legal texts.

[36] Búzás (n 6).

Despite her affinity for critical legal movements, Radha D'Souza critiques their methodological limitations, particularly their struggles with constant conjunctions in liberal theory and the occlusion of colonized and racialized peoples in legal histories. Most original is her exploration of modernity's dualistic structure, and what she terms the original sin of capitalism or land-labour dualism, ultimately calling for a radical transformation of the epistemological and methodological foundations of critical scholarship to place the relationship between racism, (neo)colonialism, and law on firmer philosophical ground. E Tendayi Achiume, Asli Ü Bâli, and S Priya Morley adopt a different outlook to D'Souza, conceptualizing the transnational dimensions of racial injustice and mobilization. They begin by highlighting how international law and organizations both perpetuate and engage with structural racism. Drawing on global movements like *I can't breathe*, they explore the racialized distributional consequences of police violence, forced migration, and climate-related harms. They argue for a scholar-activist approach towards legal scholarship, detailing a collective project aimed at building networks of scholars and advocates to develop emancipatory strategies and research agendas that resist racism in international law. For her part, Claire Smith sits somewhere between the two preceding chapters: she laments hegemonic feminist support for international law's steadfast insistence on remaining 'inside of whiteness'.[37] Highlighting the utility of White femininity and White womanhood in international law's racemaking, Smith conceptualizes the 'White women's burden' as part of any feminist debt owed. She calls for an intentional anti-racist praxis that moves beyond diversity and inclusion, instead urging for intervention to directly attend to the racial edifice international law is built upon.

Dylan Asafo brings down the curtain on our collection, proposing a sharp turn in how we conceptualize the violence of international law. He introduces two concepts—slow violence and benevolent violence—to explain how international law perpetuates the subordination of negatively racialized peoples. Rather than recognize the realities of racial injustice, key interlocutors actively obstruct these aspirations through mythmaking, posturing about the law's putative arc and gradual progress towards justice (we were reminded of Nina Simone's tongue-in-cheek ode to *going slow*). Asafo calls for the dismantling of the strategic myths that degrade the physical, psychological, and cultural well-being of negatively racialized groups through 'multidimensional acts of *counter-violence* to protect our oceans, lands, and all living beings and bring about a more just world'.

Upon reflection, we are proud to have assembled a collection that acts neither as a comprehensive critique or as a unified vision for reform. As recognized in both the prologue by Adrien K Wing and the epilogue by Christopher Gevers, this text amounts to a record of refusal and resistance—of scholars and practitioners bucking the dominant discourse about international law's racialized foundations being either accidental or soon-to-be resolved. Our contributors and their stories demonstrate that racial thinking is alive and well, continuing to shape the field's architecture and mainstream epistemology. As we have explored in this introduction, our collection is peppered with a plethora of uniting—and contrasting—themes. If we were to identify

[37] Gina Heathcote and Lucia Kula, 'Abandoning the Idealized White Subject of Legal Feminism: A Manifesto for Silence in a Lusophone Register' (2023) 12(3) Global Constitutionalism 469.

a binding agent between them, it would be our shared commitment to confronting not only international law's racialized histories but also its insistence on forgiving (itself) and forgetting (our struggle). There are no conventional solutions to the ailment of either international law or international legal scholarship. Instead, we offer a different kind of engagement where race is not presented as external to the frame, but both constitutive of its foundations and central to understanding what international law *is*. Perhaps what is most original about this text is that it also captures what international law—and scholars—have persistently refused to see.

PART I
SITUATING INTERNATIONAL LAW'S RACISM PROBLEM

1
The Racialized Epistemology of International Law
From White Ignorance to Black Dignity

Mohsen al Attar

1. The blind spots of international law: race, cognition, and epistemological failures

Modern international legal scholarship is riddled with blind spots. One of the most pervasive is its systemic neglect of racism and the associated injustices.[1] Consider, for example, that in the entire library of the American Journal of International Law (AJIL), less than 1 per cent of its documents engage substantively with issues of race.[2] Indeed, despite the frequency with which ideas of racial hierarchy were deployed to justify ethnic cleansing, enslavement, and genocide, core themes in international legal history and modern legality, publicists have eschewed engagement with the logic, preferring to deal with the outward expressions only.

Rooted in European epistemology, international law has long been shaped by a narrow Cartesian logic that privileges individual cognition above all else, thereby excluding broader social realities. Even when European scholars recognized the limits of this epistemological individualism through standpoint theory, their acknowledgement failed to extend to racial groups and their conditions.[3] This oversight has perpetuated a legal framework that remains indifferent to the structural inequities faced by racialized communities globally. WEB Du Bois may have centred the colour line in sociology but in international law, a commitment to whiteness reigned supreme.[4]

The epistemic shortcomings of international law are evident in its reliance on self-imposed boundaries where white supremacy, Eurocentrism, and other racial hierarchies such as zionism were assumed as universal truths.[5] Gradually framed as

[1] E Tendayi Achiume and James Thuo Gathii, 'Introduction to the Symposium on Race, Racism, and International Law' (2023) 117 AJIL Unbound 26.

[2] James Thuo Gathii, 'Studying Race in International Law Scholarship Using a Social Science Approach' (2021) 22 Chicago Journal of International Law 71.

[3] Luvell Anderson, 'Epistemic Injustice and the Philosophy of Race' in Ian James Kidd, José Medina, and Gaile Pohlhaus (eds), *The Routledge Handbook of Epistemic Injustice* (1st edn, Routledge 2017) <https://www.taylorfrancis.com/books/9781351814508/chapters/10.4324/9781315212043-13> accessed 26 February 2021.

[4] Robbie Shilliam (ed), *International Relations and Non-Western Thought* (Routledge 2011) 16.

[5] Christopher Gevers, '"Unwhitening the World": Rethinking Race and International Law' (2021) 67 UCLA Law Review 1652.

Mohsen al Attar, *The Racialized Epistemology of International Law* In: *Emancipating International Law*. Edited by: Mohsen al Attar and Claire Smith, Oxford University Press. © Mohsen al Attar 2026.
DOI: 10.1093/9780198935605.003.0003

universally applicable principles, these truths projected European values as an objective standard for humanity. European subjectivity—shaped by its own culture, religion, and philosophy—was equated with universal human objectivity simply because Europeans had the power to impose it, usually through colonial violence.[6] These norms were not adopted willingly by non-Europeans but enforced with cannonballs. Ultimately, non-Europeans were denied sovereignty not because of any inherent flaw but because they were not European, and only moral and cognitive traditions rooted in European thought—particularly those of Christianity, Catholicism, and later, England and France—were considered rational, moral, and universal. As a growing range of scholars have argued, these universalist claims quickly unravelled when confronted with the identities of those beyond Europe.

Epistemologically, the shortcoming of modern international law lay in the preference for idealized cognition over the complexities of actual human thought and experience. To confront real-world issues rather than uphold abstract norms, scholars needed to embed cognitive agents within their social contexts, recognizing race and racial subordination as they were lived, not just theorized. This required an acknowledgement of the messy, uneven realities of race and racial experience, rather than retreating into sanitized, aspirational frameworks. Yet, by clinging to these prescriptive norms, international legal scholars imposed what Charles Mills terms a 'cognitive handicap'—a deliberate intellectual limitation that rendered their knowledge both illogical and immoral.[7] This handicap effectively excluded the sociological and cognitive realities of non-European peoples, reinforcing a Eurocentric worldview that ignored the racialized dimensions of global injustice.[8] Indeed, by failing to engage with racial subordination, legal scholars allowed theory to morph into dogma, protecting the white core of international law and maintaining its exclusion of non-white worldviews.

In the opening chapter to this collection, which centres race in international law, I examine the underlying reasons for the regime's deliberate disregard of racial realities. In the first part, I draw on Mills's concept of 'white ignorance' to explain how European international law systematically excluded the logics and legacies of racial subordination from its analytical framework.[9] This exclusion is not merely a moral failing; it represents a cognitive distortion that prevents scholarship from confronting the entrenched racial hierarchies inherent in its modernity. In the second part, I examine the key role of whiteness and white supremacy in shaping our understanding of international law. Despite the increasing discourse on race, few scholars interrogate whiteness as an epistemic foundation, thereby limiting our understanding of how racial privilege and subordination have structured

[6] Mohsen al Attar, 'Must International Legal Pedagogy Remain Eurocentric?' (2021) 11(1) Asian Journal of International Law 176.

[7] George A Martinez, 'Law, Race, and the Epistemology of Ignorance' (2020) 17(2) Hastings Race and Poverty Law Journal 507.

[8] Matiangai Sirleaf, 'Rendering Whiteness Visible' (2023) 117 American Journal of International Law 484.

[9] Charles Mills, 'White Ignorance' in Shannon Sullivan and Nancy Tuana (eds), *Race and Epistemologies of Ignorance* (State University of New York Press 2007).

international legal norms and practices.[10] Recognizing white supremacy's role in these structures is crucial for any antiracist praxis that seeks to genuinely challenge and transform international law.[11]

I conclude with a brief exploration of epistemic resistance.[12] While various initiatives seek to address these controversies, most remain constrained by their adherence to the very status quo they aim to critique, thereby perpetuating the intellectual handicaps they challenge.[13] I argue that any serious engagement with international law's complicity in racial subordination must begin by acknowledging its white foundations and developing theories that move beyond this legacy.

2. The epistemic mechanisms of racial hierarchy in law

As research into the relationship between law and epistemology has grown, legal scholars have increasingly focused on the epistemology of ignorance.[14] Informed by the work of Charles Mills and Linda Martín Alcoff, scholars such as E Tendayi Achiume, George Martínez, and Christopher Gevers have begun to examine how white ignorance shapes both the law and our understanding of it. This form of ignorance deliberately obscures considerations of race and racial subordination within legal thought and scholarly practice, reinforcing the invisibility of racial injustice.

Epistemologists differ in their approaches towards ignorance, offering varied interpretations.[15] While some view ignorance merely as a lack of knowledge, Alcoff and Mills argue that ignorance is not a passive state, highlighting the proactive ways in which ignorance is cultivated.[16] Ignorance can be strategically maintained and structurally reproduced, evolving into an epistemic practice that preserves an unequal status quo denoted by relations of domination and subordination. When race is injected into the debate, ignorance as an epistemic practice manifests as what Mills terms 'white ignorance'—a systemic obfuscation designed to uphold the supremacy of whiteness within the law and beyond.[17]

[10] Gevers (n 5).

[11] Richard Delgado, 'Derrick Bell's Racial Realism: A Comment on White Optimism and Black Despair' (1992) 24 Connecticut Law Review 527.

[12] Andrea J Pitts, 'Decolonial Praxis and Epistemic Injustice' in Ian James Kidd, José Medina, and Gaile Pohlhaus (eds), *The Routledge Handbook of Epistemic Injustice* (1st edn, Routledge 2017) <https://www.taylorfrancis.com/books/9781351814508/chapters/10.4324/9781315212043-14> accessed 26 February 2021; José Medina, *The Epistemology of Resistance: Gender and Racial Oppression, Epistemic Injustice, and Resistant Imaginations* (Oxford University Press 2013).

[13] Mohsen al Attar, 'TWAIL: A Paradox within a Paradox' (2020) 22(2) International Community Law Review 163.

[14] Gabriella Beckles-Raymond, 'Implicit Bias, (Global) White Ignorance, and Bad Faith: The Problem of Whiteness and Anti-Black Racism' (2020) 37(2) Journal of Applied Philosophy 169; Martinez (n 7); Marzia Milazzo, 'On White Ignorance, White Shame, and Other Pitfalls in Critical Philosophy of Race' (2017) 34(4) Journal of Applied Philosophy 557.

[15] Nadja El Kassar, 'What Ignorance Really Is. Examining the Foundations of Epistemology of Ignorance' (2018) 32(5) Social Epistemology 300.

[16] ibid.

[17] Mills (n 9).

While the full scope of the philosophical debate on ignorance is beyond this chapter, two key concepts are relevant to my analysis: Alcoff's notion of ignorance as 'substantive epistemic practice' and Mills's idea of 'moral non-knowings'.[18] These concepts frame how the structural and moral dimensions of ignorance operate within the law, obscuring racial injustice by normalizing certain moral judgements and suppressing others. As Alcoff explains:

> The idea of an epistemology of ignorance attempts to explain and account for the fact that such substantive practices of ignorance—willful ignorance, for example, and socially acceptable but faulty justificatory practices – are structural. This is to say that there are identities and social locations and modes of belief formation, all produced by structural social conditions of a variety of sorts, that are in some cases epistemically disadvantaged or defective.[19]

Mills further adds:

> For me, the epistemic desideratum is that the naturalizing and socializing of epistemology should have, as a component, the naturalizing and socializing of moral epistemology also and the study of pervasive social patterns of mistaken moral cognition. Thus the idea is that improvements in our cognitive practice should have a practical payoff in heightened sensitivity to social oppression and the attempt to reduce and ultimately eliminate that oppression.[20]

As Nadja El Kassar explains, viewing ignorance as an epistemic practice highlights the role of agency, compelling us to scrutinize 'the subject's epistemic conduct, virtues, and vices'.[21] Just as epistemologies are socially embedded, so too are the epistemic agents shaped by the contexts in which these epistemologies develop.

Notwithstanding the high degree of abstraction, these ideas have direct implications for legal actors and the reasoning they deploy, as seen in the jurisprudence of the European Court of Human Rights (ECtHR) and the International Criminal Court (ICC). Both the ECtHR and ICC are emblematic of whiteness, holding a unique position in the phenomenology of international legality, and thus making them ideal sites for examining the dynamics of white ignorance and moral non-knowing in the operation of international law, even more so when we recognize that they belong to international law's self-titled benevolent wing. To explore the epistemic practice associated with international law, I use both courts to highlight some of the ways in which whiteness corrupts cognition and morality.

[18] Linda Martin Alcoff, 'Epistemologies of Ignorance: Three Types' in Shannon Sullivan and Nancy Tuana (eds), *Race and Epistemologies of Ignorance* (State University of New York Press 2007) 39; Mills (n 9) 22.

[19] Alcoff (n 18) 40.

[20] Mills (n 9) 22.

[21] El Kassar (n 15) 305.

2.1 The European Court of Human Rights

I begin with *Lautsi v Italy*, a somewhat confusing decision delivered by the ECtHR. In *Lautsi*, fifteen judges affirmed that states must be *neutral* and *impartial* when mediating the practices 'of various religions, faiths, and beliefs'.[22] A principle of neutrality and impartiality seems innocuous, even desirable. Grounded in the notion of respect, as articulated in Article 2 of Protocol No 1, the standard suggests a commitment to religious equality and freedom of religious expression. In practice, however, we immediately observe a skewed perception of neutrality.

In its judgment, the Court examined the implications of locating crucifixes in Italian classrooms, as is standard in many schools across the southern European state. The Court recognized 'that the crucifix is above all a religious symbol'.[23] Yet, applying the principle of neutrality and impartiality, it deemed this a form of protected speech as it found no evidence 'that the display of a religious symbol on classroom walls may have an influence on pupils'.[24] As such, even if the crucifix might appear to have a proselytizing effect, this does not compel its removal. Rather, because of neutrality and impartiality, states should preserve the display of the crucifix, with the capacity and responsibility to 'enlighten and advise . . . children . . . in line with [their] own philosophical convictions' falling to parents who might object to its display.[25]

In addition, the ECtHR accepted Christianity's supposed association with universal morality. The ECtHR endorsed the Italian Supreme Administrative Court's declaration that 'the crucifix symbolized the religious origin of values (tolerance, mutual respect, valorization of the person, affirmation of one's rights, consideration of one's freedom, the autonomy of one's moral conscience vis-à-vis authority, human solidarity and the refusal of any form or discrimination) which characterized Italian civilization'.[26] Going one step further, the Court intimated that the crucifix was central to a European identity, embodying 'not only . . . a religious symbol, but also . . . a cultural and identity-linked symbol, the symbol of the principles and values which formed the basis of democracy and western civilisation'.[27] In short, the ECtHR permits the display of crucifixes in public schools because, first, states must be neutral and impartial when mediating religious practices and, second, the crucifix has cultural and historical significance.

Despite revisiting the principle of neutrality and impartiality throughout its judgment, the reasoning in *Lautsi* compels us to confront a glaring contradiction in the Court's treatment of religious symbols. Since 2010, several European states have banned the wearing of either head veils or face veils in public spaces such as schools and hospitals, a policy that directly affects Muslim women.[28] In contrast to *Lautsi*, the ECtHR

[22] *Lautsi and Others v Italy* App no 30814/06 (ECtHR, 18 March 2011) [26].
[23] ibid [27].
[24] ibid [28].
[25] ibid [30].
[26] ibid [7].
[27] ibid [16].
[28] Irene Zempi, 'Veiled Muslim Women's Views on Law Banning the Wearing of the Niqab (Face Veil) in Public' (2019) 42(15) Ethnic and Racial Studies 2585.

found the veil bans lawful, declaring that Muslim women must make their heads and faces visible in public spaces to ensure that others can engage with them on their own terms.[29] Indeed, when explaining its proscription of veils, it explained that coverings hinder social interaction and make the concept of 'living together' impossible.[30] The distinct treatment afforded to crucifixes and veils raises both questions and concerns.

With crucifixes, states have a duty of respect and a responsibility to facilitate the display of overt religious symbols before putatively impressionable students. However, when the veil enters the fray, restrictions on religious practice are necessary because, as France and Belgium argued, religious symbols like the Muslim veil *could* have a proselytizing effect: 'it cannot be denied outright that the wearing of a headscarf might have some kind of proselytising effect'.[31] With crucifixes, the lack of evidence of a proselytizing effect was sufficient for it to earn protection; with veils, the possibility of a proselytizing effect was sufficient to support its banning. While Christian symbols appear benign, even invisible, Muslim symbols are omnipresent and divisive. This selective application of religious freedom reflects the entrenched biases of white ignorance, which uphold Christian dominance while pathologizing Islamic practices.

In this collection, Karla Schröter elaborates on how the Court's rulings systematically reinforced a European ontology, one that seeks to project a homogeneous vision of European identity at the expense of religious and cultural diversity. When examined through the lens of white ignorance, this issue transcends a mere lack of familiarity with Islamic practices or a denial of the agency of Muslim women. Rather, it reveals the deliberate weaponization of racialized ignorance to reinforce white epistemic dominance. For example, in *Dahlab*, the Court was vociferous in its views on the relationship between veils and (liberal) equality: '[the Muslim headscarf] is hard to square with the principle of equality' and 'the wearing of a headscarf . . . appears to be imposed on women by a precept which is laid down in the Koran (sic)'.[32] The Court dismissed the perceptions of equality held by practitioners of the Islamic faith and disregarded its own rulings about mediating religion neutrally and impartially. Indeed, by framing religious symbols worn by Muslim women as threats to *social interaction* and *living together*, the Court not only misrepresented the actual impact of these religious practices but actively contributed to the stigmatization and marginalization of Muslim communities. Rooted in a culturally biased understanding of social cohesion, the Court failed to recognize or respect the lived experiences of millions of veiled Muslim women who navigate social relations and public spaces on a daily basis without issue. Instead, as Natasha Bakht observed, the Court transformed Muslim religious attire 'from a nonexistent issue to a spectacular threat to the nation'.[33]

Moreover, the Court's perfunctory acceptance of the putative relationship between Christianity and universal morality denies Christianity's history of violence and oppression.[34] Non-Christians, for example, view Christianity not through an idealized

[29] June Edmunds, 'The Limits of Post-National Citizenship: European Muslims, Human Rights and the Hijab' (2012) 35(7) Ethnic and Racial Studies 1181.

[30] Natasha Bakht, 'In Your Face: Piercing the Veil of Ignorance About Niqab-Wearing Women' (2015) 24(3) Social & Legal Studies 419.

[31] *Dahlab v Switzerland* App no 42393/98 (ECtHR, 15 February 2001) [13].

[32] ibid.

[33] Natasha Bakht, 'Transnational Anti-Muslim Racism: Routes in Law' (2021) 20 Meridians 291, 292.

[34] *Lautsi and Others v Italy* (n 22) [45].

self-representation but through a historical record of religious wars to reclaim holy lands; the brutal persecution, torture, and execution of Muslims and Jews during the Inquisition; forced conversions, cultural erasure, and the genocide of Indigenous populations during conquest; the silencing and subordination of women, scapegoating them for 'original sin', and excluding them from church leadership.[35] Rather than recognize this comprehensive record of dehumanization associated with crucifixes, the Court retreats into ahistorical boasts about tolerance and equality, conveniently excluding the darker aspects of Christianity's movements throughout the world. These claims are more than just self-aggrandizing puffery; rather, they are crucial to white ignorance, embedding a moral self-righteousness that enables the Court to adopt a hierarchical perception of religious symbols (and religions). The crucifix can thus be venerated as a symbol of tolerance and human solidarity, even as it intensifies intolerance and racism, while the hijab can be denigrated as a symbol of female oppression.[36]

In addition to the relevance of white ignorance to understanding the contradictory reasoning of the ECtHR, its decisions also illustrate the practice of moral non-knowing. According to Mills, the failure to recognize racial biases corrupts moral judgement: moral non-knowings lead to 'incorrect judgments about the rights and wrongs of moral situations themselves'.[37] Moral non-knowing leads to the evaluation of social practices based on their alignment with a purportedly universal standard that is, in reality, steeped in European ethnocentrism, producing what Matiangai Sirleaf and others decry as white normativity. The acceptance of white normativity is central to the functioning of international law and has a dual impact: first, it embeds white perspectives as universal truths within our moral and cognitive landscapes; second, it reinforces the invisibility of its own dominance, treating alternative worldviews as marginal or pathological.[38] By legally enshrining this specific normativity, epistemic agents *rationally* deny the subjectivity and diversity inherent in moral reasoning:

> Ethnocentrism is, of course, a negative cognitive tendency common to all peoples, not just Europeans. But with Europe's gradual rise to global domination, the European variant becomes entrenched as an overarching framework, a conviction of exceptionalism and superiority that seems vindicated by the facts, and thenceforth, circularly, shaping perception of the facts.[39]

Returning to the Court's logic, the veil is proselytizing, while the crucifix is not; the veil is a symbol of gender subjugation, whereas the crucifix advances female emancipation; and while parents are entrusted with the responsibility to educate their children about aspects of Christianity with which they may disagree, children must be

[35] Sherene H Razack, *Nothing Has to Make Sense: Upholding White Supremacy through Anti-Muslim Racism* (University of Minnesota Press 2022).
[36] Sherene H Razack, 'A Site/Sight We Cannot Bear: The Racial/Spatial Politics of Banning the Muslim Woman's Niqab' (2018) 30(1) Canadian Journal of Women and the Law 169.
[37] Mills (n 9) 22.
[38] Márcio Nunes de Abreu, 'The Cultural Psychology of White Normativity: A Draft to the Concept of White Psyche' (2020) 3 Human Arenas 297.
[39] Mills (n 9) 25.

shielded from the personal practices of their Muslim teachers. These dichotomies are not mere inconsistencies, but deliberate constructions that glorify Christian symbols while denigrating Islamic ones, reinforcing a racialized hierarchy under the guise of legal reasoning. By framing Christian symbols as neutral and universal, while treating Muslim symbols as threatening and deviant, the Court distorts both legal and moral reasoning to fit a racialized narrative.[40]

2.2 The International Criminal Court

Another example that illustrates the epistemic mechanisms that enforce racial hierarchies in international law are the practices of the ICC.[41] Despite its brief history, a startling figure stands out: by 2020, the ICC had launched thirty official cases, *all* of which were against African nationals.[42] The ICC's focus on African leaders, while ignoring egregious crimes in other parts of the world, further demonstrates the operation of white ignorance within the global legal system. Practices of selective justice dictated by a racialized hierarchy enforce a worldview where violence is ascribed to non-white actors whose alleged criminality is treated as uniquely perverse.[43] Indeed, when looking at the ICC's history of warrants, prosecutions, and convictions, it appears criminality is solely the purview of the non-white world.

DeFalco and Mégret describe this selective focus as part of a broader pattern of *racial blindness* in the ICC—a wilful refusal to acknowledge the role of race in shaping legal outcomes.[44] Claims of colour-blindness or of liberal equality in the Court's operations allow the ICC to ignore how race shapes global power dynamics and the selective application of justice it produces. For example, the ICC's prosecution of African leaders reflects a legacy of colonialism wherein the vicissitudes of racialized imperialism carry forward—both in the geography of intra- and interstate conflict and in the selective prosecutions by a supposed agent of universal justice. By demanding evidence of intentional discrimination when evaluating its operations, the ICC ensures that the racially biased outcomes go unchallenged. Yet again, whiteness is made invisible, allowing the Court to reinforce global racial hierarchies while maintaining a façade of impartiality and neutrality.[45]

Mégret and DeFalco use the ICC's intervention in Libya to explore these dynamics, remarking, rightly, that the Court's treatment of Libya and its leaders has been strikingly different from its approach to *darker* African states.[46] They argue that

[40] Razack (n 35).

[41] Gregor Maučec, 'The International Criminal Court and the Issue of Intersectionality—A Conceptual and Legal Framework for Analysis' (2021) 21(1) International Criminal Law Review 1.

[42] Manisuli Ssenyonjo, 'African States Failed Withdrawal from the Rome Statute of the International Criminal Court: From Withdrawal Notifications to Constructive Engagement' (2017) 17(5) International Criminal Law Review 749.

[43] John Reynolds and Sujith Xavier, '"The Dark Corners of the World": TWAIL and International Criminal Justice' (2016) 14(4) Journal of International Criminal Justice 959.

[44] Randle C DeFalco and Frédéric Mégret, 'The Invisibility of Race at the ICC: Lessons from the US Criminal Justice System' (2019) 7(1) London Review of International Law 55.

[45] Lisa Tilley and Robbie Shilliam, 'Raced Markets: An Introduction' (2018) 23(5) New Political Economy 534.

[46] DeFalco and Mégret (n 44) 76.

the negative racialization of African subjects is central, leading to the racial blindness on display, and perpetuating the idea that Western intervention, especially in African contexts, is always salutary: 'This notion, that humanity is itself a racialised construct, strikes at the core of ICL's claims to being a cosmopolitan project in the service of protecting all human beings.'[47] While their argument about racial blindness is powerful, I believe white ignorance better captures the operations within the ICC, both in the case of Libya and in its broader operations.

In Libya, the debate centred around which African leaders to prosecute—Brown or Black, or the choice between two negatively racialized subjects—demonstrating that even the critique about ICC bias is guided by a commitment to prosecuting Africans.[48] Absent from the ICC's considerations was the role of NATO and key figures who ordered the invasion and destabilization of the country including David Cameron, Barack Obama, and Nicholas Sarkozy. Prior to the intervention, Libya was a stable state, with excellent provisions of social welfare, a high social development index, a real focus on women's rights, an antiracism agenda, and commendable diplomatic relations with virtually all states across the African continent.[49] Following the attack by NATO, the state has collapsed into civil war, with much of the population suffering from the ensuing chaos.[50] The violence of NATO and of Western states more broadly is not only invisible to the ICC, but actively disappeared by the institution. The focus on prosecuting Black-on-Black violence while disregarding white-on-Black violence is not merely an oversight, but an epistemic mechanism that reinforces a biased view of Black peoples as uniquely criminal and white peoples as uniquely moral.[51] Just as Christian symbols and norms are treated as benign, so too is the violence of whiteness ignored or justified. Like with the ECtHR, whiteness operates within the ICC as an underlying epistemic and structural force that normalizes racial hierarchies through the application of white norms and values. While Qaddafi was tortured and brutally killed and the people of Libya increasingly trafficked across (or drowned in) the Mediterranean, Cameron, Obama, and Sarkozy continue to enjoy a life of luxury on the speaker circuit.

Yet again, we are confronted with Mills's moral non-knowing—whereby the ICC's refusal to confront its racial biases leads to flawed moral judgements. The ICC's selective prosecution of Black African leaders for war crimes, while failing to address the crimes of white Euro-American leaders in Afghanistan, Iraq, Libya, or Palestine, highlights how white ignorance shapes institutional operations, ensuring that racial hierarchies remain intact within international legal frameworks. Far from being a neutral arbiter of justice, the ICC's selective focus on African leaders reinforces a racialized moral order, perpetuating the epistemic and legal hierarchies that sustain

[47] ibid 77.

[48] Katherine Fallah and Ntina Tzouvala, 'Deploying Race, Employing Force: "African Mercenaries" and the 2011 NATO Intervention in Libya' (2021) 67 UCLA Law Review 1580.

[49] Mansour O El-Kikhia, *Libya's Qaddafi: The Politics of Contradiction* (University Press of Florida 1997).

[50] Ada Peter and Innocent Chiluwa, 'Making a Case for War: CNN and the Representations of Humanitarianism, Gadhafi, and NATO in the 2011 Bombing of Libya' in Innocent Chiluwa and Oliver Ramsbotham (eds), *Discourse, Media, and Conflict: Examining War and Resolution in the News* (Cambridge University Press 2022).

[51] Fallah and Tzouvala (n 48).

white supremacy in the global legal system.[52] For example, the ICC prosecutor, Karim Khan, successfully filed two applications for warrants of arrest for Israeli representatives, the occupying state, and three warrants for Palestinian representatives of the resisting state, a curious allocation of responsibility. Moreover, the statement by Khan is replete with racialized innuendos and biased decision-making. For example, he makes no mention of Israel's occupation of Palestinian territories, the legality of resistance when engaged in anti-colonial struggle for independence, or the state of apartheid Israel is perpetrating both within and beyond its territories. He speaks to Israel's 'right to defend itself' but not of the Palestinian rights of resistance or of return. He also misrepresents the 'siege' as beginning in 2023 rather than 2006 when Israel enclosed Gaza with a wall declared unlawful by the International Court of Justice (ICJ). Last, he expresses gratitude to Israeli victims for sharing their stories, while simultaneously refusing to meet with Palestinians before drawing up the charges. It is worth noting that Israel has since assassinated two of the Palestinian leaders, making a further mockery of the notion of universal justice as well as Khan's supplication to the zionist state.

In this section, I highlighted the ECtHR and ICC's respective roles in reinforcing a racialized international legal order. Through selective reasoning and moral non-knowing, these institutions advance a prejudicial view of those it considers beyond its ontological frame, applying contradictory legal argumentation to privilege white normativity, which it then uses to judge all behaviour and experience against. This prejudicial approach deepens a historic racial hierarchy that retains whiteness as a primordial standard for all peoples, especially non-white peoples who the law is meant to civilize. Building on these reflections, in the next section, I examine the broader influence of whiteness and white supremacy in shaping international law, arguing that these constructs are not merely incidental but central to the foundation and operation of international legal norms and practices. Understanding the role of whiteness is crucial for any antiracist praxis that seeks to dismantle the deep-rooted biases within global legal structures and to challenge the persistent inequities that characterize the international legal order.

3. Whiteness and the structuring of international law

In a recent article, Oona Hathaway and John Bowers present an empirical study of international legal scholarship.[53] Relying principally on HeinOnline, an American legal database, they examine patterns of publication and citation within the field, extrapolating from the data an assessment of scholarly influence.[54] Despite the problematic methodology, their conclusion has some merit: they determined that certain journals and scholars disproportionately shape the discourse in international law, with

[52] Asad G Kiyani, 'International Crime and the Politics of Criminal Theory: Voices and Conduct of Exclusion' (2015) 48(1) New York University Journal of International Law and Politics 129.

[53] Oona Hathaway and John Bowers, 'International Law Scholarship: An Empirical Study' (2024) 49 Yale Journal of International Law 101.

[54] ibid 104.

student-run United States (US)-based journals dominating the citation landscape. Importantly for this collection, the most-cited scholars are male, white, and located in the US.[55] To illustrate, the study shows that among the top one hundred most-cited authors, ninety-one are male and ninety-one are based in the US, illustrating a concentration of recognition that contributes to the erasure of non-white perspectives from debates on international law.[56]

Notably absent from the scholarship it references, as well as the article itself, is engagement with race or the racial dynamics inherent in legal scholarship. Despite the increasing awareness of racial hierarchies within knowledge production, the article makes no mention of the absence of race in the most-cited scholarship, reflecting a broader disinterest in racial issues in the field in general. We find further evidence of the erasure of race from debates on international law in an article by James Thuo Gathii. Having analysed data from what Hathaway and Bowers identified as the most cited journal of international law— the AJIL[57]—Gathii determined that of the 5,109 documents published between 1907 and 2021, only sixty-four engaged substantially with race.[58]

The omission in the Hathway–Bowers article, as well as the record of the AJIL, is further evidence of white ignorance in the legal academy, showcasing systematic oversight of racial matters in and racial perspectives on international law. These omissions are also representative of the pervasiveness of whiteness, where whiteness is often treated as a universal standard rather than a specific, racialized perspective; consider, for example, that Hathway and Bowers identify the ninety-one scholars as individuals who write about international law rather than about US-based perspectives on international law. Incidentally, the fact that the top-cited scholars are almost exclusively white is not deemed cause for alarm. Instead, it is treated as a prosaic fact the authors simply gloss over, with the word race never appearing in the text. Their disinterest in a startling imbalance highlights how whiteness operates as an invisible norm, shaping the epistemic boundaries of the field. The overwhelming whiteness of the demographic limits the scope of legal inquiry by normalizing a narrow, Eurocentric view that is subsequently treated as universal in character. The exclusion of non-white voices from the intellectual and moral debates that define international law—meaning the exclusion of the majority of humanity—is not even worthy of a footnote in an article.

As per Mills, whiteness as a concept extends beyond racial identity to encompass a set of cultural, epistemic, and moral assumptions that shape societal structures and power dynamics on a global scale. Culturally, whiteness establishes the standard for what is considered 'normal' or 'universal', privileging Western practices, languages, and aesthetics over those from non-Western cultures.[59] This dominance manifests in the privileging of Eurocentric perspectives within knowledge production, where academic disciplines like international law have traditionally been dominated by white,

55 ibid 117.
56 ibid 123.
57 ibid 113.
58 Gathii (n 2) 75.
59 Gevers (n 5).

Western scholars. Former Cambridge international law chair John Westlake previously declared that the institute of international law 'is the international society of the white race'.[60] Yet, these scholars' works are treated as the foundation of *universal* knowledge with many of today's luminaries both recognizing their racist character yet still treating them as foundational in the field.[61] For example, while almost all mainstream international law textbooks are written by Europeans and from a European perspective, at no point is the corpus represented as Eurocentric in character; rather, these texts are presented as objective and authoritative.[62]

Equally jarring is the way non-European ways of knowing and being are dismissed as parochial or, as the ECtHR explains, an affront to modern morality. To illustrate, consider the economic and climatic inequalities that fragment the world today. Third World states have consistently challenged the dominance of Western moral and legal paradigms in the articulation of strategies towards climate and economic justice.[63] Efforts by decolonizing states to secure economic justice through demands for a New International Economic Order in the 1970s were undermined by Western powers, who prioritized free market capitalism and neoliberal economic policies over the social goals of the Global South.[64] These Western-driven economic aspirations devalued alternative economic models rooted in communal ownership and social equity, which were more aligned with the values and needs of decolonizing states, while also harming them materially through the imposition of structural adjustment programmes, debt conditionalities, and trade regimes that undermined local growth and entrenched dependency.[65] Both the International Monetary Fund and World Bank were especially egregious in their approaches, advancing a neocolonial outlook that saw legal and financial instruments deployed to compel decolonizing states to adopt Western economic orthodoxy. Through this dual strategy of delegitimizing alternative models while imposing economic governance by—and for—the First World, international law persisted in its history of predation, stifling aspirations of economic autonomy. As a result, the dialectic between the wealth of former colonial powers and the impoverishment of the formerly colonized persisted, preserving a racialized distribution of power and resources. Similarly, in the arena of climate justice, Third World states have called for a fairer distribution of the burdens and responsibilities of climate change, emphasizing the historical responsibility of industrialized nations for global

[60] ibid 1672.

[61] Martti Koskenniemi, 'Race, Hierarchy and International Law: Lorimer's Legal Science' (2016) 27(2) European Journal of International Law 415.

[62] al Attar (n 6) 184.

[63] Julia Dehm, 'Carbon Colonialism or Climate Justice: Interrogating the International Climate Regime from a TWAIL Perspective' (2016) 33(3) Windsor Yearbook of Access to Justice 129; Antony Anghie, 'Legal Aspects of the New International Economic Order' (2015) 6(1) Humanity: An International Journal of Human Rights, Humanitarianism, and Development 145; Carmen Gonzalez and Sumudu Atapattut, 'International Environmental Law, Environmental Justice, and the Global South' (2017) 26 Transnational Law and Contemporary Problems 229; Mohsen al Attar and Alexander Reay, 'Tales of Economic Warfare: The Plunder of Venezuela' (2021) 13(1) Indian Journal of International Economic Law 1.

[64] Margot E Salomon, 'From NIEO to Now and the Unfinishable Story of Economic Justice' (2013) 62(1) International and Comparative Law Quarterly 31.

[65] Mohsen al Attar and Claire Smith, 'Racial Capitalism and the Dialectics of Development: Exposing the Limits and Lies of International Economic Law' (2024) 35 Law and Critique 149.

warming.[66] Yet, international climate agreements often reflect Western priorities, such as market-based solutions like carbon trading, which frequently fail to address the immediate and disproportionate impacts of climate change on vulnerable populations in the Global South.[67] By operating at these multiple levels—cultural, epistemic, and moral—whiteness perpetuates racial and economic inequality under the guise of universality, reinforcing its dominance within international law and beyond.

Of course, as Gathii's data verifies, the embedding of whiteness in international law has a long history, operating as an epistemic framework that dictates what is considered legitimate knowledge, whose experiences are authoritative, and whose rights are worthy of protection. For example, the principle of state sovereignty, a cornerstone of international law, is often invoked to protect the interests of powerful states while ignoring the sovereignty claims of marginalized or formerly colonized ones.[68] Humanitarian intervention, ostensibly aimed at protecting human rights, can thus be used to justify military interventions in Third World states such as Libya or Afghanistan, reinforcing a neocolonial order in which Western powers impose their will on weaker states under the guise of promoting democracy and human rights. In both cases, whiteness operates as an implicit standard that determines which states and peoples are granted full legal personhood and whose sovereignty and rights are subject to conditional recognition. As per Harrison Mbori's contribution to this collection, it is not only sovereignty doctrine that reveals shades of whiteness; the doctrines of discovery, *terra nullius*, native title, and *uti possidetis*, among others, were all premised on the superiority of European civilization and the presumed inferiority of non-European ones. These legal principles justified the dispossession of Indigenous lands, the enslavement of African peoples, and the imposition of European legal systems on colonized territories. In this way, whiteness was not only a racial category but also a legal and moral justification for the material domination of non-white peoples.

As discussed earlier, white ignorance involves the systematic exclusion of non-white perspectives and the denial of the historical and ongoing impacts of racial subordination. In the context of international legal scholarship, Hathaway and Bowers verify that white ignorance is alive and well as publishing and citation practices vanish Third World voices from the debate. The consequence of this entrenched whiteness is a distorted legal and moral order that perpetuates racial and cultural hierarchies on a global scale. It also preserved a cycle of moral non-knowing, where the structural inequalities embedded in the international legal system are either ignored or rationalized for the maintenance of order. In the following section, I examine the attempts of critical scholars to contextualize and challenge the role of whiteness in international law. Alongside critiques of the ways in which whiteness shapes legal norms and practices, they have also begun to rethink the epistemic foundations of international law and to centre the voices and experiences of those who have been historically marginalized by the international legal system.

[66] Sara L Seck, 'Revisiting Transnational Corporations and Extractive Industries: Climate Justice, Feminism, and State Sovereignty' (2017)(2) 26 Transnational Law and Contemporary Problems 383.

[67] Dehm (n 63).

[68] Chhaya Bhardwaj and Abhinav Mehrotra, 'Crawford, TWAIL, and Sovereign Equality of States: Similarity and Differences' (2022) 40(1) The Australian Year Book of International Law Online 89.

4. Epistemic resistance and Black dignity: beyond counter-narratives

As I've argued throughout this chapter, the prevailing whiteness of international law acts as an epistemic filter that selectively recognizes and legitimizes some knowledge systems while dismissing or silencing others. It presumes a universal standard based on European traditions, and this standard excludes the epistemic standpoints of racialized communities. Boaventura de Sousa Santos has labelled this as 'abyssal thinking' or a form of epistemic exclusion that negates non-European forms of knowledge.[69] To illustrate, despite the long history of Islamic and Chinese reflections on international law, those same textbooks only provide ornamental references, treating them as parochial interventions with self-referential value for the practising communities, but not beyond.

Critical legal scholars, particularly those engaged with Critical Race Theory (CRT) and Third World Approaches to International Law (TWAIL), have been at the forefront of efforts to challenge the entrenched white ignorance within the international legal system.[70] By foregrounding the colonial roots of legal doctrines and the ways in which these doctrines have legitimized racial injustice and economic subordination, CRT and TWAIL scholars aim to expose the structures of white ignorance that obscure the reality of a racialized hierarchy. One of the primary strategies employed by these scholars has been the creation of counter-narratives that recentre international law's development from the perspective of colonized and marginalized peoples.[71] A pioneer of this form of scholarship was Siba N'Zatioula Grovogui. His text on sovereignty, race, and self-determination documents how concepts like sovereignty were crafted to exclude non-European peoples from the international legal community, thereby justifying their subjugation.[72] Grovogui critiques the legal discourses of international law, especially decolonization, and their entanglement with racialized tropes about African peoples. Similarly, Natsu Taylor Saito explored the links between settler colonialism and structural racism, arguing that contemporary racial injustices are continuations of historical ones, rooted in the doctrines of manifest destiny and racialized sovereignty established during the European colonization of Indigenous lands.[73] Adrien Wing, Antony Anghie, Sundya Pahuja, Arnulf Lorca, George Galindo, E Tendayi Achiume, Balakrishnan Rajagopal, and many other scholars from across

[69] Boaventura de Sousa Santos, *Epistemologies of the South Justice against Epistemicide* (Paradigm Publishers 2014).

[70] James T Gathii, 'Writing Race and Identity in a Global Context: What CRT and TWAIL Can Learn From Each Other' (2020) 67 UCLA Law Review 1610.

[71] Mohsen al Attar, 'Subverting Eurocentric Epistemology: The Value of Nonsense When Designing Counterfactuals' in Ingo Venzke and Kevin Heller (eds), *Contingency in International Law: On The Possibilities of Different Legal Histories* (Oxford University Press 2021); Ali Abdi, 'Eurocentric Discourses and African Philosophies and Epistemologies of Education: Counter-Hegemonic Analyses and Responses' (2006) 36(1) International Education 15.

[72] Siba N'Zatioula Grovogui, *Sovereigns, Quasi Sovereigns, and Africans: Race and Self-Determination in International Law* (University of Minnesota Press 1996).

[73] Natsu Taylor Saito, *Settler Colonialism, Race, and the Law*, vol 2 (NYU Press 2020) <http://www.jstor.org/stable/j.ctv1jk0hvv> accessed 1 November 2024.

the Third World have since thickened the critique, revealing the historical and ongoing impacts of whiteness on international law.[74]

Sometimes, the scholarship is directly confrontational, challenging scholars who produce work that erases race. As mentioned, Gathii conducted a study on legal scholarship, with emphasis on AJIL and AJIL Unbound, its online companion, examining their engagement with race, racism, and racial subordination. Gathii revealed that race is almost entirely absent from the discourse in both publications, a stark reflection of how deeply white ignorance is embedded in the field.[75] Both in scholarship and in episteme, academics make the overt decision to exclude race from their reflections, establishing imaginary boundaries that situate racial hierarchies beyond the purview of international law.

Yet, despite the increasing efforts by critical scholars to expose the biases and injustices within the international legal system, the reliance of these same scholars on the language and institutions of that system limits their ability to envision truly radical alternatives.[76] This paradox highlights a critical issue within the broader field of critical legal scholarship: the extent to which scholars committed to reforming the international legal system may themselves be susceptible to the very white ignorance they critique. For instance, TWAIL's dual character—offering a critique of international law's prejudicial nature and a call for its preservation-cum-reform—creates an inherent tension.[77] While scholars like Grovogui, Saito, Anghie, and Chimni expose the biases and injustices embedded in the international legal system, rarely if ever do they advocate walking away from the frame and building something anew. To the contrary, their activism often rests on a doubling down on international law—or its imagined progressive cousin—to rescue the regime from itself. In this way, critical scholarship appears inadequate, cognizant of both white ignorance and moral non-knowing but motivated by a similar idealism to what we observe in the orthodox frame.

In addressing white ignorance in international law, counter-narratives have thus proven insufficient. As Mills explained, white ignorance is a pugilistic form of ignorance, one that refuses to recognize its own failings or, to be direct, its own ignorance. Moreover, while counter-narratives are valuable for challenging dominant histories and offering alternative perspectives, they are easily subsumed into the same epistemic frameworks they seek to critique. Notice, for example, the speed at which the AJIL and the European Journal of International Law (EJIL) have sought to welcome racial and Third World perspectives onto their boards, or the same textbooks on international

[74] E Tendayi Achiume, 'Reimagining International Law for Global Migration: Migration as Decolonization?' (2017) 111 AJIL Unbound 142; George Rodrigo Bandeira Galindo and César Yip, 'Customary International Law and the Third World: Do Not Step on the Grass' (2017) 16(2) Chinese Journal of International Law 251; Arnulf Becker Lorca, *Mestizo International Law: A Global Intellectual History 1842-1933* (Cambridge University Press 2014); Sundhya Pahuja, *Decolonising International Law: Development, Economic Growth and the Politics of Universality* (Cambridge University Press 2011); Balakrishnan Rajagopal, 'Counter-Hegemonic International Law: Rethinking Human Rights and Development as a Third World Strategy' (2006) 27(5) Third World Quarterly 767; Antony Anghie, *Imperialism, Sovereignty, and the Making of International Law* (Cambridge University Press 2005); Adrien Katherine Wing, *Critical Race Feminism: A Reader* (NYU Press 1997).

[75] Gathii (n 2).

[76] al Attar and Smith (n 65) 170.

[77] al Attar (n 13).

law that effaced race now include minor homages to critical scholarship. Yet, as Tshepo Madinglozi stated, some things cannot be decolonized. In the same breath as its gestures to critical scholars, EJIL, via its online blog, EJIL: Talk!, platformed a symposium on the law of armed conflict, coordinated by the Israeli military, raising questions about the intellectual, scholarly, and moral integrity of the journal: 'By platforming a conference on the laws of armed conflict organized by the military of an occupying power that is actively colonizing another people's territory, EJIL: Talk! is compelling the scholarly community, including the undersigned, to question the integrity of the blog as a space for serious debate on international law.'[78] When confronted with the decision to privilege persistent violators of international law, the editors of the journal declared the back-and-forth a 'valuable process',[79] thereby magnifying white ignorance within the debate once more. In lieu of these facile and false forms of engagement, José Medina proposes what he terms epistemic resistance.

Medina's epistemic resistance involves a deeper engagement with the structures of knowledge production, aiming to disrupt and transform the foundational assumptions that underpin dominant epistemic systems such as international law.[80] Deriving his understanding of power dynamics from Michel Foucault, Medina views power as pervasive and relational, meaning resistance should be equally versatile.[81] He argues that epistemic resistance must involve a critical examination of these power dynamics, particularly how certain knowledges are subjugated while others are privileged, within which spaces these dynamics materialize, and how they can be co-opted to serve as sites of resistance. In contrast to the counter-narrative strategy, epistemic resistance is not merely about adding new voices but fundamentally challenging the conditions under which knowledge is produced and normalized. Medina introduces the idea of 'epistemic friction', which refers to the productive tension created when marginalized perspectives are brought into conversation with dominant discourses.[82] This friction is essential for exposing and contesting the insensitivity and active ignorance that characterize whiteness.

Epistemic friction has both parallels and differences to what TWAIL scholars advocate for. The demand is for a freedom to think, theorize, and interpret the world from one's own location, unencumbered by the hegemony of Eurocentric thinking. In the context of international law, this might involve widening or multiplying the political referents we rely upon when articulating the norms and producing the interpretations. For example, the push for recognition of Indigenous rights and self-determination within international legal forums, captured by the adoption of the UN Declaration on

[78] Letter Authors, 'Joint Open Letter to the Editorial Board of the Blog of the European Journal of International Law (EJIL: Talk!)' (*EJIL: Talk!*, 3 October 2023) <https://www.ejiltalk.org/joint-open-letter-to-the-editorial-board-of-the-blog-of-the-european-journal-of-international-law-ejil-talk/> accessed 2 November 2024.

[79] Dapo Akande and others, 'Response to the Letter to the Editors Regarding the Publication of a Symposium Based on Papers Presented at an IDF Conference' (*EJIL: Talk!*, 3 October 2023) <https://www.ejiltalk.org/response-to-the-letter-to-the-editors-regarding-the-publication-of-a-symposium-based-on-papers-presented-at-an-idf-conference/> accessed 2 November 2024.

[80] Medina (n 12).

[81] José Medina, 'Toward a Foucaultian Epistemology of Resistance: Counter-Memory, Epistemic Friction, and Guerrilla Pluralism' (2011) 12 Foucault Studies 9.

[82] ibid 21.

the Rights of Indigenous Peoples (UNDRIP) highlights an attempt to challenge the dominant frame.[83] Despite its adoption by 144 states, it is important to note that it was a long-fought battle of twenty years and only yielded a General Assembly declaration. In addition, four white settler-colonial states—Australia, Canada, New Zealand, and the United States—voted against it.

Part of their opposition was linked to epistemic departure from state-centrism and liberalism heralded by the UNDRIP. Alongside recognition of collective rights to land, culture, and self-determination, the declaration affords standing to communities devoid of the usual trappings of a nation-state. Yet, the aim of the movement was not subversive in that they did not seek to overthrow the existing frame. Rather, their resistance materialized at the epistemic level as they sought to preserve their cosmologies vis-à-vis the logic that historically aimed to eradicate them. By asserting their own legal systems and practices, Indigenous communities have forced international law to grapple with alternative epistemologies that do not conform to Eurocentric notions of sovereignty and rights. Their resistance also highlights the structural limitations of international law when confronting its overriding white ignorance—the discomfort of an international law that does not recognize an episteme beyond its own. In this way, Indigenous legal activism embodies Medina's concept of epistemic friction by insisting on the coexistence and legitimacy of multiple legal epistemologies, challenging the epistemically exclusionary character of international law.

The push for epistemic plurality in international law is complicated because it challenges the universality that international law claims to uphold. Medina's epistemic resistance is especially relevant in this context as it centres the experiences of historically oppressed communities much as Rajagopal sought to do with his research into social movements.[84] What distinguishes epistemic resistance from other forms is the assertion of an alternative epistemic frame. Vincent Lloyd conceptualizes this struggle through the lens of Black Dignity.[85] Like Medina, Lloyd argues that the Black communities he researches are not simply reclaiming a sense of self-worth in the face of oppression, but redefining the terms of moral and legal engagement. To them, resistance seeks to achieve more than plurality or facile inclusivity. They wish to reimagine international law not as a system that can accommodate difference but as one that is fundamentally transformed by it.

Taken to its logical conclusion, these approaches raise difficult, perhaps impossible questions: Does our engagement with extant international law bind us to the logic of whiteness? Can we reconcile epistemic plurality with universal legality without reinforcing the epistemic singularity plurality aims to dismantle? Or, in more abstract terms, can we escape abyssal thinking? These are questions we must grapple with if

[83] Elvira Pulitano, '"The Right to Enjoy All Human Rights": The UN Declaration on the Rights of Indigenous Peoples and the Potential for Decolonial Cosmopolitanism' in Scott Richard Lyons and Shari M Huhndorf (eds), *The World, the Text, and the Indian: Global Dimensions of Native American Literature* (State University of New York Press 2017); Michael Fakhri, 'Third World Sovereignty, Indigenous Sovereignty, and Food Sovereignty: Living with Sovereignty despite the Map' (2018) 9(3–4) Transnational Legal Theory 218.

[84] Balakrishnan Rajagopal, 'International Law and Its Discontents: Rethinking the Global South' (2012) 106 ASIL Annual Meeting Proceedings 176.

[85] Vincent W Lloyd, *Black Dignity: The Struggle against Domination* (Yale University Press 2022).

we are to upend the whiteness that has historically stifled negatively racialized communities. As Medina and Lloyd demonstrate, epistemic resistance is not a one-time effort but a dynamic process always vulnerable to co-optation. Ultimately, an antiracist praxis requires not only producing counter-narratives that nudge the dominant frame but rethinking the epistemic conditions under which legal knowledge is produced and validated.

5. From whiteness to racelessness and back again

'If originally whiteness was race, then now it is racelessness, an equal status and a common history in which all have shared, with white privilege being conceptually erased.'[86] White ignorance and white normativity rehabilitate racism and perpetuate epistemic injustice, reconstructing white memory to affirm the supposed natural order of things. Under this order, veils and crucifixes are not parallel symbols of religious expression but deviance and truth, respectively.

The individuals and communities associated with these symbols are similarly demarcated: Christians enjoy full epistemic authority, while Muslims are consistently found lacking. International law, therefore, becomes complicit in racial subordination. The epistemic practices of white ignorance are not incidental; they are central to the way legal institutions uphold a racialized moral order, privileging whiteness as the ultimate standard of knowledge and morality.

Much of international law reflects a profound white ignorance that positions the subjectivity of the non-white other outside the realm of epistemic legitimacy and rationality, and consequently, outside the realm of law. As Mills notes: '[w]hiteness is originally coextensive with full humanity, so that the nonwhite Other is grasped through a historic array of concepts whose common denominator is their subjects' location on a lower ontological and moral rung.'[87] Non-white subjectivity is thus perpetually inferior, locked into an alternate temporality that is irreconcilable with the full humanity ascribed to whiteness. In this strategic demarcation of colour, race, and religion at both epistemic and legal levels, whiteness ensures that only one race is deemed capable of truly knowing and being.

Today, we are no longer blind to the ways race is effaced from international law. Rather, those who insist on denying the frame's reification of racial hierarchies are operating within an epistemology of ignorance, actively rejecting a reckoning that would call into question what they know and are committed to. The push to provincialize Europe requires us to provincialize international law as well; to recognize the Eurocentric assumptions that underpin its structure and practices.[88] This necessitates an epistemic resistance that critiques, yes, but actively disrupts and reimagines the foundational principles of international law.

[86] Mills (n 9) 28.
[87] ibid 25.
[88] Dipesh Chakrabarty, 'The Politics and Possibility of Historical Knowledge: Continuing the Conversation' (2011) 14(2) Postcolonial Studies 243.

To move beyond whiteness, we must cultivate international law through engagement with novel political referents—concepts, norms, and values that are not beholden to Eurocentric legacies but instead draw from other universals. Such referents would allow for the constitution of legal knowledge from heterodox spaces and through distinct lenses. By embracing epistemic resistance, we can begin to understand the racialized hierarchies embedded within international law and take steps towards one that champions new epistemic lines. Only through this resistance can international law transcend its colonial past and contribute to global futures not dictated by the moral and cognitive limitations of white ignorance.

2

Disrupting International Law's Colonial Afterlives of Human Property

Educating for a World Beyond Racial Capitalism and Unending Apartheids

Folúkẹ́ I Adébísí

1. Introduction: the colonial ontology of (international) law

Euro-modern inspired legal understandings of and interactions between bodies, property, and space demonstrate how law and the social construction of race are vital to underwriting and reproducing the colonial project. These understandings continue to be implicated in the unjust use of social and political power to dictate how 'some may live, and some must die'. This necropolitical process makes the production of 'vaccine apartheid' along the abyssal line inevitable. This is because the artificed category of race has been used across space-time as the fundamental technology to abstract property through manufactured identity traits, becoming a tool both for capital accumulation and dispossession from the category 'human'. This process also demarcates areas currently designated as the Global North and Global South as evidenced by substantial material distinctions between life-making and death-making modalities and conditions in these disparate zones, as well as the hierarchical instrumentalization of the human—making things and property out of life—otherwise described as racial capitalism. Colonial logics carry on, as afterlives, by the maintenance of these distinct conditions of life in divergent zones.

Despite its triumphs on the global scene—for example, the granting of flag-independence and the introduction of the international human rights law regime—international law has more often provided the fundamental architecture to maintain unjust demarcations and necropolitical zones. In her thesis on the colonial lives of property, Bhandar explains how Lockean justifications for private property and techniques of abstraction conflate legal meanings and ontologies of property, race, subject, and object.[1] Any examination of the relationship between law, colonialism, and race very quickly reveals how entangled these are with each other. To accurately understand one, we must reflect on their interactions with the other. Excursions into legal history are not mere journeys that describe the events that authored the law we have today. Journeys into the past also force us to interrogate the nature of Euro-modern law.

[1] Brenna Bhandar, *Colonial Lives of Property: Law, Land, and Racial Regimes of Ownership* (Duke University Press 2018).

Folúkẹ́ I Adébísí, *Disrupting International Law's Colonial Afterlives of Human Property* In: *Emancipating International Law*. Edited by: Mohsen al Attar and Claire Smith, Oxford University Press. © Folúkẹ́ I Adébísí 2026.
DOI: 10.1093/9780198935605.003.0004

In this chapter, I use the concept of Euro-modern law to also denote law's intimate interplay in the legitimation and universalization of Euro-modernity. Thus, when Antony Anghie argues that imperialism is 'a crucial element of the very being, the very character of international law',[2] he is suggesting that the character and logics of colonialism are carried forward in the language and concepts of international law, illustrating how the social process of law makes those processes contingent upon human structures of coercive and authoritative power. 'Law is a social process, a complex of human activities, and an adequate legal science must deal with human activity, with cause and effect, with the past and the future.'[3] Thus, in trying to unpack the role the law plays in racial inequality, a foray into how its nature is co-constitutive of racial categorization and colonialism is indispensable.

During the European Enlightenment, racial classifications and scientific racism undergirded much of socio-legal academic thought. Many enlightenment scholars, in their articulations of key legal and jurisprudential principles, completely denied the possibility of non-white/Black rationality, unalterably linking skin colour to seemingly inexorable socio-political, socioeconomic, and sociolegal destinies. For example, throughout John Westlake's (Honorary President of the Institute of International Law) works, he identifies clear reasoning as the preserve of European men and 'natives' as impossible to civilize. He suggests that Indigenous peoples can only be governed by the laws and political structures of 'a white government, alone capable of ensuring obedience'.[4] Westlake was exceptionally influential in the crafting of Euro-modern law—Dicey called him 'the instructor of judges'.[5] Describing Westlake's approach to international law as reliant on a clearly espoused racial contract, Christopher Gevers points to Westlake's foundational contribution to a hierarchical vision of international legal order.[6]

'Race' thus emerges through this process disguised as a biologically significant category with unfortunate political uses and implications. In reality, however, it exists as a fundamentally causative socio-political force with significant socio-legal influences and outcomes.[7] It is difficult to dispute the fundamental idea of race to the legitimated and globalized practices of racialized enslavement and exploitative colonization. What often gets dismissed, especially within legal research and education, is how these intertwined processes shape the very nature of law including its mechanisms, design, capacities, and the conditions of life that it enables. As Bhandar states: 'property ownership was central to the formation of the proper legal subject

[2] Antony Anghie, 'Towards a Postcolonial International Law' in Prabhakar Singh and Benoît Mayer (eds), *Critical International Law: Postrealism, Postcolonialism, and Transnationalism* (Oxford University Press 2014) 40.

[3] Felix S Cohen, 'Transcendental Nonsense and the Functional Approach' (1935) 35(6) Columbia Law Review 809, 844.

[4] John Westlake, *International Law: Peace*, vol 1 (Cambridge University Press 1904) 92.

[5] Chas Noble Gregory, 'Review: Memories of John Westlake' (1914) 8(3) American Journal of International Law 691, 692.

[6] Christopher Gevers, '"Unwhitening the World": Rethinking Race and International Law' (2021) 67 UCLA Law Review 1652.

[7] Folúkẹ́ Adébísí, *Decolonisation and Legal Knowledge: Reflections on Power and Possibility* (Bristol University Press 2023) 65–91.

in the political sphere.'[8] The enduring and repeated dispossession of Indigenous peoples of their land as well as African people of their personhood, was underpinned by legal concepts of property ownership in ways that had a fundamental impact on our legal understanding of what it means to be human. These legal innovations also served to produce particular relations to power for those who accumulated property and those who were dispossessed of land and/or became the object of property themselves.

The central critique of this chapter is on the role and ontology of Euro-modern law. As a product and producer of present and historical colonial logics, international law is tailored to produce death-making logics that privilege property-making and property rights over earth-living. I illustrate this dynamic via what is called a 'vaccine apartheid' to explain how logics of coloniality and racial demarcations replicate themselves through legal understandings of what is property and ownership, as well as law's privileging of market imperatives over the protection of life. In other words, the colonial afterlives of property continue to make lives colonial through the co-constitution of Euro-modern law and race.

Within this colonial-necropolitical landscape, justice requires more than 'helping' the oppressed receive some succour for manufactured disadvantage. Indeed, exiting this landscape and the environmental catastrophe, systemic global racial violence, and extreme poverty it produces, requires a fundamental reconceptualization of law's normative standards, meanings, and role. Justice demands new ways of thinking about law, life, justice, and society. For example, while attempts were pursued to reverse vaccine apartheid, this reform (and similar reforms) is impossible to achieve without acknowledging how the technology of race and abstraction is a fundamental part of international law's logics. Beyond justice, decolonization is an opportunity to engage with a disruption of these logics. But this disruption has to be conceived of with a clear understanding of what decolonization is, our role within it, the nature of the world we wish to break from, and the world we want to build.

2. Law's human, abstraction, and the use of law toprivilege property over life

Euro-modern law, domestic and international, has shaped global structures, human behaviour, and norms. Law's pretensions to objectivity, neutrality, and universality conceal its dealings in injustice and its social (re)production of inequality on a global scale. A lot of this reproduction is generated almost passively—through the making of meanings that obscure hierarchies within themselves. Thus, a large part of law operates behind a veil that hides the maldistribution of power and possibility across manufactured hierarchies of life.

Euro-modern law has the power to control and punish human behaviour within and beyond the nation state. However, this is not where it displays its most destructive and effective power. This power is demonstrated in its ability to compel people globally to accept the disposability of necropolitics. Inequality, violence, and destruction

[8] Bhandar (n 1) 4.

are the outcomes of the capitalist-colonial-enslavement project yet are presented as naturally occurring, even inevitable.[9] Achille Mbembé defines necropolitics as '[t]he ultimate expression of sovereignty [that] largely resides in the power and capacity to dictate who is able to live and who must die'.[10] In other words, humanity has accepted a structure of the world that produces racial violence, extreme poverty, and environmental devastation as the only possible operating logic, enlisting the people oppressed by it towards its preservation. The necropolitical sphere even requires that premature death be, not just a possible outcome, but the seemingly-natural-yet-inevitable outcome for particular members of its population.

Such sociopolitical hierarchies are preserved by making inequality appear natural as captured by categories such as race, gender, class, and sexuality. Through a historical prism, we see how these hierarchies were created to devalue women's labour, enslave Africans, and dispossess Indigenous peoples. In this way, the contours of the category 'human' were profoundly shaped by colonial epistemes. It is not just that manufactured characteristics resulted in differential treatment under the law, but that the constitution of the category 'human' under Euro-modern law, evolving through periods of racialized enslavement and exploitative colonization, produced Euro-modern exclusions from this category. The purportedly neutral category of the 'human' is not universally open. To the contrary, as Wynter argued, there can be no disruption to the violent continuities of the 'coloniality of power' without a renewal of the human outside 'the terms of its present descriptive statement . . . Man and its over-representation'.[11]

The dehumanization of the category 'human' has produced grave and detrimental material effects. This includes the establishment of hierarchies and conditionalities within the category human, attendant overexploitation of human labour and the earth, and law's inability to protect life above material gain. This final chilling effect emanates largely from the ways in which the law has been used to make property out of everything, for the benefit of very few.

One mechanism through which law makes property out of life is the process of 'abstraction'. Abstraction is a process of conceptualization that reduces/erases the numerous properties of a phenomenon, such that its meaning is restricted to a desired instrumental use. Legal knowledge, in particular, uses abstraction to produce coterminous colonial property logics about the human, (in)tangible property, and land. Thus, Ruth Wilson Gilmore calls racism itself an abstraction.[12] 'Abstraction renders things theory, but it also can render them white possessions: it muffles the voices of Indigenous sovereign subjects, but they do not cease to speak.'[13]

Similarly, writing about the colonial lives of property, Bhandar finds the commodity logic of abstraction particularly violent in its erasure of prior interests to colonized land

[9] Adébísí (n 7) 39–40.

[10] Achille Mbembe, *Necropolitics* (Duke University Press 2019) 66.

[11] Sylvia Wynter, 'Unsettling the Coloniality of Being/Power/Truth/Freedom: Towards the Human, After Man, Its Overrepresentation—An Argument' (2003) 3(3) CR: The New Centennial Review 257, 268.

[12] Ruth Wilson Gilmore, 'Fatal Couplings of Power and Difference: Notes on Racism and Geography' (2002) 54(1) The Professional Geographer 15, 16.

[13] Elizabeth Strakosch and Alissa Macoun, 'The Violence of Analogy: Abstraction, Neoliberalism and Settler Colonial Possession' (2020) 23(4) Postcolonial Studies 505, 520.

as well as through the racial classification of human beings[14]—both of which allowed for the violent but legitimate creation, acquisition, and retention by colonial powers of the means of capital production. When bankrupt feudal landlords in Scotland and Ireland increased their rents and maximized land use, they instituted land enclosures and the removal of *othered* peoples who already inhabited the land. These removals, known as 'clearances', were supported by scholarly reconceptualizations of who could be removed from land (partial origins of racialization) and the nature of land itself. In the initial stages of colonialism, the practice of enclosure underwrote the creation of property, as coerced labour and land were also enclosed. Today, the logics of enclosure, alienation, and improvement have been masked in liberal language, now reaching well beyond enclosure of land and labour into legitimating enclosures of health, education, knowledge, social care, and other societal goods. This process, Nancy Fraser argues, goes beyond 'exploitation', and describes an 'expropriation' that indicates the perpetual entanglement between capitalism and racial oppression.[15] Law reveals itself as a past and present colonial discipline. Within law, both bodies and space-time have been revalued and redefined to meet the needs of enclosure, property-making, and capital accumulation—and not the protection of life. As I explore in the forthcoming section, 'vaccine apartheid' presents us with both an example and effect of the continuation of these logics.

Before proceeding, however, it is necessary to engage with another conundrum: the ineffectiveness of using international law to try to mitigate the results of its racial violence. If the law's nature is instrumentation and abstraction through racialization and property-fication, can we really find a solution within it? A closer look at the colonial use of law illustrates its entanglement with instrumentation for the purpose of capital accumulation. The usage of a structure changes the nature of the structure. Sara Ahmed's writings on 'use' are instructive on this point. She writes that 'use' can sometimes become a subversion of 'function' as the way a thing is used subverts or even obliterates its supposed function: 'The more a path is used, the more a path is used.'[16] 'Use' is how the past lives on in the present. Use is how lawful becomes normal, natural, the way things are, and the way things must be.

Invasion and dispossession, dehumanization and annihilation of Indigenous populations requires repeat violations of the normative foundations underpinning Euro-modern law.[17] A successful invasion demands legitimation through the introduction of the colonizer's law alongside a simultaneous de-legitimation of the law of the colonized. In the abstraction of and from time that produces the colonial moment, the laws of those colonized are rewritten as culture, custom, tradition, primitive practices, and, ultimately, non-law. Thus, Euro-modern law places Euro-America at the centre of the world; it is intimately tied to these origins and uses of law as well as the interests and desires of place.[18]

[14] Bhandar (n 1) 29.

[15] Nancy Fraser, 'Expropriation and Exploitation in Racialized Capitalism: A Reply to Michael Dawson' (2016) 3(1) Critical Historical Studies 163.

[16] Sara Ahmed, *What's the Use? On the Uses of Use* (Duke University Press 2019) 41.

[17] Charles W Mills, *The Racial Contract* (Cornell University Press 2014) 4.

[18] Eve Darian-Smith, 'Postcolonial Theories of Law' in Reza Banakar and Max Travers (eds) *Law and Social Theory* (Hart 2013) 247–64; Eve Darian-Smith, 'Postcolonial Law' in James D Wright (ed), *International Encyclopedia of the Social & Behavioral Sciences* (Oxford University Press 2015) 647–51.

Anghie charts the origins and practice of international law in the universalization of Euro-modern legality. He achieves this by examining processes of appropriation of Indigenous land, coercion of unfree labour, the administration of nation-states, and the emergence of the current global and commercial order that were made legal.[19] Thus the international legal order is characterized by various form of inequality. Linarelli, Salomon, and Sonarajah argue that international law establishes and maintains a permanence of misery, driven by capitalist need and greed, inaugurated by a world structure advancing on classifications of humanity into hierarchies, geographies, and acceptable orders.[20] In essence, the colonial encounter, 'generated a set of mechanisms . . . which operate to empower certain societies and exclude others'.[21] This contingent empowerment and disempowerment introduces and reproduces modalities of life and death, and results in profligate life for some and proximity to death for others or necropolitics.

I make very little distinction between the character of Euro-modern international law and Euro-modern domestic law. Though, for many, state law is not often thought of as an integral part of the structures of ongoing colonialism. States, and their laws, though considered to be the key agents and producers of international law, are treated as emerging mostly from the will of the people within each state's boundaries.[22] From this perspective, the law that operates within those boundaries is insulated by those boundaries and thus from the colonial-cum-misery of international law. Nevertheless, entrenched entanglements between colonialism, national legal jurisprudence, and international law have been identified by many writers.[23] Furthermore, state borders and their creation are central to international law and cannot exist without it. International law and colonial logics heavily influence law's ontology, not only beyond state borders, but also within them. As Anghie argues, the demarcation of states between sovereign and non-sovereign is a product of the universalizing logic of colonialism that establishes restrictive Eurocentric standards for 'political being' and circulated globally.[24]

Likewise, current notions of statehood are heavily inspired by principles that emerged through the processes by which European states exited from their empires, termed the political/administrative decolonization of colonies. This form of decolonization, according to Kreijen, was achieved by a 'legal trick' that attempted to normativize into states colonial territories that were no more than 'mere legal fiction'.[25] What is more appropriately called 'flag independence' is thus exposed as colonialism reifying itself, bleeding into and across fabricated borders, evolving to meet

[19] Antony Anghie, *Imperialism, Sovereignty and the Making of International Law* (Cambridge University Press 2005).

[20] John Linarelli, Margot E Salomon, and Muthucumaraswamy Sornarajah, *The Misery of International Law: Confrontations with Injustice in the Global Economy* (Oxford University Press 2018).

[21] Anghie (n 2) 140.

[22] Luis Eslava and Sundhya Pahuja, 'The State and International Law: A Reading from the Global South' (2020) 11(1) Humanity: An International Journal of Human Rights, Humanitarianism, and Development 118, 118.

[23] Kojo Koram, *Uncommon Wealth: Britain and the Aftermath of Empire* (John Murray 2022).

[24] Anghie (n 19) 196–244.

[25] Gérard Kreijen, *State Failure, Sovereignty and Effectiveness: Legal Lessons from the Decolonization of Sub-Saharan Africa* (Martinus Nijhoff 2004) 148.

the demands of a changing world, while preserving and benefiting from its powerful hierarchies. It is important to note that for states of the formerly colonized, independence and recognition within the international sphere was often dependent on adopting Euro-modern legal structures and political forms.[26] This recognition by Euro-modernity was vital for trade, travel, and development, but also served to provide narrow boundaries and formats for trade, travel, and development. Therefore, this transformation from colony to not-quite-independent state is better called 'flag independence'. This naming denotes the ways in which these states' independence extended only to their ownership of a flag, but not much else. They and their citizens' destinies are still directed by the colonial project and its rules of order—including the rules for statehood. According to Jean d'Aspremont, current principles for statehood emerged in the second part of the twentieth century. They are based on an imaginary genealogy and anthropomorphism put into service for the alleviation of the post-colonial anxieties of Euro-modern states who were facing an influx of non-European actors into the international legal sphere.[27] These anxieties were triggered by the desire to maintain the abyssal line and the colonial loot and subsequent riches abstracted from its creation.[28] Thus, state laws that cohere around the concept of natural borders rely on and reproduce the same colonial logics of instrumentalization of race and resources discussed above. The state itself is an abstraction.

As a result, for much of the world, the misery and coloniality inherent in international law create conditions within the state and the factors (such as violent borders) that keep people confined inside the state. The processes by which these world structures are produced relied on brutal and violent destruction of life—through, for example, the massive population losses occasioned by racialized enslavement.[29] The result has been to inaugurate violent modalities of life for racialized peoples, to dispossess Indigenous peoples, and to enable the unjust enrichment of those placed way 'above the line of the human'.[30] Colonial brutalities were underwritten by the law, therefore, through practices that seek to hold on to colonial gain and refuse justice for colonial violences. These brutalities have embedded within Euro-modern law, logics that continue to violently disregard the integral value of human life. This disregard includes the refusal to recognize epistemologies and jurisprudences beyond Euro-modernity that have always exercised alternative ways of being and doing in the world—including the protection of the earth and respect for all life. It is these colonial refusals to prioritize life that are both continued and exemplified by 'vaccine apartheid'.

[26] Darian-Smith, 'Postcolonial Theories of Law' (n 18) 247, 249, 255; Darian-Smith, 'Postcolonial Law' (n 18) 647.

[27] Jean D'Aspremont, 'Statehood and Recognition in International Law: A Post-Colonial Invention' in Giuliana Ziccardi Capaldo (eds), *The Global Community Yearbook of International Law and Jurisprudence* (Oxford University Press 2018) 139–52.

[28] Nadine El-Enany, *(B)ordering Britain* (Manchester University Press 2020) 74, 130–31.

[29] David Eltis, 'The Volume and Structure of the Transatlantic Slave Trade: A Reassessment' (2001) 58(1) The William and Mary Quarterly 17; James A Rawley and Stephen D Behrendt, *The Transatlantic Slave Trade: A History* (University of Nebraska Press 2005) 365; David Maybury-Lewis, 'Genocide Against Indigenous Peoples' in Alexander Hinton (ed), *Annihilating Difference: The Anthropology of Genocide* (University of California Press 2002) 43, 46–48.

[30] Ramon Grosfoguel, 'What Is Racism?' (2016) 22(1) Journal of World-Systems Research 9, 15.

3. What is 'vaccine apartheid'?

Vaccine apartheid describes unequal access to the COVID-19 vaccine, an inequality that centres the logics of abstraction, property-making, and disposability of *othered* humans in action. The Global North, an area that benefited from the colonial global economy,[31] has enjoyed broad access to the vaccine. In the areas designated the Global South, where formerly colonized nations are found, access to the vaccine has been poor. By August 2021, only 1.3 per cent of people in 'low-income countries' had received at least one dose of the vaccine, compared to 70 per cent in the United Kingdom (a 'high-income country').[32]

It should be noted that in the early days of the pandemic, a global coalition emerged to develop the vaccines. However, this 'cooperation', which pooled labour, data, and knowledge, did not extend to distribution. This disparity replicates patterns surrounding the extraction of human and capital resources from the Global South to enrich the Global North, underpinned by logics of enclosure of property. In this case, knowledge and raw materials for vaccine production were enclosed. Yet, many Global South countries were not passive observers with many actively involved in production and trials.

This apartheid also extends to practices that exploit the divergences built into the international order. In some cases, manufacturers have offered vaccines at higher prices to Global South countries—some African nations paid more than double per dose.[33] In response, Global South states petitioned for a TRIPS waiver at the World Trade Organization to permit them to produce the vaccines at affordable prices, a measure the EU and UK actively campaigned against.[34] The COVAX programme was also plagued by dubious ethical practices. For example, there have been numerous reports of donations of near-expired vaccines.[35] Results of vaccine apartheid have been devastating including the morally shattering statistic that nine out of every ten paediatric deaths due to COVID-19 occurred in 'low-income countries'. Children in low-income countries are also more vulnerable to becoming COVID orphans.[36]

The lines of vaccine apartheid bolster the global colour line. Grosfoguel uses Fanon's concepts of spatial othering to illustrate how 'there is no recognition of the humanity of the other'.[37] In the past and present 'race' and the law have enacted this unrecognition. It must be understood that the purpose of unrecognition was not 'dehumanization', understood here as the instrumentalization and thus distortion of the category 'human'. Rather, the purpose was the production and retention of property

[31] Gurminder K Bhambra, 'Colonial Global Economy: Towards a Theoretical Reorientation of Political Economy' (2021) 28(2) Review of International Political Economy 307.

[32] Vanessa S Lanziotti and others, 'Vaccine Apartheid: This Is Not the Way to End the Pandemic' (2022) 58(2) Journal of Paediatrics and Child Health 228.

[33] ibid 229.

[34] Simar Singh Bajaj Lwando Maki, and Fatima Cody Stanford, 'Vaccine Apartheid: Global Cooperation and Equity' (2022) 399(10334) The Lancet 1452, 1453.

[35] Denise N Obinna, 'Solidarity across Borders: A Pragmatic Need for Global COVID-19 Vaccine Equity' (2022) 37(1) International Journal of Health Planning and Management 21, 22.

[36] Eva Miranda Marwali and others, 'Paediatric COVID-19 Mortality: A Database Analysis of the Impact of Health Resource Disparity' (2022) 6(1) BMJ Paediatrics Open 1.

[37] Grosfoguel (n 30) 14.

and its attendant largesse. Property is legitimated and manufactured out of land, life, and labour to support the accumulation of capital. As Fraser notes, the outcome of the unrecognition of the other's humanity is to rework the largesse to which the privileged of society can legitimately lay claim. '[T]he subjection of those whom capital expropriates is a hidden condition of possibility for the freedom of those whom it exploits.'[38]

Across time and space, racialized, colonized, and Indigenous populations are marked out through logics of structured oppression. The law was and is integral to those structures. The colonial lives of property make lives colonial through the co-constitution of Euro-modern law and race. As I argued above through Anghie and Bhandar, the history of international law is littered with examples of unrecognition for accumulation. These were the social dynamics that underwrote apartheid in South Africa and the reluctance of the international community to interrupt the clear brutalities of the regime including legalized access to unfree labour, cheap resources, and boundless land. Similarly, the racialized nature of vaccine inequality and its resulting devastation provoked the adoption of the phrase 'vaccine apartheid'. This points directly to the institutionalized racial segregation legitimized by law in South Africa from 1948 to 1994. While attempts have been made to reverse vaccine apartheid, this reform (and similar reforms) is impossible without acknowledging how technologies of race and abstraction are fundamental to international law's logics. A disruption of these logics is necessary.

4. (International) law's race towards eternal apartheid and the making of everything property

As argued above, race was and continues to be a technology of political and economic domination. Race is not an objective or neutral classification of humanity, but an evolving, instrumental one that serves to identify populations for unfree labour and who could be legitimately deprived of their lives, lands, and resources. The evolving use of race further instrumentalizes bodies and resources for the accumulation of capital. It is important, however, that we pay attention to the contemporary effects of that history. These are exemplified by vaccine apartheid and how it results in the 'state-sanctioned or extra-legal production and exploitation of group-differentiated vulnerability to premature death'.[39] In other words, the manufacture, introduction, and continuation of racialization functions to produce material effects on a global scale, through racialized enslavement, commodification of land, and settler colonialism.

What we understand as modernity is underpinned by, and constitutive of, these material processes. Bhandar argues that race-making practices are entangled with property-making practices and cannot be distinguished into cause and effect. 'Abstraction functions in such a way so as to create legal forms of property and racial ontologies coterminously'[40] where the operation of this logic 'fuses property and

[38] Fraser (n 15) 166.

[39] Ruth Wilson Gilmore, *Golden Gulag: Prisons, Surplus, Crisis, and Opposition in Globalizing California* (University of California Press 2007) 28.

[40] Brenna Bhandar, 'Property, Law, and Race: Modes of Abstraction' (2014) 4(1) UC Irvine Law Review 203, 211.

race together'.[41] Legal knowledge relies on similar logics to produce meanings about property, race, and what it means to be properly human. Accordingly, racialized modalities of property-making and accumulation rely on hierarchies of humanity that 'unrecognize' the full complexity of what makes us human. Not only is race a technology of dispossession of land, resources, and liberty, but it also dispossesses racialized populations from the category 'human' and thus from living, through the distorting of the category itself. The law's role in this process is to protect privilege and access to more than equal rights to property and life. Racial capitalism is useful to understanding law's role and connection in this.

One of the first known uses of the term 'racial capitalism' was in a 1976 pamphlet. Anti-apartheid activists argued that South African racism was fortified by capitalist growth. To them, capitalism was the soil through which racism blossomed. South Africa's economic growth thus benefited from apartheid, meaning that capitalism could not resolve apartheid.[42] Cedric Robinson took this argument further by illustrating how racial violence constitutes a permanent, rather than anterior, condition of capital accumulation.[43] Through evolving modalities and racial hierarchies, racial capitalism adduces different values to life and labour, contingent on manufacturing racial categories assigned to that very life and labour.[44] Law provides the lubricant upon which racial capitalism rolls smoothly, aiding with the commodifying of everything. However, different valuations come into play, not just through the commodity, but also the differential values placed on people that make up the market. As Gilmore explains: '[c]apitalism requires inequality, and racism [and sexism, classism, ableism, etc] enshrines it'.[45] It is important to note that Gilmore recognizes the ability of capitalism to commodify anything, even the idleness of prison populations.[46] In that sense legitimate disposability still retains an accumulative aspect.

Law, therefore, as the chief regulator of capitalism is important to the normalization, rationalization, and naturalization of the hierarchies required by capitalism. Racialization enters into the discourse as the process by which the creation of race becomes a salient and normalized tool implicated in the organization of all social relations.[47] Racialization assists in the marking of bodies (and spaces) that could be legitimately colonized or commodified. In one sense, all bodies are racialized: white bodies are racialized as normal or normative just as other bodies are racialized as either exploitable or disposable. By preserving these colonial lines of differentiation and the effects thereof, the law is complicit in enshrining inequality and expropriation.

[41] ibid 205.

[42] David Ivon Jones, *Communism in South Africa: Presented to the Executive of the Third International on Behalf of the International Socialist League South Africa* (LSL Press 1921).

[43] Cedric J Robinson, *Black Marxism: The Making of the Black Radical Tradition* (University of North Carolina Press 2005) 29–44.

[44] Ida Danewid, 'The Fire This Time: Grenfell, Racial Capitalism and the Urbanisation of Empire' (2020) 26(1) European Journal of International Relations 289, 297.

[45] Ruth Wilson Gilmore, 'The Worrying State of the Anti-Prison Movement' (*Social Justice*, 23 February 2015) <http://www.socialjusticejournal.org/the-worrying-state-of-the-anti-prison-movement/> accessed 4 November 2024 (the added parentheses are mine).

[46] Wilson Gilmore (n 39) 21.

[47] Steve Garner, *Racisms: An Introduction* (SAGE 2017) 3.

Vaccine apartheid is thus created by law's entanglement with capitalism's production of bodies devalued and instrumentalized as exploitable, expropriated, and/or disposable. As stated in various ways above, the instrumentalization and commodification of bodies puts them perpetually at risk of being exploited by capital. In the field of global health, vaccine apartheid is only one among many ways in which this devaluation comes in direct conflict with the preservation of life. We see this in Robert Koch's early twentieth-century sleeping sickness concentration camps in East Africa for the harmful testing of Atoxyl,[48] and many incidents of testing of medications on Africans (Pfizer's experiments in Northern Nigeria).[49]

In the wider body of law, there are many instances where we observe the law's use as the normalization of dispossession through enslavement and colonization. In *Gregson v Gilbert*, a ship's crew confessed to the deliberate killing by drowning of 130 African captives onboard their slave ship. Despite their confession, the court refused to consider murder a relevant cause of action.[50] The case was instead determined on legal principles of insurance indicating that, alive or dead, the bodies and lives of African captives were only recognized in law as commodities. In *Re: Southern Rhodesia*, the court disregarded the jurisprudence of Indigenous peoples and their practices of land ownership.[51] This legitimized the dispossession of their land, granting ownership of it to the English settlers who had violently removed the Matabele and Mashona people from resource-rich and fertile land. Through law's 'rationality', racialized bodies are simultaneously made exploitable and disposable according to the needs of capital. Race manufacturing is essential to the social production of exploitability/disposability.

Vaccine apartheid was made inevitable. Its emergence illustrates the expansion of colonial logics and their legitimation by Euro-modern law. Property-making and race-making practices expand the concept of enclosure to include racialized labour and hegemonic knowledge. Such knowledge has never been produced solely above the abyssal line, but also through discounted contributions from below the abyssal line. However, law and legal knowledge have both been essential to reproducing these enclosures with necropolitical effect.

In the following section, I extend my argument about the racialized capitalist colonial logics of law beyond the present and the past and project into the future. The continuing colonial lives of property leave humanity unequally and cumulatively vulnerable to climate change, conflict, poverty, and racial violence.

[48] Wolfgang U Eckart, 'The Colony as Laboratory: German Sleeping Sickness Campaigns in German East Africa and in Togo, 1900-1914' (2002) 24(1) History and Philosophy of the Life Sciences 69. Koch experimented on his patients with Atoxyl, a reagent containing arsenic known to cause pain, blindness, and even death.

[49] Jacqui Wise, 'Pfizer Accused of Testing New Drug without Ethical Approval' (2001) 322 (7280) British Medical Journal 194. In *Abdullahi v Pfizer, Inc*, 2002 US Dist LEXIS 17436 at 1, Pfizer argued that it was not required to obtain informed consent for experimental drug trials in Africa. The facts of the incident inspired the book *The Constant Gardener* by John le Carré.

[50] *Gregson v Gilbert* (1783) 99 ER 629.

[51] *Re: Southern Rhodesia* (1919) AC 211.

5. Can we decolonize the Capitalocene: what lies beyond a vaccine apartheid?

The conception of the 'Anthropocene' recognizes that human activity has had a catastrophic effect on the environment. This epoch was inaugurated through humanity's unequal overemphasis on the exceptionalism of the human. Moreover, human exceptionalism proceeds unequally by casting many out of the category 'human' through varied uses of classification—race, gender, class, ability, for instance. We thus observe in the Anthropocene the evolving use of unfree/coerced labour, destruction of nature, over-consumption, and false scarcities, which are then implicated in environmental disasters and climate emergencies;[52] essentially, the redefinition of the human and 'the negation of earth'.[53] By disrupting and endangering planetary relations, the Anthropocene ushers in new challenges and thus demands new legal thinking to handle these challenges. In other words, we must consider how law can help us think beyond events such as climate devastation, racial violence, and vaccine apartheid, to consider possibilities for disrupting the logics that produce them. This must be recognized as an existential conundrum as the structure tries to free itself from itself. Decolonization is one suggested means of disruption.

However, the initial question to be answered is 'what is decolonization?' I define decolonization as the continuous and evolving refusal of colonial conditions of life which were introduced and globalized through the capitalist-colonial-enslavement project via legal, political, social, and epistemic structures of power.[54] These refusals are context-dependent and reject the meanings and uses made of bodies and space-time by this evolving project. These contexts of refusals are epistemic, spatial, and political. They include anticolonial actions by colonized nations, during and beyond the moment of colonization; Indigenous peoples' quests for sovereignty and land back within and beyond settler colonies; as well as racially minoritized peoples' quests for equality, reparation, and racial justice within imperial metropoles. In other words, due to the broad range of peoples and places that seek to engage with decolonization, 'to decolonize' encapsulates a collection of connected activities and purposes that seek to fundamentally unseat colonially produced structures of coercive power and technologies of permanent dispossession and dehumanization that threaten human and planetary survival.

In this vein, contemporary action towards decolonization in higher education borrows this framework and cannot be restricted to curricular redesign. We cannot just teach international law differently. The task of academics in the face of the foregoing is to translate varied context-dependent theories and praxes of decolonization into our academic work—teaching, research, and ancillary administration. Deep knowledge of decolonization requires academics to learn and unlearn the nature of the tool that

[52] Farhana Sultana, 'The Unbearable Heaviness of Climate Coloniality' (2022) 99 Political Geography 102638.

[53] Rolando Vázquez, 'Precedence, Earth and the Anthropocene: Decolonizing Design' (2017) 15(1) Design Philosophy Papers 77, 78. See also Mark Jackson, 'On Decolonizing the Anthropocene: Disobedience via Plural Constitutions' (2020) 111(3) Annals of the American Association of Geographers 698.

[54] Adébísí (n 7) 12.

we have made our area of expertise. Unlearning is a necessary first step that involves tracing the complicity of disciplinary dictates and conceptual methods through to the emergence and maintenance of colonialism. Next, we must consider *how* we teach and research (international) law. How do we reveal the silences within the law? Last, we must constantly ask ourselves *why* we do it. What world do we want to build? What does a study of law look like that is not headed towards eternal apartheids? Answers to these questions are beyond the space available in this chapter. Nevertheless, I proffer here a few suggestions.

First, law schools should look for ways to engage deeply and continually with the foregoing themes across the curriculum and in research. Working more thematically prevents the atomization that characterizes contemporary decolonization discourse in the legal academy. These discourses focus on adding more authors from Black or Brown backgrounds to reading lists. Working thematically could utilize reading groups, staff–student partnerships, and research projects. These allow schools to unsettle the discipline in the classroom and in research while continually crafting new strands of thought. Therefore, rather than ask: 'how do we decolonize international law?', we are able to question the possibilities that eventuate the emergence and social production of international law and its underpinning normativities, and conceptualize what future possibilities that questioning may lead us to.

Second, I suggest that law schools make legal history a fundamental part of their entire curricula and research agendas. This would enable legal scholars to give better accounts of the legal histories of racial violence within and across the curriculum and research outputs. As such, we should be able to think through, in different contexts, the multitude of ways history plays on the present, especially the cultural amnesia surrounding racialized enslavement, exploitative colonization, and their entangled afterlives. Hopefully, this would lend us a new framework for teaching and researching subjects such as international law.

Finally, we need to rethink the purposes of the law school as only a place for producing new legal practitioners. I am arguing here for a law school dedicated to a fundamentally different aim. In other words, a law school dedicated to crafting legal knowledges that turn back on death-making—legal knowledges that oversee a social order that invites, allows, and equips us to live flourishing lives in relation and not possession. That is, living in harmonious relation with other humans, the earth, and diverse temporalities, and not living in instrumental, enclosed, and extractive possession of labour, land, and time. So, rather than an invitation to decolonize the law school or the law curriculum, this chapter poses and ends on a different question: *What could it mean for you the reader to dream of new anticolonial life-making worlds from within the law school?*

6. Conclusion

In this chapter, I have argued that the nature of law in general and international law particularly revolves around a category of human that, relying on racializing logics, instrumentalizes this category for capital accumulation and contingent dispossession. The law relies on abstraction and instrumentalization in ways which produce a necropolitical/death-making world. This has resulted in various injustices including vaccine apartheid.

To disrupt law's race towards unending inequality, racial violence, and the disaster of environmental catastrophe, we need ways of thinking about law that can disrupt the colonial afterlives of property. Decolonization may offer one way of thinking beyond this present conundrum, but we must understand it as a concept that extends far beyond a tool for curricular redesign. Ultimately, we must question how and if our discipline and intellectual tradition can be put in service of remaking a world whose ways of thinking and doing and being do not reproduce the structures from which we wish to disengage.

For legal academics our task is to use our epistemic tools and academic communities to envision new understandings of value, global structure, and un-property. To survive the dangers of eternal apartheids, unrelenting racial violence, and the Anthropocene, we must conceive of new concepts of society, new ways of being and doing. In addition to this, we need to think of new strategies to bring them to life.

3

Racialized Extractivism

A Tale of Fetishism, Narcissism, Primitive Accumulation, and Expropriation

Jason Haynes

1. Introduction

For centuries, peoples from primarily capital-exporting countries have, in the words of Karl Marx, 'fetishized'[1] the expropriation of various commodities, but especially precious geological materials from the Latin American and Caribbean (LAC) region. This obsession, which stands at the core of racial/racialized capitalism,[2] has driven many investors from capital-exporting countries in the Global North on desperate 'expeditions' for these materials across the length and breadth of the LAC region. These expeditions have often resulted in the exploitation, expropriation, and expulsion of racialized peoples. By 'racialized peoples', this chapter refers to peoples, particularly from the Global South, who have been, and continue to be, systematically oppressed and subordinated by the capitalist order not simply because of their darker skin tone, but more fundamentally because of deeply entrenched perceptions, structures, and processes that conceive of these non-white or non-European populations as racially inferior and thus unworthy of equal recognition and protection.[3] These populations are only useful to investors to the extent that social and economic value can be extracted from them.

Since the 1990s the LAC region has experienced a significant expansion in mining-related activities by foreign investors from capital-exporting countries, largely due to price increases of certain minerals on international markets and the depletion of the world's main reserves.[4] Today, the Inter-American Development Bank estimates that the extractives industry accounts for nearly 26 per cent of total foreign direct

[1] Karl Marx, *The Fetishism of Commodities: Power and Inequality* (Routledge 2021) 31–32.

[2] As will be further explained in Section 2 of this chapter, there are significant similarities in the arguments advanced by 'racial capitalism' and 'racialized capitalism' scholars in the context of the extractives industry. In this regard, this chapter uses the phrase 'racial/racialized capitalism' to describe the process by which perceived racial differences between white/European people and non-white/non-European people become socially constructed and re-inscribed as being natural and necessary through social, economic, political, and legal structures that serve to extract social and economic value from the latter.

[3] UN Human Rights Council, 'Global Extractivism and Racial Equality: Report of the Special Rapporteur on Contemporary Forms of Racism, Racial Discrimination, Xenophobia and Related Intolerance' (14 May 2019) UN Doc A/HRC/41/54 [42].

[4] Laura María Carvajal, 'Extractivisim in Latin America' (*UAF—LA The Urgent Action Fund for Latin America*, September 2016) <https://genderandenvironment.org/extractivism-in-latin-america/> accessed 7 February 2026, 9.

Jason Haynes, *Racialized Extractivism* In: *Emancipating International Law*. Edited by: Mohsen al Attar and Claire Smith, Oxford University Press. © Jason Haynes 2026. DOI: 10.1093/9780198935605.003.0005

investment in the LAC region.[5] More specifically, mining-related activities account for about 10 per cent of the GDP of Mexico, Bolivia, and Colombia, and more than 15 per cent of Chile's GDP,[6] while repatriated profits in the mining sector alone are approximately $50 billion annually.[7] These mining-related activities, which have their origins in a time when European powers laid claim to LAC countries whom they considered to be *terra nullius*, have had significant adverse impacts on the region, including environmental degradation, dispossession of communal owned lands, disruption of livelihoods, the infliction of violence, and mass casualties.

This chapter argues that racial/racialized capitalism animates the social, economic, political, and legal landscapes of the LAC region, with devastating consequences for racialized peoples. It agrees with Gathii and Tzouvala[8] who have recently argued that the international investment law regime, which forms a core part of international economic law, is deeply implicated in racial/racialized capitalism, but goes further by demonstrating *how* and *why* international investment law is racialized in the specific context of the extractives industry in the LAC region. In short, the international investment law regime legitimizes, reifies, and perpetuates commodity fetishism, narcissism, primitive accumulation, and expropriation in the context of this industry, thereby resulting in the further status subordination of negatively racialized peoples.

The chapter begins by situating the LAC region in its historical context. It then moves on to argue that the complex process of racialization begins with *commodity fetishism*, involving the conceptualization of non-white or non-European peoples as racially inferior, and thus their resources, including precious metals, as liable for conscription. Investors contemplate obsessively about owning these precious metals, but do not account for the human cost associated with the extractives industry for racialized peoples. I contend that the process of racialization quickly evolves from fetishism to *narcissism*, the latter of which is characterized by investors—with the endorsement of their home states—not only *thinking* that they are racially superior, but *acting* in a manner which demonstrates that they have a right, because of their racial superiority, to control and possess racialized people and their resources. Annihilation and appropriation define the narcissistic phase, and, in this respect, investors feel no guilt for their dehumanizing treatment of racialized peoples. The paper then moves on to argue that the racialization process becomes concretized through *primitive accumulation*, which involves the unabashed accumulation of profits by dispossessing racialized peoples of their lands, and extracting their resources, quite often by means of coercion, fraud, predation, extra-economic force, and extreme violence. This complex process reaches its zenith with *expropriation*, which, among other things, is characterized by investors embedding a long-term strategy for conscripting racialized peoples' labour, capacities, and resources, while actively utilizing asymmetrical legal

[5] Martin Walter, 'Extractives in Latin America and the Caribbean: The Basics' (*Inter-American Development Bank*, January 2016) <https://publications.iadb.org/en/extractives-latin-america-and-caribbean-basics> accessed 7 February 2026, 11.

[6] Alby Aguilar-Pesantes and others, 'A Comparative Study of Mining Control in Latin America' (2021) 1(1) Mining 6, 6.

[7] Martin Walter (n 5) 11.

[8] James Gathii and Ntina Tzouvala, 'Racial Capitalism and International Economic Law: Introduction' (2022) 25(2) Journal of International Economic Law 199.

frameworks, such as international investment law and its dispute settlement system, to silence resistance from racialized peoples.

The chapter's main contribution lies in its novel use of the concepts of fetishism, narcissism, primitive accumulation, and exploitation to explain investment treaty practice in the LAC region with respect to the extractives industry. In this context, it demonstrates the extent to which international investment law is underpinned by, and reproduces, racial/racialized capitalism. It interrogates several contentious investor-state arbitral awards in this regard, concluding that international investment law has contributed to the continued status subordination[9] of racialized peoples in the LAC region.

2. Reckoning with the past, confronting the challenges of the present

Kendall Brown's work on the history of mining in Latin America methodically traces the evolution of the extractives industry in the region from the colonial era to present.[10] He argues that from 1514, when gold production began in the LAC region, and from 1545 when silver production followed, Spanish conquistadors, Christopher Columbus and Hernán Cortés, fetishized about expropriating precious metals from the region.[11] He recalls that, during this time, gold and silver worth trillions of pesos in today's currency were refined.[12] Brown contends that the fetishization of gold and silver disrupted Indigenous communities through the exploitation of their labour and forced displacement of local populations. Decades later, millions of African peoples were brought to the Americas where they, having been enslaved, were systematically oppressed through the exploitation of their labour in gold mines, especially in Brazil.[13]

Between the sixteenth and nineteenth centuries, the exploitation of African enslaved peoples continued unabated, largely through the enactment of laws which concretized a dangerous dichotomy between the propertied 'colonizers' and the property-less 'colonized', the latter being regarded as racially inferior, and thus expendable 'property'.[14] The systematic exploitation of millions, coupled with the mass displacement of Indigenous peoples and the dispossession of their lands,[15] fuelled the attendant accumulation of capital that served Europe's developmental agenda, while simultaneously leading to the underdevelopment of Africa.[16] During this period, the

[9] Nancy Fraser, 'Rethinking Recognition' (2000) 3 New Left Review 107. Fraser explains that '[when] institutionalized patterns of cultural value . . . constitute some actors as inferior, excluded, wholly other, or simply invisible—in other words, as less than full partners in social interaction—then we can speak of misrecognition and status subordination'.

[10] Kendall Brown, *A History of Mining in Latin America: From the Colonial Era to the Present* (University of New Mexico Press 2012).

[11] Kendall Brown, 'Mercury and Silver Mining in the Colonial Atlantic'(*Oxford Research Encyclopedia of Latin American History*, 29 March 2017) <https://oxfordre.com/latinamericanhistory/view/10.1093/acrefore/9780199366439.001.0001/acrefore-9780199366439-e-394> accessed 7 Feburary 2026.

[12] ibid.

[13] David Eltis, *The Rise of African Slavery in The Americas* (Cambridge University Press 2000).

[14] Eric Williams, *Capitalism and Slavery* (University of North Carolina Press 1994).

[15] Eduardo Galeano, *Open Veins of Latin America: Five Centuries of the Pillage of a Continent* (New York University Press 1997).

[16] Walter Rodney, *How Europe Underdeveloped Africa* (Verso Books 2018).

untamed extraction of various commodities from the LAC region was viewed as the natural order of things, and the use of racial difference to justify such extractivism defined the capitalist order of the day.[17]

When Spanish and Portuguese colonial rule in Latin America ended between 1808 and 1825, Brown argues that a new dispensation was ushered in, the impetus for which, according to the Rachel Carson Center, was 'the nascent industrialization of Europe'.[18] This new dispensation was characterized by the transition from the production of precious metals to the production of industrial minerals; the gradual replacement of animal power with steam; the arrival of the railroad, which allowed the entry of new producers; and the replacement of the old refining process based on mercury by separation using floating and cyanide.[19] Meanwhile, in the English-speaking Americas, slavery was only abolished in 1834, though it was not until 1838 that those formerly enslaved could be said to have been formally emancipated.[20] Notwithstanding these developments, however, extractivism did not cease in the LAC region; in fact, these countries' orientation towards extractivism was consolidated during this period.[21]

When capital-exporting nations abandoned silver and adopted gold as the monetary standard from the 1890s onward, US and British corporations began to engage in mining in the Latin American region, but with an interesting twist; they sought to involve 'local entrepreneurs',[22] such as Bolivian businessman Simon Patiño, in the process of extraction to conceal the predatory practice under a cloak of legitimacy. The active enlisting of local entrepreneurs in extractivism, and the reproduction of what came to be known as racialized capitalism, is not merely a historical fact, but also a reality in contemporary investment law and practice, where local elites today often enter into asymmetrical investment contracts that dispossess local populations of their lands and deprive them of their livelihoods.[23] However, as Gargi Bhattacharyya has noted, the involvement of 'national bourgeoisies' in extractivism did not 'signal the advent of a post-racial capitalism'.[24] Bhattacharyya highlights that the process of racialization is not exclusively tied to any particular group, and given that 'the object of racialisation may change across time or be articulated variously across space . . . the emergence of national bourgeoisies in former European colonies does not alter the logic and continuation of racial capitalism'.[25] In other words, while national

[17] Catherine Hall, 'Racial Capitalism: What's in a Name?' (2022) 94 History Workshop Journal 5. Hall argues that 'capitalism was reliant on the elaboration, reproduction, and exploitation of ideas of racial difference'.

[18] Myna Santiago, 'Extracting Histories: Mining, Workers, and Environment' in Claudia Leal, José Augusto Pádua, and John Soluri (eds), *RCC Perspectives: New Environmental Histories of Latin America and the Caribbean* (Rachel Carson Center for Environment and Society 2013) 81.

[19] Guillermo Guajardo, 'A History of Mining in Latin America: From the Colonial Era to the Present by Kendall W. Brown' (2013) 54(3) Technology and Culture 659.

[20] Douglas Hall, 'The Apprenticeship Period in Jamaica, 1834–1838' (1953) 3(3) Caribbean Quarterly 142.

[21] Matthew Himley, 'Extractivist Geographies: Mining and Development in Late-Nineteenth and Early-Twentieth-Century Peru' (2019) 45(2) Latin American Perspectives 27.

[22] Brown (n 11).

[23] Jason Haynes and Antonius Hippolyte, 'The Coloniality of International Investment Law in the Commonwealth Caribbean' (2023) 72(1) International & Comparative Law Quarterly 105.

[24] Gargi Bhattacharyya, *Rethinking Racial Capitalism: Questions of Reproduction and Survival* (Rowman & Littlefield 2018).

[25] ibid 102.

bourgeoisies are complicit in racialization, their emergence does not eviscerate the entrenched logic of racial inferiority that constructs racialized peoples as dispensable, which is so central to capitalism's very existence.

By the time Latin American countries achieved independence in the nineteenth century, strong ideological sentiments about sovereignty over natural resources had grown in the region. In fact, Arnulf Becker Lorca has noted that much of the nineteenth century was spent 'consolidating independence in the new Latin American states',[26] and that, to this end, there were concerted efforts to foster 'broader allegiances with the liberal ideals of progress and civilization generated by the independence movement'.[27] Becker Lorca further recalls that, during this period:

> International law proved critical in providing Latin American politicians with a discourse to bolster the claim of sovereign autonomy for the new nations, and the attainment of international legal autonomy emerged as a prized benchmark for civilization.[28]

Latin American countries' staunch commitment to guarding their sovereign autonomy continued well into the twentieth century, notwithstanding virulent resistance from former colonial nations. More particularly, in response to a war-like blockade against Venezuela initiated by the United Kingdom and Germany, with diplomatic support from Italy, with respect to outstanding debts owed to bondholders, the Drago doctrine was enunciated.[29] Luis Drago, Argentina's then Minister of Foreign Affairs, vehemently opposed the use of blockades and similar types of interventions by former colonial powers against weaker Latin American states for outstanding debts, arguing that such interventions were inconsistent with these states' territorial sovereignty.[30] He contended that claims over outstanding debts were better settled through arbitration or other judicial means.

To give teeth to the Drago doctrine, Latin American countries forced the 'Calvo clause' into investment instruments.[31] This clause represented a fundamental departure from previous practice by requiring that foreign investors submit their disputes and obtain appropriate remedies from the municipal judiciaries of Latin American countries, rather than pursuing claims in accordance with the rules of their home countries or the rules of international law.[32] Gathii recalls that the clause was a 'rule of equal treatment' in that foreign investors and domestic investors would enjoy the same degree of protection.[33] Only when foreign investors experienced a denial of

[26] Arnulf Becker Lorca, 'International Law in Latin America or Latin American International Law-Rise, Fall, and Retrieval of a Tradition of Legal Thinking and Political Imagination' (2006) 47(1) Harvard International Law Journal 283.

[27] ibid.

[28] ibid.

[29] Luis Drago and Edward Nettles, 'The Drago Doctrine in International Law and Politics' (1928) 8(2) The Hispanic American Historical Review 204.

[30] Amos Hershey, 'The Calvo and Drago Doctrines' (1907) 1(1) American Journal of International Law 26.

[31] James Gathii, 'War's Legacy in International Investment Law' (2009) 11(4) International Community Law Review 353.

[32] ibid.

[33] ibid.

justice were they permitted to resort to international judicial mechanisms. A failure to honour the clause would result in the termination of the investor's rights in the contract.[34] In this context, the Calvo clause succeeded in preventing foreign investors from using the diplomatic protection of their home countries as 'an instrument of oppression . . . by strong States against weak ones'.[35]

In the years that followed, Latin American countries consolidated their commitment to sovereignty by adopting policies to that end. They adopted a policy of import-substitution in the 1950s and 1960s with the aim of breaking from their previous practice of exporting food and raw materials, while importing manufactured goods from Europe and the United States. Import-substitution involved Latin American governments establishing production facilities to manufacture goods which were previously imported. Werner Baer explains that a wide range of methods were used to give effect to the policy of import-substitution, including:

> protective tariffs and/or exchange controls; special preferences for domestic and foreign firms importing capital goods for new industries; preferential import exchange rates for industrial raw materials, fuels and intermediate goods; cheap loans by government development banks for favored industries; the construction by governments of infrastructure especially designed to complement industries; and the direct participation of government in certain industries, especially the heavier industries, such as steel, where neither domestic nor foreign private capital was willing or able to invest.[36]

During the heyday of these policies, Brazil increased from 17 per cent to 28 per cent of the US GDP per capita, while Mexico increased from 25 per cent to 34 per cent, though smaller Latin American countries did not fare as well.[37]

The next epoch in the economic history of the Latin American region was the 1960s, which saw the adoption of the Declaration on Permanent Sovereignty over Natural Resources by the United Nations;[38] this Declaration was staunchly supported by LAC countries[39] and other Third World nations. This instrument required states and international organizations to respect the sovereignty of peoples and nations over their natural wealth and resources, particularly in the exploration, development, and disposition of natural resources; nationalization and expropriation; foreign investment; and the sharing of profits.[40] It was this Declaration that served as the

[34] ibid.
[35] MR Garcia-Mora, 'The Calvo Clause in Latin American Constitutions and International Law' (1950) 33 Marquette Law Review 205.
[36] Werner Baer, 'Import Substitution and Industrialization in Latin America: Experiences and Interpretations' (1972) 7(1) Latin American Research Review 95.
[37] Mauro Rodrigues, 'Import substitution and economic growth' (2010) 57(2) Journal of Monetary Economics 175.
[38] UNGA, Res 3171 (XXVIII) (17 December 1973) UN Doc A/RES/3171<https://www.refworld.org/docid/3b00f1c64.html> accessed 21 September 2023.
[39] Mats Ingulstad and Lucas Lixinski, 'Raw Materials, Race, and Legal Regimes: The Development of the Principle of Permanent Sovereignty over Natural Resources in the Americas' (2013) 29 World History Bulletin 34.
[40] Sundhya Pahuja, *Decolonising International Law: Development, Economic Growth, and the Politics of Universality* (Cambridge University Press 2011).

impetus for the subsequent adoption by the United Nations General Assembly of the Declaration for the Establishment of a NIEO and its accompanying programme of action on 1 May 1974.[41] The new international economic order (NIEO) was also vigorously championed by LAC states as representing a monumental shift in global economic relations,[42] given its emphasis on sovereign equality and full sovereignty over natural resources and other economic activities necessary for development, as well as the regulation of transnational corporations. Although the NIEO was only partly realized, leading scholars like Margot Salomon[43] and Antony Anghie[44] see it as a blueprint for achieving economic justice in an unequal world.

The ethos of the NIEO resonated with many LAC countries and influenced the implementation of restrictive policies on foreign investors operating in the extractives industry in the 1970s and 1980s. In fact, several Latin American countries enacted and/or consolidated their mining and environmental laws to regulate the sectors in which mining concessions could be granted; placed limitations on foreign ownership and the transferability of natural resources; and implemented environmental restrictions on mining activities.[45]

By the 1990s and early 2000s, however, the fetishization of precious metals from the LAC region among foreign investors peaked. In this connection, Daviken Studnicki-Gizbert recalls that since the early 1990s, Canadian mining companies have extended their presence in Latin America in 'unprecedented numbers and ways'.[46] Nicolas Perrone shares this view. He contends that the rise of neoliberalism, the decay of the industrialization project, low economic growth, and sovereign debt problems prompted most Latin American countries to favour 'a new wave of foreign-led extractivism'[47] in the 1990s. At the same time, many Latin American countries amended their legislation, including their constitutions, to allow for foreign investment in the extractives industry, and, except for Brazil, many of these countries also ratified investment treaties and accepted Investor State Dispute Settlement (ISDS), 'ending more than a century of resistance against these international standards and arbitration'.[48] Against this backdrop, with the blessing of the neoliberal international economic order, which

[41] UNGA, Res 3201 (S-VI) (1 May 1994) UN Doc A/RES/3201(S-VI) <https://www.refworld.org/docid/3b00f1e048.html> accessed 21 September 2023.

[42] Philip Golub, 'From the New International Economic Order to the G20: How the "Global South" is Restructuring World Capitalism from Within' (2013) 34(6) Third World Quarterly 1000.

[43] Margot E Salomon, 'From NIEO to Now and the Unfinishable Story of Economic Justice' (2013) 62(1) International & Comparative Law Quarterly 31; Margot E Salomon, 'Winners and Others: Accounting for International Law's Favourites' in Conor Gearty and Costas Douzinas (eds), *The Cambridge Companion to Human Rights Law* (Cambridge University Press 2012) 271.

[44] Antony Anghie, 'Legal Aspects of the New International Economic Order' (2015) 6(1) Humanity: An International Journal of Human Rights, Humanitarianism, and Development 145.

[45] Sandra Orihuela, 'Latin America: A New Era for Mining Investment' (1996) 30(1) The International Lawyer 31.

[46] Daviken Studnicki-Gizbert, 'Canadian Mining in Latin America (1990 to Present): A Provisional History' (2016) 41(1) Canadian Journal of Latin American and Caribbean Studies 95.

[47] Nicolás Perrone, 'Local Communities, Extractivism and International Investment Law: The Case of Five Colombian Communities' (2022) 19(6) Globalizations 837.

[48] ibid 842.

Gathii argues 'formally embeds racially constructed hierarchies',[49] the fetishization of precious metals by foreign investors has taken on a role similar to the one it played nearly three centuries ago in the LAC region.

Indeed, 'racialization' explains historically and today why race continues to be re-inscribed as a site of oppression in the LAC region, particularly in the extractives industry. As observed by Achiume, it is important therefore to understand racialization, including how it manifests and to what end it works. Racial equality remains a predominant concern for those who are negatively racialized—that is, non-white or non-European people who were 'formerly colonised on the grounds of false claims of their racial inferiority, and who continue to bear the greatest cost of extractivism'.[50] It is these individuals who remain 'subordinate, excluded and marginal within the global extractives economy'.[51]

For Gonzales-Sobrino and Goss, racialization is concerned with how people attach racial meanings to other people, based on a delineation of group boundaries.[52] It is borne out of social dominance and power.[53] Meanwhile, for Burden-Stelly, racialization refers to a process of regulating, organizing, and subjecting populations based on racial difference.[54] Racialization, in her view, is 'integral to and endemic in the capitalist world system',[55] as it justifies global hierarchies based on racial differences, and 'justifies inequitable distribution of resources, destabilisation of local self-sustaining economies, and the conscription of entire populations into global labour regimes'.[56] The so-called 'racial contract',[57] in her view, perpetuates an economy that is structured on the racial exploitation of the 'Other', typically manifested as white privilege and its attendant economic domination on the one hand and the exploitation of racialized labour and the expropriation of racialized peoples' lands on the other. For Burden-Stelly, 'whiteness and Blackness become metonyms for progress and stagnation, expropriator and expropriated, and exploiter and exploited, [such] that perpetual accumulation is possible'.[58] In short, racialization reinforces the presumption that racialized peoples are 'inferior, backward, and dependent, and therefore deserving of exploitation'.[59] The idea that racialized people are deserving of exploitation because they are inherently inferior to the economically dominant group is a key feature of commodity narcissism, which is discussed in the coming section.

[49] James Gathii, 'Beyond Color-Blind International Economic Law' (2023) 117 AJIL Unbound 61.

[50] UNGA (n 8) 42. Revisited in UNGA, Human Rights Council, Global Extractivism and Racial Equality (14 May 2019) UN Doc A/HRC/41/54 <https://docs.un.org/en/a/hrc/41/54> accessed 7 February 2026.

[51] ibid.

[52] Bianca Gonzalez-Sobrino and Devon Goss, 'Exploring the Mechanisms of Racialization Beyond the Black–White Binary' (2018) 42(4) Ethical and Racial Studies 507.

[53] ibid.

[54] Charisse Burden-Stelly, 'The Capitalist Foundations of Racialization' (National African-American Reparations Commission, 5 November 2021) <https://reparationscomm.org/reparations-news/the-capitalist-foundations-of-racialization/> accessed 4 March 2024.

[55] ibid.

[56] ibid.

[57] ibid.

[58] ibid.

[59] ibid.

Racialization underpins and is reproduced by what some scholars describe as 'racial capitalism',[60] 'racialized capitalism',[61] or 'race and capitalism'.[62] The central argument advanced by these schools of thought is that race is central to the capitalist order. Race is exploited by those with power to create surplus value for themselves whilst in the process subjecting non-white populations to violent dispossession of their lands and resources and expropriation of their labour. Racialized people are not simply treated in this manner because they happen to inhabit lands on which precious metals are found; rather, they are treated in this manner because, through the process of racialization, the system of capitalism reproduces a racial hierarchy in which non-white or non-European people are assigned a racially inferior status which is constructed as being natural, inevitable, and unchangeable. This inferior status is then exploited by key players in the extractives industry.

It would be a fatal mistake to think that *anybody's* labour, land, and resources are expropriated in this process of capital accumulation. Rather, it is *racialized* populations, and their labour, land, and resources that are the specific targets of capitalist tyranny precisely because the process of racialization has constructed them as racially inferior and thus available for exploitation, expropriation, and expulsion. Racialization explains why non-white or non-European people who were formerly colonized on the grounds of false claims of their racial inferiority remain subordinate, excluded, and marginalized in international investment law's domain.

3. How racial/racialized capitalism works in the extractives industry

The subordination of racialized peoples in the LAC region at the hands of racial/racialized capitalism and in the context of the extractives industry is achieved by a complex process that begins with commodity fetishism, evolves into commodity narcissism, becomes concretized by primitive accumulation, and reaches its zenith with

[60] Cedric Robinson, *Black Marxism: The Making of The Black Radical Tradition* (University of North Carolina Press 1983); Justin Leroy and Destin Jenkins (eds), *Histories of Racial Capitalism* (Columbia University Press 2021); Nancy Leong, 'Racial Capitalism' (2013) 126(8) Harvard Law Review 2151, 2155; Andrew Smolski and Matthew Lorenzen, 'Introduction: Violence, Capital Accumulation, and Resistance in Contemporary Latin America' (2021) 48(1) Latin American Perspectives 4; Ricardo Duarte, 'Drilled Mountains, Pulverised Bodies: Mining, Extractivism, and Racialisation in Brazil' (2022) 30(3) Journal of Latin American Cultural Studies 417; Adam Bledsoe, 'Foregrounding Race in Analyses of Extraction' (2021) 12(1) Dialogues in Human Geography 1; Jodi Melamed, 'Racial Capitalism' (2015) 1(1) Ethnic Studies 76.

[61] Satnam Virdee, 'Racialized Capitalism: An Account of its Contested Origins and Consolidation' (2019) 67(1) The Sociological Review 3; Nancy Fraser, 'Expropriation and Exploitation in Racialized Capitalism: A Reply to Michael Dawson' (2016) 3(1) Critical Historical Studies 163; Nancy Fraser, 'From Exploitation to Expropriation: Historic Geographies of Racialized Capitalism' (2018) 94(1) Economic Geography 1.

[62] Michael Dawson and Emily Katzenstein, 'Survey Article: Articulated Darkness: White Supremacy, Patriarchy, and Capitalism in Shelby's Dark Ghettos' (2019) 27(2) Journal of Political Philosophy 252; Michael Dawson, 'Why Race and Capitalism Not Racial Capitalism?' (Lecture, Critical Race Studies: Interdisciplinary Perspectives, Centre for Ethics, University of Toronto, 25 March 2021) <https://www.youtube.com/watch?v=3jjK3ge__ck> accessed 5 March 2024; Michael Dawson, 'Hidden in Plain Sight: A Note on Legitimation Crises and the Racial Order'(2016) 3(1) Critical Historical Studies 143.

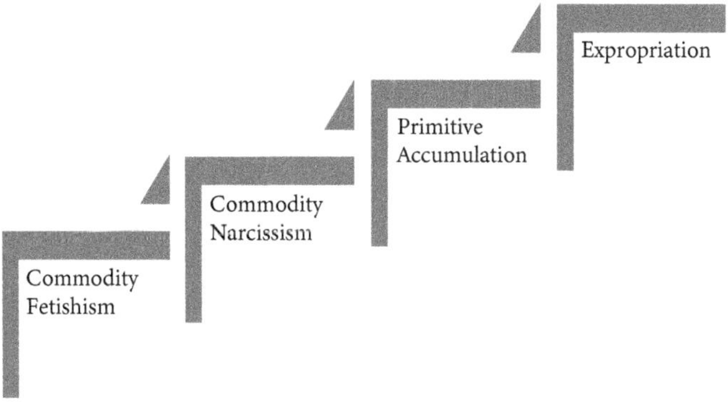

Fig 3.1 The commodity fetishism to expropriation continuum
Source: Jason Haynes

expropriation. This process, captured in the diagram in Figure 3.1, is explained in detail below, and draws on evidence from international investment law's treatment of the extractives industry.

3.1 Commodity fetishism

Although at the time of his writing, Marx did not place considerable emphasis on the extractives industry, reference to the European fetish of precious metal money does appear in some of his works, namely *Economic and Philosophic Manuscripts of 1844*. In this paper, Marx observed that European nations were 'dazzled by the sensuous glitter of precious metals, and are, therefore, still fetish-worshippers of metal money'.[63]

Marx is credited for coining the term 'commodity fetishism' in Volume I of *Capital*.[64] He defines the fetishism of commodities as consisting:

> simply in the fact that the commodity reflects the social characteristics of men's own labour as objective characteristics of the products of labour themselves, as the socio-natural properties of these things. Hence, it also reflects the social relations of the producers to the sum total of labour as a social relation between objects, a relation which exists apart from and outside the producers.[65]

Over the years, scholars have sought to decipher what Marx meant by commodity fetishism. For Bernstein and Campling, Marx's commodity fetishism represents a structural feature of the capital mode of production in which the bourgeoisie regard

[63] Karl Marx, *Economic & Philosophical Manuscripts of 1844* (Martin Mulligan tr Progress Publishers 1959) 84.
[64] ibid 164–65.
[65] Karl Marx, 'The Fetishism of the Commodity and its Secret' in *Capital: A Critique of Political Economy. Volume I: The Process of Capitalist Production*, (Charles H Kerr and Co, 1909).

commodity production as an essential condition of their social existence.[66] Fetishism is a unique form of exploitation because it not only expropriates the labour of the proletariat but appropriates the surplus value of their labour. Fetishism, they argue, is highly problematic because it makes the process of exploitation appear 'natural' to those who engage in the act.[67]

For Duncan Kennedy, Marx's concept of commodity fetishism is not simply a circumstance in which the bourgeoisie 'worship' a commodity as though it is a god; nor does he consider it to be a mere obsession with owning things. While Marx acknowledged that people can become slaves to commodities, Kennedy interprets Marx's reference to 'the definite social relation between men themselves which assumes here, for them, the fantastic form of a relation between things' as a person attributing to physical objects powers they do not possess. In Kennedy's view, 'those who suffer from commodity fetishism attribute to commodities powers to regulate relations among people that belong only to the people themselves'.[68] In other words, people who fetishize commodities believe that events they themselves bring about through concrete social activities are the necessary or natural consequences of the properties of the commodities they produce.[69]

Meanwhile, Cluley and Dunne interpret Marx's 'commodity fetishism' to mean 'more than a desire to have—it is a desire to have at the expense of others'.[70] In this regard, the person who fetishizes relates to the commodity on its own terms, mistakenly seeing it as a self-sustaining object that is imbued with qualities, characteristics, and properties of its own. Under this interpretation, commodity fetishists do not concern themselves with the journey a commodity takes to the marketplace; rather, they are *only* concerned with the commodity itself, even if it has been produced at the expense of others. In this regard, Cluley and Dunne understand commodity fetishism as a 'crucial component in the operation of capitalism and a crucial concept for understanding how capitalism works'.[71]

The foregoing description of commodity fetishism resonates in a profound way in the context of the extractives industry in the LAC region. More specifically, foreign investors, in Marx's parlance, are society's bourgeoisie, who first conceived of racialized people as inferior and thus expendable in the process of extractivism. They do not merely obsess with extracting precious metals, which are located in the Global South on former colonized lands where racialized peoples live. Rather, they attribute these metals with special powers, including the power to make them rich while simultaneously keeping the people to whom they belong—racialized peoples—in a subservient position. Remarkably, these investors are so fixated on accumulating capital from the extraction of precious metals in the Global South that

[66] Henry Bernstein and Liam Campling, 'Commodity Studies and Commodity Fetishism II: "Profits with Principles"?' (2004) 4(1) Journal of Agrarian Change 425.

[67] ibid.

[68] Duncan Kennedy, 'The Role of Law in Economic Thought: Essays on The Fetishism of Commodities' (1984) 34 American University Law Review 939, 971.

[69] ibid.

[70] Robert Cluley and Stephen Dunne, 'From Commodity Fetishism to Commodity Narcissism' (2012) 12(3) Marketing Theory 251, 253.

[71] ibid.

they are prepared to treat as 'necessary and natural' the racialization of non-white or non-European peoples in the process of extractivism. Because they not only desire racialized labour, capacities, and resources, and to have these at the expense of racialized peoples, it is not uncommon for investors to lobby governments to offer them asymmetrical concessions as a condition for investing in local communities, while bypassing environmental regulations, and Indigenous peoples' right to free, prior, and informed consent.[72] These investors are not concerned with the journey which commodities take to the marketplace, but instead are preoccupied with the commodities themselves, even if they have been produced at the expense of racialized peoples. From a racial/racialized capitalism perspective, the fetishization practised by foreign investors in this regard is not only problematic from the point of view that it makes the process of exploitation of racialized people appear natural, necessary, and inevitable, but also because of its staggering human cost to the racialized, which is either externalized or legitimized.

Illustrative of this point is the recent case of *Eco Oro v Colombia*.[73] A Canadian mining company was granted a concession to engage in extractive activities in the Santurbán Páramo, an area which provides water to around 2.5 million people in sixty-eight surrounding municipalities. In light of Colombia's renewed recognition of the area's ecological importance, it began a lengthy and expensive process aimed at delimiting the Santurbán Páramo. The investor claimed that the incomplete delimitation of the Santurbán Páramo prevented it from exploring for precious metals in areas it previously envisaged would be available. The Tribunal, while finding that the investor had not made a convincing case of expropriation, nonetheless held that the state had breached the fair and equitable treatment (FET) standard by failing to complete the delimitation. The Tribunal also considered that, notwithstanding the invocation of the environmental exception provided for under the Free Trade Agreement (FTA) between the Republic of Colombia and Canada, the state was still obliged to pay compensation to the investor.

In the context of the discussion on racial/racialized capitalism, this arbitral award provides insights into the fetishization practised by foreign investors, and the role of arbitral tribunals in further reproducing racialization. Although the Tribunal recognized that the investor exercised no due diligence in so far as their (lack of) appreciation of the environmental significance of the area in which they intended to invest was concerned, it treated the investor as the victim of non-transparent conduct by the state. While the Tribunal was critical of the state for prioritizing 'much needed royalties'[74] over the state's environmental commitments, at no point did it seek to interrogate how racial/racialized capitalism pushes desperate and vulnerable countries to compromise their environmental standards to serve the interests of foreign investors. Instead, the Tribunal entertained the investor's claim for *more* of the Santurbán Páramo, even if this was at the expense of the livelihoods of the affected racialized communities. Furthermore, the Tribunal's willingness to award compensation, even

[72] Maristella Svampa, *Neo-Extractivism in Latin America: Socio-Environmental Conflicts, the Territorial Turn, and New Political Narratives* (Cambridge University Press 2019).
[73] *Eco Oro Minerals Corp v Republic of Colombia*, ICSID Case No ARB/16/41, Award (15 July 2024).
[74] ibid 821.

when the exception in the FTA was successfully invoked, is deeply problematic from a jurisprudential perspective,[75] and indicative of a system that privileges the expropriator while delegitimizing the plight of the racialized, whom it conceives as 'inferior, backward and dependent'.[76]

3.2 Commodity narcissism

For racial/racialized capitalism scholars, the process of racialization does not end at fetishism. In fact, these scholars contend that the practice of many investors from capital-exporting countries often evolves from fetishism to narcissism. The difference between fetishism and narcissism, according to Anselm Jappe, lies in the fact that whereas the former is 'an unconscious process that hides the true nature of capitalist production',[77] commodity narcissism is deliberate and conscious. In this connection, Jappe explains that because the narcissist is keen on devaluing the 'Other', he 'is not intimately convinced of the real presence of an external world with which he has to deal with, but tries to put everything and everyone in his service'.[78] Although Jappe was not specifically addressing international investment law in his writing, it is arguable that putting racialized people and their resources in their service is the de facto modus operandi of the typical foreign investor.

Remarkably, as noted also by Jappe:

> instead of constantly reminding the subjects of their limits and their dependence on higher instances (state, religion, morals, social hierarchies), they are encouraged to overcome all limits (at least in their imagination) and to believe that the world is at their disposal: which is of course a lie.[79]

This attitude of not dissuading their nationals from perpetuating racialization when they invest in the Global South is particularly true of capital-exporting countries who in the past used the threat of force when obligations owed to their investors were not met.[80] Today, these same countries 'negotiate' international investment agreements to lock in countries from the Global South into asymmetrical investor protection standards and dispute resolution mechanisms,[81] such as umbrella clauses which elevate contractual breaches to treaty breaches. They also actively encourage their investors

[75] Laura Tremblay, 'In Need of a Paradigm Shift: Reimagining Eco Oro v Colombia in Light of New Treaty Language' (2022) 23 (5–6) The Journal of World Investment & Trade 915; Hou-chih Kuo and Jeffrey Lo, 'Runaway Tribunal? An Assessment of the Eco Oro Tribunal's Opinion on the General Exceptions' (2022) 15(1) Contemporary Asia Arbitration Journal 143.

[76] Burden-Stelly (n 54).

[77] Anselm Jappe, 'Fetishism and narcissism-the base of capitalism?' (2020) 62 Estudios de Filosofía 165.

[78] ibid.

[79] ibid.

[80] Rodrigo Polanco Lazo, 'The Changing Role of the Home and the Host State in Investor-State Arbitration: Some Conclusions' in Shaheeza Lalani and Rodrigo Polanco Lazo (eds), *The Role of the State in Investor-State Arbitration* (Brill Nijhoff 2015) 430.

[81] José Alvarez, 'Remarks by José E. Alvarez' (1988) 82 Proceedings of the ASIL Annual Meeting 552.

to overcome all limits and to believe that the world—including racialized peoples and their resources—is at their disposal.[82]

Similar sentiments have been articulated by scholars like Cluley and Dunne who situate Sigmund Freud's work on commodity narcissism in the framework of capitalism.[83] By narcissism, Freud meant a process wherein desire 'has been withdrawn from the external world and directed onto the self'.[84] This redirection of desire means that a narcissist can rarely completely satisfy their narcissistic desires with recourse to themselves alone. To this end, narcissists 'attach' their desires to external objects.[85] Using the parent–child dynamic, Freud contends that parents satisfy their own narcissistic desires through their children, thanks to consumption practices. The child fulfils their parents' wishful dreams which the parents were never able to fulfil themselves.

In a capitalist society, Cluley and Dunne argue that commodity narcissism is manifested by narcissists' wilfully ignoring exploitative social relations that create the products they consume. They argue:

> On the Freudian reading, rather, the knowledge of the reality of production, its exploitative nature and damaging environmental consequences, which we would rather deny at the moment of consumption, is actually part of what compels us to consume in the first place. When we consume, and thereby perpetuate the suffering of others, what we give expression to is a side of us that we may want to deny – a side of us that continues to exist precisely because we so actively strive to repress it. The knowledge of other people's suffering that our consumption perpetuates is precisely what satisfies our destructive and narcissistic desires, in this sense. This sadistic pleasure affords the narcissistic satisfaction of being able to think oneself better than others.[86]

In Cluley and Dunne's view, Freud's interpretation of consumption as a narcissistic practice can be further expanded to include instances where 'we consume to harm others and, consequently, elevate ourselves over them'.[87] In other words, 'not only do [narcissists] make purchasing decisions in order to satisfy their own needs, they also consume as a means of depriving and harming others'.[88] Commodity narcissism thus divides society into two groups: 'the rich, great, and the famous on the one hand and the common herd on the other'.[89] The former is privileged, while the latter's labour is exploited and their lands and precious metals are expropriated.

In the context of racialized extractivism in the LAC region, Cluley and Dunne's incisive critique is instructive. Indeed, foreign investors from capital-exporting countries, bolstered by their home states and an asymmetrical international investment law

[82] John Linarelli, Margot E Salomon, and Muthucumaraswamy Sornarajah. *The Misery of International Law: Confrontations with Injustice in The Global Economy* (Oxford University Press 2018).
[83] Sigmund Freud, 'On Narcissism: An Introduction' in *The Standard Edition of the Complete Psychological Works of Sigmund Freud*, vol XIV (The Hogarth Press 1957) 67, 91.
[84] ibid 75.
[85] ibid 85.
[86] Cluley and Dunne (n 70) 260.
[87] ibid.
[88] ibid.
[89] ibid.

regime,[90] are fully conscious of the fact that their extractives activities perpetuate the suffering of racialized people, but proceed to engage in these activities because it satisfies their destructive narcissistic desire to accumulate capital at the expense of those whom they consider racially inferior. What is particularly disturbing in this context is that through a process of re-inscription of racialization, these investors appear to obtain sadistic pleasure from not only thinking that they are better than racialized people, but also from actively depriving and harming these people. From a racial/racialized capitalism perspective, this is upsetting as it demonstrates how deeply embedded the dehumanization of racialized peoples is in the context of international investment law's legitimization of the extractives industry. The cases discussed in this chapter are merely the tip of the iceberg.

In view of the foregoing, a case can be made that many foreign investors demonstrate a 'narcissistic pathology', which James Glass identifies as having the following characteristics:

> a stance or pose of grandiosity (the self as monad); the devaluation of others; the refusal to grant to the other an autonomy that is not connected with self-gratification; a precarious inner condition that is unstable, envious, raging, and insecure. The narcissistic self projects qualities that appear to be socially functional and desirable: energy, charm, success, toughness of mind. Yet these appearances disguise a more insidious set of psychological dynamics: the rational manipulation of the other, the demand to be admired and loved, the view of the other as 'fuel' or 'supply' for egoistic needs, and ruthless and unfeeling behavior toward others the self perceives as necessary for its own interests.[91]

Added to these tendencies, Glass identifies annihilation and exploitation as key aspects of the narcissist's modus operandi when relating to the 'Other':

> relationships with other people are clearly exploitative and sometimes parasitic. The self acts without ever considering the autonomy of the other; they [the pathological narcissists] feel they have the right to control and possess others, and to exploit them without guilt feelings. Annihilation and appropriation become facts of life; it is the modern 'war of all against all'.[92]

The case of *South American Silver v Bolivia*[93] is illustrative of Glass's insightful observations. Here, the investor's mining concessions in certain Indigenous communities in Bolivia were revoked in circumstances where the investor, by its conduct, caused division among local communities, leading to demonstrations, violence, and even death. From the very outset, the investor was aware that the affected Indigenous groups made decisions by consensus. Still, the investor engaged in an aggressive strategy to

[90] Nicolás Perrone, *Investment Treaties and The Legal Imagination: How Foreign Investors Play by their Own Rules* (Oxford University Press 2021).

[91] James Glass, 'Hobbes and Narcissism. Pathology in the State of Nature' (1980) 8(3) Political Theory 335.

[92] ibid.

[93] *South American Silver Limited v Bolivia*, PCA Case No 2013-15, Award (22 November 2018).

weaken opposition to its project by offering employment and donations to its supporters, while ignoring those who opposed the project. The Tribunal found several other deficiencies in the investor's relations with community members:

> CMMK did not adequately communicate the implications of the Project, nor did it address the concerns expressed very early on by the members of the affected communities, for example, in connection with environmental pollution. The workshops held by the Company covered basic topics on mining and the environment, and did not even seem to correspond to the characteristics of the Project. The Company's contributions to the community did not seem to be tailored to the Project, rather they addressed specific requests made by certain community members. The Claimant's alleged actions and investments benefiting the community were nothing but basic instruction on what a mining project consists of, some minor investments in repairs and basic courses and, above all, an action directed to obtain the support of the majority – emphasized by the Claimant throughout its briefs – without clear evidence that an attempt was made to approach or reach consensus among the indigenous communities, respecting their indigenous decision-making processes.[94]

Nancy Leong's reference to the 'underacknowledged exchange' between the exploiter and exploited is apt in this context, in that the investor sought to offer jobs and donations for support among communities in a manner that was divisive, and which only served its unabashed economic objectives. There was no concern from the investor as to how its conduct would adversely affect community relations, and even when demonstrations and violent exchanges occurred, its aggressive communication strategy aimed at legitimizing its expropriation of racialized bodies and resources continued unabated. As highlighted by the Tribunal, the investor was blatant in its approach, seeing nothing wrong with its opportunistic and manipulative conduct, which it sought to excuse on the ground of the poverty that characterized the community. In this connection, the Tribunal ruled that it did not:

> share the Claimant's view that the Reversion did not serve a social benefit related to the internal needs of Bolivia because the Project would have brought millions of dollars of investments to one of the poorest areas of Bolivia, and that neither the Government nor the local communities have derived any benefit ever since the Reversion, and that the indigenous community representatives have requested that SAS come back to the area to continue with the Project. The Claimant cannot simply equate social benefit with purely economic benefit and expect the Tribunal to analyze compliance with this requirement from the point of view of the returns that the Project would have generated for the community, ignoring the social, cultural and political situation and the seriousness of the existing social conflict in the area.[95]

From a racial/racialized capitalism perspective, several aspects of the investor's conduct wreak of narcissism. First, the investor adopted a stance of grandiosity, seeing its

[94] ibid [481].
[95] ibid [578].

investment as the only solution to the economic challenges facing the local community. The investor, in its narcissistic mode of operation, felt that its omnipotence resided in their ability to bring millions of dollars to a poor, hapless community, and was thus unconcerned about the unique cultural and spiritual relationship the community had with the environment. This air of omnipotence has been described by Glass:

> What motivates the self is a sense of its own power, its complete omnipotence. It believes itself to have a right to dominate, to demand attention, to devour whatever it feels is necessary to satisfy appetite. The narcissistic self moves through the world as if it were in a state of nature without any inner feeling of constraint, without any sense of principle or commitment to anything other than self gratification.[96]

The investor then sought to devalue and manipulate the 'Other' by offering certain members of the community jobs, food, and related incentives to betray the trust of their fellow community members, and thus avoid the community's established decision-making processes. Relatedly, the investor refused to respect the autonomy of the community, which was grounded in their right to free, prior, and informed consent. When sections of the community resisted, the investor responded with rage, using legal action to 'scare'[97] community members, and when this failed, it initiated arbitration proceedings against the State. To use the words of Burden-Stelly, the investor's narcissist approach in this connection only reinforces the ideology in which racialization is grounded—that indigenous communities are 'inferior, backward and dependent'. Interestingly, in the course of the ensuing legal proceedings, the investor repeatedly described the affected racialized people as nothing more than 'two tiny communities',[98] a characterization which the Tribunal rightly described as problematic. Such a characterization of the affected racialized communities as insignificant and thus dispensable is consistent with Glass's argument that narcissists 'prey on and manipulate and exploit those whose appetites are either weak or who lack the social or institutional means to protect themselves'.[99]

3.3 Primitive accumulation

The process of racialization is complex, and generally non-linear. It is clear, however, that it does not end at commodity narcissism. Rather, it evolves into primitive accumulation. Primitive accumulation is not a new concept. In fact, Marx described primitive accumulation in 1887 in the following manner:

[96] Glass (n 91).
[97] *South American Silver v Bolivia* (n 93) [495]: 'The Tribunal does not deny the Company's right to take legal action to protect its interests. However, that right cannot be exercised as a means to scare the members of the community and appease the opposition, much less when there seems to be no basis for the exercise of the action, as suggested by the fact that the Company's accusations did not prevail.'
[98] ibid [501].
[99] Glass (n 91).

> The discovery of gold and silver in America, the extirpation, enslavement, and entombment in mines of the aboriginal population, the beginning of the conquest and looting of the East Indies [India], and the turning of Africa into a warren for the commercial hunting of black skins, signalised the rosy dawn of the era of capitalist production. These idyllic proceedings are the chief momenta of primitive accumulation. On their heels treads the commercial war of the European nations, with the globe for a theatre ...[100]

Marx explained that Spain, Portugal, the Netherlands, France, and England all employed 'the power of the State, the concentrated and organised force of society, to hasten, hothouse fashion, the process of transformation of the feudal mode of production into the capitalist mode, and to shorten the transition'.[101] To sustain their primitive accumulation, Marx noted that these nations employed violence, which he described as a manifestation of economic power.[102]

In contradistinction to Marx's view that primitive accumulation was a phenomenon of a period in history before capitalist production, contemporary scholars perceive primitive accumulation as an ongoing process that is integral to racial/racialized capitalism. Mark Neocleous,[103] for example, argues that 'primitive accumulation is a permanent process in the colonisation of the world by capital',[104] and that 'colonialism is achieved most effectively not simply through violence, but through law—that is, through the violence of law'.[105] Siddhant Issar similarly argues that primitive accumulation has become increasingly central to capitalist accumulation today.[106] In his view, Black and Indigenous populations are disproportionately affected by the violence of capitalism.

Issar agrees with David Harvey[107] that, since 1973, accumulation by dispossession most often entails the privatization and commodification of public assets through 'state-sanctioned, often imperialistic, "opening up" of, among other things, natural resources, public lands, social services and formerly protected markets to the profit-driven whims of private capital'.[108] The process of 'opening up' natural resources, for example, is rarely ever fair or transparent; instead, it usually involves 'coercion, fraud, predation and extra-economic force to ensure and secure capital accumulation'.[109] Issar also agrees with Saskia Sassen's account of primitive accumulation, which places considerable emphasis on the notion of 'expulsions'.[110] By expulsions, Sassen refers

[100] Karl Marx, 'Genesis of the Industrial Capitalist' in *Capital: A Critique of Political Economy. Volume I: The Process of Capitalist Production,* (Charles H Kerr and Co, 1909).
[101] ibid.
[102] Michael Grewcock, 'Settler-Colonial Violence, Primitive Accumulation and Australia's Genocide' (2018) 7(2) State Crime Journal 222.
[103] Mark Neocleous, 'International Law as Primitive Accumulation; or, the Secret of Systematic Colonization' (2012) 23(4) European Journal of International Law 941.
[104] ibid.
[105] ibid.
[106] Siddhant Issar, 'Theorising 'Racial/Colonial Primitive Accumulation': Settler Colonialism, Slavery and Racial Capitalism' (2021) 63(1) Race & Class 23, 24.
[107] David Harvey, *The 'New' Imperialism: Accumulation by Dispossession* (Oxford University Press 2003).
[108] Issar (n 106) 26.
[109] ibid.
[110] Saskia Sassen, 'A Savage Sorting of Winners and Losers: Contemporary Versions of Primitive Accumulation' (2010) 7(1) Globalizations 23.

to the violent expelling of populations through the extractive incorporation of land and natural resources for corporate profitability. In her view, 'the natural resources of much of Africa, Latin America, and central Asia are more important than the people on those lands as workers or consumers'.[111]

Issar, however, goes further than both Harvey and Sassen by treating primitive accumulation not as a colour-blind concept, but as an integral part of racial capitalism. In his critique of Harvey and Sassen's work, Issar contends that both scholars largely ignore white supremacist forms of expropriation in their account of primitive accumulation. By contrast, Issar seeks to theorize primitive accumulation within racial capitalism, better accounting for the seizure of Indigenous lands rather than just their labour.

Issar's account of primitive accumulation is timely and instructive. It is true that foreign investors have accumulated and continue to accumulate profits by dispossessing racialized peoples of their land, quite often by nefarious means. Investors' unapologetic approach in this connection is not colour-blind, but a conscious effort to reinforce the perception of racial inferiority through any means possible, including violence. In *Copper Mesa v Ecuador*,[112] for example, a dispute arose in respect of three mining concessions which had been granted by Ecuador, but were later suspended and then terminated by the respondent. Having failed to properly engage affected Indigenous communities in transparent consultation at the initial stages of the project, members of the community engaged in resistance measures, including roadblocks and arson. The state also responded to the investor's alleged failure to submit an environmental impact study, their failure to secure the approval of local communities, and the material environmental impact of mining in the area by terminating the mining concessions. The Tribunal found in favour of the investor, holding that it had jurisdiction to hear the matter because the respondent had waived its right to object to the investor's alleged unlawful conduct by not raising a complaint before the commencement of the arbitration. Further, the Tribunal found that the respondent had committed a breach of the guarantee against expropriation, the fair and equitable treatment standard, and the full protection and security standard.

The *Copper Mesa* case is fascinating from a racial/racialized capitalism perspective. Apart from its blatant conscripting of large expanses of Indigenous lands for mining, the investor failed to consult in a transparent manner the affected racialized community. Further, the investor showed no regard for the staggering human cost of its activities on the environment, which was of tremendous importance to the livelihoods of the community in question. In keeping with the sentiments expressed by Cedric Robinson, Destin Jenkins, and Justin Leroy as well as Duarte Filho that racial capitalism involves violent dispossession to secure investors' accumulation of capital, the investor in *Copper Mesa* systematically and unceremoniously recruited armed men, who fired guns and sprayed mace on members of the local community in what the Tribunal found was 'part of premeditated, disguised and well-funded plans to take the law into its own hands'.[113] This 'slow violence', to use the words of Filho, coupled

[111] Issar (n 106) 29.
[112] *Copper Mesa Mining Corporation v Republic of Ecuador*, PCA Case No 2012-2, Award (15 March 2016).
[113] ibid [6.99].

with the loss and disposability of Indigenous lands, to use the words of Jodi Melamed, should come as no surprise, however, as racial capitalism thrives on the suppression of racialized bodies, and the expropriation of their lands and its resources.

Although the Tribunal acknowledged that 'the evidence establishe[d] that several of the Claimant's senior personnel in Quito were guilty of directing violent acts committed on its behalf, in violation of Ecuadorian criminal law'[114] and that 'their resort to subterfuge and mendacity aggravated those acts',[115] remarkably, it was only prepared to reduce the quantum of damages payable by the respondent by 30 per cent. The Tribunal's approach legitimized the investor's primitive accumulation, which scholars like Issar have long warned about.

Even more troubling was the Tribunal's partial treatment of the complicity of the investor's senior management in Canada, which reinforces Burden-Stelly's argument about racial capitalism's privileging of the expropriator versus the expropriated and the exploiter versus the exploited. In this context, the Tribunal ruled:

> That is not to say that the Claimant's senior management in Canada was fully privy to the planning and execution of these acts. On the evidence, the Tribunal prefers to base its decision on the Claimant's negligence, rather than the wilful conduct of its Canadian senior management. If it were based on the latter's own wilful conduct as the Claimant's alter ego, the result, as regards Article 39, would be much graver for the Claimant's case.[116]

That the Tribunal found mere negligence, rather than wilful conduct, in circumstances where guns and sprays were purchased, armed men were recruited, and 'premeditated' and 'disguised' violence was unleashed on defenceless members of the local community is nothing short of extraordinary. This finding reinforces the view articulated by Fraser that global institutions are de facto complicit with investors in extracting value from defenceless populations, and re-inscribing racialization.

3.4 Expropriation

Expropriation is the final stage of the process of racialization. Nancy Fraser is a leading commentator on expropriation. In a debate with Michael Dawson, Fraser rejects exploitation-centred conceptions of capitalism, which she argues cannot fully explain its persistent entanglement with racial oppression.[117] Instead, Fraser provides an expanded conception of exploitation that encompasses an ongoing phenomenon she describes as 'expropriation'.[118] In her view, expropriation plays a crucial role in capital accumulation by 'conscripting unfree and dependent labour, capacities and resources into capitalists' circuits of self-expansion'.[119] In this context, racialized bodies have

[114] ibid [6.100].
[115] ibid.
[116] ibid.
[117] Fraser (n 61).
[118] ibid 166.
[119] ibid.

little choice because they are deprived of any direct access to the means of production, and therefore have no claim to the surplus value their labour generates, which accrues instead to the capitalist. She argues that class domination results in propertyless racialized peoples selling, out of necessity, their labour power and mineral-rich lands as a survival mechanism.

As a mode of accumulation, Fraser contends that expropriation is deeply entangled in racial oppression. Because the relationship between the capitalist and racialized peoples is often unmediated by a fair wage contract, the latter are treated as lesser beings who 'lack an independent legal personality'.[120] While this treatment was in the past blatant and violent, it is today veiled by a 'cloak of commerce'.[121] In Fraser's view, the primary subjects of expropriation are rural or Indigenous communities in the capitalist periphery whose 'labor, land, animals, tools, mineral or energy deposits—but also human beings, their sexual and reproductive capacities, their children and bodily organs'[122] are conscripted. These communities, far from enjoying protection, are 'defenseless and fair game for expropriation—again and again'.[123]

Fraser considers modern forms of expropriation, such as corporate land grabs associated with the 'limitless expansion and private appropriation of surplus value',[124] as linked to racial oppression and imperialism. In her view, expropriation represents 'violence and theft concealed behind the orderly facade of contractual relations and market exchanges'.[125] Regrettably, expropriation is sustained by the legal framework—treaties, general international law, and supranational governance regimes—which guarantees property rights, enforces contracts, and adjudicates disputes, often in an asymmetrical manner.[126] This legal framework operates in insidious ways by 'suppressing rebellions, maintaining order, and managing dissent'.[127]

In the context of the extractives industry in the LAC region, Fraser's rich analysis is enlightening. It is now well acknowledged that the international investment treaty regime is a central pillar in the process of racialization, and thus expropriation.[128] The international investment regime comprises a large corpus of Bilateral Investment Treaties and Regional Agreements with Investment Chapters, which typically articulate a wide range of investor protection standards, including the hugely problematic fair and equitable standard (FET),[129] the full protection and security standard, and guarantees against expropriation. These standards, often augmented by umbrella clauses,[130] are typically interpreted asymmetrically and to the disadvantage of LAC

[120] ibid 165.
[121] ibid 166.
[122] ibid.
[123] ibid 169.
[124] ibid 173.
[125] ibid 168.
[126] ibid 170.
[127] ibid.
[128] Olabisi Akinkugbe, 'Race & International Investment Law: On the Possibility of Reform and Non-retrenchment' (2023) 117(3) American Journal of International Law 535.
[129] Jason Haynes, 'The Evolving Nature of the Fair and Equitable Treatment (FET) Standard: Challenging Its Increasing Pervasiveness in Light of Developing Countries' Concerns—the Case for Regulatory Rebalancing' (2013) 14(1) The Journal of World Investment & Trade 114.
[130] Jason Haynes, 'Reforming the Bilateral Investment Treaty Landscape in the Caribbean Region: A Clarion Call' (2023) 38(1) ICSID Review-Foreign Investment Law Journal 72.

states, who have been burdened by staggering awards in damages,[131] with the potential to cause regulatory chill.[132] Fraser's assessment that international legal frameworks, like international investment law, work in insidious ways by 'suppressing rebellions, maintaining order, and managing dissent'[133] is especially relevant in this context, and resonates with Tzouvala, who argues that:

> The obligation to provide full protection and security emerges as a method of state-making, as a way to lock in through international legal standards a particular relationship between the state, its violent capabilities, capitalist accumulation, and race. This articulation demands that state resources are allocated for the protection of foreign capital to the detriment of other social goals, including other security goals. In addition, the full protection and security (FPS) demands that the host state represses violently those who refuse to participate in or worse disrupt processes of cross-border capitalist accumulation. In other words, international investment law dictates the creation and reproduction of state mechanisms that systematically subordinate, even violently, parts of their population to enable the protection of foreign investors from disruption and challenge. Another way of putting this is that the FPS standard aspires to ensure that foreign investors will benefit from the cheap labour and land of racialized peoples while being shielded from the social unrest that tends to come about when land and labour are cheapened.[134]

Perrone, in his work on local communities and extractivism in Latin America, is equally sceptical of the international investment treaty regime, which he argues was designed to promote foreign investment in the extractive industry, and, in tandem with domestic mining laws and regulations,[135] has undermined sustainable development in Latin America and compromised the livelihoods of racialized peoples in the region. He notes:

> In the Cold War, investment treaties and ISDS were a Western corporate response to the Global South's ambition to control its natural resources. They emerged from the efforts of financiers and international lawyers, who organized and promoted the investment treaty regime while simultaneously resisting the NIEO. Oil and mining companies, such as Royal Dutch Shell, Standard Oil of New Jersey and Rio Tinto, had reasons to be concerned about nationalization and the plans to put natural resources to work for industrialization. Thus, they sponsored a legal regime whereby their rights would be interpreted and disputes resolved through international arbitration. Their attempt to create a multilateral investment treaty failed, but their home

[131] Martins Paparinskis, 'Crippling Compensation in the International Law Commission and Investor–State Arbitration' (2023) 37(1) ICSID Review-Foreign Investment Law Journal 289.

[132] Anna Sands, 'Regulatory Chill and Domestic Law: Mining in the Santurban Paramo' (2023) 22(1) World Trade Review 55.

[133] ibid.

[134] Ntina Tzouvala, 'Full Protection and Security (for Racial Capitalism)' (2022) 25(2) Journal of International Economic Law 224.

[135] Nicolás Perrone, 'Local Communities, Extractivism and International Investment Law: The Case of Five Colombian Communities'(2022) 19(6) Globalizations 837.

> states began signing investment treaties, while the World Bank promoted the creation of the International Centre for Settlement of Investment Disputes and the inclusion of ISDS clauses in the treaties.[136]

Perrone further explains that in Latin America, the investment treaty regime has contributed to birthing a new wave of extractivism by enforcing foreign investors'[137] rights while locking-in domestic pro-extractive laws:

> the investment treaty regime is central to the political economy and narratives of extractivism. This international regime tilts the balance in favour of extractivism by promoting a foreign investment imperative, strengthening foreign investor rights, and making local communities invisible. When the laws of extractivism enter into tension with environmental protection or local rights, and states give in to the pressure of activists or local communities, ISDS becomes foreign investors' weapon of last resort. This way the investment treaty regime facilitates alliances between foreign investors and national elites, as ISDS represents the facts of disputes and reviews public measures through vocabularies and legal standards that have proven to be somewhat sensitive to environmental demands but unresponsive to local rights or preferences. Ultimately, the issue is not only that ISDS overlooks local rights; the situation is more complex as the investment treaty regime contributes to the ontological occupation of the territories.[138]

Perrone contends that 'what the international investment regime does in a quiet—but effective—manner is to render invisible these local entitlements and community values'.[139] Citing observations from a workshop held with five Colombian communities in 2018, Perrone recalls that members of Indigenous communities were concerned that most of the infrastructure, built either by the state or the investor, serves the investor, while environmental degradation has led to a radical transformation of the livelihoods of these communities. He recalls that many of the communities no longer produce their own food, as the lands they previously used for agriculture have been conscripted for extraction.[140] Perrone further notes that when Indigenous communities attempt to resist, national elites and investors deploy various strategies to reinforce the vulnerability of these communities, including manipulation and the fostering of division among community members.[141] In this connection, Fraser is also critical of the role played by global institutions and national elites. She argues that global institutions pressure States in the Global South to 'collude with investors in extracting value from defenseless populations',[142] even in the face of the overaccumulation of capital, and ecological degradation.

136 ibid 842.
137 ibid 837.
138 ibid 839.
139 Nicolás Perrone, 'The "Invisible" Local Communities: Foreign Investor Obligations, Inclusiveness, and the International Investment Regime Part of: Investor Responsibility' (2019) AJIL Unbound 16.
140 Perrone (n 135) 8.
141 Perrone (n 139) 16.
142 Fraser (n 61) 176.

In the context of extractivism in the LAC region, Perrone's and Fraser's sentiments are elucidating. For many decades, foreign investors have been conscripting the labour, capacities, and resources of racialized communities in the LAC region under the façade of contractual relations and market exchanges. Although these racialized communities have some appreciation that their labour, capacities, and resources are being appropriated, they have little choice but to accept this because they are disenfranchised by a capitalist legal order that privileges investors' relentless pursuit of profits, while locking local communities out of accessing the means of production or the surplus value their labour generates. The nation-state is often complicit in this regard, though as Bhattacharyya argues, this does not signal the advent of a 'post-racial capitalism'.[143]

The defencelessness of local communities to the racial oppression that is inherent in expropriation is reinforced by the international investment regime which guarantees foreign investors astounding rights and privileges,[144] all while affording them unparalleled access to international dispute settlement mechanisms, namely ICSID and the Permanent Court of International Arbitration (PCA). The case of *Bear Creek Mining v Peru*[145] is relevant. The case arose out of the cancellation of mining concessions granted to the investor in relation to the Santa Ana silver mining project in Peru. The state cancelled the concessions on the basis that, contrary to the social licence for investing in the Indigenous communities, the relevant communities had not been fully engaged or consulted prior to the project coming on stream. Furthermore, the State argued that the cancellation was justified on the basis of environmental protection. The Tribunal, however, ruled that the respondent breached the guarantee against expropriation by failing to contact and hear the investor prior to cancelling the concessions.

In the context of the discussion on racial/racialized capitalism, what is especially striking about this case is the investor's use of members of the local community to, in the words of Leong, acquire social and economic value. Without first committing to a full, transparent, and robust consultative programme of engagement with the community, the investor hurriedly offered jobs and social support programmes to members of the community in the hope of pacifying them, while relentlessly pursuing the accumulation of capital. When this strategy failed, the investor was not concerned about the ensuing externalities: the frequent protest action, the blocking of the bridge between Peru and Bolivia, injuries suffered by community members because of violent clashes, food shortages, or poor sanitation. Instead, the investor was quick to initiate proceedings before an international arbitral tribunal, which agreed with the investor, finding that the state waived the right to insist that the investor engage in full consultations because it had not objected to the lack of consultation.

While the state bears some responsibility, it is the Tribunal's lack of appreciation of the plight of members of the racialized community that is worrying, as well as its

143 Bhattacharyya (n 24).

144 Nicolás Perrone, 'Bridging the Gap between Foreign Investor Rights and Obligations: Towards Reimagining the International Law on Foreign Investment' (2022) 7(3) Business and Human Rights Journal 375.

145 *Bear Creek Mining Corporation v Republic of Peru*, ICSID Case No ARB/14/21, Award (30 November 2017).

apparent failure to find any fault in the investor.[146] In the words of Burden-Stelly, the implicit juxtaposition between the expropriator, who is painted as progressive, and the expropriated, who is presented as inferior, backward, and guilty, not only served to justify the investor's conduct in this case, but destabilized previously peaceful and self-sustaining local communities. That the Tribunal would conclude that the police powers doctrine was not applicable to shield the impugned human and/or environmental protection measures because the Canada–Peru FTA introduced all-encompassing exceptions, a view that is out of sync with contemporary understandings of the operation of the police powers exception,[147] further cements Fraser's view that global institutions like the ICSID Tribunal are complicit with investors in extracting value from defenceless populations.

4. Conclusion

This chapter concurs with Achiume's incisive assessment that racialized peoples' relationship to the extractive industry is a racial equality concern because non-white or non-European people from the Global South bear the greatest cost of extractivism. Indeed, I have argued that through a process of racialization, the age-old flawed social construction of non-white or non-European people as racially inferior continues to be reproduced and re-inscribed in novel and variable ways in the extractive industry.

Problematizing the asymmetrical relationship between foreign investors operating in the extractives industry and racialized people in the LAC region is of critical importance from a racial/racialized capitalism perspective because extractivism is yet another manifestation of how racism is hard-wired into the DNA of capitalism. That racialized people, who have endured centuries of racial subordination, marginalization, and exploitation, continue to bear the brunt of an extractive industry that re-inscribes racialization should cause us all to pause and reflect, and should inform the development of further lines of inquiry and action.

[146] ibid 412.
[147] Jason Haynes and Antonius Hippolyte, 'The Covid-19 Pandemic and The Potential for Investor-State Claims: A Caribbean Perspective' (2021) 21(2) Oxford University Commonwealth Law Journal 212.

4
The Inequalities of Sovereign Equality

Harrison Otieno Mbori

1. Introduction

Sovereignty is a foundational concept in both international law and international relations. In the mainstream of many international law discourses, sovereignty conjures up the image of the Peace of Westphalia of 1648 where the European and modern conception of the nation-state was born. However, historians have shown that this date did not mark a clear-cut beginning of the idea of sovereignty nor of modern international law.[1] Heuristically, the date is useful and finds value even among critics. Many positivist approaches to international law thus present a linear narrative of the progressive development of the doctrine of state-based sovereignty from Westphalia into the later centuries that is carefully divorced from its economic, cultural, and political contexts. For example, for the non-European 'other', the mass decolonization of African and Asian countries in the 1960s marked the beginning of their sovereign standing.

Sovereignty is not easily studied in an unbiased or dispassionate manner.[2] Through a Third World Approaches to International Law (TWAIL) lens, I see a sovereignty doctrine that is fluid, context-specific, and always contested. The concept of sovereignty is generally defined as 'the power states have at any given moment of development of the international legal system'.[3] It plays a mix of roles including imbuing states with a monopoly over political and coercive power, anchoring the idea of 'equality of nations', defining the status and rights of nation-states and their officials—sovereign immunity—and implying inviolable borders, shielding states from external intervention, at least doctrinally.[4] Ultimately, despite rising doubts about the doctrine itself,[5]

[1] See Andreas Osiander, 'Sovereignty, International Relations, and the Westphalian Myth' (2001) 55(2) International Organization 251.

[2] Pierre A Lalive, 'The Doctrine of Acquired Rights' in *The Rights and Duties of Private Investors Abroad* (Matthew Bender & Company 1965) 148–49.

[3] Antony J Colangelo, 'Spatial Legality' (2012) 107 Northwestern University Law Review 69. This Eurocentric state-based definition of sovereignty sits in contrast with alternative conceptualizations including those predicated on the status of peoples, and which exceed international law's presumptions of territoriality.

[4] John H Jackson, 'Sovereignty: Outdate Concept or New Approaches' in Wenhua Shan, Penelope Simons, and Dalvinder Singh (eds), *Redefining Sovereignty in International Economic Law* (Hart 2008).

[5] Pärtel Piirimäe, 'The Westphalian Myth and the Idea of External Sovereignty' in Hent Kalmo and Quentin Skinner (eds), *Sovereignty in Fragments: The Past, Present and Future of a Contested Concept* (Cambridge University Press 2010) 64–80 (arguing that critics of Westphalian sovereignty have discredited it on textual, historical-analytic, and normative levels. Textually, the peace treaties of Westphalia have nothing to do with the sovereignty, independence of European actors, or the principle of non-intervention.

Harrison Otieno Mbori, *The Inequalities of Sovereign Equality* In: *Emancipating International Law*.
Edited by: Mohsen al Attar and Claire Smith, Oxford University Press. © Harrison Otieno Mbori 2026.
DOI: 10.1093/9780198935605.003.0006

Westphalian sovereignty confirms a nation-state's powers over its territory and citizens.[6] Historically, it also confirmed the power of some peoples over others.[7] Antony Anghie has shown that the doctrine was formed and used by early international jurists like Francisco de Vitoria and nineteenth-century scholars such as John Austin precisely to exclude non-Europeans from the realm of sovereignty and claim sovereign rights over their territories.[8] Sovereignty is thus not a fixed doctrine established in Westphalia but was progressively produced and reproduced by European powers as a juridical tool to expand imperialism, including in its modern iteration. Despite this vital critique, sovereignty remains the essence of the nation-state, the north star towards which statehood points.[9]

In this chapter, I argue that the cultural context of sovereignty doctrine, especially in Europe's development and its subsequent engagement with other parts of the world through empire, colonialism, coloniality, and the continuities of colonialism, has created a sovereignty doctrine widely infected with racial inequalities. In contrast to positive international law's efforts to stultify the doctrine—by concealing layers of inequalities—I link it to three essential logics precisely to expose the racial inequalities that persist in the exercise of sovereignty. When fused together, the logics of race, capital, and territory show how contemporary international law tolerates sovereign inequality. These three logics operate individually, dually, and as a triad to expose the many faces of sovereign inequalities experienced in international law.

In the second section, I conceptualize the logic of race, racism, and racialization and how it has propelled racial capitalism to the fore in the structuring of racially unequal global socioeconomic and political landscapes. The third section shows how a racialized international law sustained the transatlantic trade in enslaved Africans as well as condoned colonial conquests, two direct manifestations of sovereign inequality. In contemporary international law, the mandate system in the League of Nations and the trusteeship system in the United Nations (UN) show how racial logic mutates to incorporate non-European states into the realm of Western sovereignty and its attendant inequalities. In the final section, through the concept of racial grammar, I show how the logic of race is inscribed within a frame of formal sovereign equality and how the continuities of colonialism materialize in instances of economic inequality. This section offers three specific examples: the veto power at the UN Security Council (UNSC); the Bretton Woods Institutions weighted voting system; and the economic inequalities attendant in international trade, investment, and development law.

I make one caveat before proceeding. My linking of sovereignty to statehood reflects an epistemically specific—Eurocentric—understanding of political community, privileging the state as the sole bearer of sovereignty and thus of legal personality in

Historically, the imperial estates who were supposedly to benefit from external sovereignty did not acquire it in relation to the empire).

[6] Jackson (n 4) 4, 8.

[7] Antony Anghie, 'The Evolution of International Law: Colonial and Postcolonial Realities' (2006) 27 Third World Quarterly 741.

[8] ibid.

[9] Gbenga Oduntan, *Sovereignty and Jurisdiction in the Airspace and Outer Space: Legal Criteria for Spatial Delimitation* (Routledge 2012) 21.

the modern international legal system. This framing, while necessary for engaging with international law as it operates today, reproduces some of the paradigms I critique in this chapter. A different approach that centres peoples rather than states, and imagines sovereignty beyond the state form, would offer an edifying and provocative counterpoint. Such a project, unfortunately, lies beyond the scope of this chapter.

2. Conceptualizing the logic of race: sovereign inequality constitution through racial capitalism

Race is a social construct that is included and occluded in mainstream international law.[10] This duality initially seems paradoxical but is a manifestation of an identitarian crisis in international law that evokes WEB Du Bois's concept of 'double consciousness'.[11] Du Bois argued that African-Americans were constantly oscillating in their identities between the poles of being African and being or *always becoming* American, and the puzzles and dilemmas inherent in this tension.[12] In international law, double consciousness manifests through its abhorrence of racism as a category of discrimination alongside its quotidian colour-blind applications that reaffirm the existence of a global white supremacy 'hiding in plain sight'.[13] Racialized communities remain economically, politically, and socially subordinated in many parts of the world long after international law has proscribed colonialism and discrimination on the basis of race and apartheid.[14]

The continued manifestations of racism in international relations are therefore treated as an aberration.[15] After all, international law is said to have, at best, progressively addressed or, at worst, is continuously addressing the scourge of racism. As an aberration, it is proscribed in international law via the International Convention on the Elimination of All Forms of Racial Discrimination (ICERD).[16] Its presence underscores the first frame in the international claim to progressive triumphalism over racial discrimination. Yet, race and racism remain the silent yet not-so-secret bedfellows of international law.

Race and racism are generally difficult subjects to broach in many spaces. In the United States, there is an awkward acknowledgement of its presence domestically

[10] James Thuo Gathii and Ntina Tzouvala, 'Racial Capitalism and International Economic Law: Introduction' (2022) 25 Journal of International Economic Law 199 (arguing that race and racism are categories that have been excluded for understanding International Economic Law (IEL)).

[11] See Mohsen al Attar, 'Peculiar Double-Consciousness of TWAIL' (2022) 19 Indonesian Journal of International Law 239; See also Nathaniel Berman, 'Shadows: Du Bois and the Colonial Prospect, 1925' (2000) 45(5) Villanova Law Review 959.

[12] WEB Du Bois, *The Souls of Black Folk* (AC McClurg & Co 1903).

[13] See Christopher Gevers, '"Unwhitening the World"': Rethinking Race and International Law' (2021) 67 UCLA Law Review, 1655–1656; See also: James T Gathii, 'Writing Race and Identity in a Global Context: What CRT and TWAIL Can Learn from Each Other' (2021) 67 UCLA Law Review 1622

[14] Natsu Taylor Saito, *Settler Colonialism, Race, and the Law: Why Structural Racism Persists* (New York University Press 2020).

[15] See: Charles W Mills, *Black Rights/White Wrongs: The Critique of Racial Liberalism* (Oxford University Press 2017) (describing this a form of colour-blind liberalism that is no longer overtly racist).

[16] Antony Anghie, 'Civilization and Commerce: The Concept of Governance in Historical Perspective' (2000) 45 Villanova Law Review 887.

alongside the pretence of colour-blindness. In Europe, especially continental Europe, racism and race are consistently dismissed as peripheral, shifting the focus to the other side of the Atlantic.[17] This is partially influenced by the Nazi German genocide of Jews and France's policy of assimilation in its overseas colonies, itself a form of cultural violence. In most postcolonial African nation-states (except South Africa), race and racism are also considered non-existent because of their provincialization as a phenomenon of the United States or an issue that prevails in racially heterogeneous communities. Nothing could be further from the truth. All modern, postcolonial spaces are invariably racialized, where images, institutions, and relationships of the structuring colonial moment continue to constitute and reconstitute racial hierarchies.[18]

Cedric J Robinson argued that racism was established during the early formation of European civilization as part of the oppressive institution of slavery and exacerbated with the formation of capitalism.[19] Early ninth-century Europe (the period he labels the formation of Europe) was characterized by the use of slaves among the Romans and Greeks, self-servingly labelled 'barbarians'.[20] 'Barbarians' consisted of different communities of varying races, cultures, and languages, including North Africans, Italians, and Poles.[21] They assimilated with Indigenous peoples and formed the main source of slave labour.[22] The early Greek and Roman thinkers created the totalizing construct of the barbarians, elevating the nobility above them for their putatively better blood.[23] Thus racist attitudes and constructs were first displayed among Europeans towards other Europeans (Irish, Jews, Gypsies, Slavs, etc) before being deployed phenotypically against people of colour.[24] In other words, race and racism, especially its phenotypical variant, were constructed and applied in Europe, then circulated elsewhere.

Racism is, therefore, part of the making of European civilization and politics through the projects of slavery and colonization, which echo today's 'Fortress Europe'.[25] Racism merges the three processes of prejudice, hierarchy, and power at the political, social, and ideological levels by classifying actors in racial—mainly phenotypic—categories.[26] Prejudice is founded on the construction of differences on disparate grounds: nationality, skin colour, ethnic or social origin, conscience belief, language, or birth. Hierarchical values appear when the othering and discrimination

[17] See Norimitsu Onishi, 'A Racial Awakening in France, Where Race Is a Taboo Topic' *The New York Times* (New York, 14 July 2020) <https://www.nytimes.com/2020/07/14/world/europe/france-racism-universalism.html#:~:text=With%20an%20eye%20on%20the,perceived%20challenge%20to%20France's%20universalism> accessed 29 August 2024.

[18] Jemima Pierre, *The Predicament of Blackness: Postcolonial Ghana and the Politics of Race* (University of Chicago Press 2012) xii.

[19] Cedric J Robinson, *Black Marxism: The Making of a Radical Black Tradition* (University of North Carolina Press 1983); contrast with Michael Ralph, 'Racial Capitalism' (2014) 8 Theory and Society 851.

[20] Robinson (n 19) 1–3.

[21] ibid.

[22] ibid.

[23] ibid 21.

[24] Liliana Obregon, 'Empire, Racial Capitalism and International Law: The Case of Manumitted Haiti and the Recognition Debt' (2018) 31 Leiden Journal of International Law 597.

[25] Grada Kilomba, *Plantation Memories: Episodes of Everyday Racism* (Unrast-Verlag 2010) 39.

[26] Eduardo Bonilla-Silva, 'Rethinking Racism: Toward a Structural Interpretation' (1997) 62 American Sociological Review 466 (arguing that this conception, while non-ideological, stops short of developing a structural conceptualization of racial matters).

of prejudice is 'articulated through stigma, dishonour and inferiority'.[27] This hierarchy is achieved through the denigration of a group of people as lesser, barbaric, or lazy, thereby elevating another race into a superior position.[28] Finally, these two processes are completed by the deployment of historical, political, and economic power.[29] Summoning scholars of postcolonial studies such as Edward Said, Antony Anghie has persuasively demonstrated that early and modern international law was built upon what he labelled a 'dynamic of difference': the line that culturally divided the civilized and uncivilized and the techniques used in international law to maintain this line.[30] This cultural division is done with prejudicial, inferiorizing hierarchical values and power. In this sense, Anghie's 'dynamic of difference' analytical framework can be recategorized, with some qualifications, as a manifestation of racialization in international law.[31]

Similarly, racial capitalism is based on the view that mediaeval Europe, Brazil, Africa, and the Caribbean fit together into a historical pattern that linked slavery and racism with capitalist development.[32] Robinson argued that early European civilization emerged at the same time as the arrival of barbarians.[33] The adoption of slavery as a critical basis of production continued without significant interruption into the twentieth century.[34] Slavery as a form of European agrarian production formed part of the early European feudal system between the thirteenth and sixteenth centuries and persisted to the modern era.[35] Thus, the colonization of the Americas and the transatlantic slave trade formed the material ideological foundations of capitalism as a system of extraction, accumulation through dispossession, and white supremacy or racemaking.[36] Carmen Gonzalez and Athena Mutua conclude that the merger of the logic of territory and of race—the existence of the territorial state with an integrated national market and a willingness to engage in enclosure practices and colonization—furthered capitalist development and expansion or the logic of capital.[37]

Racial capitalism and the enduring legacies of colonialism, therefore, represent profound forces shaping the contours of contemporary global socioeconomic and political landscapes. Rooted in the intersecting histories of imperialism, slavery, and capitalist exploitation, racial capitalism constitutes a system in which economic structures and practices are deeply entwined with racial hierarchies and inequalities. The

[27] Kilomba (n 25) 42.

[28] ibid; see also Bonilla-Silva (n 26) 470.

[29] Kilomba (n 25) 42–51.

[30] Antony Anghie, *Imperialism, Sovereignty and the Making of International Law* (Cambridge University Press 2005) 4.

[31] Michael Omi and Howard Winant, *Racial Formation in the United States: From the 1960s to the 1980s* (Routledge 1986) 64.

[32] Eric Williams, *From Columbus to Castro: The History of the Caribbean, 1492-1969* (London 1970) 16; contrast with Nancy Leong, 'Racial Capitalism' (2013) 126 Harvard Law Review 2151.

[33] Robinson (n 19) 11.

[34] David Brion Davis, *The Problems of Slavery in Western Civilization*, (Cornell University Press 1966) 29–61.

[35] Hugh Thomas, *The Slave Trade: The Story of the Atlantic Slave Trade: 1440-1870* (Simon & Schuster 1997) 40–64.

[36] Aníbal Quijano, 'Coloniality and Modernity/Rationality' (2007) 21 Cultural Studies 168.

[37] Carmen G Gonzalez and Athena D Mutua, 'Mapping Racial Capitalism: Implications for Law' (2022) 2(2) Journal of Law and Political Economy 132.

continuities of colonialism, manifested in patterns of ongoing domination, exploitation, and cultural subjugation, underscore the enduring impacts of historical imperial projects on present-day societies.[38] Within this framework, the exploitation of racialized bodies and lands for the accumulation of capital remains a fundamental feature, perpetuating systemic injustices and disparities along racial lines.[39] As such, an understanding of racial capitalism and the legacy of colonialism is essential for interrogating sovereignty doctrine and fostering genuine pathways towards equity, justice, and decolonization in our contemporary world. In the following section, I use three logics to explain the broad range of sovereign inequalities emerging in the process of colonialism: the logics of territory, cultural difference (race), and capital.

3. Enacting the logic of race: slavery and colonialism as manifestations of sovereign inequality

Sovereign inequalities emerged via the political and economic enactment of the logic of race during the period before and after the transatlantic slave trade, and throughout the *longue durée* of colonialism. Three logics were evident across the landscape, deployed concurrently to assert world order: the logics of territory, cultural difference (race), and capital. Each contained reflections of the sovereign inequalities that were perpetuated before and during the nineteenth century. As I argue below, they instantiate the genesis of imperialism, domination, and 'faux' sovereignty. The logic of territory was a bedrock when it came to inventing legal technologies to bolster colonialism.[40] It was of fundamental importance because international relations and international law were not 'part of a single state, but a state system'.[41] Henceforth, the territorial state would exercise jurisdiction over its controlled territory, assuming broad regulatory power of prescription, adjudication, and enforcement.[42] Imperial tendencies to expand capital are always fused with the logic of territorial control, enabling the full breadth of colonial domination.[43]

Race is the second element in our trinity. The social, economic, and cultural line that divides the civilized and uncivilized, the developed from the underdeveloped is a racial colour line. The idea that European history, achievement, and conflict birthed sovereignty doctrine, fully formed, ignores its development during the colonial encounter.[44] The European conception of non-Europeans as sub-human, barbaric, and

[38] ibid 127–201.

[39] ibid 146–47.

[40] BS Chimni, 'The International Law of Jurisdiction: A TWAIL Perspective' (2022) 35(1) Leiden Journal of International Law 29 (according to Chimni, the other logics were the 'logic of capital', the 'logic of territory', the 'logic of nature', the 'logic of culture', and the 'logic of law'); see also Guglielmo Verdirame, 'Sovereignty' in Jean D'Asperemont and Sahib Singh (eds), *Concepts for International Law: Contributions to Disciplinary Thought* (Edward Elgar 2019) 832.

[41] BS Chimni, *International Law and World Order: A Critique of Contemporary Approaches* (2nd edn, Cambridge University Press 2017) 34–35.

[42] Alex Mills, 'Rethinking Jurisdiction in International Law' (2014) 84(1) British Yearbook of International Law 187.

[43] James Thuo Gathii, 'Imperialism, Colonialism, and International Law' (2007) 54(4) Buffalo Law Review 1013.

[44] See Antony Anghie, 'Rethinking International Law: A TWAIL Retrospective' (2023) 34(1) European Journal of International Law 27.

less intellectually endowed provided the political means of racially 'othering' them and legally justifying the construction of colonial empires.[45] Racial othering had already created a large group of people available for 'enslavement' due to their putative racial inferiority. Thus, processes of enslaving non-Europeans—especially Africans—and colonization racialized these societies before practically enacting the dispossession, dehumanization, and subordination inherent in both processes.[46]

Francisco de Vitoria, the famous sixteenth-century Spanish theologian and jurist, applied the pre-existing rules of European international law to Indigenous political communities. To order the relationship between the empire and its racially collectivized Indigenous populations, Vitoria also reconceptualized the doctrines and developed new ones, helping to solve the new problems occasioned by the encounter with non-European societies.[47] This is arguably the genesis of sovereign inequality since he invented new rules to legalize the Spanish conquest. This is evident vis-à-vis sovereignty doctrine:

> [S]overeignty doctrine . . . was not already formulated and then simply applied by Vitoria to resolve the problem of creating order between different societies. Rather, for Vitoria, the sovereignty doctrine emerges through his attempts to address the problem of cultural difference.[48]

Positivism, as the secular natural law posited by early European international law thinkers, had to define a sovereignty that would conform to its methodology, theory, and identity.[49] Positivist jurists adopted the idea of territorial sovereignty to prevent non-European communities from being classified as sovereigns. Accordingly, although many non-European communities expressed some characteristics of sovereignty—among others stable government and capacity to engage in international relations—they failed because of their supposed lack of full territorial control.[50]

This juristic innovation did not fully solve the problem because it clashed with the presence of established kingdoms in Africa, such as Benin and Mali, which met this territorial control criterion.[51] To solve this dilemma, positivist jurists set another standard: to be considered sovereign, the society had to satisfy the criteria of membership in a civilized international society. This criterion was used to exclude not just African states but also extended to Asia and South America.[52] This conception of sovereignty was not to determine which society satisfies the legal status but was used by European empires to affirm their power to claim sovereignty and, critically, to make sovereignty a status they could bestow, deny, create, or fragment whenever they deemed colonized peoples ready.[53]

45 Siba N'Zatioula Grovogui, *Sovereigns, Quasi Sovereigns, and Africans: Race and Self-Determination in International Law* (University of Minnesota Press 1996) 11–42.
46 Pierre (n 18) 11–12.
47 Anghie (n 30) 15.
48 ibid 16.
49 ibid 56.
50 Thomas Lawrence, *The Principles of International Law* (DC Heath & Company 1895) 156.
51 Anghie (n 30) 58. See also TO Elias, *Africa and The Development of International Law* (AW Sijthoff and Oceana Publications 1972) 6–15.
52 Anghie (n 30) 58.
53 ibid 100.

Since then, non-European societies have engaged in an endless chase to narrow the gap. Yet, these communities can never fully acquire equal rights and obligations under international law because of some purportedly immutable differences between 'the West and the rest' that present insurmountable barriers.[54] This agenda involved the pernicious logic which provides for equal participation in international law of all sovereign powers, subject to extensive internal reform to mimic the imperatives of modern capitalism.[55] The rhetorical argument encompassed the nineteenth-century racist claim that colonization would be beneficial for Indigenous communities, improving 'their individual wealth by allowing immigration to several [Westerners] bringing their intelligence, their financial acumen and their means of enterprise'.[56]

Colonialism, merging the logic of capital and race, thus set in motion the process through which the development of international law allowed the 'specifically capitalist phenomenon of unequal and combined development that tends to generate both homogenisation and unevenness on a global scale'.[57] The logic of the racially capitalist system created a false fatalism among colonized people who came to perceive Western imperialism as a natural force that they need not resist:[58] for the oppressed, the choice was to assimilate or perish. Positivist jurists such as Westlake and Maine advocated for this idea of submissive fatalism, claiming racial destiny and civilizing barbarous societies as justifications for colonialism.[59]

Colonizers also developed a three-tier taxonomy to distinguish between the civilized and uncivilized states: the civilized, the barbarian (semi-civilized), and the savage (uncivilized).[60] This three-tier categorization was also present in racial attitudes amongst British settler colonies in Kenya, Zimbabwe, and South Africa. In colonial Kenya, for example, facilities were divided into three categories for Europeans, Asians, and Africans.[61] In contrast to French-African colonies,[62] Black Africans could never become 'British' enough to sit in parliament or be viewed as equal racially, no matter how much they imbibed in British culture, mannerisms, and education:[63] 'To have Africans in the British parliament (even under the pretext of training them in the parliamentary government) would suggest racial equality that the British were not ready for.'[64]

[54] Ntina Tzouvala, *Capitalism as Civilisation: A History of International Law* (Cambridge University Press 2020) 2.

[55] ibid 45.

[56] Rashid Khalidi, *The Hundred Years' War on Palestine: A History of Settler Colonial Conquest and Resistance, 1917-2017* (Metropolitan Books 2020) (quoting Theodor Herzl's letter response to Yusuf Diya's letter on the hidden intentions of Zionists in creating a new Jewish state in Palestine).

[57] ibid.

[58] ibid 69.

[59] ibid 69–70.

[60] James Lorimer, 'La Doctrine de la Reconnaissance, Fondement du Droit International' (1884) 16 Revue de Droit International et de Législation Comparée 333–59, 335 as cited in Tzouvala (n 54) 51.

[61] Vincent B Khapoya, *The African Experience* (Routledge 2012) 107.

[62] This should not be mistaken as a lack of racism among the French, for even its most assimilated African citizen Léopold Sédar Senghor (1906–2001) of Senegal articulated 'a philosophy of negritude', by which he and his fellow black intellectuals asserted the inherent worth of "blackness" based on his lived experiences in France; see also Frantz Fanon, *Toward the African Revolution* (Grove Press 1967) (arguing that French racism was just as pernicious, if not worse, than that of the British because they only accepted Black people as French if they gave up their own cultural identity and heritage. What he called cultural suicide).

[63] Khapoya (n 61).

[64] ibid.

This Western conception of sovereignty is well understood through the lenses of the cultural and racial diversity of the colonial encounter,[65] leading to the internalization of European culture and society and to the pursuit of the false heights of European personhood.[66] Such ontology is accurate even in current cultural representations that 'tend to idealize the desire for whiteness and devalue the presence of blackness'.[67] The Western conception of sovereignty also facilitated the extraterritorial application of European municipal law, institutions, and legal cultures in non-European societies. The imperial states used transnational companies (TNCs) as special-purpose vehicles to expand their landscape. Capital expansion was at the core of the legal formation of the East Indian and Chinese markets, American colonization, and trade with the colonies.[68]

Between the sixteenth and nineteenth centuries, the European version of the modern TNCs were the Royal Chartered companies. They were capitalist pioneers that first came into contact with Africa. Through armed intervention, they destroyed local sovereignty and laid the groundwork for colonial economies.[69] European chartered companies heralded imperialism in many parts of the Global South.[70] Before this, European imperial powers—especially Britain and Portugal[71]—claimed their interest in sub-Saharan Africa was philanthropic (to suppress the Arab slave trade).[72] While many expeditions—Burton, Speke, Livingstone, Stanley, and Cameron—were complemented with a spirit of adventure and search for knowledge,[73] the main motives were financial, chasing big gains and profits through unabashed economic exploitation.[74] Even the ending of the European slave trade was a fig leaf for the plans of the British imperial government to extend its political and economic influence to Africa.[75]

As the First World War drew to a close, the issue of managing the territories of the now-defunct German and Ottoman empires preoccupied the Allied powers. In Britain, the debate pitted Labour Party leftists who argued for international administration (to end imperialism) against advocates of annexation from the right.[76] In the next subsection, I show how the League of Nations' Mandates and the United Nations' Trusteeships systems maintained a colonial dynamic through a careful race-based

[65] ibid 102. See also, Gathii (n 13) 1617 (asserting that nineteenth-century scholars were racist).

[66] Frantz Fanon, *Black Skin, White Masks* (Charles Lam Markham trans, Grove Press 1967) 216–17.

[67] Robert Samuels, *Writing Prejudices: The Psychoanalysis and Pedagogy of Discrimination from Shakespeare to Toni Morrison* (State University of New York Press 2001) 8.

[68] Anghie (n 44) 38.

[69] Walter Rodney, 'The Colonial Economy' in Albert Abu Boahen (ed), *General History of Africa: Africa under Colonial Domination 1880-1935* (UNESCO 1985) 337.

[70] Raj Kumar Trivedi, 'The Role of Imperial British East Africa Company in the Acquisition of East African Colony in the Second Half of the Nineteenth Century' (1971) 33 Proceedings of Indian History Congress 616.

[71] Nazifa Rashid, 'British Colonialism in East-Africa during the Nineteenth Century' (2013) 1(1) International Journal of Art and Art History 23.

[72] ibid.

[73] WEB Du Bois, *The World and Africa: Color and Democracy* (Oxford University Press 2007) 71.

[74] ibid.

[75] See Rosa Luxemburg, *The Accumulation of Capital* (Routledge 2003) (arguing that imperialism is a necessary outcome of capitalism and is linked to the very survival of capitalism); see also Issa G Shivji, *The Silent Class Struggle* (Tanzania Publishing House 1973) 5.

[76] Wm Roger Louis, 'African Origin of the Mandates Idea' (1965) 19 International Organization 20.

mutation of the manifestation of sovereign inequalities, a compromise welcomed by both sides: 'viewed by the left as a limited triumph in cause of internationalization; and by the right as annexation in all but name'.[77] Its core architects, like General Jan Smuts of South African apartheid infamy, operated within a long line of Western racist thinking,[78] prolonging an 'empire of white rule through international cooperation'.[79]

3.1 The mandate and trusteeship systems as forms of sovereign inequality

The mandate system was conceptualized as a management technique to enable Third World countries to attain sovereignty under Western tutelage.[80] Using their geographic locations and economic development,[81] Smuts classified former Western colonies into three racist categories: advanced territories (mandates A),[82] semi-advanced territories (mandates B),[83] and least-advanced (mandates C),[84] which resonated with the tripartite racial categories of British colonial administration. To be clear, this portioning of sovereignty, while presented in neutral developmental language, was also a racial classification that portrayed non-European societies as bizarre, backward, disorderly, tribalistic, and lacking in political structures that Europeans would recognize.[85] Indeed, the vernacular of development in international law is racialized, deployed within a racist episteme that places Third World sovereignty below Western sovereignty and allows numerous forms of interventions into their spaces.[86]

At face value, the mandate system was a clear shift from the positivist approach of excluding non-Europeans from statehood and laid the basis for the creation of independent nation-states in the colonized territories.[87] However, the international institutions created to realize this idea were built around the logic of cultural difference.[88] Mandatories thus held a civilizational responsibility towards peoples not yet able to stand by themselves under the conditions of the modern world.[89] 'Advanced nations'

[77] ibid.

[78] Mahmood Mamdani, *Citizen and Subject: Contemporary Africa and the Legacy of Late Colonialism* (Princeton University Press 1996) 4.

[79] Mark Mazower, *No Enchanted Palace: The End of Empire and the Ideological Origins of the United Nations* (Princeton University Press 2009) 30.

[80] Antony Anghie, 'Colonialism and the Birth of International Institutions: Sovereignty, Economy and the Mandate System of the League of Nations' (2002) 34 New York Journal of International Law and Politics 513.

[81] Covenant of the League of Nations (28 April 1919) 108 LNTS 188, Article 22; see also Umozurike Oji Umozurike, *Self-Determination in International Law* (Archon Books 1972) 34–43.

[82] This included Iraq, Trans-Jordan, Palestine, Syria, and Lebanon, with Great Britain as the mandatory power for all except Syria and Lebanon, which were under French mandate.

[83] This included the Cameroons with Great Britain and France as mandatory powers; Tanganyika with Great Britain; Togoland with Great Britain and France; and Ruanda-Urundi with Belgium.

[84] This included North Pacific Islands with Japan; Nauru, New Guinea, Western Samoa with Great Britain, Australia, and New Zealand (Australia acting); and South-West Africa with Great Britain and South Africa (South Africa acting).

[85] Edward W Said, *Orientalism* (Routledge and Kegan Paul Ltd 1978).

[86] Jemima Pierre, 'The Racial Vernaculars of Development: A View From West Africa' (2019) 122 American Anthropologist 86.

[87] Anghie (n 30) 116.

[88] ibid 117.

[89] Covenant of the League of Nations (n 81) Article 22.

would assume the tutelage of such peoples because of their resources, experience, or geographical position:[90] 'The essential purpose of the system was to protect the interests of backward people, to promote their welfare and development and to guide them towards self-government and, in certain cases, independence.'[91] Tutor nations would hold these territories in trust and report annually on their progress.

The Permanent Mandates Commission (PMC) was established to review these reports. At one point, Sir Fredrick Lugard, one of the principal architects of the deeply racist indirect rule framework in Africa,[92] was one of its members.[93] Excluding the sole Japanese member, the first eight members of the Commission were all European.[94] They were all men as well, except for the Scandinavian member.[95] WEB Du Bois's efforts to convince William Emmanuel Rappard (the founder of the Graduate Institute of Geneva)[96] and the Director of the Mandates Section in the League Secretariat that a 'man of African descent' be appointed to the Commission went unheeded.[97] This outcome was to be expected as it was in the same context that the founders of the Treaty of Versailles that established the League of Nations rejected Japan's proposal that all races be declared equal and tackle the blatant racism of early twentieth-century international law.[98]

In practice, the mandated territories were governed with the same exploitation-cum-oppression dynamic of the colonies, sometimes worse.[99] Anghie offers the example of the island of Nauru, which fell to Australia, Britain, and New Zealand as a mandated territory in 1920.[100] Eventually, Australia became the main mandate power and exercised authority as something close to ownership of the island. However, the three powers divided phosphate, regarded as the island's most important resource. This partition happened even before the mandate agreement was concluded, leading to the immediate launch of phosphate mining.[101] Reasserting its imperial instinct, Usha Natarajan argued that the 2003 invasion of Iraq echoed the mandates' racialized conceptualization of Third World sovereignty.[102] The invasion displayed the

[90] ibid.
[91] Anghie (n 80) 523.
[92] Mamdani (n 78).
[93] Susan Pedersen, *Guardians: The League of Nations and the Crisis of Empire* (Oxford University Press 2015) 2.
[94] Ram Prakash Anand, 'Role of the New Asian-African Countries in the Present International Legal Order' (1962) 56 Amsterdam Journal of International Law 384.
[95] ibid.
[96] See Quinn Slobodian, *Globalists: The End of Empire and the Birth of Neoliberalism* (Harvard University Press 2018) 94 (describing him as the organizer of early neoliberalism).
[97] Anand (n 94) 3.
[98] William A Schabas, *The International Legal Order's Colour Line: Racism, Racial Discrimination, and the Making of International Law* (Oxford University Press 2023) 30–38.
[99] N'Zatioula Grovogui (n 45) 113 (arguing that the system institutionalized collective exploitation of the colonies, without the burden of collective administration, and provided alternatives to global colonial conflicts).
[100] Antony Anghie, 'The Heart of My Home: Colonialism, Environmental Damage, and the Nauru Case' (1993) 34 Harvard International Law Journal 445.
[101] Trusteeship Agreement for the Territory of Nauru (1 November 1947) 10 UNTS 3.
[102] Usha Natarajan, 'Creating and Recreating Iraq: Legacies of The Mandate System in Contemporary Understandings of Third World Sovereignty' (2011) 24 Leiden Journal of International Law 799.

West's contradictory approach to territorial integrity, arrogating to itself the power to monitor, discipline, and enforce their vision on Global South states.[103]

In its worst form, apartheid South Africa all but annexed current Namibia (then German South West Africa) under both the League's mandate and UN trusteeship. Even then, South Africa used a false emancipatory aim of safeguarding the interests of native populations—the Nama and Herero, who had suffered the first genocide in the twentieth century under the Germans—to justify their violent intervention.[104] Vasuki Nesiah uses the Namibian example to showcase a pan-European solidarity that formed the Duboisian 'colour line that belts the world'.[105] European capitals, the League of Nations and Mandate system, and the ICJ, with the heavily criticized decision in the South West Africa cases, were centres of European racial solidarity where Smut's 'white utopia' vision was formed for Global South colonies whose legacies continue to choke them today.[106]

Even among members of the League of Nations, who would have axiomatically regarded each other as sovereign equals, sovereign inequalities subsisted. Thus, the 1935 Italian invasion of the Ethiopian Empire was not widely condemned as a flagrant violation of international law.[107] Within racial logic, the mandate and trusteeship systems created mid-level civilizational standards manifested through a racialized sovereignty that was conditional on Western institutional and ideological policing. In the next section, I argue that these manifestations of sovereign inequality are a re-enactment of the logic of race through a 'racial grammar'[108] that constructs and reconstructs Global South sovereignty as peculiar, particular, inferior, and as part of the racialized 'other' of Western sovereignty which is wholesome and universal. This process reinforces patterns of racial disadvantages, global inequality, and domination.

4. Re-enacting the logic of race: colonial continuities as a form of modern sovereign inequalities

Eduardo Bonilla-Silva exposes how the logic of race exacerbates colonial continuities and deepens modern forms of sovereign inequality. He argues that 'racial domination necessitates something like a racial grammar that is used to normalize the standards of white supremacy as the standards for all sorts of everyday transactions rendering the racial domination almost invisible'.[109] International law contributed to and maintains

[103] ibid.
[104] N'Zatioula Grovogui (n 45) 135.
[105] Vasuki Nesiah, 'Solidarity in the International Court of Justice: Defining "Legal Interest" in the South-West Africa Cases' in Cecilia Marcela Bailliet (ed), *Research Handbook on International Law and Solidarity* (Edward Elgar 2024).
[106] ibid 361.
[107] Rose Parfitt, *The Process of International Legal Reproduction: Inequality, Historiography, Resistance* (Cambridge University Press 2019) 1.
[108] Eduardo Bonilla-Silva, 'The Invisible Weight of Whiteness: The Racial Grammar of Everyday Life in Contemporary America' (2011) 35 Ethnic and Racial Studies 173.
[109] ibid 174.

the distinction between civilized and uncivilized or what was previously an overt racial grammar. Today's grammar operates covertly, distinguishing between developed/ underdeveloped, good governance[110] and 'state failure',[111] 'ease of doing business', 'rule of law', and 'corruption' rankings, masked as legal indicators.[112] This new racial grammar reproduces a racial hierarchy where the logic of race is 'just the way things are'.[113]

We also observe this grammar in doctrines regarding occupation, unequal treaties, recognition, alien rights, jurisdiction, and state responsibility.[114] While a shift occurred with decolonization, perhaps counterintuitively, sovereign inequalities worsened. In neocolonial configurations, former colonial powers and TNCs wielded vast influence over ostensibly sovereign nations, structuring and manipulating their economies, governance mechanisms, and cultural narratives to serve external interests. This perpetuation of dependency and subordination sustains unequal power relations, undermining the self-determination and socioeconomic development of formerly colonized nations. Through an intricate web of economic coercion, political interference, and cultural hegemony, neocolonialism perpetuated systems of oppression and marginalization, posing formidable challenges to the realization of genuine independence, sovereignty, and equitable international relations.[115]

Chimni argues that, in the twenty-first century, we are at the cusp of a new phase that has intensified tendencies towards global imperialism. Stemming from historical traces of colonial expansion and capitalist exploitation, global imperialism manifests in various forms, including economic exploitation, political interventionism, and cultural hegemony.[116] Embedded within the structures of global capitalism, imperialism concentrates wealth and resources in the hands of a privileged few while disenfranchising and dispossessing vast populations. Through mechanisms such as unequal trade relations, military interventions, and ideological imposition, imperial powers assert control over the landscapes of subjugated nations, subverting their sovereignty and perpetuating cycles of dependency and underdevelopment, deepening unequal power relations.[117]

[110] James T Gathii, 'Retelling Good Governance Narratives on Africa's Economic and Political Predicaments: Continuities and Discontinuities in Legal Outcomes between Markets and States' (2000) 45(5) Villanova Law Review 971.

[111] Branwen Gruffydd Jones, '"Good Governance" and "State Failure": The Pseudo-science of statesmen in Our Times' in Alexander Anievas, Nivi Manchanda, and Robbie Shilliam (eds), *Race and Racism in International Relations: Confronting the Global Colour Line* (Routledge 2015) 62.

[112] See Melike Arslan, 'Differentiating and Connecting Indicators: The Quality and Performance of Law in the World Bank's Doing Business Project' (2020) 16 International Journal of Law in Context 17.

[113] Bonilla-Silva (n 108) 174; see also Charles W Mills, *The Racial Contract* (Cornell University Press 1999).

[114] Anghie (n 30) 4; see also BS Chimni, 'Articles on Responsibility and the Guiding Principles of Shared Responsibility: A TWAIL Perspective' (2020) 31(4) European Journal of International Law 1211.

[115] Kwame Nkrumah, *Neo-Colonialism: The Last Stage of Imperialism* (International Publishers Co, Inc 1965)

[116] BS Chimni, 'Capitalism, Imperialism, and International Law in the Twenty-First Century' (2012) 14 Oregon Review of International Law 17.

[117] BS Chimni, International Institutions Today: An Imperial Global State in the Making' (2004) 15(1) European Journal of International Law 18, 28.

I offer three examples that drive this subversion of sovereignty through its inscribed racial grammar: the veto power at the UNSC, the Bretton Woods Institutions (BWIs) weighted voting system,[118] and the unequal international economic system.[119]

4.1 Inscribing international law's racial grammar: the UNSC veto

One of the markers of a racial ideology is what Bonilla-Silva has called abstract liberalism.[120] Contextualizing the false colour-blindness of the US, abstract liberalism 'involves using ideas associated with political liberalism (e.g., "equal opportunity," the idea that force should not be used to achieve social policy) and economic liberalism (e.g., choice, individualism) in an abstract manner to explain racial matters'.[121] He argues that liberalism as a modern political philosophy is denoted by four distinctive features: individualism, universalism, egalitarianism, and meliorism (the idea that people and institutions can be improved).[122] Within this framework and in agreement with Charles W Mills' idea of a racial contract,[123] Bonilla-Silva argues that these libertarian ideals were limited to the mainly white, male, and middle-class owners of property. Notably for international law, the liberal project excluded colonized countries that were seen as outposts for raw materials and racialized workers, either as slaves, indentured servants, or precarious labourers.[124]

In its various iterations, abstract liberalism has continued many discriminatory practices and actively co-opted various new regimes of imperial racial rule, with a devastation far greater than the ancient class-based regimes it sought to replace.[125] The Euro-American foreign affairs tradition also frames its 'humanitarian' commitments in libertarian language. This framing includes 'a commitment to multilateralism and intergovernmental institutions, a renunciation of power politics, militarism, and imperial aspirations, a commitment to moral idealism and projects of ethical, spiritual and political betterment for other nations, and a commitment to cosmopolitanism'.[126] Yet, like the American libertarian project, when this racial international emancipatory project is transcribed into international laws like human rights, global trade, and humanitarian warfare, the inscription generates a grammar that helps to reproduce a racial order as simply the way things are.

[118] James Thuo Gathii and Harrison Otieno Mbori, 'Sovereign Debt as Subordination to Global Finance' in Antony Anghie, Vasuki Nesiah, and Karin Michelson (eds), *TWAIL Reader* (Edward Elgar 2025).

[119] James Thuo Gathii and Harrison Otieno Mbori, 'Reform and Retrenchment in International Investment Law: Introduction to a Special Issue' (2023) 24 Journal of World Investment and Trade 535; Harrison Otieno Mbori, 'International Trade Solidarity Governance Splits: Bretton Woods Solidarity vs. Bandung Solidarity' in Cecilia Marcela Bailliet (ed), *Research Handbook on International Law and Solidarity* (Edward Elgar 2024).

[120] Eduardo Bonilla-Silva, *Racism without Racists: Color-Blind Racism and the Persistence of Racial Inequality in America* (Rowman & Littlefield 2006) 39.

[121] ibid 40.

[122] ibid 39.

[123] See Charles W Mills, *Black Rights/White Wrongs: The Critique of Racial Liberalism* (Oxford University Press 2017).

[124] Bonilla-Silva (n 120) 40.

[125] See Domenico Losurdo, *Liberalism: A Counter-History* (Verso 2011).

[126] David Kennedy, 'Reassessing International Humanitarianism: The Dark Sides' in Anne Orford (ed), *International Law and Its Others* (Cambridge University Press 2006) 131–32.

The UN system affirms the sovereign equality of all members within the abstract liberal frame.[127] Within a colour-blind frame of racial politics, this affirmation underlines formal equality, using neutral language that keeps intact the underlying racial grammar. While the overt racial ideology of the civilizing mission was dropped, the current orthodoxy perpetrates a colour-blind form of racism that manifests indirectly.[128] The formal invocation of sovereign equality exists contemporaneously with other incidents of formal sovereign inequality existing in the UN Charter itself.[129] The Westphalian conception of sovereignty officially extends special rights to the five permanent members (P5) of the UNSC—the United States, the United Kingdom, China, France, and Russia—in facially neutral language.[130]

The veto power is embodied in the UNSC voting process in Article 27(3) of the UN Charter, providing that 'all substantive decisions of the Council must be made with the concurring votes of the permanent members'.[131] The P5 are thus formally allowed to nullify any non-procedural resolutions regarding the maintenance of international peace and security with their negative vote, irrespective of majority support for the resolution.[132] The basic structure of arguably the most powerful organ in the UN system and a bastion of hope for international peace and security maintains a hierarchical order initially adopted by the US, the UK, and the USSR, and imposed an unequal system derived from a colonial model of governance.[133] The veto power of the P5 did not just appear out of thin air:[134] it is an affirmation of state inequality supported by a strong dose of racial superiority using racially neutral language that has direct racial outcomes. At its core, the UN system is therefore designed to be formally racist by an institutional racial grammatical design. The permanency of the P5 membership and the veto power easily expose the faux underbelly of sovereign equality.

The veto power creates an unequal playing field within the UN architecture, making the P5 'guardians of the holy temple', invoking former US President Franklin D Roosevelt's vision of the US, the UK, the USSR, and China as the 'four policemen'.[135] This power imbalance can lead to decisions that serve the interests of a few powerful nations—or one—rather than the collective good. Other peace and security issues are simply sidelined due to the lack of representation at the UNSC. It can also lead to

[127] Charter of the United Nations (adopted 26 June 1945, entry into force 24 October 1945) 1 UNTS XVI, Article 2; see also Guy Fiti Sinclair, *To Reform the World: International Organizations and the Making of Modern States* (Oxford University Press 2017) 118 (arguing that the US projected the structure of its domestic welfare-administrative state onto global institutions).

[128] Bonilla-Silva (n 120).

[129] Jack Donnelly, 'Sovereign Inequalities and Hierarchy in Anarchy: American Power and International Society' (2006) 12(2) European Journal of International Relations 162.

[130] Jennifer Trahan, *Existing Legal Limits to Security Council Veto Power in the Face of Atrocity Crimes* (Cambridge University Press 2020) 9–52.

[131] Charter of the United Nations (n 127) Article 27(3).

[132] Fakiha Mahmood, 'Power Versus the Sovereign Equality of States: The Veto, the P-5 and United Nations Security Council Reforms' (2013) XVII Perceptions 117.

[133] Giorgia Papalia, 'A Critique of the Unqualified Veto Power' (2017) 2 Perth International Law Journal 56; see also Mazower (n 79) 60.

[134] Martti Koskenniemi and Ville Kari, 'Sovereign Equality' in Jorge E. Viñuales (ed), *The UN Friendly Relations Declaration at 50* (Cambridge University Press 2020) 175-176.

[135] Francine McKenzie, *GATT and Global Order in the Post-war Era* (Cambridge University Press 2020) 27-30.

decisions that do not (contextually) serve the situation at hand or are mismatched due to limited representation, input, and the matter of making compromises to balance P5 interests. And because they also wield enforcement power, there is little or no accountability or check when they violate their resolutions.

In light of the unfairness associated with veto powers, there have been increasing calls for its restructuring. One suggestion is to limit or eliminate the veto power, as it can hinder the organization's ability to respond effectively to global crises or serious global conflicts. Indeed, the Cold War and post-Cold War politics between the US and Russia have variously coloured the system's effectiveness. A lack of responsiveness to mass atrocities in the Global South in Rwanda, Darfur, Syria, Sri Lanka, Myanmar, Yemen, and Palestine has added to the persistent accusation of the UNSC ignoring some of the most severe atrocities.[136] The fact that the calls for reforms have not yielded any tangible progress over seven decades is further evidence of this inequality. And so are the legal barriers to democratization of the UNSC in the UN Charter since change to the veto power requires unanimous endorsement from the P5. In this sense, the racial grammar within the core of the UN system remains intact and affirms the words of Du Bois at the formation of the UN: 'We have conquered Germany . . . but not their ideas. We still believe in white supremacy, keeping Negroes in their place and lying about democracy when we mean imperial control of 750 million human beings in colonies.'[137] The inscription of international law's racial grammar does not just stop at the UNSC but finds an even stronger presence within the BWIs.

4.2 Inscribing international law's racial grammar: Bretton Woods Institutions weighted voting system

The presence of weighted voting rights within the World Bank Group (WBG)[138] and the IMF, the two post-war international financial institutions (IFIs), provides an additional instance of international law's racial grammar. The World Bank began initially as the International Bank for Reconstruction and Development (IBRD), which intended to repair the damage wrought by the Second World War in Europe and then later develop resources and productive capacities of the less developed countries.[139] The IMF, on the other hand, started as an international institution intended to stabilize and monitor the global monetary order to promote seamless international trade.[140] Known as the BWIs, the IFIs furthered the primary economic and

[136] See Yasmine Nahlawi, *The Responsibility to Protect in Libya and Syria: Mass Atrocities, Human Protection, and International Law* (Routledge 2020).

[137] Mazower (n 79) 61.

[138] The WBG now includes five separate 'arms': the International Bank for Reconstruction and Development (IBRD), the International Development Association (IDA), the International Finance Corporation (IFC), the International Center for Settlement of Investment Disputes (ICSID), and the Multilateral Investment Guarantee Agency (MIGA).

[139] Edward S Mason and Robert E Asher, *The World Bank Since Bretton Woods* (The Brooking Institution 1973); see also International Bank for Reconstruction and Development Articles of Agreement (27 December 1945) 2 UNTS 134, OXIO (IBRD Articles of Agreement) Article I(1).

[140] International Monetary Fund, 'Articles of Agreement of the International Monetary Fund July 22, 1945' (*IMF*) <https://www.imf.org/> accessed 13 August, 2024 (the IMF is created to promote 'international monetary cooperation' and inspire fiscal confidence by making the Fund's resources temporarily available to IMF members under adequate safeguard) Article I(i), I(v).

geopolitical interests of the United States and other leading Global North states. From a racial viewpoint, this hierarchical system maintained a racial hierarchy 'through [the] production and transformation of post-imperial economic integration, stabilization, and domination by Western states'.[141] Institutionally, this hierarchical structure was formalized through a weighted voting system.

In the Bank, voting power is distributed according to basic votes and share votes.[142] In the Fund, voting power is distributed according to basic votes and quota-based votes.[143] For both the Bank and the Fund, all decisions are made by a majority of the votes cast.[144] As of August 2024, in the IMF, the US enjoys the largest percentage of the total voting power at 17.43 per cent, followed by Japan at 6.47 per cent, China at 6.40 per cent, Germany at 5.59 per cent, and France at 4.23 per cent, respectively. If the G7 nations (the US, Japan, Germany, France, the UK, Italy, and Canada) combine their votes, they reach a total of approximately 41 per cent of the entire vote. Comparatively, the combined voting power of all the fifty-four African states is approximately 7.38 per cent, that of Asian countries, including China, Japan, India, and Saudi Arabia, is approximately 26-27 per cent, and that of Latin America is approximately 7–8 per cent.[145] The situation is not much different at the World Bank; the US holds the largest total share of voting power at 15.49 per cent, followed by Japan at 7.08 per cent, China at 5.91 per cent, Germany at 4.21 per cent, and France at 3.86 per cent.[146] This basic structure creates the infamous weighted voting system of the BWIs that inscribes a racial grammar that directly favours the US and other Western nations.

This outlook also influences the colour of the Executive Board of the IMF, which currently has twenty-four directors, with each of the financially strong members (the US, China, Japan, Germany, France, the UK, and Saudi Arabia) having its own director while the rest of the countries are grouped into seventeen clusters each with one director.[147] This voting power outlay, in addition to the racialized informal and practice-based rule of having the Managing Director of the IMF selected from Europe and the President of the World Bank from the US, embeds a personified form of racist institutionalization (despite one non-American and two people of colour having held the position of President).[148] Recent reforms to increase the representativeness of the

[141] Mbori (n 119) 181.

[142] IBRD Articles of Agreement, Article V(3). The basic votes of each member are the number of votes that result from the equal distribution among all members of 5.55 per cent of the aggregate sum of the voting power of all members, provided that there shall be no fractional basic votes, while the share votes are the number of votes that result from the allocation of one vote for each share of stock held.

[143] IMF Articles of Agreement XII, section 5. The basic votes of each member are the number of votes that result from the equal distribution among all the members of 5.502 per cent of the aggregate sum of the total voting power of all members, provided that there shall be no fractional basic votes, while the quota-based votes are the number of votes that result from the allocation of one vote for each part of its quota equivalent to 100,000 special drawing rights (SDRs).

[144] IBRD Articles of Agreement, Article V(3)(b); IMF Articles of Agreement XII, section 5(c).

[145] IMF, 'IMF Members' Quotas and Voting Power, and IMF Board of Governors' (*IMF*, 17 November 2024) <https://www.imf.org/en/About/executive-board/members-quotas> accessed 17 November 2024.

[146] World Bank Group, 'Voting Powers' (*World Bank Group*) <https://www.worldbank.org/en/about/leadership/votingpowers> accessed 13 August 2024.

[147] IMF, 'IMF Members' Quotas and Voting Power, and the IMF Board of Governors' (*IMF*, 17 November 2024) <https://www.imf.org/en/About/executive-board/eds-voting-power> accessed 17 November 2024.

[148] Alexander Mayer and Stefan Napel, 'Weighted Voting on the IMF Managing Director' (2020) 21 Economics of Governance 237.

Board by adding a twenty-fifth directorship intended for Sub-Saharan Africa[149] do little to erase the racial grammar imprinted in this structure and can be credibly described as racially tokenistic.[150]

The 1980s provide a concrete example of how the racial grammar of the BWIs can manifest devastating racial outcomes. On 21 October 1982, the UN General Assembly resolved that the IMF should refrain from granting the apartheid South African government any financial credit.[151] The UNGA resolution was adopted by 121 votes to 3 (the US, the UK, and West Germany voting against and twenty-three abstentions).[152] The context was that the government of South Africa had applied for a $1.07 billion loan from the IMF to address its budgetary deficits. At that point, the weighted voting system of the IMF meant that just three dissenting states in the UNGA—the US, the UK, and West Germany—possessed 31.38 per cent of the votes.[153] What looked like an overwhelming majority in the UNGA turned up short in the IMF as the South African loan was approved by the voting coalition of Western countries (forming 51.6 per cent of the votes).[154]

For the World Bank, a similar racially charged debate ended with an eerily identical outcome. In 1965, the UNGA approved resolutions by a special committee established under the Declaration on the Granting of Independence to Colonial Countries and Peoples. The committee appealed to:

> all the specialized agencies of the United Nations, and in particular the International Bank for Reconstruction and Development and the International Monetary Fund, and requests them to refrain from granting Portugal any financial, economic or technical assistance so long as the Portuguese Government fails to renounce its colonial policy, which constitutes a flagrant violation of the provisions of the Charter of the United Nations.

and later in softer language:

> request all States and international institutions, including the specialized agencies of the United Nations, to withhold assistance of any kind to the Governments of Portugal and South Africa until they renounce their policy of colonial domination and racial discrimination.[155]

[149] IMF, 'IMF Board of Governors Issues a Resolution to Create a 25th Chair at the IMF Executive Board' (*IMF*, 2 August 2024) <https://www.imf.org/en/News/Articles/2024/08/02/pr-24299-imf-board-of-governors-issues-resolution-to-create-a-25th-chair-at-the-imf-exec-board> accessed 17 November 2024.

[150] Glenda Marisol Flores, 'Racialized Tokens: Latina Teachers Negotiating, Surviving and Thriving in a White Woman's Profession' (2011) 34 Qualitative Sociology 313 (arguing that racial tokenism occurs when coloured individuals are added among a predominantly white group without reaching a 'tipping point' number that can cause a cultural transformation).

[151] UNGA RES/37/2 (21 October 1982) UN Doc A/RES/37/2.

[152] HML Beri, 'IMG Loan to South Africa' (1982) Strategic Analysis 549.

[153] Jonathan Kwitny, 'An IMF Happening' (*CSIS Africa Notes*, 6 June 1983) <https://csis-website-prod.s3.amazonaws.com/s3fs-public/legacy_files/files/publication/anotes_0683.pdf> accessed 13 August 2024.

[154] Rob Clark, 'Quotas Operandi: Examining the Distribution of Voting Power at the IMF and World Bank' (2017) 58 Sociological Quarterly 595.

[155] UN Document A/AC 109/124 (10 June 1965); UNGA Res 2105(XX) (20 December 1965) para 11.

In classic legal technicalist stance, the World Bank defied these requests, arguing that Article IV of its Articles of Agreement absolved it of abiding by UN Resolutions.[156] Consequently, between 1958 and 1968, World Bank loans financed 'pro-White' projects in apartheid South Africa, such as a thermal power plant which supplied electricity to only white peoples and a railway network only usable by Black peoples upon travel authorization.[157]

One way to explain away these inscriptions of racial grammar is what Bonilla-Silva calls 'the anything but racism' methodology.[158] This methodology explains the institutional setup of the UN generally, the UNSC specifically, and the Bretton Woods Institutions weighted voting system as forms of legal constructive ambiguity,[159] a natural promotion of self-interest by powerful states,[160] an indispensable compromise reached in treaty negotiations to save the institution's formation, or as a lack of democratic legitimacy and representativeness.[161] In many deliberations, interlocutors examine every reason for this unfair, unequal, and hegemonic institutional setup except for racism. Additionally, it is possible to argue that, since some Western nations that were implicated in racist policies domestically, like Australia, vehemently opposed the UNSC permanency and veto powers, the setup cannot be racist.[162] Yet, these countries were not invoking a claim against the unequal racial grammar of the current institutional setup but more protesting their own exclusion from global institutional white supremacy. Thus, the argument itself would affirm the claim of racialization, as other nations that considered themselves part of the racial hegemony protested their exclusion. The racial grammar of this institutional setup enforces the production of 'deep and malleable systems of global white supremacy'.[163]

4.3 Economic sovereign inequalities

In the economic governance of sovereign authority, the processes of an institutionalized racial grammar produce economic outcomes that directly undermine sovereign equality. This is mainly achieved through a global governance process that extends economic governance tools extraterritorially. The BWIs and the WTO models thus

[156] Eric Toussaint and Patrick Bond, 'South Africa: The Support of the World Bank and the IMF to the Apartheid Regime' (*CADTM*, 29 April 2019) <https://www.cadtm.org/spip.php?page=imprimer&id_article=17364> accessed 13 August 2024.

[157] ibid.

[158] Eduardo Bonilla-Silva and Gianpaolo Baiocchi, 'Anything but Racism: How Sociologists Limit the Significance of Racism' in Tukufu Zuberi and Eduardo Bonilla-Silva (eds), *White Logic, White Methods: Racism and Methodology* (Rowman & Littlefield Publishers 2008) 137–52.

[159] Fiti Sinclair (n 127) 121–24.

[160] David Kennedy, *The Dark Sides of Virtue: Reassessing International Humanitarianism* (Princeton University Press 2004) 157.

[161] Ariel Buira, 'The Bretton Woods Institutions: Governance without Legitimacy?' in Ariel Buira (ed), *Reforming the Governance of the IMF and the World Bank* (Anthem Press 2005) 7–42.

[162] This opposition to the veto powers continues today from a broad spectrum of UN members, UN, 'General Assembly adopts Landmark Resolution aimed at holding Five Permanent Security Council members Accountable for Use of Veto' (*UN*, 26 April 2022) <https://press.un.org/en/2022/ga12417.doc.htm> accessed 12 August 2024.

[163] Michelle Christian, 'A Global Critical Race and Racism Framework: Racial Entanglements and Deep and Malleable Whiteness' (2019) 5(2) Sociology of Race and Ethnicity 169.

naturalize a racial grammar by promoting liberal and neoliberal ideas such as free trade, development, good governance, and rule of law as universally beneficial. The outcome indirectly disperses Western political and economic norms in the Global South. Unfortunately, such dispersal reinforces patterns of racial disadvantage already visible in Global North countries, including racialized impoverishment and cultural racism that sees many Global South countries as naturally underdeveloped. The racial grammar of development and the rule of law discourse is an excellent example of how Western sovereignty is dispersed through neutral normative standards that naturalize and minimize racism.[164]

A racial grammar of development operates mainly by using neutral ideas associated with liberalism to sanction the incursion into the internal domestic affairs of 'other' sovereigns. Since its inception, the development project has been an 'othering' process that sets out to project most of the Global South as possessing 'particularized lack'. Development has two dimensions: internal or domestic and external or international. At the domestic level, the developmental state is a construct of the Global South's engagement with postcolonialism. While the primary mode of governance of the colonial state was socially, economically, and environmentally extractive,[165] the postcolonial state aimed at creating cohesive national identities using the idea of 'development'. The development ideology was synonymous with European industrialization, progress, and modernization,[166] encouraging global transformation via 'human intervention [science and technology], industrial production, the harnessing of nature, and the establishment of a market economy'.[167] The emergent state in the Global South, while reacting to the extractive nature of the colonial state and aiming at national unity, used the idea of development as the bridge between the traditional and the modern. This dichotomy, as we have seen before, is racialized.

In the colonial years, the colour line demarcated civilized and uncivilized. The colonial powers rhetorically justified their extractive intervention using the image of the civilizing mission, while in many cases pursued overt racist policies.[168] In the postcolonial phase, the dynamic of difference acquired a new form: mimicking the developmental trajectory of Europe.[169] Civilized and uncivilized morphed from cultural to economic, further justifying European intervention in the underdeveloped countries of the world.[170] Simply put, Global South countries are 'increasingly dominated by imposed economic controls that make a mockery of their right to self-determination'.[171]

[164] Pierre (n 86).

[165] See Luis Eslava, 'The Developmental State: Independence, Dependency, and the History of the South' in Jochen von Bernstorff and Philipp Dann (eds), *The Battle of International Law: South-North Perspectives on the Decolonization Era* (Oxford University Press 2019) 73–74.

[166] Anghie (n 32) 205; see also Karin Mickelson, 'South, North, International Environmental Law, and International Environmental Lawyers' (2000) 11 Yearbook of International Environmental Law 52.

[167] Anthony Giddens, *Conversations with Anthony Giddens: Making Sense of Modernity* (Stanford University Press 1998).

[168] See generally Anghie (n 30).

[169] ibid 202.

[170] ibid 203.

[171] Faye V Harrison, 'Global Apartheid, Foreign Policy, and Human Rights' (2002) 4(3) Souls 48.

Decolonization was, therefore, simultaneously an emancipatory awakening of the Global South and a heteronomous process of imperial economic restructuring.[172] The Global North countries, propped-up by the BWIs, have systematically underdeveloped countries in the Global South through economic and militaristic interventionist policies.[173] The implementation of IMF and World Bank neoliberal economic interventions/reforms have led to increased sovereign debt distress; poverty; reduced access to healthcare, education, and other social services; and created mass displacement.[174] The austerity design for lending implemented by the IMF is not a design flaw but a carefully woven mechanism to undermine, control, and influence domestic policies of debtor countries.[175] Furthermore, 'the perverse effects of the foreign aid allocation to countries from the 1960s to the early 2000s, mostly as a function of the Structural Adjustment Programmes (SAPs) since the 1980s, were obviously in direct relation with the sovereign debt crisis in African countries and the persistence of poverty'.[176]

To understand the decolonization process and its relationship to sovereignty, we must acknowledge that political decolonization was incomplete; it only transferred rudimentary political powers but maintained the structures of domination of Western hegemony.[177] On the other hand, the colonial governance system—indirect rule by the British and French empires—established a system of differentiation or institutional segregation in colonial Africa.[178] This system partially reformed with decolonization, through only artificial de-racialization.[179] The view that emerges from the logic of neocolonialism is that economic domination and exploitation of the colonized remained intact. Mohammed Bedjaoui, the towering Algerian jurist, judge, diplomat, and politician[180] argued 'that international law had long concealed flagrant economic inequalities between states under the cover of sovereign equality'.[181] His outline of

[172] Gary Wilder, *Freedom Time: Negritude, Decolonization, and the Future of the World* 241 (Duke University Press 2014) 241.

[173] See Jamie Martin, *The Meddlers: Sovereignty, Empire, and the Birth of Global Economic Governance* (Harvard University Press 2022).

[174] Antony Anghie, 'Time Present and Time Past: Globalization, International Financial Institutions and the Third World' (2000) 32 New York Journal of International Law and Politics 243; Antony Anghie, 'International Financial Institutions' in Christian Reus-Smit (ed), *The Politics of International Law* (Cambridge University Press 2009).

[175] See Olufunmilayo Arewa, 'Colonial Hangover in Global Financial Markets: Eurobonds, China, and African Debt' in Ndogo Samba Sylla (ed), *Imperialism and the Political Economy of Global South's Debt* (Emerald Publishing 2023) 61–62.

[176] Toussaint Kafarhire Murhula, 'United States Foreign Policy Toward HIV/AIDS in Africa: The Role of Pharmaceutical Companies in the Formulation and Implementation of the President's Emergency Plan for AIDS Relief (PEPFAR) 2003-2008' (PhD Thesis, Loyola University Chicago Faculty of Graduate School 2016) 232–54.

[177] N'Zatioual Grovogui (n 45).

[178] Mamdani (n 78).

[179] ibid.

[180] Antony Anghie and BS Chimni, 'Third World Approaches to International Law and Individual Responsibility in Internal Conflicts' (2003) 2 Chinese Journal of International Law 77.

[181] Mohammed Bedjaoui, *Towards a New International Economic Order* (UNESCO 1979) 61. The legal manifestation of the NIEO was in three important but non-binding UNGA Resolutions: *Permanent Sovereignty over Natural Resources*, UNGA Resolution 1803 (XVII) (14 December 1964); *Declaration on the Establishment of a New International Economic Order*, UNGA Resolution 3201 (1 May 1974); and *The Charter of Economic Rights and Duties of States*, UNGA Resolution 3281 (XXIX) (12 December 1974). Scholars of the twenty-first century view the NIEO model as a failure, even though some TWAIL II scholars have taken the opportunity to unravel globalization and the neoliberal economic model to remind the

the NIEO demanded that formerly colonized states must enjoy a right 'to dispose of their own natural resources, the prohibition of all forms of illegitimate interference in their economic affairs, and the banning from economic affairs of force and all forms of constraints'.[182]

Latin American decolonization, starting in the early nineteenth century, was already following the trajectory of European modernity.[183] The transformation of the world represented this modernity through human intervention, industrial production, harnessing nature, and establishing a market economy.[184] The state was the enabler of this process in Europe.[185] The international developmental institutions offered a push to link European modernity to developmentalism and the Global South's desire for the fruits of development. From then onwards, it has been a perpetual chase of development for the Global South. The developmental state as bureaucratic centralized machinery geared towards economic and social modernization was institutionalized in the international order and consolidated into a right globally.[186] Since decolonization, states in the Global South have become 'modernizing dispositifs'[187] programmed on Western-based conditionalities to enact international requirements and aspirations in their domestic administrative actions, norms, and ethos.[188]

If colonialism has many forms and manifestations, then decolonization is equally varied. Economically, Kwame Nkrumah defined neocolonialism as the condition in which 'the state which is subject to it is, in theory, independent and has all outward trappings of international sovereignty but in reality, its economic system and thus its political policy is directed from outside'.[189] Nkrumah argued that African states had gained territorial and political independence but were still colonized economically. Until economic decolonization happened, African states would remain neocolonial.[190]

world of the aspirations, values, and hopes of the NIEO. Samual Moyn, 'The High Tide of Anticolonial Legalism' (2021) 23 Journal of the History of International law 5; Antonius R Hippolyte, 'Aspiring for a Constructive TWAIL Approach Towards the International Investment Regime' in Stephan W Schill, Christian J Tams, and Rainer Hofmann (eds), *International Investment Law and Development: Bridging the Gap* (Edward Elgar 2015); see also Margot E Salomon, 'From NIEO to Now and the Unfinishable Story of Economic Justice' (2013) 62 International & Comparative Law 41 (arguing that any claims of the normative success of the PSNR principle are merely of sentimental historical value since the efforts of poor countries in the shaping of international rules show them to be instruments of the powerful); Karin Mickelson, 'Hope in a TWAIL Register' (2020) 1 Twail Review 14; Christopher J. 'Weeramantry, International Law and the Developing World: A Millennial Analysis, Keynote Address' (2000) 41 Harvard International Law Journal 280.

[182] Bedjaoui (n 181) 87.

[183] Luis Eslava, 'The Developmental State: Independence, Dependency, and the History of the South' in Jochen von Bernstorff and Phillip Dann (eds), *The Battle for International Law: South-North Perspectives on the Decolonization Era* (Oxford University Press 2019) 71.

[184] Giddens (n 167).

[185] ibid.

[186] Eslava (n 183) 74.

[187] ibid 76 (citing Foucault's definition of dispositif: an 'ensemble consisting of discourses, institutions, architectural forms, regulatory decisions, laws, administrative measures, scientific statements, philosophical, moral and philanthropic propositions— in short, the said as much as the unsaid').

[188] ibid.

[189] Nkrumah (n 115).

[190] See Bedjaoui (n 181).

As the Global North's resistance to the NIEO mostly succeeded, the world has become more unequal for the peoples of the developing world. In 1960, Africa's share of world poverty was 15 per cent; in recent years (2016–2020), more than 40 per cent of people in Africa live below the poverty line.[191] In his final report, former Special Rapporteur on Extreme Poverty Philip Alston severely criticized this international poverty line as seriously flawed.[192] He argued that 'the international community mistakenly gauges the progress in eliminating poverty by reference to a standard of miserable subsistence rather than an even minimally adequate standard of living'.[193] He strongly cautioned against the pre-COVID-19 pandemic triumphalism that extreme poverty has been eradicated, pointing out that the international poverty line by the World Bank relies on a measure that has been misappropriated for a purpose it was never intended for.[194] He additionally shows that extreme poverty has only marginally decreased in the past thirty years if a more realistic yardstick is used. Billions (1.4 billion in 2013)[195] worldwide still face few opportunities, countless indignities, unnecessary hunger, and preventable death, remaining too poor to enjoy basic human rights.[196]

Importantly, for over three decades, Upendra Baxi has advocated against using the term poverty. The word has since become a buzzword, and instead, Baxi insists we should use the term impoverished.[197] This continuous usage of poverty embeds a racial grammar through abstract liberalism as it abhors the use of more relational terms that easily show hierarchy, such as impoverishment and immiseration.[198] He argued that poverty is a passive word that hides the real ways it is considered just, right, and fair that some people become and generationally remain impoverished.[199] Baxi noted that our focus should be on reducing impoverishment and excessive affluence.[200]

5. Conclusion

Twenty-first-century international law is purported to be universal, neutral, and equal, providing and securing sovereignty as a fundamental doctrine. Yet, the analysis

[191] Zachary Donnenfeld, 'What is the future of Poverty in Africa' (*Institute for Security Studies*, 2 March 2020), <https://issafrica.org/iss-today/what-is-the-future-of-poverty-in-africa#:~:text=Roughly%2040%25%20of%20people%20in,the%20next%20poorest%20region%20globally> accessed 13 August 2024.

[192] UNHRC, 'The Parlous State of Poverty Eradication—Report of the Special Rapporteur on Extreme Poverty and Human Rights' (3 July 2020) UN Doc A/HRC/44/40.

[193] ibid.

[194] ibid; see also Steven Pinker, *Enlightenment Now* (Penguin Books 2018) 116.

[195] Salomon (n 181).

[196] Pinker (n 194) 116.

[197] Upendra Baxi, 'Introduction in Law and Poverty' in Upendra Baxi (ed), *Law and Poverty: Critical Essays* (NM Tripathi 1989); See also Upendra Baxi, 'Global Development and Impoverishment' in Mark Juergensmeyer and others (eds), *The Oxford Handbook of Legal Studies* (Oxford University Press 2005); Upendra Baxi, 'International Development, Global Impoverishment, and Human Rights' in Scott Sheeran and Sir Nigel Rodley (eds), *Routledge Handbook of Human Rights Law* (Routledge 2013).

[198] John Linarelli, Margot E Salomon, and Muthucumaraswamy Sornarajah, *The Misery of International Law: Confrontations* (Oxford University Press 2018).

[199] Upendra Baxi 'Impoverishment in the Anthropocene' in Mark Juergensmeyer and others (eds), *The Oxford Handbook Of Global Studies* (Oxford University Press 2018) 456.

[200] ibid.

of race shows how the principle of sovereign equality propelled racial capitalism through its racialized grammar and abstract liberalism, fundamentally structuring an unequal global socioeconomic and political landscape along the global colour line. Its origin within the Westphalian tradition is tied to a biological and naturalized conception of race that overtly demarcated Europeans as sovereign and non-Europeans as non-sovereign. The racial grammar that supported such sovereign inequalities includes fundamental doctrines such as discovery, terra nullius, and enforcement of unequal treaties. Abstract liberalism facilitated the mutation of racialized sovereigns as novel legal technologies while vocabularies exacerbated an extant global racial hierarchy. The paradigm of developed and developing countries is an example of this dynamic, concretizing a racially unequal international order. Others include principles like good governance, democracy, and the rule of law, all of which are invariably summoned as pretexts to undermine the sovereignty of countries in the Global South whether politically, economically, or militarily.

Analytically, merging the logics of territory, capital, and race shows how the sovereign doctrine has produced a litany of racial exclusions, expropriations, and injustices. The concept of racial capitalism, which joins the logic of race and capitalism when analysed against the background of the logic of territory, helps identify the historical instances of sovereign inequalities, including slavery, colonialism, and the quasi-sovereign control systems of international law such as the mandate and trusteeship system. This chapter demonstrates the importance of engaging with the logics of race closely as well as its ongoing implications, including the institutionalized hierarchies in the UNSC and the BWIs. International law's racialized and racializing grammars produces a litany of economic sovereign inequalities packaged through concepts such as free trade, development, and good governance presented as universal values yet carefully packaged to facilitate incursions into the Global South and extraction of value from negatively racialized states.

5

The Colour of *Jus Cogens*

Sarah Riley Case and Frédéric Mégret[*]

1. Introduction

The international law doctrine of *jus cogens* recognizes that some prohibitions—such as those against slavery, genocide, and torture—have peremptory status above other international norms and cannot be negotiated away by treaty. However, in their 1993 article 'The Gender of Jus Cogens' Hillary Charlesworth and Christine Chinkin claimed that 'the concept of *jus cogens* is not a properly universal one as its development has privileged the experiences of men over those of women, and it has provided a protection to men that is not accorded to women'.[1] The definition of *jus cogens* in spaces dominated by men, they argued, entrenched gendered experiences with distributive consequences. *Jus cogens* norms did not address the impacts of violence, poverty, food insecurity, and inaccessible health care on women.[2] They are biased and have been used to reinscribe benefits that men accrue from oppressing women.

Charlesworth and Chinkin published their article as part of early engagements with Feminist Approaches to International Law across the Global North, which foregrounded how international law is socially constructed to produce gender disparities. Sources of inspiration for these approaches included literature on colonialism and Third World feminisms.[3] In their discussion, Charlesworth and Chinkin used the term 'women' to refer to persons 'around the world' whose experiences *jus cogens* should reflect.[4] Nonetheless, proposals to accommodate women in international law coming from the Global North have been critiqued for eclipsing alternate feminisms and perspectives concerned with racism, colonialism, gender normativity, and economic inequality, with important consequences.[5]

Acknowledging these nuances, we wish to focus on whether *jus cogens* reinforces hierarchies associated with multiple forms of imperialism. This has led us to ask whether *jus cogens* might be associated with the dominance of people who have

* We are grateful to the editors for inviting us to contribute to the book and to Christopher Gevers for his helpful comments on parts of the chapter.

1 Hilary Charlesworth and Christine Chinkin, 'The Gender of Jus Cogens' (1993) 15 Human Rights Quarterly 63, 65.

2 ibid.

3 For this critical reflection, see Karen Knop, 'Re/statements: Feminism and State Sovereignty in International Law' (1993) 3(2) Transnational Law and Contemporary Problems 293.

4 Charlesworth and Chinkin (n 1). See this observation in Karen Engle, Vasuki Nesiah, and Dianne Otto, 'Feminist Approaches to International Law' in Jeffrey Dunoff and Mark Pollack (eds), *International Legal Theory: Foundations and Frontiers* (Cambridge University Press 2022).

5 Engle, Nesiah and Otto (n 4).

Sarah Riley Case and Frédéric Mégret, *The Colour of* Jus Cogens In: *Emancipating International Law*. Edited by: Mohsen al Attar and Claire Smith, Oxford University Press. © Sarah Riley Case and Frédéric Mégret 2026.
DOI: 10.1093/9780198935605.003.0007

benefited from and have reproduced the white supremacy of colonialism and trans-atlantic slavery.[6] The question is whether *jus cogens* might be defined by processes of racialization simultaneously caught up with gender and class. As Charlesworth and Chinkin did, we recognize that *jus cogens* norms are largely symbolic in practice, although this symbolism has real power under international law. Our intuition is that *jus cogens* has, at times, been evoked for its symbolic value in disciplining racialized people across a gender spectrum,[7] while their appeals to *jus cogens* have often been excluded from its ambit of protection.

Our choice of the title 'the colour of *jus cogens*' signals to this economy that diminishes the inherent worth of non-white people. Referring to 'colour' in this context borrows from the great intellectual WEB DuBois, who described the colour line, including under international law (here, *jus cogens* as a colour line).[8] Colour recalls the observations of critical race theorists that 'colourblind'[9] standards, such as formal equality, will not realize substantive equality for racialized people under structural conditions of whiteness (the false neutrality of *jus cogens*). Colour also evokes hegemonic processes that 'invisibilize' the demands and experiences of racialized people. In this chapter, we therefore suggest that *jus cogens* norms that are purported to be universal and neutral may reinforce the global colour line, including by invisibilizing calls from racialized people for transformative justice through *jus cogens*.

It merits emphasizing that subaltern proposals for *jus cogens* are not invisible but are actively ignored, altered, and dismissed by those who can afford to do so.[10] Racialized people may even feel hyper-visible as they/we assert conceptions of international law, and their/our humanity 'against a sharp white background'.[11] Invisibility is best understood in the verbal tense of *invisibilization*, denoting a relation of dispossession and obfuscation. Ralph Ellison depicted this in his poignant novel *Invisible*

[6] 'Whiteness' denotes worldviews and ways of life that are Eurocentric, while these travelled to and developed across colonies and the New World, multiplying and globalizing iterations that consolidate in conceptual and material structures. Privileges associated with whiteness consolidate around people socially constructed as 'white', excluding peoples racialized otherwise. White privileges often pass from one generation to the next through complex regimes of nationality, wealth transfer, education, employment, culture . . . Whiteness also consolidates in the privileges and operations of European and settler colonial states as well as institutions dominated by them. By 'white supremacy' we mean the dominance of such conceptual and material whiteness, conscious and unconscious, including under international law. See especially for our purposes '*The Souls of White Folk*' in WEB Du Bois, *Darkwater: Voices from Within the Veil* (Harcourt, Brace and Company 1920); Cheryl Harris, 'Whiteness as Property' (1993) 106(8) Harvard Law Review 1707; Charles Mills, 'White Supremacy as Sociopolitical System: A Philosophical Perspective' in Ashley Doane and Eduardo Bonilla-Silva (eds), *White Out* (Routledge 2003); Christopher Gevers, '"Unwhitening the World": Rethinking Race and International Law' (2020) 67 UCLA Law Review 1652; María Teresa Garzón Martínez, 'Whiteness' in Olaf Kaltmeier and others (eds), *The Routledge Handbook to the History and Society of the Americas* (Routledge 2019).

[7] Although there are important gender dynamics caught up with geopolitical racialization, this chapter cannot undertake an intersectional analysis, due to research and space constraints.

[8] WEB Du Bois, 'To the Nations of the World' (Speech at the Pan African Conference, London, 1900) drawing on Frederick Douglass, 'The Color Line' (1881) 132 North American Review 566.

[9] Because of the ableist connotations of the term 'colourblind', throughout this chapter we use the term 'false neutrality' explained below.

[10] Vasuki Nesiah, 'A Double Take on Debt: Reparations Claims and Regimes of Visibility in a Politics of Refusal' (2022) 59(1) Osgoode Hall Law Journal 153.

[11] Zora Neale Hurston, 'How It Feels to Be Colored Me (1928)' in Zora Neale Hurston, *Folklore, Memoirs and Other Writings* (Library of America 1995).

Man when he wrote: 'I am a man of substance, of flesh and bone, fiber and liquids—and I might even be said to possess a mind. I am invisible, understand, simply because people refuse to see me.'[12]

We are mindful of the paradox that *jus cogens* norms may be used to invisibilize and entrench racial dispossession and hierarchy, even as they may be aimed at prohibiting racial injustices such as genocide. This chapter therefore describes *how* some racialized people have been excluded from the protective ambit of *jus cogens* in practice. It also describes how some proposals for the content of *jus cogens* norms were universalized, while transformative proposals to upend structural white supremacy were minimized, sidelined, or effaced. The progressive quality of *jus cogens* norms helps cloud this unequal access. White-dominated states and lawyers of the Global North may even evoke humanitarian ideals underlying *jus cogens* prohibitions to justify international shaming and interventions that further entrench the racial divisions of the world.

Our intuitions are grounded in the histories of *jus cogens* that we describe throughout the chapter. In the first section we develop a theoretical argument that discursive legal qualities of *jus cogens* may be used to sustain and obscure racial injustices. In the second part, we revisit how the doctrine of *jus cogens* originally crystallized in international law as a radical initiative of Third World states to achieve decolonization, including racial justice, but was co-opted by white-dominated states and international lawyers after the end of the Cold War in ways that effaced anticolonial proposals. In the third section, we narrate further histories of *jus cogens* concerning the dismissal of primarily Black and Indigenous calls for justice rooted in *jus cogens* norms that *have* become generally accepted as international law, namely slavery, genocide, and apartheid. Overall, we show that subaltern appeals to *jus cogens* have repeatedly been excluded from its definitions, re-entrenching racial dispossession.

2. Invisibilizing racial injustices through *jus cogens*

Jus cogens norms prohibit injustices based in racism. Still, an Indigenous-led commission was met with backlash when it used the language of genocide to denounce the fact of missing and murdered Indigenous women, girls, and 2SLGBTQ+ people across a settler colonial state.[13] This is one account we raise to show that there is an economy of *jus cogens* that has discounted the appeals of racialized people. Before turning to these appeals, we explore how discursive legal qualities of the doctrine of *jus cogens* may be used to reinforce and obscure white supremacy, even as *jus cogens* is held out to be progressive.

To explore how *jus cogens* is caught up in international law's promise and predation, we draw on critical race theory, Third World Approaches to International Law, Indigenous critique, and Black Studies. These theoretical traditions and sources of praxis inspire overlapping intuitions about the white supremacy of international law and subaltern resistance. We pursue three intuitions relevant to our focus on *jus*

[12] Ralph Ellison, *Invisible Man* (Random House 1952) prologue.
[13] See Umut Özsu, 'Genocide as Fact and Form' (2020) 22 Journal of Genocide Research 62.

cogens: the false neutrality of international law, the erasure of subaltern international legal histories, and the retrenchment of racial oppression through international law discourses of benevolence. Being attentive to these processes of racialization highlights how dominant states and international lawyers may reproduce racial injustices under the guise of progress, including when *jus cogens* norms are defined and put into practice unequally.

2.1 The false neutrality of international law

Our first intuition about how *jus cogens* invisibilizes racial hegemony is captured by the concept of 'false neutrality'.[14] This concept underscores that although legal standards are often presented as rational and objective, they are historically contingent. False neutrality tends to be associated with the rise of formal equality during the twentieth century across Western democratic states, which was a means to address explicit racial discrimination that had been previously legislated. Instead of redressing historical inequities, formal equality failed to transform structural disparities and hid persistent racial injustices under the guise of facial non-discrimination.

If we look to international law, similar qualities of false neutrality uphold and obscure racial hegemony. Contemporary international law standards are formulated without express distinctions on racial grounds and are generally applicable to formally equal states and people. Formal equality is a basic precept of the post-Second World War liberal international order that coexisted with colonization and then constrained the possibilities for postcolonial flourishing, as European-American powers denied redress for colonialism and maintained their hegemony intact, including in settler colonies. International law's appearance of neutrality is therefore misleading and oppressive because structural conditions sustained by international law distribute benefits and precarities according to underlying racial stratifications.

Take border regimes, which E Tendayi Achiume refers to as 'racial borders' to foreground practices of discrimination.[15] Achiume shows how facially neutral categories of 'nationality' and 'citizenship' restrict the mobility of racialized people through place-of-birth criteria, passports, visas, and other means of controlling migration while simultaneously promoting white mobility. Racially disparate border regimes could not be more consequential. The Mediterranean Sea is one example—a site where death is made inevitable. Racial borders, in turn, perpetuate white supremacy and racial capitalism writ large by policing access to labour, health, education, and other benefits reserved for citizens of white-dominated states, often forcing racialized people into precarious living.

We suggest that *jus cogens* provides another means through which racism operates under the disguise of false neutrality. The doctrine of *jus cogens* epitomizes formal

[14] Khiara Bridges, *Critical Race Theory: A Primer* (Foundation Press 2019); E Tendayi Achiume and Devon Carbado, 'Critical Race Theory Meets Third World Approaches to International Law' (2020) 67 UCLA Law Review 1462; James Thuo Gathii, 'Writing Race and Identity in a Global Context: What CRT and TWAIL Can Learn from Each Other' (2021) 67 UCLA Law Review 1610.

[15] E Tendayi Achiume, 'Racial Borders' (2022) 110(3) Georgetown Law Journal 445.

equality, given that it embodies norms purported to apply to all without distinction. *Jus cogens* standards are formally universal by definition. At the same time, the doctrine of *jus cogens* does not require positive obligations to realize substantive equality in the face of structural disparities.[16] Instead, the false neutrality of *jus cogens* may help obscure substantive inequalities that are indissociable from the conduct that *jus cogens* norms prohibit.

2.2 The historical erasure of subaltern engagements

Our second intuition concerns the erasure of subaltern experiences. This intuition overlaps with false neutrality insofar as international law doctrines may appear ahistorical in form. Even when mainstream scholars pierce this veneer to trace histories of international law, their accounts are often one-sided. Dominant histories of international law foreground the perspectives of white Global North nations and lawyers and obscure fraught circumstances leading to the relative acceptance of norms in the international system. This erasure can be understood as a kind of whitewashing, as norms are presented as part of a linear evolution, obscuring the initiatives of racialized people and making the status of white Northern norms appear objective.

A pathbreaking account of sovereignty by Siba N'Zatioula Grovogui in the 1990s paved the way for historical approaches that foreground the Western dominance of international law.[17] Antony Anghie developed similar histories of the sovereignty doctrine, which he traced to the colonial encounter.[18] There is now a growing number of scholars committed to recovering alternative histories of slavery and colonialism, including their contemporary forms, which have largely been expunged from mainstream education.[19] Given that historical erasure invisibilizes subaltern engagements, scholars have also revitalized counter-narratives of international law to share attempts at transformation. Nonetheless, these accounts have been marginalized in mainstream international legal scholarship.

When it comes to *jus cogens,* mainstream histories of its genesis and operations tend to reproduce the whitewashing of international law. For example, many accounts highlight the acceptance of *jus cogens* prohibitions among Western powers within European-American contexts, such as the condemnation of genocide after the

[16] Arguably a remedy for a *jus cogens* violation could entail positive redress; however, later in the chapter, we show how racialized people have been denied remedies. We also show how Third World states were unsuccessful in advocating for *jus cogens* norms requiring affirmative action.

[17] Siba N'Zatioula Grovogui, *Sovereigns, Quasi Sovereigns, and Africans* (University of Minnesota Press 1996).

[18] Antony Anghie, *Imperialism, Sovereignty and the Making of International Law* (Cambridge University Press 2005).

[19] eg Adelle Blackett, 'Theorizing Emancipatory Transnational Futures of International Labour Law' (2012) 113 AJIL Unbound 390; Sundhya Pahuja, *Decolonising International Law: Development, Economic Growth and the Politics of Universality* (Cambridge University Press 2011); Noura Erakat, *Justice for Some: Law and the Question of Palestine* (Stanford University Press 2019); Nesiah (n 10); Sheryl Lightfoot, *Global Indigenous Politics: A Subtle Revolution* (Routledge 2016); Henry J Richardson III, *The Origins of African-American Interests in International Law* (Carolina Academic Press 2008); Darrel Li, 'Genres of Universalism: Reading Race into International Law with Help from Sylvia Wynter' (2021) 67 UCLA Law Review 1686.

Second World War and the British prohibition against slavery during the nineteenth century. Although these histories may be 'true', they gloss over complicity with imperialism, past and ongoing, while erasing subaltern advocacy for alternative visions of *jus cogens.*

2.3 Retrenchment under international law's liberal promise

Our last intuition is that racial oppression may be reinscribed under international laws that are commonly said to be beneficent. We begin with Saidiya Hartman's work that described how the recognition of Black people as legal persons after the abolition of slavery often bound them to plantations no less through contractual relations that were formally equal but substantively unequal, emblematic of liberal transactions.[20] Kimberlé Crenshaw described similar processes as 'retrenchment', referring to the *continuity* and *deepening* of white supremacy in the United States, following Black civil rights gains.[21] The concept of retrenchment captures how liberal legalism 're-packages racism' under reforms that appear to be progressive.[22]

Retrenchment can also be understood as the 'co-optation' of Third World politics[23] to use the language of Sundhya Pahuja or as 'moves to innocence', which Tuck and Yang associate with the appropriation of 'decolonization' discourses in the settler context.[24] Glen Coulthard explores this idea, drawing on Frantz Fanon, when he explains that Indigenous struggles for self-determination have been subverted under domestic and international laws that channel colonial violence into the liberal governmentality of 'recognizing' Indigenous identity rights within the state.[25] For us, the concept of retrenchment suggests that racism may lurk behind postures and standards that are purported to overcome racial injustices.

Classical international law's civilizing mission instantiates this, given European international lawyers justified colonization and imperialism through the elaboration of doctrines that they claimed would assist Indigenous peoples. The ascendency of liberal internationalism after the Second World War, and its shift into neoliberalism after the Cold War, then consolidated the 'false promises'[26] of international law in important ways. The dominance of Western liberal and neoliberal projects of human rights, free trade, good governance, and foreign investment continues to overshadow

[20] Saidiya Hartman, *Scenes of Subjection: Terror, Slavery and Self-Making in Nineteenth-Century America* (Oxford University Press 1977).

[21] Kimberlé Crenshaw, 'Race, Reform and Retrenchment: Transformation and Legitimation in Antidiscrimination Law' (1988) 101 Harvard Law Review 1331.

[22] ibid.

[23] Pahuja (n 19).

[24] Eve Tuck and K Wayne Yang, 'Decolonization Is Not a Metaphor' (2012) 1 Decolonization: Indigeneity, Education and Society 1.

[25] Glen Coulthard, *Red Skin, White Masks: Rejecting the Colonial Politics of Recognition* (University of Minnesota Press 2014).

[26] Mari Matsuda, 'Looking to the Bottom: Critical Legal Studies and Reparations' (1987) 22 Harvard Civil Rights-Civil Liberties Law Review 323, 324.

subaltern proposals that may be related, but meaningfully different, perpetuating racial hegemony under the cover of progress.[27]

We suggest that the doctrine of *jus cogens* may be used similarly. For example, the *jus cogens* prohibition against the use of force, for all of its insistence on sovereignty, is saturated with racial hierarchies when it comes to whose sovereignty is sacrosanct and whose sovereignty can be violated through international interventions ostensibly based on human rights.[28] International humanitarian law and international criminal law, which are similarly bound up with *jus cogens* values, exemplify this erasure of racial hegemony through discourses of benevolence premised, in these cases, on representations of Black and Brown criminality.[29] The liberal promise of *jus cogens* to overcome heinous conduct therefore minimizes and obscures how this symbolism can be racializing.

In short, the liberal promise of achieving progress should be understood alongside false neutrality and historical erasure as legal techniques that may be used to perpetuate and distract from injustices associated with *jus cogens*.[30] This whiteness of *jus cogens* may be brought into relief by (re)centring transgressive engagements of racialized people with *jus cogens*. In the remaining sections, we recover such self-assured engagements and their invisibilization.

3. Anticolonial proposals for *jus cogens* and western capture

One history of *jus cogens* that is often neglected in mainstream scholarship concerns the advocacy of leaders from newly independent nations in bringing the doctrine to prominence.[31] These Third World leaders proposed *jus cogens* to dismantle hegemonic Western legal structures by establishing norms that former and lasting colonial powers could not violate: norms against racial discrimination, for full decolonization, and for meaningful sovereignty through the global redistribution of wealth and decision-making.

As we show, their efforts were successful in the sense that the doctrine crystallized in the 1969 Vienna Convention on the Law of Treaties. This did not stop Western states and scholars from deriding the doctrine and subverting its anticolonial purposes. However, within a generation, at the end of the Cold War, white-dominated

[27] See, eg, Pahuja (n 19); James Thuo Gathii, 'Reform and Retrenchment in International Investment Law' (Lecture at Sander Roundtable Discussions on International Economic Law, Cologne, 13 January 2021); Anna Spain Bradley, 'Human Rights Racism' (2019) 32 Harvard Human Rights Journal 1.

[28] Robert Knox, 'Civilizing Interventions? Race, War and International Law' (2013) 26(1) Cambridge Review of International Affairs 111; James T Gathii and Henry J Richardson III, Symposium on TWAIL Perspectives on ICL, IHL and Intervention (2015) AJIL Unbound 252.

[29] Gathii and Richardson III (n 28); Frédéric Mégret, 'From "Savages" to "Unlawful Combatants": A Postcolonial Look at International Humanitarian Law's "Other"' in Anne Orford (ed), *International Law and its Others* (Cambridge University Press 2006); Randle DeFalco and Frédéric Mégret, 'The Invisibility of Race at the ICC: Lessons from the US Criminal Justice System' (2019) 7(1) London Review of International Law 55.

[30] Toni Morrison, 'A Humanist View' (Lecture at Portland State University, Portland, 30 May 1975).

[31] Umut Özsu, 'An Anti-Imperialist Universalism? Jus Cogens and the Politics of International Law' in Martti Koskenniemi, Walter Rech, and Manuel Jiménez Fonseca (eds), *International Law and Empire: Historical Explorations* (Oxford University Press 2017).

states and lawyers of the Global North embraced peremptory norms, skewing their radical potential to renew longstanding humanitarian narratives. These were then deployed against postcolonial states, where racialized people live out the consequences in the everyday life of international law.

3.1 *Jus cogens* as a Third World strategy and Western resistance

The doctrine of *jus cogens* was one among several techniques that Third World jurists and statesmen used to dismantle and rebuild international law during the decolonization era, culminating in their campaign for a New International Economic Order (NIEO).[32] Upon the accession of postcolonial nations to the existing international order, Western states had constrained participation to formal equality among substantively unequal states. There would be no redress for centuries of racist imperial plunder. Transnational companies would maintain their grip on Third World resources acquired through coercive treaties. The General Agreement on Tariffs and Trade would sustain the 'plantation logics'[33] of concentrating raw commodity production in the 'Darker Nations'.[34] Western states maintained that the doctrine of international law's sources prohibited newly independent states from changing the rules that legitimized these injustices because changes to treaty and custom required consent, which Western states withheld.[35]

For Third World jurists and statesmen, the doctrine of *jus cogens* was a means to confront these legal structures by establishing a list of peremptory norms as a new source of international law. *Jus cogens* rules would supersede liberal relations of formal equality, including the façade of consent, and reconfigure international law through affirmative redistribution.[36] *Jus cogens* was therefore a project of what Umut Öszu has described as 'anti-imperialist universalism'.[37] It was proposed to reinvent foundational values for an emergent international community, in which universal international law would no longer oppress colonized peoples through the false neutrality of statehood but would respect solidarity across difference.[38]

Although Third World leaders were inspired by many visions of independence—including nationalism, federalism, socialism, and capitalism—they expressed solidarity in forms such as non-alignment, Pan-Africanism, and Afro-Asian solidarity. They also worked in coalitions on projects that included embedding *jus cogens* into sources of international law, an effort that reached boiling point during the ILC's work, and the Vienna Conference on the Law of Treaties.

[32] For other anticolonial legal techniques, see Antony Anghie, 'Legal Aspects of the New International Economic Order' (2015) 6(1) Humanity: An International Journal on Human Rights, Humanitarianism, and Development 145; Sarah Riley Case, 'Climate Change, Anticolonial International Law, and the Universality of the Commons' (Doctoral thesis, University of Toronto 2023).

[33] Katherine McKittrick, 'Plantation Futures' (2013) 17(3) Small Axe 1.

[34] Vijay Prashad, *The Darker Nations: A People's History of the Third World* (LeftWord Books 2007).

[35] Anghie (n 32).

[36] Riley Case (n 32).

[37] Özsu (31).

[38] Riley Case (n 32).

The point was not only to recognize *jus cogens* as a source of international law, but also to imbue *jus cogens* norms with anticolonial content that might transform the international order.[39] For example, Third World leaders passed General Assembly resolutions on the *self-determination of all colonial peoples*, the *elimination of all forms of racial discrimination*, and the right of Third World peoples to *freely exploit natural resources* within their territories. They articulated an expansive understanding of *non-intervention*. They formulated norms of *ecological protection* over the global commons (said to be 'common heritage'). They insisted on a strict *prohibition against the use of force* to thwart multifarious imperialist incursions. And they sought *international economic justice* through the 1974 Charter of Economic Rights and Duties of States. They then pushed for the entrenchment of these demands through *jus cogens* status.[40]

This vision was bound to be resisted and, during the Vienna negotiations on the law of treaties, Western states sought to rein in the 'unruly horse' of *jus cogens*.[41] The French legal advisor at the time proclaimed, '[w]hen I hear of *jus cogens* I reach for my revolver'.[42] This statement captures the depth of historical Western enmity towards *jus cogens*, while threats of imperial violence loomed against the background of recent and ongoing anti-independence wars. Faced with such opposition, Nigerian jurist Taslim Olawale Elias helped negotiate a compromise in Article 53 of the Vienna Convention,[43] although Third World and supporting Soviet states held most of the votes anyway.

This did not prevent scholars of the Global North from persisting in the denigration of *jus cogens*. They argued that peremptory norms would undermine state autonomy and the principle of consent, and thus the ideal of formal equality. Peremptory norms were vague, incoherent, unrealistic, and counterproductive to the rule of law. Anthony d'Amato mocked the concept's idealism in 'It's a Bird, It's a Plane, It's Jus Cogens!', deploring the 'kitchen-sink approach to the sources of international law'.[44] Prosper Weil insisted that *jus cogens* would weaken international normativity, arguing that it would violate law's neutrality.[45] Georg Schwarzenberger endorsed classical notions of sovereignty, bemoaning the doctrine of *jus cogens* with 'all the trappings of fashionable "progressive" if unrealistic, thinking'.[46] In response to this kind of liberal positioning, much like critical race theorists would later do, Third World jurists, such as Mohammed Bedjaoui, exposed Western preferences for neutrality, objectivity, and formal equality as no less political in a world marked by racism and structural power.[47]

[39] ibid.

[40] See ibid.

[41] Kirsten Sellars, 'Reining in the "Unruly Horse" of Jus Cogens' (*Australian Institute of International Affairs*, 20 May 2019) <https://www.internationalaffairs.org.au/australianoutlook/reining-in-the-unruly-horse-of-jus-cogens/> accessed 20 July 2022.

[42] Hélène Ruiz Fabri, 'Enhancing the Rhetoric of Jus Cogens' (2012) 23(4) European Journal of International Law 1049, 1050.

[43] Taslim Olawale Elias, *New Horizons in International Law* (Brill Academic Publisher 1979) 50–51; CL Lim, 'Neither Sheep nor Peacocks: T. O. Elias and Post-Colonial International Law' (2008) 21(2) Leiden Journal of International Law 295.

[44] Anthony D'Amato, 'It's a Bird, It's a Plane, It's Jus Cogens Essay' (1990) 6 Connecticut Journal of International Law 1.

[45] Prosper Weil, 'Toward Relative Normativity in International Law?' (1983) 77 American Journal of International Law 413.

[46] Georg Schwarzenberger, 'International Jus Cogens' (1964) 43 Texas Law Review 455, 477–78.

[47] Mohammed Bedjaoui, *Towards a New International Order* (UNESCO 1978) 139, 63, 186.

3.2 The ascendency of *jus cogens* at the end of the Cold War

By the 1990s, however, *jus cogens* had been widely accepted by Western states and international lawyers. This reversal is rarely explained, except as rallying around a more progressive understanding of international law following the end of the Cold War.[48] Such expressions of reconciliation and the approval of *jus cogens* did not testify to a Third World victory as much as a process of co-optation that invisiblized its origins and distanced the doctrine from a reckoning with international law's racist imperialism.[49]

The Western co-optation of *jus cogens* can be understood through the selective inclusion and exclusion of what counted as *jus cogens* norms after the doctrine had crystallized in the Vienna Convention. Western statesmen and jurists were especially opposed to anticolonial *jus cogens* norms that focused on substantive racial justice, preferring the peremptory status of a subset of international crimes represented as 'atrocities' (notably, genocide, crimes against humanity, and war crimes). As one contemporary commentator put it, 'when Western nations refer concretely to peremptory norms ... they tend to emphasize in the liberal tradition negative prohibitions against the official use of force, genocide, slave trade, state torture, or arbitrary state murder' rather than prohibiting 'ordinary, Euro-centric rules'.[50]

The evolution in *jus cogens* norms tilted the project away from its moorings in anti-racism, self-determination, postcolonial sovereignty, and global economic justice towards understandings consistent with liberal and, increasingly neoliberal, ideologies. Third World demands for collective responsibility—to foster wellbeing, the common heritage of humankind, and independence from transnational corporations—were to be clearly excluded from *jus cogens*.[51] *Jus cogens* would instead serve ascendant neoliberal internationalism marked by white Western conceptions of human rights and the rule of law.[52]

Human rights, underpinned by peremptory norms, were increasingly deployed to condemn grave violence within postcolonial states characterized as illiberal. This condemnation was detached from legacies of colonialism, notably quasi-sovereignty, impoverishment, and the consolidation of diverse political communities within *uti possiditis* borders. Although mainstream international lawyers are guarded when it comes to justifying humanitarian interventions through *jus cogens*, allusions to *jus cogens* values have saturated their commentary,[53] while reinforcing liberal

[48] Riley Case (n 32).

[49] ibid.

[50] Gordon Christenson, 'Jus Cogens: Guarding Interests Fundamental to International Society' (1987) 28 Vanderbilt Journal of International Law 585, 597.

[51] See, eg, Thomas Weatherall, 'The Content of Jus Cogens' in *Jus Cogens: International Law and Social Contract* (Cambridge University Press 2015) 263.

[52] See, eg, Markus Petsche, 'Jus Cogens as a Vision of the International Legal Order' (2010) 29 Penn State International Law Review 233, 269–70.

[53] Spiermann, 'Humanitarian Intervention as a Necessity and the Threat or Use of Jus Cogens' (2002) 71 Nordic Journal of International Law 523; Manuel J Ventura, '17 The Prevention of Genocide as A Jus Cogens Norm? A Formula for Lawful Humanitarian Intervention' in Charles Chernor Jalloh and Olufemi Elias (eds), *Shielding Humanity Essays in International Law in Honour of Judge Abdul G. Koroma* (Brill 2015) 289.

exceptionalism. In this respect, not only Western men but also women played a role in legitimizing international interventions, militarization, and prosecutions aimed at the Global South, focusing, for example, on Third World women's experiences of sexual violence during conflicts.[54] Overall, the Western liberal redirection of *jus cogens* took a carceral turn with racializing consequences.

4. Racialized exclusions from the protective ambit of *jus cogens*

We therefore think of *jus cogens* as operating within a racialized economy in which the determination of claims to *jus cogens* is subject to white elite capture. Historically, anticolonial aspirations for *jus cogens* were resisted, then co-opted and deployed in ways that reimposed 'neocolonial empire'[55] through a combination of false neutrality, historical erasure, and liberal beneficence. One result has been that while there is nominal agreement on the categorical significance of *jus cogens* under international law, there remains little agreement over its content. Importantly, by consistently objecting to anticolonial and antiracist norms, dominant lawyers and governments stripped *jus cogens* of its radical potential.

In this section, we shed light on how the doctrinal edges of even accepted *jus cogens* norms—namely, slavery, genocide, and apartheid—have been policed to invisibilize the appeals of primarily Black and Indigenous people against settler colonial and formerly colonial governments. Again, we follow our three intuitions about legal techniques that have invisibilized (reinforced and concealed) white supremacy through *jus cogens*.

4.1 Slavery

The *jus cogens* status of slavery is not disputed; however, international law histories of the prohibition against slavery suffer from a similar invisibilization to histories of *jus cogens* generally. The dominant history of prohibitions against slavery props up a narrative about emancipation, according to which white governments—especially the British—abolished slavery during the nineteenth century through European-American positive law.[56] Global prohibitions against slavery were then affirmed (*after* transatlantic slavery ceased), for example in the 1926 Slavery Convention.[57] In this narrative, European-American states redeemed harms of the past through the finality of legal emancipation.[58]

[54] Engle, Nesiah, and Otto (n 4).
[55] Achiume (n 15).
[56] On our line of reasoning in this section, see Christopher Gevers 'Refiguring Slavery through International Law: the 1926 Slavery Convention, the 'Native Labour Code' and Racial Capitalism' (2022) 25(2) Journal of International Economic Law 312.
[57] Albeit proceeded by such normative processes as the Congress of Vienna, 1814–1815. Frédéric Mégret, 'Droit international et esclavage: pour une réévaluation' (2010) 18 African Yearbook of International Law 121.
[58] Gevers (n 56).

Subaltern histories of abolition and reparations, by contrast, focus on the long processes of resistance by enslaved persons themselves, free Black abolitionists, and allies.[59] The supposed progression towards the prohibition against slavery by European-Americans has obscured these insurrections, 'everyday transgressions',[60] and legal engagements against colonial powers by Black people, especially, in the patchwork unfolding of abolition. The obfuscating quality of mainstream histories makes events such as the Haitian revolution 'unthinkable', as Michel-Rolph Trouillot described.[61] This has promoted a narrative about saviours and salvation, even as white-dominated states and institutions continue to benefit from the harms inflicted by slavery.[62]

However, well into the twentieth century, a European state used the prohibition against slavery to justify renewed incursions into an African nation.[63] The Berlin Conference of 1884–1885 had framed war against slavery as a humanitarian cause, while European powers negotiated partition. As a humanitarian intervention, emancipation was then wielded for another half century in racially disparate ways against and supposedly on behalf of African peoples, obscuring the motive of material exploitation. Early twentieth-century international law rules meanwhile distanced many unfree labour practices from slavery, which Black intellectuals and leaders had framed as a continuum.[64] This distancing legitimized unfree racialized labour in colonies and the New World, including forced prison labour.[65]

The long-term material consequence of this historical erasure and narrative of white emancipation has been the denial of claims for reparations that seek redress for the afterlives of slavery, which is to say the weight of the transatlantic slave trade on persistent anti-Black racism. Saidiya Hartman describes these afterlives as 'skewed life chances, limited access to health and education, premature death, incarceration, and impoverishment'.[66] Although Hartman writes in the United States context, the influence of the transatlantic slave trade on anti-Black racism solidified over centuries, affecting African and African descendant peoples globally in different and overlapping ways.

In this context, calls for reparations have been transnational, coming from the African diaspora since at least the nineteenth century, when the Haitian revolution and abolition movements took hold,[67] while Pan-African and Black Power movements

[59] Sarah Riley Case, 'Homelands of Mary Ann Shadd' in Immi Tallgren (ed), *Portraits of Women in International Law: New Names and Forgotten Faces?* (Oxford University Press 2023).

[60] Adelle Blackett, *Everyday Transgressions: Domestic Workers' Transnational Challenge to International Labour Law* (Cornell University Press 2019).

[61] Michel-Rolphe Trouillot, *Silencing the Past: Power and the Production of History* (Beacon Press 2015).

[62] Gevers (n 56).

[63] Adom Getachew, *Worldmaking After Empire: The Rise and Fall of Self-Determination* (Princeton University Press 2019) (writing about Italy's invasion of Ethiopia in 1935).

[64] See, eg, Adelle Blackett, 'On the Presence of the Past in the Future of International Labour Law' (2020) 43(2) Dalhousie Law Journal 94; WEB Du Bois, *Black Reconstruction in America, 1860-1880* (Harcourt, Brace and Company 1935).

[65] ibid.

[66] Saidiya Hartman, *Lose Your Mother: A Journey Along the Atlantic Slave Route* (Farrar, Straus & Giroux 2007) 6.

[67] Sarah Riley Case, 'Looking to the Horizon: The Meanings of Reparations for Unbearable Crises' (2023) 117 AJIL Unbound 49.

called for reparations in the twentieth century.[68] In the 1990s, African intellectuals organized to embed these demands into the work of the Organization of African Unity, also focusing on slavery across the continent.[69] African and Caribbean governments then supported calls for reparations during the 2001 Durban Conference against racial discrimination. Some years later, the Caribbean Community initiated a reparations claim against European governments.[70] And racialized lawyers, scholars, communities, and allies have consistently pursued transnational and local reparations.

Like the obfuscation of subaltern histories of abolition, these reparations claims have been invisibilized by mainstream international lawyers and implicated states. One formal argument is that the violation of *jus cogens* norms cannot give rise to a remedy if the impugned act was legal at the time it occurred (the intertemporal principle).[71] This argument about non-retroactivity is presented as rational and objective; however, it is steeped in liberal theories of what fairness across generations requires.[72] For example, it requires empirical proof of individual wrongdoer–wronged relationships and rejects any consideration of the structural hierarchies among collectives that arise from the past.[73]

Dominant interpretations of the intertemporal principle on this issue can be contrasted against the willingness of Western lawyers to pursue *jus cogens* norms retroactively for *some* criminal responsibility (for example, the Allies after the Second World War). Falsely neutral interpretations of reparations therefore deny intergenerational justice for Black people, while preserving white Western domination.[74]

In response, people struggling for reparations have proposed anti-imperial interpretations of the intertemporal principle, highlighting that claims are not doctrinally barred when there are ongoing consequences of the wrongful act.[75] The notion of 'continuing violations' provides a doctrinal foothold to address legacies of slavery, because structural and institutional anti-Black racism did not cease with abolition. Advocates for reparations also argue that the principle does not bar crimes against humanity, and Black jurists and leaders have worked to have slavery recognized as such, reinforcing its *jus cogens* status, for example under the Durban Declaration.

Despite such legal engagements, reparations for slavery are characterized by mainstream international lawyers as a political issue rather than a legal one, which one of us has observed is a classic technique of racial obfuscation used previously to counter anti-apartheid campaigns.[76] This falsely neutral bar to claims for reparations is racializing in perspective and effect, retrenching the legacies of slavery by avoiding redress for harms that cannot be disentangled from present-day anti-Black racism.

[68] ibid.

[69] Rhoda Howard-Hassmann, 'Reparations to Africa and the Group of Eminent Persons' (2004) 173–74 Cahiers d'Études africaines 81.

[70] CARICOM Reparations Commission, 'Ten Point Action Plan' (CARICOM Preparations Commission, 2013) <https://caricomreparations.org> accessed 20 December 2024.

[71] UNGA, 'Report of the Special Rapporteur on contemporary forms of racism, racial discrimination, xenophobia and racial intolerance' (2019) UN Doc A/74/321.

[72] Riley Case (n 67).

[73] ibid.

[74] ibid.

[75] UNGA (n 71) [32]; Riley Case (n 67).

[76] Riley Case (n 67).

4.2 Genocide

As with slavery, genocide is a *jus cogens* violation. Moreover, the prohibition against genocide acknowledges that racism has inspired attempts to destroy a people. The Holocaust preceded the international acceptance of genocide as a *jus cogens* norm that formally captured racial intent in the Genocide Convention. Nonetheless, what counts as genocide is contested in ways that often reinscribe white supremacy. Here, we focus on attempts by Black and Indigenous people living on Turtle Island (North America) to hold settler colonial states accountable for genocide, which have been sidelined from dominant international law histories and avenues of recourse.

Soon after states adopted the 1948 Genocide Convention, Black lawyers and activists sought to frame mass killings and systemic premature deaths of African Americans as a form of genocide. The *We Charge Genocide* petition was brought at a time when interpretative possibilities seemed wide-open and linked anti-Black violence in the United States to structural harms that persisted after the abolition of slavery.[77] The petition documented thousands of lynchings, police killings, widespread death row sentences, and policies that contributed to deaths, such as the denial of health care and unfit housing. The petitioners chose the charge of genocide to highlight the US government's intent to destroy a people in part, and to challenge the nascent UN, which had ignored earlier African American appeals under the emerging human rights regime.[78]

However, mainstream lawyers and diplomats dismissed this African American framing. Eleanor Roosevelt—then Chairperson of the UN human rights Commission—rebuffed the petition at the UN, and spoke against it publicly, using language that exemplifies the liberal erasure of racism as aberrational, rather than systemic.[79] She mocked the petition, saying it was 'ridiculous' in terms of the UN definition of genocide.[80] Perversely, she argued that, although the death rate of African Americans was high, the birth rate was too.[81] Roosevelt blamed the petitioners for *inspiring* violence against Black people, which is a racializing technique of reversing the blame.[82]

Raphael Lemkin—the foremost advocate of the prohibition—also publicly lambasted the petition, stating 'the accusations were a manoeuvre to divert attention from the crimes of genocide committed against . . . Soviet-subjugated peoples.'[83] He

[77] Civil Rights Congress, *We Charge Genocide: The Historic Petition to the United Nations for Relief from a Crime of the United States Government against the Negro People* (1st edn, Civil Rights Congress 1951).

[78] Carol Anderson, *Eyes off the Prize: The United Nations and the African American Struggles for Human Rights, 1944-1955* (Cambridge University Press 2003).

[79] UNGA, 371st Meeting of the Third Committee (20 December 1951) UN Doc A/C.3.SR.371 [28].

[80] William Rutherford, 'Mrs. Roosevelt Claims Progress' *New York Amsterdam News* (New York, 26 January 1952).

[81] Steven Leonard Jacobs, 'We Charge Genocide: A Historical Petition All But Forgotten and Unknown' in Scott Murray (ed), *Understanding Atrocities: Remembering, Representing, and Teaching Genocide* (University of Calgary Press 2017).

[82] Eleanor Roosevelt, 'My Day (28 Dec 1951) The Eleanor Roosevelt Papers, Digital Edition' (*The George Washington University*, 2017) <https://www2.gwu.edu/~erpapers/myday/displaydoc.cfm?_y=1951&_f=md002103> accessed 24 August 2024.

[83] Raphaël Lemkin, 'Nature of Genocide; Confusion with Discrimination Against Individuals Seen' *New York Times* (New York, 14 June 1953).

acknowledged that Black communities experienced discrimination, but not genocide, as they were 'increasing in condition of evident prosperity and progress'.[84]

Scholars explain the denunciation of Roosevelt and Lemkin as tactical moves as they wanted the United States to ratify the treaty, the petitioners were Black communists, and the context was the Cold War.[85] Such dismissals nonetheless denied anti-Black violence by presenting African Americans as threatening, better-off, beyond the remit of international law, and offside rational thinking. Despite this, the language of *We Charge Genocide* resonated among activists supporting Black life, most recently in a submission to the UN Committee on Torture.[86] However, this framing of genocide has been erased from mainstream international law discourses.[87]

White-dominated states and international lawyers have also discounted Indigenous claims of genocide against settler governments and institutions. Just before the African American appeal, the language of 'cultural genocide' was excluded from the Genocide Convention, partly because this language might provide recourse to Indigenous peoples.[88] Indigenous peoples persisted in using this concept to describe their experiences, culminating in advocacy for its inclusion in the 2007 UN Declaration on the Rights of Indigenous Peoples.[89] To no avail, however, as states opposed including the term in that instrument. In both cases, the concept was assailed in the racially infused, 'neutral' language of vagueness.[90] This outcome would not prevent the Truth and Reconciliation Commission of Canada from finding that Canada's 'residential school' system for Indigenous children consisted of cultural genocide,[91] although this finding led to a mainstream public outcry and dismissal by politicians.[92]

Some years later, Indigenous lawyers and the Native Women's Association of Canada requested the ICC investigate governmental and church-led crimes against humanity, after evidence was released showing unmarked residential school graves.[93] The petitioners omitted the claim of genocide from their requests, likely because of concerns about the retroactive application of that norm under the Rome Statute.[94]

[84] Douglas Irvin Erikson, *Raphaël Lemkin and the Concept of Genocide* (University of Pennsylvania Press 2016) 207.

[85] Indeed, Lemkin's denunciation is in tension with his work on colonial genocide.

[86] We Charge Genocide, 'Police Violence Against Chicago's Youth of Color: A report prepared for the United Nations Committee Against Torture on the occasion of its review of American's Third Periodic Report to the Committee Against Torture' (2014) <http://report.wechargegenocide.org/> accessed 23 August 2024.

[87] Sarah Riley Case, 'Black Life under the Genocide Convention and Third World Solidarity' (2022) Draft Paper Loyola International Law Seminar.

[88] Sheryl Lightfoot and David MacDonald, 'The UN as Both Foe and Friend to Indigenous Peoples and Self-Determination' (*E-International Relations*, 12 March 2020) <https://www.e-ir.info/2020/03/12/the-un-as-both-foe-and-friend-to-indigenous-peoples-and-self-determination/#google_vignette> accessed 23 August 2024.

[89] Sandra Prium, 'Ethnocide and Indigenous Peoples: Article 8 of the Declaration on the Rights of Indigenous Peoples' (2014) 35 Adelaide Law Review 269.

[90] ibid.

[91] Selen Kazan, 'Residential School Graves, Canada's "Slow" Genocide and the International Criminal Court' (*Yellowhead Institute*, 4 May 2022) <https://yellowheadinstitute.org/2022/05/04/residential-school-graves-canadas-slow-genocide-the-international-criminal-court/> accessed 23 August 2024.

[92] Emmanuel Guematcha, 'Genocide Against Indigenous Peoples: The Experiences of the Truth Commissions of Canada and Guatemala' (2019) 10 The International Indigenous Policy Journal 1.

[93] Kazan (n 91).

[94] ibid; Office of the Independent Special Interlocutor for Missing Children and Unmarked Graves and Burial Sites associated with Indian Residential Schools, 'Sacred Responsibility Searching for the Missing

The ICC declined to investigate their claim of crimes against humanity, however, in part citing a temporal bar,[95] which again reflects liberal conceptions of fairness that discount non-Western interpretations of intertemporality in the context of intergenerational harms that racialized people experience.

Other Indigenous-led efforts have come under attack for asserting that governmental policies, laws, and practices facilitate the systemic killing and abuse of Indigenous peoples in the present. Scholars and public figures openly contested this finding from an expert report on missing and murdered Indigenous women, girls, and 2SLGBTQ+ persons in Canada.[96] Mainstream media outlets hosted commentators who used formalistic reasoning to argue that genocide could not include such harms.[97] These arguments are emblematic of a culture of denial that invisibilizes Indigenous women, men, and 2SLGTQ+ people across settler colonies constructed as white through Indigenous dispossession and selective immigration.

The dominant 'atrocity' reading of *jus cogens* norms, discussed before, has helped to invisibilize such richer understandings of genocide committed structurally by colonial and settler colonial governments. Although some white-dominant governments have occasionally acknowledged mass violence within their jurisdictions as genocide—for example, Canada and Germany—it is not surprising that they have continued to circumvent calls to redress the continuing structural inequalities implicit in their *jus cogens* violations.[98]

4.3 Apartheid

A third case of the racial economy of *jus cogens* is apartheid. Apartheid overlaps with genocide, forced labour, land dispossession, and other racial injustices that we have discussed, while a distinctive feature is its institutionalization in state policy. Even with evidence of state policy, international lawyers and states have thwarted subaltern appeals for relief from violations of this *jus cogens* norm. Although apartheid is a general prohibition under international law—one that is evoked in contexts such as

Children and Unmarked Burials Interim Report' (June 2023) <https://osi-bis.ca/wp-content/uploads/2023/06/OSI_InterimReport_June-2023_WEB.pdf> accessed 23 August 2024, 122.

[95] Office of the Independent Special Interlocutor (n 94).

[96] National Inquiry into Missing and Murdered Indigenous Women and Girls, 'A Legal Analysis of Genocide: Supplementary report of the National Inquiry into Missing and Murdered Indigenous Women and Girls (2019) <https://publications.gc.ca/site/eng/9.877097/publication.html> accessed 23 August 2024.

[97] See, eg, Özsu (n 13).

[98] Yellowhead Institute, 'Calls to Action Accountability; A 2022 Status Update on Reconciliation'(December 2022) <https://yellowheadinstitute.org/wp-content/uploads/2022/12/TRC-Report-12.15.2022-Yellowhead-Institute-min.pdf> accessed 23 August 2024; Kate Connolly, 'UN Representatives Criticise Germany over Reparations for Colonial Crimes in Namibia' *The Guardian* (Berlin, 28 April 2023) <https://www.theguardian.com/global-development/2023/apr/28/un-representatives-criticise-germany-over-reparations-for-colonial-crimes-in-namibia#:~:text=UN%20representatives%20criticise%20Germany%20over%20reparations%20for%20colonial%20crimes%20in%20Namibia,-This%20article%20is&text=UN%20special%20rapporteurs%20have%20criticised,colonial%20crimes%20against%20their%20ancestors> accessed 24 August 2024.

Kosovo and Palestine[99]—its status as a *jus cogens* norm must be traced to anticolonial struggles in southern Africa and their persistent denials by white colonizers.

An early effort in this direction was the case that Liberia and Ethiopia brought to the ICJ against South Africa for its conduct in the Mandate of South West Africa (Namibia).[100] The Mandate was established under the League of Nations, of which Liberia and Ethiopia were the only independent Sub-Saharan African members given European colonization. After World War II, South Africa maintained its grip on South West Africa and expanded its apartheid policy to the territories. Although the ICJ found in 1950 that South Africa's Mandatory duties to Indigenous peoples remained, South Africa shirked this Opinion with the support of white Allied powers.[101] By 1960, independent African governments resolved to submit South Africa's conduct to binding proceedings at the ICJ.[102] The pleadings were saturated with emerging Third World principles of self-determination, human rights, and racial non-discrimination. Importantly for the evolution of *jus cogens*, those states argued that South Africa 'may not claim exemption from a legal norm which has been created by the overwhelming consensus of the international community'.[103]

Notwithstanding, seven white judges of the ICJ rejected the claim for reasons of standing, with the President casting the deciding vote. Specifically, the Court held that Liberia and Ethiopia had no legal interest in the case, which the Court said rested with the League, not its members. Strikingly, the ICJ's ruling contradicted the 1962 decision made under more diverse judicial membership.[104] Between the earlier decision, where the ICJ affirmed its jurisdiction to hear the merits, and the 1966 decision, where it refused standing to the applicants, several judges of the Third World had left the Court due to death, illness, and retirement. Judge Spender, who vehemently dissented in 1962, became President of the Court by 1966, and he pressured Judge Zafrulla Khan of Pakistan not to sit for specious reasons, giving himself the casting vote.[105] Thus constituted, the ICJ articulated a legal rule against the standing of League members, which the parties had not pleaded.[106]

Third World and African leaders, especially, denounced the decision as 'totally unsound from both the legal and moral standpoints' and a 'perversion of justice'.[107] The President of Liberia condemned the dismissal as a manifestation of 'racism and the old game of colonialism'.[108] Discursively, we understand the ICJ's interpretation of

[99] John Dugard and John Reynolds, 'Apartheid, International Law, and the Occupied Palestinian Territory' (2013) 24(3) European Journal of International Law 867.

[100] *South West Africa, Second Phase, Judgment* (1966) ICJ Rep 6 and related documents.

[101] Jean Allain, 'Decolonization as the Source of the Concepts of Jus Cogens and Obligations Erga Omnes' (2017) Ethiopian Yearbook of International Law 2016.

[102] Victor Kattan, 'Decolonizing the International Court of Justice: The Experience of Judge Sir Muhammad Zafrulla Khan in the *South West Africa* Cases' (2015) 5 Asian Journal of International Law 310.

[103] GM Danilenko, *Law-Making in the International Community* (Martinus Nijhoff 1993) 220 (citing the oral pleadings of Ethiopia and Liberia).

[104] Makane Moïse Mbengue and Najib Messihi, 'The South West Africa Cases: 50 Years Later' (2017) 1 Ethiopian Yearbook of International Law 11.

[105] Kattan (n 102).

[106] ibid.

[107] ibid.

[108] Christopher Gevers, 'Prosecuting the Crime against Humanity of Apartheid: Never, Again' (2018) African Yearbook on International Humanitarian Law 25 (citing the President of Liberia).

standing in this case as reflecting a technique that is routinely used to subvert the legal claims of racialized people by characterizing them as purely political. Moreover, the *political* manoeuvring of some white judges—notably Judge Spender, an Australian with a record of supporting colonialism—went beyond the legal remit of the ICJ to secure South Africa's possession.[109] In other words, *South West Africa* was a white apology for apartheid.

Years later, while Namibia was gaining independence—and after sustained transnational anticolonial struggles[110]—the dismantling of apartheid in South Africa would suffer from further racial obfuscation, albeit mediated by the progress narratives of transitional justice. For all of its successes, the constitutional process in South Africa was a deep compromise between the apartheid National Party and the ANC.[111] If the interests of these parties converged—to use Derrick Bell's concept—around a peaceful road to democratic government, their compromise sacrificed remedies that were vital to the Black majority.[112]

For one thing, constitutional negotiations paved the way for amnesty from prosecution. Amnesty was adopted in extremely difficult conditions, in part because there was no successful revolution against 'internal colonialism'.[113] The amnesty provisions were contested from below by Black victims of apartheid, but the Constitutional Court in *AZAPO* upheld the mandate of the newly established Truth and Reconciliation Commission (TRC) to extend amnesty, prioritizing the interest convergence around a peaceful transition to a unified state.[114]

The decision also ignored efforts among African leaders to prosecute apartheid dating back to the 1960s, which affirmed its *jus cogens* status by designating it a crime against humanity.[115] Although the TRC's mandate included the capacity to recommend *limited* prosecutions (of perpetrators who refused to come forward), scant prosecutions followed.[116] No pursuit of international prosecutions for apartheid would be forthcoming either at a time when anti-impunity narratives were otherwise pervasive.[117]

[109] Kattan (n 102).

[110] Frédéric Mégret, 'The Liberation of Nelson Mandela: Anatomy of a « happy event » in International Law' in Fleur Johns, Richard Joyce, and Sundhya Pahuja (eds), *Events: The Force of International Law* (Routledge 2010).

[111] Mahmood Mamdani, 'Beyond Nuremberg: The Historical Significance of the Post-Apartheid Transition in South Africa' in Karen Engle, Zinaida Miller, and DM Davis (eds), *Anti-Impunity and the Human Rights Agenda* (Cambridge University Press 2016).

[112] ibid.

[113] See ANC, 'Statement at the Conference of the African Liberation Movement' (Statement at the Conference of the African Liberation Movement, Lisbon, 1977); DM Davis, 'The South African Truth Commission and the AZAPO Case: A Reflection Almost Two Decades Later' in Karen Engle, Zinaida Miller, and DM Davis (eds), *Anti-Impunity and the Human Rights Agenda* (Cambridge University Press 2016).

[114] *AZAPO v South Africa*, 4 SA 672 (South Africa Constitutional Court). See also Li (n 19).

[115] Gevers (n 108).

[116] Davis (n 113).

[117] See Gevers (n 108); Li (n 19). Recently, a prosecution under international charges has been secured for the killing of and serious injury to members of the Congress of South African Students. See Foundation for Human Rights, 'The Case of the COSAS 4' (*Foundation for Human Rights*, 24 May 2024) <https://unfinishedtrc.co.za/future-cases/#COSAS-3-Zandisile-Musi> accessed 24 August 2024.

Our point here is not to advocate for criminal responsibility, which itself has structural limitations, but to foreground the invisibilization of subaltern demands for remedies for violations of *jus cogens*. In terms of structural transformation, it is just as important to observe the economic and social compromises made during the transitional justice process. For example, the Constitution was drafted to protect a fundamental human right to private property, while the repatriation of land was placed outside the Bill of Rights, giving white settlers the upper hand in disputes around land redistribution.[118] Moreover, when it came time for the TRC to define its mandate, the Commission focused on discrete human rights violations such as murder and torture, rather than on the regime of apartheid and how it dispossessed millions.[119]

The TRC further defined human rights violations narrowly as the violation of an individual's 'bodily integrity', which minimized dehumanizing practices of apartheid that often had deathly consequences, such as forced labour, the pass system, land theft, and violent relocation.[120] These official apartheid policies were acknowledged, but relegated to the social context against which individual harms occurred.[121] In addition, the TRC process resulted in scant reparations to individuals,[122] which took the form of monetary compensation and avoided a systemic reckoning with apartheid's distribution of benefits along a racial hierarchy.[123] The 'double closure' of liberal progress, both 'constitutional and narrative',[124] thus diminished subaltern experiences of apartheid and associated calls for reparations.

With transitional justice in South Africa also came the overall erasure of the crime of apartheid under international law. UN bodies charged with investigating apartheid were dismantled,[125] and the push by African states to eventually embed the crime of apartheid in the Rome Statute of the ICC has been described as largely 'symbolic'.[126] Although we focused on the example of southern Africa, the *jus cogens* prohibition against apartheid has been broadly neglected,[127] or repressed, by white-dominant states and international lawyers. Apartheid was confined to the status of an aberration, rather than an ongoing colonial project.

A clear example of this has been the denial by white-dominated states and many international lawyers that Israel has instituted an apartheid regime in the occupied Palestinian territories. Scholars who support Palestinian self-determination, or even academic freedom on this matter, have been persecuted by universities and governments. This invisibilization of apartheid in Palestine has persisted in the face of mass

[118] Mamdani (n 111).
[119] ibid.
[120] ibid.
[121] ibid.
[122] Davis (n 113).
[123] Mahmood Mamdani, 'A Diminished Truth' in Wilmot James and Linda Van De Vijver (eds), *After the TRC: Reflections on Truth and Reconciliation in South Africa* (David Phillip Publisher 2000).
[124] Mamdani (n 111).
[125] Dugard and Reynolds (n 99).
[126] Gevers (n 108) citing Roger S Clark, 'History of Efforts to Codify Crimes Against Humanity: From the Charter of Nuremberg to the Statute of the Rome' in Leila Nadya Sadat (ed), *Forging a Convention for Crimes Against Humanity* (Cambridge University Press 2011) 25.
[127] Dugard and Reynolds (n 99).

violence in Gaza, ongoing at the time of writing, which Palestinians, allied activists, and many other international lawyers have described as genocide that conditions of apartheid facilitated. Here again, white-dominated states with significant power (US, UK, Germany, France, etc) and lawyers of the Global North have opposed the charge of genocide at every turn, as if a Global North settler colonial state[128] and its allies could not possibly perpetuate genocide against Palestinians.

5. Conclusion

The colour of international law is unmistakable. Our chapter extends this insight from subaltern legal traditions to describe the colour of *jus cogens*, which has barely been concealed through tools of racial obfuscation. *Jus cogens* exemplifies the invisibility of racialization in international law, acknowledging that racialization is not factually invisible, as Ralph Ellison's novel illustrates, but is *invisibilized* to benefit white-dominated states and institutions at the expense of racialized people.

The idea of *jus cogens* expresses an aspiration for substantive commitments that are beyond state voluntarism and applicable to the entire international community. Yet, the elite capture of *jus cogens* towards liberal and neoliberal human rights, including an 'atrocity' reading of international crimes, has moved the concept in different directions, reinforcing racial hierarchies and exceptionalism under the cover of progress.

In this chapter, we describe how this was made possible through dominant appeals to objectivity and rationality, which fit well with the emphasis of *jus cogens* on universality and peremptory qualities. Specifically, we emphasize the need to think critically about what is included in and excluded from the category and by whom. We suggest that dominant international lawyers, states, and commentators police the racial borders of *jus cogens*, imparting onto the doctrine a specific hue. This colour line cuts across even generally agreed *jus cogens* norms by trivializing the claims of racialized people in terms of what *really* counts as slavery, apartheid, and genocide. It betrays an economy of racial ordering operating through *jus cogens* norms that has often re-entrenched the imperialism of international law.

Recall the situatedness and global expanse of the few stories that we have told from the Vienna Convention debates on the law of treaties to silencing around Palestine. The examples that we shared illustrate the persistence of white supremacy through legal techniques that simultaneously subvert and obscure racial oppression: the false neutrality of *jus cogens* norms, the historical erasure of racialized peoples' appeals to *jus cogens*, and the retrenchment of oppression under the *jus cogens* guise of benevolence.

At the same time, we acknowledge that *jus cogens* could express a radical commitment. The genesis of *jus cogens* in Third World solidarity around self-determination, and the many histories of subaltern advocacy around *jus cogens*, illuminate the emancipatory potential of anticolonial and antiracist international law rooted in popular

[128] ICJ, *Legal Consequences arising from the Policies and Practices of Israel in the Occupied Palestinian Territory, including East Jerusalem*, Advisory Opinion (19 July 2024).

struggles. We therefore sought to foreground not only the persistence of white supremacy under international law but also the endurance of racial justice struggles. These struggles are no less adaptable or sustained (from abolition to decolonization to anti-apartheid . . .). Anchored in transnational praxis, they *visibilize* the structures and intimacies of racism under international law, providing some measure of reparation.[129]

[129] Nesiah (n 10).

PART II

THE TOOLS, TECHNIQUES, AND TECHNOLOGIES OF LEGALIZED RACIAL INEQUALITY

6
Race as Citizenship Personified
Illuminating the Ghosts of Racial Discrimination in International Law

*Shahab Saqib**

1. Introduction

Imagine an organization limits its admission to those who are white and therefore rejects a Black applicant (X). On being challenged that this classifies as racial discrimination, the organization argues that the refusal is not because X is Black but, rather, because X is not white. Would such an argument succeed in a court adjudicating a case of racial discrimination? Surely not. The criterion of 'only white' is based on an implicit preference that is designed to exclude people of colour, even if such a preference is not explicitly stated. Such an argument, therefore, would not only be rejected but viewed as morally reprehensible as well.

We must therefore ask why these arguments convince when applied to citizenship. In *Diop v France*, a Senegalese citizen—residing in France and married to a French citizen—was refused admission to a French bar association.[1] He satisfied all the requirements to practise law in France, except the nationality one. The state made a similar argument to what I illustrated above. To quote verbatim, the state argued that 'the rejection of his application by the Bar Council of Nice was . . . not because he was Senegalese but because he was not French within the meaning of article 1, paragraph 2 (of ICERD)'.[2] The Committee on the Elimination of Racial Discrimination (CERD) accepted the argument, ultimately rejecting the discrimination claim by Mr Diop.

Since the hypothetical would amount to racial discrimination yet the latter does not, a dispute arises over the parameters of race and the connection it has with colour and not citizenship. This chapter does not provide comprehensive answers to these questions.[3] Instead, it demonstrates that the concept of race has always been

* I am indebted to numerous scholars who have provided guidance throughout the process of producing this chapter. Some of them deserve a special mention, such as the editorial team of this volume, including Mohsen and others, as well as Audrey Macklin, Anver Emon, Maleiha Malik, Satvinder Juss, and Jonathan Gingerich. I open this chapter with a hypothetical to address certain audiences who essentialize colour as a sacred classification for the prohibition of racial discrimination. Examining the case of Mr Diop afterwards challenges this essentialism by showing other operative modes of racial exclusion.

[1] *Diop v France*, Communication No 2/1989, UN Doc CERD/C/39/D/2/1989 (18 March 1991).

[2] ibid [6.6].

[3] This is primarily the case because this difference cannot be explored in full without examining the political and territorial dimension of the current world order—a task that exceeds the limited scope of this chapter.

Shahab Saqib, *Race as Citizenship Personified* In: *Emancipating International Law*. Edited by: Mohsen al Attar and Claire Smith, Oxford University Press. © Shahab Saqib 2026. DOI: 10.1093/9780198935605.003.0009

an imperial-cum-colonial project to establish a dividing line between those who belong and those who did not—*us and them*.[4] In the creation of this division, race acted as a malleable instrument that was used, or perhaps abused, by imperialistic actors.[5] The racial logic of exclusion acted as an imagined platform on which the rationale of 'only white' fooled the audiences through different disguises.[6] International law operated as an imagined platform of exclusion where the 'only white' logic could be reconstituted under the veil of citizenship,[7] splitting the world into heaven and hell,[8] the good West and bad Third World,[9] the white and the darker worlds,[10] and, as the High Representative of the European Union recently declared, the garden and the jungle.[11] Racial boundaries between these worlds were (and remain) demarcated through a boundary of exclusion known as the global colour line.[12] In this split, citizenship was the new colour, which functioned as an intermediary to fulfil the desires of imperial states, providing means to legitimize practices of racial discrimination.[13]

I refer to this phenomenon as the *personification of race into citizenship*. Race may have been a fluid concept; however, its classification for the purpose of exclusion was a colonial construct.[14] Through its Eurocentric and colonial foundations, international law inherited this racial classification but mystified it to prohibit certain forms of racial discrimination while simultaneously justifying others, primarily, as I argue, through the concept of citizenship. Citizenship thus developed into a persona through which practices of racial discrimination were concealed and buried in a graveyard. In this context, the metaphorical articulation of a 'graveyard' and of 'ghosts'

[4] Achiume makes a similar observation as she states that 'theorizing the system of imperial racial borders is understanding race itself as a border'. E Tendayi Achiume, 'Racial Borders' (2022) 110(3) Georgetown Law Journal 450. For the purposes of my work, I refer to it as a border of exclusion.

[5] As Hannah Arendt states, 'racism has been the powerful ideology of imperialistic policies since the turn of our century. It certainly has absorbed and revived all the old patterns of race opinions which, however, by themselves would hardly have been able to create or, for that matter, to degenerate into racism as a Weltanschauung or an ideology'. Hannah Arendt, *The Origins of Totalitarianism* (Penguin Books 2017) 158.

[6] The 'only-white' policies were an integral part of the history of imperial states. For instance, the White Australia Policy restricted the entry of non-Europeans into the country to make it a racially insulated white society. Similar discourses were prevalent in other imperial states as well. See David Atkinson, 'The White Australia Policy, the British Empire, and the World' (2015) 8(2) Britain and the World 204.

[7] Christopher Gevers, 'Unwhitening the World: Rethinking Race and International Law' (2021) 67 UCLA Law Review 1652.

[8] Obiora Okafor and Shedrack Agbakwa, 'Re-Imagining International Human Rights Education in Our Time: Beyond Three Constitutive Orthodoxies' (2001) 14(3) Leiden Journal of International Law 563.

[9] Obiora C Okafor, 'On the Patchiness, Promise and Perils of "Global" Human Rights Law' [2011] Nigerian Institute of Advanced Legal Studies 1.

[10] WEB Du Bois, 'Of the Culture of White Folk' (1917) 7(4) The Journal of Race Development 434, 439.

[11] Ben Norton, 'In neocolonial rant, EU says Europe is "garden" superior to rest of world's barbaric "jungle"' (*MR online*, 15 October 2022) <https://mronline.org/2022/10/19/in-neocolonial-rant-eu-says-europe-is-garden-superior-to-rest-of-worlds-barbaric-jungle/> accessed 31 July 2024.

[12] Charles W Mills, 'The Illumination of Blackness' in Moon-Kie Jung and João H Coasta Vargas (eds), *Antiblackness* (Duke University Press 2021) 26.

[13] I am using the term 'colonial/imperial' in the sense of European colonial powers, which includes European settlers such as Australia, Canada, and the United States. This meaning is used in this sense elsewhere as well. For instance, see Balakrishnan Rajagopal, 'Locating the Third World in Cultural Geography' (2000) 15 Third World Legal Studies 1.

[14] Ivan Hannaford, *Race: The History of an Idea in the West* (Johns Hopkins University Press 1996); Nell Irvin Painter, *The History of White People* (Illustrated edn, WW Norton 2011); George M Fredrickson and Albert Camarillo, *Racism: A Short History* (Princeton University Press 2015).

gestures to the necropolitics of international law that, due to its liberal expression, seeks to bury the histories of racial discrimination, yet ultimately reincarnates the same teleology through the persona of citizenship. The 'ghosts' of racial discrimination are resurrected from the graveyard, shaping international legal practice and the lives of racialized peoples,[15] but consistently concealed by imperial powers lest they expose the racial illiberalism of the liberal era.[16]

I explore this argument in three parts. The first deconstructs the notion of colour as something unique or exceptional. It shows that colour was merely one of the means by which the colonial powers classified race as 'differentiable' to justify the legalization of discrimination against people of colour. In this process, colours were often imagined, racially assigned, and deployed against different races according to the colonial powers' racial thinking. Since the hypothetical treats colour as a relevant characteristic when prohibiting racial discrimination, by examining the roots of colour and deconstructing its connection with race, this part builds a platform to showcase the ghosts of racial discrimination and lay the groundwork for the personification of race into citizenship.

Next, I map the process of personification. By focusing on the provisions relating to the prohibition of discrimination in different international human rights law (IHRL) instruments, particularly the International Convention of the Elimination of All Forms of Racial Discrimination (ICERD), this part demonstrates how race was constructed as a concept independent from citizenship.[17] This separation made citizenship a legal characteristics or *persona* that was then used to enable racial discrimination via international law. In the concluding section, I connect colour and citizenship by arguing that, as a racial imaginary, international law transformed the 'only white' logic to the 'only white nations', where citizenship operated as the new colour and citizenship rules demarcated a new global colour line. As I demonstrate, the unequal value allocated to citizenship across the world maps eerily onto the same colour line WEB Du Bois lamented a century ago, effectively achieving a lawful and sanguine form of racial discrimination, thus resurrecting the ghosts of the past to haunt the present.

2. Deconstructing the connection between race and colour

What is black, red, white, yellow, or brown? A scientist sees them as a distribution of waves on the electromagnetic spectrum, while someone who suffers from achromatopsia would call them little more than shades. How do they materialize into

[15] In this sense, the metaphor of a 'graveyard' refers to the necro characteristic of international law which transforms racial discrimination from one form into another.

[16] The use of metaphors in this article is intentional, even though it may seem abstract or poetic at some points. The main purpose of doing so is not to distract the reader but to instigate reimagination of a concept which is primarily understood through doctrinal means. Such metaphorical illustrations are found in other works as well. See, for instance, Avery F Gordon, *Ghostly Matters: Haunting and the Sociological Imagination* (2nd edn, University of Minnesota Press 2008).

[17] Since the provisions related to the prohibition of discrimination in international law are found mostly in the IHRL instruments, the terms international law and IHRL are used interchangeably in this chapter.

racial colours? Charles Hirschman offers a possible answer, arguing in *The Origins and Demise of the Concept of Race* that the diversity of phenotypes provides an approximate guide to the geographical allocation of humans.[18] The difference in physical features arises through natural selection when populations are geographically separated from each other for longer periods of time.[19] The phenotypical diversity results from this separation which became salient when boundaries overlapped, through migration, invasion, or by other means.[20] This helps explain why imperialists used colour to establish racial boundaries in line with geographical location. As I argue below, they also used colour to expand, exploit, and regulate the boundaries of racial exclusion. In that sense, the reification of colours into racial boundaries was an effective method of racial stratification.

A classic example of racialization through colour was the invention of the term 'red Indians', used to demarcate Native Americans as a different race because of an alleged difference in colour.[21] Some historical accounts suggest this colour was associated with Indigenous people because they used red paint as war symbolism, wore red dresses, or used red plant pigment as protection from the sun.[22] However, these explanations are neither reliable nor convincing.[23] Similarly, Michael Keevak shows how yellow colour had nothing to do with the skin colour of East Asians either. In *Becoming Yellow*, Keevak argues that yellow was a product of imperial racial thinking, used to racially designate Mongolians.[24] Colour assignment, therefore, was a common technique employed by imperialists to separate those who belonged from those who did not.

The Hollywood film *Megamind* (2010) provides a useful illustration of colour assignment in action. The two main characters, Metro Man and Megamind, are alien children who, after the destruction of their planets, reach Earth on separate spaceships. Metro Man lands in an aristocratic mansion, destined to become a hero, while Megamind lands in a prison, condemning him to a life of villainy. One feature of this film stands out: Metro Man was white whereas Megamind was purple. Deploying the riddle of the egg or the chicken, did the creators assign the characters roles based on skin colour or did they just presume them? These were fictional characters making an immutable skin colour impossible. Even in fiction, their classification only vindicated an imperialistic racial ordering, deploying non-whiteness to exclude.[25]

[18] Charles Hirschman, 'The Origins and Demise of the Concept of Race' (2004) 30(3) Population and Development Review 385, 386.

[19] ibid 387.

[20] For a general overview of the history of colour and race, see Nina G Jablonski, 'Skin Color and Race' (2021) 175(2) American Journal of Physical Anthropology 437. See also CB Davenport, *The Skin Colors of the Races of Mankind* (1926) 26 Natural History 44.

[21] Nancy Shoemaker, 'How Indians Got to Be Red' (1997) 102(3) The American Historical Review 625.

[22] These are not the only explanations for the derivation of the red colour. The linkage is also often made to 'the red crawfish' that created the earth, made of 'red blood'. See ibid 634 for details.

[23] Nancy Shoemaker, 'Race' in Nancy Shoemaker (ed), *A Strange Likeness: Becoming Red and White in Eighteenth-Century North America* (Oxford University Press 2004).

[24] Michael Keevak, *Becoming Yellow: A Short History of Racial Thinking* (Princeton University Press 2011) 2.

[25] The preference of white in Hollywood is not a new phenomenon. See Nancy Wang Yuen, *Reel Inequality: Hollywood Actors and Racism* (Illustrated edn, Rutgers University Press 2016).

These examples echo with the opening hypothetical. If 'only white' means skin colour, could X have painted his body to satisfy the criteria of inclusion? If not, was it a matter of pigmentation instead? Or does it mean natural whiteness, implying that X could have qualified if he were Albino, irrespective of the underlying ethnicity? The answer to these questions depends on the taxonomy of acceptable and unacceptable degrees of whiteness and how imperialists construct the boundaries of 'only white' through their racial thinking (the historic one-drop rule comes to mind). They can define colour as paint, skin pigment, or a health condition; or as illustrated previously, they can racially assign colours, such as yellow or red, create characters based on colour, or do whatever is necessary to advance an ethos of stratification and exclusion. The 'only white' logic, therefore, was less about colour, or a particular conception of colour, and more about the boundary of exclusion that separated imperialists from their identified others. Rather than being inherent, blackness or colour—and the ensuing separation—resulted from an imperial gaze.

Karen Brodkin illustrates the dynamics of this exclusionary boundary in *How Jews Became White Folks*. Brodkin explains the history of racial change through which Jews were assigned colours, often white or off-white, to define their ethno-racial identities.[26] She recounts how the anti-Semitic environment that racialized her parents was not the one she spent her life in.[27] After the Second World War, the American Jewry was granted 'many institutional privileges of white racial assignment',[28] resulting in some of her children preferring to classify themselves as generic whites rather than Jews.[29] As observed by Du Bois elsewhere,[30] this gave her a kind of *second sight* that came from what Brodkin defines as 'an experience of marginality vis-a-vis whiteness, and an experience of whiteness and belonging vis-à-vis blackness'.[31] Whiteness, in her story, was never about colour. Rather, it was about the distribution of privileges and crossing the boundary of exclusion; it was a certificate of entitlement that others—including previous generations of her family—were denied.

'Only white' logic, therefore, connoted a special form of racial thinking that emerged in a different time and space to impose and regulate the racial boundaries of exclusion. It was never about skin colour, but exclusion, domination through separation, and the ongoing maintenance of the privileges it created. As Charles W Mills explained, whiteness was 'constructed not by the inclusion of the other colors but by their official exclusion, an "Optic White" for "Keeping America Pure", even if an unacknowledged Black base lied at the heart of its purity'.[32] In this sense, colour was not something racialized people were born with;[33] rather, colour assignment is part of the process of racialization.

[26] Karen Brodkin, *How Jews Became White Folks and What That Says About Race in America* (Rutgers University Press 1998) 1.
[27] ibid 2.
[28] ibid 3.
[29] ibid 2.
[30] WEB Du Bois, *The Souls of Black Folk* (Revised edn, Dover Publications 1994).
[31] Brodkin (n 26) 1–2.
[32] Mills further writes that 'figuring whiteness in this way demystifies its chromatic pretensions and the related illusions of the Eurocentric worldview that has biased objective inquiry into the workings of the world'. Mills (n 12) 18.
[33] Du Bois (n 30) 8.

If this is the peculiarity of 'only white' logic, the peculiarity of *only French* citizenship does not appear much different. It is structured on the same boundary of exclusion in which, instead of colour, citizenship is deployed to justify separation. The logic of 'non-white are not a part of us' was transmuted into the logic of 'non-citizens are not a part of us'; it just happens that non-citizens are predominantly racialized. The paths overlapped and justified various exclusions and discriminations. One example of this overlap can be found in *Dred Scott v Sandford*, where the majority of the Supreme Court of the United States of America opined that 'a free negro of the African race, whose ancestors were brought to this country and sold as slaves, is not a citizen of this country (the United States of America).'[34] The majority further stated that members of African descent were 'not included, and were not intended to be included, under the word "citizens" in the Constitution, and can therefore claim none of the rights and privileges which that instrument provides for and secures to citizens of the United States.'[35] The boundary of exclusion operated in the same way. The only difference was the transformation of language from colour to citizenship.

Building on Benjamin Isaac's *The Invention of Racism in Classical Antiquity*[36] and Charles W Mills's *The Illumination of Blackness*,[37] I argued in this section that race was a defining line of colour more than colour a defining line of race. This contrasts with the hypothetical I opened with where discrimination based on skin colour was considered racial but not when based on citizenship. Yet, in both cases, the denominator is exclusion, allowing me to challenge the exceptionality of colour in identifying race. Colouring or pigmentocracy[38] was an invention with a purpose, an alienating technique to designate racial superiority and inferiority and demarcate the boundaries of inclusion and exclusion.

In the following section, I argue that a similar dynamic applies to citizenship and international law. As Christopher Gevers has noted, 'international law was a racial imaginary—a White International that emerged from and reinforced Global White Supremacy'.[39] International law was another platform through which the racial epistemologies of modernity gained traction, with the logic of 'only white' transformed into 'only white nations'.[40] The boundaries of exclusion were adjusted, as was the mode of deployment from the assignment of colour to the assignment of citizenship. In a world of international law where the particularities of whiteness masqueraded as

[34] *Dred Scott v Sandford* 60 US 393 (1856) 393.

[35] The shift from colour to citizenship in the context of the United States can be found in this statement of the judgement: 'it is true that the course of events has brought the Indian tribes within the limits of the United States under subjection to the white race; and it has been found necessary, for their sake as well as our own, to regard them as in a state of pupilage, and to legislate to a certain extent over them and the territory they occupy. But they may, without doubt, like the subjects of any other foreign Government, be naturalized by the authority of Congress, and become citizens of a State, and of the United States'. ibid.

[36] Benjamin Isaac, *The Invention of Racism in Classical Antiquity* (Princeton University Press 2006).

[37] Mills (n 12).

[38] The word is taken from Jemima Pierre, *The Predicament of Blackness: Postcolonial Ghana and the Politics of Race* (University of Chicago Press 2012) xiv.

[39] Gevers (n 7) 1652.

[40] See Marilyn Lake and Henry Reynolds, *Drawing the Global Colour Line: White Men's Countries and the International Challenge of Racial Equality* (1st edn, Cambridge University Press 2008).

universality,[41] 'citizenship' walked as a persona, concealing an underlying teleology of racial discrimination.

3. Personification of race into citizenship in international law

The term 'race' lacks a concrete definition in international law. Despite this, provisions within international law often include a reference to race under the laws concerning the prohibition against discrimination. For instance, Article 2 of the Universal Declaration of Human Rights (UDHR),[42] Article 26 of the International Covenant on Civil and Political Rights (ICCPR), and Article 2 of International Convention on Economic, Social and Cultural Rights (ICESCR) all prohibit discrimination on the basis of race, among other factors. Even ICERD does not provide any explicit definition of the term race but insists on prohibiting racial discrimination on the grounds of 'race, colour, descent, or national or ethnic origin'.[43] In other words, while international law insists on protecting against racial discrimination, the term 'race' remains undefined in its core instruments.

The use of protected categories to conceptualize discrimination does not effectively convey its meaning. Each of the categories in IHRL instruments is independently recognized and therefore needs to be proven separately to claim protection against discrimination.[44] An individual who has suffered discrimination on the basis of their skin colour, for instance, cannot claim protection on the ground of political opinion unless that is proven independently. Within this conceptualization of discrimination in IHRL, if ethnicity, colour, national or social origin, descent, language, and even religion are separately protected, what is left for race to include? Stated otherwise, if race is something other than the above grounds—that are independently protected—is it an empty concept in international law?

Perhaps race serves as a general category, with colour or other characteristics constituting further subclassifications or dimensions of it. Alternatively, race may be understood to encompass what other categories do not.[45] However, this is a separate inquiry. In this text, I contend that the failure to recognize citizenship as a protected ground against discrimination obscures the connection between race and citizenship, rooted in the same racial thinking that underpinned the manipulation of race to sustain 'only white' logic. The classification of race as an independent category and the omission of

[41] Linda Martín Alcoff, *The Future of Whiteness* (Polity 2015).

[42] Universal Declaration of Human Rights (adopted 10 December 1948) UNGA Res 217 A(III) (UDHR) Article 2.

[43] Convention on the Elimination of All Forms of Racial Discrimination (adopted 21 December 1965) 660 UNTS 195 (ICERD) Article 1(1)

[44] This single-axis dimension of discrimination has generated problems for the claims of intersectional discrimination as well. See Shreya Atrey, *Intersectional Discrimination* (Oxford University Press 2019) 85.

[45] See *Williams Lecraft v Spain*, Communication No 1493/06, CCPR/C/96/D/1493/2006 (27 July 2009) in which the identification of 'coloured people' was classified as a case of racial discrimination. Otherwise, it has been very rare for race to be invoked as an individual ground which, as Wouter Vandenhole mentions, has been invoked only twice in individual communications to the Human Rights Committee (HRC) (in which both complaints were found inadmissible) and exceptionally to the Committee on Economic, Social and Cultural Rights (CESRC). See Wouter Vandenhole, *Non-Discrimination and Equality in the View of the UN Human Rights Treaty Bodies* (Intersentia 2005) 89, 105.

citizenship as a protected ground divorce both categories from each other. Since citizenship is treated as something other than race through this separation, its persona becomes a platform on which practices of racial discrimination are legitimized.

The issue of recognizing citizenship as a protected ground against discrimination did not emerge in the early IHRL instruments in relation to race, but, rather, through the category of nationality and national origin. The *travaux préparatoires* of the foundational document of IHRL—the UDHR—reveal that the debate to include members of different nationalities was pursued in its initial drafts. During the fifth meeting of the Sub-Commission on Prevention of Discrimination and Protection of Minorities,[46] Mr AP Borisov, a Russian delegate, proposed the addition of the term 'national' along with 'social origin' to protect individuals from different nationalities living under the same government. The Australian, French, and British delegates objected, contending that 'national origin' was synonymous with 'nationality' and could lead to confusion.[47] The Sub-Commission thus had to clarify that 'national origin' would be interpreted in the sense of national characteristics and not in the sense of citizens of a state.[48] It eventually adopted 'social or national origin' as a ground of protection against discrimination, rather than citizenship. Similar discussions on the recognition of citizenship as a protected ground of discrimination can also be found in the *travaux préparatoires* of the ICERD, where it is mostly discussed in connection with nationality and national origin, rather than race.[49]

Ironically, a clear dissociation between race and citizenship is made by the ICERD. Where Article 1(1) of ICERD prohibits racial discrimination on the grounds of race, colour, descent, or national or ethnic origin, Article 1(2) provides that this prohibition does not apply to distinctions, exclusions, restrictions, or preferences between citizens and non-citizens.[50] Ion Diaconu rightly criticizes this formulation, arguing that this provision is exclusionary and, if taken literally, 'would have compelled the Committee to avoid any discussion on the situation of stateless populations or those of a foreign citizenship living on the territories of the States parties'.[51] The CERD, therefore, has to clarify in General Recommendation (GR) 30 that Article 1(2) 'must be construed so as to avoid undermining the basic prohibition of discrimination'.[52] However, it did not repair the fragmentation between race and citizenship created by Article 1(2) of the ICERD.

Viewed with a focus on citizenship, the structure of conceptualizing race through the grounds of discrimination begins to rupture. On one end, race is and is not

[46] UN Commission on Human Rights 'Sub-Commission on Prevention of Discrimination and Protection of Minorities First Session: Summary Record of Fifth Meeting' UN Doc E/CN 4/Sub.2/SR/5 (27 November 1947).

[47] ibid 7–8.

[48] Johannes Morsink, *Inherent Human Rights: Philosophical Roots of the Universal Declaration* (University of Pennsylvania Press 2012) 157.

[49] See Patrick Thornberry, *The International Convention on the Elimination of All Forms of Racial Discrimination: A Commentary* (Oxford University Press 2016) 101, 142. See also Anna Spain Bradley, 'Human Rights Racism' (2019) 32 Harvard Human Rights Journal 22.

[50] ICERD (n 43) Article 1(2).

[51] Ion Diaconu, *Racial Discrimination* (Eleven International Publishing 2011) 152.

[52] CERD, 'General Recommendation 30 on Discrimination Against Non-Citizens' UN Doc CERD/C/64/Misc.11/rev.3 (1 October 2002) [2].

associated with the grounds protected against discrimination due to its recognition as an 'independent' ground. On the other end, citizenship is divorced from race and connected with national origin and nationality instead. Between these two ends, ICERD proclaims that racial discrimination shall not be associated with citizenship, confronting the narrative that it may as well be. International law thus ends up in a bizarre play with racial epistemologies. It endeavours to address discrimination with a protective strategy that aims to cure the past. However, it does so without acknowledging that the present world has been demarcated through a global colour line, where citizenship is the new modus operandi to justify exclusions. The dissociation of race from citizenship creates a filter through which 'racial discrimination' receives legitimacy simply because it is justified on the ground of citizenship and not race.

There is also a broader problem associated with this conceptualization of race and citizenship. The fact that citizenship is tied to nationality rather than race means that exclusions stemming from it are scrutinized through the lens of nationality as well. Article 1(3) of the ICERD states that, 'nothing in this convention may be interpreted as affecting in any way the legal provisions of States Parties concerning nationality, citizenship or naturalization, provided that such provisions do not discriminate against any particular nationality'.[53] The word 'nationality' is used twice in this provision, but it is unclear what it means in either instance. According to Egon Schwelb, the first use of 'nationality' is in an ethnic sense, whereas the second refers to a politico-legal sense.[54] Diaconu, on the other hand, writes that nationality in the first sense means citizenship, whereas he and Lerner agree that the second equates with national origin.[55] The ambiguity surrounding the term is often extended to race as a general category. James A Goldston, for instance, writes that Article 1(3) of the ICERD 'grants states discretion in applying race-based distinctions when it comes to citizenship rules'.[56] Peter Spiro also observes that Article 1 'brackets the use of race as a criterion for citizenship'.[57] Nationality is thus a mystery term which seems to be lost in different epistemic classifications of race. Without a clear definition, it remains uncertain whom it is intended to safeguard from discrimination. However, what seems clear is that it creates a boundary line between race and citizenship, separating one from the other.

International law, in this way, begets the persona of citizenship to obscure cases of racial discrimination. It allows, as Patrick Wolfe stated, colonialism to speak in idioms[58] and disorientates the epistemic roots of race so deeply that anything without

[53] ICERD (n 43) Article 1(3).

[54] See Egon Schwelb, 'The International Convention on the Elimination of All Forms of Racial Discrimination' (1966) 15(4) International & Comparative Law Quarterly 996, 1009.

[55] See Diaconu (n 51); Warwick A McKean, *Equality and Discrimination Under International Law* (Clarendon Press 1983) 157; Thornberry (n 50).

[56] James A Goldston, 'Holes in the Rights Framework: Racial Discrimination, Citizenship, and the Rights of Noncitizens' (2006) 20 Ethics & International Affairs 321, 333.

[57] Peter J Spiro, 'A New International Law of Citizenship' (2011) 105 American Journal of International Law 694, 716. For a detailed and thorough discussion on Article 1(3) of the CERD, see Michelle Foster and Timnah Rachel Baker, 'Racial Discrimination in Nationality Laws: A Doctrinal Blind Spot of International Law?' (2021) 11 Columbia Journal of Race and Law 83, 107; Theodor Meron, 'The Meaning and Reach of the International Convention on the Elimination of All Forms of Racial Discrimination' (1985) 79 American Journal of International Law 283.

[58] Patrick Wolfe, *Traces of History: Elementary Structures of Race* (Verso Books 2016) 21.

the label of white citizenship is excluded straight away. The eroticism of an imperial past is resurrected on a still-racialized world in which international law blindfolds itself with a cloth of citizenship. The practices of racial discrimination are buried in the graveyard where citizenship acts as a veil to conceal the inequalities that exist in the present world. The irony of this personification is that while international law and the ICERD in particular aim to eliminate 'all' forms of racial discrimination, limited by its vision, the protections available extend only to those classifications inherited from imperialism.

The outcome of this personification is tragic. The discriminations that international law buries through citizenship do not vanish. Rather, they re-emerge as spectres that haunt the structure of international law. International law may be blind to the persona of citizenship, but these ghosts are real, at least for those affected by them. In the following section, I showcase the reincarnation of these ghosts of racial discrimination. Given that this operates through an imperialistic construction of race, the protection against racial discrimination in international law becomes a myth as skin colour is transmuted into passport colour.

4. Ghosts of racial discrimination in international law

Following the period of formal decolonization, the world was not only left unequal but *racially unequal*, with Anglo-American centralization of resources starving the rest.[59] The Global South—including its ethnicities, cultures, and citizens—stood economically, socially, and politically disadvantaged.[60] Political or economic opportunities were fundamentally unequal since decolonizing states stood far behind the starting line of the global race. Even then, they may still have flourished if it was not for the predatory policies of imperial powers and their financial 'meddlers' (the International Monetary Fund and World Bank).[61] As Jason Hickel rightly puts it, the Global South remained poor 'because they were integrated into the global economic system on unequal terms'.[62] Among those unequal terms, citizenship contributed to the inequality of the racialized Global South. In this section, I illustrate how citizenship demarcated a colour line in a globally racialized world.

Dimitry Kochenov and Justin Lindeboom recently developed a Quality Nationality Index (QNI) to measure the internal and external value of nationality vis à vis citizenship. The index measures quality of life in one's country of citizenship, alongside the opportunities made available via this citizenship beyond it. It was composed of seven sub-elements:

[59] Harsha Walia, *Border and Rule: Global Migration, Capitalism, and the Rise of Racist Nationalism* (Haymarket Books 2021).

[60] Jason Hickel, *The Divide: Global Inequality from Conquest to Free Markets* (Illustrated edn, WW Norton 2018).

[61] Jamie Martin, *The Meddlers: Sovereignty, Empire, and the Birth of Global Economic Governance* (Harvard University Press 2022) 6.

[62] ibid 2 (italics added).

the level of human development in the nationality-conferring country; the economic strength of the nationality-conferring country; the degree of peace and stability in the nationality-conferring country; the diversity of settlement freedom; the weighed value of settlement freedom; the diversity of travel freedom; and the weighed value of travel freedom.[63]

The map they came with, in contrast to the value of citizenship, is shared below in Figure 6.1.

The map presents a disintegrated view of the world, divided through the value of citizenship. Borders of exclusion are evident, where nations of non-white populations predominantly occupy disadvantaged positions. In this polarized world, citizenship determines the value and rights of a person. Those who have white citizenship get what Branko Milanovic calls a 'citizenship premium', whereas those who have coloured citizenship suffer a 'citizenship penalty'.[64] The citizens of predominantly white nation-states have won the 'birthright lottery'[65] when compared to those from the Global South, who are treated as the 'children of a lesser state'.[66] Given the role of citizenship in enabling global inequality, Kochenov describes it as a tool of 'hypocrisy, and blunt domination, all dressed up as agency and the pursuit of the common good . . . a very effective abstract legal tool to justify essentially random violence, humiliation, and exclusion'.[67]

IHRL reserves certain rights exclusively to the citizens of a state. While this may have initially meant that all citizens were guaranteed equal, though separate, rights, citizenship's intrinsic inequality meant that the approach also legitimized forms of discrimination against those who possessed non-white citizenship—a global Jim Crow.[68] For instance, where Article 25 of ICCPR reserves political rights only for the citizens of a state, the General Comment (GC) 25 of the HRC interprets the term 'public services' under this article to include 'executive, judiciary, legislature, and other areas of state administration'.[69] Similarly, Article 12 and 13 of ICCPR read with

[63] See Dimitry Kochenov and Justin Lindeboom, 'Empirical Assessment of the Quality of Nationalities: The Quality of Nationality Index (Qni)' (2017) 4 European Journal of Comparative Law and Governance 314, 322, 329.

[64] Branko Milanovic, *Global Inequality: A New Approach for the Age of Globalization* (Harvard University Press 2016) 222.

[65] Ayelet Shachar, *The Birthright Lottery: Citizenship and Global Inequality* (Harvard University Press 2009).

[66] Ayelet Shachar, 'Children of a Lesser State: Sustaining Global Inequality through Citizenship Laws' (2003) 44 Nomos 345.

[67] Dimitry Kochenov, *Citizenship* (MIT Press 2019) xii, xiii.

[68] By using the term 'a new Jim Crow' I follow the rationale used by Michelle Alexander as she writes 'in the era of colorblindness, it is no longer socially permissible to use race, explicitly, as a justification for discrimination, exclusion and social contempt. So we don't. Rather than rely on race, we use our criminal justice system to label people of color 'criminals' and then engage in all the practices we supposedly left behind. Today it is perfectly legal to discriminate against criminals in nearly all the ways that it was once legal to discriminate against African Americans'. In my case, however, I am referring to the labelling of 'citizenship' instead of 'criminals'. Michelle Alexander and Cornel West, *The New Jim Crow* (Revised edn, New Press 2012) 14.

[69] UN HRC, 'General Comment No 25: Article 25 (Participation in Public Affairs and the Right to Vote)' (27 August 1996) UN Doc CCPR/C/21/Rev1/Add 7 [5]. See also Sarah Joseph and Melissa Castan, *The International Covenant on Civil and Political Rights: Cases, Materials, and Commentary* (3rd edn, OUP Oxford 2013) 728.

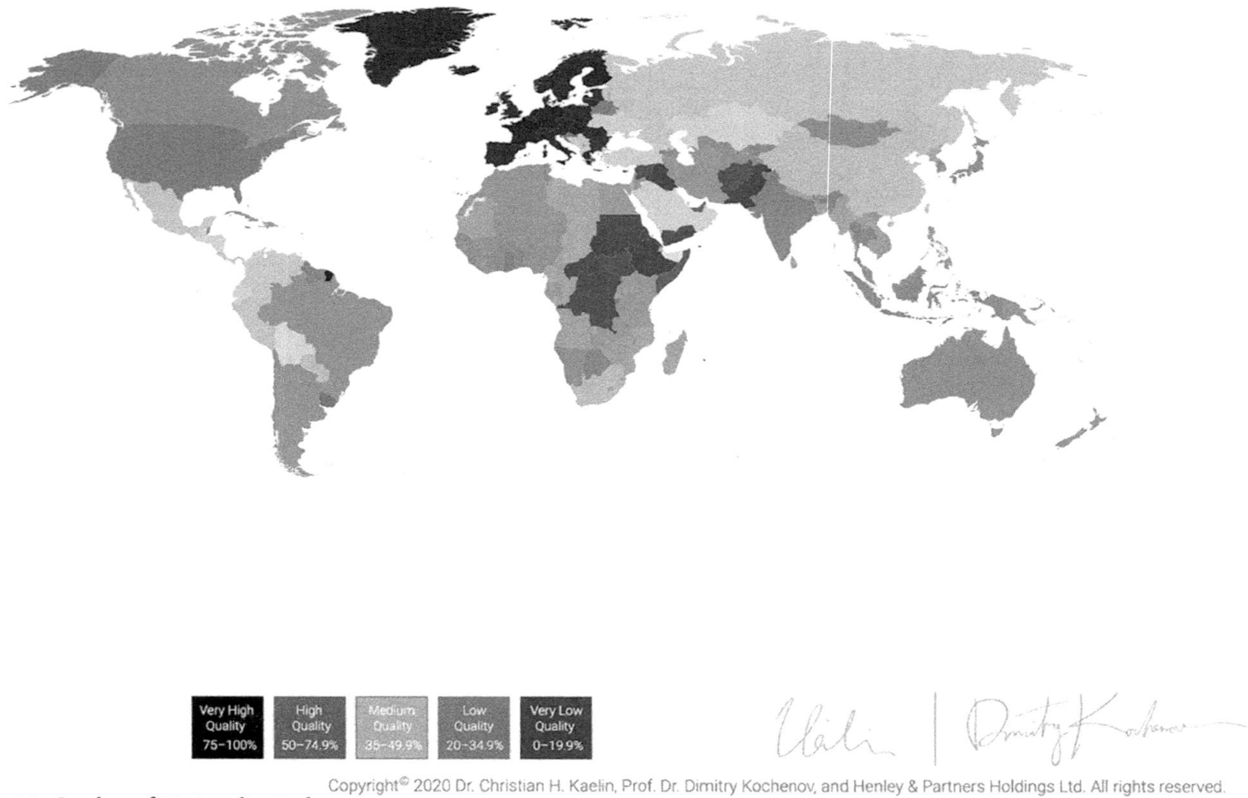

Fig 6.1 Quality of Nationality Index map

Source: Kälin and Kochenov's Quality of Nationality Index[a]

[a]Quality of Nationality Index, Map of Quality of Nationality Index (*Quality of Nationality Index* 2020) <https://www.nationalityindex.com> accessed 31 July 2024.

GC 15 of the HRC position borders as exclusionary fields, allocating to states discretion in the regulation of inclusion, deportation, and processing of non-citizens (residence, movement, and migration).[70] General Recommendation (GR) 30 on Article 1(2) of ICERD, ironically titled discrimination against non-citizens, also authorizes states to revoke job offers to those non-citizens who do not have a work permit.[71]

Compare the exclusivity of these rights in a globally racialized world with the European Union, an 'only white' region, which shows an eerie resemblance to the American Jim Crow model. Article 20 of the Treaty on the Functioning of the European Union establishes the 'Citizenship of the Union' while Articles 21 and 22 obliterate the nation-state borders and extend to other white citizens, albeit with some limits,[72] political rights, freedom of movement, and residency.[73] In addition, Article 18 prohibits discrimination based on nationality (understood as citizenship), especially for workers (Article 45),[74] while certain directives and regulations emphasize upholding these rights.[75] The European Union (EU) thus becomes a magnified version of the 'only white' institution where the litmus test for inclusion is white citizenship rather than skin colour.

The jurisprudence of the IHRL treaty bodies and of the EU regarding these rights is certainly complex. Each article and the rights it grants carry different legal technicalities and limitations.[76] However, the use of the EU as a comparator, or an alternate prism, as Mills terms it,[77] gives a bird's eye view of the racialized world of imagination that regulates the boundary of exclusion. Mills argued that the social contract tradition 'is not a contract between everybody (we the people), but between just the people who count, the people who really are people (we the white people)'.[78] The racialized contract Mills describes maps neatly onto the racialized citizenship argument I have developed in this chapter. Similarly, Achiume and others have detailed the racialized

[70] UN HRC, 'General Comment No 15: The Position of Aliens Under the Covenant' (11 April 1986) UN Doc HRI/GEN/1/Rev 1.

[71] ICERD (n 43) [35].

[72] See, for instance, European Council Directive 2004/38/EC on the right of citizens of the Union and their family members to move and reside freely within the territory of the Member States [2004] OJ L158/77, which regulates the right to exit (Article 4), the right to entry (Article 5), the right to residence (Articles 6 and 7), and the residence permit with its own limitations (Articles 8–11).

[73] See Consolidated version of the Treaty on the Functioning of the European Union [2012] OJ C326/1, Articles 20–25.

[74] However, as David Fennelly and Clíodhna Murphy point out: 'this principle is erected on a fundamental distinction between nationals of EU Member States, on the one hand, and nationals of non-member countries, on the other hand. Thus, the fundamental principle prohibiting nationality discrimination stops at the EU's own borders.' David Fennelly and Clíodhna Murphy, 'Racial Discrimination and Nationality and Migration Exceptions: Reconciling CERD and the Race Equality Directive' (2021) 39 Netherlands Quarterly of Human Rights 308, 318.

[75] Council Directive 2014/54/EU of 28 April 2014 on measures facilitating the exercise of rights conferred on workers in the context of freedom of movement for workers [2014] OJ L128/8; Council Regulation No 492/2011 on freedom of movement for workers within the Union [2011] OJ l 141/1.

[76] See Hermann-Josef Blanke and Stelio Mangiameli (eds), *Treaty on the Functioning of the European Union—A Commentary: Volume I: Preamble, Articles 1-89* (1st edn, Springer 2021) for issues related with these rights, such as proportionality, cross-border element, public policy, public security, and public health limitations.

[77] In the words of Mills, 'through this alternative prism, whiteness is a willed darkness; whiteness is segregated investigation; whiteness is the particular masquerading as the universal'. Mills (n 12) 18.

[78] Charles W Mills, *The Racial Contract* (1st edn, Cornell University Press 1999) 22.

character of neocolonial borders.[79] They argue that national borders operate as instruments for exclusion in matters related to migration, asylum seeking, and visas, among others.[80] I go further, however. While I agree that understanding the formation of national borders is crucial in addressing issues of racialized exclusions, I argue that citizenship transcends borders, operating as a boundary of exclusion within the racialized division of the world. It functions as a persona to justify those cases of racial discrimination that may have little to do with the national borders or sovereignty of white nations. In this sense, it creates a boundary of exclusion around imperial states (though coloured citizenship is also disadvantageous to the racialized groups within those internal boundaries as well).

Returning to *Diop v France*, in which Diop was excluded from practising law in Nice,[81] it is important to note that he was not seeking to subvert the validity of national state boundaries. He had no interest in the political rights reserved only for citizens by IHRL instruments. Diop was married to a French citizen, resided in France, and his child lived in Monaco. He argued that the Bar of Paris had already licensed six non-citizen lawyers,[82] and therefore the practice should remain consistent.[83] It is worth noting that both the CERD and the French government agreed that Diop met all the statutory requirements to gain admission to the profession, except French nationality. In the given context, there was no material reason for his rejection. However, the persona of citizenship blinded the CERD from reflecting on the racial element of his case. The citizenship defence raised by France obscured Diop's skin colour, Senegalese origin, and disadvantaged background.[84]

Likewise, in *AMM v Switzerland*, a Somali national began residing in Switzerland in 1999 under the 'F' category (giving him temporary admission status) after his refugee application was refused on the ground that he had not personally suffered

[79] Achiume (n 4); Walia (n 59). Antony Anghie, *Imperialism, Sovereignty and the Making of International Law* (Cambridge University Press 2005).

[80] E Tendayi Achiume, 'Migration As Decolonization' (2019) 71(6) Stanford Law Review 1509. Cathryn Costello and Michelle Foster, '(Some) Refugees Welcome: When is Differentiating between Refugees Unlawful Discrimination?' (2022) 22(3) International Journal of Discrimination and the Law 244; Frédéric Mégret, 'The Contingency of International Migration Law: "Freedom of Movement", Race, and Imperial Legacies' in Ingo Venzke and Kevin Jon Heller (eds), *Contingency in International Law On the Possibility of Different Legal Histories* (Oxford University Press 2021); Audrey Macklin, 'Can We Do Wrong to Strangers?' in David Dyzenhaus and Mayo Moran (eds), *Calling Power to Account* (University of Toronto Press 2016); E Tendayi Achiume, 'Reimagining International Law for Global Migration: Migration as Decolonization?' (2017) 111 American Journal of International Law 142; E Tendayi Achiume, 'Governing Xenophobia' (2018) 51 Vanderbilt Journal of Transnational Law 333; Ayelet Shachar, *The Shifting Border—Legal Cartographies of Migration and Mobility: Ayelet Shachar in Dialogue* (Manchester University Press 2020); Radhika Viyas Mongia, 'Race, Nationality, Mobility: A History of the Passport' (1999) 11 Public Culture 527.

[81] *Diop v France* (n 1).

[82] ibid [3.1].

[83] ibid [4.5].

[84] The fact that this decision came from an international body—one that claimed to be universal in granting protection against discrimination—makes it more contentious when even a national court (Supreme Court of Canada) could see beyond the veil of citizenship. In somewhat similar facts, the Supreme Court of Canada allowed the admission of David Andrews 'a British subject permanently resident in Canada' who met all the requirements for admission to the British Columbia bar except that of Canadian citizenship. See *Andrews v Law Society of British Columbia* [1989] 1 SCR 143. The same case was, however, differentiated in *Lavoie v Canada* [2002] 1 SCR 769, in which Lavoie was barred from federal public service employment due to her citizenship.

persecution. He applied for jobs, performed well in interviews,[85] and was deemed competitive for admission to university,[86] but all opportunities were refused because of his coloured citizenship and F category visa. He disputed the implicit racism in his application processing,[87] arguing that the F category system was designed to deter foreigners from remaining on Swiss territory, and was prejudicially applied according to physical characteristics, language, national and cultural origin, and categorically distinguished between (i) Swiss; (ii) Europeans and American, Canadian, Australian, and New Zealand citizens; and (iii) nationals of third countries.[88] Even the committee noted that 'the petitioner's claims have been abundantly supported by specific examples of decisions the author considers to be discriminatory against him . . . in particular the petitioner's claims regarding obstacles to access to work, to vocational and university training and to health'.[89] However, the committee ultimately declared that the discrimination was based on foreign nationality (coloured citizenship) and not 'race, colour, descent, or national or ethnic origin' within the meaning of Article 1 of the Convention.[90]

In various other cases, the persona of citizenship muddied the conception of race in a similar way by impacting the outcome of the cases. In *D. F v Australia and D. R v Australia*, the committee found no wrong in levelling down the rights for New Zealand citizens, arguing that 'it did not result in the operation of a distinction, but rather in the removal of such a distinction'.[91] In *BMS v Australia*, the committee observed that even if the quota benefited 'those who have attended Australian and New Zealand medical schools, such persons are not characterized by a national origin. Instead, they would be likely to share citizenship, a factor outside the realm of the Convention (ICERD)'.[92] In *Benon Pjetri v Switzerland*, the state contended that the petitioner's application for naturalization was not refused on grounds relating to his race, colour, descent, or national or ethnic origin, but under Article 1(2) of the ICERD, and therefore should not amount to racial discrimination.[93] The CERD concurred that such rejection was not based on the discriminatory grounds and therefore was not a violation.[94]

85 *AMM v Switzerland*, Communication No 050/2012, CERD/C/84/D/50/2012 (18 February 2014) [2.5].
86 ibid [2.9].
87 ibid [2.13].
88 ibid [5.1].
89 ibid [8.3].
90 ibid [8.6].
91 *DF v Australia*, Communication No 39/2006, CERD/C/72/D/39/2006 (3 March 2008) [7.1]; *DR v Australia*, Communication No 42/2008, CERD/C/75/D/42/2008 (15 September 2009).
92 *BMS v Australia*, Communication No 8/1996, CERD/C/54/D/8/1996 (12 March 1999) [7.21].
93 *Benon Pjetri v Switzerland*, Communication No 53/2013, CERD/C/91/D/53/2013 (5 December 2016) [4.2].
94 ibid [7.7]. Only in exceptional cases, did the CERD look beyond the veil of citizenship. In *Qatar v Kingdom of Saudi Arabia*, UN Doc CERD/C/99/6 (27 August 2019) and *Qatar v United Arab Emirates*, UN Doc CERD/C/99/4 (30 August 2019), the committee decided in the favour of racialized non-citizens when the issue was about 'collective expulsion'. In *LK v Netherlands*, Communication No 4/1991, CERD/C/42/D/4/1991 (16 March 1993); *Saada Mohamad Adan v Denmark*, Communication No 43/2008, CERD/C/77/D/43/2008 (21 September 2010); *MB v Denmark* Communication No 20/2000 CERD/C/60/D/20/2000 (13 March 2002), the committee addressed the cases of racialized harassment/threats/attacks against non-citizens. In *Habassi v Denmark*, Communication No 10/1997, CERD/C/54/D/10/1997 (17 March 1999), the committee decided that the requirement of citizenship was not necessary for getting a loan.

These are but a few cases. Many of those who face racial discrimination do not come forward and those who do must navigate the hierarchical structure of the state's judicial system before seeking relief from international human rights bodies. This process deters many from pursuing justice. While some cases of racial discrimination do rise to the surface, they are consistently met with resistance and dismissed under the guise of citizenship. The result is abhorrent. The final report of David Weissbrodt, Special Rapporteur on the Rights of Non-Citizens, classified non-citizens as the most 'disadvantaged group', documenting a range of practices in which non-citizens were discriminated against in almost every sector due to their coloured citizenship, including health care, property, social security housing, employment, education, and detention.[95] The CERD itself, on many occasions, expressed concerns of xenophobic treatment of non-citizens.[96] However, in the cases presented above, it condoned the same through the persona of citizenship. The fact that their treatment went unchecked due to their 'coloured' citizenship, obfuscated all the racially discriminatory practices associated with it.

These prejudicial outcomes beg to challenge the structure of international law and the adopted approach towards addressing racial discrimination. The cases illustrated earlier are not coincidental. They result from a structural premise that characterizes citizenship as fundamentally different from race. However, the most problematic feature of this personification is the epistemic ripples it creates. The remedies of the IHRL committees, and specifically CERD, are mostly compensatory. The jurisprudence they create and the message they send are more impactful for understanding race than a payout conferred upon a petitioner. By treating citizenship and race as dissociated, international law becomes an assenting stamp for the racial thinking of white imperial states.

Deploying this background to the hypothetical I began with is revelatory. It shows that seeking the distinction between colour and citizenship for a case of racial discrimination is the wrong premise. What is worth probing are the similarities between both, which we can use to demystify or 'illuminate'[97] 'only white' as a racial logic of superiority and exclusion. With this new lens, the connection between blackness, citizenship, and the blindness of international law is revealed, and the ghosts of racial discrimination become visible. They can be seen haunting the very institutions established to bring racial discrimination to an end.

5. Conclusion

International law's reincarnation and resurrection of racialized teleology through the persona of citizenship remain ever ongoing. As this chapter has shown, citizenship acts as a persona that legitimizes instances of racial discrimination. It began by

[95] OHCHR, 'Prevention of Discrimination: The Rights of Non-Citizens Final Report of the Special Rapporteur, Mr. David Weissbrodt. Addendum Examples of Practices in Regard to Non-Citizens' (26 May 2003) UN Doc E/CN.4/Sub 2/2002/25/Add 3.

[96] CERD, 'Response of the Committee on the Elimination of Racial Discrimination to the questionnaire' (2003) UN Doc CERD/C/62/Misc 17 rev 3, 2.

[97] Mills (n 12) 18.

analogizing a case of racial discrimination on 'colour' with 'citizenship' and questioning the distinction between the two. Subsequently, it deconstructed the notion of colour as something exceptional, arguing that colour was one of the modi operandi of imperialism used to classify those slated for exclusion. Thereafter, it explored the construction of citizenship as a persona in international law. This persona was constructed by separating race and citizenship into two distinct entities. In the last part, it presented international law as a racial imaginary which transformed the 'only white' logic to the 'only white nations'. In this transformation, citizenship became the new colour. The value of citizenship, and the rights and privileges that accompany it, were divided by the colour of citizenship, providing a logic to perpetuate the exclusion of people in the Global South from the Global North. Bodies such as the CERD that were meant to give protection against all forms of racial discrimination became an assenting mechanism for states. Against this background, the distinction between the hypothetical case of racial discrimination based on colour (X) and the one based on citizenship (*Diop v France*) remains nothing but the reincarnation of the former into the latter.

7
A Racialized Existence
Lessons from Palestine and the Genocide Convention

Dimitrios A Kourtis

1. Introduction

Genocide is a powerful word[1] and a highly contested legal concept.[2] Over seventy years have passed since the term emerged and came to inform the Convention on the Prevention and Punishment of the Crime of Genocide.[3] Despite a vast literature on the crime and its constitutive elements, relatively little attention[4] has been paid to identifying, analysing, and theorizing the basic characteristics of the protected groups, which are the ultimate victims of the crime and the right-holders of the underlying primary right of existence.[5] For instance, it is unclear whether the four protected groups (national, ethnic, racial, and religious) should be construed subjectively or objectively.[6] Even more controversial is the definitional question: namely, how each of the protected tetrad must be defined and whether the groups represent one broader protected category or a plurality of separate yet interconnected collectivities.[7]

These definitional challenges are particularly notable when tackling race, which is mirrored in Article II of the Convention[8] and proscribes the perpetration of genocide against, inter alia, racial groups. The idea that a group defined by race forms part of the

[1] Mark A Drumbl, 'Sixtieth Anniversary of the Genocide Convention: The Power of a Word' (2009) 40 Studies in Transnational Legal Policy 97, 104–16.

[2] Larissa van den Herik, 'The Schism between the Legal and the Social Concept of Genocide in Light of the Responsibility to Protect' in Ralph Henham and Paul Behrens (eds), *The Criminal Law of Genocide* (Ashgate 2007) 75.

[3] Raphael Lemkin, *Axis Rule in Occupied Europe* (Carnegie Endowment for International Peace 1944) 79; Convention on the Prevention and Punishment of the Crime of Genocide (adopted 9 December 1948, entered into force 12 January 1951) 78 UNTS 277.

[4] See, however, Carola Lingaas, 'Conceptualizing the National Group for the Crime of Genocide: Is Law Able to Account for Identity Fault Lines?' (2021) 49(2) Nationalities Papers 240; Carola Lingaas, 'The Elephant in the Room: The Uneasy Task of Defining 'Racial' in International Criminal Law' (2015) 15(3) International Criminal Law Review 485; Nigel Eltringham, *Accounting for Horror* (Pluto Press 2004).

[5] Dimitrios A Kourtis, 'The *Ultimate Victim* of Genocide and the Question of Collective Reparations' (2023) 31(1) International Journal on Minority and Group Rights 1.

[6] Christian J Tams, Lars Berster, and Björn Schiffbauer, *Convention on the Prevention and Punishment of the Crime of Genocide: A Commentary* (Beck and Hart 2014) 79, 103–07.

[7] William A Schabas, *Genocide in International Law: The Crime of Crimes* (2nd edn, Cambridge University Press 2009) 129–33; Diane Marie Amann, 'Group Mentality, Expressivism, and Genocide' (2002) 2 International Criminal Law Review 93, 95, 103–13.

[8] Carola Lingaas, *The Concept of Race in International Criminal Law* (Routledge 2020) 2.

Dimitrios A Kourtis, *A Racialized Existence* In: *Emancipating International Law*. Edited by: Mohsen al Attar and Claire Smith, Oxford University Press. © Dimitrios A Kourtis 2026. DOI: 10.1093/9780198935605.003.0010

'crime of crimes' seemingly defies international criminal law's predilection for objectivity.[9] Given that race is widely considered an unhelpful (even discredited) category in contemporary scientific debate,[10] it might appear odd or even dangerous to reintroduce it as the qualifying characteristic of a protected group. Moreover, even though racial groups are included in the definitions of genocide and crimes against humanity (notably apartheid and persecution),[11] few scholars offer an analytical framework to address the challenges posed by an idea that 'has become virtually obsolete'.[12] On the other hand, most of the existing interpretations are primarily subjectivist and perpetrator-based.[13] As such, they offer little clarity as to how a group arbitrarily racialized by the perpetrator(s) can claim the right to exist.[14]

In this chapter, I hypothesize that the inclusion of racial groups among the protected tetrad connotes a distinct and identifiable normative message: that the four ascriptive collectivities are more than permanent, stable, or inescapable. They are dynamic and relational social constructs conferring a collective identity with strong links to both in-group and out-group perceptions.[15] Arguing that racialized realities under conditions of social control might trigger conventional protection is no longer original. For example, in its early jurisprudence on Tutsi grouphood, it is well-established that the International Criminal Tribunal for Rwanda (ICTR) sought to label the group as permanent and stable and thus protected by Article 2 of the ICTR's Statute based on an *ejusdem generis* formula, without classifying it as either ethnic or racial.[16] Yet, even under this approach, the trial chamber in *Akayesu* conceded that the Tutsi were considered a distinct ethnic group[17] by everyone, including their victimizers.[18] This

[9] ibid 3–4.

[10] Indicatively, see American Association of Biological Anthropologists, 'Statement on Race and Racism' (*American Association of Biological Anthropologists*) <https://bioanth.org/about/aaba-statement-on-race-racism/> accessed 10 June 2024; Joan H Fujimura and others, 'Clines without Classes: How to Make Sense of Human Variation' (2014) 32(3) Sociological Theory 208; William JT Mitchell, *Seeing Through Race* (Harvard University Press 2012) 11.

[11] International Criminal Court, Elements of Crimes (2002/2010) Article 7(1)(h)(3) and 7(1)(j)(4) (*International Criminal Court*, 2011) <https://www.icc-cpi.int/sites/default/files/ElementsOfCrimesEng.pdf> accessed 12 June 2024; Gerhard Kemp and Windell Nortje, 'Prosecuting the Crime against Humanity of Apartheid: The Historic First Indictment in South Africa and the Application of Customary International Law' (2023) 21(2) Journal of International Criminal Justice 405.

[12] Schabas (n 7) 142.

[13] See works cited in n 4.

[14] UNGA Res 96(I) (11 December 1946) UN Doc A/RES/96(I) Preamble cl 1; *Application of the Convention on the Prevention and Punishment of the Crime of Genocide (Bosnia and Herzegovina v Serbia and Montenegro)* (Merits) [2007] ICJ Rep 43, 110–11 [161]; *Application of the Convention on the Prevention and Punishment of the Crime of Genocide (Croatia v Serbia)* (Merits) [2015] ICJ Rep 3, 46–7 [87]; *Application of the Convention on the Prevention and Punishment of the Crime of Genocide (The Gambia v Myanmar)* (Provisional Measures: Order) [2020] ICJ Rep 3, 26 [69]; *Application of the Convention on the Prevention and Punishment of the Crime of Genocide in the Gaza Strip (South Africa v Israel)* (Provisional Measures: Order) (26 January 2024) 20–21 [65] <https://www.icj-cij.org/sites/default/files/case-related/192/192-20240126-ord-01-00-en.pdf> accessed 14 June 2024; *Prosecutor v Akayesu* (Judgment) ICTR-96-4-T, T Ch I (2 September 1998) [469]; *Prosecutor v Krstić* (Judgment) IT-98-33-T, T Ch (2 August 2001) [553].

[15] Christopher Powell, 'What Do Genocides Kill? A Relational Conception of Genocide' (2007) 9(4) Journal of Genocide Research 527, 538–41.

[16] *Akayesu* (n 14) [511].

[17] ibid [82], [170]–[171], [702].

[18] Eltringham (n 4) 18, 27–31.

chapter adds to the debate a standalone analysis of racial groups as a protected category under the law against genocide and a more detailed discussion of what it means for a racial (or racialized) collective to be brought under conventional protection in the context of collective violence.

In the following sections, I will first explain how the racial groups were envisaged during the drafting of the Convention and discuss the normative iterations of the concept in theory and praxis after its adoption. Next, I will present an alternative interpretation, making use of social science scholarship on the processes of racialization and collective identity formation. I will apply this theoretical framework to the Palestinians and show how they are constituted as racialized subjects. Following this, I will connect these processes to an evolving atrocity spectrum. Here, I will also employ exegetic tools borrowed from the criminology and victimology of genocide to describe the various alterations that a racialized collective identity undergoes as a society moves closer to the eruption of genocidal violence. This chapter will conclude with some remarks regarding the debate on genocide labelling vis-à-vis the humanitarian catastrophe unfolding in the Gaza Strip.

Ultimately, this chapter underscores how the concept of race, despite its ambiguous definition during the drafting of the Convention, remains pivotal in identifying and understanding genocidal conditions. Historical and legal perspectives reveal that racialized collective identities are often construed through universal and localized racial contracts that are subsequently used to legitimize and normalize systemic oppression, dispossession, and violence. Through these processes, the individual and collective racialized subject emerges. This subject, despite being the outcome of a subjugating and violent condition, is the primary holder of the collective right of existence, which the Convention guarantees through measures aiming at the prevention and punishment of its breaches. The inclusion of racialized collective subjects under conventional protection necessitates a nuanced approach that delineates the processes involved in forming this collective identity. These processes often include oppression, domination, and exclusion, which constitute the *actus reus* and *mens rea* of distinct international crimes, including apartheid and persecution.

Before I proceed, a caveat is necessary. As this chapter deals with the connection between the racialized existence of the Palestinians and the epistemological categories of the Convention, it does not delve into the intricacies of the apartheid regime, which is established and perpetuated by Israeli authorities against the Palestinians.[19] Still, it acknowledges the existence of a system of racialized oppression and domination and seeks to complement analyses of apartheid with a long overdue discussion focused on genocide.

[19] See Victor Kattan and Gerhard Kemp, 'Apartheid as a Form of Genocide: Reflections on South Africa v Israel' (*EJIL: Talk!*, 25 January 2024) <https://www.ejiltalk.org/apartheid-as-a-form-of-genocide-reflections-on-south-africa-v-israel/> accessed 14 June 2024.

2. The multiple meanings of race: from the Genocide Convention to post-1948 international law

The idea that an inextricable link exists between race, racism, and genocide is fairly established in legal literature.[20] For example, Tawia Ansah has argued that the very concept of genocide was called into existence by drawing a definite line between civilized warfare and barbarous (racial) blood wars.[21] In the same vein, Dirk Moses has shown that the idea of persecution against racial grounds was decisive in the concept's early formation.[22] Still, it might be argued that the connection runs even deeper.

Firstly, the intellectual father of the word and the idea, Raphael Lemkin, explained his neologism by reference to the Greek notion of *genos*. He identified it with 'race' or 'tribe' and uncovered genocide as the racial masterplan of Nazi Germany,[23] a way to win the war and all future wars by achieving the 'vantage point' of racial superiority.[24] Even though Lemkin's notion of race was distinctly cultural, if not ethnonational,[25] at the early stages of the concept's formation, he espoused a biopolitical understanding, grounding his idea of race on both blood and peoplehood. Citing the Nazi ideologue Alfred Rosenberg, he argued that the German vision for a new world order was, in reality, a plan of racial domination.[26] This was no coincidence. This ambiguous and latently biopolitical idea of race played a key role in distinguishing Lemkin's new crime from prior contentious debates of the interwar period, including the frustrated anti-terrorism convention and the minorities treaties.[27] By presenting genocide as a technique motivated by racial supremacy and grounding his concept linguistically on the notion of race, he established a direct link between the prevailing understanding of German aggression as a plan for a new racial order imposed against the 'captive nations' of Europe.[28] Thus, at the beginning of genocide's long journey towards the 'crime of crimes',[29] race de-politicized and essentialized the debate on Nazi criminality.

In the same vein, the inclusion of racial groups among the protected collectives of Article II of the Genocide Convention, as discussed in a moment, was met with practically no resistance as it dovetailed with prevailing ideas of permanence, stability, and inescapability.[30] The drafters also employed these elements to exclude more variable human figurations such as political groups, liberation movements, and peoples under colonial domination.[31]

[20] John K Roth, 'Genocide and the "Logic" of Racism' in John K Roth (ed), *Genocide and Human Rights* (Palgrave Macmillan 2005) 255; Alexander Laban Hinton, *It Can Happen Here* (New York University Press 2021).

[21] Tawia Ansah, 'Subject to Surveillance: Genocide Law as Epistemology of the Object' (2010) 3(1) Washington University Jurisprudence Review 31, 38.

[22] A Dirk Moses, *The Problems of Genocide* (Cambridge University Press 2021) 138–43.

[23] Lemkin (n 3) 79–90.

[24] ibid 81.

[25] A Dirk Moses, 'Raphael Lemkin, Culture, and the Concept of Genocide' in Donald Bloxham and A Dirk Moses (eds), *The Oxford Handbook of Genocide Studies* (Oxford University Press 2010) 19, 22–36.

[26] Lemkin (n 3) 81.

[27] Moses (n 22) 156–61, 173.

[28] Lemkin (n 3) 80–81, 92–93.

[29] *Prosecutor v Kambanda* (Judgment & Sentence) ICTR 97-23-S, T Ch I (4 September 1998) [16].

[30] Nehemiah Robinson, *The Genocide Convention: A Commentary* (Institute of Jewish Affairs 1960) 59.

[31] UNGA Sixth Committee 107th Meeting (15 November 1948) UN Doc A/C.6/SR.107UNGA; UNGA Sixth Committee 128th Meeting (29 November 1948) UN Doc A/C.6/SR.128.

Likewise, the idea of race—complemented by that of religion—appeared in a series of communications from the World Jewish Congress (WJC) to the Economic and Social Council during the late 1940s, alerting the United Nations (UN) about the 'extreme and imminent danger'[32] faced by Jewish communities in the Middle East. The WJC sought to concern the international community with a 'racial and religious group whose human rights and fundamental freedoms are being violated'[33] while protesting Arab resistance to the implementation of the 1947 Partition Plan for Palestine.[34] This resistance was framed as a 'declaration of war' against the Jewish population of Palestine, signalling a serious 'peril of annihilation'.[35] In reality, the communications were a constellation of genocide/discrimination claims against the Jews in Palestine and the 'Near East' purportedly committed by Arab states.[36] The strategy of this activist organization was to deploy the concept of genocide as an antidote to the extreme politicization of the situation in Palestine, while the Zionist leadership could continue fighting to establish the Jewish State.[37] As its representative observed, the question was distinct from the political future of Palestine and, therefore, had to be considered separately.[38] Allegations of racism and genocide quickly emerged, if only to conceal the true political and colonial character of the conflict.

These early encounters between the concepts of genocide, race, and racial violence underline the complex relationship between the offence standing at the apex of international criminality and the political struggles unfolding since its inception. Even though Article II extended conventional protection against genocide to racial groups, neither the drafters nor the UN system was willing to accept that systemic violence grounded on racialized realities of oppression, domination, and dispossession could be labelled 'genocide'.[39] That said, the protection of racial groups became the *chapeau* of the fundamental norm codifying the crime of genocide.

Even so, the constitutive elements of a racial group received little attention during the drafting of the Convention. The idea that racial groups must be protected was present in all relevant drafts submitted during the negotiations, including the original tripartite proposal of Cuba, India, and Panama and Resolution 96(I),[40] but it was never analysed or extensively discussed. Records are largely limited to the objection

[32] ECOSOC, 'List of Communications Received from Non-governmental Organizations Granted Category (b) or (c) Consultative Status' (5 February 1948) UN Doc E/C.2/75.

[33] ibid.

[34] ibid; ECOSOC, 'List of Communications Received from Non-Governmental Organizations Granted Category (b) or (c) Consultative Status' (25 August 1948) UN Doc E/C.2/125; ECOSOC, 'List of Communications Received from Non-Governmental Organizations Granted Category (b) or (c) Consultative Status' (11 February 1949) UN Doc E/C.2/143.

[35] ECOSOC, 'Statements on International Non-Governmental Organizations whose Applications for Consultative Status are to be Considered by the Council NGO Committee' (27 May 1948) UN Doc E/C.2/W.10; ECOSOC, 'NGO Committee Summary Record of the 32nd Meeting'(16 February 1948) UN Doc E/C.2/SR.32.

[36] James Loeffler, 'Three Days in December: Jewish Human Rights between the United Nations and the Middle East in 1948' (2022) 17(2) Journal of Global History 312, 319.

[37] ibid.

[38] ECOSOC (n 35).

[39] As also evinced by the fate of the historic petition of the Civil Rights Congress in 1951 against the United States; see Civil Rights Congress, *We Charge Genocide* (Civil Rights Congress 1951).

[40] UNGA, 'The Crime of Genocide: Request from the Delegations for Cuba, India and Panama' (2 November 1946) UN Doc A/BUR/50; UNGA (n 14).

of certain delegates to the inclusion of the qualifier 'ethnical' since it was thought to be identical to 'racial'.[41] However, Norway and Haiti thought racial groups could be distinguished from their ethnic counterparts, espousing a biological understanding of race.[42] As the Haitian delegate explained: the 'intermingling between races in certain regions has made the problem of race so complicated that it might be impossible, in certain cases, to consider a given group as a racial group, although it could not be denied classification as an ethnical group'.[43] Even more troubling is the fact that the term carried a colossal ideological burden, given the recent experience of racial persecution and genocide and the extreme racial violence exercised by Europeans against colonized peoples.[44] Nevertheless, both early post-war jurisprudence[45] and the framers of the Convention endorsed its use.[46]

The *travaux préparatoires* do not offer an unequivocal answer about what race or racial groups meant either. For example, we can surmise that for certain drafters, race differed from nationality and that it was understood partly as a biological concept—for instance, by the Haitian delegate who spoke of the 'intermingling' of races and the Swedish delegate who distinguished race from traditions and cultural heritage.[47] Race was presented as something immutable and racial groups as a by-product of fortune. As the British delegation noted, conventional protection should include racial groups since '[n]o one should be persecuted because of the accident of his birth'.[48] By contrast, racial groups were not completely separated from the ideas of nationhood and ethnicity. The Egyptian delegate saw 'no great difference' between racial and ethnic groups.[49] The Chinese, Czechoslovakian, and Mexican representatives referred to their respective peoples as 'races'.[50] The British delegate explained the practical importance of the Convention by reference to 'the six million human beings [that] had been coldly and deliberately exterminated with a view to destroying the Jewish race'.[51] The Belgian delegate explained that he saw no point in adding the qualified 'ethnical' in the draft convention. He argued that the adjectives 'racial' and 'ethnical' were identical and completed his statement with a general reference to the language employed by the interwar minorities treaties.[52] In the same vein, the Iranian delegate posited that the qualifiers 'racial' and 'national' were equivalent, noting that their 'distinctive features were permanent'.[53] In a similar manner, the Dutch representative placed race

41 UNGA Sixth Committee 75th Meeting (15 October 1948) UN Doc A/C.6/SR.75 115–16.

42 ibid.

43 ibid 116.

44 See, more generally, Nathan A Kurz, '"Hide a Fact Rather than State it": The Holocaust, the 1940s Human Rights Surge, and the Cosmopolitan Imperative of International Law' (2021) 23(1) Journal of Genocide Research 37; AW Simpson, 'Britain and the Genocide Convention' (2002) 73 British Yearbook of International Law 5.

45 See, eg, *Judgment of the Nuremberg International Military Tribunal* (1946) 1 TMWC 272, 302.

46 Schabas (n 7) 139.

47 UN Doc A/C.6/SR.75 (n 41) 115–16.

48 UNGA Sixth Committee 69th Meeting (7 October 1948) UN Doc A/C.6/SR.69 60.

49 UN Doc A/C.6/SR.75 (n 41) 115.

50 UN Doc A/C.6/SR.69 (n 48) 59; UNGA Sixth Committee 24th Meeting (29 November 1946) UN Doc A/C.6/SR.24 114-5; UNGA 123rd Meeting (2nd session) (21 November 1947) UN Doc A/PV.123 1296.

51 UNGA, Sixth Committee 22nd Meeting (22 November 1946) UN Doc A/C.6/SR.22 102.

52 UN Doc A/C.6/SR.75 (n 41) 116.

53 UNGA, Sixth Committee 74th Meeting (14 October 1948) UN Doc A/C.6/SR.74 99.

and nationality on an equal footing, highlighting the need for conventional protection for both national and racial groups based on practical and historical considerations.[54] Finally, the Russian delegate considered race and nationality as cognates that established 'distinct, clearly determinable communities'.[55]

Moreover, we should remain mindful of the previous legal use of the term in minorities treaties.[56] During the interwar period, no one ever seriously argued that racial groups constituted different biological communities. As Anthony Eden explained, the problem of minorities 'is not the existence of different races or religions within one country, but the fact that a minority in one country is adjacent to a majority of its own race, language or religion in a neighbouring country from whose territory it has recently been transferred'.[57] Similarly, the European Jews were described as 'a race scattered through all countries'.[58] Therefore, it is quite possible that the use of the qualifier 'racial' was premised on cultural nationality or ethnicity considerations. This understanding is further supported by the practice of the framers, both parallel and subsequent to the adoption of the Convention. For instance, in 1948, Greece officially denounced its northern communist neighbours and its own nationals, who were not considered part of the 'Greek race' anymore, for devising a plan to 'destroy the Greek race', which was, at the time, envisaged as a distinct ethnonational and biopolitical collective.[59] In 1950, during the first round of ratification debates before the Senate of the United States, Deputy Under-Secretary of State Dean Rusk referred to the Holocaust as the 'organized butchery of racial groups'.[60] Finally, a similar expression was used during the ratification debate in the English House of Commons.[61] Therefore, it is reasonable to suggest that the idea of race *qua* ethnonational identity was not discredited during the drafting of the Genocide Convention.

A consequence of this drafting process was the tautological relationship established between race as a conceptual category and the idea of racial groups.[62] Genocide was originally envisaged as a crime of motive.[63] Motives were considered an essential element of the crime,[64] without which genocide could not exist.[65] As the Lebanese

[54] ibid 100.
[55] ibid 105.
[56] Schabas (n 7) 129, 140–41.
[57] LoN Assembly Sixth Committee 10th Meeting (21 September 1934) 130 LoN OJ Spec Supp 60.
[58] LoN Assembly Sixth Committee, 5th Meeting (3 October 1933) 120 LoN OJ Spec Supp 29.
[59] Dimitrios A Kourtis, 'The Greek Civil War and Genocide by Forcible Transfer of Children' (2023) 26(2) Journal of Genocide Research 142.
[60] Marjorie M Whiteman, *Digest of International Law*, vol 11 (USGPO 1968) 858.
[61] HC Deb 5 February 1969, vol 777, col 481.
[62] See, more generally, Lingaas (n 8) 60–63.
[63] Ad Hoc Committee on Genocide 2nd Meeting (5 April 1948) UN Doc E/AC.25/SR.2; Ad Hoc Committee on Genocide 4th Meeting (7 April 1948) UN Doc E/AC.25/SR.4; Ad Hoc Committee on Genocide 5th Meeting (8 April 1948) UN Doc E/AC.25/SR.5; Ad Hoc Committee on Genocide 6th Meeting (9 April 1948) UN Doc E/AC.25/SR.6; Ad Hoc Committee on Genocide 9th Meeting (14 April 1948) UN Doc E/AC.25/SR.9; Ad Hoc Committee on Genocide 10th Meeting (16 April 1948) UN Doc E/AC.25/SR.10; Ad Hoc Committee on Genocide 11th Meeting (16 April 1948) UN Doc E/AC.25/SR.11; Ad Hoc Committee on Genocide 12th Meeting (19 April 1948) UN Doc E/AC.25/SR.12; Ad Hoc Committee on Genocide 13th Meeting (20 April 1948) UN Doc E/AC.25/SR.13; Ad Hoc Committee on Genocide 18th Meeting (23 April 1948) UN Doc E/AC.25/SR.18; Ad Hoc Committee on Genocide, 'Report of the Committee and Draft Convention Drawn up by the Committee' (24 May 1948) UN Doc E/794 4.
[64] E/AC.25/SR.10 (n 63) 10; E/AC.25/SR.11 (n 63) 1–2.
[65] E/AC.25/SR.18 (n 63) 6.

delegate noted, 'there was . . . nothing to correspond to the racial hatred or religious fanaticism which usually motivated acts of genocide'.[66] The motive that fuelled the specific intent of genocide gave the crime its distinct collective dimension. Thus, racial, national, and religious fanaticism could acquire a genocidal tendency when a collectivity targets another collectivity.[67] This element distinguished genocide from common law crimes, transforming it into a 'collective crime'[68] or a 'crime *sui generis*'.[69] Consequently, the constellation of genocidal persecution[70] based on, inter alia, racial grounds, as the crime was defined at the beginning of the drafting process, introduced the idea that race was the qualifying characteristic and the reason for slating a certain group for annihilation.[71] As a result, a racial group was a collectivity defined by this fundamental characteristic, which sealed its fate, exposing it to an existential threat of annihilating violence.[72] Even though the element of motives was later suppressed,[73] the tautological relationship between race and racial groups persisted.[74] Race, no matter how defined, was the distinctive element of a racial group, and a racial group was a collective distinguished by race, a condition that made its members 'defenceless'[75] because it was 'inevitable'[76] and, as such, could be used to single out and target 'human beings whom chance alone had grouped together'.[77]

It is impossible to find the common denominator between the perceptions of the drafters or assess whether the biological or sociocultural understanding of race was the dominant element both before and during the drafting of the Convention. Early commentators, like Antonio Planzer, oscillated between biological and cultural understanding, embedding the concept of race into the overall framework of racial discrimination.[78] Many years later, India submitted before the International Court of Justice (ICJ) that '[t]he people of Dadra and Nagar Aveli are of Indian race, the great majority being Hindus, speaking the same language as the inhabitants of the surrounding Indian territory in the State of Bombay'.[79] However, a biological conceptualization of race was never entirely abandoned in international law.[80] For example, in *South West Africa*, Judge Tanaka opined that 'as a matter of common-sense [the] criteria to distinguish one race from the other, are the appearance, particularly physical characteristics such as colour, hair, etc'.[81] Resonating with this approach, the

[66] E/AC.25/SR.13 (n 63) 2.
[67] See George P Fletcher and Jens David Ohlin, *Defending Humanity* (Oxford University Press 2008) 192–93.
[68] UNGA Sixth Committee 66th Meeting (4 October 1948) UN Doc A/C.6/SR.66 32.
[69] UNGA Sixth Committee 73rd Meeting (13 October 1948) UN Doc A/C.6/SR.73 97.
[70] Ad Hoc Committee on Genocide, 'Commentary on Articles adopted by the Committee' (26 April 1948) UN Doc E/AC.25/W.1 2–3.
[71] Ad Hoc Committee on Genocide 24th Meeting (28 April 1948) UN Doc E/AC.25/SR.24 4, 14–6.
[72] ECOSOC 218th Meeting (26 August 1948) UN Doc E/SR.218 718.
[73] Schabas (n 7) 297–301
[74] See, eg, the debate in UNGA 178th Meeting (3rd Session) (9 December 1948) UN Doc A/PV.178.
[75] A/C.6/SR.75 (n 41) 111.
[76] A/C.6/SR.74 (n 53) 99.
[77] ibid.
[78] Antonio Planzer, *Le crime de génocide* (Schwald 1956) 97.
[79] *Right of Passage over Indian Territory (Portugal v India)*, Counter-Memorial of the Government of India, 1958 ICJ Pleadings, Oral Arguments, Documents Vol II [218].
[80] EW Viedrag, *The Concept of Discrimination in International Law with Special Reference to Human Rights* (Nijhoff 1973) 89.
[81] *South West Africa (Ethiopia & Liberia v South Africa)* (Second Phase) [1966] ICJ Rep 6, 308.

European Court of Human Rights noted that 'the notion of race is rooted in the idea of biological classification of human beings into subspecies according to morphological features such as skin colour or facial characteristics.'[82]

The lack of relevant practice regarding the definition of racial groups under the Convention and the Rome Statute is also noticeable,[83] despite the attention that race has gained in human rights and antidiscrimination law. Human rights law focuses on discrimination on grounds of race,[84] with the latter being conceptualized in the broadest sense. For example, the ICERD defines racial discrimination as 'any distinction, exclusion, restriction or preference based on race, colour, descent, or national or ethnic origin.'[85] The CERD has also opined that membership of racial or ethnic groups is primarily a matter of self-identification.[86] Similarly, the existing scholarship[87] adopts a rather liberal interpretation of race. Egon Schwelb, who played a paramount role in the formation of postwar international human rights law, argued that racial discrimination was broader, encompassing colour, descent, and national/ethnic origin, even though, in his understanding, race was a much narrower conceptual category.[88] Michael Banton, a former member of the Committee on the Elimination of Racial Discrimination, posited that race was the outcome of subjective ascriptions and socially construed realities, giving prevalence to the ascriptions of the discriminator.[89] As a result, we can argue that much like other scientific fields, human rights law treats the idea of race, especially in its biological conceptualization, as a falsity,[90] inseparable from racist ideologies and hatred,[91] whereas the law against genocide deals with race as a specific characteristic ascribing an identity that demands protection.

The normative corpus of human rights aspires to stigmatize, police, and tackle discrimination and prejudice on grounds of race. In contrast, the Convention aims to protect the physical existence of groups defined by such grounds. In simple words, in human rights law discourse, race is the by-product of discrimination,[92] whereas, in the law against genocide, it is the reason for recognizing the group's collective right to exist and be free from annihilating violence. The two *corpora juris* serve different purposes and quite possibly define race differently. The same analysis applies to definitions of race advanced under the anti-apartheid law as a crime against humanity. In apartheid,

[82] *Timishev v Russia*, App nos 55762/00 and 55974/00 (ECtHR, 13 December 2005) [54].

[83] Claus Kress, 'The Crime of Genocide under International Law' (2006) 6 International Criminal Law Review 461, 478.

[84] See, eg, International Convention on the Elimination of All Forms of Racial Discrimination (adopted 21 December 1965, entered into force 4 January 1969) 660 UNTS 195.

[85] ibid Article 1(1).

[86] Committee on the Elimination of Racial Discrimination, 'General Recommendation VIII' (22 August 1990) UN Doc A/45/18 79.

[87] Walter Kälin and Jörg Künzli, *The Law of International Human Rights Protection* (2nd edn, Oxford University Press 2019) 356–57.

[88] Egon Schwelb, 'The International Convention on the Elimination of All Forms of Racial Discrimination' (1966) 15(4) International and Comparative Law Quarterly 996, 1002.

[89] UN Commission on Human Rights, 'The Causes of, and Remedies for, Racial Discrimination—Background paper prepared by Mr. Michael Banton' (26 February 1999) UN Doc E/CN.4/1999/WG.1/BP.6 [1].

[90] UNESCO First Statement on Race (July 1950); UNESCO Fourth Statement on Race (September 1967); UNESCO Declaration on Race and Racial Prejudice (November 1978).

[91] Roth (n 20) 257–58.

[92] Wenke Brückner, *Minderheitenschutz im Völkerstrafrecht* (Nomos 2018) 182.

the critical issue is the domination of one racial group over another within a system of institutionalized oppression and subjugation.[93] In this context, the racial identity of the oppressed group is qualified by the very system the crime presupposes. If one focuses on the experience of South Africa,[94] as the Apartheid Convention explicitly does,[95] then racial groups must be construed in the broadest social sense with prevalence given to the perceptions of the oppressors.[96] The differentiated understanding of race in human rights law and the law against apartheid highlights the *aporia* of legal interpretation when dealing with the protection of racial groups under Article II of the Convention.[97]

Nevertheless, a legal concept of race exists for better or worse, and international criminal lawyers try to find content and fill the term accordingly.[98] In the relevant legal debate, we can discern three trends. Following the Proxmire Act,[99] the first trend articulated most clearly in *Akayesu*[100] identifies race with externally visible hereditary characteristics.[101] Scholars espousing objectivist approaches would usually also demand a connection between group members beyond the commonality of such traits. However, or so the argument goes, this sense of 'togetherness' is looser in racial groups compared to national, ethnic, or religious groups.[102] A second trend treats race as a subjective concept established exclusively by the ascriptions of the perpetrators.[103] A third, historically more accurate trend, with William Schabas as its leading authority, posits that race should be conceptualized based on its historical and linguistic context, that is, as the framers understood the term in the 1940s.[104] Otherwise, we risk restricting the Convention's protective scope and neutralizing the intention of the drafters, namely to afford the broadest possible protection.[105]

3. A critique of the existing interpretations

The first reading sees racial groups as biological figurations with intergroup solidarity *lite* or 'visible minorities'.[106] The second reading solves the Gordian knot by

[93] International Convention on the Suppression and Punishment of the Crime of Apartheid (adopted 30 November 1973, entered into force 18 July 1976) 1015 UNTS 243.

[94] Gerhard Kemp, 'The Crime of Apartheid' in Sergey Sayapin and others (eds), *International Conflict and Security Law* (TMC Asser 2022) 1073.

[95] ibid 1084.

[96] John Dugard and John Reynolds, 'Apartheid, International Law, and the Occupied Palestinian Territory' (2013) 24(3) European Journal of International Law 867, 885–91.

[97] Lyal S Sunga, *Individual Responsibility in International Law for Serious Human Rights Violations* (Nijhoff 1992) 68.

[98] Brückner (n 92) 183.

[99] 18 US Code §1093(6).

[100] *Akayesu* (n 14) [514].

[101] Kai Ambos, *Treatise on International Criminal Law*, vol II (2nd edn, Oxford University Press 2022) 6; Kress (n 83) 478.

[102] Tams and others (n 6) 110 fn 55.

[103] Lingaas (n 8) 96–141; Caroline Fournet, *The Crime of Destruction and the Law of Genocide* (Ashgate 2007) 58–60.

[104] Schabas (n 7) 139–43.

[105] ibid 143.

[106] Patrick Thornberry, *The International Convention on the Elimination of All Forms of Racial Discrimination: A Commentary* (Oxford University Press 2016) 97, 126.

suppressing the trans-subjective status of the group, pinpointing its existence in the minds of the perpetrators. The third espouses the holistic 'four corner posts' approach,[107] which solves the problem of race by merging it into an even greater entity equivalent to the concept of minorities in the interwar treaties. Moreover, by suggesting that race should be understood in the light of its early twentieth-century meaning, this reading removes the inconvenience of dealing with a notion inextricably linked with racism. Put another way, unlike today, in the 1940s, the logic of race was still valid, at least to some.

Each one of these interpretations faces several challenges. The 'visible minority' thesis espouses the common everyday meaning of race and follows international jurisprudence but fails to explain how pigmentation can foster solidarity without any other bond.[108] The allure of the reading based on pure subjectivism ends as soon as the discussion about the right to exist begins. Right-holders cannot be hypothesized. They can either exist in a trans-subjective socially verified way or can be aggregates of victimized individualities whose rights come into play only once violated. Finally, Schabas's thesis has the most merit from a historical perspective. Indeed, the idea of race was less monolithic as a concept in the 1940s compared to our times. The fact that the drafters were unable to agree on whether race was based on biological or ethnic and cultural characteristics, but were persistent on the inclusion of racial groups, lends support to this understanding. However, it is conditioned on too many assumptions. *Primo*, this theory assumes that the drafters expected the referent to remain unalterable. The expression 'racial group' does not refer to a single referent (eg the Armenians of the Ottoman Empire) or even to an identifiable group of referents (eg the Armenians, the Greeks, and the Assyrians of the Ottoman Empire), but rather to a whole class of phenomena. It is a generic referencing expression that can have either an alterable or an unalterable referent.[109] Both the object and purpose of the Convention and especially the drafters' decision to omit references to their contemporary atrocities and legal milestones, including, inter alia, fascism, Nazism, the Nuremberg trial, and the notion of crimes against humanity[110]support the view that, when the terms of the Convention were articulated, the referents were not assumed fixed.

Secundo, it assumes that all delegates understood race in the same way. However, as explained above, there is evidence that certain drafters, such as Swedish and Haitian delegates, had a more biological understanding of race, whereas others—including the Egyptian, Uruguayan, and Belgian representatives—espoused a sociocultural understanding.[111] *Tertio*, it considers that the term's ordinary meaning must be identical to the one the term had at the time of the utterance. This interpretation presupposes that the linguistic anachronism it proposes is in line with the established principles of interpretation. However, this is not necessarily the case. Generally, we must interpret a conventional term following its everyday meaning, placing it 'within the framework

[107] Schabas (n 7) 129.

[108] Tams and others (n 6) 110–12 fns 55–56; Claus Kress, 'VStGB §6' in *Münchener Kommentar zum Strafgesetzbuch*, vol 9 (4th edn, Beck 2022) fn 41.

[109] Ulf Linderfalk, *On the Interpretation of Treaties* (Springer 2007) 78.

[110] A/C.6/SR.22 (n 51) 5; UNGA Sixth Committee 110th Meeting (18 November 1948) UN Doc A/C.6/SR.110 508.

[111] A/C.6/SR.75 (n 41) 115–16.

of the entire legal system prevailing at the time of interpretation',[112] and presuming that the drafters intended to 'follow the evolution of the law and to correspond with the meaning attached to the expression by the law in force at any given time'.[113] This is particularly true for treaties that remain in force for a very long time, like the Genocide Convention. As the ICJ held more recently:

> where the parties have used generic terms in a treaty, the parties necessarily having been aware that the meaning of the terms was likely to evolve over time, and where the treaty has been entered into for a very long period or is 'of continuing duration', the parties must be presumed, as a general rule, to have intended those terms to have an evolving meaning.[114]

Since race is such a notion, that is, a temporal and dynamic concept whose meaning and content vary drastically over time, the applicable rules of interpretation suggest that we must construe it from today's perspective, following the term's meaning in the contemporary vernacular. It must be recalled that the same rule applies to the other generic notions used to describe the remaining collectives. For example, it can hardly be said that the drafters intended to exclude less traditional religious groups that emerged after the adoption of the Convention by 'freezing' in time the meaning of the respective referent.

4. The racialized subject

All three approaches capture essential aspects of the main issue. The historical thesis suggests that the term should be construed per its everyday meaning, even though race has been scientifically discredited.[115] The subjectivist thesis posits that racial groups are the products of ascription, who do not have an immutable or objectively verifiable existence outside their social context.[116] Finally, the 'visible minority' thesis describes some of the anchor points of such ascriptions, arbitrarily chosen external characteristics considered hereditary or proof of a person's ancestry. Societal actors use these visible characteristics to ascribe a distinct identity to the group, and so does the group to self-identify.[117]

As a result, race implies visibility and interaction. It is not a natural given or a dispassionate depiction of reality. It may appear like a 'norm' (eg some physical traits), however, it is a 'normative phantasm', a set of identification practices attached to the

[112] *Legal Consequences for States of the Continued Presence of South Africa in Namibia (South-West Africa) notwithstanding Security Council Resolution 276 (1970)* (Advisory Opinion) [1971] ICJ Rep 16, 31 [53].

[113] *Aegean Sea Continental Shelf* (*Greece v Turkey*) (Jurisdiction & Admissibility) [1978] ICJ Rep 3, 32 [77].

[114] *Dispute Regarding Navigational and Related Rights* (*Costa Rica v Nicaragua*) [2009] ICJ Rep 213, 243 [66].

[115] Francisco J Gil-White, 'Are Ethnic Groups Biological "Species" to the Human Brain?: Essentialism in Our Cognition of Some Social Categories' (2001) 42(4) Current Anthropology 515, 534–36.

[116] Linda Martín Alcoff, 'Philosophy and Racial Identity' (1997) 41(1) Philosophy Today 67.

[117] Lawrence Blum, "*I'm Not a Racist, But...*" (Cornell University Press 2002) 100–01.

racialized subject regardless of their true nature and agency.[118] The racialized subject is the normative outcome of a process that has been aptly described as the 'racial contract'. This is a heuristic device[119] employed to make sense of a 'set of formal or informal agreements or meta-agreements' between the members of a human subset designated by shifted criteria as racially superior compared to other human subsets that are debased racially inferior.[120] The racial contract is political, moral, and epistemological,[121] but also highly juridified and mediated by legal institutions, both domestic and international.[122] Even though the racial contract is global, localized contracts might also exist, especially on the fringes of the political, historical, and social spaces occupied by the allegedly superior group. Spaces like the Mediterranean, the Balkans, and the Middle East demonstrate the limits of a global racial contract.[123] Still, the contract as an analytical framework can also operate in these *topoi* as well, but in a modified version.

In the case of Palestine, which is the focal point of this chapter, the foundations of the racial contract can be traced back to the projects of colonialism and European domination over the political, economic, and social stratifications of the *Orient*, as expressed, inter alia, through the mandates system of the League of Nations.[124] Both the 1917 Balfour Declaration[125] and the Mandate for Palestine[126] linguistically erased the existence of an Arab Palestinian community.[127] The Arab Palestinians were either one of the 'existing non-Jewish communities' or one of the 'sections of the population' whose rights were to be preserved.[128] Thus, the preamble of the racial contract between a community that was not present in the territory but sought to claim it and one that was there but was subject to textual elision and political silencing was sanctioned and institutionalized in international law by dint of the Mandate.[129]

Nevertheless, the racial contract in Palestine remained uncertain for much of the Second World War and the subsequent events until the newly established UN decided to pursue the Partition Plan.[130] That said, during this crucial period, distinct articulations of the localized racial contract can also be discerned in the work of specialized UN bodies. For instance, in the 1947 report of the UN Special Committee on Palestine

[118] Judith Butler, *Bodies that Matter* (Routledge 1993) 3.

[119] Yasmeen Abu-Laban and Abigail B Bakan, 'The Racial Contract: Israel/Palestine and Canada' (2008) 14 Social Identities 637.

[120] Charles W Mills, *The Racial Contract* (25th anniv edn, Cornell University Press 2022) 11.

[121] ibid 14–16.

[122] See generally Christopher Gevers, '"Unwhitening the World": Rethinking Race and International Law' (2021) 67(6) UCLA Law Review 1652.

[123] Mills (n 120) 78–9.

[124] Noura Erakat, *Justice for Some* (Stanford University Press 2019).

[125] Balfour Declaration (2 November 1917).

[126] Mandate for Palestine (22 July 1922) reproduced in UN Doc A/292 (18 April 1947).

[127] Erakat (n 124) 39.

[128] Mandate (n 83) Preamble cl 2, Article 6.

[129] John Strawson, 'Mandate Ways: Self-Determination in Palestine and the "Existing Non-Jewish Communities"' in Sanford R Silverburg (ed), *Palestine and International Law* (McFarland & Co 2002) 251–70; Yasmeen Abu-Laban and Abigail B Bakan, *Israel, Palestine and the Politics of Race* (Bloomsbury Academic 2020).

[130] UNGA Res 181(II) (29 November 1947) UN Doc A/RES/181(II).

(UNSCOP),[131] the denial of the Indigenous community's right to self-determination and its practical exclusion from the essence of the mandate was justified and rationalized by citing the 'antagonistic' national claim of the Jewish community and the prospect of establishing a Jewish 'National Home'.[132] Even at the beginning of the post-Holocaust era, the issue of Palestine was still depicted as a purported conflict between two opposing groups, wherein one had to be suppressed for the other to prosper. The Partition Plan, which was included in UNSCOP's recommendations,[133] similarly amounted to a process of erasure; the obligations of both the Mandatory Power and the international authority overseeing the mandate were completely disregarded, and the proposed solution institutionalized the inequalities and injustices that fractured Palestinian society and fuelled tensions and hostility between the two communities.[134]

In UNSCOP's vision of an ideally structured two-state Palestine, the racialized perspective was glaringly evident. Both communities were assigned specific 'national' characteristics, which could flourish and reach their highest potential if edified under the solution proposed by an ostensibly impartial and benevolent international authority.[135] However, this idealized racial Palestine was destined to remain a contingency story of international law. The establishment of the State of Israel was accompanied by the application of policies of persecution, uprooting, and ethnic cleansing against the Arab Palestinian population,[136] and the enactment of rigorous policies solidifying the localized racial contract.[137] The Declaration of Independence presented the state as a Jewish National Home open to immigration and citizenship for every person who can claim Jewish heritage.[138] While stipulating 'full social and political equality of all its citizens, without distinction of race, creed or sex',[139] the Declaration commanded into political and legal existence a state and a political community based on a bond of allegiance qualified by ethnic, spiritual, and even racial characteristics.[140] Citizenship became a question of association by this narrative of belonging, producing uneven citizenry and proliferating lines of segregation and non-belonging.[141] This has been indirectly confirmed by the Israeli Supreme Court, which held in 1972 and 2013 that the only nationality recognized in the state of Israel is a Jewish one.[142] In

[131] UNSCOP Report (31 August 1947) UN Doc A/AC.13/82.
[132] ibid 88–90; Erakat (n 124) 45.
[133] UNSCOP Report (n 131) Ch VI.
[134] Walid Khalidi, 'Revisiting the UNGA Partition Resolution' (1997) 27 Journal of Palestine Studies 5.
[135] UNSCOP Report (n 131) 135.
[136] Ilan Pappé, *The Ethnic Cleansing of Palestine* (Oneworld Publications 2011) Ch 3.
[137] Abu-Laban and Bakan (n 129) 33, 67, 116; Yair Bäuml, 'Israel's Military Rule over Its Palestinian Citizens (1948–1968): Shaping the Israeli Segregation System' in Nadim M Rouhana (ed), *Israel and its Palestinian Citizens* (Cambridge University Press 2017) 103–31.
[138] Declaration of the Establishment of the State of Israel (14 May 1948), Operative cl 2.
[139] ibid.
[140] Noura Erakat, 'Whiteness as Property in Israel: Revival, Rehabilitation, and Removal' (2015) 31 Harvard Journal on Racial & Ethnic Justice 69, 84.
[141] Nimer Sultany, 'The Making of an Underclass: The Palestinian Citizens of Israel' (2012) 27 Israel Studies Review 190; Shira Robinson, *Citizen Strangers* (Stanford University Press 2013) 68–112.
[142] CA 8573/08 *Ornan v Ministry of the Interior* (6 October 2013) <https://versa.cardozo.yu.edu/opinions/ornan-v-ministry-interior> accessed 20 April 2024.

other words, there is no single political and legal concept of Israeli nationality separate from the Jewish identity[143] of the holder.[144]

While Palestinians forcibly driven out of their hearths were barred from acquiring the citizenship of the new state and those who continuously resided in Israel since the establishment of the state were effectively denationalized,[145] the 1950 Law of Return and the 1952 Citizenship Law[146] granted every *oleh* (Jewish immigrant to Israel) entitlement to citizenship and all the privileges attached thereto.[147] Notably, the Citizenship Law of Israel outlines four pathways through which citizenship may be granted by the state: return, residence in Israel, birth, and naturalization.[148] The provision regarding 'return' is exclusively extended to individuals of Jewish heritage, based on a racialized construction of the 'right to return' and the tradition of the ingathering of the exiles.[149] In contrast, the 'residence in Israel' pathway is available to Palestinians. However, such eligibility is contingent upon demonstrating residency before 1948, inclusion in the population registry, and continuous presence or lawful entry during the period spanning from 1948 to 1952.[150] Therefore, Arab Palestinians and their descendants who were forcibly uprooted from their ancestral lands during the 1940s and those who were not included in the population registry because of the haphazard procedure that was followed remain 'citizen strangers'.[151]

In the same vein, the Basic Law ('Israel—The Nation State of the Jewish People'[152]) constitutionalizes the condition of non-belonging as the quintessence of the racial contract.[153] Israel is labelled the *foyer national* of the Jewish people.[154] This collective agent is also proclaimed the sole bearer of the right to self-determination.[155] Jerusalem, *united and complete*, is recognized as the capital of the state.[156] The 'ingathering of the exiles' acquires constitutional supremacy[157] and Israeli settlements, illegal under international law,[158] are made the object of preferential state treatment and concern.[159] As an Israeli court held in 2020, interpreting this law, which is part and parcel of Israel's apartheid policies, 'the development and establishment of Jewish settlement

[143] Jewish identity has in and of itself a complex relationship with race; see Efraim Sicher (ed), *Race, Color, Identity: Rethinking Discourses about 'Jews' in the Twenty-First Century* (Berghahn Books 2013).
[144] Roselle Tekiner, 'Race and the Issue of National Identity in Israel' (1991) 23 International Journal of Middle East Studies 39–55.
[145] Victor Kattan, 'The Nationality of Denationalized Palestinians' (2005) 74 Nordic Journal of International Law 67.
[146] The Law of Return, 5710-1950 [LR]; Citizenship Law, 5712-1952 [CL].
[147] LR (n 146) Article 1; CL (n 146) Article 2; Erakat (n 124) 58–59.
[148] CL (n 146) Article 1.
[149] Tekiner (n 144) 48.
[150] Robinson (n 141).
[151] ibid.
[152] Basic Law: Israel as the Nation State of the Jewish People (2018) [NSBL].
[153] Yousef Jabareen, 'The Nation-State Law and Jewish Supremacy' (2018) 23 Palestine-Israel Journal of Politics, Economics & Culture 16.
[154] NSBL (n 152) Article 1B.
[155] ibid Article 1C.
[156] ibid Article 3.
[157] ibid Article 5.
[158] *Legal Consequences of the Construction of a Wall in the Occupied Palestinian Territory* (Advisory Opinion) [2004] ICJ Rep 136, 181 [120].
[159] NSBL (n 152) Article 7.

is a national value enshrined in [this] Basic Law and is a worthy and dominant consideration' in administrative decision-making processes.[160]

Still, a constitutional statute lending legal and moral support to policies of appropriation does not tell the whole story. Israel has enacted a series of legislative provisions aimed at securing the permanent dispossession of Palestinian refugees and internally displaced persons. The Absentees Property Law of 1950, the flagship of these policies,[161] encompassed the territories of Arab Palestinians who had fled across borders, becoming refugees, as well as those who were displaced internally within the nascent state. It delineated four circumstances under which private land could be subject to confiscation and transfer into state custodianship. These conditions included (i) ownership by citizens or nationals of specific enemy countries, (ii) location in designated hostile countries or parts of Palestine beyond Israel's control and jurisdiction, (iii) departure from Palestine by Palestinian citizens before September 1948, or (iv) relocation within Palestine to areas held by forces who sought to prevent the establishment of the state or fought against it post-independence.[162] The crucial period to apply this was the period between 29 November 1947 and the official end of Israel's state of emergency regime.

The law of 1950, along with subsequent amendments, even created a legal category of 'present-absentees' covering internally displaced Palestinians, some of them residing near their former properties.[163] Based on subsequent legislation, administrative, and judicial practices, Israel not only appropriated the properties but also transferred effective ownership to state and quasi-state entities for the benefit of Jewish nationals.[164] The 1967 war and the occupation of the Palestinian Territories further solidified these policies through measures of appropriation, forced eviction, and confiscation, eroding Palestinian land ownership over five decades.[165]

Land seizure, denial of entry, and de facto denationalization thus constitute the essence of the Palestinian racialized subject.[166] This identity is further shaped by the state's active cultivation of a perception of Palestinians as 'state enemies' and by emergency regulations in force since Israel's inception that severely constrain the fundamental rights of both Palestinian citizens in Israel and in the West Bank and Gaza Strip.[167] Policies of biopolitical control and surveillance also play a dominant role in constructing the Palestinian racialized subject.[168] Control over movement, communications, and everyday life activities, the institution of exclusionary barriers, the construction of the Wall, and the system of checkpoints and movement permits[169] are but

[160] *Nezar Bakri v Karmiel Municipality* (Krayot Magistrate's Court, 24 November 2020), reported in Human Rights Watch, 'A Threshold Crossed: Israeli Authorities and the Crimes of Apartheid and Persecution' (April 2021) 150 [HRW].

[161] Absentees Property Law 5710-1950 [APL]; Noura Erakat, 'Taking the Land without the People: The 1967 Story as Told by the Law' (2017) 47 Journal of Palestine Studies 18, 28.

[162] APL (n 161) Article 1(b).

[163] Erakat (n 124) 56; Erakat (n 140) 92.

[164] Erakat (n 124) 55–56.

[165] HRW (n 160) 196–98.

[166] Rashid Khalidi, *Palestinian Identity* (Columbia University Press 1997) 193.

[167] Erakat (n 124) 57–58; Abu-Laban and Bakan (n 129) 197–210, 46–47, 60–61, 71.

[168] Elia Zureik, 'Constructing Palestine through Surveillance Practices' (2001) 28 British Journal of Middle Eastern Studies 205.

[169] Elia Zureik, 'Colonialism, Surveillance, and Population Control: Israel/Palestine' in Elia Zureik, David Lyon, and Yasmeen Abu-Laban (eds), *Surveillance and Control in Israel/Palestine* (Routledge 2011).

iterations of this racial contract.[170] Israeli laws and practices vis-à-vis the Palestinians constitute a form of the 'law of the enemy',[171] which articulates what David Theo Goldberg has described as 'racial Palestinianization', a condition that denies the Palestinians agency, makes them suspect by definition, ontologically threatening, and perennially foreign.[172]

Strikingly, Israeli penal law retains one of the most comprehensive definitions of the 'enemy', which dovetails with ascriptions feeding into the identity of the racialized subject. For Israel, an enemy is 'anyone who is a belligerent, maintains a state of war against Israel or declares himself one of those, whether or not a war was declared and whether or not armed hostilities are in progress, and [is] also a [member of a] terrorist organisation'.[173] Domestic law also penalizes interactions with persons deemed to be part of the 'enemy' collectivities.[174] This practice has significant indirect consequences. For instance, starting from 2003 onwards, Israeli authorities have adopted special provisions effectively barring family reunification between Israeli citizens and their Palestinian spouses.[175] The legislation and the administrative practice stemming from it neutralize the possibility of a normal spousal life between Israelis and Palestinians by negating the possibility of establishing a common residence in Israel. This impediment, which further evinces an apartheid system, is not premised on an individualized security assessment but rather on the mere fact of belonging to the Palestinian communities of the 'areas', as the law calls the West Bank and the Gaza Strip.[176]

Consequently, the multilayer collective identity of the Palestinians has been forged through persecution, ethnic cleansing, displacement, and a precarious existence either outside the Palestinian Territories in the form of diasporic communities and/or communities of refugees or within them in the juridical and social condition of the racialized subject.[177] Therefore, racialized ascriptions have also affected how Palestinians see themselves. For example, the Palestinian National Covenant of 1968 defines the Palestinian identity as 'a genuine, essential, and inherent characteristic', which 'is transmitted from parents to children'.[178] In the same vein, the Election Law by Decree of 2007 disenfranchises all persons who would normally be considered Palestinians if they have acquired Israeli citizenship.[179] The constitution of the

[170] Yasmeen Abu-Laban and Abigail B Bakan, 'The "Israelization" of Social Sorting and the "Palestinianization" of the Racial Contract: Reframing Israel/Palestine and the War on Terror' in Elia Zureik, David Lyon, and Yasmeen Abu-Laban (eds), *Surveillance and Control in Israel/Palestine* (Routledge 2011).

[171] Rachel Noah Hefetz, 'Understanding Conflict Penality: Dominant Themes and the Case of the Israeli–Palestinian Conflict' (2023) 27(4) Theoretical Criminology 619, 627.

[172] David Theo Goldberg, 'Racial Palestinianization' in Ronit Lentin (ed), *Thinking Palestine* (Zed Books 2008) 25.

[173] Penal Law 5737–1977, Article 91.

[174] Sharon Weinblum, *Security and Defensive Democracy in Israel* (Routledge 2015) 67–68.

[175] The latest version of this 'temporary' law is: The Citizenship and Entry into Israel Law (Temporary Order), 5782-2022.

[176] HRW (n 160) 201–02.

[177] Richard Falk and Virginia Tilley, 'Israeli Practices Towards the Palestinian People and the Question of Apartheid' (UN ECOSOC Economic & Social Commission for Western Asia Report, 2017) UN Doc E/ESCWA/ECRI/2017/1 37–48.

[178] Palestinian National Covenant (1–17 July 1968) Article 4.

[179] Decree of 2 September 2007 Pertaining the General Elections, Article 29(d).

racialized subject in the law of Israel as 'citizen' (at least nominally) thus disqualifies them from the Palestinian national community in its most sovereign manifestation, the body politic competent to elect its political leadership.[180]

Mediated through the law, both domestic and international, this identity becomes decisive for the individual and collective existence of the racialized subject. For example, even though the tripartite right of Palestinian refugees to return, restitution, and/or compensation has been unequivocally articulated in the UN General Assembly (UNGA) resolution 194(III),[181] one of the most widely reaffirmed resolutions in UNGA's record,[182] which evinces a juridical consensus on the question at hand,[183] Israeli legislation subordinates this right to the exigencies of the *raison d'état*. By alluding to the idea of racial dispossession, the Israeli legal order embeds the racial contract into the very foundations of the state, whose territorial character is undeniable. Under the Basic Law 'Israel Lands', much of the Palestinian land appropriated by the state apparatus is rendered *res extra commercium*, that is, excluded from the real estate market and the freedom of contract.[184] Therefore, title to these properties cannot be purchased or transferred to private persons, including their original Palestinian owners, but will remain in perpetuity under the control of state agencies whose mandate explicitly discriminates against non-Jewish persons and entities.[185] Thus, both international law and Israeli domestic law mediate a racialized Palestinian identity grounded in displacement and exclusion.

Double standards also apply to the personal status of people residing not only in Israel but also in the Palestinian Territories. For instance, Israeli settlers are constituted as legal subjects under civil/regular law, whereas Palestinians are relegated to the realm of military/emergency law.[186] The application of even these laws is also subject to a wide margin of discretion and arbitrariness. [187] Thus, the racialized subject is not only banned from the ambit of regular law/the 'law of the friend' but is also debased by the double standards of the 'law of the enemy'.[188] While the legal category of the Jewish subject is singular and uniform, the racialized Palestinian subject is fragmented and conditional.[189]

This fragmented racialized subject has become the norm through a system of oppression and domination, tantamount to the crime of apartheid. Once institutionalized and

[180] Israel follows the same rule. Amendment no 9 (Authority for Revoking Citizenship) to Article 11 of the Citizenship Law (2008).

[181] UNGA Res 194(III) (11 December 1948) UN Doc A/RES/194(III) Operative cl 11.

[182] Francesca Albanese and Lex Takkenberg, *Palestinian Refugees in International Law* (2nd edn, Oxford University Press 2020) 349.

[183] Susan M Akram, 'Myths and Realities of the Palestinian Refugee Problem' in Susan M Akram and others (eds), *International Law and the Israeli/Palestinian Conflict* (Routledge 2011) 13, 28–30.

[184] Basic Law: Israel Lands (1960) Article 1.

[185] Erakat (n 140) 92–93; John Reynolds, 'Apartheid and International Law in Palestine' in Nada Kiswanson and Susan Power (eds), *Prolonged Occupation and International Law* (Nijhoff 2022) 104, 117.

[186] Reynolds (n 185) 118; HRW (n 160) 27; Falk and Tilley (n 177) 5, 44–46.

[187] See, eg, Matthew Zagor, '"I Am the Law!"—Perspectives of Legality and Illegality in the Israeli Army' (2010) 43 Israel Law Review 551.

[188] Silvia Pasquetti, 'Legal Emotions: An Ethnography of Distrust and Fear in the Arab Districts of an Israeli City' (2013) 47 Law & Society Review 461.

[189] Russell Tribunal on Palestine, 'Findings of the South African Session' (Russell Tribunal on Palestine, 5–7 November 2011) <https://www.russelltribunalonpalestine.com/en/wp-content/uploads/2011/09/RToP-Cape-Town-full-findings2.pdf> accessed 19 June 2024, [5.19].

forcibly imposed,[190] racialized ascriptions might prompt the subject to act or be used to interpret the subject's actions. This is because racialized ascriptions always have an agenda. They serve some purpose or project;[191] for example, racialized ascriptions can be used to justify dispossession, feeding into the project of racial capitalism.[192] More accurately, they are connected with a set of expectations or presuppositions regarding the racialized subject's actions. As Linda Martín Alcoff posits '[r]aces may have indeterminate borders . . . but many people believe that . . . *if one peers* long enough at, or observes carefully enough, the person's physical features and practiced mannerisms'.[193]

Thus, racialized subjectivity is not an absolute concept; it is rather a *focus* of a specific performative identity.[194] In this sense, racialized subjectivity is not a static category but a practice espoused by the out-group and in-group, which performs an identity and denotes what one is expected to do rather than what one necessarily is.[195] For example, the *idée fixe* of the Palestinian *qua* terrorist, which permeated Israeli legal, political, and administrative discourse, especially after the 1988 and 2000 uprisings and the subsequent extreme securitization of the Palestinian Territories are paramount for the construction of the 'norm' vis-à-vis the racialized subject.[196] The subject is expected to be a de-civilianized security threat.[197] This prompts the agents of the system, including police forces and even judicial institutions, to treat them (even pre-emptively) as such. In addition, this ascription affects the fabric of self-consciousness of the racialized subject. People growing up in the West Bank or the Gaza Strip have internalized these collective conditions. Practices of suspicion, fear, disobedience, and outsmarting the system have become part and parcel of their individual and collective identities. Such elements reveal the establishment of a 'double-consciousness',[198] a dual self-perception of the racialized subject, who defines themselves through the eyes of the oppressor.[199] Even when such subjects leave the Palestinian Territories, the practices attached to their identity *qua* racialized subjects retain their social and psychological reverberations.[200]

[190] Eloisio Moulin de Souza, 'Intrinsically Intersectional: Difference, Performativity, and Hybridity' in Shirley Anne Tate and Encarnación Gutiérrez Rodríguez (eds), *The Palgrave Handbook of Critical Race and Gender* (Palgrave Macmillan 2022) 633, 643.

[191] Lucius Outlaw, 'In Defense of WEB Du Bois' in Bernard W Bell, Emily R Grosholz, and James B Stewart (eds), *WEB Du Bois on Race and Culture* (Routledge 1996) 15, 20–1.

[192] David G Embrick and Johnny Eric Williams, 'Alienation, Racial Capitalism, and the Racialization of Palestinians' (2023) 49 Critical Sociology 939.

[193] Linda Martín Alcoff, *Visible Identities* (Oxford University Press 2006) 196.

[194] Shirley Anne Tate, 'Performativity and 'Raced' Bodies' in Karim Murji and John Solomos (eds), *Theories of Race and Ethnicity* (Cambridge University Press 2014) 180, 180–81.

[195] Shirley Anne Tate and Encarnación Gutiérrez Rodríguez, 'Critical Race and Gender: Dialogues between Decoloniality and Intersectionality' in Shirley Anne Tate and Encarnación Gutiérrez Rodríguez (eds), *The Palgrave Handbook of Critical Race and Gender* (Palgrave Macmillan 2022) 1, 8.

[196] Abu-Laban and Bakan (n 170) 283–89; Marya Al-Hindi, 'Criminalising Palestinians: History and Borders in the Construction of the Palestinian Threat' (2023) 12 International Journal for Crime, Justice and Social Democracy 36.

[197] UNHRC, '"Arbitrary Deprivation of Liberty in the Occupied Palestinian Territory" Report of the Special Rapporteur on the situation of human rights in the Palestinian territories occupied since 1967, Francesca Albanese*' (28 August 2023) UN Doc A/HRC/53/59 [95].

[198] WEB Du Bois, *The Souls of Black Folk* (Oxford University Press 2007) 8.

[199] Lara Sheeh and Stephen Sheehi, *Psychoanalysis Under Occupation* (Routledge 2022) 179.

[200] Dominika Blachnicka-Ciacek, 'Occupied from within: Embodied Memories of Occupation, Resistance and Survival among the Palestinian Diaspora' (2020) 34 Emotion, Space & Society 100653.

Moreover, race is situational and contingent.[201] Racial definitions are about power as much as belonging. Thus, Jews of Arab descent, the communities collectively referred to as the Mizrahi Jews,[202] could be reconstituted as proper legal and political subjects in post-1967 Israel. The emergence of the racialized other allowed these persons to be incorporated into the national community. As Yehouda Shenhav pointedly notes, referring to Jewish Arab intelligence operatives employed by Israel during the 1950s and 1960s, '[b]y working for the state against the Arab enemy, [they] earned [their] entry ticket into Israeliness'.[203]

Race is also hybrid.[204] Thus, a racialized subject can deviate from normative schemas that perform their identity.[205] A pertinent example is offered by the Israel debate on national loyalties and Palestinian representation in the Knesset. Per Article 7A, added in 2008 to the 1958 Basic Law 'The Knesset',[206] Israeli parliamentarians redefined the limits between what is acceptable in a Jewish democratic state (which, ultimately, is democratic because it is Jewish) and the participation of the racialized 'other' in the political life of said state.[207] By invoking the imperative of democracy to defend itself, the 2008 provision barred individuals from participating in the elections if they opposed the 'existence of the state of Israel as a Jewish and democratic state' or visited 'unlawfully' an 'enemy country' in the preceding seven years.[208] Denationalization laws are motivated by the same policy.[209] Thus, 'loyal' citizens can be provisionally included in the body politic, but only if they concede the basic characteristics of the state, including prominently its non-negotiable Jewish identity. As John Reynolds observes, this practically means that Palestinians willing to be re-labelled as 'loyal' are expected to legitimize the very juridical and political order that racializes and subordinates them.[210]

Finally, race's hybridity means that it can be negotiated.[211] Studies about the Israeli public discourse show that a distinction between 'good Arabs, who accept the Jewish rules of the game, and bad Arabs, who do not accept these rules' is a recurring pattern.[212] Similarly, in 1996, Matti Kaminsky and Daniel Bar-Tal showed that slight alterations in the conditions of the racialized subject might significantly affect their positionality.[213] In their research, 'Arab Israelis' was the least dehumanized social category compared to 'Palestinian supporters of the PLO', even though both labels

[201] Michael Omi and Howard Winant, 'Blinded by Sight: The Racial Body and the Origins of the Social Constructions of Race' (2016) 41(4) Law & Social Inquiry 1062, 1067.

[202] The Mizrahi collective identity is in itself controversial; see Ella Shohat, 'The Invention of the Mizrahim' (1999) 29 Journal of Palestine Studies 5.

[203] Yehouda A Shenhav, *The Arab Jews* (Stanford University Press 2006) 3.

[204] Shirley Anne Tate, *Black Skins, Black Masks* (Routledge 2017).

[205] de Souza (n 190) 644.

[206] Basic Law: The Knesset Amendment no 39 (2008) [KBLA].

[207] Weinblum (n 174) 75–81.

[208] KBLA (n 206).

[209] Nimer Sultany, 'The Legal Structures of Subordination' in Nadim M Rouhana (ed), *Israel and its Palestinian Citizens* (Cambridge University Press 2017) 191, 211–13

[210] Reynolds (n 140) 117.

[211] Tate (n 204) 2; de Souza (n 190) 644.

[212] Daniel Bar-Tal and Yona Teichman, *Stereotypes and Prejudice in Conflict* (Cambridge University Press 2009) 152.

[213] Matti Kaminsky and Daniel Bar-Tal, 'Stereotypical Perceptions of the Israeli Arabs with Different Labels as a Function of Age and Religiosity' (1996) 1 Studies in Education 121.

ostensibly referred to overlapping social identities.[214] Similarly, the racialized subject's subordination can be inversely proportional to their willingness to comply. In this constellation, social control over the very acts of remembering and forgetting becomes essential.[215] Members of the Palestinian minority in Israel are prompted to forget the memory of the *Nakba* for fear of their organizations and associations facing budgetary restrictions, namely withholding of state funding by the Finance Ministry.[216] The message communicated by such legal provisions is clear, at least on the abstract level: disseminating memories of an event considered constitutive of the racialized subject's existence will result in further subordination. 'Forced forgetting',[217] however, will be rewarded.

Taking into account our previous analysis and the three existing trends in legal scholarship, we can argue that a racial group constitutes a human figuration whose members are perceived and perceive themselves as having some different characteristics ascribing to them a distinct identity, the latter being hybrid, situational, fragmentary, and negotiable. In the following section, I demonstrate how this definition affects the constitution of the Palestinians as a protected group under the Convention by addressing the ways in which Palestinian racialization might increase the risk of them suffering genocidal violence.

5. A racialized existence: genocidal priming and activation

Framing the plight of the Palestinians as genocide is neither new nor unheard of. During the drafting of the Convention, the Syrian delegate unsuccessfully sought to add another subparagraph to Article II, classifying as genocide the imposition of measures 'intended to oblige members of a group to abandon their homes in order to escape the [serious][218] threat of subsequent ill-treatment'.[219] Some thirty years later, the UNGA would classify as 'genocide' the massacres of Palestinian refugees in the refugee camps of Sabra and Shatila.[220] This resolution marked the first post-1948 engagement of the UNGA with the concept of genocide and was fraught with symbolism, rhetorical accusations, and conflicting political motivations.[221] Instead of summarily applying the genocide label to the traumatic experiences of the Palestinians and the atrocities Israel has committed (and is still committing) against them, as with the 1948 and 1982 genocide claims, this section will focus on how the processes of Palestinian racialization increase the risk of genocide.

[214] Bar-Tal and Teichman (n 212) 222.

[215] Yifat Gutman and Noam Tirosh, 'Balancing Atrocities and Forced Forgetting: Memory Laws as a Means of Social Control in Israel' (2021) 46 Law & Social Inquiry 705.

[216] Amendment no 40 to the Budgets Foundations Law (2011).

[217] Gutman and Tirosh (n 215).

[218] UNGA Sixth Committee 82nd Meeting (23 October 1948) UN Doc A/C.6/SR.82.

[219] UNGA Sixth Committee 'Syria: Amendment to Article 2' (15 October 1948) UN Doc A/C.6/234; UNGA Sixth Committee 81st Meeting (22 October 1948) UN Doc A/C.6/SR.81.

[220] UNGA Res 37/123D (16 December 1982) UN Doc A/RES/37/123D.

[221] Antonio Cassese, *Violence and Law in the Modern Age* (Princeton University Press 1988) 82–84.

Genocide does not take place *in vacuo* and is not the outcome of a spontaneous decision.[222] Moreover, genocide as a process does not create identities *ex nihilo*.[223] However, it makes its collective identity visible through processes of dichotomization and stigmatization, and finally, it transforms this identity through extreme othering and dehumanization.[224] Such processes turn collective identities into singularized notions and establish hard lines between a dominant group and the group(s) they subordinate. Social or racial enmity can be manipulated to justify inter-group domination and oppression, but it also has the potential to induce genocidal violence, thus leading to the destruction of the oppressed collective.[225]

Of course, the constitution of the racialized subject does not demand genocidal violence. However, racialization entails complex processes of othering and inter-group patterns of interaction which can lead to antagonism, conflict, or genocide, but this process is neither linear nor deterministic,[226] especially when there is room for de-escalation and the establishment of some *modus vivendi*.[227] Furthermore, othering can result in encompassment, subsuming the 'othered' group into a new dominant community, a practice that usually falls short of physical destruction but can lead to cultural erasure.[228]

As Alexander Hinton suggests, we must distinguish between essentializing othering and annihilating othering.[229] Essentializing entails the construction of false dichotomies based on putative differences between the in-group and the out-group. One important parameter of essentializing othering is the perception of a certain collective identity as self-reproducing, which is generally the case with, inter alia, racialized identities.[230] Annihilating othering encompasses practices intended to cleanse the dominant group of an 'alien' presented as an existential threat.[231] In this context, the inter-group patterns of collective violence increases the risk of genocide and might even consolidate the quintessence of the crime of genocide, the intent to destroy the targeted group in whole or in part.

Othering processes and the representation of the targeted group as an existential threat often climaxes with the occurrence of a critical event.[232] This 'trigger event' is framed as either an external or an internal necessity, making the survival discourse much more urgent and tangible.[233] Of course, the singularity of the event

[222] Nicole Rafter, *The Crime of All Crimes* (New York University Press 2016) 131.
[223] Maureen S Hiebert, *Constructing Genocide and Mass Violence* (Routledge 2017) 141.
[224] Rowan Savage, 'Modern Genocidal Dehumanization: A New Model' (2013) 47(2) Patterns of Prejudice 139, 143; David Moshman, 'Us and Them: Identity and Genocide' (2007) 7(2) Identity 115, 120–21.
[225] Gideon Boas, 'What Is International Criminal Justice?' in Gideon Boas, William A Schabas, and Michael P Scharf (eds), *International Criminal Justice* (Edward Elgar 2012) 1, 21.
[226] Henri Tajfel and John C Turner, 'The Social Identity Theory of Intergroup Behavior' in John T Jost and Jim Sidanius (eds), *Political Psychology* (Psychology Press 2004) 367, 374–86.
[227] Deborah Mayersen, 'On the Timing of Genocide' (2010) 5(1) Genocide Studies & Prevention 20, 30.
[228] Gerd Baumann 'Grammars of Identity/Alterity: A Structural Approach' in Gerd Baumann and Andre Gingrich (eds), *Grammars of Identity/Alterity* (Berghahn Books 2006) 18, 25–7.
[229] Alexander Laban Hinton, 'The Dark Side of Modernity: Toward an Anthropology of Genocide' in Alexander Laban Hinton (ed), *Annihilating Difference* (University of California Press 2022) 1, 12, 18.
[230] Daniel Chirot and Clark McCauley, *Why Not Kill Them All?* (Princeton University Press 2006) 82.
[231] Moshman (n 224) 123.
[232] Jacques Semelin, *Purify and Destroy* (Columbia University Press 2007) 47–51.
[233] Hiebert (n 223) 8, 11.

is an illusion.[234] It is better understood as a series of events that facilitate a broader societal change and bring the targeted group closer to an existential threat that can activate the protective regime of the Genocide Convention. These triggering conditions are parts of a genocidal sequence moving from priming to activation.[235] Genocidal priming refers to the processes by which various factors come together, influencing the likelihood of genocide in certain historical and sociopolitical contexts.[236]

'Specific situations will become more or less "hot" and volatile—or more likely to be "set off"—as certain processes unfold'.[237] These latter processes are epitomized by the repercussions of the racial contract and the construction of the racialized subject.[238] Otherwise put, the processes of racialization, marginalization, securitization, and dehumanization, essential to the constitution of the racialized subject, are also indispensable conditions of genocidal priming.[239] The intensity and speed of priming is dynamic and situational[240] with both domestic and international events affecting this process.[241] Sometimes, it might be more accurate to describe the various primers as 'incremental' or 'slow-boiling' pathways to the eruption of genocidal violence, a set of *escalating commitments* on behalf of the dominant group that facilitates the crescendo.[242] This process normalizes the theoretical underpinnings of genocide (eg ideology or a preferred historical narrative) as well as the commission and consequences of dehumanizing violence.[243] The historical record of the Israeli–Palestinian conflict offers several such candidates. The Nakba and the establishment of the state of Israel,[244] the various phases of the conflict from the 1960s to the 1980s,[245] the blockade

[234] Alexander Laban Hinton, *Why Did They Kill?* (University of California Press 2005) 280–81.

[235] Alexander Laban Hinton, 'Genocide and Anthropology' in Alexander Laban Hinton (ed), *Genocide: An Anthropological Reader* (Blackwell Publishers 2002) 1, 14.

[236] Hinton (n 229) 29; see also Hinton (n 234) 280.

[237] Hinton (n 229) 29.

[238] John Hagan and Wenona Rymond-Richmond, 'The Collective Dynamics of Racial Dehumanization and Genocidal Victimization in Darfur' (2008) 73 American Sociological Review 875.

[239] Hinton (n 234) 282; Hinton (n 235) 14–15; Hagan and Rymond-Richmond (n 238) 881; Jeylan Wolyie Hussein, 'Discursive and Processual Socialization of the Mass into Acts of Violence: the Case of Rwandan Genocide' (2013) 36 Ethnic Studies Review 77, 78–96.

[240] Hinton (n 235) 14.

[241] Hinton (n 229) 20; Leo Kuper, *Genocide: Its Political Use in the Twentieth Century* (Yale University Press 1981) 46, 183–84, 208.

[242] James Waller, *Becoming Evil* (Oxford University Press 2007) 232; Ilan Pappé, 'A Brief History of Israel's Incremental Genocide' in Noam Chomsky and Ilan Pappé (eds), *On Palestine* (Haymarket 2015) 147.

[243] Nancy Scheper-Hughes, 'Coming to Our Senses' in Alexander Laban Hinton (ed), *Annihilating Difference* (University of California Press 2022) 348, 373; Omar Shahabudin McDoom, 'Radicalization as Cause and Consequence of Violence in Genocides and Mass Killings' (2020) 1 Violence 123, 127.

[244] Ilan Pappé, 'Israel's Incremental Genocide in the Gaza Ghetto' (*The Electronic Intifada*, 13 July 2014) <https://electronicintifada.net/content/israels-incremental-genocide-gaza-ghetto/13562> accessed 14 June 2024; Ilan Pappé, 'New-Old Thinking on Palestine' in Ian Parker (ed), *For Palestine: Essays from the Tom Hurndall Memorial Lecture Group* (Open Book Publishers 2023) 41, 47; Martin Shaw, 'Palestine in An International Historical Perspective on Genocide' (2010) 9 Holy Land Studies 1, 13–20.

[245] A Clare Brandabur, 'Roadmap to Genocide' (2008) 5(3) Nebula 25, 25–49; Edward Said, 'Permission to Narrate' (1984) 13 Journal of Palestine Studies 27; see also 'Israel in Lebanon: Report of the International Commission to Enquire into Reported Violations of International Law by Israel during Its Invasion of the Lebanon' (1983) 12 Journal of Palestine Studies 117.

of Gaza,[246] and Israel's Operation Cast Lead (2008–2009)[247] can all be considered equally critical for the genocidal priming of the Palestinian case.

Genocidal priming is necessary but not sufficient. A society under priming might need decades to reach the apex of genocidal violence. All through the various phases, the 'heat' increases and the targeted group is gradually brought closer and closer to an existential precipice. This risk, finally, materializes through the process of 'genocidal activation'.[248] Activation takes place under circumstances of extreme social control[249] when an event or a series of events is manipulated by societal leaders to present genocide as a—if not 'the'—rational choice.[250] 'Architects' are responsible for the emergence, proliferation, and gradual heating of the priming process.[251] They use such means as ideology, opportunity, communication, and distortions of social reality to establish both a grand narrative moving from priming to activation and a contextual level that can foster genocidal acts once the process is activated.[252] In such constellations, the criticality of the activation event(s) is contingent on the perceptions of the architects and their audience, that is, the collectivity with which the perpetrators identify themselves.[253] Therefore, events that can be framed as evidence of the existential threat posed by the stigmatized group *en bloc*, provided that the internal and external constraints are non-existent or ineffective,[254] can result in activation, even if they appear to be a continuation of prior instances of violence and subjugation against the targeted collective.[255]

Genocidal activation does not always boil down to a single historical conjuncture. To the contrary, the aggregation and concentration of racial dehumanization through a chain of events spanning a significant period can be sufficient to ignite the flames of genocide.[256] In the Palestinian case, this process—set into motion since the establishment of the state of Israel—could have led to genocidal activation in various instances.[257] Nevertheless, as activation needs impetus and organization,[258] it can

[246] Iyas Ashour, 'Does the Blockade of Gaza Constitute Genocide?' (MPhil Thesis, University of Western Cape 2013).

[247] Haifa Rashed and Damien Short, 'Genocide and Settler Colonialism: Can a Lemkin-Inspired Genocide Perspective Aid our Understanding of the Palestinian Situation?' (2012) 16 International Journal of Human Rights 1142, 1155–60.

[248] Hinton (n 234) 280–81; Hinton (n 235) 14–15.

[249] Bradley Campbell, 'Genocide as Social Control' (2009) 27(2) Sociological Theory 150.

[250] Helen Fein, *Accounting for Genocide* (Free Press 1979) 9–10; Maureen S Hiebert, 'The Three "Switches" of Identity Construction in Genocide: The Nazi Final Solution and the Cambodian Killing Fields' (2008) 3(1) Genocide Studies & Prevention 5, 6–9; Antonius CGM Robben and Alexander Laban Hinton, *Perpetrators: Encountering Humanity's Dark Side* (Stanford University Press 2023) 8; Semelin (n 232) 43–48.

[251] Robben and Hinton (n 249) 8, 15.

[252] ibid.

[253] Mayersen (n 227) 29; Semelin (n 232) 45–48; Nicole Rafter, *The Crime of All Crimes* (New York University Press 2016) 47–48; Alette Smeulers and Fred Grünfeld, *International Crimes and other Gross Human Rights Violations* (Nijhoff 2011) 175–6.

[254] Hinton (n 235) 14.

[255] See more generally Maryam Jamshidi, 'Genocide and Resistance in Palestine under Law's Shadow' (2024) Journal of Genocide Research 1, 3 https://doi.org/10.1080/14623528.2024.2348377.

[256] Hagan and Rymond-Richmond (n 238) 881.

[257] Jamshidi (n 255) 3.

[258] Hinton (n 229) 36 (n 26).

only take place when the leadership of the dominant group abandons the existing constraints—either normative or ethical—and unleashes the forces of annihilating violence against the dehumanized other.

Such a decision might be traced to the 7 October 2023 Hamas-led attacks, including killings of Israeli soldiers, civilians, and foreigners, rocket hits, and hostage-taking.[259] Even though this is yet another chapter in Israel's recourse to excessive force against the Palestinians in Gaza,[260] it is chosen as the milestone of genocidal activation precisely due to the relative 'success' of the previous phases of genocidal priming and the existential rhetoric developed by Israeli authorities immediately after the attacks. The settler-colonialism mentality of Zionism;[261] the international isolation of Gaza due to Israel's policies of occupation and apartheid;[262] the normalization of the disproportionate, selective, and punitive use of force;[263] the realignment of international and regional political synergies fostering impunity;[264] and the massive demographic alterations in the Palestinian territories that Israel has caused over the decades[265] are all primers that brought about the 'ripening' of the conditions necessary for genocidal activation.[266]

The sense of urgency created by these events allowed Israeli authorities and officials to neutralize the existing constraints and single-handedly frame all Palestinians, irrespective of age, status, or participation in the hostilities, as immediate threats to the survival of the Israeli state, thus justifying their indiscriminate targeting and the mounting annihilating violence.[267] For example, Giora Eiland, a former Israel Major General and special advisor to the Minister of Defence, explicitly referred to Israel's war on Gaza as an existential conflict.[268] Minister of Settlements and National Missions Orit Strook labelled the existence of a Palestinian state an 'existential threat'.[269] With

[259] OHCHR, 'Gaza: UN Experts Call on International Community to Prevent Genocide against the Palestinian People' (*OHCHR*, 16 November 2023) <https://www.ohchr.org/en/press-releases/2023/11/gaza-un-experts-call-international-community-prevent-genocide-against> accessed 22 April 2024.

[260] Mohammed Nijim, 'Genocide in Palestine: Gaza as a Case Study' (2023) 27 International Journal of Human Rights 165, 177.

[261] Edward Said, 'Zionism from the Standpoint of its Victims' in Moustafa Bayoumi and Andrew Rubin (eds), *The Edward Said Reader* (Granta 2000) 114–68; Patrick Wolfe, 'Settler Colonialism and the Elimination of the Native' (2006) 8 Journal of Genocide Research 387.

[262] Ilan Pappé, *The Biggest Prison on Earth: A History of Gaza and the Occupied Territories* (Simon and Schuster 2017).

[263] Ravi Bhavnani, Dan Miodownik, and Hyun Jin Cho, 'Three Two Tango: Territorial Control and Selective Violence in Israel, the West Bank, and Gaza' (2011) 55 Journal of Conflict Resolution 133.

[264] Colter Louwerse, '(Un)Limited Force: Regional Realignments, Israeli Operations, and the Security of Gaza' in Philipp O Amour (ed), *The Regional Order in the Gulf Region and the Middle East* (Palgrave Macmillan 2020) 217.

[265] Nur Masalha, *Expulsion of the Palestinians: The Concept of 'Transfer' in Zionist Political Thought, 1882–1948* (Institute for Palestine Studies 1992).

[266] Jamshidi (n 255) 3.

[267] Abdelwahab El-Affendi, 'The Futility of Genocide Studies After Gaza' [2024] Journal of Genocide Research 1–8, 2 <https://doi.org/10.1080/14623528.2024.2305525> accessed 1 July 2024; Zoé Samudzi, '"We are Fighting Nazis": Genocidal Fashionings of Gaza(ns) After 7 October' (2024) Journal of Genocide Research 1–10 <https://doi.org/10.1080/14623528.2024.2305524> accessed 1 July 2024.

[268] Law for Palestine, 'Database with 500+ Instances of Israeli Incitement to Genocide' (*Law for Palestine*, 4 January 2024) <https://law4palestine.org/law-for-palestine-releases-database-with-500-instances-of-israeli-incitement-to-genocide-continuously-updated/> accessed 1 July 2024 [LfPDB].

[269] ibid.

a similar tone, the Israeli Prime Minister framed the war as a battle between civilization (Israel) and barbarism (Palestinians).[270] Strikingly, even judge ad hoc Aharon Barak, through his separate opinions in *Genocide in the Gaza Strip* (provisional measures phase), framed the conflict as a war against an 'existential threat'[271] equivalent to a 'second war of independence'.[272] This existential rhetoric articulated even in the chambers of the ICJ evinces the immense importance of the October events as a point of consummation of the decades-long genocidal priming.

It is a truism that Israeli officials have long portrayed Palestinians as security threats and enemies of the state, justifying patterns of dispossession, marginalization, systematic oppression, and sociopolitical degradation.[273] However, all these phases of priming and racialized dehumanization can be seen as stepping stones towards genocidal activation. During the decades of priming, the precarity of the Palestinians' collective existence intensified, and their status as 'less than human' became increasingly consolidated. This led to the ultimate activation of the genocidal process once both the organization, a collective formation bent on apartheid and violence, and the impetus (a presumed existential threat justifying the abrogation of legal and moral constraints) were put into place. After the activation event, Yoav Gallant, Israeli Minister of Defence, explicitly stated that he 'removed all restraints' regarding troop conduct in Gaza.[274] This statement is paradigmatic of how genocidal activation is connected to the apparatus entrusted with the execution of a genocidal campaign. The troops, long trained in violence, subjugation, and dispossession or what Kjell Anderson has described as the 'humanity gap',[275] are now used to effect 'Gaza's Nakba'.[276]

After activation, the Palestinians *qua* people are stigmatized as existential threats[277] and re-imagined as *pariahs*[278] or 'others in excess',[279] ontologically different, dangerous, and unworthy of survival. To this end, symbolic imagery, including such references as the 'people of darkness' or 'the children of Amalek',[280] normalize and verbalize the racialization and dehumanization of the Palestinian people. Of course, these

[270] ibid; see further *The Times of Israel*, 'Netanyahu: "We Are in an Existential War, Israel Has to Win"' *The Times of Israel* (7 March 2024) <https://www.timesofisrael.com/liveblog_entry/netanyahu-we-are-in-an-existential-war-israel-has-to-win/> accessed 1 July 2024.

[271] *Genocide in the Gaza Strip* (n 14) Dissenting Opinion of Judge ad hoc Barak (24 May 2024) [2], [8].

[272] ibid [34].

[273] See, eg, Center for Constitutional Rights, 'The Genocide of the Palestinian People: An International Law and Human Rights Perspective' *Center for Constitutional Rights* (25 August 2016) <https://ccrjustice.org/genocide-palestinian-people-international-law-and-human-rights-perspective> accessed 1 July 2024; Yasmeen Abu-Laban and Abigail B. Bakan, 'Anti-Palestinian Racism: Analyzing the Unnamed and Suppressed Reality' (*Project on Middle East Political Science*, 16 September 2021) <https://pomeps.org/anti-palestinian-racism-analyzing-the-unnamed-and-suppressed-reality> accessed 1 July 2024; Center for Security, Race and Rights (Rutgers University Law School), 'Presumptively Antisemitic: Islamophobic Tropes in the Palestine-Israel Discourse' (*Center for Security, Race and Rights*, November 2023) <https://csrr.rutgers.edu/wp-content/uploads/2023/11/csrr-presumptively-antisemitic-report.pdf> accessed 1 July 2024.

[274] LfPDB (n 268).

[275] Kjell Anderson, *Perpetrating Genocide* (Routledge 2019) 28.

[276] LfPDB (n 268).

[277] ibid.

[278] Compare with Anderson (n 275) 195.

[279] Semelin (n 232) 37–38.

[280] LfPDB (n 268).

patterns have a long history in shaping Israeli perceptions vis-à-vis the Palestinians and consolidating anti-Palestinian racism.[281] However, their use in an emerging context of genocidal activation highlights a significant alteration in both their aetiology and teleology. These tropes of anti-Palestinian racism now justify Israel collectively and indiscriminately destroying a racialized and dehumanized group without much nuance or distinction.[282] In victimological terms, these alterations increase the targeted group's potential for victimization.[283] Thus, racialization and dehumanization initiated during the various stages of genocidal priming and solidified through a system of institutionalized oppression (apartheid) were turned into instruments of legitimization[284] justifying the initiation of a genocidal campaign subsequent to the activation event.

The prior phases of genocidal priming and especially the institution of an apartheid regime in the Palestinian territories established the foundation for the subsequent activation and execution of the crime of genocide. The 1973 Apartheid Convention recognized that systems of racial domination and institutionalized racial discrimination could foster conditions conducive to the physical destruction of a targeted group.[285] A regime of racial oppression effectively laid the groundwork for genocide by systematically dehumanizing and marginalizing the Palestinian people.[286] This dehumanization process was pivotal for genocidal priming, as it conditioned both the oppressors and the wider society to accept and even endorse extreme measures against the stigmatized group.[287]

The interdependence between apartheid and genocide becomes apparent when considering the structural similarities in their definitions.[288] South Africa's submissions to the ICJ against Israel elucidate this connection, referencing numerous instances of Israel's apartheid policies and contextualizing them within the framework of genocidal actions, particularly in Gaza.[289] These policies, including the extensive

[281] Silvana Rabinovich, *Biblical Figures in Israel's Colonial Political Theology* (Palgrave Macmillan 2022) 887–113.

[282] See the emphasis placed on these statements by both states and international actors: *Genocide in the Gaza Strip* (n 14) Public Sitting (11 January 2024) CR 2024/1 [20]–[32]; Public Sitting (16 May 2024) CR 2024/27 [5], [24]–[26]; UNHRC, 'Anatomy of a Genocide Report of the Special Rapporteur on the situation of human rights in the Palestinian territories occupied since 1967, Francesca Albanese*' (25 March 2024) UN Doc A/HRC/55/73; see further Yoav Di-Capua, 'Genocidal Mirroring in Israel/Palestine' (2024) Journal of Genocide Research 1 <https://doi.org/10.1080/14623528.2024.2361978> accessed 4 July 2024; Chris McGreal, 'The Language Being Used to Describe Palestinians Is Genocidal' *The Guardian* (16 October 2023) <https://www.theguardian.com/commentisfree/2023/oct/16/the-language-being-used-to-describe-palestinians-is-genocidal> accessed 4 July 2024.

[283] See more generally Nicole Rafter and Sandra Walklate, 'Genocide and the Dynamics of Victimization: Some Observations on Armenia' (2012) 9(5) European Journal of Criminology 514.

[284] Tom Van Hout and others, 'Claiming Genocidal Intent: A Discourse Analysis of South Africa's ICJ Case against Israel' (*Diggit Magazine*, 19 January 2024) <https://www.diggitmagazine.com/articles/claiming-genocidal-intent-discourse-analysis-south-africa-s-icj-case-against-israel> accessed 4 July 2024.

[285] Kattan and Kemp (n 19).

[286] Richard Falk, 'Slouching Toward a Palestinian Holocaust' in William A Cook (ed), *The Plight of the Palestinians* (Palgrave Macmillan 2010) 55–61; Nimer Sultany, 'A Threshold Crossed: On Genocidal Intent and the Duty to Prevent Genocide in Palestine' (2024) Journal of Genocide Research 1, 3–4, 16–18 <https://doi.org/10.1080/14623528.2024.2351261> accessed 12 July 2024; see also Nijim (n 260) 175–89.

[287] Savage (n 224).

[288] Kattan and Kemp (n 19).

[289] See, eg, *Genocide in the Gaza Strip* (n 14) Application Instituting Proceedings and Request for the Indication of Provisional Measures (29 December 2023) [2], [4], [35].

destruction of infrastructure and large-scale killing of civilians, aim to subjugate and set the stage for potential annihilation.[290] The transition from apartheid to genocide is, of course, marked by a shift in intent. Whereas apartheid's special intent is to sustain an oppressive regime,[291] genocide's *dolus specialis* is to annihilate a group, in whole or in part.[292] However, apartheid can act as a prelude to genocide,[293] creating a context where genocidal intent can emerge. Prolonged racial oppression and systematic discrimination under apartheid can lead to conditions where the oppressed group is viewed as expendable or as an existential threat that can be eliminated with impunity. Historical contexts such as Rwanda exemplify how prolonged discrimination and oppression eventually escalated into genocidal violence.[294]

From a victimological perspective, apartheid as a condition of genocidal priming has augmented the propensity for genocidal victimization of the Palestinian people, heightening their collective existential risk.[295] The systematic dehumanization and prolonged oppression under apartheid have rendered the Palestinian people more susceptible to extreme measures, facilitating the transition to genocidal actions.[296] In a sense, the system of apartheid not only enhanced the 'humanity gap', allowing for the emergence of new societal norms[297] that effectively barred Palestinians from equal participation in the dominant group's community, but also offered the Israeli leadership the means necessary to induce and justify the eruption of genocidal violence. As Edward Said astutely observed, the thought that the other 'is not quite as human as we' forms the foundation of systems of oppression and violence but may also entail a denial of agency or even of independent and meaningful existence,[298] a sobering reality underscored by the current plight of the Palestinian people.

6. Conclusion

The analysis presented explored the complex interplay between race, racialization, and genocide, using the Palestinian experience as a focal point. The Palestinians, as a racialized group, fit the criteria for protection under the Genocide Convention. The current circumstances, especially following the events of 7 October 2023 and the subsequent Operation Swords of Iron, exhibit conditions alarmingly consistent with

[290] Kattan and Kemp (n 19).
[291] Max Du Plessis, 'International Criminal Law: The Crime of Apartheid Revisited' (2011) 24 South African Journal of Criminal Justice 423, 427.
[292] *Bosnian Genocide* (n 14) [187]; *Croatian Genocide* (n 14) [132]; *Myanmar Provisional Measures Order* (n 14) [56].
[293] Winston P Nagan, John AC Cartner, and Robert J Munro, *Human Rights and Dynamic Humanism* (Nijhoff 2017) 358.
[294] See Scott Strauss, *The Order of Genocide: Race, Power, and War in Rwanda* (Cornell University Press 2006).
[295] A/HRC/55/73 (n 282) [10]–[13]; Judith Butler, 'Precarious Life, Vulnerability, and the Ethics of Cohabitation' (2012) 26 Journal of Speculative Philosophy 134; Mikko Joronen, 'Negotiating Colonial Violence: Spaces of Precarisation in Palestine' (2019) 51 Antipode 838.
[296] Stephen Bennett, 'On the Dehumanization of the Palestinians' (*Institute for Palestine Studies*, 23 October 2023) <https://www.palestine-studies.org/en/node/1654481> accessed 12 July 2024.
[297] Anderson (n 275) 195.
[298] Edward Said, *Orientalism* (Penguin Books 2003) 108.

established genocidal processes.[299] The Palestinians *qua* racialized collective have long faced the repercussions of genocidal priming. The precarity of their collective existence has steadily increased through systemic oppression, domination, and exclusion. The racial contract established and perpetuated by both domestic (Israeli) and international law provided the necessary framework to legitimize the subjugation and denial of agency and self-determination. This process has facilitated both genocidal priming and activation by systematically dehumanizing the Palestinian people and framing them as existential threats. The racial contract's legal and social mechanisms have entrenched discriminatory practices, ensuring the continuous marginalization of Palestinians and setting the stage for extreme measures threatening both the political and physical existence of the group. This environment of legitimized oppression coupled with the necessary ingredients of genocidal activation, the impetus created by the October attacks, and the pre-existing power structure utilized to implement the apartheid system, has allowed for the escalation of violence, leading to a context where genocidal actions are more readily justified and consummated.

Moreover, the abundance of statements of Israeli officials used to incite and morally ground the attacks against the collective existence of the Palestinians reveal a grim reality for students of genocide law as they evince a high probability of genocidal intent.[300] This has not gone unnoticed by the ICJ in the case between South Africa and Israel regarding the application of the Genocide Convention in the Gaza Strip. In the provisional measures order, the Court made use of the statements of the Israeli leadership to render its judgment on the plausibility of the rights and violations alleged by South Africa.[301] The presence of clear evidence of incitement to commit genocide is particularly alerting as the 'crime of crimes' is, by all accounts, a collective endeavour, where foot soldiers, who might or might not share the intent to destroy, operate within an overall atrocity context targeting the collective existence of a group slated for annihilation by a power structure.[302] The emergence of such a context in the case of the Gaza Strip must make us extremely careful in documenting and analysing its characteristics. As Stephan Kirsch aptly notes, sometimes we only need nuance to ascribe to some purposeful action an entirely new meaning.[303] A murder between civilians during an armed conflict does not seem like an act of genocide, even if we assume that the offender harboured an eliminatory intent. The same murder committed within an overall context of genocidal incitement and propaganda calling on civilians to 'take action' might be seen with more suspicion. In the final analysis, there is some distance to be covered between subjugating and annihilating the racialized subject, and this distance can be bridged even by a single architect *spiritus rector* provided that 'willing executioners' are placed at their disposal.[304]

[299] A/HRC/55/73 (n 282) [46]–[54].

[300] ibid.

[301] *Genocide in the Gaza Strip* (n 14) Order (26 January 2024) [51]–[54].

[302] See, eg, Kai Ambos, 'Criminologically Explained Reality of Genocide: Structure of the Offence and the 'Intent to Destroy' Requirement' in Alette Smeulers (ed), *Collective Violence and International Criminal Justice* (Intersentia 2010) 153.

[303] Stefan Kirsch, 'The Two Notions of Genocide: Distinguishing Macro Phenomena and Individual Misconduct' in Christoph Safferling and Eckart Conze (eds), *The Genocide Convention: The Legacy of Sixty Years After its Adoption* (TMC Asser 2010) 141, 148–49.

[304] Kress (n 108).

8
Settler Colonialism, Race, and International Law
Lessons from the Frontier

Faisal al-Asaad

1. Introduction

In this chapter, I consider the relationship between international law (IL) and race from the perspective of settler colonialism. I argue that this perspective offers a useful and distinct starting point for understanding how IL and legal discourse work together to produce an adjacent discourse on race. I begin by outlining what I mean by race, drawing on Marxist theory to define race as a process of abstraction. This definition will help us frame IL as a 'raced discourse' insofar as it elaborates juridical categories which are premised on a set of anthropological presuppositions. I then turn to the work of historian Patrick Wolfe, who offers a crucial thesis on settler colonialism: exception. I use Wolfe's theory of exception to outline a settler colonial perspective on race and IL and illustrate how IL works as an abstracting discourse on race.

With this analysis, it becomes possible to highlight a politico-juridical dynamic for which the critique and critical theory of law are well placed as a site of intervention. This can be understood as the metapolitical project of hegemonic states: a dynamic with historical provenance in settler colonial conquest, but with ongoing and rapidly evolving consequences in the historical present. Recent work on international humanitarian law (IHL) in the war on terror has been crucial for critically interrogating this dynamic. I thus conclude by reflecting on this scholarship and its implications for reconsidering and transforming IL in the context of the 'frontier'.

2. Race and/as abstraction

To specify the meaning of race, it is useful to draw a conceptual distinction between 'race' and 'racism' or 'racialization'. This distinction has been theorized by scholars working across various disciplinary traditions.

Cultural theorist WJT Mitchell defined race as the medium through which racial difference is perceived or denied.[1] Critical legal theorist Nasser Hussain critically reworked Hannah Arendt's famous distinction between race and race thinking 'to move

[1] WJT Mitchell, *Seeing Through Race* (Harvard University Press 2012) 13.

Faisal al-Asaad, *Settler Colonialism, Race, and International Law* In: *Emancipating International Law*.
Edited by: Mohsen al Attar and Claire Smith, Oxford University Press. © Faisal al-Asaad 2026.
DOI: 10.1093/9780198935605.003.0011

analysis away from understandings of race centered around bodies and presumptively stable identities . . . to a more discursive analysis that emphasizes the interplay between typology and ontology'.[2] For Hussain, race 'refers primarily to an impersonal, discursive arrangement, the brutal result of the raciological ordering of the world, not its cause'.[3] Understanding it as such 'directs attention toward the manifold structures of racial nomos—a legal, governmental, and spatial order'.[4] Likewise, comparative historian Patrick Wolfe traces distinct forms of racialization to illustrate 'race in action'.[5] While race is seen as a discursive formation or an ideological 'doctrine' with a measure of coherence, racialization is how this ideology is expressed 'as an assortment of local attempts to impose classificatory grids on a variety of colonised populations, to particular though coordinated ends'.[6]

Important differences exist between these approaches and the traditions to which they belong. However, I invoke them here to highlight what they share in common by distinguishing race from a specific category with distinct analytic consequences. Most importantly, they suggest that this distinction reveals a fundamental relationship between the more obvious material and contingent aspects of colonialism and its appearance as a consistent or structured discursive whole. We might say that in and through this discursive structure, the contextual and concrete realities of race are abstracted via the 'analytics of raciality'[7] or interpretive and theoretical work. Racism is historically contingent, harnessed to various strategic ends, be it the plunder of land, resources, labour, or a combination of all three. However, race can be identified as the way these historically contingent practices of domination derive a set of metahistorical narratives, rules, axioms, principles, or laws. This sense-making project gives colonialism the appearance of an overarching totality with onto-epistemic content. Indeed, and as the very process of 'articulating' racist practices, I argue that race entails a set of anthropological presuppositions.[8]

Why theorize race in this way and what does this definition contribute to the critique of IL and settler colonialism? For starters, this approach helps us attribute anthropological presuppositions to colonialism without going so far as to anthropomorphize it. Colonial and racist practices, after all, have nothing to say about humanity (though they say much about human behaviour). It is ultimately an exercise of violence premised on an arbitrary calculus of power at a given moment. As Frantz Fanon put it, 'colonialism is not a thinking machine, nor a body endowed with reasoning faculties. It is violence in its natural state'.[9] However, and insofar as we can speak of 'social logics', it is possible for colonialism to have a form of thought. In Marxist value-form theory, this has been conceptualized as a 'real abstraction': a process of abstraction that takes place

[2] Nasser Hussain, 'Hyperlegality' (2007) 10 New Criminal Law Review 516.
[3] ibid.
[4] ibid.
[5] Patrick Wolfe, *Traces of History: Elementary Structures of Race* (Verso 2016) 10.
[6] ibid.
[7] Denise Ferreira da Silva, *Toward a Global Idea of Race* (Minnesota University Press 2007).
[8] Stuart Hall, 'Race, Articulation, and Societies Structured in Dominance' in Houston A Baker Jr, Manthia Diwara, and Ruth A Lindeborg (eds), *Black British Cultural Studies: A Reader* (Chicago University Press 1996).
[9] Frantz Fanon, *The Wretched of the Earth* (Grove Press 1963) 61.

in social reality and material practice rather than in the mental faculties of individuals. This concept can shed considerable light on race's presuppositions.

The idea of real abstraction is experiencing a revival in critical theory.[10] It has also found purchase further afield, travelling from its traditional abode in Marxist theories of exchange to new frontiers in race, gender, and even nature itself.[11] Mobility aside, the concept's strength is its specificity as a critique of thought rooted in Marx's theory of abstract labour,[12] which is the transformation of qualitatively different acts of concrete labour into quantitatively commensurable units of exchange. This process results in abstract labour, a peculiar feature of capitalist modernity, and a substance of surplus value. For Marx, this 'social' substance is completely at odds with the 'material' substance of individual products of labour. 'The value of commodities', he observed in an oft-quoted passage, 'is the very opposite of the coarse materiality of their substance, not an atom of matter enters into its composition'.[13] Thus, capitalist production is a process of abstraction, since its mode of commodity exchange—imposed as a precondition for the realization or 'socialization' of value—retains nothing of the concrete materiality of individual or private acts of labour.

A vital consequence is that human labour becomes thinkable as a homogeneous or 'identical social substance' of which every commodity is seen as an expression.[14] However, the fact that this idea becomes thinkable does not mean that its origin can be traced to an individual philosopher or political economist, although it certainly finds expression in and through them. Rather, it is a general presupposition that is immanent to capitalist social relations or, in Marx's terms, it results from an 'abstraction in actu'.[15] Thus, the virtue of real abstraction theory is to extrapolate from Marx's critique of political economy, a thesis explicitly concerned with the onto-epistemic implications of abstract labour.

In the same way that the abstract categories of political economy provided Marx with a means of investigating the real abstractions of capital, so too can race and its critiques provide a means of unearthing the presuppositions immanent to colonialism. This understanding is already evident in the way that historically contingent practices of racial domination seem to evince a more consistent and totalizing social logic. Beyond analogy, however, the relationship between abstract labour and race can be seen as mutually constitutive and mediated by human labour. This 'identical

[10] See Chris O'Kane, 'The Critique of Real Abstraction: From the Critical Theory of Society to the Critique of Political Economy and Back Again' in Antonio Oliva, Angel Oliva and Ivan Novara (eds), *Marx and Contemporary Critical Theory: The Philosophy of Real Abstraction* (Palgrave Macmillan 2020) 265.

[11] Brenna Bhandar and Alberto Toscano, 'Race, Real estate, and Real Abstraction' (2015) 194 Radical Philosophy 8; Maya Gonzalez and Jeanne Neton, 'The Logic of Gender' (*Endnotes: Gender, Class, Race, and Other Misfortunes*, September 2013) <https://endnotes.org.uk/issues/3> accessed 17 July 2024; Jason W Moore, 'Nature/Society & the Violence of Real Abstraction' (*Jason W Moore World-Ecological Imaginations: Power and Production in the Web of Life*, 4 October 2016) <https://jasonwmoore.wordpress.com/2016/10/04/naturesociety-the-violence-of-real-abstraction> accessed 17 July 2024.

[12] See Elena Louisa Lange, 'Real Abstraction' in Beverley Skeggs and others (eds), *The Sage Handbook of Marxism* (Sage 2022) 593.

[13] Karl Marx, *Capital: Volume 1* (Penguin Books 1990) 138.

[14] ibid.

[15] See Mauricio Vieira Martins, 'On Real Objects that are not Sensuous: Marx and Abstraction *in actu*' in Antonio Oliva, Angel Oliva, and Ivan Novara (eds), *Marx and Contemporary Critical Theory: The Philosophy of Real Abstraction* (Palgrave Macmillan 2020) 191.

social substance'—realized through exchange relations and formalized through institutional and philosophical discourse—is the reason for pointing to anthropological presuppositions as the uniqueness of race. In other words, a particular discourse is *raced* through the anthropological claims it maintains, which can be illuminated in and through it. Resulting from capital's peculiar tendency for abstraction, an 'idea' of humanness comes to preoccupy modern thought without actually originating in it, and at the same time it acquires highly active and versatile institutional forms.[16]

In addition to avoiding the analytic pitfall where colonialism is anthropomorphized, this way of theorizing race is also useful for identifying a discursive form as *raced* even when it is not explicitly or expressly 'racist'. As we will see below when discussing IHL, the relationship between this discourse and race is not borne out of its adoption of a racial narrative or racially loaded terms, or even in its implication in racist practice. In fact, it is precisely the capacity to obscure a race that gives a particular discourse such as IL its *raced* character. Instead of sifting through its anthropological presuppositions, we can better position our critique of *raced* discourse to examine its material conditions and possibilities irrespective of its racial character.

To this end, we must trace the notion of 'sovereign humanness' in settler states' constitutional discourse. This notion is peculiar to colonial modernity, and this peculiarity derives from the way it allows the nation-state to claim universality *through*, rather than despite, its own particularity.[17] Race, as a form of thought subject to the law of abstraction, enables the conflation of a group's particular self-identity (eg Aryans) with universal human essence. Far from hindering racist practice, this contradiction facilitates it by institutionalizing indefinite categories such as 'humanity' and outlining the contours within which racist and colonial practice can take shape.

As critical legal scholars have observed, inclusion within these encompassing anthropological categories makes certain groups of human beings subject to the most inhumane practices, including conquest, dispossession, and enslavement.[18] The social logic of racism and racial violence transpires within the formal logic of race. However, in the process, what is taken for granted in one traverses the other as contradictory propositions with indeterminate political consequences.

3. Settler colonialism, elimination, and exception

In the previous section, I argue for distinguishing *raced* discourse from racist practice in order to highlight the process of abstraction which is immanent to capitalist social relations and grants colonialism a globalizing power that stretches beyond its

[16] For the relationship between capital, colonialism, and anthropological speculations in Western thought, see Sylvia Wynter, 'Unsettling the Coloniality of Being/Power/Truth/Freedom: Towards the Human, After Man, Its Overrepresentation—An Argument' (2003) 3(3) CR: New Centennial Review 257; Alberto Toscano, 'By Contraries Execute All Things: Figures of the Savage in European Philosophy' (2019) 204 Radical Philosophy 9.

[17] Kalpana Seshadri-Crooks, *Desiring Whiteness: A Lacanian Analysis of Race* (Routledge 2000) 55.

[18] Anthony Anghie, *Imperialism, Sovereignty, and the Making of International Law* (Cambridge University Press 2005); Ayça Çubukçu, 'Thinking against Humanity' (2017) 5(2) London Review of International Law 251.

particularities in specific contexts. IL is such a *raced* discourse, and its categories work to translate the social logics of racism and colonial violence into a more formal (and abstract) institutional logic which can travel with ease and evolve with versatility. As philosopher Etienne Balibar puts it, law's categories 'become more and more abstract, in order to apply to every possible place and situation'.[19]

There is additional value in describing this process as an abstraction. The historical specificity of capitalist abstraction is abstract labour, which allows us to conceive *human* labour as universal and fungible. Our critique of race can benefit from accounting for this anthropological presupposition that makes a discourse *raced*. While I examine the value of this critique in the context of the war on terror in the concluding section, I outline the specificity of settler colonialism as an analytic tool to highlight two values. First, the analysis of settler colonialism is generative for critical race and legal scholarship. Second, it provides a unique historical perspective on the abstraction process described above, the permutations of which resonate today. To this end, I focus on two 'theses' in settler colonialism derived from the work of Patrick Wolfe: the 'elimination' and 'exception' theses.

A useful starting point is the seminal article in which Wolfe discusses the concept of elimination, theorizing it as the organizing principle and structural logic of settler colonialism. Since its publication, *Settler colonialism and the elimination of the native* has become a landmark text and a crucial reference for readers of both Wolfe and settler colonial studies.[20] In the process of elaborating the relationship between the specifics of elimination and genocide, the article outlines some of the defining features for which settler colonialism has come to be recognized analytically. The results can be summarized as follows:

- The irreducible specificity of settler colonialism as a social formation—'Settler colonialism is inherently eliminatory but not invariably genocidal'.
- The centrality of indigenous lands and their dispossession—'Territoriality is settler colonialism's specific, irreducible element'.
- The temporal dimension of elimination—'It is both as complex social formation and as continuity through time that I term settler colonialism a structure rather than an event'.
- The 'positive' dimension of elimination—'Settler colonialism destroys to replace'.

This minimalistic outline suffices to reflect the key conceptual building blocks on which a growing edifice of literature is built.

The formative role of IL and critical legal theory in theorizing elimination is evident in Wolfe's critique of European state sovereignty and its realization through the doctrine of discovery. To him, the doctrine is a misnomer insofar as it is 'misleadingly referred to in the singular' and understood as a discourse about 'relations between Europeans and natives' rather than about 'relations between European sovereigns'.[21]

[19] Etienne Balibar, 'Hegel, Marx, Pashukanis and the Idea of Abstract Right as a Bourgeois Form' in Cooper Francis and Daniel Gottlieb (eds), *Institution: Critical histories of Law* (CRMEP Books 2023) 74.
[20] Patrick Wolfe, 'Settler Colonialism and the Elimination of the Native' (2006) 8(4) Journal of Genocide Research 387.
[21] ibid 390.

Noting some crucial differences in the way that colonizers formalized recognition or rejection of local Indigenous authority, Wolfe suggests that the 'rights accorded to natives tended to reflect the balance between European powers in any given theatre of colonial settlement'.[22] For example, while 'Aborigines were accorded no rights to their territory' because of British dominance in Australia, the use of treaties in the North American context 'reflected Indians' capacity to permute local alliance networks from among the rival Spanish, British, French, Dutch, Swedish and Russian presences'.[23] Despite these historical differences, what persists as a constitutive premise of European sovereignty is the supposition that the dominion inhered in this sovereignty from the moment of discovery, while Indigenous peoples retained the rights of occupancy at best.

By focusing on this distinction, Wolfe argues that dominion and occupancy simply express 'the pragmatics of the doctrine of discovery'.[24] Far from being 'an assertion of native rights', occupancy acted instead as a 'pragmatic acknowledgement of the lethal interlude that would intervene between the conceit of discovery, when navigators proclaimed European dominion over whole continents . . . and the practical realization of that conceit in the final securing of European settlement, formally consummated in the extinguishment of native title'.[25] Observing a structural homology in the logics subtending the extinguishment of native title in one century and its recognition in the next, Wolfe concludes by noting that 'the logic of elimination continues into the present'.[26]

Before turning to the exception thesis, it is worth noting that Wolfe is not the only theorist to take an interest in the concept, for which philosophers Schmitt and Agamben are the most famous.[27] For instance, Mark Rifkin argued that Agamben's use of an 'inside/outside' tropology in demarcating subjects excluded from juridical orders appears as a 'metaphor divorced from territoriality', privileging biopolitics at the expense of geopolitics.[28] Discussing US Indian policy, Rifkin suggests that the articulation of state sovereignty is contingent on the production of a territorially specific jurisdiction that negates Indigenous political authority. In contrast to the presumption of 'inherent sovereignty' as a positive set of powers, he considers the negation of Indigenous political will as the condition of state sovereignty. In this sense, the 'exception' can be understood as the creation of the authority to define jurisdiction and law itself by rendering extant polities as juridically anomalous and thus inadmissible as separate political entities.

Rifkin's revision of the exception thesis is helpful in illustrating the role of settler state sovereignty as but an 'empty placeholder' denoting an ongoing process

[22] ibid.
[23] ibid 391.
[24] ibid 392.
[25] ibid 393.
[26] ibid.
[27] See Julie Evans and others, *Sovereignty: Frontiers of Possibility* (University of Hawai'i Press 2013); Ronit Lentin, 'Palestine/Israel and State Criminality: Exception, Settler Colonialism and Racialization' (2016) 5 State Crime Journal 32; David Lloyd, 'Settler Colonialism and the State of Exception: The Example of Palestine/Israel' (2012) 2 Settler Colonial Studies 59; Mark Rifkin, 'Indigenizing Agamben: Rethinking Sovereignty in Light of the "Peculiar" Status of Native People' (2009) 73 Cultural Critique 88.
[28] Rifkin (n 27) 90.

of consolidating a 'monopoly on legitimacy'.[29] The key to this process is the idea of 'domestic dependent nations', which exempted Indigenous polities as independent foreign nations subject to IL, while at the same time facilitating their simultaneous incorporation and exclusion as extranational non-citizens. Turning to Wolfe's exception thesis, however, we find a gap in Rifkin's critique. While Rifkin's shift in emphasis from biopolitics of race to geopolitics of territory is instructive, it goes too far in the opposite direction. How do we clarify the role of race in the ongoing business of establishing a settler state's authority in the contemporary world?

As with elimination, this exception begins with critical references to legal theory. It challenges the view that so-called 'legal black holes' such as Guantánamo Bay present 'a constitutional anomaly' that exemplify the contradiction between 'the domestic realm of constitutional propriety' and 'a lack of constitutional restraint in the realm of international relations'.[30] Building on his earlier discussion of discovery, Wolfe sets out to demonstrate that US constitutional discourse is 'inherently—rather than accidentally—exclusionary'.[31] To illustrate this, he defines *exception* as a 'nullificatory component of US constitutional discourse', and one which is a 'necessary consequence of the set "we the people of the United States" being a subset of the universal set "we the people"'.[32] This principle, Wolfe argues, complements US exceptionalism since, while the latter 'inscribes a positivist repudiation of international accountability', the former 'maintains a universalism that . . . derives from natural-law thinking'.[33] A peculiar and hybrid logic, exception is the outcome of 'a set of historically specific practices and discursive formations' produced in the context of settler colonial conquest, which affected the incorporation of the territories of Native Americans concomitantly with their constitutional effacement both as national citizens as well as independent nations.

Wolfe distinguishes exception 'from the secondary or less intense otherings and marginalisations experienced by migrant groups' and strictly refers to an 'outer limit of othering that is reached when, as in the case of nineteenth century US Indian policy, particular humans are excepted from the general requirements that govern the treatment of humanity as a whole'.[34] Wolfe treats the 1831 *Cherokee v Georgia* decision as a watershed moment signalled by the notion of *domestic dependent nations*. As a formula that stripped Native Americans of independent national sovereignty, the judgment sanctioned the incorporation and conversion of their territories into 'so many parts of the United States', at the same time as it barred them from 'applying for the treaties that they had signed to be upheld by the US Supreme Court'.[35] This

[29] ibid 108.

[30] Patrick Wolfe, '*Corpus Nullius*: The Exception of Indians and Other Aliens in US Constitutional Discourse' (2007) 10 Postcolonial Studies 127.

[31] ibid 128. This is in keeping with arguments found in critical legal scholarship challenging the 'exceptionality' of Guantánamo Bay. See, eg, Fleur Johns, 'Guantánamo Bay and the Annihilation of the Exception' (2005) 16 European Journal of International Law 613. Yet, while the latter focuses on the 'norm-producing' effects of Guantánamo Bay in the specific context of the war on terror, Wolfe's focus is on its historical precedents in the longue durée of American settler colonialism. In the final section below, this chapter will bring the two foci into the same lens.

[32] ibid 129–30.

[33] ibid.

[34] ibid 127–30.

[35] ibid 139–40.

was historically unique and consequential since the 'resulting civic limbo—whereby Indians were neither citizens nor foreigners and, in consequence, had no qualities to which rights might attach—constitutes a juridical forerunner to Guantánamo Bay, only on a much larger scale'.[36]

The exception thesis is instructive here for several reasons. First, while US jurisprudence and constitutional discourse are central, the aim of exception is to highlight 'the pretextual conditions of the Constitution's own possibility', as well as the extra-discursive implications which extend well beyond the domestic realm.[37] Insofar as 'the Constitution acknowledged Indian sovereignty by default', the novel form of popular sovereignty it invokes is premised on the subsumption of international law to the 'national interest'.[38] As Wolfe pithily declares, this settler colonial presupposition 'constructs the world as potential: in the end, all the world is potentially American'.[39] Second, the argument concludes with an important qualifier, pointing out that 'the status of the exception is not . . . defined in relation to given communities'.[40] Rather, it is better understood 'as a versatile property of US constitutionalism that is available to be applied to different groups at different times'.[41] This thesis presents an avenue for exploring the articulation of race and IL from the perspective of settler colonialism. Not only does it raise the question of whether US foreign policy can be understood 'as the continuing containment and domestication of the world outside its borders, an endlessly expanding frontier',[42] it allows us to recentre the treatment of First Nations by juridical settler discourse as the precondition of international law and to examine the extra-discursive exclusions it produces as the condition for inscribing a general category of the human.

This close reading of Wolfe's theses was intended to highlight how legal discourse functions as a process of abstraction which inscribes the anthropological presuppositions of colonialism into juridical categories. It further reveals an essential feature of settler colonialism by clarifying how 'sovereignty' is the exercise of metapolitical authority that is *negative* in content. That is, it is premised on the elaboration of juridical categories that express a *lack* of political authority, and it is the process of negating these categories which realizes state sovereignty.[43] It follows that, as a 'negative articulation', metapolitical authority requires the enumeration of juridical categories which underwrite its existence. 'Peculiar' statuses (eg dependent domestic nations and unlawful enemy combatants) attest to the state's monopoly on the determination of the legitimate use of force and of 'the legitimate exercise of legitimacy' itself, 'an exclusive uncontestable right to define what will count as a viable legal or political form(ul)ation'.[44] Therefore, the exercise of metapolitical authority involves the maintenance of

[36] ibid 142.
[37] ibid 143.
[38] ibid.
[39] ibid 145.
[40] ibid 146.
[41] ibid.
[42] ibid 147.
[43] There is no space to adequately discuss it here, but the idea of 'counter-sovereignty' is an apt description, as discussed in Manu Karuka, *Empire's Tracks: Indigenous Nations, Chinese Workers, and the Transcontinental Railroad* (University of California Press 2019).
[44] Rifkin (n 27) 91.

a discursive framework through which juridical categories can be developed, modified, and expanded to provide new grounds for realizing state sovereignty. From this perspective, 'an endless frontier' can be understood as a consequence of this dynamic, whereby new spaces are continuously opened up by settler colonialism and its juridical grammar.

So far, I have defined race as a process of abstraction that highlights how IL can be understood as *raced* discourse. I have illustrated this through Wolfe's theses on settler colonialism, which offer a generative reading based on a twin critique of race and IL. While his reading is based on historical vignettes specific to conventional settler colonialism, it produces a far-reaching critique of metapolitical authority. This critique can reframe settler colonialism to shed light on an important sociolegal dynamic. In the next section, I explore IHL in the context of the war on terror to demonstrate this potential, suggesting that framing settler colonialism in this way can prove enlightening for a critique of anthropological presuppositions, and hence the *raced* discourse, immanent to IL in our contemporary era.

4. International law and the frontier-making project of settler colonialism

The earlier emphasis on settler colonialism as a historically determinate social form is worth reiterating. While the Anglosphere provides an exemplary terrain for the study of settler colonial policies, it is not an exceptional domain of this phenomenon. Beyond (commonwealth) nation-state formations, we trace the shifting contours of a versatile logic moving between different spaces and towards different geopolitical ends. Versatility notwithstanding, what gives this logic consistency is its tendency to produce frontiers, wherein the process of reproducing the metapolitical authority of the state form appears as a *historical process* and not a given fact. This is particularly evident within scholarship in political theory and critical international relations, which has provided important conceptual markers to help identify this logic. Namely, it operates across a transnational 'archipelago' of often (para)militarized hotspots which act as 'laboratories' and 'nodes of transmission' for material and discursive technologies of state-making.[45] For our purposes, however, it is worth focusing on critical interventions which link this logic to its peculiar legal form: the interplay between the juridical categories of IL and extrajudicial practices and spaces. As observed by political theorist Mark Neocleous in his critique of IL, 'the act of violence that constitutes accumulation is always already a politico-juridical act'.[46]

[45] See Paul Amar, *Human-Security States, Sexuality Politics, and the End of Neoliberalism* (Duke University Press 2013); Darren Byler, *Terror Capitalism: Uyghur Dispossession and Masculinity in a Chinese City* (Duke University Press 2021); Stephen Graham, 'Laboratories of War: United States-Israeli Collaboration in Urban War and Securitization' (2010) 17 Brown Journal of World Affairs 35; Laleh Khalili, 'The Location of Palestine in Global Counterinsurgencies' (2010) 42 International Journal of Middle East 413; Rhys Machold, 'Reconsidering the Laboratory Thesis: Palestine/Israel and the Geopolitics of Representation' (2018) 65 Political Geography 88.

[46] Mark Neocleous, 'International Law as Primitive Accumulation; or, the Secret of Systematic Colonization' (2012) 23 European Journal of International Law 954.

In addition to Guantánamo Bay, scholars have historicized this legal form in different contexts, from the Americas to Kashmir to Palestine.[47] Lisa Hajjar's work on IHL is particularly relevant to this discussion.[48] By developing the idea of IHL as a juridical field, Hajjar traces the continuities and ruptures between different paradigms of law-making that involve the pioneering of unconventional legal interpretations in settler colonial frontiers, which are then normalized and transformed into 'custom' through interpretive labour and legal work. Additionally, this process is shown to hinge on the elaboration of peculiar juridical categories which in turn work through and reinscribe the meanings and 'legal foundation of "humanity" itself'.[49] Hajjar's work shows how IL performs the kind of abstractions which are characteristic of race.

While her investigation is broadly concerned with IHL, its main object of inquiry is a distinct politico-juridical paradigm developed in the context of the war on terror. Specifically, it is concerned with the emergence of the counterterrorism paradigm as an 'alternative legality' through which hegemonic states, such as the US and Israel, pursue the 'domestication of international law'.[50] In an important sense, this idea of 'domestication' is consistent with the thesis of exception discussed earlier, since it denotes the subordination of IHL conventions and norms to the domestic political agendas and interests of hegemonic states. Hajjar argues that these states do not simply ignore IHL, but instead seek to reinterpret it such that it accords with an evolving set of prerogatives, particularly in the context of 'asymmetrical' warfare. Of course, the history of armed conflict between state and non-state actors in the wake of the two world wars, and the role of the international community in defining such conflicts and their rules of engagement, serves as an important backdrop for tracing the process of domestication. However, the latter only comes into sharp relief when our attention is drawn to the legal work that states such as Israel and the US put into carving out exceptions to IHL—exceptions which are simultaneously extrapolated as the basis for alternative legal rules. As Hajjar puts it: 'Many states violate and deny people's rights, but few have gone to such lengths to frame their policies and practices as legal, just, and necessary.'[51]

This observation is made while examining Israel's policies and legal doctrines after the 1967 war and its occupation of Gaza and the West Bank. As noted, the notion of a paradigm highlights how disparate policies and doctrines evolve into a cohesive framework which becomes unmoored from its origin. It is this gradual but systematic process of unmooring or abstracting that illuminates Hajjar's account. Having

[47] See Noura Erakat, *Justice for Some: Law and the Question of Palestine* (Stanford University Press 2019); J Kehaulani Kauanui, 'Hawaiian Nationhood, Self-Determination, and International Law' in Florencia E Mallon (ed), *Decolonizing Native Histories: Collaboration, Knowledge, and Language in the Americas* (Duke University Press 2012); Nimer Sultany, 'International law's Indeterminacy and 1948 Palestine: Two Comments on Aeyal Gross's *The Writing on the Wall*' (2018) 6 London Review of International Law 315; Shaiba Rather, 'Falling through the Cracks: Kashmir's Resistance against Settler Colonialism and the Limits of International Law' (2022) 63 Harvard International Law Journal 1; Juan Pablo Scarfi, *The Hidden History of International Law in the Americas* (Oxford University Press 2017).

[48] Lisa Hajjar, 'International Humanitarian Law and "Wars on Terror": A Comparative Analysis of Israeli and American Doctrines and Policies' (2006) 36 Journal of Palestine Studies 21.

[49] ibid 37.

[50] ibid 22.

[51] ibid 26.

explored the efforts of Israeli jurists and courts to sanction extrajudicial practices in the years following the war—including a 'pioneering venture to "legalize" torture'[52]—Hajjar turns to the Second Intifada. She explains how Israel deployed a versatile interpretive schema, evidenced by the elaboration of novel concepts such as 'armed conflict short of war' to describe the uprising or the casting of Palestinians as 'foreign armed adversaries'. This represented a turning point in the consolidation of a 'new paradigm', formalized by the US-led 'war on terror', for which it paved the way. This is a new paradigm in the sense that it casts the net wide, encompassing a global theatre where a diverse cast of existing and *potential* adversaries exist. In this sense, it expressed both rupture and continuity with Israel's legal work, insofar as it widened the scope of the paradigm by abstracting from its context, while at the same time developing its content, including the reinterpretation and authorization of torture, assassination, and forms of collective punishment. Israel justified these practices by asserting 'that *this war* was "unprecedented" and thus constituted a legal *terra nulla*'.[53] Redolent as the nomenclature is, it also speaks to the recursive logic at play, given the precedent in Israel's own juridical discourse.

Thus, while Hajjar's account is comparative, focusing on Israel and the US, there is an implicit unity in the paradigm. In a recent revision of her thesis, Hajjar used Bourdieu's field theory to conceptualize this unity.[54] As a juridical field, the counterterrorism war paradigm is an interpretive project with a systemic dimension, operating on the basis of shared 'military, security, and strategic interests'.[55] Moreover, it is sustained as a politico-juridical project through the recruitment of a vast pool of cultural and social capital and a wide array of 'legal entrepreneurs' who actively produce conceptual innovations 'not against but rather *through* law'.[56] As in Israel's alternative and 'operational' legality, these conceptual innovations produce mutable categories which, depending on context, aim to modify the rules of engagement based on the hegemonic state's strategic interests. These include novelties such as 'unlawful enemy combatants', which erase the distinction between combatants and civilians; the legitimation of torture based on the status of those administering it (US state agents and contractors); and the creation of subjects (terror suspects) who are right-*less* and susceptible to any form of violence.

As Hajjar observes, what is striking about these innovations is the underlying logic that shifts the focus of juridical discourse from the overall balance of power in an armed conflict and the legal status of the actors to their ontological status. It is not so much the nature of the conflict and its larger context but rather 'the nature of the enemy [which] determines the applicability or inapplicability of law'.[57] As a

[52] ibid 27.
[53] ibid 32.
[54] Lisa Hajjar, 'The Counterterrorism War Paradigm versus International Humanitarian Law: The Legal Contradictions and Global Consequences of the US "War on Terror"' (2019) 44 Law and Social Inquiry 922. An added benefit of Bourdieu's field theory which is not explicated in Hajjar is its emphasis on the 'relative autonomy' that a social (and in this case juridical) field acquires, which is consistent with the level of abstraction that characterizes the counterterrorism paradigm of IHL. See Yves Dezalay and Mikael Rask Madsen, 'The Force of Law and Lawyers: Pierre Bourdieu and the Reflexive Sociology of Law' (2012) 8 Annual Review of Law and Social Sciences 433.
[55] Hajjar (n 54) 929.
[56] ibid.
[57] ibid 926.

consequence, the 'practical effects of this post-9/11 interpretative process included forging new categories of being'.[58] It is these juridical innovations and their inscription on ontological categories that make it possible to view the discourse of IL as a discourse of race, not least since they double as anthropological categories. In other words, they are a medium through which the kinds of human, nonhuman, and *potential* humans created through colonial violence are given conceptual and institutional forms.[59] In this form, the arbitrary calculus underlying colonial violence becomes legible as a politico-juridical framework, and even a moral imperative. As Hajjar puts it, it sets the stage for extrajudicial practices and their justifications to '"ripen" into custom and thus become legal for all'.[60]

This is not a foregone consequence but a potential one. As noted by Hajjar, this paradigm has 'not yet garnered international credibility, let alone ripened into custom ... and there have been significant examples of international pushbacks'.[61] As a 'field', the paradigm is a space of contestation and struggle. However, there are other consequences clarified by the racial settler colonial lens. While an alternative legality has failed to displace the more conventional, internationally mandated framework of IHL, it has consolidated the metapolitical authority of hegemonic states insofar as it has formalized their insistence on defining the exercise of legitimacy *despite* contravening international consensus; hence, the investment of these states in legal work and the embrace of their imperialist and settler colonial status.[62]

Rather than expressing an ideological strategy to appease their constituencies by appearing as law-abiding, the politico-juridical projects of these states welcome their existence as expansionist entities committed to making their own law on their own terms and to the exclusion and *negation* of other mandates. As observed earlier, negation is a constitutive element of these projects since the sovereignty of these states has no necessary or positive content. Accordingly, 'frontier' expansion is productive not simply because it enacts the political will and (para)military power of the state, but also because its violence provides the very terms and grammar through which the latter *articulates* its monopoly on legitimacy.

Vis-à-vis Hajjar's account of the juridical discourse of the war paradigm, I have highlighted how frontiers are recursively conceptualized as legal *terra nullas* that justify exemptions from conventional IHL. I have also emphasized how one frontier produces discursive conditions for the making of another: Israel's alternative legality paved the way for the globalization of the paradigm via the US-led war on terror. Legal work provided a powerful medium for abstracting and formalizing the anthropological presuppositions of colonial violence. Hajjar recognizes the stakes of

[58] ibid 928.

[59] As Çubukçu argues, the term 'dehumanization' would be misleading, since it is not the exclusion but rather the inclusion within the anthropological category of humanness that subjects particular groups to violence and inhumane treatment: Çubukçu (n 28) 262; see also Samera Esmeir, 'On Making Dehumanization Possible' (2006) 121 Publications of the Modern Language Association of America 1544.

[60] Hajjar (n 54) 924.

[61] ibid 948.

[62] Hajjar (n 48) 22. Critical theorists of law as well as settler colonialism have attributed liberal democratic consensus in Western societies for motivating efforts by hegemonic states to reinterpret the law and legally justify extrajudicial practices or colonial projects. Indeed, both Hajjar and Wolfe have suggested this in different ways.

this project: '[w]hat hangs in the balance is not only the future of humanitarian law but the very meaning of humanity in times of war.'[63]

5. Conclusion

The war paradigm is now bearing horrid fruit. At the time of writing, Israel's war of extermination in Gaza has entered its ninth month. During this period, the Israeli state has acted with complete impunity, circumventing or simply disregarding historically significant challenges such as the International Court of Justice case brought by South Africa. While the Israeli military has undoubtedly acted in violation of IHL, committing numerous and well-documented war crimes, its capacity to continue doing so is perhaps symptomatic of the legal and metapolitical dynamics outlined throughout this discussion. Not least among these is the extreme and unembellished dehumanization of Palestinians by Israeli politicians, lawmakers, and military officials.

Defined as a politico-juridical project, therefore, settler colonialism may offer a generative paradigm for thinking about IL and its relationship to race. This is particularly so when examined as an iterative and versatile historical process, whereby a particular kind of hegemonic state formation is constituted through the assertion of metapolitical authority. As such, it redirects our attention from nationally bounded historical legacies of conquest to the 'frontier': a transnational, shifting, and dynamic state-making process. While seemingly exceptional, the frontier is crucial and constitutive since it enables expansionist 'settler' states to *renew* their monopoly on the legitimate use of legitimacy. This is because frontier violence is the basis on which sovereignty is articulated. As we have seen, this negative articulation involves the production of peculiar juridical categories which derive their efficacy through negation. It is the capacity to legitimize practices *despite* other existing sources of legitimacy which realizes the metapolitical authority of states. As discussed earlier, as an axiomatic principle for these states, this exception is therefore dependent on, rather than indifferent to, the law, a discursive framework of legitimacy.

Thus, the relationship between law and colonial violence is systemic and not superstructural. As such, the legal innovations of war paradigms do not simply provide extrajudicial state practices with ideological cover. By formalizing the presuppositions of colonial violence, IL also transforms its conditions of possibility. As evident in the globalized expansion of Israel's legal paradigm through the war on terror, the legal innovations of the frontier are powerful abstractions which do not simply justify past violations but also *anticipate* and pave the grounds for future ones. By insisting on the unprecedented nature of a particular frontier context, settler colonial states fashion precedents for their replication in other contexts.

What becomes apparent when focusing on this frontier-making project is that its anticipatory logic is premised on anthropological conjectures of the war paradigm. The construction and elaboration of peculiar subjects and statuses—of novel but abject 'categories of being'—acquires its consistency of sense from a framework that

[63] Hajjar (n 48) 37.

presumes a generic notion of sovereign humanness. It plays a fundamental role in the discursive reproduction of this framework which warrants its characterization as a discourse of race.

Politically and methodologically, this IL framework is instructive. In keeping with critical legal scholars, it points to the significance of the frontier as a site which is equally as productive for critical and political intervention as it is for legal 'innovation'.[64] When framed as part of the metapolitical projects of settler colonial states, the emergence of alternative legalities suggests that alternatives in the proper plural sense are both possible and necessary for emancipatory movements and counterhegemonic frameworks of legitimacy. In this regard, IL is critical, especially when it is understood as a mode of abstraction. As Ntina Tzouvala has recently argued, for example, South Africa's International Court of Justice case can be understood as an attempt to make 'legible', through the Genocide Convention, the political economy of Israeli settler colonialism and its eliminationist policies.[65]

Legal work and interpretive juridical labour are therefore arguably imperative for movements seeking to abolish the frontier as a precondition for imperialist and settler colonial states. What makes this labour an alternative is, I suggest, its capacity to radically reformulate the anthropological premises on which the law rests. Whether such labour can be geared to emancipatory ends is determined by its capacity to inscribe alternative 'genres' of the human which are rooted precisely in the terrain where they are denied: the frontier.

[64] Dezalay and Madsen (n 54).

[65] Ntina Tzouvala, 'Genocide and Political Economy: Reconstructing the Relationship' (*LPE Project*, 24 June 2024) <https://lpeproject.org/blog/genocide-and-political-economy-reconstructing-the-relationship/> accessed 17 July 2024.

9

Survive the Journey Only to Succumb to International Refugee Law

Jinan Bastaki

1. Introduction

Outside of critical scholarship, the 1951 Refugee Convention (Convention) is often portrayed as a panacea to the various refugee crises around the world. The promotion of universal adherence to the 1951 Convention and encouragement of new accessions have been endorsed by signatory states in various official declarations.[1] If more states ratified the Convention, and if those who did took their obligations seriously, refugees in territories of states parties would find the protection they needed—or so the narrative goes. When international refugee law works, it works well.

However, the Convention is problematic in many ways. For example, it does not offer extensive practical guidance on how states should treat individual refugees.[2] In fact, ratification or accession to the Convention is not a pledge to take in refugees, but a commitment to maintaining certain standards if they are admitted, including not to return them to where they may be persecuted.[3] Many of the states parties thus externalize refugee processing to politically weaker states in exchange for financial or political incentives. Partner states may or may not be party to the Convention, and in recent years, these have included Malaysia, Papua New Guinea, Rwanda, and Turkey.[4]

Moreover, refugees who do not strictly qualify under the Convention, but remain at risk of serious harm if returned, are given *subsidiary* protection. Rights under subsidiary protection vary depending on the state. With border control shifting outside the metropole, those in need are prevented from fully accessing protections. This has been a common predicament for refugees from Africa, the Middle East, and South Asia. While some have suggested this is the most that can be expected of states, the recent reception of Ukrainian refugees has highlighted the different *possibilities* in

1 eg UNHCR, 'Declaration of States Parties to the 1951 Convention and/or its 1967 Protocol Relating to the Status of Refugees' endorsed during the Ministerial Meeting of States Parties in Geneva, Switzerland, on 12–13 December 2001, <https://www.unhcr.org/news/latest/2001/12/3c18e6054/declaration-reaffirming-principles-1951-refugee-convention-adopted.html> accessed 25 April 2021.

2 Alexander Betts and Paul Collier, *Refuge: Transforming a Broken Refugee System* (Penguin Books 2017).

3 Hirotaka Fujibayashi, 'When an Arab State Entered into International Refugee Instruments: Behind the Scenes of Egypt's Accession to the 1951 Refugee Convention' (2022) 35(1) Journal of Refugee Studies 220.

4 Jennifer Hyndman and Alison Mountz, 'Another Brick in the Wall? Neo-Refoulement and the Externalization of Asylum by Australia and Europe' (2008) 43 Government and Opposition 249, 256–68; Lori A Nessel, 'Externalized Borders and the Invisible Refugee' (2008) 40 Columbia Human Rights Law Review 625.

Jinan Bastaki, *Survive the Journey Only to Succumb to International Refugee Law* In: *Emancipating International Law*. Edited by: Mohsen al Attar and Claire Smith, Oxford University Press. © Jinan Bastaki 2026.
DOI: 10.1093/9780198935605.003.0012

treatment and application of refugee protection, at least when the incoming group is not from the Global South. To illustrate, Poland erected a border wall to keep Syrian asylum seekers out, yet in 2022 it welcomed some two million Ukrainian refugees.[5] In less than ten years, Poland went from building walls to keep refugees out, to becoming one of the world's foremost refugee host states.

Observers have offered a range of theories to explain the stark difference of treatment, ranging from 'moral realism' to a shared history and future, to xenophobia and racism.[6] Is this difference attributable to the politics of individual states, showing how 'far-right politics have changed the scope of refugee protection in Europe'?[7] Or, is this differentiation inherent to the global refugee regime? This chapter will analyse how the 1951 Convention and its universalizing 1967 Protocol bolster racial borders and enable the exclusion of certain categories of people, achieving a macabre balancing act between state sovereignty and humanitarian concerns.[8]

I begin by interrogating the concept of sovereignty and the Refugee Convention, showing how the latter was designed almost exclusively to care for European refugees. While some advocated for a thoughtful yet pragmatic conception of refugees—especially former refugees[9] —powerful states ultimately insisted on retaining discretion over who to admit or reject. Next, I argue that the Convention was adopted in a colonial context heavily coloured by conceptions of race. Even seemingly neutral terms, such as sovereignty, have race embedded in them, as only certain states were perceived as truly sovereign and free. Since sovereign states open their borders to some while closing them to others, who is included and excluded illustrates the racialization of borders.[10] In protecting a state's sovereignty, the Convention reifies and even bolsters racial borders.

Two case studies help highlight the manifestations of racialization and racism in international refugee law, as well as the techniques of international refugee law that embody racializing practices. The first explores Palestinian refugees, implicitly addressed by Article 1(D) of the Convention. While Palestinian refugees were a hot topic during the Conference of Plenipotentiaries, they were ultimately excluded from

[5] UNHCR, 'Poland Welcomes More than Two Million Refugees from Ukraine' (*UNHCR*, 18 March 2022) <https://www.unhcr.org/news/press/2022/3/6234811a4/poland-welcomes-million-refugees-ukraine.html> accessed 18 July 2024.

[6] Karolina Wigura and Jarosław Kuisz, 'Poland's Door Is Wide Open to Ukrainians—We Know These Refugees Could Be Us' *The Guardian* (9 March 2022) <https://www.theguardian.com/world/commentisfree/2022/mar/09/poland-ukrainians-refugees-history> accessed 18 July 2024; James Traub, 'The Moral Realism of Europe's Refugee Hypocrisy' (*Foreign Policy*, 21 March 2022) <https://foreignpolicy.com/2022/03/21/ukraine-refugees-europe-hyporcrisy-syria/> accessed 18 July 2024; Bryan Chan Yen Johnson, Kevin Ah-Sen, and Philip SS Howard, 'Ukraine Refugee Crisis Exposes Racism and Contradictions in the Definition of Human' (*The Conversation*, 21 March 2022) <http://theconversation.com/ukraine-refugee-crisis-exposes-racism-and-contradictions-in-the-definition-of-human-179150> accessed 18 July 2024.

[7] Kemal Kirişci, 'The 1951 Refugee Convention Is Falling Short of Its Mission. Could the Global Compact on Refugees Help?' (*Brookings*, 26 July 2021) <https://www.brookings.edu/blog/order-from-chaos/2021/07/26/the-1951-refugee-convention-is-falling-short-of-its-mission-could-the-global-compact-on-refugees-help/> accessed 18 July 2024.

[8] James C Hathaway, 'A Reconsideration of the Underlying Premise of Refugee Law' (1990) 31 Harvard Journal of International Law 129.

[9] Irial Glynn, 'The Genesis and Development of Article 1 of the 1951 Refugee Convention' (2012) 25 Journal of Refugee Studies 134, 136–38.

[10] E Tendayi Achiume, 'Racial Borders' (2021) 110 Georgetown Law Journal 445.

the Convention's ambit, reflecting the geopolitical power dynamics of the time rather than any definitional distinction. The second case study examines externalizing regimes, where refugees are relocated to so-called safe third countries. To better identify their racializing dimensions, I compare what Europe termed a 'refugee crisis' in 2015 with the support offered to Ukrainian refugees in 2022. As an extension of the modern refugee framework, externalizing regimes are not an exception but representative of the original exclusionary teleology of international refugee protections. There are other considerations such as, inter alia, international political interests and domestic electoral contexts that influence the preferred demarcations.[11] The desire to control borders and the policies enacted towards this aim create a 'hierarchy of the excluded' that intersects with race, class, and gender.[12]

2. All states are sovereign, but some are more sovereign than others

To modern international law, sovereignty is the fundamental *state* of states, with its foundations in the 1648 Treaty of Westphalia.[13] While Europe developed its conception of sovereignty—including the right of a state to exercise jurisdiction over its territory and population, to use force in certain circumstances, and to reciprocal non-interference in the internal affairs of other sovereign states—it colonized lands and peoples across the world. European powers saw themselves as possessing the intrinsic standard of civilization and thus sovereignty, while non-European peoples came up short.[14] Since they were not sovereign, 'they lacked rights under international law and could thus be legally attacked and conquered, all in the name of transforming and civilizing them'.[15] Colonialism produced and depended upon racial hierarchies, denigrating cultures that were distinct from European civilization.[16] Within a racialized dynamic, there was no contradiction between purported European objectivity and non-European subjectivity.[17]

Racial colonial rule entrenched exclusive territorial sovereignty which, although it began in Westphalia, only took hold in the nineteenth century. Positivist jurists broke with the idea of a universally valid natural law and settled on a position that international law was the exclusive domain of civilized societies.[18] In defining sovereignty, jurists relied on the presumed inferiority of colonized peoples which they related to

[11] Lamis Elmy Abdelaaty, *Discrimination and Delegation: Explaining State Responses to Refugees* (Oxford University Press 2021).
[12] Liza Schuster, 'Common Sense or Racism? The Treatment of Asylum-Seekers in Europe' (2003) 37(3) Patterns of Prejudice 233.
[13] See discussion in Antony Anghie, 'Rethinking Sovereignty in International Law' (2009) 5 Annual Review of Law and Social Science 291, 291.
[14] Francisco Vitoria (1480–1546) maintained that the Indigenous people of South America ('Indians') should be regarded as nations, but even here, not as equals. He also acted on behalf of the Spanish Inquisition.
[15] Antony Anghie, *Imperialism, Sovereignty and the Making of International Law* (Cambridge University Press 2005).
[16] Kerem Nisancioglu, 'Racial Sovereignty' (2020) 26 European Journal of International Relations 39, 43.
[17] ibid 44.
[18] ibid 48; Anghie (n 15) 53.

a lack of territorial control, society, or law.[19] Distinctions were made between the societies of Asia, Africa, and the Pacific,[20] with the lack of capacity to enjoy sovereignty also manifesting around extraterritoriality—the application of European laws beyond Europe—an issue I return to in the second case study.[21]

European sovereignty evolved, albeit in different forms. By the advent of the First World War, the discourse had shifted from non-sovereignty of the uncivilized to protecting the sovereign interests of 'backward' peoples previously under the control of the defeated Germans and Ottomans. As they declared, the League of Nations mandate system would guide the inhabitants of these territories to self-government and, in some circumstances, even to independence. By the end of the Second World War, several formerly colonized peoples achieved independence and *became* sovereign in international law. Anti-colonial nationalist movements also asserted themselves, forcing the doctrine of self-determination onto the United Nations (UN) agenda. Founding imperial members of the UN, we should mention, only had the peoples of Eastern Europe in mind when the concept was first articulated. Nevertheless, anti-colonial struggles soared, aided by European economic exhaustion, the emergence of the United Nations as a deliberative forum, and Third World alliances which combined to orient global society towards a decolonizing imperative.

The move towards sovereign equality, with formerly colonized nations declaring independence in their territory and claiming the right to self-rule, may appear to 'right the wrong' of racialized non-sovereignty. But the entrenchment of Eurocentric sovereignty as a fundamental doctrine ignores the fact that 'the evolution of sovereignty doctrine toward a more absolutist conception of the right to exclude non-nationals was driven by racist colonial ambitions'.[22] Indeed, with sovereignty comes borders, and with borders comes the right to include and exclude.

3. Establishing racial borders

By the end of the First World War, it was evident certain colonized territories would become 'sovereign', but not before border control was entrenched. European sovereignty demarcated borders that established an 'inside' and an 'outside' dichotomy, which included the unlimited power to decide and regulate admissions, while colonial rule perfected the restriction of the movement of Indigenous populations.[23] Borders emerged to police movement along a racialized spectrum. On one hand,

[19] For how jurists dealt with the fact that some European nations had treaties with Indigenous authorities, see discussion in Anghie (n 15) 56–74.

[20] ibid 84–86.

[21] Siba N'Zatioula Grovogui, *Sovereigns, Quasi Sovereigns, and Africans: Race and Self-Determination in International Law, vol 3* (University of Minnesota Press 1996) 44.

[22] Achiume (n 10) 488.

[23] T Alexander Aleinikoff, 'State-Centered Refugee Law: From Resettlement to Containment' (1992) 14 Immigration and Nationality Law Review 186, 187; Lucy Mayblin and Joe Turner, *Migration Studies and Colonialism* (John Wiley & Sons 2020) 67–70.

they contained Indigenous mobility while facilitating the forced movement of slaves and indentured servants; on the other, they enabled the migration of settler colonial populations. Indeed, in the late 1800s, settler colonial states formalized immigration and citizenship law around race to 'stratify the movement and rights of people across empires'.[24] For example, between the 1880s and 1910s, white settler colonies formed border controls to restrict Asian migration, and by the 1930s these controls were universalized as part of the foundation of sovereignty.[25] Likewise, nationality also tied colonized peoples to their regions and precluded their movement to the metropole.[26]

The UK established infrastructure for some intra-imperial mobility, but colonial subjects were legally re-categorized between 1905 to 1971 from subjects to citizens to migrants and were no longer permitted to enter the UK freely.[27] The French, however, were always suspicious of intra-imperial mobility and suppressed it through a series of controls, while the Dutch regulated the movement of non-native Asians to and within Indonesia.[28] These controls and exclusions were justified by 'racism and fears of the bad influence of "uncivilized" peoples' that eventually expanded globally.[29] As Haddad observes, First World states always claimed the right to exclude others from entry, enabling the hostile response to migrants, including refugees:[30]

> [R]efugees are not the consequence of a breakdown in the system of separate nation-states; rather, they are an integral part of the system—as long as there are political borders constructing separate states and creating clear definitions of insiders and outsiders, there will be refugees. Without the modern state there could be no refugees. It is a characteristic of sovereignty that the attempt to place all individuals within (homogeneous) territorial spaces will inevitably force some between the borders, into the gaps and spaces between states and thus outside the normal citizen-state-territory hierarchy. As such, refugees are victims of an international system that brings them into being, then fails to take responsibility for them.[31]

Racial sovereignty, then, did not just manifest in controlling one's borders, but dictating the degree to which others could control theirs. As I explain in the following section, the interplay between sovereignty, borders, race, and refugees is evident and nefarious.

[24] Mayblin and Turner (n 23) 70–71.

[25] Adam M McKeown, *Melancholy Order: Asian Migration and the Globalization of Borders* (Columbia University Press 2008) 2–3.

[26] Achiume (n 10) 459–62.

[27] Thom Davies and Arshad Isakjee, 'Ruins of Empire: Refugees, Race and the Postcolonial Geographies of European Migrant Camps' (2019) 102 Geoforum 214, 215.

[28] Adam McKeown, 'A World Made Many: Integration and Segregation in Global Migration, 1840–1940' in Donna R Gabaccia and Dirk Hoerder (eds), *Connecting Seas and Connected Ocean Rims Indian, Atlantic and Pacific Oceans and China Seas Migrations from the 1830s to the 1930s* (Brill 2011) 52.

[29] ibid 55.

[30] Mayblin and Turner (n 23) 88.

[31] Emma Haddad, 'The Refugee: The Individual between Sovereigns' (2003) 17 Global Society 297, 297.

4. Roots of the current regime: race, sovereignty, and borders

The modern international refugee regime is tied to the governance of borders and migration. A person is only a prima facie refugee when they have crossed an international border for reasons that warrant international protection, activating the legal procedures that may recognize them as a refugee. Borders function as gateways of inclusion and exclusion, and the manner in which exclusion is enforced is 'racially disparate'.[32]

The racialization of the refugee regime is tied to colonialism, the emergence of sovereignty as a fundamental right of states, and the regulation of borders. Colonialism refers to the subjection of peoples to alien rule and exploitation, while racism describes a system of domination and of power, based on the racialization of bodies that occurs through markers such as ethnicity, colour, culture, and/or religion where people are stratified into classifications of superior or inferior.[33] These function alongside socially constructed notions of race or act as proxies for them.[34]

In connecting the two, Fanon stated that in the colonial context:

> [I]t is evident that what parcels out the world . . . is . . . the fact of belonging to . . . a race . . . [In] the colonies the economic substructure is also a superstructure . . . The governing race first and foremost are those who come from elsewhere, those who are unlike the original inhabitants, 'the others'.[35]

Xenophobia, as a separate but related concept, also applies to refugees since they are literal 'outsiders', and face backlash from host populations because of their outsider status. Xenophobia intersects with race, influencing which people are viewed as outsiders and to what degree, but can be distinct from it, 'challeng[ing] the status of non-nationals as beneficiaries of the goods of national membership'.[36] Both are tied to sovereignty and borders. For instance, anti-refugee rhetoric in Lebanon, within the context of an economic crisis and rising sectarianism, became much more palpable in 2023, and Lebanese Armed Forces had been carrying out discriminatory raids against Syrians since April of that same year.[37] Refugees in particular, regardless of race or colonial encounter, have been made problematic.

Building on Fanon and other Afro-Caribbean scholars, Grosfoguel explains that certain subjects are racialized as inferior and live in the 'zone on non-being', while those racialized as superior live in the 'zone of being'. While they can still experience class, gender, sexual, and/or national discrimination, they do not experience racial oppression but racial privilege.[38] For those in the zone of non-being, 'the multiple

[32] Achiume (n 10) 448.

[33] Mayblin and Turner (n 23) 50–55.

[34] E Tendayi Achiume, 'Race, Refugees and International Law' in Catherine Costello, Michelle Forster, and Jane McAdam (eds), *The Oxford Handbook of International Refugee Law* (Oxford University Press 2021) 45.

[35] Frantz Fanon, *The Wretched of the Earth* (Grove Press 1968) 40.

[36] Achiume (n 34) 47.

[37] Amnesty International, 'Lebanese Authorities Must Halt Summary Deportations of Syrian Refugees' (*Amnesty International*, 11 May 2023) <https://www.amnesty.org/en/latest/news/2023/05/lebanon-halt-summary-deportations-of-syrian-refugees/> accessed 26 May 2023.

[38] Ramon Grosfoguel, 'What Is Racism?' (2016) 22 Journal of World-System Research 9, 11.

oppressions are aggravated by racial oppression'.[39] Conflicts that occur in the zone of being are regulated, largely, through non-violent means, and violence is the exception; in contrast, those in the zone of non-being are dehumanized, and conflicts are managed through violence and dispossession.[40]

To illustrate, Eastern Europeans, particularly the Polish, have experienced xenophobia in Britain. Processes of racialization stratify groups of people with the Polish racialized as *not-quite-white* and *not-quite-European.* Indeed, Larry Wolff shows that Western Europe 'invented' Eastern Europe in order to demonstrate its own superiority in comparison.[41] In the US, both Eastern and Southern Europeans were deemed less white than Northern Europeans, but they were positioned above those who were more obviously non-white.[42] Yet, the desire to dehumanize Middle Eastern and African refugees has resulted in the repositioning of Poles 'as white and European enough'.[43] In the end, Polish refugees are represented as lesser than British, but better than Africans.

The racism that emerged from the history of colonialism and organized the world along racial lines did not dissolve with the end of formal colonialism.[44] Even after decolonization, 'race persists as a neo-colonial structure, one that still allocates benefits and privileges to the advantage of some and the disadvantage of others'.[45] While decolonized states achieved independence and hence formal sovereignty in international law, it is precisely sovereignty that laid the foundation for racialized modes of exclusion that materialize via the Convention.

5. The adoption of the Convention

Throughout history, involuntary movements of people were common and arriving peoples experienced a range of receptions. Roman citizens fleeing a massacre in 88 BCE found sanctuary in a temple on the island of Kos, and advocated for their protection.[46] The Christian King of Ethiopia (*al-Habasha*) welcomed persecuted Muslims from Mecca, just as the new Muslim converts of Medina welcomed the Prophet Muhammad and his followers, circa 400 ACE, and promised them protection. This was after the people of the city of Ta'if rejected the new religious community.[47] In 1492, Ottoman ships travelled to Spain to collect Jewish refugees who were persecuted during the Inquisition; in fact, one third of Jewish refugees who left Spain settled in

[39] ibid 12.

[40] Ramon Grosfoguel, Laura Oso, and Anastasia Christou, '"Racism", Intersectionality and Migration Studies: Framing Some Theoretical Reflections' (2015) 22 Identities 635, 639.

[41] Larry Wolff, *Inventing Eastern Europe: The Map of Civilization on the Mind of the Enlightenment* (Stanford University Press 1994) 4.

[42] Matthew Frye Jacobson, *Whiteness of a Different Color* (Harvard University Press 1999).

[43] Alina Rzepnikowska, 'Racialisation of Polish Migrants in the UK and in Spain (Catalonia)' (2023) 49 Journal of Ethnic and Migration Studies 1517, 1517–21.

[44] Grosfoguel, Oso, and Christou (n 40) 641.

[45] Achiume (n 10) 45.

[46] David Scott FitzGerald, *Refuge Beyond Reach: How Rich Democracies Repel Asylum Seekers* (Oxford University Press 2019) 1.

[47] Khadija Elmadmad, 'Asylum in Islam and in Modern Refugee Law' (2008) 27 Refugee Survey Quarterly 51.

the Ottoman Empire.[48] In the mid and late 1800s, Great Britain had a liberal immigration policy and many European revolutionary exiles fled there. Between 1823 and the Alien's Act of 1905, no foreigner was refused entry or expelled.[49]

The international legal regulation of refugees, however, developed after the First World War, and initially a group approach reigned, with various treaties regulating Russian, Armenian, and other refugees. Early refugee law 'constituted a largely humanitarian exception to the protectionist norm, with the screening of immigrants eliminated for large groups of fleeing persons'.[50] This group approach applied to European and European-adjacent refugees. However, between the 1930s and 1950, refugee protection became more selective.[51]

With the unprecedented numbers of refugees in Europe, China, India, Pakistan, and Palestine after the Second World War, the newly established UN convened the Conference of Plenipotentiaries to discuss the adoption of a convention. The discussions at the Conference reveal that a more limited definition of a refugee was adopted, despite a greater number of states advocating a broader definition (though even the latter was qualified). The states invited to discuss the convention were those considered sovereign. This included recently independent states such as India, Pakistan, Egypt, and Iraq, but the discussions were mostly dominated by colonial and imperial states. Colonized territories were excluded altogether, and this coloured the discussions. While India and Pakistan were initially motivated about adopting a convention, their enthusiasm waned when it became clear the most dominant voices wanted to focus on European refugees.[52] Indeed, after recognizing the racial dynamics at play and that their refugees would be excluded from the ambit of the Convention, India and Pakistan withdrew from the discussions and never signed it.

France and the US were the most supportive parties to a Europe-centred definition, arguing that the parameters would cover those most in need of international protection.[53] The French delegate insisted that Europe was the centre of the refugee population and, in any case, most representatives attending the conference would be from Europe. The US delegate acknowledged the scope of the global refugee issue, but was dismissive of non-European refugee populations.[54] This was partly ideological: an individualized definition that focused on persecution would embrace East Bloc dissidents and embarrass the Soviet Union.[55] By contrast, and despite their colonial holdings at the time, the delegations of Belgium, the Netherlands, and the UK

[48] Kemal Kirisci, 'Refugee Movements and Turkey' (1991) 29 International Migration 545, 545.

[49] John Saville, '1848—Britain and Europe' in Sabine Freitag and Rudolf Muhs (eds), *Exiles From European Revolutions: Refugees in Mid-Victorian England* (Berghahn Books 2003).

[50] Hathaway (n 8) 137.

[51] ibid 140.

[52] Pia Oberoi, 'South Asia and the Creation of the International Refugee Regime' (2000) 19 Refuge 36.

[53] ibid 41.

[54] Ulrike Krause, 'Colonial Roots of the 1951 Refugee Convention and Its Effects on the Global Refugee Regime' (2021) 24 Journal of International Relations and Development 599, 601.

[55] James C Hathaway, 'International Refugee Law: Humanitarian Standard or Protectionist Ploy?' in Alan E Nash (ed), *Human Rights and the Protection of Refugees Under International Law: Proceedings of a Conference Held in Montreal, November 29-December 2, 1987* (Institute for Research on Public Policy 1988) 185–86.

promoted a universal definition.[56] Yet, what they meant by universal and international requires some unpacking.

The International Refugee Organization (IRO) was established by the ECOSOC in 1946. Despite the name, it was devised to deal with the refugees created by the Second World War, and one might assume this meant it operated solely in Europe. However, they were tasked with helping European refugees in other parts of the world as well. The IRO operated in India for the benefit of some 4,000 Second World War Polish refugees, despite the massive refugee movements resulting from partition.[57] The IRO then relocated the remaining 700 Polish refugees to East Africa when the British withdrew from India in 1948. The IRO also took over the British administered camps for Polish refugees in Southern Rhodesia. Tellingly, international meant European, wherever in the world Europeans happened to be. I note that Polish refugees were partially privileged as Europeans and afforded a certain standard of living in the camps; less than (Western) European settlers, but much better than the Indigenous Africans. They were kept separate from Africans, as Poles were perceived as not understanding the need for social distinctions.[58] Even after the establishment of the United Nations Refugee Agency (UNHCR), which took over the tasks of the IRO, imperial governments were reluctant to recognize Africans as refugees, despite the UNHCR's eagerness to expand its activities.[59]

The UK's support for a universal definition focused on the ability of the UK and Europe to control the movement of refugees, potential economic gains from immigration, and border controls.[60] Thus, even when 'events occurring in Europe *or elsewhere* before 1 January 1951' was included as an option—as a compromise between States that wanted a limited definition and those that wanted a more expansive one—Europe was still at the centre, and the default was the exclusion of those in the colonies. The very category of universal 'privileges [the] "European man" in the production of universal knowledges' as Grosfoguel argued.[61] That the universal was, in fact, particular had to be made explicit at an international conference of more than just European states. To emphasize the exclusion of colonial holdings, the UK extended the Convention only to the Channel Islands and the Isle of Man, despite holding significant overseas territories.[62] Article 40(1) enabled signatory states to extend the Convention to 'all or any of the territories for the international relations of which it is responsible'. The Netherlands, another state favouring the 'universal' definition, also insisted that the Convention did not apply to its Indonesian colonies.[63] The international and the universal ended at European borders.

[56] Krause (n 54) 607; Edwin O Abuya, Ulrike Krause, and Lucy Mayblin, 'The Neglected Colonial Legacy of the 1951 Refugee Convention' (2021) 59 International Migration 265, 266.

[57] Jochen Lingelbach, 'Refugees in the Imperial Order of Things: Citizen, Subject, and Polish Refugees in Africa (1942–50)' (2022) 69 Africa Today 14, 26.

[58] ibid.

[59] ibid.

[60] Krause (n 54) 611.

[61] Ramón Grosfoguel, 'Decolonizing Western Universalisms: Decolonial Pluri-Versalism from Aime Cesaire to the Zapatistas 1' in João M Paraskeve (ed), *Towards a Just Curriculum Theory* (Routledge 2017) 90.

[62] Lucy Mayblin, 'Colonialism, Decolonisation, and the Right to be Human:Britain and the 1951 Geneva Convention on the Status of Refugees' (2014) 27(3) Journal of Historical Sociology 423, 433.

[63] Krause (n 54).

It is worth mentioning that these States were not averse to sending humanitarian aid to refugee populations outside their territory. For example, the UK supported Korean refugees financially in the 1950s.[64] But there is a material difference between discretionary aid for political or humanitarian purposes, and the granting of fundamental rights and the right of access. While providing valuable assistance, these agencies helped contain refugees outside the borders of European states.

Ultimately, the Convention imagined one type of refugee: the individual refugee fleeing persecution in Europe, despite many refugee crises around the world at the same time. It was supportive of Western political and ideological goals, and by default excluded all other types of refugees. The 1967 Protocol removed the temporal and geographical limitations, opening up Convention protection to everyone regardless of their national origins, but the individualized definition remained intact. This narrowness of what is to be considered 'fear of persecution' would be used to stem the arrival of Third World refugees for generations.[65]

6. The thread of exclusion and modern-day manifestations

Refugee law has come a long way since 1951. For example, juridical interpretations of the Convention and developments in human rights law have expanded the scope of grounds for claiming asylum.[66] Yet, as Behrman points out, key aspects that enable exclusion remain intact. These include: the lack of a *right* to asylum; states' inherent power to decide on access to their territories; the burden on refugees to prove their claim; and states' retention of the right to decide on the procedures for assessing any asylum claim. Alongside a Europe-centred definition, these aspects have produced 'a two-tiered protection scheme that shields Western states from most Third World asylum seekers'.[67] As Hathaway explains, the narrow and individualized definition could be conveniently interpreted to align with States' interests, while expanding the humanitarian activities of international agencies to ensure that refugees are contained within their regions.[68] This duality is inherent to a regime born from existing structures of racial sovereignty and border control. In the following subsections, I examine how this regime enables the exclusion of Palestinian refugees and the externalization of refugee processing.

[64] Mayblin (n 62) 432.

[65] Hathaway (n 55) 186.

[66] For example, many states now include gender within the meaning of 'membership of a particular social group', enabling women suffering from some forms of gender-based violence to claim asylum. This is not without its problems, as it is far from uniform, and it is women who suffer from more exoticized forms of violence that are accepted. See Catherine Dauvergne, 'Women in Refugee Jurisprudence in Cathryn Costello, Michelle Foster, and Jane McAdam (eds), *The Oxford Handbook of International Refugee Law* (Oxford University Press 2021); Susan Musarrat Akram, 'Orientalism Revisited in Asylum and Refugee Claims' (2000) 12 International Journal of Refugee Law 7.

[67] Hathaway (n 8) 144.

[68] ibid 187.

6.1 Palestinian refugees

Palestinian refugees were discussed during the Conference of Plenipotentiaries, in large part because Arab states advocated for them (particularly Egypt). At the time, two temporary UN Agencies were established to aid with the plight of some 750,000 Palestinian refugees forced to flee their homes in what became Israel: the United Nations Relief and Works Agency (UNRWA), which was to direct relief and works for 'Palestine refugees' registered by the Agency,[69] and the UN Conciliation Commission for Palestine (UNCCP), which was tasked with achieving a final settlement of the Palestine question. UNRWA operates in five territories and continues to have its mandate renewed to provide aid to Palestine refugees; the UNCCP is now defunct as it was prevented from carrying out its mandate.[70]

Both the Arab and European states wished to exclude Palestinians from the ambit of the Convention for different reasons. The Saudi Arabian delegate declared:

> The Arab States desired that those refugees should be aided pending their repatriation, repatriation being the only real solution of their problem. To accept a general definition [of a refugee] . . . would be to renounce insistence on repatriation.[71]

Western states, on the other hand, wished to exclude Palestinian refugees because the Convention would otherwise bind them to protect what they perceived as a new and large group of refugees.[72] What was new and large about them for European states was implied: 750,000 non-European refugees. The French delegate was more direct, stating that the problems of Palestinian refugees were 'different from those of the refugees in Europe'.[73] While they also fled their homes because of ethnic cleansing, the difference was not in their plight but their identity.

In an effort to ensure that Palestinian refugees would be cared for pending their return, the Egyptian representative suggested an amendment to 'make sure that Arab refugees from Palestine who were still refugees when the organs or agencies of the United Nations at present providing them with protection or assistance ceased to function, would automatically come within the scope of the Convention'.[74] This was the foundation for the inclusion of Article 1D, which reads:

[69] UNRWA is mandated to help 'Palestine' refugees, who are defined as those whose 'normal place of residence was Palestine during the period 1 June 1946 to 15 May 1948 and who lost both home and means of livelihood as a result of the 1948 conflict'.

[70] For more on the UNCCP, see Lex Takkenberg and Francesca Albanese, *The Status of Palestinian Refugees in International Law* (Oxford University Press 2020); Michael Fischbach, *Records of Dispossession: Palestinian Refugee Property and the Arab-Israeli Conflict* (Columbia University Press 2003).

[71] UNGA Third Committee (328th meeting), 'Statement of Mr. Baroody of Saudi Arabia' (27 November 1950) UN Doc A/C.3/SR.328, 359.

[72] James C Hathaway, *The Law of Refugee Status* (Butterworths 1991) 512.

[73] UNGA, 'Conference of Plenipotentiaries on the Status of Refugees and Stateless Persons: Summary Record of the Nineteenth Meeting' (26 November 1951) UN Doc A/CONF.2/SR.19, 11.

[74] UNGA, 'Conference of Plenipotentiaries on the Status of Refugees and Stateless Persons: Summary Record of the Twenty-Ninth Meeting' (28 November 1951) UN Doc A/CONF.2/SR.29.

> This Convention shall not apply to persons who are at present receiving from organs or agencies of the United Nations other than the United Nations High Commissioner for Refugees protection or assistance.
>
> When such protection or assistance has ceased for any reason, without the position of such persons being definitively settled in accordance with the relevant resolutions adopted by the General Assembly of the United Nations, these persons shall ipso facto be entitled to the benefits of this Convention.

According to Qafisheh and Azarov, these clauses were inserted to make Palestinian refugees' exclusion from the UNHCR's mandate temporary, as long as they were receiving protection or assistance from another UN agency, and to eliminate any kind of interpretation that would permanently exclude Palestinian refugees from international protection pending their return.[75] As Akram observes, this clause was 'intended as a contingent inclusion clause'[76] to affirm the particular circumstances of Palestinian refugees. This may indeed have been the intention of the Egyptian delegate, but once the debate began, the Iraqi delegate assuaged Western participants, noting that Palestinians were unlikely to emigrate to Western Europe because of the cost. The UK delegate agreed and, if they were to face such a situation, each European country would deal with it individually—a nod to their sovereign power to exclude, especially when aimed at non-European populations.[77]

As Charles Mills shows, racial categories are continually socially and politically reconstructed.[78] Neither domestic nor international law are neutral; the sovereign state and the law are 'part of the racial polity's apparatus of subordination, codifying whiteness and enforcing racial privilege'.[79] Palestinians, indeed, are negatively racialized, and the refugee regime, though outwardly and seemingly race-neutral, reproduces racial categories through the exercise of sovereignty and state power. Hence, Palestine refugees continue to be victimized by the international refugee regime through its exclusions.[80] What was meant to be a temporary condition has morphed into three generations of camp living, occupation, secondary displacement, and instability—a way of life rather than an 'aberrative blip'.[81] As the *other* of the Refugee Convention, Palestinians are confined to camps in the states where they first fled, and this

[75] Mutaz M Qafisheh and Valentina Azarov, 'Article 1 D' in Andreas Zimmermann and Terje Einarsen (eds), *The 1951 Convention Relating to the Status of Refugees and its 1967 Protocol: A Commentary* (Oxford University Press 2011) 547.

[76] Susan Akram, 'Palestinian Refugees and Their Legal Status: Rights, Politics and Implications for a Just Solution' (2002) 31 Journal of Palestine Studies 36, 39.

[77] Krause (n 54) 615.

[78] Charles W Mills, *The Racial Contract* (Cornell University Press 2019).

[79] Charles W Mills, 'Racial Liberalism' (2008) 123 Publications of the Modern Languages Association 1380, 1389.

[80] Noura Erakat, 'Palestinian Refugees and the Syrian Uprising: Filling the Protection Gap during Secondary Forced Displacement' (2014) 26(4) International Journal of Refugee Law 581; Jinan Bastaki, 'The Legacy of the 1951 Refugee Convention and Palestinian Refugees: Multiple Displacements, Multiple Exclusions' (2017) 8(1) Berkeley Journal of Middle East and Islamic Law 1; Thomas McGee, 'From Syria to Europe: Experiences of Stateless Kurds and Palestinian Refugees from Syria Seeking Protection in Europe' (*Institute on Statelessness and Inclusion*, January 2019), <https://files.institutesi.org/from_Syria_to_Europe.pdf> accessed 19 July 2024.

[81] Diana Allan, 'The Long Turning: A Palestinian Refugee in Belgium' (2020) 35 Cultural Anthropology 225, 226.

containment is accepted and normalized; indeed, early interpretations of Article 1D insisted that it was solely an exclusion clause, unless UNRWA was *fully* terminated.[82] Various courts have limited the interpretation of Article 1D, effectively confining Palestinians to UNRWA camps in host territories, unless they were being individually persecuted or their lives were at risk.[83]

Moreover, UNRWA suffers severe funding shortfalls, and with the exception of Jordan, Palestinians are stateless in their host states, being victim to the various governments that privilege or scapegoat them, making their mobility in a world of citizenship, status, passports, and visas even more precarious. Abu Laban and Barkan argue that these categories are not race-neutral but are 'part of the continued exercise and reproduction of state power. In particular, these categories are part of the continued imperialism and an ideological privileging of a constructed and hegemonic whiteness.'[84] Camps are not a temporary measure to keep refugees alive, 'but rather to park and guard all kinds of undesirable populations'.[85]

More recent European jurisprudence acknowledges the inclusion paragraph of Article 1D, interpreting the cessation of protection and assistance as the responsible agency's *inability* to provide protection or assistance.[86] Lawyers and advocates for Palestinian refugees continue to critique what they view as a restrictive application of Article 1D, but the reality is that the Convention was designed to enable sovereign states to decide how to interpret its provisions. Western states' misgivings about granting Palestinians access to signatories of the Convention are reflected in the interpretations we find today, notwithstanding challenges by civil society, advocates, and some courts. Due to the conditions in the Gaza Strip resulting from the Israeli blockade—implemented in 2007—and several large-scale attacks, the UNHCR stated in 2022 that these conditions may constitute an objective reason for bringing Palestine refugees from Gaza within the scope of Article 1D(2)—meaning that they should *ipso facto* benefit from the Convention in whichever state party they flee to.[87] With the genocide in Gaza unfolding since October 2023 and into 2025, those in Gaza—the majority of whom are refugees and descendants of the refugees of 1948—have been unable to flee due to deliberate border closures. Those who have managed to escape have not been met with the same reception as other groups; Australia was criticized for not creating specific visas like they did for Ukrainians for example.[88] In December 2023, the Netherlands paused its work on applications from Palestinian asylum-seekers,

[82] Takkenberg and Albanese (n 70) 107.

[83] Gábor Győző, 'Palestinians and Article 1D' *(Rights in Exile*, 1 March 2013) <http://rightsinexile.tumblr.com/post/44317910924/palestinians-and-article-1d> accessed 19 July 2024; Qafisheh and Azarov (n 75).

[84] Yasmeen Abu-Laban and Abigail B Bakan, 'The Racial Contract: Israel/Palestine and Canada' (2008) 14 Social Identities 637, 638.

[85] Michel Agier, *Managing the Undesirables* (Polity 2011) 3.

[86] Case C-31/09 *Bolbol v. Bevándorlási és Állampolgársági Hivatal* [2010] ECR I-05539; Case C-364/11 *El Kott (Mostafa Abed El Karem) and Others v Bevándorlási és Állampolgársági Hivatal* (Judgment of 19 December 2012), EU:C:2012:826

[87] UNHCR, 'UNHCR Position on Returns to Gaza' (UNHCR, March 2022) <https://www.refworld.org/policy/countrypos/unhcr/2022/en/124067> accessed 26 May 2024.

[88] Rafqa Touma, 'Fleeing Bloodshed in Gaza, Palestinians Arriving in Australia Find They Have No Place to Call Home' *The Guardian* (26 March 2024) <https://www.theguardian.com/australia-news/2024/mar/26/gaza-palestine-immigrants-australia-cancelled-visas> accessed 8 July 2024.

necessitating an order from the highest administrative court to compel the state to resume processing in April the following year.[89] Advocate General Nicholas Emiliou advised in January 2024 that for the purposes of Article 1D, UNRWA's aid and assistance in Gaza can be considered to have ceased.[90] It remains to be seen whether Palestinians will be able to benefit from Convention protections in the EU.

6.2 Externalizing 'protection'

The removal of the geographical and temporal limitations by the 1967 Protocol resulted in a marked increase in 'remote controls', as the removal of the geographical limitation made it more difficult for Global North states to select refugees according to their geopolitical interests and racial preferences.[91] Indeed, use of remote controls intensified after the end of the Cold War,[92] which also coincided with the rise of Third World refugees.

Remote controls refer to processes outside a state's territories that keep people away from their borders.[93] They are a mechanism for externalizing refugee processing on non-entrée regimes. Indeed, since the Convention limits state sovereignty, however minimally, and places obligations upon states when refugees reach their borders and apply for asylum, many states with the resources opt for externalization. The measures include containment, extraterritorial processing and detention, third country and maritime interception, and international agreements with transit countries.[94] The profile of states with such measures is staggering.[95] Denmark was one of the first states to advocate for exporting camps outside of Europe.[96] The idea took root and was picked up by the UK, Spain, and the Netherlands, who lobbied to make it official EU policy. One of the reasons for containing refugees in camps outside of Europe was that they would have a 'similar environment and people'.[97]

[89] Molly Quell, 'Dutch High Court Orders Immigration Office to Restart Claims Process for Palestinians' (*Courthouse News Service*, 24 April 2024) <https://www.courthousenews.com/dutch-high-court-orders-immigration-office-to-restart-claims-process-for-palestinians/> accessed 8 July 2024.

[90] Case C-563/22 *SN, LN v Zamestnik-predsedatel na Darzhavna agentsia za bezhantsite*, ECLI:EU:C:2024:494 (Opinion of AG Emiliou, 11 January 2024).

[91] FitzGerald (n 46) 44.

[92] Asher Lazarus Hirsch, 'The Borders beyond the Border: Australia's Extraterritorial Migration Controls' (2017) 36 Refugee Survey Quarterly 48, 54; FitzGerald (n 46) 18.

[93] Coined by Aristade Zolberg. See Aristide Zolberg, 'The Archaeology of Remote Control' in Andreas Fahrmeir, Olivier Faron, and Patrick Weil (eds), *Migration Control in the North Atlantic World: The Evolution of State Practices in Europe and the United States from the French Revolution to the Inter-War Period* (Berghahn Books 2003).

[94] FitzGerald (n 46).

[95] David Scott FitzGerald and David Cook-Martín, *Culling the Masses: The Democratic Origins of Racist Immigration Policy in the Americas* (Harvard University Press 2014); Laura Madokoro, *Elusive Refuge: Chinese Migrants in the Cold War* (Harvard University Press 2016); FitzGerald (n 45).

[96] Martin Lemberg-Pedersen, 'Losing the Right to Have Rights: EU Externalization of Border Control' in Erik André Anderson and Eva Maria Lassen (eds), *Europe and the Americas: Transatlantic Approaches to Human Rights* (Brill Nijhoff 2015) 400.

[97] ibid.

It would be beyond the scope of this chapter to cross-examine all measures and trace their development,[98] so I will focus on the deportation of asylum seekers to so-called safe third countries or for offshore processing and the legal justifications that purport to be consistent with the Convention. Several safe third country regimes currently exist: the EU–Dublin Regulation, the EU–Turkey Deal, the United States–Canada Safe Third Country Agreement, and other individual state measures, such as Australia's numerous offshore processing regulations, and the UK's Rwanda programme.[99] It is commonly seen that since the Convention does not explicitly bind states to process asylum cases on their territory and does not expressly prohibit reliance on protection elsewhere, such measures are, at best, legal and, at worst, neutral.

6.2.1 Legal justifications

Australia has notorious non-entrée policies targeted specifically at people who arrive by boat. Through legal manipulation, Australia's Christmas Island is classified as *excised territory* where those seeking asylum are not able to apply for protection under Australian law. Other measures include imposing indefinite mandatory detention on asylum seekers. To better understand Australia's questionable approach towards refugee protection, we turn to the 2011 High Court decision regarding the 'Malaysia Solution'.

In 2011, Australia signed an agreement with Malaysia to transfer up to 800 asylum seekers. Assessment claims would be carried out by the UNHCR in Malaysia, and Australia would in return resettle a greater number of refugees who were in Malaysia. Malaysia is not a party to the Convention and therefore deported refugees cannot apply for asylum. Though Malaysia was declared to have satisfied the requirements of an 'offshore processing country' set out under the 1958 Migration Act, the High Court ruled to the contrary. They stated that the relevant law speaks of countries that provide protections to those recognized as refugees including, but not limited to, protection against refoulement.[100] The Court decided that Malaysia did not satisfy these requirements. However, the Court also stated that Article 33.1 of the Convention 'nevertheless permits removal of a refugee to a "safe" third country'.[101] Indeed, the Australian Parliament subsequently passed legislation in 2013 removing the requirements set out in the Migration Act,[102] while passing further laws to enable offshore processing. Australia has since implemented several policy changes due to legal challenges, deteriorating human rights conditions, and reputational impact, but it remains that Australia does not permit those who arrive by boats to access asylum, a

[98] Moreno-Lax has traced the development as well as the legal arguments: Violeta Moreno-Lax, 'The Legality of the "Safe Third Country" Notion Contested: Insights from the Law of Treaties' in Guy S Goodwin-Gill and Philippe Weckel (eds), *Migration & Refugee Protection in the 21st Century: Legal Aspects* (Martinus Nijhoff 2015).

[99] Before it was scrapped by the Labour government.

[100] *Plaintiff M70/2011 v Minister for Immigration and Citizenship; and Plaintiff M106 of 2011 v Minister for Immigration and Citizenship* [2011] HCA 32, 31 August 2011, [123].

[101] ibid [5].

[102] Australia Migration Amendment (Unauthorised Maritime Arrivals and Other Measures) Act 2013 (No 35, 2013).

position construed as legal by the Australian courts.[103] In the end, it is the condition of offshore processing and detention, and neither the concept itself nor the racial dynamics at play, that may render it illegal.

A similar measure was announced by the UK in 2022. Instead of processing applicants on British territory, the UK would deport anyone who arrived there to seek asylum without a visa or permission to enter. The UK signed an memoranda of understanding (MoU) with Rwanda, bypassing Parliamentary scrutiny of the instrument. The policy was challenged, but the UK High Court ruled that the Rwanda option was legal and consistent with the Convention and the UK's human rights obligations.[104] The judges disagreed that the Convention imposed an obligation upon states to examine asylum applications, rather, the only commitment was not to return the individual to where they might be threatened on the basis of a Convention ground. They stated:

> . . . Article 31 *does not prevent a state expelling a refugee.* States must not act in breach of article 33; removal that is not contrary to article 33 is not a penalty for the purposes of article 31.[105]

In concluding that Article 31 (impermissibility of penalizing a refugee for unauthorized entry) does not prohibit deportation to a safe third country, the judges considered the *travaux préparatoires*, and quoted the Colombian, Dutch, and Canadian delegates during the Conference of Plenipotentiaries that expulsion was permitted.[106] The judges allowed an appeal on some grounds, including whether the Rwanda plans constitute a penalty under the Convention. The Court of Appeal found that, in fact, it was not a safe third country, making the removal of asylum seekers to Rwanda unlawful. Still, the principle of removing asylum seekers to a safe third country was not proscribed, and doing so would be compatible with the Convention.[107] While the new Prime Minister announced that he would scrap the Rwanda scheme after the victory of the Labour party in the 2024 elections, his reasoning was that '[i]t's never been a deterrent'.[108] The issue was not that it violated refugee rights or that it was inhumane, but that it would not actually deter asylum seekers.

The 1967 Protocol's undoing of the geographical or racial limitation has pushed states to turn the Convention into a discretionary instrument, allowing them to pick and choose their worthy refugees based on geopolitical and racial considerations.

[103] Azadeh Dastyari and Asher Hirsch, 'Australia's Extraterritorial Border Control Policies' in Jillian Robin Chambers, Kathryn Rae Libal, and Molly Katrina Land (eds), *Beyond Borders: The Human Rights of Non-Citizens at Home and Abroad* (Cambridge University Press 2021); Helen Davidson, 'Almost 300 Asylum Seekers Prevented from Sailing to Australia in Past Year' *The Guardian* (11 November 2018) <https://www.theguardian.com/australia-news/2018/nov/12/hundreds-of-asylum-seekers-disrupted-while-trying-to-sail-to-australia-in-past-year> accessed 28 August 2019.

[104] *AAA and others v Secretary of State for the Home Department* [2022] EWHC 3230 (Admin).

[105] ibid [121]–[125] (emphasis added).

[106] ibid [124].

[107] *R (AAA) v SSHD* [2023] EWCA Civ 745.

[108] Al Jazeera, 'Keir Starmer Says Scrapping UK's Rwanda Migrant Deportation Plan' (*Al Jazeera*, 6 July 2024) <https://www.aljazeera.com/news/2024/7/6/keir-starmer-says-scrapping-uks-rwanda-migrant-deportation-plan> accessed 7 July 2024.

The reception of Ukrainian refugees verifies this. The same states enacting safe third country protocols have authorized more generous treatment of Ukrainian refugees. Like some other countries, Australia adopted the Temporary Humanitarian Concern Visa, providing Ukrainians with working rights, free English language tuition, and support under the government funded Humanitarian Settlement Programme for six months. The Department of Home Affairs intended to transition Ukrainian nationals to another type of visa (subclass 786 visa), which grants expanded benefits for three years. The EU also granted temporary protection to all Ukrainians and long-term foreign residents and invoked, for the first time, a 2001 directive that allowed displaced people the opportunity to stay, work, and send children to school, something notably missing for the refugees that came before. This directive was not applied to Syrians in 2015, and the EU's rhetoric towards Afghans fleeing in 2021 after the US and coalition withdrawal was about containment.[109] While the UK has been criticized for its response to Ukrainian refugees in comparison to EU countries (the UK still required a visa for Ukrainian nationals), it did not place a cap on the number of Ukrainians eligible to be sponsored by a UK resident (Homes for Ukraine scheme), and has issued over 119,000 visas.[110] Sponsored Ukrainians were allowed to work, receive public funds, and access public services for an initial period of three years.

Most stark in contrast is the Visegrad states' response to Ukrainian refugees compared to their response to previous groups of Syrians and Afghans. In the context of non-white refugees, Hungary erected a 13-foot razor-wire fence along its border with Serbia in order to keep them out. Prime Minister Victor Orban stated that: 'we do not want to be multi-colored by being mixed . . . with others . . . The experience of slow migration which we see in Western Europe if we go to a city like one of your cities, frankly, I see nothing attractive in that . . . We do not want to be a multi-colored country.'[111] Poland also built a border fence, started to build a wall, and passed legislation to make entry more difficult. Jaroslaw Kaczynski, leader of the ruling conservative Law and Justice Party, stated that immigrants could bring 'parasites . . . and diseases' to Poland.[112] Hungary, Poland, and two other central and eastern European Union states, rejected participation in a mandatory EU responsibility-sharing resettlement scheme.

However, these same states opened their doors to Ukrainian refugees. In Poland, the federal government passed the Act on Aid for Ukrainian citizens, which allowed Ukrainian refugees the right to live, work, and access health care and government benefits. Both media and political rhetoric have focused on how Ukrainian refugees

[109] Human Rights Watch, 'EU's Generous Response to Ukraine Refugees Shows Another Way is Possible' (*Human Rights Watch*, 9 March 2022) <https://www.hrw.org/news/2022/03/09/eus-generous-response-ukraine-refugees-shows-another-way-possible> accessed 29 May 2023.

[110] United Kingdom Government, 'Homes for Ukraine Scheme: Frequently Asked Questions' (29 July 2022) <https://www.gov.uk/guidance/homes-for-ukraine-scheme-frequently-asked-questions> accessed 19 January 2026.

[111] Tom Miles, 'U.N. Human Rights Chief Calls Hungarian PM Orban a Racist' *Reuters* (6 March 2018) <https://www.reuters.com/article/uk-hungary-un-idUKKCN1GI272> accessed 29 May 2023.

[112] Henry Foy and Zosia Wasik, 'Immigrants Pay for Poland's Fiery Rhetoric' *Financial Times* (15 September 2016) <https://www.ft.com/content/9c59ba54-6ad5-11e6-a0b1-d87a9fea034f> accessed 29 May 2023.

were different from the 'other' refugees, frequently referring to their 'blue eyes' or European origins.[113]

Generalized xenophobia and host-state fatigue are also a reality. Many states stopped some of the benefits by mid-2022. Poland ended subsidies to Polish families supporting Ukrainian refugees in their homes in the summer of 2022. After 10,000 Ukrainians benefited from the scheme, Australia stopped applications for humanitarian visas from 31 July 2022, but other types of visas remained open, including the Protection visa.[114] It appears that the Global North is retreating to the group-approach to supporting refugees, while bypassing the Convention through ever-expanding extraterritorialization. The result is that most non-white refugees will be contained in the Global South, with some exceptions for select refugees, and European refugees will be able to access a better range of benefits.

7. Conclusion

In this chapter, I attempted to trace the thread of racialized exclusion in international refugee law, starting with state sovereignty, border regimes, and the inception of an international refugee regime that regarded the archetypal refugee as European and white. Initially adopted in a colonial context, the Convention perpetuates the racialization of borders by reinforcing the notion of certain states as truly sovereign and free, while excluding others. Its limitations, coupled with historic and ongoing racial biases within the refugee regime, hinder the provision of adequate protection for all refugees. Since the removal of the geographical and temporal limitations in 1967, and subsequently the end of the Cold War, states have intensified the use of non-entrée regimes, and domestic courts have more recently interpreted the Convention's provisions as allowing the removal of refugees to other states for any reason, effectively removing a state's obligations to refugees. The 2015 refugee crisis, largely Syrian but including Afghans, Iraqis, Liberians, and others from the Global South, exposed the flimsiness of the international refugee regime, while the 2022 Ukrainian refugee crisis affirmed its strength, a stark division erected along racial lines.

By contrast, the UNHCR, non-governmental organizations, lawyers, and activists have championed a more humanitarian approach to refugees. As Hathaway states,

> While laudable efforts are made by a variety of agencies to attend to the immediate needs of refugees often unmet by the narrow scope of legal protection, both emergency assistance and durable solutions are beyond their exclusive control and can be frustrated by the exercise of negative state discretion.[115]

[113] Moustafa Bayoumi, 'They Are "Civilised" and "Look like Us": The Racist Coverage of Ukraine' *The Guardian* (2 March 2022) <https://www.theguardian.com/commentisfree/2022/mar/02/civilised-european-look-like-us-racist-coverage-ukraine> accessed 29 May 2023.

[114] Australian Government, 'Ukraine Visa Support' (*Department of Home Affairs*) <https://www.homeaffairs.gov.au/help-and-support/ukraine-visa-support> accessed 29 May 2023.

[115] Hathaway (n 8) 133.

The adoption of the non-binding Global Compact on Refugees in 2018 was a further attempt by the UNHCR to address some of the limitations of the current regime. While it could help provide basic relief to greater numbers of refugees, it does not address the underlying racial foundation of the refugee regime; indeed, many have critiqued it as watering down what refugee rights do exist.[116] As always, those bearing the brunt of these policies are negatively racialized refugees from the Global South.

[116] T Alexander Aleinikoff, 'The Unfinished Work of the Global Compact on Refugees' (2018) 30 International Journal of Refugee Law 611; Bhupinder S Chimni, 'Global Compact on Refugees: One Step Forward, Two Steps Back' (2018) 30 International Journal of Refugee Law 630; James C Hathaway, 'The Global Cop-out on Refugees' (2018) 30 International Journal of Refugee Law 591.

10

How the UN Guiding Principles on Internal Displacement Fail Climate and Racial Justice

Time for the Kampala Convention?

Nciko wa Nciko[*]

1. Introduction

In the face of climate change, internally displaced persons in the Third World have been normalized as disposable.[1] I define climate-induced internally displaced persons (climate IDPs) as those forced to flee their homes because of environmental shifts precipitated by climate change, but who do not cross an internationally recognized border. Their disposability is palpable when we situate them within the broader history of international migration and asylum.

Both migration and asylum have consistently operated as tools of racial governance, with whiteness or proximity to whiteness determining who enjoys the privileges of international mobility.[2] From the nineteenth to the mid-twentieth century, roughly 62 million Europeans emigrated to colonial territories in the Third World, a process that international law facilitated and celebrated.[3] In stark contrast, the same international law has obstructed the mobility of Third World peoples. From the first contact with Europeans, through the slave trade, to colonialism and now globalization, the mobility of Third World peoples has always been contingent on its ability to generate profit for the First World. The slave trade, for example, forcibly transported able-bodied Africans to lands from which Native Americans had been expropriated—and then expelled—so as to exploit their bodies and labour (while some writers exclude the Americas from the category of the Third World, I adopt a more inclusive framing—one that allows for engagement with Indigenous resistance and the colonial structures that continue to shape the region). Expropriation, expulsion, and exploitation were violent processes that provided the foundation for the world's economic regime, while also establishing a racialized migration and asylum framework.[4]

[*] The views expressed in this chapter are solely the author's own and should not be attributed to any of the institutions with which he is affiliated.

[1] Adapted from the definition IDPs in the Guiding Principles on Internal Displacement. OHCHR, 'The Guiding Principles on Internal Displacement' (1998) UN Doc E/CN.4/1998/53/Add 2.

[2] E Tendayi Achiume, 'Racial borders' (2022) 110 The Georgetown Law Journal 445.

[3] E Tendayi Achiume, 'Migration as Decolonization' (2019) 71 Stanford Law Review 1517, 1518.

[4] Carmen G Gonzalez 'Climate Change, Race, and Migration' (2020) 1 Journal of Law and Political Economy 109, 116.

Nciko wa Nciko, *How the UN Guiding Principles on Internal Displacement Fail Climate and Racial Justice* In: *Emancipating International Law*. Edited by: Mohsen al Attar and Claire Smith, Oxford University Press. © Nciko wa Nciko 2026.
DOI: 10.1093/9780198935605.003.0013

Throughout Europe's colonization of Africa and after political decolonization, the international mobility of Third World peoples continued to be circumscribed by this same violent triad,[5] normalized by and normalizing of a global racial hierarchy. A white episteme divided humanity into a hierarchy of *races*, based upon imagined phenotypical differences.[6] In the five centuries of the slave trade and colonialism, for example, 'black skins' were racialized as devoid of souls, sentiments, and societies:[7] "They could be bartered for beads; gunned down like wild animals; packed like sardines; shipped like cattle and harnessed to a plough like horses without any compunction."[8] The devastating impacts of this history of international (im)mobility have become impossible to ignore.[9] As the bodies and labour of Third World peoples were ruthlessly exploited, endless industrial production, consumption, and excretion of commodities for the First World went beyond the natural resource base.[10] Capitalist processes produced unimaginable volumes of greenhouse gas emissions that have surpassed our ecosystem's regenerative capacity, leading to an unsafe increase in global surface temperatures and triggering the current climate crisis.

Today, the most pressing impact of this crisis has been a new wave of mass migration among people from developing countries.[11] Indeed, Europe built its wealth and technological power through brutal, climate-destructive projects, leaving Third World states underdeveloped, with limited economic and technological capabilities to adapt to the climate crisis or address its resulting losses and damages.[12] Due to the increasing frequency of droughts, cyclones, rising sea levels, and floods, scores of Third World citizens are forced to abandon their homes, continuously relocating in an ongoing search for survival.[13] By 2050, climate change is expected to have displaced one billion people.[14]

However, in morbid fashion, one of the defining features of the present wave of climate change induced migration has been the further expansion of profit for the First World via the exacerbation of a racial hierarchy.[15] Young, light-skinned, able-bodied, and skilled migrants are preferred, while darker-skinned, poorer, older, or

[5] Achiume (n 3) 1519.

[6] Carmen G Gonzalez and Athena Mutua, 'Mapping Racial Capitalism: Implications for Law' (2022) 2(2) Journal of Law and Political Economy 127, 145.

[7] Issa Shivji, *The Concept of Human Rights in Africa* (1st edn, Codesria Book Series 1989) 1.

[8] ibid.

[9] Gonzalez and Mutua (n 6) 173; see also Achiume (n 3) 1518.

[10] Gonzalez and Mutua (n 6) 148.

[11] Intergovernmental Panel on Climate Change, *Climate Change: The 1990 and 1992 IPCC Assessments: IPCC First Assessment Report Overview and Policymaker Summaries and 1992 IPCC Supplement* (World Meteorological Organisation and United Nations Environment Programme 1992) 103. I recognize that the terms *developed* and *underdeveloped* carry significant ideological baggage. Tied to a discourse that has naturalized a linear evolutionary trajectory as well as global hierarchies and interventions—always at the expense of the Third World—these categories reinforce Eurocentric models of progress and obscure the structural violence of the international framework. My use of these terms is not uncritical nor should be read as an endorsement of the assumptions. Rather, I seek to reflect the dominant language within discourses I am analysing. Throughout I am attentive to the need for alternative framings that acknowledge the plurality of human societies.

[12] Julia Dhem, 'Carbon Colonialism or Climate Justice? Interrogating the International Climate Regime from a TWAIL Perspective'(2016) 33(3) Windsor Yearbook 129, 140.

[13] Achille Mbembe, *Necropolitics* (1st edn, Duke University Press 2019) 3.

[14] Gonzalez and Mutua (n 6) 173.

[15] ibid 158–59.

disabled are sequestered and repelled.[16] The vast disposable majority of climate migrants tragically perish from shipwrecks or electrocution on barbed wire fences at the borders of First World nation-states.[17] Many of them are contained within militarized encampments (to be) established by Third World states like Morocco,[18] Libya,[19] and Rwanda[20] at the behest of their First World counterparts and in exchange for an array of baubles. Those who survive the journey are fed into First World economies, populating sectors like agriculture, health care, and social care in France, Germany, Italy, Spain, and the United States that depend heavily on migrant workers.[21] Yet, they too are disposable, admitted only in numbers that align with the First World's demands, which fluctuate with every economic upswing or downturn.[22] In addition, even the favoured ones are usually only granted seasonal or temporary visas and in deplorable working conditions that would be illegal if applied to the local white population.[23]

Of course, the biggest volume of the disposable majority remains internally displaced within the borders of their own states.[24] It is this latter group of climate IDPs that I focus on in this chapter. I argue that the 1998 United Nations Guiding Principles on Internal Displacement (UNGPID or Guiding Principles)—a text that was never negotiated but *articulated* and *adopted*—were partly designed to control the movement of climate IDPs. Predominantly concentrated in the Global South or Third World states, the principles are designed to keep IDPs away from the borders of wealthy, First World nations. Moreover, the architects of these principles, Francis Deng and Roberta Cohen, two individuals I discuss at length later in the text, intentionally structured them to prevent climate IDPs from receiving reparations from the First World states who are largely responsible for the climate crisis. By restricting their movement and denying them reparations, Deng and Cohen relegated climate IDPs to a status of disposability, leaving them stranded in the so-called 'sacrifice zones', areas marked by neglect, hardship, and abandonment. Deng and Cohen's influence over the system is evident in the Guiding Principles as well as in their journal articles, books, and commissioned studies. These works often employed racist discourses that normalized the suffering and disposability of climate IDPs. In contrast to the racialized approach of the Guiding Principles, I propose the 2009 African Union Convention for the Protection and Assistance of Internally Displaced Persons in Africa (the Kampala

[16] Gonzalez (n 4) 126.

[17] Mbembe (n 13) 3.

[18] European Union, 'EU migration support in Morocco' (*European Union*, February 2023) <https://neighbourhood-enlargement.ec.europa.eu/system/files/2023-03/EU_support_migration_morocco.pdf> accessed 9 August 2024.

[19] Romain Philips, 'EU signs controversial migration agreements in Africa' (*InfoMigrants*, 21 May 2024) <https://www.infomigrants.net/en/post/57175/eu-signs-controversial-migration-agreements-in-africa#:~:text=Brussels%20has%20provided%20logistical%20and,ships%20to%20the%20Libyan%20authorities> accessed 9 August 2024.

[20] Peter William Walsh, 'Q&A: The UK's former policy to send asylum seekers to Rwanda' (*The Migration Observatory*, 25 July 2024) <https://migrationobservatory.ox.ac.uk/resources/commentaries/qa-the-uks-policy-to-send-asylum-seekers-to-rwanda/> accessed 9 August 2024.

[21] Gonzalez and Mutua (n 6) 156.

[22] Gonzalez (n 4) 125.

[23] ibid 126.

[24] ibid 121.

Convention) as a more humane and equitable pathway, one that could better address the needs of climate IDPs.

2. Containment and the denial of claims

Based on available estimates, climate IDPs constitute nearly 90 per cent of all IDPs.[25] Their true scale, however, is often underreported or overlooked in data collections, which typically focus on sudden-onset events like hurricanes, floods, wildfires, and other extreme weather events. This narrow focus excludes climate IDPs displaced by slow onset events, such as sea level rise, desertification, ocean acidification, glacial retreat, salinization, land and forest degradation, or loss of biodiversity, among others. These forms of displacement are not viewed as urgent or life-threatening, resulting in less attention and thus less data.[26] The fact that climate change is a threat multiplier—frequently accelerating displacement—complicates further the determination of the true scale of climate IDPs.[27] Despite the data-gathering challenges, the Internal Displacement Monitoring Centre has shown that climate IDPs are mostly in Third World states.[28]

Consistent with the racialized approach that dominates the regulation of international migration and asylum, the Guiding Principles indicate a clear priority: to keep Third World peoples far from First World borders. While seemingly cynical, Deng and Cohen admitted as much, declaring that preventing refugee flows played a pivotal role in the design of the principles:

> [The] international preoccupation with preventing refugee flows has also brought increased attention to the internally displaced . . . This spurred greater interest in protecting and assisting persons displaced within their own countries as a means of discouraging them from seeking asylum.[29]

As I argue later, notwithstanding the humanitarian tone presented in the Guiding Principles, the objective was anything but humanitarian. Rather, the containment of climate IDPs in Third World states is consistent with two mutually reinforcing desires of white supremacy: first, to safeguard the resources of life for First World peoples, which international mobility is believed to threaten and, second, to deny claims

[25] Kristy Siegfried, 'Climate change and displacement: the myths and the facts' (*UNHCR*, 15 November 2023) <https://www.unhcr.org/uk/news/stories/climate-change-and-displacement-myths-and-facts> accessed 9 September 2024.

[26] Advisory Group on Climate Change and Human Mobility and the Loss and Damage and Challenges of Human Mobility and Displacement Working Group, 'How to quantify and measure loss and damages associated with displacement' (*Loss and Damage Collaboration*, 16 May 2024) <https://www.lossanddamagecollaboration.org/publication/how-to-quantify-and-measure-loss-and-damage-associated-with-displacement> accessed 9 September 2024, 5–7.

[27] Siegfried (n 25).

[28] Internal Displacement Monitoring Centre, 'Displacement, disasters and climate change' (*Internal Displacement Monitoring Centre*, 31 December 2023) <https://www.internal-displacement.org/focus-areas/Displacement-disasters-and-climate-change/> accessed 10 September 2024.

[29] Roberta Cohen and Deng Francis, *Masses in Flight: The Global Crisis of Internal Displacement* (1st edn, Brookings Institution Press 1998) 3.

for reparations, either as financial support or access to environmentally sound technologies.[30] Third World states advocated for reparations to enable them to invest in adaptation mechanisms and provide direct support to IDPs.[31] In the absence of such reparations, climate IDPs are often displaced from their informal agrarian and pastoralist livelihoods.[32] Moreover, as informal agrarian and pastoralist groups, they were not groomed for industrial production and consumption, rendering them useless for employment in the formal economy and thus redundant within the frame of global capitalism.[33] As peripheral communities, they are treated as disposable, justifying their containment far from the centres of capital.[34]

To illustrate, consider the case of an 18-year-old Malagasy from the Antandroy community in the drought-stricken south of Madagascar as the archetype of a climate IDP. He lost his cattle and access to agricultural land because of severe drought and had little access to inadequate humanitarian aid. As a result, this young man was forced to flee, made homeless in a country where actions related to homelessness such as petty theft are criminal offences. Each night, he struggled to find a place to sleep in dignity, and each morning, he awoke to the grim reality that he could be harassed by the gendarmes because his situation violated the law, potentially leading to imprisonment in one of Madagascar's overcrowded prisons where inhumane and degrading treatment is common and survival is uncertain.[35]

The story of our 18-year-old Malagasy mirrors that of many displaced by climate change extremes in Madagascar. Yet, the Guiding Principles appear tone deaf, failing to recognize climate change as a cause of internal displacement and thus denying reparations for their forced displacement.[36] In 2022, for example, the International Organization for Migration (IOM) reported that only 8 per cent of the 90,219 individuals displaced from the southern part of Madagascar returned, with the majority compelled to re-establish themselves elsewhere.[37] The story is the same for many climate IDPs across Africa, where states still possess colonial-era laws criminalizing homelessness and petty offences related to it.[38] After being displaced, they survive as street

[30] Gargi Bhattacharyya, *Rethinking Racial Capitalism: Questions of Reproduction and Survival* (Rowman & Littlefield 2018) 178; UN General Assembly, 'Report of the Special Rapporteur on contemporary forms of racism, racial discrimination, xenophobia and related intolerance, E. Tendayi Achiume - Ecological crisis, climate justice and racial justice' (25 October 2022) UN Doc A/77/549, 11.

[31] Jordi Jaria Manzano and others, 'Measuring Environmental Injustice: How Ecological Debt Defines a Radical Change in the International Legal System' (2016) 23(1) Journal of Political Ecology 386. To understand which states, per UN language, fall into the 'Third World', see Dire Tladi, 'Representation, Inequality, Marginalization, and International Law-Making: The Case of the International Court of Justice and the International Law Commission' (2022) 7(60) UC Irvine Journal of International, Transnational & Comparative Law 60, 66–68.

[32] Michelle Yates 'The Human-As-Waste, the Labor Theory of Value and Disposability in Contemporary Capitalism' (2011) 43(5) Antipode 1679, 1680.

[33] Gonzalez and Mutua (n 6) 158–59.

[34] Yates (n 32) 1680.

[35] The author led field research on the internal displacement of the Antandroy community in 2024.

[36] Cohen and Deng (n 29) 16.

[37] IOM, 'Displacement Tracking Matrix, Madagascar—Baseline Mobility Assessment, Grand Sud' (*IOM*, September 2022) <https://dtm.iom.int/datasets/madagascar-baseline-assessment-drought-grand-sud-sep-2022> accessed 20 November 2024.

[38] See Southern African Litigation Center, 'Vagrancy-related provisions in various criminal laws and criminal procedure laws in Africa' (*ICJ*, 28 January 2018) <https://icj-kenya.org/wp-content/uplo

vendors and vagabonds, often falling afoul of the law,[39] with their livelihood and habitation as squatters placing them in a permanent state of illegality.[40] Climate IDPs are at risk of being displaced from one sacrifice zone to another.

Sacrifice zones are regions made dangerous or uninhabitable due to environmental degradation including, for example, the ancestral lands of the Antandroy in Madagascar.[41] While some climate IDPs reside in camps, a study commissioned by the UN Secretary General António Guterres verified that the majority live in slums, where they are exposed to further hazards that often lead to cumulative displacements.[42] As the World Bank noted, the suffering of IDPs is exacerbated in slums:

> Residents, especially the poor, are increasingly exposed to the impacts of landslides, sea level rise, flooding and other hazards, increasing risks in already vulnerable communities and impacting health and the spread of disease, livelihoods, and the very limited assets of the poor.[43]

It is also worth noting that an estimated 64.6 per cent of climate IDPs are between the ages of 5 and 24,[44] and half are women and girls, vulnerable to 'heightened levels of sexual and gender-based violence', common to other crises.[45]

Regrettably, the Guiding Principles contribute to the consignment of climate IDPs to a slow death.[46] Indeed, Deng and Cohen deployed racist discourses while working on the Guiding Principles, despite—or perhaps because of—their awareness of climate change as a major cause of internal displacement across the Third World, as I detail in the following section.

3. Intentional denial of claims

Before working on the Guiding Principles, Cohen held senior positions in human rights non-governmental organizations (NGOs) and the US government.[47] In the late

ads/2018/01/Vagrancy-laws-in-Africa-by-Southern-Africa-Litigation-Center-SALC.pdf> accessed 20 November 2024.

[39] Gonzalez and Mutua (n 6) 159.
[40] ibid 160.
[41] UNGA (n 30) 3.
[42] ibid 11.
[43] Judy L Baker (ed), *Climate Change, Disaster Risk, and the Urban Poor: Cities Building Resilience for a Changing World* (World Bank 2011) 1.
[44] United Nations, 'The United Nations Secretary-General's Action Agenda on Internal Displacement Follow-Up to the Report of the UN Secretary-General's High-Level Panel on Internal Displacement' (June 2022) <https://www.un.org/en/content/action-agenda-on-internal-displacement/assets/pdf/Action-Agenda-on-Internal-Displacement_EN.pdf> accessed 20 November 2024, 5.
[45] ibid 3.
[46] Jason Hickel, 'Reimagining the Human Environment Relationship: A New Political Economy for a Healthy Planet' (United Nations University Centre for Policy Research and UN Environment Programme, May 2022) <https://collections.unu.edu/eserv/UNU:8832/UNUUNEP_Hickel_RHER.pdf> accessed 20 November 2024.
[47] Francis Deng, 'Putting IDPs on the Map: A personal tribute to Roberta Cohen' (*Forced Migration Review*) <https://www.fmreview.org/brookings/deng> accessed 18 January 2024.

1980s, she joined the Refugee Policy Group, an independent centre for policy analysis and research on refugee issues.[48] This role allowed her to study the escalating crisis of internal displacement. She identified three main obstacles to meaningful collaborative intervention: (i) a strong adherence to state sovereignty that treated internal displacement as a domestic issue; (ii) the lack of an international legal framework to address the rights and needs of IDPs; and (iii) inadequate institutional responses to provide aid and protection.[49] Cohen concluded that internal displacement was not only a humanitarian crisis but also a human rights issue that warranted the attention of the UN Commission on Human Rights.[50]

In 1990, Cohen rallied support among other NGOs around her assessment and advocated for the recognition of internal displacement as a human rights crisis. Together, they urged the Commission to establish a mechanism for an international response.[51] Their agitation succeeded, leading the Commission to request that UN Secretary-General Boutros Boutros-Ghali investigates internal displacement, resulting in the appointment of Deng as the Secretary-General's Representative on Internal Displacement.[52] Deng's selection was influenced by his African origins as well as Africa's high number of IDPs. In fact, Deng's home country of Sudan had the highest number of IDPs globally, and his village, Dinka, was among the most severely affected by the crisis.[53]

It is also worth noting that, in 1992, Sudan was under a theocratic government seeking to impose Islamic rule over the predominantly Christian and animist southern region. This government employed starvation as a weapon of war, causing significant internal displacement within Sudan.[54] However, these violations were not the only cause of internal displacement. According to a report by the United States Agency for International Development:

> Droughts are one of the most frequently cited reasons for climate-induced migration, particularly country-specific internal displacement. Droughts can lead to temporary migration as individuals seek food and water to improve their livelihoods, as seen in western Sudan in the 1990s. Severe and persistent droughts can also result in permanent migration if livelihoods are abandoned, as observed in the Darfur [in Sudan] region in the 1980s.[55]

[48] Roberta Cohen, 'Developing an International System for Internally Displaced Persons' (2006) 7(2) International Studies Perspectives 87.

[49] ibid 88.

[50] ibid.

[51] ibid.

[52] ibid.

[53] OHCHR, 'Statement by Mr Francis M Deng Representative of the Secretary-General on Internally Displaced Persons - Commission on Human Rights—57th Session' (12 April 2001) <https://www.ohchr.org/en/statements/2009/10/statement-mr-francis-m-deng-representative-secretary-general-internally> accessed 18 January 2024.

[54] Roberta Cohen, 'Commentary: The Global Crisis of Internal Displacement' (*Brookings*, 11 November 2001) <https://www.brookings.edu/articles/the-global-crisis-of-internal-displacement-2/> accessed 18 January 2024.

[55] USAID, 'South Sudan Climate Vulnerability Profile: Sector- and Location-Specific Climate Risks and Resilience Recommendations' (*USAID*, May 2019) <https://www.climatelinks.org/sites/default/files/asset/document/USAID_The%20Cadmus%20Group_South%20Sudan%20Climate%20Vulnerability%20Profile%20to%20Improve%20Resilience.pdf> accessed 18 January 2024.

Deng and Cohen were aware of drought as a major cause of displacement. By 1992, when Deng's mandate was established,[56] an average of 239 annual natural disasters had been recorded throughout the 1980s, including droughts, floods, and wildfires.[57] Additionally, substantial scientific evidence had already linked drought to climate change, strongly supported by states worldwide. Indeed, while Cohen was advocating for the recognition of internal displacement as a human rights crisis, the Intergovernmental Panel on Climate Change (IPCC), the scientific body advising the UN on climate matters, released its First Assessment Report. This report connected the displacement crisis to climate change, forewarning that forced migration, including internal displacement, could become one of the greatest impacts of climate change.[58] The report highlighted that vast human migration was inevitable 'as millions are displaced by shoreline erosion, coastal flooding, and severe drought'.[59]

The IPCC Report played a crucial role in bringing countries together for the Earth Summit in Brazil in 1992. At the Summit, participants agreed on the United Nations Framework Convention on Climate Change (UNFCCC),[60] which recognized the connection between climate change and displacement, while acknowledging the responsibility of First World states. Under the UNFCCC, participants recognized that First World states had a greater responsibility to develop and implement integrated plans to protect and rehabilitate areas affected by drought, desertification, and floods, particularly in Africa.[61] Yet, Deng chose to ignore both the IPCC Report and the UNFCCC's articulation of the various causes of internal displacement.

In 1995, the UNFCCC held its first Conference Of Parties (COP), followed by COP 2 in 1996, and COP 3 in 1997,[62] each of which took place before the adoption of the Guiding Principles in 1998. Media coverage of the COPs and negotiations had a mobilizing effect:

> [W]ith the creation of the COPs, a routine was established that continuously brings the topic of climate change back into the media and public agenda, thereby applying pressure on political actors to prioritize it. This, without doubt, is the main function of the COPs.[63]

[56] OHCHR, 'Report of the Representative of the Secretary-General, Mr. Francis M DEng, submitted pursuant to Commission resolution 1997/39. Addendum: Guiding Principles on Internal Displacement' (11 February 1998) UN Doc E/CN.4/1998/54/Add 2.

[57] UN (n 44) 6.

[58] Intergovernmental Panel on Climate Change (n 11) 103.

[59] ibid 24, 42.

[60] Intergovernmental Panel on Climate Change, 'History of the IPCC' (*IPCC*) <https://www.ipcc.ch/about/history/> accessed 18 January 2024.

[61] United Nations Framework Convention on Climate Change (adopted 9 May 1992, entered into force 21 March 1994) 1771 UNTS 107, Article 4.

[62] United Nations Climate Change, 'Past Conferences Overview' (*United Nations Climate Change*) <https://unfccc.int/process-and-meetings/conferences/past-conferences/past-conferences-overview> accessed 18 January 2024.

[63] Jens Wolling and Dorothee Arlt, 'Media Coverage of International Climate Summits and Negotiations' (*Oxford Research Encyclopedia of Climate Science*, 26 September 2017) <https://oxfordre.com/climatescience/view/10.1093/acrefore/9780190228620.001.0001/acrefore-9780190228620-e-362> accessed 18 January 2024.

Each COP reaffirmed First World responsibility to address the effects of climate change including internal displacement.[64] Moreover, when Deng began his mandate, he was presented with a UN working definition that included natural and human-made disasters as causes of internal displacement. By 1998, this recognition was still reflected in the definition of who qualifies as an IDP.[65] Yet, Deng and Cohen still failed to connect 'natural and human-made disasters' to climate change.

A key element of the COP negotiations was the principle of Common but Differentiated Responsibilities and Respective Capabilities (CBDR-RC), which Third World states began advocating for at the UNFCCC.[66] Central to Third World advocacy was their desire to have the same developmental opportunities enjoyed by the First World. They argued that they had the right to develop but to do so in a manner that would allow them to adapt to the consequences of climate change.[67] To illustrate, a developmental strategy cognizant of internal displacement in the Guiding Principles might include planned relocations programmes financed by First World states to help climate IDPs rebuild their lives rather than being reduced to disposable populations.[68] Ultimately, the adoption of the CBDR-RC principle in the Guiding Principles would have highlighted the racial vulnerabilities and inequalities at the heart of the internal displacement crisis, and assigned greater responsibility for climate change mitigation, adaptation, and funding to First World states.[69] Yet, this too was excluded from the Guiding Principles.

Considering the global interests at stake, some readers will be surprised to learn that, contrary to standard practice, the Guiding Principles did not emerge from a compromise between states; in fact, they were never negotiated.[70] Rather, Cohen and Deng independently drafted the principles, including the containment of climate IDPs within national borders and the blanket denial of reparations. In the following section, I examine some of the racist discourses they deployed to get away with this.

4. Normalizing climate IDPs as disposable populations

Deng and Cohen are decorated diplomats, policy makers, and scholars. Yet, they ultimately succumbed to a familiar racist discourse in their conceptualization of the Guiding Principles. Rather than engaging the concerns of Third World states, Deng and Cohen replaced the responsibility of the First World with a fantasy. This fantasy posits that the problem of internal displacement, including when it is climate change induced, is cultural and civilizational and can only be resolved through the spread of

[64] United Nations Climate Change (n 62).
[65] See Guiding Principles (n 1).
[66] Dhem (n 12) 141.
[67] ibid.
[68] UN Human Rights Council, 'Planned relocations of people in the context of the adverse effects of climate change and disasters Report of the Special Rapporteur on the human rights of internally displaced persons, Paula Gaviria Betancur' (11 July 2024) UN Doc A/HRC/56/47.
[69] Dhem (n 12) 141.
[70] Adama Dieng, 'Protecting Internally Displaced Persons: The Value of the Kampala Convention as a Regional Example' (2017) 99(1) International Review of the Red Cross 270.

democracy and human rights in Third World states, the sites of the internal displacement crisis.[71]

To advance this familiar colonial narrative, Deng and Cohen abandoned their earlier understanding of internal displacement as a post-Cold War phenomenon. Initially, they noted:

> [I]n the four decades of their struggle, the United States and the Soviet Union contributed to the development and intensification of internal conflicts in Africa, in Asia and in Latin America. The two superpowers enlisted client governments and political or opposition movements in their 'cause', supplying them with arms, often directly, sometimes through proxies, and usually in large quantities . . . Many of the major instances of internal displacement during the 1970s and 1980s took place in regions and states that were the locus of cold war proxy wars.[72]

With the end of the Cold War, they were prompted to locate another culprit:

> If a preponderant number of situations of internal displacement are related to external political developments such as the cold war or its end, then internal displacement could decline as the world gradually adjusts to a new post-cold war equilibrium. On the other hand, if deep-rooted issues of collective identity are at the base of many conflicts, then the number of internally displaced persons might rise as the demand grows for local and regional autonomy and independence.[73]

Then, in an era where natural (and human-made) disasters were already displacing millions, Deng and Cohen reached the following startling conclusion:

> Thus, the hope remains that the spread of democracy and respect for human rights may yet show the way toward the easing of crises of national identity and internal displacement.[74]

For Deng and Cohen, internal displacement is a crisis of Third World states which requires their maturation into democracies and human rights-respecting polities. Before unpacking the racist undertones, it is crucial to reiterate that they applied this conclusion to both conflict and climate-induced displacement. In other words, to Deng and Cohen, even climate IDPs are victims of sociopolitical conditions. As per the Guiding Principles:

> Persons uprooted by natural disasters would not, however, qualify as refugees. They were included in the definition [of who are IDPs in the Guiding Principles] because in some natural disasters governments respond by discriminating or neglecting

[71] Mbembe (n 13) 98; Cohen and Deng (n 29) 23.
[72] Cohen and Deng (n 29) 19.
[73] ibid 23.
[74] ibid.

> certain groups on political or ethnic grounds, or by violating their rights in other ways.[75]

Some critics view climate change as a human-made disaster, and it is important to note that Deng and Cohen included this term in the Guiding Principles for reasons similar to those expressed in the above quotation.[76]

Returning to Deng and Cohen's colonial narrative, some may recognize a familiar form of racial prejudice. Their conclusion hints that the First World generally does not face crises of internal displacement because they are mature democracies with a strong human rights record, in stark contrast to Third World states. Moreover, as is common with civilizational discourses, the implication is that Third World states cannot do for themselves and must accept Western tutelage towards 'the spread of democracy and respect for human rights' rather than the accountability of First World nation-states for climate change-inducing industrial practices and lifestyles.[77] Deng and Cohen perpetuate a colonial-era racial dynamic.[78] Until Third World states mature, the Guiding Principles leave climate IDPs to survive on the charity of First World states and humanitarian organizations.

Masses in Flight: The Global Crisis of Internal Displacement, co-authored by Deng and Cohen,[79] captures the historical processes behind the Guiding Principles, as well as their preferred response to the crisis.[80] They note that humanitarian and development organizations should coordinate the delivery of aid to IDPs while regional organizations, such as the then Organisation of African Unity, should monitor and safeguard humanitarian relief operations, ensuring that charitable goods are not commandeered for strategic objectives.[81] *Masses in Flight* advocates for restating existing international human rights, humanitarian, and refugee law, excluding First World responsibility from the equation.

Rather than accountability, Deng and Cohen prefer to provide for the humanitarian needs of IDPs.[82] Seemingly benevolent, this approach perpetuates a racialized framework that prioritizes charity over justice, painting Third World states as savages and their IDPs as victims, with salvation appearing in First World principles and

[75] ibid 16. See Cohen reiterating this point in Roberta Cohen and Megan Bradley, 'Disasters and Displacement: Gaps in Protection' (2010) 1(1) Journal of International Humanitarian Legal Studies 1, 6–7.

[76] Cohen and Deng (n 29) 16.

[77] Walter Rodney, *How Europe Underdeveloped Africa* (Howard University Press 1982) 21.

[78] Dhem (n 12) 143.

[79] Two books were critical to Deng and Cohen's work on the Guiding Principles, one of which they co-authored. The other, which they co-edited, was a compilation of ten case studies of internal displacement, which was also silent on climate change as a cause of internal displacement. The case studies in question were on Burundi, Rwanda, Liberia, and Sudan in Africa; the former Yugoslavia and the Caucasus in Europe; Tajikistan and Sri Lanka in Asia; and Colombia and Peru in the Americas. The two books were *The Forsaken People: Case Studies of the Internally Displaced* and *Masses in Flight: The Global Crisis of Internal Displacement*. The co-authored *Masses in Flight* (n 29) was however more influential in defining the content and the structure of the Guiding Principles. See Cohen (n 48); Roberta Cohen and Deng Francis, *The Forsaken People: Case Studies of the Internally Displaced* (1st edn, Brookings Institution Press 1998).

[80] Cohen and Deng (n 29).

[81] ibid, ch 6.

[82] ibid ch 3.

NGOs. Deng and Cohen did not shy away from identifying the saviours, naming the European Union and other Western institutions:

> The European Union . . . in recent years has become involved in extending humanitarian aid in emergency situations, mediating political disputes, and contributing monitors to UN human rights and humanitarian operations in the field. The [Office for Democratic Institutions and Human Rights] would do well to seek out the European Union's expertise and support, particularly for its monitoring missions that involve the displaced. By coordinating its activities with those of the EU, it would also be able to put pressure on states that cause mass displacement.[83]

Deng and Cohen believed the purpose of developing a normative instrument on internal displacement was twofold: first, to strengthen existing protections by consolidating relevant norms into a single coherent document and, second, to address gaps and ambiguities in these protections.[84] They retained a team of experts to help them with this agenda. Walter Kalin and Robert Kogod Goldman played pivotal roles in outlining the factors to be considered as well as identifying the gaps. Like Deng and Cohen, they too did not attribute any responsibility to First World states and proposed two factors to guide the content and structure of the Guiding Principles: whether humanitarian assistance exists under international law as a right for IDPs and whether the international community has a duty to intervene in Third World states experiencing internal displacement that are either unwilling or unable to resolve the underlying crisis.[85] Principle 30 wraps these factors in diplomatic language:

> All authorities concerned shall grant and facilitate for international humanitarian organizations and other appropriate actors, in the exercise of their respective mandates, rapid and unimpeded access to internally displaced persons to assist in their return or resettlement and reintegration.[86]

Curiously, neither Kalin nor Goldman, Deng nor Cohen considered the UNFCCC regime, the COPs, or the CBDR-RC principle. They also did not engage with the idiosyncrasies of charity, as both an unpredictable and inadequate response to internal displacement,[87] nor with the many questions surrounding humanitarian intervention as new wine in the old, discredited bottles of manifest destiny and white man's burden. Last, they also dismissed the agency of climate IDPs, who possess valuable situated knowledge for managing their situation.[88]

83 ibid ch 6.
84 ibid 76.
85 ibid.
86 Guiding Principles (n 1) Principle 30.
87 Ugochi Daniels, 'As climate change drives displacement, what could ease the risks?' (*Reliefweb*, 17 December 2023) <https://reliefweb.int/report/world/climate-change-drives-displacement-what-could-ease-risks> accessed 9 August 2024.
88 Carmen G. Gonzalez, 'Racial Capitalism, Climate Justice, and Climate Displacement' (2021) 11(1) Oñati Socio-Legal Series 108, 124–28.

Absent a rigorous examination of the lives of Deng and Cohen, we are left to speculate about their motives.[89] Why did they scupper the momentum building around the CBDR-RC principle and ignore the UNFCCC in their deliberations? How did the Guiding Principles gain international recognition despite the absence of negotiations? Such an investigation could perhaps reveal why the figures behind the Guiding Principles reverted to racist discourses that relegated IDPs to a disposable status. Tellingly, Deng's personal tribute to Cohen reveals much about the hierarchies within their professional relationship:

> Our personalities were different but complementary. Anyone with a fraction of wisdom would not want to be on the opposite side from Roberta [Cohen], and I was fortunate enough to be naturally on her side and she on mine. Her challenge to my acknowledged tendency to favour a diplomatic, constructive engagement with governments contrasted with her inclination to be a more aggressive defender of human rights. This was always a source of creative tension between us but we both realised the value of our complementarity and, over the years, inched toward one another.[90]

Understanding whether their 'different but complementary' personalities influenced the final product of the Guiding Principles is something that a thorough life-writing investigation might uncover. Also revelatory are Cohen's declared views of Deng:

> Deng's position, like that of other representatives and rapporteurs emanating from the Commission on Human Rights, was a voluntary one with only limited human and material resources made available by the UN. Although governments had requested him to undertake a major legal analysis for the world community, it was basically left up to him to find the people and the funds to do it. When Deng travelled to New Haven to meet with legal scholars assembled from Yale and Harvard, the UN did not even pay his train fare; nor did it fund the meetings that brought together experts to discuss the relevant legal issues. It was from their offices at the Brookings Institution that the representative and I directly contacted individual lawyers and institutions to seek their pro bono involvement and solicited foundations and donor governments for funds to carry through the process of developing a legal framework.[91]

Much can be gleaned from these two statements alone: each appears to be fond of the other, albeit with important reservations. Ultimately, however, Deng's preferred approach was overshadowed by Cohen's, and, perhaps more importantly, by the Brookings Institution that bankrolled their efforts.[92]

[89] See generally David Sugarman, 'The Legal Boundaries of Liberty: Dicey, Liberalism and Legal Science' (1983) 46(1) Modern Law Review 102; Andrew Lang and Susan Marks, 'People with Projects: Writing the Lives of International Lawyers' (2013) 27 Temple International & Comparative Law Journal 437.

[90] Deng (n 47).

[91] Roberta Cohen, 'The Guiding Principles on Internal Displacement: An Innovation in International Standard Setting' (2004) 10 Global Governance 459, 462.

[92] While further investigation into their dynamics would be elucidative, such an exercise is beyond the remit of this chapter.

One element left out of their spirited engagement with IDPs is the race of the victims. Despite the absence of any mention of a racial hierarchy and climate IDPs not crossing the borders of their own states, racial injustices are embedded within the Guiding Principles, preserving both white innocence and white epistemic authority within international law.[93] I thus devote my concluding section to exploring an alternative approach that eschews the racial politics of the Guiding Principles.

5. An alternative framework: the Kampala Convention

The Kampala Convention offers potential pathways towards disrupting the denial of climate IDPs' rightful claims and their relegation to a disposable status. In 2006, African states determined that the Guiding Principles were inadequate for addressing the internal displacement crisis on the continent. Unsurprisingly, the two core criticisms were the failure to provide either an accountability framework or, curiously, any solutions.[94] Their dissatisfaction culminated in the adoption of the Kampala Convention in 2009.[95]

The Kampala Convention unequivocally identifies 'climate change' as a leading cause for internal displacement in Africa and provides for a framework within which to bring about accountability.[96] Conscious that an African Union treaty could not impose binding obligations on First World states, they established a competent authority that could hear claims of climate losses, damages, and adaptation needs as well as mobilize support for African states undergoing internal displacement. In this regard, the Kampala Convention empowers African states to convene their own COPs to deliberate bespoke approaches towards internal displacement.[97] The deliberations of this African COP (A-COP) can play a critical role in organizing African states around policy positions absent from First World mechanisms. Such positions might involve official condemnations of African states that collaborate in the containment of climate IDPs, comprador gatekeepers if you will.[98] Additionally, the A-COP could serve as a platform for actions such as collective refusals to repay sovereign debt, a quid-pro-quo for the First World's refusal to pay their climate debt, including reparations for displacement.[99]

The Kampala Convention is critical because Africa is experiencing the fastest rate of warming, leading to accelerating (internal) displacement.[100] To illustrate, instead of

[93] Achiume (n 2).
[94] Dieng (n 70) 272.
[95] ibid.
[96] African Union, Kampala Declaration on Refugees, Returnees and Internally Displaced Persons in Africa (adopted 23 October 2009, entered into force 6 December 2012) Ext/Assembly/AU/PA/Draft/Decl (1) Rev 1 (Kampala Convention) Article V(4).
[97] Kampala Convention, Article XIV.
[98] E Tendayi Achiume, 'Empire, Borders, and Refugee Responsibility Sharing' (2022) 110 California Law Review 1011, 1013–19.
[99] Manzano and others (n 31) 386.
[100] See for instance Agence Française de Développement (AGD), 'Climate change in Africa in numbers' (AGD, November 2023) <https://www.afd.fr/en/ressources/coping-climate-change-africa-numbers#:~:text=Africa%20is%20particularly%20exposed%20to,faster%20than%20the%20global%20average> accessed 4 August 2024.

investing in well-planned relocation programmes, African states such as Mozambique and Ethiopia are forced to prioritize debt servicing. In 2021, Mozambique spent $855 million on paying off its debt, which was more than the $759 million it needed for climate-related expenses.[101] Similarly, Ethiopia set aside $810 million for climate adaptation, but it was projected to spend three times that amount on debt payments between 2021 and 2022.[102]

There is thus an urgent need for all African countries to ratify the Kampala Convention and for other Third World states to adapt it to their contexts. Currently, only thirty-three out of fifty-four African states have ratified it. Equally crucial is the regular convening of A-COPs as envisioned by the Convention. Since the Kampala Convention was adopted in 2009, it is disheartening that only one A-COP was held in 2017.[103] Notably, the responsibility of First World states for climate change-induced internal displacement was not on the agenda.[104] Without addressing climate change as a cause of internal displacement and emphasizing an accountability framework, the Kampala Convention risks falling into the same stasis as the Guiding Principles. Much like climate IDPs, the Kampala Convention's future depends on the courage and commitment of African states to break with the Eurocentrism of international law.

6. Concluding remarks: escaping sacrificial zones

International law projects like the Guiding Principles on Internal Displacement are both desirable to and necessary for the First World.[105] Not only are they designed to keep climate IDPs away from First World borders, but they seek to prevent a reckoning with international law's racialized past and present. These principles are integral to the racial governance regimes of international migration and asylum, which demand that whiteness or proximity to whiteness determine who enjoys the privileges of international mobility or, in this instance, the privileges of livelihood and life. Indeed, these principles relegate climate IDPs to a disposable status, abandoned in racial sacrifice zones, where survival is precarious and death imminent.

Like the Guiding Principles, much of international law remains enamoured with itself, self-proclaiming its benevolence and humanitarianism.[106] Curiously, this fantasy cannot withstand the slightest scrutiny, yet is part of the same historical matrix

[101] Afronomiclaw, 'Debt, Climate Finance and Vulnerability: A Brief on Debt and Climate Vulnerable Countries in Africa' (November 2022) <https://www.afronomicslaw.org/sites/default/files/pdf/A%20Brief%20on%20Debt%20and%20Climate%20Vulnerable%20Countries%20in%20Africa.pdf> accessed 9 August 2024, 13.

[102] ibid.

[103] African Union, '1st Meeting of the Conference of States Parties to the Kampala Convention' (*African Union*, 3 April 2017) <https://au.int/en/newsevents/20170403/1st-meeting-conference-states-parties-kampala-convention#:~:text=Harare%2C%20Zimbabwe%205%20April%202017,implementation%20of%20the%20Kampala%20Convention> accessed 19 July 2024.

[104] African Union, 'Concept Note: First Session of Conference of States Parties for the African Union Convention for the Protection and Assistance of Internally Displaced Persons in Africa (Kampala Convention)' (3–5 April 2017) <https://au.int/web/sites/default/files/newsevents/conceptnotes/32304-cn-concept_note_-_cosp_meeting_2017.pdf> accessed 19 July 2024.

[105] Mbembe (n 13) 117.

[106] ibid 16.

that afflicts climate IDPs.[107] The slave trade, colonialism, and their enduring legacies concentrated the world's wealth within the borders of First World states and at the cost of a burning planet. Our unwillingness to confront international law's dubious past thus forces interlocutors of the regime to give in to the same racialized thinking that mis-colours the present.

I do not think Deng and Cohen were malicious; their approach and outlook were consistent with the state of international law and practice, developed in a manner to preserve a racially unequal status quo.[108] Today, this inequality in lawmaking demands the sacrifice of climate IDPs to protect First World societies from the climate-warming lifestyles they have come to expect.[109] In the face of accelerating climate displacement and its racialized dimensions, we are left to ponder if international law can transcend the entrenched Eurocentric biases that deny the humanity and rights of climate IDPs. Without such a transformation, these laws will continue to codify racial hierarchies and shield the First World from responsibility. By recognizing the racial inequalities perpetuated by the Guiding Principles, states could begin to dismantle the sacrificial logic that relegates climate IDPs to a disposable status. Only then might we move towards an international legal order that prioritizes the dignity and survival of all peoples over the selective security of a privileged few.

[107] ibid 22.

[108] Rodney (n 77) 10.

[109] Antony Anghie and JR Robert G Real, 'Teaching and Researching International Law in Asia (TRILA) Project: 2020 Report' (*Centre for International Law, National University of Singapore*, 28 May 2020) <https://cil.nus.edu.sg/wp-content/uploads/2020/06/TRILA-Project-Report-Final-compressed-v2.pdf> accessed 14 October 2024.

PART III

A RIGHT TO BE FREE FROM RACISM

11
The Intersection of Race and Economic, Social, and Cultural Rights

Raghavi Viswanath

1. Introduction

'The plunder of Black life was not incidental to America's rise; it was instrumental.'[1] Te-Nehisi Coates' powerful words are a scathing reminder of what racialized peoples have always known: that racism constitutes and is constituted by economic and social exploitation. It took a long time for this lived knowledge to be spoken; understandably so because racialized peoples' voices were suppressed.[2] In 1952, Frantz Fanon—one of the most influential anticolonial thinkers—remarked that 'the economic infrastructure is also a superstructure. The cause is the consequence; you are rich because you are white, you are white because you are rich.'[3] Fanon's observation is a window into the relationship between racism and economic structures, where racism can be explained as a systemic and structural phenomenon rooted in white supremacy.[4] It creates a hierarchy[5] that justifies the commodification of people belonging to oppressed races, including through economic, social, and cultural exploitation.[6]

This chapter argues that this understanding of the reciprocal relationship between economic and social structures and racism has yet to translate into economic, social, and cultural *rights* (ESCRs) within human rights law. ESCRs are legal entitlements necessary for survival, such as 'housing, food, clothing, water, health care,

[1] Ta-Nehisi Coates, 'The Case for Reparations' (*The Atlantic*, 22 May 2014) <https://www.theatlantic.com/magazine/archive/2014/06/the-case-for-reparations/361631/> accessed 23 April 2024. In its linguistic style, this chapter draws inspiration from the language protocol subversions attempted in the brilliant Italian translation of Grada Kilomba's book *Plantation Memories* by Marie Moïse and Mackda Ghebremariam Tesfau' (Capovolte 2021). Moïse and Tesfau' play with the protocols of the Italian language, particularly its rigidly gendered spellings and its rules of capitalization. Illustratively, their Italian translation capitalizes the N of Nero (Blackness) in order to signify that is a self-assertive label, and uses a small case b for bianca (whiteness) to signify that whiteness is merely a social construction. This chapter similarly capitalizes the B of Black or the I of Indigenous and uses small case for the w of whiteness (and similar terms such as eurocentrism embodying imperial or racial domination) to refuse the social superiority of whiteness.

[2] Anna J Cooper, *A Voice from the South: By a Black Woman of the South* (University of North Carolina Press 2017).

[3] Frantz Fanon, *Black Skin, White Masks* (Pluto Classics edn, Pluto Press 2002).

[4] Charles W Mills, *The Racial Contract* (Cornell University Press 1997).

[5] ibid.

[6] CLR James, *The Black Jacobins: Toussaint l'Ouverture and the San Domingo Revolution* (2nd edn, Vintage Books 1989).

Raghavi Viswanath, *The Intersection of Race and Economic, Social, and Cultural Rights* In: *Emancipating International Law*. Edited by: Mohsen al Attar and Claire Smith, Oxford University Press. © Raghavi Viswanath 2026.
DOI: 10.1093/9780198935605.003.0015

social security, and an adequate standard of living'.[7] The genesis of ESCRs in contemporary international human rights law can be credited to the sustained efforts of the 'Third World' movement, born in proud contrast to the 'U.S.-aligned West (the First World) and the Soviet-aligned Eastern Bloc (the Second World)'.[8] Following the end of the Second World War and the formal demise of colonialism in some parts of the world, newly independent states convened in Bandung in 1955 to forge a new vision of the 'Third World'. The 'Bandung ethic' rested on South–South cooperation, anti-imperialism, and the restoration of the agency of colonized peoples.[9] The centrepiece of the Bandung vision was human rights praxis, particularly recognition of the ESCRs of colonized peoples.[10]

An important victory for the Third World was the adoption of the International Covenant for Economic, Social, and Cultural Rights (ICESCR) in 1966, the first ever binding treaty to give teeth to ESCRs. For Third World states, the ICESCR represented an opportunity to remedy the economic inequities wrought by colonialism by introducing collective rights, imposing positive duties on states, and codifying a redistributive vision of justice.[11] Because Third World states were so actively involved in designing ESCRs, the ICESCR was also uncritically accepted as an 'anticolonial' instrument.[12] As more and more states ratified the Covenant,[13] its anticolonial status was elevated to an *antiracist* one more broadly.[14] This label is often validated by citing evidence of the Covenant's commendable recognition of the intersectionality of racial discrimination and violations of ESCRs. However, this chapter argues that despite their anticolonial origins, ESCRs are not antiracist. A study of the drafting history of the ICESCR and the contemporary interpretations of the Covenant reveals that it *entrenches* rather than combats racism.

The chapter proceeds in three parts. Section 2 contextualizes the racial state of the world in which the ICESCR was adopted and maps the Covenant's present engagement with racial discrimination when delineating state obligations towards ESCRs. Section 3 explains how the Covenant's engagement with race is informed by eurocentrism. It

[7] Claire-Michelle Smyth, 'Social and Economic Rights: The Struggle for Equivalent Protection' in Sean Egan (ed), *The Routledge History of Human Rights* (Routledge 2019).

[8] Michael Galant and Aude Darnal, 'Who's Afraid of the Global South?' *Foreign Policy* (15 August 2024) <https://foreignpolicy.com/2024/04/14/global-south-united-nations-new-international-economic-order/> accessed 23 April 2024.

[9] Obiora C Okafor, 'The Bandung Ethic and International Human Rights Praxis: Yesterday, Today, and Tomorrow' in Luis Eslava, Michael Fakhri, and Vasuki Nesiah (eds), *Bandung, Global History, and International Law: Critical Pasts and Pending Futures* (Cambridge University Press 2017).

[10] ibid; David Kimche, *The Afro-Asian Movement: Ideology and Foreign Policy of the Third World* (Praeger 1966).

[11] Matthew CR. Craven, *The International Covenant on Economic, Social and Cultural Rights: A Perspective on Its Development* (Oxford University Press 1998).

[12] Maya H Randall, 'The History of the Covenants: Looking Back Half a Century and Beyond' in Daniel Moeckli, Helen Keller, and Corina Heri (eds), *The Human Rights Covenants at 50: Their Past, Present, and Future* (Oxford University Press 2018).

[13] Ben Saul, David Kinley, and Jacqueline Mowbray, 'Introduction' in Ben Saul, David Kinley, and Jacqueline Mowbray (eds), *The International Covenant on Economic, Social and Cultural Rights: Commentary, Cases, and Materials* (Oxford University Press 2014).

[14] Daniel J Whelan, *Indivisible Human Rights: A History* (University of Pennsylvania Press 2011; Steven LB Jensen, 'Twentieth-Century Economic and Social Rights: Decolonization and the Global South' in Malcolm Langford and Katharine G Young (eds), *The Oxford Handbook of Economic and Social Rights* (Oxford University Press 2022).

theoretically teases out the relationship between eurocentrism and racism in international law, analysing how the genocide unfolding in Gaza lays bare the analytical and epistemic links between the two. Section 4 uncovers evidence of eurocentrism within the ICESCR both in the discourse on civilizing and economic development as well as in the epistemic makeup of those engaged in drafting the Covenant. These strains—rooted in the originary and the contemporary life of the Covenant—the section argues, sustain the 'racial international legal imaginary' within the Covenant.[15] Section 5 concludes by proposing ways through which the ICESCR can meaningfully engage with racism, invoking existing tools in its institutional toolbox, taking inspiration from the better practices of contemporaneous institutions.

The chapter's diagnosis emerges from its study of the contemporary interpretive and adjudicative practices of the chief interpretive bodies of the ICESCR to understand the extent of official engagement with the racial dimensions of ESCRs. Of special interest is the interpretive practice of the Covenant bodies within the United Nation's (UN) framework. Chief among these is the Committee on Economic Social and Cultural Rights (CESCR), the body tasked with interpreting the ICESCR and overseeing its implementation. The Committee has been central in developing the normative definitions of key ESCRs, interpreting the obligations of states parties to the ICESCR, and monitoring protections and violations of the ICESCR. Also relevant is the interpretive practice of the Human Rights Council and the Special Procedures, both of which are universal procedures aimed at addressing gross violations of human rights by any of the 193 UN member states.[16]

2. Locating race in the substantive content of ESCRs

Following the adoption of the Universal Declaration on Human Rights (UCHR) in 1948—a non-binding resolution that many describe as having acquired the status of a supreme law within the lexicon of human rights law[17]—the Commission of Human Rights was tasked with drawing up a 'binding international human rights treaty'.[18] At that time, the socialist bloc teamed up with the Third World states to propose a separate binding treaty for ESCRs,[19] firmly resisting the pushback from the United States and the United Kingdom, both of whom were concerned about ESCRs curbing market freedoms.[20] Ultimately, concerns about market freedoms were put to rest, and

[15] Frederick Douglass, 'The Color Line' (1881) 132 North American Review 567; Douglass describes the colour line as the gate to personhood in society. He compares the situation of Black people in the United States with those living outside the states, noting that abroad is 'where this malignant prejudice, as we know it in America, does not prevail; where character, not color, is the passport to consideration; where the right of the Black man to be a man, and a man among men, is not questioned; where he may, without offense, even presume to be a gentleman'.

[16] OHCHR, 'Human Rights Council Complaint Procedure' (*OHCHR*) <https://www.ohchr.org/en/hr-bodies/hrc/complaint-procedure/hrc-complaint-procedure-index> accessed 23 April 2024.

[17] Mary A Glendon, 'Knowing the Universal Declaration of Human Rights' (1998) 73 Notre Dame Law Review 1153.

[18] ECOSOC Resolution 1/5 (16 February 1946) E/RES/5(I).

[19] UNGA Resolution 543 (VI) UN Doc A/RES/543(VI) (1952).

[20] Eric D Weitz, 'The Human Rights Surges of the 1940s and 1990s: A Commentary on Margaret E McGuinness and William A Schabas' (2011) 35 Diplomatic History 794.

the ICESCR was adopted in 1966, together with the International Covenant on Civil and Political Rights.[21]

Because newly independent states heavily lobbied for ESCRs,[22] the Covenant was seen as an accomplishment of the anticolonial coalition.[23] In part, this attribution was a product of the anticolonial politics of the time. The negotiations for the Covenant followed closely on the heels of the Asian–African conference in Bandung in 1955, hailed as the birthplace of an 'impregnable Asian-African alliance'.[24] Although it would be presumptuous to credit Bandung for facilitating ideological agreement amongst the participating Third World states, what Bandung definitively did was offer a platform for newly independent states to express their 'determination to share more fully with the west in decisions affecting the interests of their countries'.[25]

The drafting history of the Covenant reveals that postcolonial states did steer the formulation of many ESCRs. States such as the Philippines, Mexico, and Egypt[26] took important strides to prevent western imperial powers from blocking the drafting of the Covenant.[27] For Third World states, ESCRs presented an opportunity to lay stakes to power and knowledge in the same way as their western counterparts did. As James Gathii writes, it was an opportunity for Third World states to challenge the eurocentrism of international law and rescript the Third World as a site of epistemic production.[28] Third World states 'saw socioeconomic rights as a way of moving beyond the age of colonialism in which human livelihood was sacrificed for the economic gain of the metropole'.[29]

Racial discrimination was a notable fixture in this postcolonial lawmaking strategy,[30] or as Bertrand Ramachandran notes, racial discrimination was the 'dominant single theme' of the ICESCR.[31] This is no surprise given that the postcolonial

[21] Helen Keller and Daniel Moeckli, 'Introduction' in Corina Heri (ed), *The Human Rights Covenants at 50: Their Past, Present, and Future* (Oxford University Press 2018).

[22] As Carozza notes, the human rights traditions of Latin American states married the individualistic and socioeconomic dimensions of human dignity. See Paolo G Carozza, 'From Conquest to Constitutions: Retrieving a Latin American Tradition of the Idea of Human Rights' (2003) 25 Human Rights Quarterly 281.

[23] Roland Burke, *Decolonization and the Evolution of International Human Rights* (University of Pennsylvania Press 2018); Aiah Hasan, 'Report by Aiah Hasan (Algeria)' in *Afro-Asian Peoples' Solidarity Conference Cairo, December 26, 1957–January 1, 1958* (Foreign Languages Publishing House 1958); Katharine McGregor and Vannessa Hearman, 'Challenging the Lifeline of Imperialism: Reassessing Afro-Asian Solidarity and Related Activism in the Decade 1955–1965' in Luis Eslava, Michael Fakhri, and Vasuki Nesiah (eds), *Bandung, Global History, and International Law: Critical Pasts and Pending Futures* (Cambridge University Press 2017).

[24] Departemen Penerangan Republik Indonesia, *Pidato-Pidato Peringatan Ulang Tahun ke-V Konperensi Asia-Afrika: tahun 1960 [Speeches for the Commemoration of the Fifth Year since the Asia Africa Conference: 1960]* (Departemen Penerangan RI 1960).

[25] George M Kahin, *The Asian-African Conference: Bandung, Indonesia, April 1955* (Cornell University Press 1956).

[26] Jensen (n 14).

[27] ibid.

[28] James T Gathii, 'The Promise of International Law: A Third World View' (Grotius Lecture, American Society of International Law Virtual Annual Meeting, 25 June 2020).

[29] Christopher NJ Roberts, *The Contentious History of the International Bill of Human Rights* (Cambridge University Press 2015).

[30] Jensen (n 14); Steven LB Jensen, *The Making of International Human Rights Law: The 1960s, Decolonization, and the Reconstruction of Global Values* (Cambridge University Press 2017).

[31] Bertrand G Ramcharan, 'Equality and Non-discrimination' in Louis Henkin (ed), *The International Bill of Rights: The Covenant on Civil and Political Rights* (Columbia University Press 1981).

bloc first catapulted to international visibility because of its concerted condemnation of the apartheid regime of South Africa.[32] Indeed, in the very first meeting of the Commission of Human Rights in 1947, the postcolonial delegation succeeded in persuading the Commission to recognize that the apartheid regime perpetrated 'racial persecution and discrimination'.[33] On this basis, securing the 'unity of the human race' became the Commission's ambition.[34] Many postcolonial states advanced this agenda in the drafting of the ICESCR as well, particularly advocating that the prohibition of racial discrimination be incorporated into the recognition of ESCRs.

One example is the right to work, as recognized in Article 6 of the ICESCR. Much of the groundwork for the recognition of the right to work was done by Asian states such as Pakistan and Afghanistan,[35] clarifying how unjust work conditions result from existing social prejudices against racialized communities.[36] This is reflected in the practice of relegating racialized peoples to low-skilled employment[37] and requiring fluency in colonial languages to prevent racialized employees[38] from obtaining identity documents.[39] In more contemporary readings of the right to work, monitoring bodies such as the CESCR and the Human Rights Council have found that racial discrimination continues to be the highest contributor to national unemployment.[40] Racial discrimination has been placed at the centre of other rights too. In the case of the right to health, for instance, early negotiations led by the Philippines and Afghanistan[41] invited attention to how racialized communities were disproportionately disadvantaged in terms of access to health care.[42] First introduced in the Covenant by the state of Jamaica, since the adoption of the Covenant, many interpretive bodies such as the Special Rapporteurs on Health and on Racism have condemned states for enabling health inequities between dominant and oppressed racial groups.[43] Racialized peoples are reported to have been denied access to emergency care, subjected to forced

[32] UNGA Third Committee (112th Meeting) 'Summary Record' (25 October 1948) UN Doc A/C.3/SR.1127.

[33] UN Commission on Human Rights (1st Meeting) 'Summary Record' (27 January 1947) UN Doc E/CN.4/SR.1.

[34] UN Commission on Human Rights (13th Meeting) 'Summary Record' (4 February 1947) UN Doc E/CN.4/SR.13.

[35] UNGA Third Committee (710th Meeting) 'Summary Record' (13 December 1956) UN Doc A/C.3/SR.710.

[36] Constitution of the International Labour Organization (adopted 1 April 1919, entered into force 28 June 1919) 15 UNTS 40.

[37] CESCR, 'Concluding Observations: Ukraine' (4 January 2008) UN Doc E/C.12/UKR/CO/5

[38] *Jean-Louis Ramiaranjatovo v Fitsaboana Maso* (2004) Antsirabe Labour Court No 58 (Madagascar).

[39] CESCR, 'Concluding Observations: Russian Federation' (12 December 2003) UN Doc E/C.12/1/Add.94.

[40] CESCR, 'Concluding Observations: Bosnia and Herzegovina' (24 January 2006) UN Doc E/C.12/BIH/CO/1; 'Concluding Observations: Estonia' (19 December 2002) UN Doc E/C.12/1/Add.85; 'Concluding Observations: Macedonia' (15 January 2008) UN Doc E/C.12/MKD/CO/1; 'Concluding Observations: Hungary' (16 January 2008) UN Doc E/C.12/HUN/CO/3.

[41] UNGA Third Committee 'Draft International Covenants on Human Rights: Amendments to Article 13 of the Draft Covenant on Economic, Social and Cultural Rights' (1956) UN Doc A/C.3/L.589.

[42] ibid; UN Commission on Human Rights, 'Report of the Special Rapporteur on the Right of Everyone to the Enjoyment of the Highest Attainable Standard of Physical and Mental Health' (11 February 2005) UN Doc E/CN.4/2005/51.

[43] UNGA 'Report of the Special Rapporteur on the right of everyone to the enjoyment of the highest attainable standard of physical and mental health - racism and the right to health' (20 July2022) UN Doc A/77/197.

sterilization, offered poor medicines, and even non-consensually treated as subjects of clinical trials.[44] No doubt, facially, the ICESCR's engagement with race appears to be quite progressive. However, behind the veneer of an easy acceptance of the normative immorality of *racial discrimination*, the Covenant's engagement with *racism* proves to be normatively dubious and theoretically suspect.

Firstly, in spite of including race within the enumerated grounds of discrimination, the Covenant chooses not to define race at all, unlike other identity categories such as gender, religion, and national origin, which are considerably theorized. When the list of enumerated protected grounds was being drawn up, Covenant drafters shared that the grounds—taken together—were *intended* to address the rampant racial discrimination in the United States, particularly against Indigenous peoples.[45] Yet, race itself was left unspoken. The historical records of the Covenant are equally helpful. At the Universal Declaration of Human Rights (UDHR) negotiations, delegates from India proposed the addition of the word 'colour' as an enumerated ground for non-discrimination. In deliberating the conceptual boundaries of colour, delegates shed light on its relationship with race, with delegates from Lebanon, the Philippines, and China clarifying that race *included* colour and ethnicity—all of which are immutable features of one's birth.[46] Their comments implied that race was considered to have a more social rather than scientific basis.[47]

By failing to define race as such, the Covenant confers race with *naturality*, treating it as a *pre-existing difference* between rightsholders.[48] The naturality of race, as Christopher Gevers argues, is not coincidental. It is a deliberate construction of fiction that nurtures the racial imaginary of international law as a system of values and rules made by and for white subjects.[49] Naturalizing race in this way makes it impossible to historicize or explain racism,[50] a disadvantage imposed purely on those *subjugated by* racism. This is only exacerbated by the incorporation of colour into the category of race.[51] Colour, as Shahab Saqib's chapter in this collection explains, was another work of fiction that was imported into social hierarchies both in the west and in postcolonial societies simply to vindicate the racial thinking of international law by colouring those that international law was looking to exclude.[52]

[44] ibid [35]; OHCHR 'Communication to Special Procedures' (*OHCHR*, 3 May 2024) <https://spcommreports.ohchr.org/TMResultsBase/DownLoadPublicCommunicationFile?gId=28751> accessed 23 April 2024; CESCR 'General Comment No 17' (12 January 2006) UN Doc E/C.12/GC/17.

[45] Johannes Morsink, *'Nondiscrimination' in the Universal Declaration of Human Rights for a New Generation* (University of Pennsylvania Press 2022).

[46] UN Commission on Human Rights (35th Meeting) 'Summary Record' (12 December 1947) UN Doc E/CN.4/SR.35; see remarks of the Belgian delegation raising the minority view of race being a scientifically justifiable.

[47] UN Commission on Human Rights Sub-Commission on Prevention of Discrimination and Protection of Minorities (426th Meeting) 'Summary Record' UN Doc E/CN.4/Sub.2/SR.4/2.

[48] Robert Knox, 'International Law, Race, and Capitalism: A Marxist Perspective' (2023) 117 AJIL Unbound 55.

[49] Christopher Gevers, 'Unwhitening the World: Rethinking Race and International Law' (2021) UCLA Law Review 1652.

[50] Knox (n 48).

[51] UNGA Third Committee (659th Meeting) 'Summary Record' (9 November 1955) UN Doc A/C.3/SR.659. Israel, too, described apartheid as a colour-based identity discrimination, noting that 'men are deprived of rights and opportunities because of the colour of their skin'.

[52] See Saqib, ch 6 in this volume.

Secondly, the Covenant is marked by a conspicuous silence on *racism*, where racism can be understood—invoking Derrick Bell's conceptualization—as a tool of socioeconomic stratification in which white people enjoy supremacy via the oppression of Black people.[53] Throughout the ten-year drafting discussions of the Covenant, there is only one fleeting reference to racism: that of the Lebanese delegate describing 'nazism' and 'zionism' as forms of racism.[54] This is not to say that the spectre of racism did not loom large over the minds of the Covenant drafters. Famously, Soviet delegate Alexi Pavlov strongly opposed South Africa's bid to prevent the proscription of racial discrimination from being included in the Covenant, inviting attention to the systemic ways in which Asians and Black South Africans were systematically eviscerated from economic and social life in South Africa by application of the apartheid regime. Pavlov remarked how 'Indians were forced to live in restricted areas, where there was a shocking mortality rate. The colour line was strictly drawn in theatres, parks, restaurants, cafés, and railway trains. Millions of people paid in blood and tears for the policy of discrimination pursued by the Government of the Union of South Africa.'[55] The Soviet delegate was actually describing racism, but he hesitated to call it by that name. Compared to racism, the Covenant is liberal in its proscription of racial discrimination. The drafting history is replete with examples of how racial discrimination was credited as the inspiration for the Covenant. As the previous paragraphs note, it was also inserted into the formulation of multiple ESCRs.

Although racial discrimination seems to be an adjectival form of racism, the differences between the two are far from slight. Racial discrimination can be understood as 'any distinction, exclusion, restriction or preference based on race, colour, descent, or national or ethnic origin which has the purpose or effect of nullifying or impairing the recognition, enjoyment or exercize, on an equal footing, of human rights and fundamental freedoms in the political, economic, social, cultural or any other field of public life'.[56] Racial discrimination, however, does not address the culpability of structures and institutions of the state in the way that racism does. If racial discrimination penalizes the visible conduct of individuals, racism proscribes the *ideology* of segregating people on the basis of race. Racial discrimination places guilt on select individuals, whereas racism implicates larger systems of power, knowledge, and thought. Scholars like Anna Spain Bradley argue that the Covenant's silence on racism and visibly insistent commitment to racial discrimination are by design.[57] The few and far mentions of racism in the drafting of the Covenant ensure that racism is confined to the realm of an *extreme ideology* that rears its head only in an exceptional, totalitarian state. By locating racism in the exceptional and the extreme such as the nazi or apartheid state, a broader understanding of 'the interaction between racism as a modern political project and the European nation-state' is lost.[58] This works to the advantage of western

[53] Derrick Bell, *Faces at the Bottom of the Well: The Permanence of Racism* (Basic Books 1992).

[54] UNGA Third Committee (649th Meeting) 'Summary Record' (1 November 1955) UN Doc A/C.3/SR.649.

[55] UNGA Third Committee (112th Meeting) 'Summary Record' (25 October 1948) UN Doc A/C.3/SR.1127.

[56] ICERD (adopted 21 December 1965, entered into force 4 January 1969) 660 UNTS 195 (ICERD), Article 1.

[57] Anna Spain Bradley, 'Human Rights Racism' (2019) 32 Harvard Human Rights Journal 1.

[58] Alana Lentin, *Racism and Anti-racism in Europe* (Pluto Press 2004).

liberal states that have historically benefited from structures of racism. These benefits are fastened more securely by the Covenant's visibly insistent commitment to the prohibition of racial discrimination, which succeeds in diverting attention away from the Covenant's complicity in naturalizing race and diminishing the everyday impact of racism.

The Covenant's damning relationship with racism points to a more systemic feature of international human rights law, one that leaves little capacity within international law to interrogate the discipline's complicity in sustaining the apparatus that enables racism. This feature is better known as eurocentrism.

3. Eurocentrism as the enabler of racism

Originating from European imperialism, eurocentrism describes the centring of European or white ways of knowing and defining the world.[59] In Egyptian thinker Samir Amin's words, 'eurocentrism's manifestations, like those of other prevailing social phenomena, are expressed in the most varied of areas: day-to-day relationships between individuals, political information and opinion, general views concerning society and culture, social science'.[60]

Eurocentrism shares a peculiar relationship with racism, serving as a foundation for enabling and legitimizing racism by positioning European thought as normal and superior. In the early eighteenth century, racial difference was predicated on abjection. Racial abjection, as Charles Mills and Juliet Hooker explain, creates white identity from the disgust and desire felt towards Blackness and the pain of Black people.[61] The repulsiveness of the Black body was the reasoning offered to justify that higher forms of life were meant to dominate the lower.[62] 'Racial abjection simultaneously constructs racial difference and renders it incoherent by exposing its arbitrary and ambiguous nature.'[63] However, these assertions proved to be quite precarious. As imperialism came to be challenged in many parts of the world, it was no longer sufficient to evoke the abjection of race alone. The biological horrors of co-existing with coloured peoples could not explain why the labour of coloured peoples could be exploited. To do so, race had to transition from being a marker of biological difference to a grammar of political economy.

Eurocentrism was the method used to achieve this shift: placing European thought at the centre allowed racial *worldmaking*. Because European thought dictated the political economy, free labour was considered a birthright of white employees or what David Roediger calls the 'wages of whiteness'.[64] Moreover, because sovereignty was

[59] Samir Amin, *Eurocentrism* (2nd edn. Monthly Review Press 2009).

[60] ibid 179.

[61] Charles Mills, *Blackness Visible: Essays on Philosophy and Race* (Cornell University Press 1998); Juliet Hooker, 'Black Protest/White Grievance: On the Problem of White Political Imaginations Not Shaped by Loss' (2017) 116(3) South Atlantic Quarterly 483.

[62] Mills (n 61).

[63] Brandon R Davis, 'The Politics of Racial Abjection' (2023) 20(1) Du Bois Review 143.

[64] David R Roediger, *The Wages of Whiteness: Race and the Making of the American Working Class* (Rev edn, Verso 2007).

seen as the provenance of European states alone, the colonization of coloured peoples was understood to be legally permissible. In this way, race rapidly 'became the ideological medium through which people posed and apprehended basic questions of power and dominance, sovereignty and citizenship, justice and right'.[65]

International law was one of the first and the most successful laboratories of this analytical experiment using eurocentrism and racism, a critique that was first vocalized by Third World Approaches to International Law (TWAIL) scholars. By reconfiguring international law through the lens of colonialism,[66] TWAIL scholars showed how imperialism and later colonialism erased the contributions of those outside Europe, both to the originary encounters of international law and to its contemporary praxis.[67] A number of critical scholars have pointed to the eurocentrism ingrained in the list of sources of international law,[68] the jurisdiction of international courts,[69] the publishing preferences of international legal journals,[70] the rules permitting use of force,[71] and even the teaching of international law.[72] The impact of eurocentrism in international law is not confined to the epistemic realm alone.[73] Eurocentrism incorporates 'prejudice against the Other' into the political, cultural, and social world of international law as well.[74] It is no surprise that racialized peoples are the most frequent victims of human rights abuses by states and state institutions.

The ongoing Israeli genocide in Gaza makes the links between eurocentrism and racism in international law more apparent than ever. Since the Hamas-led offensive of 7 October 2023 and the genocidal destruction that Israel has wreaked ever since in Gaza, the West Bank, and East Jerusalem, mainstream media, international legal institutions, academics, and states have rushed to invoke the language of international law.[75] Media channels have reported on the ongoing 'humanitarian conflict' or 'crisis', 'calling on 'both sides' to use 'restraint' and, partly, 'blaming the Palestinian Resistance

[65] ibid.

[66] Andrew F Sunter, 'TWAIL as Naturalized Epistemological Inquiry' (2007) 20 Canadian Journal of Law & Jurisprudence 475.

[67] Georges Abi-Saab, 'The Third World and the Future of the International Legal Order' (1973) 29 Revue Egyptienne de Droit International 27; JJG Syatauw, *Some Newly Established Asian States and the Development of International Law* (Martinus Nijhoff 1961).

[68] Ntina Tzouvala, 'The Specter of Eurocentrism in International Legal History' (2021) 31 Yale Journal of Law & Humanities 413.

[69] BS Chimni, 'The International Law of Jurisdiction: A TWAIL Perspective' (2022) 35 Leiden Journal of International Law 29.

[70] Mohsen al Attar and Claire Smith, 'Racial Capitalism and the Dialectics of Development: Exposing the Limits and Lies of International Economic Law' (2024) 35 Law Critique 149.

[71] Ntina Tzouvala, 'TWAIL and the "Unwilling or Unable" Doctrine: Continuities and Ruptures' (2015) 109 AJIL Unbound 266.

[72] Makane M Mbengue and Olabisi D Akinkugbe, 'The Criticism of Eurocentrism and International Law: Countering and Pluralizing the Research, Teaching, and Practice of Eurocentric International Law' in Anne van Aaken and others (eds), *The Oxford Handbook of International Law in Europe* (Oxford University Press 2023) and Mohsen al Attar, 'Must International Legal Pedagogy Remain Eurocentric' (2021) 11 Asian Journal of International Law 176.

[73] Arturo Escobar, *Territories of Difference: Place, Movements, Life, Redes* (Duke University Press 2008) 310–11.

[74] Gloria Anzaldúa, *Borderlands: The New Mestiza = La Frontera* (Aunt Lute Books 2007).

[75] Tor Krever and others, 'On International Law and Gaza: Critical Reflections' (2024) 12(2) London Review of International Law 217.

for the ongoing Israeli massacres'.[76] Legal scholars have engaged in pages of debates about the principles of distinction and necessity within international humanitarian law, the permissible limits of the use of force *in jus in bello*, and the reasonable restrictions that can be placed on the enjoyment of human rights.[77] This coverage is a marked departure from the resolute silence of the western liberal fraternity towards Israel's historical occupation of Palestine and the longstanding decolonial struggles for resistance by Indigenous Palestinians.[78] The events of 7 October 2023 and the shuddering carnage that Israel launched presented a moment of moral reckoning for the western liberal powers, all of whom rushed to express solidarity with Israel. International law and its eurocentric design proved crucial in articulating this 'malleable morality' of western liberalism.[79]

Despite confirmation from the highest international court (the International Court of Justice) that Israel has occupied Gaza and the West Bank,[80] ministers, lawyers, and news channels have unabashedly cited international law to deny that Israel's conduct meets the standard of genocidal intent.[81] News channels continue not to mention who carried out the bombing of schools, homes, museums, and hospitals in Gaza; the sexual crimes against men and women in Gaza; or the plunder of Gazan homes.[82] Citing the international laws of war, the western world has conveniently concluded that Israel is at best 'only culpable for the ongoing "war" in Palestine, just as much as Palestinians themselves are'.[83] The genocide of Palestinians is 'en brera' or 'the only choice available to Israelis to defend themselves against the violence used by Hamas'.[84]

As Robert Knox writes, the sanitization of Israeli guilt is not an example of hypocrisy or inconsistent application of international law, but the very objective of international law.[85] The genocide in Gaza unmasks the *structural racism* within international law. Gaza makes clear that the rules of necessity in international humanitarian law were

[76] Ramzy Baroud, '"Watering Down" Genocide: No More Moral Compromises on Palestine, Please' (*CounterPunch*, 30 July 2024) <https://www.counterpunch.org/2024/07/30/watering-down-genocide-no-more-moral-compromises-on-palestine-please/> accessed 23 April 2024.

[77] Shahd Hammouri, 'The Commission of Inquiry on Palestine and Israel: To Speak of Genocide from a European Liberal Lens' (2024) Peace Human Rights Governance 1; Justina Uriburu, 'On Gaza, International Law, and Future Conversations' (2024) 12(2) London Review of International Law 298.

[78] 'Watershed Moment: Hundreds of Academics Equate Israel Occupation with Apartheid' (*Middle East Eye*, 24 January 2024) <https://www.middleeasteye.net/news/watershed-moment-hundreds-academics-equate-israel-occupation-apartheid> accessed 23 April 2024.

[79] 'War on Gaza: From Decades of Colonialism to a Genocidal Moment' (*Middle East Eye*, 15 October 2023) <https://www.middleeasteye.net/opinion/war-gaza-israel-decades-colonialism-genocidal-moment> accessed 23 April 2024.

[80] Legal Consequences arising from the Policies and Practices of Israel in the Occupied Palestinian Territory, Including East Jerusalem (Advisory Opinion) [2024] ICJ Rep.

[81] Jeremy Scahill and Ryan Grim, 'Leaked NYT Gaza Memo Tells Journalists to Avoid Words "Genocide," "Ethnic Cleansing," and "Occupied Territory"' (*The Intercep*, 15 April 2024) <https://theintercept.com/2024/04/15/nyt-israel-gaza-genocide-palestine-coverage/> accessed 23 April 2024.

[82] Natalie Khazaal, 'Bias Hiding in Plain Sight: Decades of Analyses Suggest US Media Skews Anti-Palestinian' (*The Conversation*, 29 February 2024) <http://theconversation.com/bias-hiding-in-plain-sight-decades-of-analyses-suggest-us-media-skews-anti-palestinian-216967> accessed 23 April 2024.

[83] Baroud (n 76).

[84] 'Israel's Preventative War' (*Politico*, 10 October 2023) <https://www.politico.eu/article/israel-gaza-preventative-war/> accessed 23 April 2024.

[85] Robert Knox, 'Hypocrisy, Race, and International law' (2024) 12(2) London Review of International Law 224.

always intended to disadvantage technologically challenged, racialized parties to an armed conflict. International criminal law—in requiring endorsements from known depredators such as the United States (through the device of the Security Council authorization)—was always intended to immunize white perpetrators from prosecution.[86] Similarly, international human rights law was always intended to free western states from the traps of fixed obligations towards securing the rights of minorities. That is why economic, social, and cultural rights were made contingent on state capabilities and executive discretion.

As Nahed Samour and Ntina Tzouvala note, the genocide unfolding in Gaza can only be explained if we acknowledge the 'racialised and, more broadly, hierarchical elements of the international (legal) order that authorise excessive, often eliminationist violence as a response to the violence (justified or not, legitimate or not) of subaltern actors'.[87] This hierarchy and the drunken power that those beholden to international law enjoy emerges from a deep-seated eurocentrism within international law. In the white world in which international law resides, there can be no genocide when a white state eliminates ethnic minorities, in the same way that Israel has full license to eliminate 'human animals' such as Palestinians.[88] Even if one produces evidence of schools, refugee camps, and hospitals being burnt with thousands of Palestinians inside, it would not meet the standard of proof unless 'internationally accredited investigators' are able to attest to the veracity of such proof.[89] In this hierarchical world, even time, space, and feeling are dictated by European thought.[90] The humanitarian crisis in Gaza and the West Bank is temporally affixed to 7 October 2023, rendering consideration of the historical continuities between the Nakba of 1948, the interim occupation of the West Bank, and the events of the present day impossible.[91] The spatial narrative is similarly controlled.[92] Gaza is spatially classified as an isolated conflict zone, caught in the crossfire between two warring powers: Hamas and Israel.[93] Such a spatial framing disconnects Gaza from the histories of Palestinian struggle and invisibilizes the everyday lived experiences of Palestinians under occupation outside of the active hostilities. Each of these assaults on time and space and ontology occurs through law. In this way, the eurocentrism of international law nurtures racism in its

[86] Rugenge wa Nciko, 'Symposium on Unbroken Bond: Solidarity Between the Palestinian Al-Haq and Congolese Action Youth Platform's Campaigns against Genocide' (*Opinio Juris*, 31 July 2024) <https://opiniojuris.org/2024/07/31/symposium-on-unbroken-bond-tracing-the-ties-between-african-and-palestinian-anti-colonial-struggles/> accessed 23 April 2024; see also John Reynolds, 'Genocide and/as Civilisation' (2024) 12(2) London Review of International Law 279.

[87] Nahed Samour and Ntina Tzouvala, 'Self-Defence in Israel and Palestine: Unsuspending Disbelief' (*Research Society of International Law*, 27 November 2023) <https://rsilpak.org/2023/self-defence-in-israel-and-palestine-unsuspending-disbelief/> accessed 23 April 2024.

[88] Brett Wilkins, 'Israeli Defense Minister Calls Palestinians "Human Animals" in Vow to Cut Off All Food, Fuel to Gaza' (*HuffPost*, 9 October 2023) <https://www.huffpost.com/entry/israel-defense-minister-human-animals-gaza-palestine_n_6524220ae4b09f4b8d412e0a> accessed 23 April 2024.

[89] William A Schabas, *The International Legal Order's Colour Line: Racism, Racial Discrimination, and the Making of International Law* (Oxford University Press 2023).

[90] Ilan Pappé, *The Ethnic Cleansing of Palestine* (Oneworld Publications 2006).

[91] Noura Erakat, 'The Limits and Potential of International Law in Gaza' (Lecture, Georgetown University Center for Contemporary Arab Studies, Washington DC, 8 March 2024) <https://ccas.georgetown.edu/2024/03/08/the-limits-and-potential-of-international-law-in-gaza/> accessed 23 April 2024.

[92] Chandler (n 76).

[93] ibid.

most terrifying proportions. The net effect is that eurocentrism enables international law to exist as a racist regime.[94] The racist structures of international law, in turn, allow for white domination to thrive. It is the thirst for domination that motivates white people and institutions to be betrothed to the international legal project.[95]

4. Finding evidence of eurocentrism in the ICESCR

The ICESCR is no stranger to eurocentrism. Within the Covenant, two pools of evidence of eurocentrism are covertly available: one, the recurring use of rhetorical devices such as civilization and economic development, and second, the epistemic make-up of the voices who participated in the treaty's making.

4.1 The grammars of civilization and economic development

Described by many as the 'founding ideal' of international law,[96] civilization appears in many international treaties in the form of 'civilized nations', 'civilized worlds', and 'civilized peoples'.[97] Having originated as a justification for settler colonialism, the valence of civilization remains undiminished, as it helps western liberal states rely on eurocentrism to validate the economic and epistemic suppression of the non-western world.[98] Analytically and normatively, civilization draws on regressive racial classifications.[99] Civilization is seen as the anathema for the savagery of racialized peoples. Throughout history, racist regimes have justified zionist and apartheid projects as attempts to 'save western civilization from uncivilized savages'.[100] What makes civilization even more insidious is how it is dressed in a morally defensible, *improvement-oriented* narrative. As Sarah Krakoff writes, civilization is framed as an opportunity offered to racialized peoples 'to become white',[101] and this is how it is made resistant to challenge. The construction of this narrative reveals that it is eurocentrism through the centring of the white standard of life that facilitates the racist civilizing mission to fester.

[94] See Saqib, ch 6 in this volume.

[95] More generally, see Kyoko Kishimoto, 'Anti-Racist Pedagogy: From Faculty's Self-Reflection to Organizing within and beyond the Classroom' (2018) 21(4) Race Ethnicity and Education 540.

[96] William E Hall, *A Treatise on International Law* (3rd edn, Clarendon Press 1890).

[97] Schabas (n 89).

[98] Antony Anghie and BS Chimni, 'Third World Approaches to International Law and Individual Responsibility in Internal Conflicts' (2003) 2 Chinese JIL 77; Patrick Thornberry, *The International Convention on the Elimination of All Forms of Racial Discrimination* (Oxford University Press 2016).

[99] Jean Allain, 'Slavery and the League of Nations: Ethiopia as a Civilised Nation' (2006) 8 Journal of the History of International Law 213. Hathaway and Shapiro find the interconnections between racism and civilization in the early writings of Grotius justifying private wars against the Portuguese. Oona Hathaway and Scott Shapiro, *The Internationalists* (Simon & Schuster 2018).

[100] 'Gallant: "This is a War Between Light and Darkness"' (*Jerusalem Post*, 15 October 2023) <https://www.jpost.com/israel-news/article-768470> accessed 23 April 2024.

[101] Sarah Krakoff, 'They Were Here First: American Indian Tribes, Race, and the Constitutional Minimum' (2017) 69 Stanford Law Review 491.

Like other fields of international law, ESCRs have also routinely employed the discourse of civilization. Particularly in the ICESCR, civilization has been a fixture since some of the earliest iterations of the Covenant. Even though postcolonial states succeeded in inserting race into the Covenants, ESCRs were accepted solely because their protection was considered the prerogative of 'civilized nations'.[102] Hernán Santa Cruz, the Cuban delegate to the Commission of Human Rights observed: 'Europeans colonized portions of Africa or Asia in order to preserve the indigenous peoples from barbarism, to convert them to Christianity, or to bring to them the "benefits" of civilization.'[103] The only critical voice raising the alarm about using the grammar of civilization was the Soviet delegation, but as a lone dissenter it was unable to mobilize much support.[104] The systematic invocation of civilization forced a universal acceptance that it was the burden of the 'civilized' white man to ensure this improvement occurred.[105]

The drafting records of the ICESCR reveal that it was infact often postcolonial states that invoked the discourse of civilization. The Pakistani and Guatemalan delegations linked the protection of the right to work to the protection of human civilization. The Pakistani delegate noted that recognition of the right to work was important because it enabled each citizen to 'contribute to the enrichment of the civilization to which he belonged and to the production of the goods and services which were essential to the life of his country'.[106] Similarly, Uruguay proposed the introduction of annual paid leave because 'this was the minimum guarantee in all civilized countries'.[107] Even the debate about cultural rights and the right to science was attached to civilization, with the Czechoslovakian delegate claiming that cultural rights were in service of the 'creation of a world civilization'.[108]

By the mid-twentieth century, the explicit invocation of the grammar of civilization had become 'untenable in a world witnessing antiracist, anti-imperialist and anti-capitalist struggles'.[109] In the bid to rescue civilization from antiracist struggles, the international legal community started to search for less suspect alternatives. The framework of economic development emerged as the most suitable disguise for the civilizing mission. First invoked in technical standard-setting organizations such as the Permanent Mandates Commission and the International Labor Organization,[110]

[102] Glenda Sluga, 'René Cassin: Les droits de l'homme and the Universality of Human Rights, 1945-1966' in Stefan Ludwig Hoffman (ed), *Human Rights in the Twentieth Century* (Cambridge University Press 2011); Burke (n 23).

[103] Hernán Santa Cruz, *Racial Discrimination* (United Nations 1977) [40].

[104] UN Commission on Human Rights Drafting Committee (2nd Meeting) 'Summary Record' (11 June 1947) UN Doc E/CN.4/AC.1/SR.2.

[105] See the Belgian and American delegates' comments at EECOSOC (151st Meeting) 'Report of the Commission on Human Rights' (10 August 1950) UN Doc E/AC.7/SR.151.

[106] UNGA Third Committee (709th Meeting) 'Summary Record' (13 December 1956) UN Doc A/C.3/SR.709 (Pakistan's comments); UNGA Third Committee (742nd Meeting) 'Summary Record' (25 January 1957) UN Doc A/C.3/SR.742.

[107] UNGA Third Committee (713th Meeting) 'Summary Record' (17 December 1956) UN Doc A/C.3/SR.713.

[108] UNGA Third Committee (797th Meeting) 'Draft International Covenants on Human Rights' (31 October 1957) UN Doc A/C.3/SR.797.

[109] Tzouvala (n 68).

[110] Guy Fiti Sinclair, 'A "Civilizing Task": The International Labour Organization, Social Reform, and the Genealogy of Development' (2018) 20 Journal of the History of International Law 145.

economic development was quickly absorbed into the broader ideal of improvement.[111] Given its technically dense and neutral-seeming language, economic development enjoyed more immunity from critique than the doctrine of civilization as such, even though the former was merely a reincarnation of the latter. At its core, the grammar of economic development—much like its predecessor—was entangled in eurocentrism. Effectively, the objective of securing economic development through human rights justified the 'global expansion and reproduction of capitalism in ways that denied non-Europeans any form of historical agency and commanded them into Europeanising themselves at the pains of irreversible social and cultural decline'.[112]

When the ICESCR was being negotiated, participating states were hesitant to assent to a universal and absolute obligation to secure ESCRs, noting that the degrees of performance were contingent on each state's resource capabilities.[113] This reservation was not completely ill-founded, as not all states have equally and evenly benefited from economic development.[114] In the ICESCR, differentiated economic capacities were addressed by introducing the 'progressive realisation' standard, according to which states' performance of their obligations would be assessed in proportion to their means. With these caveats formalized within the text of the Covenant, the added *discourse* of economic development was no longer about moderating responsibility based on economic capacity. Instead, development was simply utilized to affirm the colour line, separating the world into the 'disproportionately poor and relatively powerless'[115] and the developed, without acknowledging the former's complicity in creating and sustaining the latter, and the Covenant offers ample evidence of this.[116] The standard of 'productive and full employment' is interpreted differently in developing vis-à-vis developed countries.[117] Forced labour is recognized as a social menace that only developing states grapple with.[118] Developed states are obliged to offer assistance to 'poorer developing states' to discharge their obligations towards the right to health.[119] State obligations towards education—especially towards eliminating illiteracy and offering vocational education—are also segregated based on the degree of development.[120] As the Soviet delegate at the Commission of Human Rights

[111] Ntina Tzouvala, *Capitalism As Civilisation: A History of International Law* (Cambridge University Press 2020).

[112] Amin (n 59).

[113] See Argentina's comments in UNGA Third Committee (299th Meeting) 'Draft First International Covenant on Human Rights and Measures of Implementation' (31 October 1950) UN Doc A/C.3/SR.299; UN Commission on Human Rights (184th Meeting) 'Proposals for Additional Articles to be Inserted in Part II of the Draft Covenant' (19 May 1950) UN Doc E/CN.4/SR.184.

[114] Cristina Lafont, 'Global Justice and Economic and Social Rights' in Malcolm Langford and Katharine G Young (eds), *The Oxford Handbook of Economic and Social Rights* (Oxford University Press 2022).

[115] Ruth Gordon, 'Critical Race Theory and International Law: Convergence and Divergence' (2000) 45 Villanova Law Review 827.

[116] Anibal Quijano, 'Colonialidad del poder y clasificación social' (2000) 1(2) Journal of World-Systems Research 342; Jessica Whyte, *The Morals of the Market: Human Rights and the Rise of Neoliberalism* (Verso 2019).

[117] Krzysztof Drzewicki, 'The Right to Work and Rights in Work' in Asbjorn Eide, Catarina Krause, and Allan Rosas (eds), *Economic, Social and Cultural Rights: A Textbook* (2nd edn, Kluwer 2001).

[118] ibid.

[119] CESCR 'General Comment No 14: The Right to the Highest Attainable Standard of Health' (11 August 2000) UN Doc E/C.12/2000/4.

[120] CESCR 'General Comment No 13: The Right to Education' (8 December 1999) UN Doc E/C.12/1999/10.

remarked, economic development was actually intended to emphasize that 'races and nations did not have equal rights'.[121]

Clearly, not all references to development relate exclusively to economic *capabilities*; they also draw on the correlations between poverty and race.[122] It shows how European states and Third World states naturalized white modes of capitalist accumulation, embracing it as the universal standard of progress.[123] By centring white modes of production and ordering of labour and land, the rhetoric of economic development allowed race to become the primary means of ordering human bodies and their relationship with the economy, enabling dehumanizing practices such as slavery.[124] In so doing, developmentalism ensured the continuation of racism.

As this section shows, contrary to mainstream claims, the Covenant has struggled to rid itself of the eurocentric grammars of international law, particularly concerning race. Instead, from the time of its conception, the Covenant has provided fertile ground for states—European and Third World—to naturalize race as a means of policing human bodies and their social and economic interactions. On some occasions, race is naturalized through protective measures such as the prohibition of racial discrimination. On other occasions, race is naturalized through the repeated invocation of civilization and economic development as objectives that the protection of ESCRs ought to achieve. What connects all these grammars is the emphasis on white ways of reading race. The following section finds an explanation for the ubiquity of eurocentric grammars in the Covenant in the racial and epistemic dynamics of those representing the participating states in the Covenant.

4.2 Finding evidence in the privileges of racialized representation

As a successor to the UDHR—an instrument widely maligned for its birth defects[125] and its loyalty to European-origin natural rights theories[126]—the ICESCR is not unfamiliar with the critique of eurocentrism. As Georges Abi-Saab, a prominent Third World jurist, remarked: 'countries inhabited by people of colour were, by and large, "objects" of international law rather than its "subjects"'.[127] Today, a diverse group of scholars continues this critique, arguing that international law has benefited from European states positioning themselves as standard-setters.[128]

[121] UNGA (183rd Plenary Meeting) 'Verbatim Record' (10 December 1948) UN Doc A/PV.183169.

[122] OHCHR 'Report by Maurice Glélé-Ahanhanzo, Special Rapporteur on Contemporary Forms of Racism, Racial Discrimination, Xenophobia and Related Intolerance, on His Mission to Brazil' (23 January 1995) UN Doc E/CN.4/1996/72/Add.1.

[123] Robert Knox, 'Haiti at the League of Nations: Racialisation, Accumulation and Representation' (2020) 21 Melbourne Journal of International Law 299.

[124] Eric Williams, *Capitalism and Slavery* (University of North Carolina Press 1994).

[125] Christian Tomuschat, *Human Rights Between Idealism and Realism* (Oxford University Press 2003).

[126] Howard Langer, 'Human Rights: A Documentary on the United Nations Declaration of Human Rights Featuring an Interview with Mrs Eleanor Roosevelt' (Folkways Records 1958).

[127] Georges Abi-Saab, 'The Newly Independent States and the Rules of International Law: An Outline' (1962) 8 Howard Law Journal 95.

[128] Tzouvala (n 111); Makau Mutua, *Human Rights Standards: Hegemony, Law and Politics* (State University of New York 2016); Susan Marks, *The Riddle of All Constitutions: International Law, Democracy, and the Critique of Ideology* (Oxford University Press 2000).

Typically, however, attempts to redress the eurocentrism of international law focus on improving the representation of racialized people in international legal spaces. Representation has been a moot point in conversations about the UDHR for many years. The Declaration came to life in an imperial world; there is no denying this. It was drafted at a time when half of the world was still colonized. Including apartheid South Africa, only four of the fifty-four states that exist in Africa today participated in the negotiations and voted on the Declaration.[129] Famously, in 1947, the civil rights organization National Association for the Advancement of Coloured Peoples (NAACP) led by WEB Du Bois called out the hypocrisy of the UDHR: that Black Americans were both central to the democratic promise of the Declaration and yet remained firmly outside of the rooms where the Declaration was drafted.[130] Carol Andersen credits Du Bois's appeal and the highly publicized condemnation of NAACP's demands for representation of racialized peoples in the UDHR drafting process for ushering what she calls their 're-enfranchisement'.[131] In the face of the lack of non-European voices in the making of the UDHR, many scholarly efforts started to rescript the Declaration by amplifying the instrumental role played by Asian delegates like Charles Malik from Lebanon, Vijayalakshmi Pandit from India, PC Chang from China, and Carlos Romulo from the Philippines.[132]

Compared to the UDHR, the twin Covenants saw a significantly higher number of Third World states participating.[133] Between 1948 and 1966, UN membership had increased from 58 to 122 states, many of whom were newly independent Asian and African states.[134] Consequently, the authorship of the Covenants was more *representative* compared to the UDHR, even though important states like China, Malaysia, and Saudi Arabia did not participate.[135] Postcolonial states led by Liberia, Jamaica, the Philippines, Ghana, and Costa Rica formed the biggest voting bloc at the General Assembly[136] allowing the Covenants to support the recognition and codification of a number of important protections including the right to be free from racial discrimination, the right to health,[137] and the right to self- determination.[138]

[129] Aristoteles Constantinides, 'Questioning the Universal Relevance of the Universal Declaration of Human Rights' (2008) 62/63 Cuadernos Constitucionales de La Cátedra Fadrique Furió Ceriol 49.

[130] WEB Du Bois (ed), *An Appeal to the World* (NAACP 1947).

[131] Gerald Horne, *Black and Red: WEB DuBois and the Afro-American Response to the Cold War, 1944-1963* (State University of New York 1986); Carol Anderson, *Bourgeois Radicals: The NAACP and the Struggle for Colonial Liberation, 1941-1960* (Cambridge University Press 2015).

[132] Johannes Morsink, 'Article 1: Born Free and Equal' in Article by Article: The Universal Declaration of Human Rights for a New Generation (University of Pennsylvania Press 2022).

[133] Jensen (n 30).

[134] UN, 'Growth in United Nations Membership, 1945-Present' <www.un.org/en/sections/member-states/growth-united-nations-membership-1945-present/index.html> accessed 23 April 2024.

[135] Yogesh Tyagi, 'Influence of the ICCPR in Asia' in Daniel Moeckli, Helen Keller, and Corina Heri (eds), *The Human Rights Covenants at 50: Their Past, Present, and Future* (Oxford University Press 2018); Sarah Joseph, Melissa Castan, and Jenny Schultz, *The International Covenant on Civil and Political Rights: Cases, Materials, and Commentary* (2nd edn, Oxford University Press 2005).

[136] Jean H Quataert, *Advocating Dignity: Human Rights Mobilizations in Global Politics* (University of Pennsylvania Press 2009).

[137] Daniel Ricardo Quiroga-Villamarin, '"An Atmosphere of Genuine Solidarity and Brotherhood": Hernan Santa-Cruz and a Forgotten Latin American Contribution to Social Rights' (2019) Journal of the International History of Law 71

[138] Article 1 of both the ICCPR and ICESCR recognize the right to self-determination. The fight against racism and apartheid was also the driving force behind the first human rights treaty to be adopted after the UDHR—the ICERD.

However, the emphasis on the participation of negatively racialized delegates confuses tokenism for *epistemic inclusion* of those who are negatively racialized.[139] By placing reliance merely on facial representation, such accounts both conflate the mere 'representation' of postcolonial states with the epistemic representation of those marginalized because of their race[140] and blur counter-stories of those who were not allowed to reach the hallowed halls of the Commission of Human Rights where the UDHR was negotiated precisely because of their racial status.[141] Illustratively, the Indian delegation that was involved in drafting the UDHR and later the ICESCR was led by delegates including Vijayalakshmi Pandit, Hansa Mehta, R Venkataraman, and MR Masani[142]—all of whom were privileged caste, affluent diplomats trained in law in elite schools abroad.[143] The success of Pandit (the sister of India's first Prime Minister Jawaharlal Nehru)—with many lauding her for combining the 'best of the East' with a familiarity of the west[144]—inspired the selection of similarly elite diplomats, all of whom fit the moulds of worldly European diplomats while still embracing their Indian origins.[145] The most famed Chinese delegate to the Commission of Human Rights, PC Chang, has often been credited for bringing 'antiracist Asian values such as Confucianism' to the Commission's drawing board when drafting ESCRs.[146] However, Chang's contributions during the drafting were all geared towards advancing the developmental interests of the Chiang Kai-shek government—much less towards importing Confucianist teachings into the UDHR.[147] Chang was chosen as China's delegate on account of his training in American universities, his expertise in cultural translations, and his diplomatic experience, as opposed to his grounding in Confucian thought.[148] In her sociological study of the contemporary state of Indian diplomatic services, Kira Huju notes how Asian diplomats were merely Asian in 'blood and colour, but English in taste, opinions, morals, and intellect'.[149]

[139] Balakrishnan Rajagopal, 'Counter-Hegemonic International Law: Rethinking Human Rights and Development as a Third World Strategy' (2006) 27 Third World Quarterly 767.

[140] Jensen (n 30).

[141] Rajagopal (n 139).

[142] Miloon Kothari, 'Remembering India's Contributions to the Universal Declaration of Human Rights' (*The Wire*, 20 December 2018) <https://thewire.in/rights/remembering-indias-contributions-to-the-universal-declaration-of-human-rights> accessed 23 April 2024.

[143] ibid; Sanjoy Ghose, 'Rights For "Human Beings", Not Just for "Men": The Amazing Life of Hansa Mehta' (*The Wire*, 28 December 2020) <https://thewire.in/rights/hansa-mehta-universal-declaration-of-human-rights> accessed 23 April 2024; Granville Austin, *The Indian Constitution: Cornerstone of a Nation* (Oxford University Press 1966).

[144] RL Khipple, *The Woman Who Swayed America* (Lion Press 1946).

[145] Niraja Gopal Jayal, 'Hansa Mehta: An Early Indian Feminist' (*South Asia @LSE*, 12 September 2022); Sanjoy Hazarika, 'Man in the News: India's Mild New President: Ramaswamy Venkataraman' *The New York Times* (New York, 17 July 1987); V Lawrence Sundaram, *A Great Indian Jesuit, Fr Jerome D'Souza, 1897-1977: Priest, Educationist, and Statesman* (Gujarat Sahitya Prakash 1986).

[146] Fernand de Varennes, 'The Fallacies in the "Universalism versus Cultural Relativism Debate" in Human Rights Law' (2006) 1 Asia-Pacific Journal on Human Rights and the Law 71.

[147] Piérre-Etienne Will, 'The Chinese Contribution to the Universal Declaration of Human Rights, 1947-48' in Mireille Delmas-Marty and Pierre-Étienne Will (eds), *China, Democracy, and Law: A Historical and Contemporary Approach* (Brill 2012).

[148] ibid.

[149] Thomas B Macaulay, 'Minute on Indian Education (1835)' in Mia Carter and Barbara Harlow (eds), *Archives of Empire, Volume I: From the East India Company to the Suez Canal* (Duke University Press 2003).

A closer inspection reveals that the selection of such local elites was also informed by colour, an identity category that imports the same eurocentric logic as race, to ensure that communities disadvantaged by birth are placed at the bottom of socio-economic and epistemic hierarchies.[150] Evidence of this motive can be found in the circumstances of Pandit's appointment as the leader of the Indian delegation to the Commission of Human Rights. Pandit was selected by snubbing other equally competent but caste-oppressed Indian thinkers such as Dr BR Ambedkar.[151] Ambedkar was the chairman of the drafting committee of the Indian constitution. He was an internationally renowned spokesperson for equality and the abolition of caste in India, his impassioned advocacy drawing from his own lived experiences as a caste-oppressed Dalit.[152] Around the time of the negotiations of the UDHR, Ambedkar was actively mobilizing with Black civil society organizations and forming networks of antiracism activists including sociologist Du Bois to invite the UN's attention to the shared struggles of Black Americans and Dalits.[153] However, Ambedkar was restrained from speaking on behalf of India at diplomatic forums by former Prime Minister Jawaharlal Nehru.[154] The story of Pandit's selection at the expense of Ambedkar's voice shows that while material representation of non-European faces and voices certainly challenges the whiteness of international legal spaces, it is unconcerned with challenging the eurocentrism ingrained within postcolonial societies. This is further corroborated by the contents of the contributions made by postcolonial delegates. As the previous section showed, it was primarily postcolonial states that were eager to embed grammars of civilization and developmentalism into human rights. Postcolonial delegations were also often issued specific instructions not to invite attention towards their state's own colour-based discriminatory practices.[155]

5. Steps forward

Seeing the ICESCR through the lens of race exposes the eurocentrism of the Covenant, and shows how the Covenant has failed to challenge the racist framework of international law. It also prompts questions about how—if at all—the ICESCR can be reimagined as an antiracist instrument.

[150] Ahmed Memon, 'English in Taste, Indian in Blood': Caste Hegemony in the Making of British International Legal Thought' (2024) 12 London Review of International Law 23.

[151] Khushi Rathore, 'Excavating Hidden Histories: Indian Women in the Early History of the United Nations' in Rebecca Adami and Dan Plesch (eds), *Women and the UN: A New History of Women's International Human Rights* (Routledge 2021).

[152] Anurag Bhaskar, *The Foresighted Ambedkar* (Penguin Books 2024).

[153] BR Ambedkar, 'Letter to WEB Du Bois' (1946) in Dr Ambedkar Life and Mission (Ministry of Culture, Government of India) <http://indianculture.gov.in/ebooks/dr-ambedkar-life-and-mission> accessed 23 April 2024.

[154] Bhaskar (n 152); Team Dharma, 'How Prime Minister Jawaharlal Nehru Ousted Dr BR Ambedkar from the Cabinet: The Full Story' (*The Dharma Dispatch*, 14 April 2019) <https://www.dharmadispatch.in/history/how-prime-minister-jawaharlal-nehru-ousted-dr-b-r-ambedkar-from-the-cabinet-the-full-story> accessed 23 April 2024.

[155] Indian delegate Hansa Mehta was specifically instructed not to raise internal issues such as caste at the Commission of Human Rights. GS Bajpai, 'Letter to Hansa Mehta' (22 January 1947) Nehru Memorial Museum and Library, New Delhi.

For this to happen, it is imperative for the Covenant's interpretive bodies to *name* racism. As Theo van Boven explains, 'only when named and acknowledged can racism be recognized, identified, and addressed effectively'.[156] Following the adoption of the Covenant, seldom do the interpretive bodies of the Covenant illuminate the links between racism and large-scale violations of ESCRs. In the context of Kenya, the Committee on Economic, Social, and Cultural Rights—the chief interpretive body of the ICESCR—ruled that the marginalization of ethnic minorities, especially nomadic pastoralists, was violative of the Covenant.[157] Similarly, responding to Bolivia's periodic reports, the CESCR noted that Indigenous populations 'suffer from inadequate access to basic education, adequate housing, and health services'.[158] In both cases, the Committee stopped short—arguably deliberately—from characterizing such marginalization as racism. As a principle, the Committee's deliberate sparse references to racism ensure that racism continues to be relegated to the extraordinary rather than the everyday of international law. The Covenant is not alone in taking this position, as most states themselves prefer to deny racism altogether. In 1994, when the Special Rapporteur for Racism surveyed states in preparation for their report, sixteen out of thirty states denied the existence of racism in their territories altogether.[159] Nonetheless, simply because racism is unspoken does not mean that states remain unaware of racism. Indeed, claims rooted in racism have come before the CESCR and Special Procedures on several occasions.[160] Giving name to racism is therefore the first step to take.

There is no doubt that defining racism is challenging and has to be undertaken with great care. It is crucial not to be too ascriptive with the definition of racism, as it is likely to risk reifying eurocentric notions of discrimination, identity, and thought itself. The contemporaneous practice of sister institutions within and outside of the UN framework can prove quite instructive in this respect. In 1978, for instance, the UNESCO defined racism as including 'racist ideologies, prejudiced attitudes, discriminatory behaviour, structural arrangements and institutionalised practices resulting in racial inequality as well as the fallacious notion that discriminatory relations between groups are morally and scientifically justifiable'.[161] By contrast, the Inter-American Convention against Racism, Racial Discrimination and Related Forms of Intolerance defined racism as 'any theory, doctrine, ideology, or set of ideas that assert a causal link between the phenotypic or genotypic characteristics of individuals or groups and their . . . traits, including the false concept of racial superiority' and acknowledges that racism leads to 'racial inequalities, and to the idea that discriminatory relations between groups are morally and scientifically justified'.[162] Specifically for the ICESCR,

[156] Cohen, *Denial and Acknowledgement: The Impact of Information about Human Rights* Violations' (Stanley Center for Human Rights, Hebrew University 1995); Theo van Boven, 'Discrimination and Human Rights Law: Combating Racism' in Sandra Fredman (ed), *Discrimination and Human Rights: The Case of Racism* (Oxford University Press 2001).

[157] CESCR, 'Concluding Observations: Kenya' (3 June 1993) UN Doc E/C.12/1993/6.

[158] CESCR, 'Concluding Observations: Bolivia' (21 May 2001) UN Doc E/C.12/1/Add.60.

[159] UNGA Resolution 49/147 (23 December 1994) UN Doc A/RES/49/147.

[160] The Special Procedures alone have received nearly 500 complaints alleging human rights violations rooted in racism. <https://spcommreports.ohchr.org/TmSearch/Results> accessed 22 January 2026.

[161] Declaration on Race and Racial Prejudice (adopted by the General Conference of UNESCO at its 20th Session, Paris, 27 November 1978).

[162] Inter-American Convention against Racism, Racial Discrimination and Related Forms of Intolerance (adopted 5 June 2013) OAS Treaty Series A-68, Article 1.

it is important to highlight the links between racism and economic and social discrimination, a complementarity that the former Special Rapporteur of Racism Glele Ahanhanzo from Benin has already explored.[163] Ahanhanzo's report also clarified how racism is perpetuated by state institutions through economic and social segregation. Since Ahanhanzo's report, the Council of Europe,[164] the Organization of American states,[165] and domestic courts[166] have followed suit.

In naming racism, interpretive bodies such as the CESCR must engage with their own racist origins as well and acknowledge that international law has historically, if not also in present time, benefited from racist ideologies.[167] Some might say that international law is incapable of being antiracist. As Cheryl Harris notes, 'the law has established and protected an actual property interest in whiteness itself'.[168] Even if ridding itself of its racial origins is impossible for the law, a genuine acceptance of the ways in which international human rights law constitutes racism is still achievable. Indeed, on some occasions, the CESCR and Special Procedures have flagged the racism entrenched in domestic legal systems.[169] A similar understanding of how international legal systems entrench racism is what is missing. Acknowledging international law's complicity in sustaining racism in such a way is crucial to decentre white epistemologies and find ways to offer space for racially marginalized epistemologies in international legal discourse.[170]

This chapter is an effort to peel back the laudatory and emancipatory narrative associated with the Covenant, only to find that the Covenant—in spite of proscribing racial discrimination in the protection of ESCRs—retains eurocentric grammars, and in combination, these grammars do very little to challenge racism itself. Whether it is racial amnesia or the reification of race as an identity or the continued invocation of civilization and economic development, the Covenant joins the ranks of many international legal instruments that are hard-wired to facilitate white domination over racialized peoples. Despite these antecedents, this chapter is a nudge for us all to hold on to the Covenant's promise of antiracial solidarity and attempt to rescript its purposes rather than allowing it to remain a relic of its eurocentric origins.

163 UNGA, 'Report on Contemporary Forms of Racism, Racial Discrimination, Xenophobia and Related Intolerance by Maurice Glélé-Ahanhanzo, Special Rapporteur' (1 July 1994) UN Doc E/CN.4/1994/66.

164 Council Directive 2000/43/EC of 29 June 2000 implementing the principle of equal treatment between persons irrespective of racial or ethnic origin [2000] OJ L180/22.

165 Inter-American Convention against Racism, Racial Discrimination and Related Forms of Intolerance (n 163), Article 4(xii) recognizes the race-based denial of access to economic, social, and cultural rights as an act of racism.

166 *R v Parks* [1993] 15 OR (3d) 324; *R v Hamilton* [2004] OJ No 3252 (CA).

167 Bradley (n 57); Kimberlé Williams Crenshaw, 'Race Liberalism and the Deradicalization of Racial Reform' (2017) 130 Harvard Law Review 2298.

168 Cheryl I Harris, 'Whiteness as Property' (1993) 106 Harvard Law Review 1707; Kimberlé Crenshaw, 'Mapping the Margins: Intersectionality, Identity Politics, and Violence Against Women of Color' (1991) 43 Stanford Law Review 1241.

169 OHCHR, 'Communication to the United States of America' (2024) AL USA 7/2024 <https://spcommreports.ohchr.org/TMResultsBase/DownLoadPublicCommunicationFile?gId=28835> accessed 23 April 2024.

170 Michelle Staggs Kelsall, 'Disordering International Law' (2022) 33(3) European Journal of International Law 729.

12

Racialized Ableism and the Need for Intersectional Discourse and Action

Tess Sheldon, Ruby Dhand, and Roxanne Mykitiuk

1. Introduction

The development of international human rights law has progressed from a universal declaration to the recognition and protection of the rights of historically marginalized groups or population-specific protections relating to identities including race, gender, childhood, and Indigeneity.[1] Human rights instruments are often celebrated as tools for advancing the rights of the oppressed as states parties are required to implement legal reforms in compliance with their obligations under individual conventions.

The Convention on the Rights of Persons with Disabilities (CPRD) is the most recent international human rights legal instrument.[2] Disabled People's Organisations (DPOs), advocates, and academics praise the CRPD for its ability to facilitate the inclusion and participation of persons with disabilities (PWD) through rights protections. Yet, many people occupy multiple and intersecting identity categories and concomitantly experience discrimination and derogation of their rights based on intersecting categories. Under the current international human rights regime, however, it remains difficult for an individual to advance claims of discrimination on intersecting grounds, as none of the international treaties expressly recognize the concept of intersectional discrimination.[3] Notwithstanding the discrete vulnerabilities confronted by an individual who experiences discrimination as a person who is racialized and disabled, for example, their encounter will remain largely siloed to have their specific experience addressed within the current international human rights framework. Indeed, despite including the concept of multiple discrimination in the CRPD—the first time in a UN human rights convention—the Convention is remarkably silent on addressing the intersecting vulnerabilities that lie at the critical juncture of disability, race, and Indigeneity.

In this chapter, we discuss how race and Indigeneity are rendered visible or invisible by the CRPD. In doing so we examine the CPRD Committee's approach to multiple

[1] See, eg, ICERD (adopted 21 December 1965, entered into force 4 January 1969) 660 UNTS 195; CEDAW (adopted 18 December 1979, entered into force 3 September 1981) 1249 UNTS 13; CRC (adopted 20 November 1989, entered into force 2 September 1990) 1577 UNTS 3; UNDRIP (adopted 13 September 2007) UNGA Res 295 A (61).

[2] CRPD (adopted 13 December 2006, entered into force 3 May 2008) UNGA Res 106 A (61).

[3] As we discuss later, the language of multiple discrimination rather than intersectional discrimination is used in the text of the CRPD.

Tess Sheldon, Ruby Dhand, and Roxanne Mykitiuk, *Racialized Ableism and the Need for Intersectional Discourse and Action*
In: *Emancipating International Law*. Edited by: Mohsen al Attar and Claire Smith, Oxford University Press.
© Tess Sheldon, Ruby Dhand, and Roxanne Mykitiuk 2026. DOI: 10.1093/9780198935605.003.0016

discrimination, as it is principally through the inclusion of this concept in the CRPD that a space for the consideration of race and Indigeneity has been made. In addition, to understand the scant attention paid to race and Indigeneity in the Convention, we outline relevant historical deliberations regarding its negotiation and the place of race and Indigeneity within it. We then offer two brief case studies from Canada that demonstrate the significant ways in which disability and race create intersectional discrimination, the risk of using a race-evasive approach to disability discrimination, and the possibility of adopting an intersectional analysis using the CRPD. First, we rely on the rights claims of Nell Toussaint, who challenged Canada's refusal to fund health care for migrants with an irregular status. We then consider a constitutional claim to British Columbia's (BC) Mental Health Act, where legal counsel uses the CRPD as a tool for advocacy to increase access to justice for Indigenous and racialized people with mental health disabilities experiencing involuntary detention and treatment. This chapter aims to analyse the limitations of the CRPD's ability to confront systemic racism and what an intersectional disability discrimination approach would require in Canada.

2. The CRPD's approach to intersecting forms of discrimination

Building on the International Covenant on Civil and Political Rights (ICCPR) and the International Covenant on Economic, Social and Cultural Rights (ICESCR), the CRPD establishes an extensive regime of civil, political, economic, social, and cultural rights across a range of life activities within a disability-focused context. Its mandate is to protect the full and equal enjoyment of rights and freedoms by all persons with disabilities and to ensure that states parties enable the exercise of those rights. As Beth Ribet affirms, the CRPD achieves this through an emphasis on individual rights protection, advanced through an equal protectionist approach within an antidiscrimination framework.[4] Within this framework, disability is an identity which 'functions to designate membership in a class of persons protected from discriminatory treatment'.[5] This approach, however, precludes the inclusion of collective rights and the integration of the socio-structural dimensions of disability subordination which a Convention that recognizes Indigeneity and race could have embraced.[6]

The CRPD adopts a model of disability that regards disability as an evolving concept arising from the interactions between persons with impairments and the attitudinal and environmental barriers that hinder their full participation in society.[7] Referred to as a human rights model of disability in General Comment No 6 on Equality and Non-Discrimination (General Comment No 6), the CRPD Committee recognizes

[4] Beth Ribet, 'Emergent Disability and the Limits of Equality: A Critical Reading of the UN Convention on the Rights of Persons with Disabilities' (2011) 14 Yale Human Rights and Development Law Journal 101, 103, 125.

[5] ibid 106.

[6] Huhana Hickey, 'Chapter 10. Indigenous People with Disabilities: The Missing Link' in Maya Sabatello and Marianne Schulze (eds), *Human Rights and Disability Advocacy* (University of Pennsylvania Press 2013) 157.

[7] CRPD (n 2) Preamble (e).

disability as a social construct and only one of the many layers of identity, thus requiring policies to account for the diversity of persons with disabilities.[8] However, language about the prevention of disability and some text about the interrelationship between poverty, conflict, and the high incidence of disability were omitted from the CRPD. For example, a Venezuelan proposal (which was not adopted) in response to the Mexican proposal contained the following language:

> Concerned at the fact that extreme poverty, marginalization, social exclusion, war and underdevelopment contribute to the existence of high disability rates, since the great majority of persons with disabilities live in developing countries,
>
> Bearing in mind that, in many cases, disability can be prevented by creating conditions of equity and thus by increasing the level of development and quality of life of the world's people,
>
> Recognizing that the strength of international peace and security and the prevention of conflict help reduce the high rates of disability in the world.[9]

Representatives of DPOs and some governments were highly critical of the prevention language, viewing it as supporting an understanding of disability that is problematic and a condition to be eliminated, thereby reinforcing a medical model of disability, and detracting from the social model thrust that animates the Convention. Moreover, the language of prevention was considered inappropriate in a convention to be applied to persons who already had disabilities.[10]

Ribet argues that the exclusion of disability prevention from the CRPD has the effect of 'vacat[ing] any analysis of disability that acknowledges its social origins' and negates the recognition that subordination is involved in the production of disabilities.[11] Attention to the forces that lead to disablement—poverty, war, abuse, environmental degradation, lack of education, employment, and health care—reveals that those who experience deprivation and disablement in a globalized and colonial order are disproportionately racialized and Indigenous. Racism is a cause of disablement, racism is disabling, and 'disability discrimination' requires recognition that race, Indigeneity, and disability are intersectional and, in the context of colonialism and white supremacy, inextricable.

[8] UN Committee on the Rights of Persons with Disabilities, 'General Comment No 6 on Equality and Non-Discrimination' (26 April 2018) UN Doc CRPD/C/GC/6/.

[9] Ad Hoc Committee on a Comprehensive and Integral International Convention on Protection and Promotion of the Rights and Dignity of Persons with Disabilities, 'Draft submitted by the Bolivarian Republic of Venezuela' (New York, 16–27 June 2003) UN Doc A/AC265/2003/WP/. The Bangkok proposal also contained language in the Preamble (i) referencing social circumstances that contribute to the increased incidence of disability and the relationship between disability and poverty. *Ad Hoc* Committee on a Comprehensive and Integral International Convention on Protection and Promotion of the Rights and Dignity of Persons with Disabilities, 'Bangkok Draft: Proposed Elements of a Comprehensive and Integral International Convention to Promote and Protect the Rights and Dignity of Persons with Disabilities' (Bangkok 14–17 October 2003) <https://www.un.org/esa/socdev/enable/rights/bangkokdraft.htm> accessed 2 December 2024.

[10] Janet E Lord, 'Preamble' in Ilias Bantekas, Dimitris Anastasiou, and Michael Ashley Stein (eds), *The UN Convention on the Rights of Persons with Disabilities: A Commentary* (Oxford University Press 2018) 1, 6.

[11] Ribet (n 4) 105.

Although the CRPD did not explicitly address the concept of disablement, it has been argued that the principle of intersectionality is implied within its provisions. As clarified in General Comment No 6, the CRPD is animated by a substantive model of equality that 'seeks to address structural and indirect discrimination' in addition to direct discrimination 'and takes into account power relations'.[12] Referred to as inclusive equality, this understanding of equality includes a 'distributive dimension to address socioeconomic disadvantages', a recognition of intersectionality, a participative dimension, and accommodations to make space for difference.[13]

Elaborating on the legal requirements for achieving equality and protection against discrimination,[14] General Comment No 6 further recognizes that discrimination can be based on multiple and/or intersecting characteristics and clarifies that protection against 'discrimination on all grounds' under Article 5 'means that all possible grounds of discrimination and their intersections must be taken into account'.[15] General Comment No 6 adopts the definitions of multiple and intersectional discrimination advanced by the CRPD committee in its earlier General Comment No 3 on Article 6: Women and Girls with Disabilities (General Comment No 3).[16] The CRPD Committee confirmed that Article 6 requires states parties to recognize that 'multiple discrimination' as an obstacle to the full enjoyment of the rights and freedoms of women and girls with disabilities embodies two distinct dynamics.[17]

First, multiple discrimination is a situation in which a person experiences discrimination on two or more grounds, with one compounding or aggravating others. Second, intersectional discrimination is a 'situation where several grounds operate and interact with each other at the same time in such a way that they are inseparable and thereby expose relevant individuals to unique types of disadvantage and discrimination'.[18] It is noteworthy that, while both General Comment No 3 and General Comment No 6 refer to and distinguish the concepts of multiple and intersectional discrimination, the text of the CRPD includes references to multiple discrimination only.[19] While it is the first international human rights convention to

[12] CRPD (n 8).

[13] ibid.

[14] The CRPD also refers to equality and non-discrimination in Article 5 as rights and in Article 3 as principles. Therefore, they are both principles and rights within the CRPD.

[15] CRPD (n 8).

[16] UN Committee on the Rights of Persons with Disabilities, 'General Comment No 3 on Women and Girls with Disabilities' (25 November 2016) UN Doc CRPD/C/GC/3.

[17] ibid. 4(c) notes that the '[g]rounds for discrimination include, but are not limited to: age, disability, ethnic, indigenous, national or social origin, gender identity, political or other opinion, race, refugee, migrant, or asylum status, religion, sex, or sexual orientation'. It is interesting to note that this list of grounds for discrimination differs from that contained in the Preamble (p) of the CRPD which includes: race, colour, sex, language, religion, political or other opinion, national, ethnic, indigenous or social origin, property, birth, age or other status.

[18] CRPD (n 16) [4].

[19] While the language of multiple discrimination is used in the final text of the CRPD, language of intersectionality was used in various documents during the negotiation process. For examples see Ad Hoc Committee on a Comprehensive and Integral International Convention on the Rights and Dignity of Persons With Disabilities, 'Compilation of proposals for a Comprehensive and Integral International Convention to Promote and Protect the Rights and Dignity of Persons with Disabilities' (New York, 16–27 June 2003) <https://www.un.org/esa/socdev/enable/rights/a_ac265_2003_crp13.html> accessed 2 December 2024; Ad Hoc Committee on a Comprehensive and Integral International Convention on the Rights and Dignity of Persons With Disabilities, 'Daily summary of discussion at the fourth session'

include references to multiple discrimination in its binding text, in its application the CRPD falls short of protecting all relevant forms of multiple and intersectional discrimination.[20] As demonstrated below, because the concept is articulated in relation to multiple grounds of disability, gender, disability, and age (childhood), none of the direct benefits of the twin-tracking approach that women and children with disabilities receive within the CRPD are available based on race or Indigeneity. Moreover, similar to all other grounds of discrimination, these terms are relegated to one paragraph of the preamble.

With a focus on multiple discrimination faced by women and children with disabilities, the provisions of the CRPD are highly reflective of the draft negotiation process by the Ad Hoc Committee on a Comprehensive and Integral Convention on the Protection and Promotion of the Rights of Persons with Disabilities. Throughout this process, most discussions on multiple and intersectional discrimination have focused on the experiences of both women and girls.[21] It was largely agreed that the specific rights of women and children with disabilities should be addressed within the CRPD, and the question was how to do so. Early in the negotiations, parties considered the double disadvantage or multiple discrimination that women with disabilities experienced in areas of pregnancy, health care, employment, education, sexual exploitation, and abuse.[22] Eventually, the final version of Article 6 and the twin-track approach were settled upon, whereby gender protections and issues were mainstreamed into a number of substantive provisions. The inextricable way in which disability and gender subordination are co-constructed was built into the Convention. To a lesser

(New York, 25 August 2024) <https://www.un.org/esa/socdev/enable/rights/ahc4sum25aug.htm> accessed 2 December 2024.

[20] Wiebke Ringel, 'Non-Discrimination, Accommodation, and Intersectionality under the CRPD: New Trends and Challenges for the UN Human Rights System' (2016) 20 Max Planck Yearbook of United Nations Law 98, 103; Theresia Degener, 'Intersections between Disability, Race and Gender in Discrimination Law' in Anna Lawson and Dagmar Schiek (eds), *European Union Non-Discrimination Law and Intersectionality* (Routledge 2011).

[21] See the discussion of the Ad Hoc Committee on a Comprehensive and Integral International Convention on the Rights and Dignity of Persons With Disabilities in relation to gender and multiple and/or intersectional discrimination in its negotiation sessions 3–8: 'Report of the third session of the Ad Hoc Committee on a Comprehensive and Integral International Convention on the Protection and Promotion of the Rights and Dignity of Persons with Disabilities' (9 June 2004) UN Doc A/AC.265/2004/5; 'Report of the fourth session of the Ad Hoc Committee on a Comprehensive and Integral International Convention on the Protection and Promotion of the Rights and Dignity of Persons with Disabilities' (14 September 2004) UN Doc A/59/360; 'Report of the Ad Hoc Committee on a Comprehensive and Integral International Convention on the Protection and Promotion of the Rights and Dignity of Persons with Disabilities on its fifth session' (23 February 2005) UN Doc A/AC.265/2005/2; 'Report of the Ad Hoc Committee on a Comprehensive and Integral International Convention on the Protection and Promotion of the Rights and Dignity of Persons with Disabilities on its sixth session' (17 August 2005) UN Doc A/60/266; 'Report of the Ad Hoc Committee on a Comprehensive and Integral International Convention on the Protection and Promotion of the Rights and Dignity of Persons with Disabilities on its seventh session' (13 February 2006) Un Doc A/AC.265/2006/2; 'Final report of the Ad Hoc Committee on a Comprehensive and Integral International Convention on the Protection and Promotion of the Rights and Dignity of Persons with Disabilities on its eighth session' (1 September 2006) UN Doc A/AC.265/2006/4. See also Roxanne Mykitiuk and Ena Chadha, 'Article 6: Women with Disabilities' in Elias Bantekas, Dimitris Anastasiou, and Michael Ashley Stein (eds), *The UN Convention on the Rights of Persons with Disabilities A Commentary* (Oxford University Press 2018).

[22] ibid.

extent, this approach was also taken with children; however, it was not pursued with race or Indigeneity.

When examining the history of the draft negotiation process through the lens of disability, race, ethnicity, and Indigeneity, we observe a consistent rejection of the proposals made to enhance their inclusion in the CPRD. Huhana Hickey documents how Indigenous peoples were excluded from the negotiations and how the lack of representation impacted the outcome. According to Hickey, only a small online network—the Indigenous Disability Convention Working Group—was invited to join the International Disability Caucus (IDC), and two individuals (including her) were appointed representatives of Indigenous people with disabilities in the IDC.[23] However, there was no Indigenous representation at any of the Ad Hoc Committee sessions, nor did states include Indigenous persons with disabilities in their delegations: '[r]equests made by indigenous persons with disabilities to the state representatives from New Zealand, Australia, and Canada went unheeded.'[24] This absence, Hickey contends, precluded the CRPD from reflecting an Indigenous understanding of disability and the collective concept of rights in addition to a separate article on Indigenous persons.

During the sixth session of negotiations, the IDC proposed a standalone article regarding 'Indigenous, tribal, ethnic and cultural minorities'.[25] If adopted, Harpur and Stein argued that this provision would have elevated the protection of Indigenous persons with disabilities to the same level as women and children.[26] Furthermore, in the seventh session, Australia proposed draft Article 5bis, which addressed the vulnerability of specific population groups of persons with disabilities, including persons from racial, ethnic, linguistic, and/or religious minority groups, as well as those who are Indigenous.[27] This article received support from the IDC, but was not adopted again. Thus, the negotiation process first established a hierarchy of concern for persons at vulnerable intersections of certain identities intertwined with disability and then cemented this hierarchy within the Convention.

The CRPD has adopted a twin-track approach to address the multiple and compounding forms of discrimination faced by women and girls with disabilities. As set out above, this framework includes the adoption of a distinct article—Article 6 on 'women with disabilities', together with their mainstreaming throughout the Convention. In addition to Article 6, gender equality is a founding principle (Preamble and Article 3) that is specifically referenced in several thematic articles, including those dealing with violence and sexual and reproductive health (Articles 8, 16, 25, and 28), and

[23] Hickey (n 6) 165–66.

[24] ibid 166.

[25] Ad Hoc Committee on a Comprehensive and Integral International Convention on the Protection and Promotion of the Rights and Dignity of Persons with Disabilities (6th session) 'International Disability Caucus Draft Article: Indigenous, tribal, ethnic and cultural minorities' (24 January–4 February 2005) <https://www.un.org/esa/socdev/enable/rights/documents/ahc6idcdaprop.doc> accessed 3 December 2024.

[26] Paul Harpur and Michael Ashley Stein, 'Indigenous Persons with Disabilities and the Convention on the Rights of Persons with Disabilities: An Identity without a Home' (2018) 7(2) International Human Rights Law Review 165, 179.

[27] Ad Hoc Committee on a Comprehensive and Integral International Convention on the Protection and Promotion of the Rights and Dignity of Persons with Disabilities (7th Session) 'Australian Proposed Article 5bis - Specific Population Groups' (*UN Enable*, 2006) <https://www.un.org/esa/socdev/enable/rights/ahcstata5sevscomments.htm#australia> accessed 3 December 2024.

mandatory gender parity is established for the configuration of the CRPD Committee (Article 31). A similar twin-track approach was adopted within the CRPD to address the intersectional discrimination faced by children with disabilities. Article 7 focuses on the rights of children with disabilities, whereas Article 24 refers to the rights of children in education. We note, however, that the provisions relating to children with disabilities do not mention 'multiple discrimination'.[28]

By contrast, the CRPD is almost entirely silent on race and Indigeneity. As Achiume and Carbado suggest, legal instruments crafted without any mention of race reinforce Eurocentrism and racial subordination.[29] The CRPD contains only one mention of race and one of Indigeneity within subsection (p) of its Preamble, which provides that 'persons with disabilities are subject to multiple or aggravated forms of discrimination on the basis of race, colour, sex, language, religion, political or other opinion, national, ethnic, indigenous or social origin, property, birth, age or other status'.[30] Indeed, reference to Indigeneity as grounds for discrimination in the Preamble was a late addition by Venezuela.[31] As noted, the CRPD failed to include the language of race or Indigeneity in any of its substantive articles directed at state action or responsibility. The only other mention of the term 'racial' is also in the Preamble in Subsection (d) which references the ICERD as one of several human rights treaties.

With these absences, the CRPD falls short of recognizing the ways in which race impacts the meaning of and access to disability rights, the forms of discrimination faced by persons at the nexus of disability and race, and the way in which race, in some instances, creates disability. By failing to draw attention to the specificities that lie at the intersection of disability and race, and of race and Indigeneity, the CRPD runs the risk of eliding a significant portion of the population to whom it most needs to apply.

3. Case study: Nell Toussaint's international human rights claims towards disability justice for migrant workers in Canada

The *Toussaint* case exemplifies deficiencies in the approach to the rights claims of racialized workers with disabilities. For the purposes of this chapter, we imagine what would have happened if *Toussaint* had been a CRPD case. Since Canada did not sign the CRPD's Optional Protocol until December 2018, well after Nell Toussaint launched her constitutional challenge, our examination is principally intellectual.[32] We use this case as a warning against race-evasive and/or disability-evasive arguments.

[28] Gauthier de Beco, 'Intersectionality and Disability in International Human Rights Law' (2020) 24(5) International Journal of Human Rights 593.

[29] Tendayi Achiume and Devon W Carbado, 'Critical Race Theory Meets Third World Approaches to International Law' (2021) 67(6) UCLA Law Review 1462, 1477.

[30] CRPD (n 2).

[31] Hickey (n 6) 166.

[32] Employment and Social Development Canada, 'Canada accedes to the Optional Protocol to the United Nations Convention on the Rights of Persons with Disabilities' *(Employment and Social Development Canada*, 3 December 2018) <https://www.canada.ca/en/employment-social-development/news/2019/01/canadaaccedes-to-the-optional-protocol-to-the-united-nations-convention-on-the-rights-of-persons-with-disabilities.html> accessed 18 July 2024.

Nell Toussaint was a Black woman with disabilities. She faced barriers normalizing her residency and remained in Canada without 'regular' migrant status. She experienced health problems, and was refused access to public health benefits because of her immigration status. She alleged that her exclusion from the Interim Federal Health Program (IFHP) was discriminatory on the grounds of disability and citizenship and resulted in serious long-term health impacts.

Toussaint applied for judicial review of the federal government's decision to deny her request to cover her medical and hospital charges. She raised the constitutionality of this denial, asserting that the overt denial of entitlement to public health for people with uncertain or precarious immigration status violated their rights to life; to be free from torture and cruel, degrading, and inhuman treatment; and to liberty and security. She also argued that her exclusion from the IFHP violated her rights to non-discrimination, although she did not raise the ground of race. Instead, her equality claims raised the analogous ground of 'immigration status'.[33]

In 2010, the Federal Court rejected her application.[34] While Justice Zinn found that her exclusion from the IFHP engaged her *Charter* rights to both life and to security of the person, the denial was not 'arbitrary', since it was consistent with the government's objective of preventing Canada from becoming a 'health care safe haven'.[35] The Federal Court easily dismissed her equality arguments, finding that she was not excluded from the IFHP because of her 'disability'.[36]

In 2011, the Federal Court of Appeal also found against Toussaint.[37] Stratas JA concluded that her rights to life and to security of the person had been put at risk, but that her own conduct was the 'operative cause' of any injury to those rights.[38] On equality, Stratas JA did not accept that 'immigration status' qualified as an analogous ground and refused to consider her 'intersecting grounds' argument.[39] Race was not raised. Most concerning, Stratas JA proposed that even if the equality argument had been persuasive, ameliorative programmes such as the IFHP may be immune from a finding of

[33] Applicant's Memorandum of Argument, 'Nell Toussaint and Attorney General of Canada and Minister of Health (Federal Court)' (Social Rights Canada) <https://www.socialrights.ca/documents/Toussaint%20M%20o%20A.pdf> accessed 18 July 2024.

[34] *Toussaint v Canada* (Attorney General) [2010] FC 810.

[35] ibid [94]

[36] ibid [83].

[37] Appellant's Memorandum of Fact and Law, 'Nell Toussaint v Attorney General of Canada and The Minister of Health' (Federal Court of Appeal) (10 November 2010) <https://www.socialrights.ca/litigation/toussaint/IFH%20APEAL/appellant's%20memorandum%20of%20fact%20and%20law%20FCA.pdf> accessed 28 January 2026: 'A secondary intersecting ground relates to what is being denied in this case—healthcare for needs related to a disability. The applicant has unique healthcare needs related to complications from diabetes that she has developed in recent years. She is differentially affected by the disqualification from healthcare because of her disability. On this secondary comparison, the policy creates a distinction between undocumented migrants with disabilities, who are adversely affected by the policy, and those without disabilities, who are similarly disqualified from coverage, but who do not have serious disabilities or related healthcare needs, therefore experiencing a differential effect.'

[38] *Toussaint v Canada (Attorney General)* [2011] FCA 213, [2013] 1 FCR 374 [72]–[73].

[39] ibid [100]; 'The "secondary intersecting ground" is said by the appellant to be "a distinction between undocumented migrants with disabilities, who are adversely affected by the policy, and those without disabilities, who are similarly disqualified from coverage, but who do not have serious disabilities or related healthcare needs, therefore experiencing a differential effect". Intersecting grounds can affect the quality of the alleged discrimination and influence the section 15 analysis.'

discrimination. It is worth noting that in 2011 the Supreme Court of Canada denied her leave to appeal and, as usual, without reasons.[40]

Toussaint persisted, bringing a petition to the UN Human Rights Committee pursuant to the *Optional Protocol* to the ICCPR.[41] She alleged violations of Articles 6 (Right to Life) and 26 (Non-Discrimination) of the ICCPR.[42] Her petition regarding Article 26 did not raise race or disability but focused on her exclusion from IFHP coverage based on her particular 'citizenship status' or 'immigration status'.[43] As an intervener at the hearing, the International Network for Economic, Social and Cultural Rights submitted that Canada's refusal to provide health care because of migration status was discriminatory ('Immigration status has been widely recognized as a prohibited ground of discrimination'). There were no references to the grounds of disability or race. The balance of the intervener's submissions focused on Canada's failure to fulfil its positive obligation to protect Toussaint's right to life.[44]

In 2018, the UN Human Rights Committee found violations of Articles 6 (Right to Life)[45] and 26 (Non-Discrimination).[46] The Committee concluded that health care is inherent to the right to life, which is too often 'narrowly interpreted' to exclude the positive obligation of States to 'adopt positive measures'.[47] The Committee ordered Canada to compensate Toussaint and 'to take all steps necessary to prevent similar violations in the future'.[48]

Toussaint is often seen as a case about positive rights. Remarkably, the Human Rights Committee's decision is the first instance in which a UN treaty body considered the claims of an irregular migrant who was refused essential health care. Traditionally, claims of socioeconomic rights, including those relevant to health justice, have not yet been heard. In November 2018, the UN Special Rapporteur on the Right to Health drew specific attention to the UN Human Rights Committee's decision.[49]

40 *Toussaint v Canada (Attorney General)* (Leave to appeal refused) [2011] SCCA No 412 (SCC); Appellant's Memorandum of Fact and Law, 'Nell Toussaint v Attorney General of Canada and Minister of Health' (application for leave to the Supreme Court of Canada) (23 September 2011) <https://www.socialrights.ca/litigation/toussaint/IFH%20APEAL/Applicants%20memorandum%20of%20argument%20for%20leave%20SCC.pdf> accessed 28 January 2026.

41 Optional Protocol to the International Covenant on Civil and Political Rights (adopted 16 December 1966, entered into force March 23, 1976) 999 UNTS 171.

42 International Covenant on Civil and Political Rights (adopted 16 December 1966, entered into force 23 March 1976) 999 UNTS 171.

43 *Nell Toussaint v Canada* (Communication Submitted for Consideration Under the First Optional Protocol to the International Covenant on Civil and Political Rights) 28 December 2013 Communication No 2348/2014 <https://socialrightscura.ca/documents/legal/tousaint%20IFBH/Toussaint%20v%20Canada%20HRC%20No%202348-2014.pdf> accessed 28 January 2026.

44 The International Network for Economic, Social and Cultural Rights, 'Nell Toussaint v. CANADA Communication No. 2348/2014 Legal Opinion' (*ESCR-Net*, 22 August 2015) <https://socialrightscura.ca/documents/international/toussaint/ESCR-Net%20Opinion.pdf> accessed 28 January 2026.

45 ICCPR (n 41) Article 6.

46 ibid Article 26.

47 *Toussaint v Canada* (24 July 2018) Communication No 2348/2014 CCPR/C/123/D/2348/2014, [11.3].

48 ibid [14].

49 UN Special Rapporteur on the right of everyone to the enjoyment of the highest attainable standard of physical and mental health Mr. Dainius Pūras, 'Preliminary Observations—Country Visit to Canada, 5–16 November 2018' (*OHCHR*, 16 November 2018) <https://www.ohchr.org/en/statements/2018/11/preliminary-observations-country-visit-canada-5-16-november-2018> accessed 28 January 2026.

The Committee's decision is also remarkable for its failure to address disability or race. Toussaint's arguments about non-discrimination focused entirely on the ground of 'immigration status', which Canada argued was not a prohibited ground.[50] While we are unsure why her team excluded race and disability from their strategy, we speculate that the pursuit of legal claims centred on a single basis of oppression often results in a more straightforward litigation process.

In light of the Committee's decision, Toussaint applied in 2019 to the Supreme Court of Canada to reconsider its earlier 2011 decision to refuse leave to appeal, but was denied once again.[51] She then brought a Statement of Claim in 2022 for Canada's refusal to implement the recommendations of the UN Human Rights Committee.[52] The Attorney General's motion to strike her Statement of Claim was dismissed by the Ontario Superior Court. Justice Perell criticized Canada for bringing 'a dog whistle argument that reeks of the prejudicial stereotype that immigrants come to Canada to milk the welfare system'.[53] Canada's failure to implement, Justice Perrell opined, may be subject to judicial review in a domestic court for 'the purpose of modern international human rights law is to identify and remedy breaches of internationally accepted norms in a global war on human rights' abuses'.[54]

We celebrate Toussaint's extraordinary victory, ensuring that her claim proceeds in domestic courts. Her claim about the constitutionality of the exclusion of migrants with irregular statuses may still see the light of day. Thus, she was successful. We wonder, however, if her success might have accounted for the complexity of her experience of discrimination. To confront disability and racial oppression, clarity regarding their true character is essential. In particular, we wonder if Toussaint might have fared better at the CPRD Committee because, according to Kirichenko and Król, a 'key feature' of the CRPD is its strong emphasis on intersectionality.[55]

The UN Human Rights Committee made its final decision on 24 July 2018 while Canada acceded to the Optional Protocol to the CRPD only a few months later on 3 December 2018. Sadly, Toussaint passed away on 9 January 2023,[56] meaning there was only a short window wherein she might have made a petition to the UNCRPD. Even if the CRPD had been available to her, very few persons with disabilities from Canada have had their matters heard by the Committee. Indeed, as of April 2023, there have been no Canadian matters brought to the UNCRPD under the CRPD's Optional Protocol.

[50] *Toussaint* (n 47)

[51] Appellant's Memorandum of Argument, 'Nell Toussaint and Attorney General of Canada (In The Supreme Court of Canada, 5 June 2019) (Social Rights Canada) <https://www.socialrights.ca/2019/nt-moa-sccrecon.pdf> accessed 28 January 2026.

[52] *Toussaint v Canada* (Attorney General) 2022 ONSC 4747.

[53] ibid [134].

[54] ibid [182].

[55] Kseniya A Kirichenko and Agnieszka Król, 'Intersectionality and the CRPD: An Analysis of the CRPD Committee's Discourse and Civil Society Advocacy at the Intersections of Disability and LGBTI' (2022) 17 Global Public Health 11.

[56] Nicholas Keung, 'She went from undocumented to undeniable. Advocate whose fight against Canadian government reached the UN remembered as an "inspiration"' *Toronto Star* (21 January 2023) <https://www.thestar.com/news/canada/2023/01/21/she-went-from-undocumented-to-undeniable-advocate-whose-fight-against-canadian-government-reached-the-un-remembered-as-an-inspiration.html> accessed 28 January 2026.

If she had been able—in a procedural sense—to bring her complaint to the UNCRPD, she might have raised Article 25 (health), which sets out that persons with disabilities have the right to the enjoyment of the highest attainable standard of health without discrimination because of disability. Displaced persons with disabilities, many of whom are racialized, confront 'additional burden'[57] including those that arise from hazardous employment and workplace accidents in construction and manufacturing sectors and from toxic exposures in nail salons or agricultural settings, which increase their risk of acquiring disabilities. Migrant workers are often excluded from access to quality health care services, including disability support.[58] Toussaint might also have raised Article 5 (equality and non-discrimination). The claims of racialized women with disabilities who have been forcibly displaced are rejected because of ableist perceptions of the economic costs of disability, prioritizing economic considerations over human rights and equality and perpetuating the marginalization of individuals with disabilities.[59] In 2010, the Office of the United Nations High Commissioner for Refugees recognized that the protection of refugees with disabilities, particularly women, is necessary as they are exposed to discrimination, exploitation, violence, and sexual and gender-based violence.[60]

Would the CPRD Committee have understood Toussaint's intersectional claims in such a way that the UN Human Rights Committee did not? While Toussaint could not have raised the CRPD, the facts may have lent themselves to an application to the UNCRPD nevertheless. That Committee would have had General Comment No 6 (right to life) available to it, unlike the Human Rights Committee, which governs complaints under the Optional Protocol to the ICESCR.

The CPRD Committee has heard similar positive rights claims in the context of health justice. In 2022, the Committee found that Australia breached the human rights of Grainne Sherlock, a woman with a disability, wanting to migrate to Australia.[61] She alleged that Australia denied her a work sponsored visa, and the Committee agreed that her application for a work visa was 'rejected solely due to her diagnosis of multiple sclerosis and the economic cost it could represent'.[62] While Sherlock's petition did not explicitly raise arguments about race, it touched on her argument about intersecting

[57] United Nations Department of Economic and Social Affairs, 'Refugees and migrants with disabilities' (*UN Department of Economic and Social Affairs*, 4 April 2016) <https://www.un.org/development/desa/disabilities/refugees_migrants_with_disabilities.html> accessed 18 July 2024.

[58] United Nations High Commissioner for Refugees, 'Conclusion on Refugees with Disabilities and Other Persons with Disabilities Protected and Assisted by UNHCR' (*UNHCR*, 10 October 2010) <https://www.unhcr.org/publications/conclusion-refugees-disabilities-and-other-persons-disabilities-protected-and-assisted> accessed 18 July 2024.

[59] Women's Refugee Commission 'Refugees with Disabilities: Fact Sheet' (*Women's Refugee Commission*, 22 September 2023) <https://www.womensrefugeecommission.org/research-resources/disabilities-program-fact-sheet/> accessed 15 October 2023.

[60] UNHCR (n 58).

[61] *Grainne Sherlock v Australia*, Communication No 20/2014, CRPD/C/24/D/20/2014 (19 March 2021); NEDA, 'UN CRPD finds Australia in breach of human rights of woman with disability: NEDA shares recommendations on how to make our migration system fairer' (*NEDA*, 10 June 2021) <https://neda.org.au/un-crpd-finds-australia-in-breach-of-human-rights-of-woman-with-disability-neda-shares-recommendations-on-how-to-make-our-migration-system-fairer/> accessed 5 July 2024.

[62] Mary Crock and others, 'Cases before International Courts and Tribunals concerning Questions of Public International Law Involving Australia 2021' (2023) 40(1) The Australian Year Book of International Law Online 475, 493.

grounds and cited General Comment No 6.[63] Toussaint may have made a similar argument.

If *Toussaint* was reconstructed to engage the CRPD, her complaint might have been heard differently. Upon reflection, this is more than an intellectual exercise and is deeply relevant to the 2023 provincial cuts to health care funding for uninsured Ontarians.[64] Without careful attention to the lived experience of discrimination, forthcoming challenges such as Toussaint's will fail to sufficiently describe, resist, and challenge their experiences of injustice.[65] It is impossible to know how the UNCRPD would have decided a petition from Toussaint. As with all claims from persons with disabilities, there is a massive gap between law on the books and law in action. Additionally, this gap is doomed to persist if it is left up to counsel and/or interveners to require decision-makers to 'see' race or make connections between disability and race.

Toussaint illustrates the risk of a race-evasive approach to understanding the claims of disabled people and warns future claimants. This investigation might guide strategic decisions to challenge recent cuts to health care for migrants in Ontario, ultimately avoiding what Crenshaw calls 'racial perspectivelessness'.[66] The decision-makers in Toussaint's case appear to have overlooked the intricate and intersecting nature of her claims. This oversight concerns the capacity of international legal frameworks, whether the ICESR or the CRPD, to address the specific intersectional inequalities that Toussaint endured. The question arises whether international laws are equipped to deliver disability justice in cases involving intersecting identities.[67] While important, these frameworks might not provide comprehensive solutions for individuals who face compounded discrimination due to their disabilities, along with other factors such as race, gender, or socioeconomic status. Achieving disability justice for

[63] *Sherlock* (n 61) [8.5]: 'The Committee notes that treatment is indirectly discriminatory if the detrimental effects of a rule or decision exclusively or disproportionately affect persons of a particular race, colour, sex, language, religion, political or other opinion, national or social origin, property, birth or other status. Being a woman with a disability falls within such categories.'

[64] Ritika Goel, Vanessa Redditt, and Michaela Beder, 'Ford's health-care cuts risk lives of society's most vulnerable' *Toronto Star* (28 March 2023) <https://www.thestar.com/opinion/contributors/2023/03/28/fords-health-care-cuts-risk-lives-of-societys-most-vulnerable.html> accessed 18 July 2024; Jesse McLaren, 'Stop Ford's cuts to healthcare for all' (*Spring*, 29 March 2023) <https://springmag.ca/stop-fords-cuts-to-healthcare-for-all> accessed 18 July 2024.

[65] See in general Vasanthi Venkatesh, '"No Status, No Race": *Toussaint* and The Erasure of Race in Immigration Judicial Making' [2023] unpublished cited in Vasanthi Ventakesh, 'Radical Resistance in the Penumbra of the Law: Legal Mobilization for Migrant Farmworkers under Neo-Colonial Capitalism' (2025) 37 Journal of Law and Social Policy 22 at 32.

[66] Kimberle Williams Crenshaw, 'Toward a Race-Conscious Pedagogy in Legal Education' (1988) 11(1) National Black Law Journal 1.

[67] Catalina Devandas-Aguilar, 'End of Mission Statement by the United Nations Special Rapporteur On rights of persons with disabilities' (*OHCHR*, 12 April 2019) <https://www.ohchr.org/en/statements/2019/04/end-mission-statement-united-nations-special-rapporteur-rights-persons> accessed 15 October 2023. Devandas-Aguilar notes, 'The situation of indigenous persons with disabilities is particularly worrisome, as they are far behind in the enjoyment of their rights, and they do not have access to the same services and opportunities, many of which are only provided outside the reserves and in non-cultural sensitive ways . . . In addition, I am very concerned about the overrepresentation of persons with disabilities, particularly those belonging to indigenous or other minority communities, in both prisons and the juvenile justice system. I have also received alarming information that persons with psychosocial disabilities are diverted to mental health courts for minor offences where they are subjected to higher penalties and stricter regimes.'

such individuals may require a more nuanced and inclusive legal framework (and an understanding and application of intersectionality) that considers the full spectrum of their experiences.

In the following section, we provide another case study to assess the potential of the CRPD to support access to justice for Indigenous and racialized people with mental health disabilities who experience intersectional discrimination.[68]

4. Case study: British Columbia's Mental Health Act and the CRPD's potential to address intersectional discrimination

In the context of mental health laws, disability scholars have recognized that involuntary detention and treatment of people with mental health disabilities violate multiple sections of the CRPD. According to Gooding (2013), the United Nations Office of the High Commissioner for Human Rights adopted a view that:

> ... [M]ental health legislation is unjustly discriminatory against people with psychosocial disability because it systematically uses mental disorder as criteria to limit legal capacity, a view echoed by the CRPD Committee. The proposition of applying supported decision-making to mental health legislation is therefore problematic, given that the principles of non-discrimination and equality underpin supported decision-making. Particular sections of the CRPD will create ongoing challenges to the operation of mental health legislation: in particular, Article 14, as relates to detention ('the existence of a disability shall in no case justify a deprivation of liberty'); Article 17, as relates to involuntary treatment ('(e)very person with disabilities has a right to respect for his or her physical and mental integrity on an equal basis with others'), and 25, and, again, Article 12, as relates to restrictions on legal capacity on the basis of a disability.[69]

Canada's Supreme Court has found that 'international human rights treaties, such as the CRPD',[70] are a 'relevant and persuasive factor in Charter interpretation'[71] and directed 'that Canadian laws should be interpreted and applied in a manner that is consistent with Canada's international human rights obligations'.[72] Article 4(1)(a) of

[68] See, eg, Theresia Degener and Gerald Quinn, 'A Survey of International, Comparative and Regional Disability Law Reform' in Mary Lou Breslin and Sylvia Yee (eds), *Disability Rights Law and Policy: International and National Perspectives* (Transnational Publishers 2002) 3.

[69] Piers Gooding, 'Supported Decision-Making: A Rights-Based Disability Concept and Its Implications for Mental Health Law' (2013) 20(3) Psychiatry, Psychology and Law 431, 440; Tina Minkowitz, 'The United Nations Convention on the Rights of Persons with Disabilities and the Right to be Free from Nonconsensual Psychiatric Interventions' (2007) 34(2) Syracuse Journal of International Law and Commerce 405; Tina Minkowitz, 'Abolishing Mental Health Laws to Comply with the Convention on the Rights of Persons with Disabilities' in Bernadette McSherry and Penelope Weller (eds), *Rethinking Rights-Based Mental Health Laws* (Hart 2010).

[70] Ruby Dhand and Kerri Joffe, 'Involuntary Detention and Involuntary Treatment Through the Lens of Sections 7 and 15 of the Canadian Charter of Rights and Freedoms' (2020) 43(3) Manitoba Law Journal (Criminal Law Edition) 207.

[71] *Reference re Public Service Employee Relations Act (Alberta)* (1987) 1 SCR 313, 38 DLR (4th) 161, Dickson CJC dissenting.

[72] Dhand and Joffe (n 70) at 210 citing *R v Hape* (2007) SCC 26 [35].

the CRPD requires that 'States Parties undertake to ensure and promote the full realization of all human rights and fundamental freedoms for all persons with disabilities without discrimination of any kind on the basis of disability. To this end, States Parties undertake: (a) To adopt all appropriate legislative, administrative and other measures for the implementation of the rights recognised in the Convention.' [73] Following this, 'any *Charter* analysis of Canadian mental health legislation must consider the implications of the CRPD'.[74]

British Columbia's Mental Health Act is an important case study for our analysis of the potential of CRPD. *Maclaren v British Columbia (Attorney General)*[75] challenges the constitutionality of the 'deemed consent provisions' of BC's Mental Health Act. It was brought forward by individual plaintiffs first and public interest litigants subsequently, including Community Legal Assistance Society (CLAS) and the Council of Canadians with Disabilities (CCD). The 'action has yet to be determined on its merits, as the collateral issue of the test for public interest standing was recently decided in favour of the Canadian Council of Canadians with Disabilities in the Supreme Court of Canada's case of *British Columbia (Attorney General) v Council of Canadians with Disabilities*'.[76]

Section 31(1) of the BC *Mental Health Act* is the 'deemed consent' provision. It states:

> If a patient is detained in a designated facility under section 22, 28, 29, 30 or 42 or is released on leave or is transferred to an approved home under section 37 or 38, treatment authorized by the director is deemed to be given with the consent of the patient.[77]

In other words, people with mental health disabilities who are involuntarily detained under BC's Mental Health Act regime are 'administered compulsory treatment by the director of the facility and deprived of their right to a capacity assessment, the right to a substitute decision-maker and/or representative and other legal safeguards'.[78]

Following the Ontario Court of Appeal's decision in *Fleming v Reid*,[79] the litigants in *Maclaren* and CCD's case argued that BC's Mental Health Act's deemed consent provisions harm people with mental health disabilities: they are 'subjected to

[73] CRPD (n 2) Article 4(1).

[74] Dhand and Joffe (n 70) at 210; In 2018, Canada acceded to the Optional Protocol enabling Canadians to make human rights complaints under the CRPD.

[75] *British Columbia (Attorney General) v Council of Canadians with Disabilities* (2022) SCC 27; *Council of Canadians with Disabilities v British Columbia (Attorney General)* (2020) BCCA 241, 2. The trial addressing the merits of the case continues in the BC Supreme Court (2026).

[76] Anita Szigeti and Ruby Dhand, *Law and Mental Health in Canada: Cases and Materials* (Lexis Nexis Canada 2022) at 138.

[77] Mental Health Act, RSBC 1996, c 288, section 31(1).

[78] D'Arcy Hiltz, Anita Szigeti, and Ruby Dhand, *Halsbury's Laws of Canada Mental Health Law* (3rd edn, Lexis Nexis Canada 2019) at 21; Also, see *Mental Health Act*, RSBC 1996, c 288, s 8(a). Anita Szigeti and Ruby Dhand, *Law and Mental Health in Canada: Cases and Materials* (LexisNexis 2022) 90; Anita Szigeti and Ruby Dhand, 'British Columbia's Mental Health Act: Deemed "Consent" is not Consent,' in Anita Szigeti, Ruby Dhand, and Dena Bonnet (eds) *Canadian Anthology on Mental Health and the Law* (1st edn, Lexis Nexis Canada 2024).

[79] *Fleming v Reid and Gallagher* (1991) 48 OAC 46 (CA).

forced psychiatric treatment [that] has caused severe psychological pain and stress'.[80] According to the plaintiffs, these actions are unconstitutional under sections 7 and 15 of the Canadian Charter of Rights and Freedoms. Counsel also argued that the deemed consent provisions contravene Articles 12 and 13 of the CRPD,[81] which Canada signed in 2007 and ratified in 2010. Article 12 of the CRPD recognizes that 'persons with disabilities are presumed to have legal capacity on an equal basis with others in all aspects of their lives'.[82]

As summarized in 'Operating in Darkness: B.C.'s *Mental Health Act* Detention System', a study conducted by the Community Legal Assistance Society (CLAS) in 2017:

> BC's deemed consent model permits treating physicians to make psychiatric treatment decisions unilaterally, without assessing whether a detainee is capable of making his own treatment decisions and without recourse to any other decision maker. Representatives reported many negative impacts of forced psychiatric treatment, including increased feelings of helplessness and fear, failure to involve individuals in an autonomous and collaborative recovery plan, adversarial relationships with mental health care professionals, avoidance of voluntary mental health services, and minimisation and disregard of reported experiences and side effects with psychiatric treatment. The exclusion of family members and friends from psychiatric treatment decisions contributes to the isolation of individuals with mental disabilities and discounts the valuable role that personal support networks play in recovery. The prohibition on Mental Health Act detainees using planning tools like Representation Agreements means individuals with mental health problems are not permitted to put a legal plan in place to prevent or ameliorate future mental health crises. BC is the only deemed consent model of psychiatric treatment in Canada and while there are diverging opinions about which model is the most effective, it is widely recognised that the BC deemed consent model does not comply with the rights guaranteed by the Charter and the UN CRPD.[83]

Through the lens of intersectionality, the CRPD could help address the disproportionate adverse impacts of BC's deemed consent provisions on Indigenous and racialized people with mental health disabilities. Empirical evidence in Canada highlights that 'people from ethnic minorities are also more likely to experience mental health

[80] Mary Louise MacLaren, DC, 'Canadian Council with Disabilities v. Attorney General', *Amended Notice of Civil Claim*, Vancouver Registry, No S-168364 (BC SC) [*CCD v BC*]; Community Legal Assistance Society, 'Charter Challenge of Forced Psychiatric Treatment Filed in BC Supreme Court' (Community Legal Assistance Society, 13 September 2016) <https://clasbc.net/charter-challenge-of-forced-psychiatric-treatment-filed-in-bc-supreme-court/> accessed 28 January 2026; Ruby Dhand and Isabel Grant, 'Charter challenge to B.C. Mental Health Act long overdue' (*Vancouver Sun*, 23 September 2016) <http://vancouversun.com/opinion/opinion-charter-challenge-to-b-c-mental-health-act-long-overdue> accessed 28 July 2024.

[81] CRPD (n 2).

[82] ibid.

[83] CLAS, 'Operating in Darkness: BC's Mental Health Act Detention System' (September 2017) <https://d3n8a8pro7vhmx.cloudfront.net/clastest/pages/1794/attachments/original/1527278723/CLAS_Operating_in_Darkness_November_2017.pdf> accessed 18 July 2024.

stigma and legal barriers than the majority group'.[84] In the mental health context, 'legal barriers faced by ethno-racial psychiatric consumer/survivors are complex; factors such as racism, poverty, unemployment, separation from family and community support, socio-cultural mental health stigmas, misdiagnosis, mistrust of the mental health system and culturally inappropriate care often define experiences'.[85] When interacting with the mental health system, Indigenous and racialized people with mental health disabilities experience a 'higher rate of involuntary admission, a higher likelihood of misdiagnosis', and barriers to accessing justice and culturally appropriate care.[86]

Johnston and Milne found the following in BC:[87]

> While there is little data publicly available on the use of the statutory powers and safeguards pursuant to civil mental health legislation in British Columbia, available evidence indicates that the impacts of detention and involuntary treatment may be disproportionate based on factors such as age, sex, Indigeneity, and race . . .
>
> British Columbia does not track disaggregated race-based data with respect to mental health detention and involuntary treatment, however, disproportionate impacts documented in other jurisdictions indicate there are significant reasons to responsibly monitor this data. Jurisdictions that do track impacts based on race, ethnicity, and Indigeneity have shown that Indigenous, Black, and other racialised communities experience detention and involuntary treatment at disproportionately higher rates and are subject to higher levels of coercion while detained . . .
>
> [Reports have documented] a number of discriminatory stereotypes that are applied to Indigenous people in the health care system. Many of these racist stereotypes, including that Indigenous people are less capable and compliant, may directly impact how authorized health care staff assess the appropriateness or necessity of detention and involuntary treatment for an Indigenous person. Often there are stories [and cases] from Indigenous people who went to hospital seeking physical health care who were detained under the Mental Health Act, with police and security involvement. The Ministry of Health has stated that it believes 'Indigenous children and youth are detained at higher rates in British Columbia under the *Mental Health Act*, despite the absence of data on that question.
>
> . . . McKenzie has also noted that Black and other racialised people are less likely to be offered mental health support, such as counselling and psychotherapy, and are more likely to be offered prescription drugs and subjected to coercive health care.[88]

Disability advocates have long recognized that models of involuntary detention disproportionately impact Indigenous and racialized people with mental health disabilities interacting with BC's deemed consent provisions. The CRPD could help address

[84] Ruby Dhand, 'Access to Justice for Ethno-Racial Psychiatric Consumer/Survivors in Ontario' (2011) 29 Windsor Yearbook of Access to Justice 127, 128.

[85] ibid.

[86] ibid 129; World Health Organization, 'WHO Resource Book on Mental Health', *Human Rights and Legislation* (World Health Organization, 2005) 85.

[87] Laura Johnston and Kendra Milne, 'Why Have We Left Human Rights Out of Mental Health and Substance Use Health Care' (2021) Continuing Legal Education Society of BC, 2.1.3–2.1.5.

[88] ibid.

the 'increased vulnerability'[89] and 'root causes'[90] of intersectional and aggravated forms of discrimination experienced by Indigenous and racialized people with mental health disabilities. The CRPD articulates that it 'must combat stereotypes, prejudices and harmful practices relating to persons with disabilities, including those based on sex and age, in all areas of life'.[91] By embracing an intersectional and social model of disability, the CRPD provides that people with disabilities receive 'recognition and support of their specific cultural and linguistic identity'.[92]

Maclaren and CCD's case provide Canadian courts with the opportunity to strengthen and legitimize the CRPD as a legitimate source of law. Using a positive rights approach, the courts can draw from the CRPD, the Optional Protocol, and its accompanying work, including the General Comments, Observations, consultative reports, and proceedings, to explicitly address intersectional disability discrimination. Pursuant to the CRPD Articles 12, 13, 14, 17, and 25, there is a clear recognition of the entrenched patterns of systemic disability discrimination, increased vulnerabilities, and harm that Indigenous and racialized people with mental health disabilities experience as a result of forced psychiatric treatment and involuntary detention. A robust implementation of the CRPD in this case could result in the expansive interpretation of the following provisions: Article 12 (prohibition restricting legal capacity via BC's deemed consent provisions); Article 13 (recognition of intersectional barriers to accessing justice), Article 14 (recognition of the significant deprivation of liberty in psychiatric detention experienced by Indigenous and racialized people with mental health disabilities), Article 17 (recognition of the disproportionate harm and impact of involuntary detention and forced treatment for Indigenous and racialized people with mental health disabilities), and Article 25 (recognition of the profound impact access to culturally appropriate psychiatric treatment, mental health support, and care can have for Indigenous and racialized people with disabilities).

In this section, we sought to illustrate the potential of the CRPD to address the 'multiple and aggravated forms of discrimination' experienced because of BC's deemed consent provisions. If the CRPD is used as a tool for advocacy in cases such as this one, it may trigger the courts to examine the intersectional and unique barriers to accessing justice and culturally appropriate care for Indigenous and racialized people with mental health disabilities involuntarily detained under BC's *Mental Health Act*.

5. Conclusion: the CRPD as a tool for advocacy to address intersectional discrimination

Disability injustice for Indigenous and racialized people with disabilities is intertwined with other structural injustices, particularly colonialism and systemic racism. Intersectionality requires us to understand how our identities shape our relationship

[89] Gauthier de Beco, 'Protecting the Invisible: An Intersectional Approach to International Human Rights Law' (2017) 17(4) Human Rights Law Review 633, 642.
[90] ibid
[91] CRPD (n 2) Article 8.
[92] ibid.

with patterns of oppression and dynamics of power. Patricia Hill Collins argues that intersectionality operates within a matrix of domination, which refers to the organization of power within a society.[93] According to Collins, each matrix of domination contains a range of intersecting forms of oppression. This naming of the complexities of the experiences of intersectional discrimination is necessary to transform them.[94]

The CRPD 'provides an excellent opportunity to examine how international human rights law can accommodate intersectionality'.[95] As this chapter suggests, while there is scope within international human rights law—and the CRPD in particular—to recognize claims of intersectional discrimination, some groups and identities, especially cisgender women and children with disabilities, are centred while the experiences of others are all but absent. Therefore, we do not propose that an application to the Committee on the Rights of Persons with Disabilities would serve as a panacea. Indeed, analysis based on intersectional discrimination has very minimal application in our home jurisdiction of Canada, despite being first embedded in domestic law.[96] Moreover, our review of the Committee's Concluding Observations in relation to Canada indicates that, while concerns about intersectionality and multiple discrimination are raised in relation to Indigeneity, there is no mention of race.

Notwithstanding these limitations, international human rights norms, including the CRPD, can provide a broad range of remedies to address systemic injustices underlying intersectional disability discrimination (in contrast to domestic litigation).[97] The two case studies illustrate the challenges of bringing forth claims of intersecting disability discrimination in domestic legal fora and international human rights mechanisms outside the CRPD.

While there is potential to advance intersectional claims, the realization of that potential depends on lawyers and advocates who are prepared to use the CRPD as a tool to address intersectional discrimination for Indigenous and racialized people with disabilities. Lawyers and advocates should attend to the complex forms of intersectional discrimination, and to do so must advance a robust intersectional interpretation of the CRPD's articles. Such an interpretation should contextualize the 'underlying causes of increased vulnerabilities'[98] and the complex factors which contribute to the injustices they suffer such as colonialism, systemic racism, poverty, stigma, and culturally inappropriate services and supports.[99] As de Beco explains, '[w]hat intersectionality requires is that social complexities be taken into account and the reassembling of various dimensions of identity from the artificially constructed monolithic identities be questioned'.[100] As highlighted in the case studies, the CRPD must be used to address

[93] Patricia Hill Collins, *Black Feminist Thought: Knowledge, Consciousness and the Politics of Empowerment* (Unwin Hyman 1990).

[94] ibid.

[95] de Beco (n 89) 642.

[96] Grace Akele and Jena McGill, 'Intersectionality in Law and Legal Contexts' (Women's Legal Education and Action Fund 2020) <https://www.leaf.ca/publication/intersectionality-in-law-and-legal-contexts> accessed 3 December 2024.

[97] de Beco (n 89) 642.

[98] ibid 641.

[99] Dhand (n 84) 128; Ruby Dhand, 'Creating a Cultural Analysis Tool for the Implementation of Ontario's Civil Mental Health Laws' (2016) 45 International Journal of Law & Psychiatry 25.

[100] de Beco (n 89) 640.

the systemic racism and attitudinal barriers experienced by Indigenous and racialized people with disabilities interacting with Canadian laws and policies.

Devoid of an intersectional lens, disability justice is not justice for Indigenous and racialized peoples with disabilities. The potential cannot be realized with a colour-evasive approach. Structural and systemic changes require more than bringing claims of intersecting discrimination by lawyers and advocates. It also requires multiple stakeholders in the domestic and international spheres to identify intersectional forms of discrimination and prioritize accountability and enforcement.

13

De-essentializing Race

Intersectionality as a Feminist Approach in International Human Rights Law

Paulina Jimenez Fregoso

1. Intersectionality meets international human rights law

Nowadays, intersectionality is slowly being mainstreamed into international human rights law. However, two major issues have arisen; first, intersectionality has the massive task of challenging the status quo of international human rights law (IHRL), which as I explain, is a heavily gendered and racialized system. Second, the implementation of intersectionality theory in IHRL adjudication tends to take place independently of the discussions and debates of the same feminist scholars that developed the theory, bringing about mixed results.

In this chapter, I explore whether the use of intersectionality by international human rights adjudicative bodies addresses and redresses the harm experienced by multiply burdened individuals, with a special focus on cases related to race, racism, colourism, and racial discrimination. In the first sections, the research demonstrates how human rights adjudicative processes have used tools to address discrimination cases that conceptualize victims as homogenous individuals that are discriminated against on the basis of one identity alone. When single-axis tools were proven to be ineffective to tackle human rights violations experienced by multiply burdened individuals, intersectionality rose as a possible way to obtain a more comprehensive justice. The case studies included in this chapter illustrate that when the victim is thought of as a complex individual, it is possible to more accurately assess their different qualitative experiences of harm. The final section highlights the potential of taking intersectionality seriously to provide tools for multiply burdened racialized individuals to achieve meaningful reparation within the human rights framework.

2. Combating discrimination; when the white and male lens becomes the norm

In theory, the systems and laws devised to protect and guarantee the rights of individuals are meant to be neutral and objective. However, in practice, this has been proven incorrect with scholars arguing that legal systems are very much gendered and white.[1]

[1] See, eg, Hilary Charlesworth, Christine Chinkin, and Shelly Wright, 'Feminist Approaches to International Law' (1991) 85(4) American Journal of International Law 613; Hilary Charlesworth, 'What

Paulina Jimenez Fregoso, *De-essentializing Race* In: *Emancipating International Law*. Edited by: Mohsen al Attar and Claire Smith, Oxford University Press. © Paulina Jimenez Fregoso 2026. DOI: 10.1093/9780198935605.003.0017

IHRL has not been exempted from these criticisms. While there is no need to condemn the entirety of the discipline, we must also acknowledge that because of the context in which international law was devised, certain aspects reproduce unequal social dynamics.[2]

When the modern concept of human rights was adopted in 1948, Western 'values' were embedded into the Universal Declaration of Human Rights,[3] values that for many years did not apply to Black people, Indigenous people, or even women. As Becker explains:

> Colonised subjects were excluded from the human rights texts of the 1940s . . . Even during the 1950s, colonial powers inserted a clause in policies to ensure that human rights were not applicable in colonies . . . Anticolonial human rights movements only started in the 1960s, when the UN General Assembly Resolution 1514 condemned colonisation . . .[4]

From tolerance to apartheid to the disproportionate investigations launched by the International Criminal Court (ICC) against predominantly Black African countries, 'the history of human rights . . . has largely been constructed by nations, leaders, and scholars who are overwhelmingly from Western Europe and North America and who identify racially as white'.[5] Then, one can assume safely that tackling racism using tools, such as mechanisms, laws, and even research methodologies with a racist history will either achieve its objective slowly or will fail to do so completely.

What is considered normal and standard in everyday life has referred to the identifications, norms, and interests of white people,[6] and as such, laws have implicitly considered a white, straight, Western man as the default 'neutral' individual.[7] Kanter explains that '[W]hen the issue is gender, men are treated but never acknowledged, as the norm, while women are considered the deviation'.[8] This is similar to what occurs

are 'Women's International Human Rights?' in Rebecca J Cook (ed), *Human Rights of Women: National and International Perspectives* (University of Pennsylvania Press 1994).

[2] Bhupinder Chimni, 'Third World Approaches to International Law: A Manifesto' (2006) 8 International Community Law Review 3, 3.

[3] See Rebecca Adami, 'On Subalternity and Representation: Female and Post-Colonial Subjects Claiming Universal Human Rights in 1948' (2016) 6 Journal of Research on Women and Gender 56; Mukua Mutua, *Human Rights: A Political and Cultural Critique* (University of Pennsylvania Press 2002).

[4] Anne Becker, 'Decolonial Human Rights Education: Changing the Terms and Content of Conversations on Human Rights' (2021) 4(2) Human Rights Education Review 49, 53.

[5] Anna Spain Bradley, 'Human Rights Racism'(2019) 32 Harvard Human Rights Journal 1, 16.

[6] Gloria Ladson-Billings and William F Tate 'Toward a Critical Race Theory of Education' (1995) 97(1) Teachers College Record 47.

[7] Lynn Roseberry, 'Multiple Discrimination' in Malcolm Sargeant (ed), *Age Discrimination and Diversity: Multiple Discrimination from an Age Perspective* (Cambridge University Press 2011) 33; Joan C Williams, 'Dissolving the Sameness/Difference Debate: A Post-Modern Path beyond Essentialism in Feminist and Critical Race Theory' (1991) 2 Duke Law Journal 296; Lisa A Crooms, 'Indivisible Rights and Intersectional Identities or, "What Do Women's Human Rights Have to Do with the Race Convention' (1997) 40 Howard Law Journal 619, 620; Charlotte Helen Skeet, 'Intersectionality as Theory and Method. Human Rights Adjudication by the European Court of Human Rights' in Naomi Creutzfeldt, Marc Mason, and Kirsten McConnachie (eds), *Routledge Handbook of Socio-Legal Theory and Methods* (Routledge 2020) 277.

[8] Arlene S Kanter, 'The Law: What's Disability Studies Got to Do with it or an Introduction to Disability Legal Studies' (2010) 42 Columbia Human Rights Law Review 403, 406.

when the issue is race. While it is not openly acknowledged, human rights theory treats whiteness as the norm and thus has failed to properly develop antiracist strategies that do not take whiteness as their starting point.

Therefore when marginalized social groups fail to match the neutral standard, they must be brought in line with white standards. In other words, they must overcome their marginalization and discrimination by aspiring to have and experience what their white Western counterparts have and do. Moreover, traditionally, legal regimes have considered discrimination as a single event meaning that a person was discriminated against on one ground, such as race, exclusively.[9]

Anti-discrimination laws have the notion of formal equality at their centre, treating likes alike.[10] To bring forward a successful claim of discrimination on the basis of race, one must demonstrate how their situation is unfair when compared to another individual who is not of that race. As discussed, this other hypothetical individual is a white person. Theoretically, the victim must pick a social group that possesses the same relevant circumstances as them in order to compare both social groups and demonstrate that unfair or disadvantageous treatment has occurred.[11] This single-axis approach to identities builds its analysis on the idea that person A would not have been discriminated against if they did not have that specific identity—race in the context of this chapter—and ignores all other identities that might have been impacted by the discriminatory act or that were also relevant to the decision of discriminating against the person.[12]

Instead of recognizing that some individuals might experience further marginalization because they belong to several excluded social categories concurrently, the single-axis approach uses the experiences of the most privileged within the discriminated social category as the experience of all its members: '[i]t is assumed that everyone in a particular pocket [ie protected ground] has no other relevant characteristics, it is not possible to articulate differences between those within a pocket'.[13] For example, discrimination on the basis of race is endowed with specific characteristics that can prove inaccurate when facing racist misogyny, yet it will guide the result of a discrimination claim. Even when the individual suffers discrimination on the basis of more than one ground, they are forced to frame the discriminatory treatment within one single ground at a time. This accentuates the 'atomized' application of antidiscrimination law, favouring one ground to the exclusion of others.[14] As David Gillborn points out, 'to understand how racism works, we need to appreciate how race intersects with other axes of oppression at different times and in different contexts, but we must try

[9] Timo Makkonen, 'Multiple, Compound and Intersectional Discrimination: Bringing the experiences of the most marginalised to the fore' (LLM Thesis, Åbo Akademi University 2002).

[10] Jess Bullock and Annick Masselot, 'Multiple Discrimination and Intersectional Disadvantages: Challenges and Opportunities in the European Union Legal Framework' (2012–2013) 19 Columbia Journal of European Law 57, 61.

[11] Sarah Hannet, 'Equality at the Intersections: The Legislative and Judicial Failure to Tackle Multiple Discrimination' (2003) 23 Oxford Journal of Legal Studies 65.

[12] Nitya Iyer, 'Categorical Denials: Equality Rights and the Shaping of Social Identity' (1993–1994) 19 Queen's Law Journal 179, 193.

[13] ibid.

[14] Hannet (n 11) 67.

to find a balance between remaining sensitive to intersectional issues without being overwhelmed by them'.[15]

In a nutshell, the single-axis approach is ideal for cases in which the individual only suffers from discrimination on the basis of a single identity; that is, individuals who are in a position of privilege but for one identity. The theory of antidiscrimination has traditionally considered the experiences of exceptions rather than the rule, and in a way it has downplayed or ignored the experiences of those who are marginalized at the intersection of two or more grounds. With this in mind, it was necessary to rethink the work done so far as it does not fully capture such a complex phenomenon as discrimination or oppression; cue intersectionality.

3. When the single-axis approach fails: what then?

As discussed, there is a very narrow conceptualization of the effects racial discrimination has on individuals. The 'but-for' approach that has been used for this type of discrimination has done very little to fully comprehend the root causes of racism and the extent of its harms.[16] With the indiscriminate use of single-axis tests to demonstrate discrimination, adjudicative bodies have obscured the historical and systematic inequalities endured by multiply burdened individuals[17] who are also racialized. Intersectionality can therefore contribute to understanding how racialized individuals who suffered discrimination at the intersection of two or more personal characteristics experience inequality not in comparison to a white, straight person but in terms of domination and marginalization more broadly.[18]

Kimberlé Crenshaw coined the term 'intersectionality', understood as a 'concept that enables us to recognise the fact that perceived group membership can make people vulnerable to various forms of bias. Yet, because we are simultaneously members of many groups, our complex identities can shape the specific way we each experience that bias',[19] and it takes its name from the analogy of a road intersection:

> This apparent contradiction is but another manifestation of the conceptual limitations of the single-issue analyses that intersectionality challenges. The point is that Black women can experience discrimination in any number of ways and that the contradiction arises from our assumptions that their claims of exclusion must be unidirectional. Consider an analogy to traffic in an intersection, coming and going in all four directions. Discrimination, like traffic through an intersection, may flow in one direction and it may flow in another. If an accident happens in an intersection, it can be caused by cars travelling from any number of directions and, sometimes, from all

[15] David Gillborn, 'Intersectionality, Critical Race Theory, and the Primacy of Racism: Race, Class, Gender, and Disability in Education' (2015) 21(3) Qualitative Inquiry 277, 279.

[16] Bradley (n 5) 7.

[17] Colleen Sheppard, 'Grounds of Discrimination: Towards an Inclusive and Contextual Approach' (2001) 80 Canadian Bar Review 893.

[18] Catharine A MacKinnon, *Feminism Unmodified: Discourses on Life and Law* (Harvard University Press 1987) 123.

[19] African American Policy Forum, *A Primer on Intersectionality* (Columbia Law School, 2008)

of them. Similarly, if a Black woman is harmed because she is in the intersection, her injury could result from sex discrimination or race discrimination.[20]

To illustrate this point, one needs to look at the waves of migration experienced on the Mexico–United States border. The xenophobia that was displayed, particularly in the city of Tijuana, is not something that can be fully understood without addressing classism alongside racism. When the first wave of migrants from Haiti and Central America arrived in Tijuana in October 2018, seeking to cross into the United States, they experienced high levels of discrimination and violence due to their skin tone, their nationality, and their perceived poverty, all of this at the hands of Mexican institutions and citizens. On the contrary, when the wave of Ukrainian and Russian migrants arrived in the city, also seeking to cross into the United States, their being European, white, and with better economic resources translated into a warm welcome from State authorities and the population alike.[21] The intersections of the first group made them vulnerable to aggravated forms of discrimination and other human rights violations, and thus it is not possible to use a single-axis framework to understand their harm, to compare them to the discriminatory acts experienced by white migrants, or to compare them to the discrimination endured by racialized men or women in their country of origin.

Intersectionality is useful because it plays with the idea that identities are properties of a person that cannot be physically separated from them or from each other.[22] For our discussion on race, 'a black woman is not the intersection to be considered but rather a black woman is in an intersection of gender and race'.[23] The purpose of using intersectionality when addressing and redressing racism is to recognize the common situations experienced by individuals and then dig deeper to see their differences.[24] All of the above does not mean that an individual's identity will be fragmented and multiplied ad infinitum, but rather, highlighting those intersections will allow potential adjudicators to understand the dynamic and interactive nature of these identities[25] and their relationship to historical, political, cultural, social, and geographical contexts.[26]

[20] Kimberlé Crenshaw, 'Demarginalizing the Intersection of Race and Sex: A Black Feminist Critique of Antidiscrimination Doctrine, Feminist Theory and Antiracist Politics' (1989) 1 University of Chicago Legal Forum 139, 149.

[21] See, eg, Inés García Ramos, 'Tijuana para los ucranianos: los migrantes "sofisticados"' *Gatopardo* (11 May 2022) <https://gatopardo.com/reportajes/ucranianos-tijuana-migrantes/> accessed 26 April 2023; CNN, '"Fuera hondureño, aquí no te queremos": Tijuana, la ciudad que no quiere a la caravana de migrantes' *CNN* (19 November 2018) <https://cnnespanol.cnn.com/2018/11/19/fuera-hondureno-aqui-no-te-queremos-tijuana-la-ciudad-que-no-quiere-a-la-caravana-de-migrantes/> accessed 26 April 2023; Kate Morrissey, 'Para los migrantes haitianos, la espera en Tijuana conlleva miedo, discriminación e incluso muerte' *Los Angeles Times* (14 June 2022) <https://www.latimes.com/espanol/mexico/articulo/2022-06-14/dos-migrantes-haitianos-en-tijuana-han-sido-los-ultimos-en-morir-en-circunstancias> accessed 26 April 2023.

[22] Maria Rodó-Zárate and Marta Jorba, 'Metaphors of Intersectionality: Reframing the Debate with a New Proposal' (2022) 29(1) European Journal Of Women's Studies 23, 29–31.

[23] ibid 27.

[24] Dimitrina Petrova, 'Equal Rights Review: Special Focus: Intersectionality' (2016) 16 Equal Rights Review 5.

[25] Nira Yuval-Davis, 'Intersectionality and Feminist Politics' (2006) 13(3) European Journal of Women's Studies 193.

[26] Kathryn Sorrells and Sachi Sekimoto, *Globalising Intercultural Communication: A Reader* (SAGE Publications 2015) 85.

Crenshaw's work reinforces the idea that the identity of a group cannot be constructed by the identities of a few members. As such, when trying to understand complex systems of oppression like racism, one must ask the 'other question':

> The way I try to understand the interconnection of all forms of subordination is through a method I call 'ask the other question'. When I see something that looks racist, I ask, 'Where is the patriarchy in this?' When I see something that looks sexist. I ask, 'Where is the heterosexism in this?' When I see something that looks homophobic, I ask, 'Where are the class interests in this?'[27]

All things considered, understanding what differences matter when dealing with racial discrimination and racism via intersectionality is an added value, not only to possible IHRL judgments but also to understanding these phenomena, as it provides a more precise analysis of the character and/or extent of harm. The subsequent case studies will help illustrate in practice not only the importance of accurately addressing the harm, but also the possible improvement in the reparations ordered to redress it.

4. Intersectionality at play: addressing the harm

In order to understand how intersectionality exposes the consequences of racial discrimination, the seriousness of the violence perpetrated against racialized individuals, and consequently how it can contribute to the enforcement of human rights, this section will draw from cases decided by different IHRL systems in order to illustrate the benefits of using this theory. Intersectionality can expand the knowledge of race, racism, racial discrimination, and other related forms of intolerance. As Anna Spain Bradley argues, IHRL needs to adopt an explicit race consciousness which would recognize the harms unique to racism 'alongside other harms of discrimination on the basis of other features of identity including national origin, religion, sexual orientation, gender, and more'.[28]

Moreover, avoiding the fragmentation of personal characteristics of a racial discrimination victim will also contribute to the understanding that the oppression directed towards a racialized individual may occur only because of their race. However, due to the close interactions of all their identities, the harm can trigger other pre-existing systems of oppression, such as discrimination on the basis of their sexual orientation or ageism; thus a new and aggravated dimension of disempowerment will manifest.[29] Consequently, using intersectionality to understand, for example, how the gender dimension of racism or the racist implications on ableist policies is important in and of itself, as naming the harm accurately raises awareness of these issues but also pushes a more effective agenda to address them.[30]

[27] Mari J Matsuda, 'Beside My Sister, Facing the Enemy: Legal Theory out of Coalition' (1991) 43 Stanford Law Review 1183.

[28] Bradley (n 5) 50–51.

[29] Kimberle Crenshaw, 'Mapping the Margins: Intersectionality, Identity Politics, and Violence against Women of Color' (1991) 43(6) Stanford Law Review 1241.

[30] Bradley (n 5) 48.

The work of the International Criminal Tribunal for Rwanda (ICTR) is an example of the importance of using intersectionality to make visible the different dimensions of crimes such as rape. In the case of *Akayesu*, the ICTR Trial Chamber considered that the rape experienced by Tutsi women on the basis of their gender and their ethnicity was 'an integral part of the process of destruction' of the Tutsi.[31] As Greene recounts, scholars supported the determination of 'genocidal rape' because:

> First, rape as an act of genocide conveys the surplus of intent and the aggravated nature of SGBV [sexual and gender-based violence] when committed (in addition to harm women) to eradicate a protected group. Second, genocidal rape more accurately represents the multiple harms of women without compartmentalizing their identities and experiences. For instance, regarding Tutsi women, it expresses their experiences as women, as Tutsi, and as Tutsi women. Third, if rape is only emphasized as an individual (sexual) harm, delinked from the group harm, it risks perpetuating the gender binaries that have hamstrung women's agency by representing women as victims of sexual violence.[32]

Furthermore, in IHRL, intersectionality can also serve the purpose of determining whether a discriminatory act has taken place, while also explaining how and why this intersectional discrimination creates a qualitatively different experience of harm. For example, the case of *Cuscul Pivaral et al v Guatemala*, issued by the Inter-American Court of Human Rights (IACtHR) will be used. This case refers to forty-nine people diagnosed with HIV between 1992 and 2003, where the Court found that the State had violated the rights to health, life, personal integrity, judicial process, and non-discrimination of the victims, most of whom were multiply burdened.[33] Amongst the victims, there were individuals who were in a relationship with people of the same sex, victims who belonged to Indigenous groups and did not speak Spanish, women who were illiterate, and individuals who had limited economic resources.[34]

In the judgment, the judges used intersectionality to examine the situation of women who were pregnant at the time of their diagnosis. This effort was commendable as it recognized that the violation of the right to health that had already been identified was different from the rest as it affected not only the lives of the mothers but also those of the offspring they were carrying. In this sense, the IACtHR analysed the character of the violation in light of the intersecting characteristics to also conclude that the extent of the harm went beyond the mother. Later, this analysis also played a significant role in establishing the reparations ordered for these women.[35]

The judges of the IACtHR decided to include an intersectional lens since the representatives of the victims argued 'that the State had failed to adopt measures to provide

[31] *Prosecutor v Jean Paul Akayesu* (Trial Judgment) ICTR-96-4-T (2 September 1998) 731.

[32] Llezlie Green, 'Gender Hate Propaganda and Sexual Violence in the Rwandan Genocide: An Argument for Intersectionality in International Law' (2002) 33 Columbia Human Rights Law Review 16.

[33] *Cuscal Pivaral et al v Guatemala*, Judgment, Inter-American Court of Human Rights Series C No 359 (23 August 2018).

[34] ibid Annex 3.

[35] ibid.

comprehensive care to the presumed victims that took into account the different factors of vulnerability that coalesced and resulted in a specific form of discrimination owing to their intersection'.[36] Consequently, the Court decided that it '[would] analyze whether discrimination existed in this case . . . [understanding] that the combination of factors of discrimination in an intersectional manner resulted in a discriminatory experience that differs from the simple accumulation of different reasons for the discrimination against a person'.[37]

However, in a case characterized by the numerous intersections that played a role in the violations experienced by the forty-nine victims, the IACtHR fell short and constrained itself to just one specific group, ignoring the rest of the intersections. It is particularly noticeable that a court known for championing Indigenous peoples' rights does very little to address how the high incidence of HIV/AIDS in Indigenous populations and their lack of medical access is linked to the historic discrimination they have endured. For example, if the interlocking systems of oppression are taken into account by adjudicators and intersectionality is implemented to understand the harm, the *Cuscul Pivaral* judgment could have assessed and taken into account the literacy rates among Indigenous groups in Latin America—the lowest among all social groups—and the causes and impact on the information they received regarding sexual and reproductive health, for both purposes of prevention and appropriate treatment.[38]

Furthermore, in the particular case of Guatemala, there has been a significant increase in the rates of people living with HIV/AIDS in regions where there is a majority of Indigenous peoples. According to UNAIDS, 21 per cent of people living with HIV/AIDS are individuals who belong to the Maya Indigenous groups—especially those who belong to the K'iche, Queqchi, Mam, and Kaqchiquel linguistic groups[39]—and live in discrete departments and speak a variety of languages.[40] Some of the victims in Cuscul Pivaral align perfectly with the diagnosis made by UNAIDS. However, the IACtHR does very little to address how living in the abovementioned departments and belonging to certain linguistic groups complicates their ability to prevent contracting HIV, and their access to health once they have been given the diagnosis. Not understanding the effect the HIV/AIDS epidemic has on certain groups based on their location contributes to the underestimation of the real effect that HIV/AIDS has on the wider communities.[41]

[36] ibid [128].

[37] ibid.

[38] Patricia Ponce and others, 'Estado del Arte sobre VIH y Pueblos Indígenas en América Latina' (Secretariado Internacional de Pueblos Indígenas frente al VIH, la sexualidad y los derechos humanos (SIPIA) y ONUSIDA – Latina 2016) 52.

[39] ibid 68.

[40] Abana-Yala Kunarinaki, 'Promoción de la salud sexual y prevención del VIH/sida y de las ITS en los pueblos indígenas de las Américas' (Organización Panamericana de la Salud y Asociación Mundial de Sexología 2003).

[41] Ministerio de Salud Pública y Asistencia Social, Organización Panamericana de la Salud y Organización Mundial de la Salud en Guatemala, 'Perfil de salud de los pueblos indígenas de Guatemala' (2016) <https://reliefweb.int/report/guatemala/perfil-de-salud-de-los-pueblos-ind-genas-de-guatemala> accessed 22 November.

Additionally, when the court argues that the economic power of the victims made them more vulnerable to a denial of medical treatment, it does not account for the extra barriers that Indigenous peoples have. For example, it is true that the cost of transportation affected most victims in the case, but the fact some Indigenous persons do not speak Spanish results in the cost of transportation being even higher, as the person living with HIV might require someone else to accompany them for translation purposes.[42]

Finally, while most human rights adjudicative bodies have addressed how the right to health entails availability, accessibility, adaptability, and quality of medical services, it is still conceptualized with a Eurocentric lens. Authors Angel Romeo Solval, Janet Midori Ikeda, and Norman Hearsch have established that between 70 and 90 per cent of Indigenous people have an understanding of health issues and treatment that differs from that of Western medicine.[43] This means that awareness campaigns related to sexual and reproductive rights might not have been as effective in Indigenous populations because these campaigns have a linguistic and cultural codification envisioned for white or *mestizo* recipients.[44] Moreover, the understanding of the different cultural codifications could also extend to the care received by people living with HIV/AIDS, allowing for treatments that take into account their cosmovision and traditional medicine, and not only impose a care service that is racially coded to favour *mestizo* understandings of medicine. Thus, when it comes to Indigenous peoples, taking into account all these interlocking systems of oppression is fundamental to understanding their risk of contracting HIV and their ability to access subsequent treatment.[45]

International human rights adjudicators should focus not on what intersectionality is, but on what it does when addressing and redressing racism. According to David Gillborn, intersectionality has two key elements: firstly, an empirical basis which is focused on understanding the systems of oppression that individuals endure, and how they are created and sustained; and secondly, a core activist component, with the objective 'of resisting and changing the status quo'.[46] Additionally, if intersectionality has been identified as a different qualitative experience, for the purpose of determining the harm, it is natural to assume that intersectionality can also contribute to providing more tailored reparations than the current practice provides.

With this in mind, there is only left to assess whether the claims made about intersectionality can actually produce reparations that are specifically tailored to the situation of vulnerability of the victims of racism and racial discrimination and their intersecting identities.

[42] ibid 117.

[43] Ponce and others (n 38) citing Solval, Ikeda, and Hearst who noted: 'Culturally appropriate integrated care is essential for the Adherence of Indigenous Persons Infected with HIV in Guatemala'.

[44] Ponce and others (n 38) 110.

[45] Organización Panamericana de la Salud y Organización Mundial de la Salud, *Incorporación del Enfoque Intercultural de la Salud en la Formación y Desarrollo de Recursos Humanos* (Organización Panamericana de la Salud 1998).

[46] Gillborh (n 15) 279.

5. Repairing the interlocking experiences of harm

When a serious IHRL violation can be attributed to the state, it is the state's legal obligation to provide the victim with all necessary means to repair the damage caused in accordance with the severity and the circumstances of the violation.[47] However, when it comes to the harm experienced by multiply burdened individuals, the reparations offered have not been very effective.

IHRL provides a combination of resources that act as reparations: *restitutio in integrum*, compensation, rehabilitation, just satisfaction, *proyecto de vida* (life project), and guarantees of non-repetition, and these mechanisms take different forms on a case-by-case basis.[48] To provide more comprehensive justice, the importance of an intersectional analysis for the determination of reparations relies on the possibility of tailoring those measures to the real harm that took place. Reparations must go above and beyond the immediate reasons and consequences of the crimes and violations; they must aim to address 'the political and structural inequalities that negatively shape ... lives.'[49] This means that, if the court orders reparations without taking into account the larger context that further marginalizes the victims, then whatever they obtain from the judgment will be futile. Intersectionality can contribute to determining the ideal reparation in cases where the victim was already in a disadvantaged situation that allowed the violation to happen, thereby avoiding restoring them to the same position.

Concrete examples of the use of intersectionality can be seen in the guarantees of non-repetition ordered by IHRL adjudicative bodies. This type of reparation aims to ensure that all policies, legislations, practices, and societal conducts have a deterrence effect and, as such, courts can order that the state changes its policies and laws in order to prevent similar violations from occurring in the future.[50] Here, intersectionality can guide human rights adjudicative bodies to repair the harm on a personal level, but also more broadly, since individuals and social groups exist at intersections and are not isolated from each other.

By contrast, the Peace and Reconciliation Process in Colombia is a great example of how not using an intersectional approach to repair the damage done to Afro-descendant and Indigenous women can do little to remedy their harm. According to González y Bueno-Hansen, the Colombian Peace Process (CPP) has failed to include the cosmologies of these groups of women because they were considered too 'family-centered'. Furthermore, the CPP provided reparations modelled not on the social fabric of these communities but in alignment with a Western nuclear family model that, in the case of Colombia, refers to white or *mestizo* family values and compositions. Yet, with 115 distinct Indigenous groups, a 'one size fits all' approach to

[47] UNGA, 'Basic Principles and Guidelines on the Right to a Remedy and Reparation for Victims of Gross Violations of International Human Rights Law and Serious Violations of International Humanitarian Law' (16 December 2005) UN Doc A/RES/60/147 paras 15–18.
[48] Dinah Shelton, *Remedies in International Human Rights Law* (2nd edn, Oxford University Press 2010).
[49] 'Nairobi Declaration on Women's and Girl's Right to a Remedy and Reparation' Nairobi, 22 May 2007.
[50] Shelton (n 48) 315.

reparations was certain to flounder.[51] Similarly, Afro-descendant communities also think of family as a collective; the 'big family', as they call it, is fundamental to their everyday life. So, in reality, what was supposed to be a programme made only to help these affected communities has turned into an imposition of Western 'values' that does little to respond to their needs. In this sense, what intersectionality could contribute to is to ensure that the remedies available to Indigenous and Afro-descendant women meet their particular needs, even if that includes tailoring the individual right to reparations to also respond to the collective realities of these communities.

Furthermore, intersectionality can contribute to the establishment of social programmes and services that respond to the suffering of multiply burdened individuals. Instead of ordering social programmes of a general application that follow a single-axis framework, intersectionality could contribute to the creation of highly flexible programmes that avoid grouping victims into single-axis clusters. In this way, the user would have agency 'to best use the resources the state makes available to them' as they would take active participation in the development of these reparation programmes.[52] Continuing with the example of Colombia, Butti and McGonigle Leyh analysed whether the inhabitants of the town of San Carlos, who were heavily affected by the Colombian conflict, were as successfully compensated as has been argued. What they discovered is that the Victims' and Land Restitution Law (VLRL) created in Colombia had an essentialist notion of children, as the legal frameworks thought of young victims as passive 'vulnerable' subjects and ignored the different situations of marginalization.[53] 'By failing to appreciate these youths' multifaceted identities, and the specific impacts the armed conflict had on them, the differential approach foreseen by the Victims' Law results in interventions that are ineffective at best, and furthering exclusion at worst.'[54]

Additionally, reparations aimed at rehabilitating victims—not only physically or mentally but also through any social programmes or services that have accounted for the intersecting characteristics of individuals—can provide more tailored reparations. This was done in the case of the *Fireworks Factory v Brazil*, where the IACtHR found 'patterns of structural and intersectional discrimination' within the merits section of the judgment as well as in the identities of the victims, since most who died in the explosion were Afro-descendant women and girls who lived in a situation of poverty that forced them to work under terrible conditions. The judges ordered Brazil to create a socioeconomic programme, in consultation with the victims and their representatives, to provide safe alternative work opportunities, especially for young people above the age of 16 and women who are also Afro-descendants. This included workshops that would help them gain work experience in safer lines of work,[55] and, eventually, remove them from the interlocking systems that oppressed them.

[51] Juliana González Villamizar and Pascha Bueno-Hansen, 'The Promise and Perils of Mainstreaming Intersectionality in the Colombian Peace Process' (2021) 15(3) International Journal of Transitional Justice 553, 572.

[52] Elena Butti and Brianne McGonigle Leyh, 'Intersectionality and Transformative Reparations: The Case of Colombian Marginal Youths' (2019) 19(5) International Criminal Law Review 753, 778.

[53] ibid 757.

[54] ibid 775.

[55] *Employees of the Fireworks Factory of Santo Antônio de Jesus and their families v Brazil* (Judgment) Inter-American Court of Human Rights Series C No 427 (21 June 2021) para 289.

Lastly, compensation is perhaps the reparation where an intersectional approach could be deemed less relevant, as compensation is awarded in the presence of any economically assessable damage proportional to each case's severity and the facts.[56] One example of a compensation programme that takes into account the interlocking systems of oppression experienced by individuals is the Brazilian programme 'Bolsa Familia' (PBF). While PBF is not, per se, compensation in the terms used by IHRL adjudicative bodies, it shows how economic stipends can effectively remedy the harm endured by multiply burdened people. The PBF is a welfare programme that gives money to families who live in poverty. However, this monetary stipend changes in accordance with the intersecting characteristics of the beneficiary. To start, families enter the PBF depending on the group to which they belong. The first group of beneficiaries comprises families considered to be '*prioritárias*', meaning families that belong to *quilombolas* and are presumably Afro-descendants, Indigenous families, families whose main breadwinner works in recycling, families whose children work, and families whose members have been freed from contemporary forms of slavery. The second group comprise families with a very low income. The third group comprises families whose children are mostly under the age of 17.

Furthermore, it is not just the money that will help improve the lives of the beneficiaries. In the PBF, there are also certain conditions that the families must comply with in order to keep receiving money. These conditions are aimed at improving the health and education of the children of the family, and thus they must have a minimum attendance record at school and complete their vaccination. If there are pregnant or lactating women among the beneficiaries, then they also must attend their prenatal and post-natal medical check-ups.[57]

In short, reparations need an intersectional approach to take account of the extreme marginalization of multiply burdened victims and the particular barriers they face in access to justice, especially if they are poor or belong to minority or excluded groups. Ordering public policies and norms that provide remedies is not enough; adjudicators must ensure that, in practice, reparation programmes can be accessed by everyone in an equal, adequate, effective, and prompt manner. As the Centre for Reproductive Rights eloquently puts it:

> This means that special measures must be taken to guarantee that marginalized or disadvantaged groups of women who are often unable to access justice are able to do so in practice. Marginalized groups must be provided with free legal aid and targeted measures must be adopted to ensure that they are aware of their rights and that they receive necessary support in access to justice and states have a duty to ensure that victims are adequately informed of their right to seek redress. Barriers that can have a particular impact on marginalized groups of victims' access to justice include inequities in practical access to complaint procedures and judicial bodies, failure to provide

[56] UNGA (n 47) para 20.

[57] Inter-American Development Bank, 'How does Bolsa Familia Work? Best Practices in the Implementation of Conditional Cash Transfer Programs in Latin America and the Caribbean' (*Inter-American Development Bank*, September 2015) <https://publications.iadb.org/es/publications/english/viewer/How-Does-Bolsa-Familia-Work-Best-Practices-in-the-Implementation-of-Conditional-Cash-Transfer-Programs-in-Latin-America-and-the-Caribbean.pdf> accessed 27 April 2023.

legal aid and the impact of costs of bringing a complaint, and evidentiary burdens and other procedural requirements.[58]

The abovementioned examples are in no way exhaustive and more can be said and done with regard to the manner in which intersectionality provides tools so that multiply burdened racialized individuals can achieve substantive equality. 'By ensuring that a rich range of experiences is brought before judicial and quasi-judicial authorities, intersectionality offers a framework to comprehensively prevent and remedy inequalities.'[59] Sometimes, the specificity demanded by an intersectional analysis tends to be interpreted as making it impossible to implement any measure that answers to the needs of those intersectional subjects. However, the purpose of using intersectionality in cases of racism, racial discrimination, or other forms of related intolerance is to effectively realize a human rights practice that can transform the lives of the victims. Finding the proper balance between the recognition of the suffering of, for example, Black transgender women collectively, and the specific harm endured by the victim of a specific case is the challenge that lies ahead.

6. Conclusion

IHRL has sought to combat racial discrimination, racism, and related forms of intolerance, but it still has a pending debt both with racialized individuals and multiply burdened ones. By failing to acknowledge its role in sustaining social hierarchies, IHRL has struggled to name and address the harms faced by multiply burdened individuals. While intersectionality has helped move beyond a single-axis framework, much work remains before adjudicative bodies can fully articulate the interlocking systems of oppression that shape qualitatively different experiences of harm.

In order to fully address and redress the harms that people suffer based on the intersection of their race with other identities, adjudicative bodies must stay away from the single-axis model recognized in human rights instruments which atomizes the individual by categorizing them on mutually exclusive grounds. The cases examined in this chapter illustrate how intersectionality can be operationalized to account for the vulnerabilities created by overlapping identities and to assess the compounded impact of human rights violations. In short, they demonstrate which differences matter in understanding both the nature and extent of harm.

Recognizing intersectionality is not just a symbolic gesture; it is a necessary step towards delivering meaningful justice. Using an intersectional approach will produce reparations that generate momentum towards a broad range of laws, policies, and practices flexible enough to accommodate the complexity of the lives of the victims, while also making them active agents in the transformation of their lived realities.

[58] Centre for Reproductive Rights, 'Expert Opinion submitted by the Center for Reproductive Rights in the case of J.D. et al. v. the Czech Republic' CEDAW Communication No 102/2016' (24 November 2017) <https://reproductiverights.org/wp-content/uploads/2021/04/CRR-Expert-Opinion_JD-et-al.-v.-Czech-Rep_Final.pdf> accessed 22 November 2024, 8.

[59] Ivona Truscan and Joanna Bourke-Martignoni, 'International Human Rights Law and Intersectional Discrimination' (2016) 16 The Equal Rights Review 103, 130–31.

14
Colonial Fantasies in the European Court of Human Rights

*Karla Schröter**

1. Introduction

This chapter examines how white and patriarchal ontologies guide the European Court of Human Rights (the 'Court' or ECtHR) in its decision-making. I aim to show how these ontologies are based on fantasies about Europe's violent colonial past, which simultaneously glamorize and deny its horrors. Even if repressed, violent memories haunt European states, compelling the Court to systematically repeat actions of epistemic violence against Europe's Others; here, Muslim women.

To demonstrate this, I analyse case law in which the Court has opined on prohibitions of the practice of veiling under the European Convention on Human Rights (ECHR). In the cases *Köse and Others v Türkiye*,[1] *Leyla Sahin v Türkiye*,[2] and *Dogru v France*,[3] pupils and a university student were refused entry to their educational institutions for wearing the hijab. In *Dahlab v Switzerland*[4] and *Ebrahimian v France*,[5] a teacher and a social worker lost their respective jobs for the same reason. The Court based its decisions on the principle of secularism, presented as a guarantor of equality and neutrality. In *SAS v France*[6] and *Dakir v Belgium*,[7] face veils were banned from public spaces under threat of a fine and, in Belgium, imprisonment. In this instance, the Court relied on the principle of 'living together'. The legal question that guides this chapter is thus whether the prohibitions constitute an illegitimate infringement on the applicants' religious freedoms and rights granted under Article 9 of the ECHR. This chapter does not engage with the legal technicalities of the case law,[8] but the discursive processes that occur in the Court's argumentation.

* I would like to wholeheartedly thank the editors Professor Mohsen al Attar and Claire Smith for their constructive and encouraging feedback as well as their kind support throughout the writing process. I also want to thank the participants of the doctoral workshop organized at Åbo Akademi University in connection to the Annual Minority Seminar 2024 for their engagement with my early draft and the valuable discussions held during that session. Moreover, I thank my supervisor Pamela Slotte Russo for her continuous support and for always asking the right questions to push me further.

1 *Köse and 93 Others v Türkiye* App no 26625/02 (ECtHR, 24 January 2006).

2 *Leyla Şahin v Türkiye* App no 44774/98 (ECtHR, 10 November 2005).

3 *Dogru v France* App no 27058/05 (ECtHR, 4 December 2008).

4 *Dahlab v Switzerland* App no 42393/98 (ECtHR, 15 February 2021).

5 *Ebrahimian v France* App no 64846/11 (ECtHR, 26 November 2006).

6 *SAS v France* App no 43835/11 (ECtHR, 1 July 2014).

7 *Dakir v Belgium* App no 4619/12 (ECtHR, 11 July 2017).

8 Such as questions arising from the legitimate aim test, proportionality test. or Member State's margin of appreciation.

Karla Schröter, *Colonial Fantasies in the European Court of Human Rights* In: *Emancipating International Law*. Edited by: Mohsen al Attar and Claire Smith, Oxford University Press. © Karla Schröter 2026.
DOI: 10.1093/9780198935605.003.0018

When criticizing the veil cases, scholars often scrutinize religion and gender in relation to secularism.[9] For my part, I wish to shift attention from religion and secularism to the epistemic structures of whiteness and its intersection with patriarchy. The chapter assesses the case law through the psychoanalytic concept of fantasies to interrogate how 'Whiteness as an epistemological and ontological *a priori*',[10] rooted in colonial narratives, informs the Court's argumentation. When whiteness is adopted as a point of departure, deviations in appearance, language, or cultural/religious practices become Othered and risk being deemed 'unworthy' of human rights protection.[11] While race and religion are separate categories in many contexts, the colonial project consolidated the two to create a double bind and dichotomy between the Christian white *civilizer* and the *savage*, defined through non-whiteness and lack of Christian faith.[12] Europe arrogated to itself the right to colonize due to its putative civilizational-*qua*-racial superiority, linking the 'saviour-colonizer psyche' to race.[13] In short, the racialization of Europe as civilized whites and Others as savage non-whites was necessary to legitimize colonial conquest,[14] while the ensuing unequal power structures ensured the endless reproduction of racialized categories.[15]

As the word race has fallen out of fashion in the European context, religion and culture have emerged as covert ways of expressing racism,[16] while the savage has been replaced by Muslim as the absolute opposite of whiteness.[17] As observed by Sahar Aziz, Muslim women are further disadvantaged, placed in a triple bind of religion, race, and gender, as all three combine to facilitate their oppression under postcolonial white male dominance. To illustrate, a Muslim woman who wears the hijab is often perceived as oppressed by her patriarchal religion and family. If she challenges this stereotype by being assertive and critical, she is equally denigrated and delegitimized as unappreciative or dangerous, triggering another battery of religious and racialized stereotypes of Muslim terrorists and angry women of colour.[18]

[9] See Carolyn Evans, 'The Islamic Scarf in the European Court of Human Rights' (2006) 7(1) Melbourne Journal of International Law 52; Kati Nieminen, 'Eroding the Protection against Discrimination: The Procedural and De-Contextualized Approach to S.A.S. v France' (2019) 19(2) International Journal of Discrimination and the Law 69; Lourdes Peroni, Religion and Culture in the Discourse of the European Court of Human Rights: The Risks of Stereotyping and Naturalising' (2014) 10(2) International Journal of Law in Context 195; Anastasia Vakulenko, 'Islamic Headscarves' and the European Convention on Human Rights: An Intersectional Perspective' (2017) 16(2) Social & Legal Studies 183.

[10] Aileen Moreton-Robinson, *Whitening Race: Essays in Social and Cultural Criticism* (Aboriginal Studies Press 2004) 84.

[11] Makau Mutua 'Savages, Victims, and Saviors: The Metaphor of Human Rights' (2001) 42(1) Harvard International Law Journal 201, 203.

[12] Rabiat Akande, 'An Imperial history of Race-Religion in International Law' (2024) 118(1) American Journal of International Law 1; Mutua (n 11).

[13] Mutua (n 11) 204.

[14] Mahmud Tayyab, 'Colonialism and Modern Constructions of Race: A Preliminary Inquiry' (1999) 53(4) University of Miami Law Review 1219.

[15] Mahfoud Bennoune, 'Maghribin Workers in France' (1975) 34 MERIP Reports 1.

[16] David Theo Goldberg, 'Racial Europeanization' (2006) 29(2) Ethnic and Racial Studies 331; Farah Elahi and Omar Khan, 'Introduction: What Is Islamophobia' in Farah Elahi and Omar Khan (eds) *Islamophobia: Still a Challenge for Us All* (Runnymede Trust 2017) 5–13; Burak Erdenir, 'Islamophobia Qua Racial Discrimination: Muslimophobia' in Anna Triandafyllidou (ed), *Muslims in 21st Century Europe: Structural and Cultural Perspectives* (Routledge 2010).

[17] Edward Said, *Orientalism* (Vintage Books 1979); Goldberg (n 16).

[18] Sahar Aziz, 'Coercing Assimilation: The Case of Muslim Women of Color' (2015) 24 Transnational Law & Contemporary Problems 341, 343.

To explore this dynamic, I examine the case law through the concept of fantasies, identifying ontologies that centre the white male saviour-colonizer as a morally superior agent in the Court's argumentation. In addition, I assess the epistemic tools and gymnastics deployed to uphold the authority of these fantasies/ontologies. I argue that colonial fantasies enable European institutions to offer, yet again, 'their pseudo-knowledge of the colony' and former colonized peoples to bolster their interpretations. The White Man acts as a personification of white and patriarchal ontological structures that define European states, functioning as a type of 'fertilizer of the colonial vision'.[19] By pathologizing her gender, race, and religion, the Muslim Woman is also instrumentalized, created as a counterbalance to the White Man and his self-representation.

Through my reading of the cases, I have identified three fantasies of the Muslim Woman and the veils. First, she is portrayed as a victim awaiting liberation by the White Man from both Islam and the savage Muslim Man. *Her* female and racialized victimhood reflects *his* role as the saviour. Second, freeing her from the veil and the Muslim Man is fetishized as a realization of the White Man's dominance over her. As a target of sexual conquest, the veil must be conquered for the White Man to actualize his civilizing role. Third, where she rejects salvation, she becomes the savage driven by the destruction of the White Man's empire. Discipline becomes the avenue to civilization. I argue that the Court's commitment to these fantasies dehumanizes the Muslim Woman, who is rendered incapable of being anything other than the caricature imagined. As I conclude, this practice constitutes forms of epistemic and material violence perpetrated against Muslim women.

2. The theoretical frame: the meaning of fantasies and desires

Meyda Yeğenoğlu argues that studies on colonialism are incomplete if we do not recognize the fundamental role that 'fantasy and desire as unconscious processes' play within the colonial project.[20] To her, fantasies operate 'at the cross-roads of psychoanalysis and social history, inhabiting the threshold of both personal and historical memory'.[21] Indeed, when examining fantasies in colonial relations, Yeğenoğlu observes a 'historically specific construction of a collective process' rather than 'individual psychological motivations'.[22] In concrete terms, the White Man's 'unconscious fantasies, dreams, and desires . . . structure his relation to the Oriental other',[23] constituting 'the so-called autonomous and rational Western subject' while simultaneously exposing 'this position as structurally male' and white.[24]

19 Malek Alloula, *The Colonial Harem* (Myrna Godzich and Wlad Godzich tr, University of Minnesota Press 1986) 3.
20 Meyda Yeğenoğlu, *Colonial Fantasies: Towards a Feminist Reading of Orientalism* (Cambridge University Press 1998) 2.
21 Anne McClintock, *Imperial Leather: Race, Gender and Sexuality in Colonial Contest* (Routledge 1995) 184.
22 Yeğenoğlu (n 20) 2.
23 ibid 11.
24 ibid.

Relying on the work of Jacques Lacan, Slavoj Žižek argues that fantasies are often based on repressed traumatic experiences.[25] For national communities, it is the traumatic and violent establishment of the nation-state that its citizens are 'obliged to forget'.[26] For European states, this necessarily includes the horrors of colonialism, perpetrated to establish economic domination and cultural superiority over non-white peoples: 'Acts of terror make the nation and the empire, and as such they will continue to happen.'[27] The past is thus split into multiple Histories,[28] one that represses the violent and traumatic past, substituting it with fantasies of civilizing missions and human rights, helping to preserve a narrative of moral superiority.[29] A second History is the one that remembers the horrors visited upon others.[30]

Malek Alloula illustrates this divide. In his description of the colonization of Algeria, he points to two contrasting representations: while the French speak of civilization and women's liberation, for Algerians, French colonialism was 'less [of] a conquest than a deformation of the social order'.[31] History 1 is told by the French to cleanse themselves of the barbarities they inflicted on Algerians. History 2 is told by Algerians to recall the violence they suffered and, as Alloula aptly describes, to centre the deformation of their social order.

When split, the traumatic part that is repressed produces gaps in our understanding of the present. As a space of imagination and meaning making, fantasies offer an opportunity to fill these gaps, resolve ambivalences, and manipulate realities.[32] Information about the past and present is henceforth measured against the fantasy and interpreted in a way that rationalizes the latter.[33] The fantasy eventually evolves into an ontology, allowing for the construction of coherent narratives and the maintenance of imagined identities.[34] The gaze supports the fantasy in its selection of what is gazed upon and in its search for objects relevant to one's desire,[35] much like epistemologies buttress ontologies. Thus, the gaze is determined by the agent and the teleology it aims to validate, whether this involves sexualizing, judging, or surveilling the Other.[36]

[25] Both Bhabha and Žižek focus on how societies work out their trauma. See Slavoj Žižek, *The Plague of Fantasies* (Verso 2008) 10. See also Homi Bhabha 'DissemiNation: Time, Narrative, and the Margins of the Modern Nation' in Homi K Bhabha (ed), *Nation and Narration* (Psychology Press 1990). In contrast, Fanon's psychiatric work shows that French colonizers as individuals were also traumatized by their own actions of violence. Thus, trauma is not necessarily connected to the position of a victim in this context. Frantz Fanon, *The Wretched of the Earth* (Constance Farrington tr, Grove Press 1963).

[26] Bhabha (n 25) 310; Žižek (n 25) 74–75.

[27] Sherene Razack, *Casting Out: The Eviction of Muslims from Western Law and Politics* (University of Toronto Press 2008) 19.

[28] Bhabha (n 25) 295.

[29] Dierk Walter and Peter Lewis, *Colonial Violence: European Empires and the Use of Force* (Oxford University Press 2017) on the patterns of continuous violence of European states from the start of imperialism until the early 2000s; McClintock (n 21).

[30] See Bhabha (n 25) on the split and counter histories.

[31] This is how Harlow defines Alloula's work in her Foreword to the book (Alloula (n 20) xiii).

[32] Žižek (n 25) 10–12; Bhabha (n 25); McClintock (n 21) 184.

[33] Žižek (n 25) 62.

[34] ibid 48.

[35] ibid 21.

[36] ibid 39; Yeğenoğlu (n 20) 40–46.

Makau wa Mutua provides a framework similar to Yeğenoğlu's and Žižek's. In a well-known article, he explained that '[t]he saviour-colonizer psyche reflects an intriguing interplay of both European superiority and manifest destiny over the subject. The 'othering' project degrades although it also seeks to save.'[37] Mutua thus demonstrates what Žižek warns us of: 'desire's *raison d'être* is not to realize its goal... but to reproduce itself as desire.'[38] Mutua has noted that human rights regimes are often based on a savage-victim-saviour (SVS) narrative that reinforces a colonial perspective where the saviours are white while negatively racialized peoples and cultures are both savages and victims of their savagery. Mutua argued that human rights law was another tool of white supremacy that sought to 'civilize' by 'correcting' the 'non-European person, cultural practice, or state'[39] based upon white standards.[40] Thus, the SVS narratives are simultaneously degrading while 'saving' the Other.[41] As the colonial fantasy conceals the 'horror of the Real', consistent with Mutua's SVS narrative, the White Man is compelled to create a substitute savage.[42] Historically, this role was played both by 'the Jew'[43] and 'the Muslim',[44] of which the latter is increasingly carrying the burden. Moreover, because a fantasy 'presupposes as already given what it purports to produce',[45] the White Man narrates a past and future where he is legitimized to violently discipline the savage.[46]

The fantasy dictates one's desires.[47] For the White Man, he wishes to be recognized as the *universal*.[48] The fantasy is thus about who he is (in relation to Others) and how he is perceived by Others, reflecting the need for recognition and love rather than the Real. For the White Man to live out his fantasy of a conqueror who civilizes the savage, he must penetrate the 'new' world; the land, body, and mind of the savage must be 'uncovered', both metaphorically and literally. As 'bearers of the collective',[49] 'biological reproducers of the nation' and 'the body of the nation',[50] the colonized female body becomes the gateway and battleground for control.[51] Moreover, because of the White Man's obsession with visual and physical access to the colonized, the hijab has been a source of infinite frustration since his first encounter with Muslims.[52] As the White Man desires 'to master, control, and reshape the body of the subjects by making them visible',[53] the veil constitutes a form of emasculation, blocking both fantasy and identity, preventing him from 'fantasi[sing] himself as a full subject'.[54] He becomes

37 Mutua (n 11) 235.
38 Žižek (n 25) 53.
39 Mutua (n 11) 216.
40 ibid 224.
41 ibid 207.
42 Žižek (n 25) 7, 32, 40.
43 ibid 32, 40.
44 Goldberg (n 16); Razack (n 27) 19.
45 Žižek (n 25) 12.
46 Yeğenoğlu (n 20) 27.
47 Žižek (n 25) 7.
48 Yeğenoğlu (n 20) 8.
49 Nira Yuval-Davis, 'Women and the Biological Reproduction of the Nation' in *Gender & Nation* (Sage 1997) 26.
50 Floya Anthias and Nira Yuval-Davis, *Women-Nation-State* (Macmillan 1989) 287.
51 Alloula (n 19) 15.
52 Fanon (n 25) 35, 44.
53 Yeğenoğlu (n 20) 12.
54 ibid 63.

embittered as the veil renders 'her body completely invisible to the European observer except for her eyes, *the veiled woman can see without being seen*'.[55] Through the hijab, the colonizer is the one who is gazed upon, 'dispossessed of his own gaze'.[56]

Neither Yeğenoğlu, Žižek, nor Mutua engages with the 'ghost' that haunts the fantasizer, but rather each focuses on the effects of the fantasy (such as the obsession with removing the veil). I understand the past and memories as things that flash 'incessantly through the film: a dangerous repetition in the present of the cinematic frame; the edge of human life that translates what will come next and what has gone before in the writing of History'.[57] To reiterate, traumatic events are split into multiple Histories of which one contains the suppressed event, while the other creates a hero and a savage. Fantasies keep the trauma operational, while leaving it forgotten and unconfronted and legitimating endless violence, both material and epistemic. In other words, the split is where white epistemologies flow from, sustaining their ontology and suppressing other forms of being. The White Man is thus simultaneously a character, creator, and consumer of his fantasies.[58] Of course, these fantasies need a basis in the Other, the one who lacks what the White Man cl/aims to be/come, as his unique motives legitimize oppressive policies European states and actors enact. In the hijab cases, the Muslim Woman is called into being by the White Man both through discursive practices and their material effects as her gendered, religious, and racialized otherness 'confirm[ing] his identity' as a White Man and master, and as the civilizing agent.[59] As Sara Farris notes, 'the racist imagery operates through the powerful sexual metaphors and desires' in which race and gender intertwine as 'racist ideologies express the desire to dominate the Other through fantasies of possessing the body of the racialized woman'.[60]

In the forthcoming sections, I aim to reconnect suppressed memories with the fantasies designed to conceal them; an act of 'painful re-membering' which Homi Bhabha described as 'putting together . . . the dismembered past to make sense of the trauma of the present'.[61] Only this way can we understand the epistemological choices that are made by the Court in its aim to sustain the White Man's fantasy while invalidating the Muslim reality in human rights law.

When analysing the case law, I talk about characters within imagined dreams created by the collective memory of Europe. For example, French photographers used Algerian actresses to stage distorted versions of Algerian women and their homes, presenting *French fantasies about Algerian women* and Algerian society, rather than their lived experiences.[62] In the same manner, this chapter refers to these essentialized, distorted characters when referring to 'the Muslim Man', 'the Muslim Woman', or 'the White Man'. The White Man is the conqueror, the saviour, and the hero that

[55] ibid 43; as was originally expressed in Fanon (n 25) 44.
[56] Alloula (n 19) 14.
[57] Bhabha (n 25) 306.
[58] Yeğenoğlu (n 20) 6.
[59] ibid 3–4, 49; as Fanon noted: 'The black soul is a white man's artifact' (Fanon (n 25) 16) as is the Orient and the Muslim (Said (n 17)).
[60] Sara Farris, *In the Name of Women's Rights: The Rise of Femonationalism* (Duke University Press 2017) 74.
[61] Homi Bhabha, *The Location of Culture* (Routledge 1995) 90.
[62] Alloula (n 19) 21.

European policy-makers, states, and international institutions identify with.[63] These subjectivities or 'fictive characters' are produced retrospectively through the 'historical inscription of a particular identity'.[64] They also constitute a future oriented process of becoming that identity. Regimes consistently recreate their violent pasts, as the narrative forms the very heritage that 'survives and haunts the regime'.[65] To break free from Europe's and human rights institutions' desire to reproduce the savage and white superiority, we must expose the fantasies they are part of.

3. The dream: the Muslim Woman waiting to be saved by the White Man

In the hijab cases, the bans were partly argued for due to the hijab's presumed denigration of Muslim women. In *Dahlab*, the Court noted that the hijab 'appears to be imposed on women by a precept which is laid down in the Koran and which . . . is hard to square with the principle of gender equality',[66] a conclusion which was later referred to in *Sahin*[67] and *Dogru*.[68] In *Sahin*, the Grand Chamber relied on the Chamber's previous judgment, in which it had stated that restrictions would be necessary to protect rights and freedoms of others and public order 'in a country [Türkiye] in which the majority of the population, while professing a strong attachment to the rights of women and a secular way of life, adhere to the Islamic faith'.[69] The Court's statements and outcome-oriented logic reveal that being Muslim is an inherent threat to secularism. In a country where Muslims are the minority (in *Dogru* France and *Dahlab* Switzerland), state institutions and women (including the applicants) must be protected from the influence of Muslims; where Muslims are the majority (in Türkiye), the state must be especially careful to uphold secular values and gender equality.

Even if a population was acknowledged to embrace both, Muslims were assumed to eventually undue secularism and gender equality. The greater the number, the greater the threat. The fact of being Muslim is enough for the Court to draw this conclusion, as it does not ponder the diversity in how Muslims position themselves in relation to religion, secularism, and gender equality. For example, in *Sahin*, the applicant resented the ban's dismissal of women's capacity to decide for themselves 'what was appropriate conduct'.[70] She rejected the notion of being forced to wear the hijab, emphasizing instead that she did it 'based on religious conviction', which she should be 'free to choose whether or not to comply with',[71] a freedom which the Court deprived her of because of its application of secularism.

[63] Yeğenoğlu (n 20); Mutua (n 11).
[64] Yeğenoğlu (n 20) 3–4.
[65] Žižek (n 25) 76. See also Bhabha (n 25) 295.
[66] *Dahlab* (n 4) 13.
[67] *Sahin* (n 2) [111].
[68] *Dogru* (n 3) [64].
[69] *Sahin* (n 2) [115].
[70] ibid [101].
[71] ibid [101].

In all three cases, adhering to set standards of secularism was deemed to guarantee gender equality in public institutions, which Islam, Muslim men, and the hijab collectively threaten. The Court thus took the assumption of secularism being gender-neutral as a self-evident fact, although this assumption is historically wrong. Before the Enlightenment, gender differences were justified through religion and religious practice. Post-Enlightenment, the secularization of societies provided *science-based* justifications for gender differences, mostly by locating them in nature.[72] Moreover, secularism has not currently established gender equality.[73] In *Dahlab*, the Court only engages in a superficial inquiry into the religious roots of the hijab through passing references to the Qur'an, a theological undertaking which would perhaps better be left to theologians. By contrast, it does not critically engage with the claim that secularism protects gender equality, even though Ms Sahin raised the reality of her now diminished freedoms. Her access to both religion and education were not limited by Islam, a religion she freely chose to practise, but by secularism which curbed her rights.

Through the lens of secularism, Sahin's choices are condemnable precisely because of her gender: as a woman, she could not wear a symbol of a religion that is believed to suppress her. Without acknowledging it, the Court relies on a white episteme in which secularism's History and current effects of gender discrimination are omitted, preferring to apply scrutiny to Islam only. This is a common deflection often used by European states, which makes it possible for them to brand Christianity as an enabler of gender equality, while Other(ed) religions, specifically Islam, are declared to be in existential opposition to gender equality.[74] These discourses do not only focus on Islam as a religion (as was done in *Dahlab*), but also on Islamic culture, representing it as patriarchal and describing Muslim men as dangerous and oppressive (in *Sahin*, the Court even commented on the danger a Muslim *population* posed).[75] Within the colonial context, the triangle of Christianity, secularism, and gender equality were integral to the French '*mission civilisatrice*',[76] a legacy which secularism has inherited.[77] Thus, secularism has become an epistemic tool, an instrument that locates Muslims on a span between the savage and the civilized. Because of the applicants' and the Turkish population's Islamic faith, the Court found it necessary to allow bans against the hijab, ostensibly to protect Muslim women from their avowed faith.

To muddy the waters, the Court appeared to change its approach in *SAS*. In defending its ban on face veils, the French government argued that the proscription was based on the 'respect for equality between men and women' and 'respect for human dignity'.[78] To the French government, the face veil was an 'effacement'

[72] Joan Wallach Scott, *Sex and Secularism* (Princeton University Press 2018) 21.
[73] ibid 14.
[74] ibid.
[75] Saba Mahmood, 'Feminism, Democracy and Empire: Islam and the War on Terror' in Joan Wallach Scott (ed), *Women's Studies on the Edge* (Duke University Press 2018).
[76] Paul Silverstein, *Algeria in France: Transpolitics, Race, and Nation* (Indiana University Press 2004) 44–45.
[77] ibid; Ruth Maas, 'Compelling the Muslim Subject: Memory as Post-Colonial Violence and the Public Performativity of "Secular and Cultural Islam"' (2006) 96(4) The Muslim World 585; Talal Asad, 'Trying to Understand French Secularism' in Hent de Vries and Lawrence E Sullivan (eds), *Political Theologies: Public Religions in a Post-Secular World* (Fordham University Press 2006).
[78] *Sahin* (n 2) [116].

that 'was necessarily dehumanising and could hardly be regarded as consistent with human dignity'.[79] Finally, the Court dismissed the two aims, opining that 'a State Party cannot invoke gender equality in order to ban a practice that is defended by women'.[80] Diverging from its previous rulings, it went on to proclaim that women could not 'be protected on that basis from the exercise of their own fundamental rights and freedoms'.[81]

While the Court's new approach might be seen as a positive change, I believe this conclusion would be misguided for it hides the Court's failure to take any meaningful action to improve the human rights protection of Muslim women. It must be emphasized that the deliberations surrounding the face veil bans were largely based on racist tropes of Muslim women being victims of Islam and Muslim men,[82] an assumption the applicant in *SAS* denounced as 'paternalistic'.[83] While the Court acknowledged the concern over gender equality, it dismissed this legitimation as insufficient, thus leaving harmful stereotypes unchallenged.[84] I return later to the legitimate aim of 'living together', which ultimately solidified France's defence.

For now, I wish to highlight that a breach of the face veil ban could be followed by criminal sanctions, either through fines[85] or even imprisonment in Belgium.[86] In the French context, criminal sanctions could be avoided if the woman claimed victimhood by naming who had forced her to wear the face veil.[87] Worrisomely, the Court welcomed this part of the law, stating that 'a State Party which, in the name of gender equality, prohibits anyone from forcing women to conceal their face pursues an [legitimate] aim'.[88] In its putative defence of women's rights, the Court effectively confirmed the stereotype of the domineering Muslim Man and passive Muslim Woman, indirectly confirming liberal perceptions of gender equality as a legitimate justification for criminalizing the hijab.

The narrative of France *bringing* dignity, civilization, freedom, and equality to the 'oppressed' and 'denigrated' women of Algeria helped justify the brutal violence committed by France during colonial exploitation and the Algerian War of Independence.[89] During this time, 'the symbol of the "falling veil" anchored official French efforts to present their fight against the FLN [the National Liberation Front of Algeria] as a crusade for modernity'.[90] Women were to be freed from their proverbial prison by the French government and its military, which included the veil, their

[79] *SAS* (n 6) [82].
[80] ibid [119].
[81] ibid [119].
[82] See the non-governmental organizations Open Society Justice Initiative (*SAS* (n 6) [103] and Amnesty International (*SAS* (n 6) [90]–[91]) stating that the ban was based on the assumption that Muslim women who wear a face veil are oppressed.
[83] *SAS* (n 6) [78].
[84] ibid [119].
[85] ibid [28].
[86] In Belgium the women could be fined or a repeated offence could lead to several days of imprisonment: *Dakir* (n 7) [17].
[87] *SAS* (n 6) [31].
[88] ibid [119].
[89] Todd Shepard, *The Invention of Decolonization: The Algerian War and the remaking of France* (Cornell University Press 2008) 187.
[90] ibid 180.

families, religion, and culture.[91] Not unique to France, these perceptions pervade both international and domestic programmes that assume that gender equality as a value must be instilled by Western (white) institutions into Muslim communities, whether through integration programmes for Muslim immigrants and citizens of European states,[92] or as foreign military intervention in Afghanistan and Iraq, which subjected ordinary citizens to 'educational' campaigns in their 'war on terror'.[93] Several scholars have noted how these narratives racialize Muslims both outside and within Europe.[94]

In *Sahin,* the Court first lumped the Turkish applicant together with a large unknown mass that was perceived to risk turning against secularism and gender equality if not restricted. The Court then declared in *SAS* that Muslim women needed to be protected from the coercion of Muslim men by prohibiting the face veil. Across its rulings, the Court legitimized the SVS narrative. In the Court's argumentation, the language of civilization was substituted with gender equality, either in connection with secularism or alone, but the structure of the dream in which 'White men save brown women from brown men'[95] remains intact. In no case did the applicants confirm the Court's assumption that they were victims. To the contrary, they explicitly contested it, asserting their agency by claiming their right to religious freedom before an international court.

The Court's denial of these facts can be understood through the fantasy. Is the problem that Islam poses a threat to secularism and gender equality, or that the Court's perceptions are based on white epistemologies, including the notion of white superiority, making it impossible for it to envision other forms of gender equality? If the Court recognized that Islam and gender equality can coexist, or even support each other, it would not confirm the special status that whiteness enjoys as a guarantor of gender equality. The White Man will not be the saviour of the Muslim Woman, as there is no one needing to be saved, and thus whiteness loses its moral superiority, causing the ontology to collapse. By preserving her fantasized status as a victim, the White Man remains the saviour, however concrete (saving Muslim women from Muslim Men) or abstract (saving European values from Islam).

In other words, the gaze searches for evidence that supports the fantasy. As Spivak notes, '"White men are saving brown women from brown men" is a sentence indicating a *collective* fantasy symptomatic of a *collective* itinerary of sadomasochistic repression in a *collective* imperialist enterprise.'[96] The saviour-narrative is needed for white men and liberal-democratic states to repress the violence they have inflicted

[91] Fatima El-Tayeb, *European Others: Queering Ethnicity in Postnational Europe* (University of Minnesota Press 2011) 83; Alloula (n 19) 21.

[92] Farris (n 60) 2–3.

[93] As Mahmood (n 75) notes, this war is not only waged against the 'terrorist' and 'fundamentalists' through physical violence, but also through campaigns that target ordinary Muslim civilians and women, thus also penetrating the minds of people.

[94] Étienne Balibar, *Secularism and Cosmopolitanism: Critical Hypothesis on Religion and Politics* (Columbia University Press 2018); Goldberg (n 16); El-Tayeb (n 91).

[95] Christine M Jacobsen and Dag Stenvoll, 'Muslim Women and Foreign Prostitutes: Victim Discourse, Subjectivity, and Governance' (2010) 17(3) Social Politics: International Studies in Gender, State & Society 270, 289.

[96] Gayatri Chakravorty Spivak, 'Can the Subaltern Speak?' in Carrie Nelson and Lawrence Grossberg (eds), *Marxism and the Interpretation of Culture* (University of Illinois Press 1988) 92.

upon Muslim women. Some examples of this silenced History is the colonial impoverishment and destruction of societal structures that drove Algerian women out of their lands into cities, where due to the lack of options, some were forced to work in brothels serving European male settlers.[97] Silence also surrounds the sexual harassment, rape, gendered violence, and killings of Muslim women and civilians by white men during colonialism,[98] the Algerian War of Independence,[99] and during the Afghan and Iraq wars,[100] all of which were legitimized via the narrative of saving Muslim women. Likewise, current violent attacks perpetrated by white men against Muslim women in the streets of Europe, including ripping off veils or threatening violence, are frequently ignored.[101]

The omission of the racism, Islamophobia, and misogyny within European societies and institutions exposed by these crimes is essential to the preservation of the saviour-narrative intact.[102] While gender-based violence by white men against (racialized) women is explained as the action of problematic individuals, violence by Muslim men is framed as inherent to 'Islamic culture'.[103] As Mahmood observes, the biased framing means that the solution demands either the reform or eradication of Islamic culture.[104] As mentioned above, the Court determined that simply 'adher[ing] to the Islamic faith' posed a danger to secularism, compelling its restriction. Rather than engage critically with the power dimensions that emerge in religion, race, and gender, the Court confirmed a biased picture, focusing on the *threat* of Islam and Muslim men, which they purport to resolve by restricting how Muslim women dress,

[97] David C Gordon, *Women of Algeria: An Essay on Change* (Harvard University Press 1972); Alloula (n 19).

[98] On rape as a means of conquest all over Africa, see Amina Mama, 'Sheros and Villains: Conceptualising Colonial and Contemporary Violence Against Women in Africa' in M Jacqui Alexander and Chandra Talpade Mohanty (eds), *Feminist Genealogies, Colonial Legacies, Democratic Futures* (Routledge 1996); in Algeria, see Frantz Fanon, *A Dying Colonialism* (Haakon Chevalier tr, Grove Press 1965) 45; Gordon (n 97).

[99] For how violence against Algerian women was used as a weapon of war both as a form of targeted torture of visibly active women as well as a systematic form of violence against rural women, see Gordon (n 97).

[100] Mason notes the disturbing irony of sending an inherently violent and patriarchal institution to 'protect' women and criticizes the 'feminist and liberal concerns for equality and women's rights are co-opted for imperialist projects'. For Mason, the increased hiring of women is an attempt to 'look less as a rapist' against the 'horrific acts of physical and sexual violence perpetrated against female civilians and others by US military personnel and their associates'. Corrine L Mason 'Global Violence Against Women as a National Security "Emergency"' (2013) 14(5) Feminist Criminology 540, 63–70.

[101] Tell Mama, 'A Decade of Anto-Muslim Hate' (*Tell Mama*, 2023) <https://tellmamauk.org/wp-content/uploads/pdf/A-Decade-of-Anti-Muslim-Hate-TellMAMAReport.pdf> accessed 21 July 2024, 78–81; Hanna Mason-Bish and Irene Zempi, 'Misogyny, Racism, and Islamophobia: Street Harassment at the Intersections (2019) 14(5) Feminist Criminology 540; Barbara Perry, 'Gendered Islamophia: Hate Crime against Muslim Women'(2014) 20(1) Social Identities 74; Irene Zempi and Neil Chakraborti, '"They Make Us Feel Like We're a Virus": The Multiple Impacts of Islamophobic Hostility Towards Veiled Muslim Women' (2015) 4(3) International Journal for Crime Justice and Social Democracy 44.

[102] As expressed in most of the sources listed in the previous footnotes as well as in Sheila Jeffreys, 'Double Jeopardy: Women, the US Military and the War in Iraq' (2007) 30(1) Women Studies International Forum 16; Elisabeth Jean Wood and Nathaniel Toppelberg, 'The Persistence of Sexual Assault within the US Military' (2017) 54(5) Journal of Peace Research 620; Vivian C Fox, 'Historical Perspectives on Violence Against Women' (2002) 4(1) Journal of International Women's Studies 15.

[103] Mahmood (n 75) 96. Mahmood also notes that gender-based violence is even sometimes naturalized as a way of expressing jealousy, instead of understanding it as a problem in Western culture.

[104] ibid.

forcing them, yet again, to undress in public and limiting their access to livelihood and education. Descendants of the formerly colonized encounter the same violence, now perpetrated by the same states, but also by Türkiye and the Court.

In the next section, I examine how the violent sexual fantasies of white men about Muslim women are integral to the project of civilizing the savage.

4. The fantasy: the Muslim Woman as an object of conquest

In *SAS*, the Court accepted France's argument that a face veil could be perceived as a 'barrier raised against others' that would 'fundamentally call into question the possibility of open interpersonal relationships', which is an 'indispensable element of community life'.[105] The face veils could thus be interpreted as 'breaching the right of others to live in a space of socialisation'.[106] The Court accepted without further discussion the French government's assertion that concealing one's face was incompatible with French society's way of 'living together', grounded in the ideal of fraternity and 'the minimum requirement of civility'.[107] The Court viewed the face veil as antithetical to these principles, despite third-party interventions which demonstrated that some Muslim women experienced the face veil as a means of actively participating in society in the first place, and instead feared further isolation due to the effects of the ban.[108] Moreover, the applicant made this very argument, explaining that face veils did not hinder her participation in society.[109] In this instance, the Court viewed the abstract desire of the majority to *live together* to be more valuable than the social interaction of the small number of Muslim women affected by the ban.

After the success of the principle of 'living together' in *SAS*, Belgium leveraged the same argument in *Dakir*. While the Court underlined the importance of 'fraternity' and 'civility' as 'fundamental requirements' of 'living together' in French society in *SAS*,[110] in *Dakir* it was enough for Belgium to rely on 'ground rules of social communication and more broadly the establishment of human relations that are essential for living together'.[111] The Court did not question the weight of these principles or why face-to-face contact was essential for 'the establishment of human relations'.[112] To the Court, Belgium 'sought to protect a form of interaction between individuals which was essential in the respondent state's view to the functioning of a democratic society'.[113] Both states could thus dictate a certain kind of interaction and form of dress which, combined, afforded the White majority greater access to Muslim women.[114] A stranger's right to see a Muslim woman's face and to interact with her on

105 *SAS* (n 6) [122].
106 ibid.
107 ibid [141].
108 ibid [96]; *Dakir* (n 7) [43].
109 *SAS* (n 6) [77].
110 ibid [141].
111 *Dakir* (n 7) [56]. The non-governmental organization Liberty noted this in its third-party submission to the Court, stating that Belgium had no tradition comparable to that of France. See [36].
112 ibid [56].
113 ibid.
114 *SAS* (n 6) [141]; *Dakir* (n 7) [56].

the stranger's terms was deemed more important than the applicants' religious rights and freedoms. Moreover, as the bans now extend to swimsuits that cover the whole body,[115] it is essential to reflect on the French *mission civilisatrice* as 'a violent cultural rape',[116] that continues to reverberate in present-day jurisprudence. To scrutinize the Court's assessment, we must understand the fantasy and ontology that guided it.

For the success of the colonial project, the White Man's physical access to the Muslim Woman was key.[117] In orientalist fantasies, the conquest of land and the female body merge, manifesting in a moment where the White Man unveils the Muslim Woman, who submits to him and welcomes the 'seed' of civilization.[118] The land was conquered by the flag, and her body would now mirror the colonizing nation.[119] While for some Indigenous peoples this meant 'dressing up', 'Arab women were to be "civilized" by being undressed'.[120] Between the 1900s and 1930s, these orientalist fantasies circulated via French postcards where Algerian women were presented unveiled and undressed. Alloula understands the postcards as an extension of the colonial violence inflicted on Algerians, portraying the Muslim Woman as the White Man fantasized.[121] Displaying her exposed body amounted to 'an imaginary revenge upon what had been inaccessible until then'. These fantasies persist in European pornography, which continues to depict the White Man undressing the Muslim Woman, either with her consent or through coercion.[122]

The seclusion of women through veiling or her refusal to interact grates the White Man because it unravels his perception of himself as a benevolent and civilizing conqueror.[123] To regain his self-esteem, he reinterprets the act of locking the colonizer *out* of her private sphere as her being locked *into* the private sphere.[124] Moreover, him being denied access to her is represented as a barrier imposed by the Muslim Man, preventing the White Man from living out his fantasy of being desired by the Muslim Woman.[125] As the veil blocks the White Man's access, removing it becomes 'the most powerful expression of the symbolic overcoming of the obstacle'[126] and redeems his heroic status. Ultimately, the denial of access invokes anxiety and frustration as it obstructs the White Man's 'ability to achieve self-realization',[127] and, instead, forces him to confront the History he refuses to acknowledge.

[115] See also van de Graaf on the lodged complaint against Belgium on the burkini bans (*Missaoui and Akhandaf v Belgium*). Catherine van de Graaf, 'Banning body-covering swimwear: the Human Rights Centre submitted a Third Party Intervention to the ECtHR in Missaoui and Akhandaf v. Belgium' *Strasbourg Observer* (Strasbourg, 28 October 2022) <https://strasbourgobservers.com/category/cases/missaoui-and-akhandaf-v-belgium> accessed 21 July 2024.

[116] Silverstein (n 76) 47; see also *Leila Ahmed, 'New Discourses' in Women and Gender in Islam: Historical Roots of the Modern Debate* (Yale University Press 1992).

[117] Fanon (n 98) 35, 44; Yeğenoğlu (n 20) 12.

[118] McClintock (n 21) 26.

[119] ibid.

[120] ibid 31.

[121] Alloula (n 19) 5; Mama (n 98).

[122] Mehammed Amadeus Mack, *Sexagon: Muslims, France, and the Sexualization of National Culture* (Fordham University Press 2017) 223–42.

[123] McClintock (n 21) 26; Alloula (n 19) 26.

[124] Alloula (n 19) 21.

[125] Alloula writes: 'If the women are inaccessible to sight (that is, veiled), it is because they are imprisoned.' ibid 21.

[126] ibid 26.

[127] ibid.

As the Court leans into the White Man's fantasies, it could resolve the White Man's anxiety only by allowing him to break into the Muslim Woman's private sphere and by enforcing state rules on her body against her will. Whether the applicants were capable of interacting with others while wearing the face veil was ultimately insignificant; the Court leaned into the dominant fantasies, painting veiling as a violation of French 'fundamental requirements' and Belgian 'ground rules' for a 'democratic society'. In other words, while pontificating about equality and freedom, European states seek to transfer the imagined control and authority of the Muslim Man over the Muslim Woman to the White Man.[128] Her submission legitimizes the civilizing mission and the supremacy of whiteness as she is saved from her savage tormentor, whether person, religion, or culture.[129] Through bans on religious freedoms, the Court reaffirms the greatness of European 'fraternity', 'civility', 'equality', and 'ground rules of a democratic society'. Looking at the Court's arguments through the lens of these fantasies, human rights law appears at risk of becoming the postcard: a tool of revenge and self-realization for the White Man through the enforcement of his violent sexual fantasies, here conveyed via the violence of law.

5. The nightmare: the hijab is a threat to the empire

So far, the Muslim Woman has had two options for her storyline in the examined white and patriarchal ontologies. The first option is to remain victimized by the Muslim Man and the Islamic faith. The second is to denounce them by embodying white epistemologies, that is, secularism, which reasserts the backwardness of her ontology while confirming the superiority and universality of Europe's. However, if she rejects white representations of the discussed values, a third option is foisted upon her: she becomes a threat to the White Man's empire.[130]

According to the Court, the hijab threatened multiple values within European states. In *Dahlab*, the hijab contravened 'the message of tolerance, respect for others and, above all, equality and non-discrimination that all teachers in a democratic society must convey to their pupils'.[131] It also threatened 'religious harmony' in the classroom.[132] In *Ebrahimian*, the hijab was interpreted as 'an ostentatious manifestation of her religion, incompatible in this case with the neutral environment required in a public service'[133]and 'amounted to a culpable breach of her duty of neutrality'.[134] In *Sahin*, the hijab was framed as a 'symbol of political Islam',[135] meaning that 'the Court must have regard to what is at stake, namely the need to protect the rights and freedoms of others, to preserve public order and to secure civil peace and true religious

[128] Fanon (n 98) 40; Alloula (n 19) 21 26; Evans (n 9).

[129] Jacobsen and Stenvoll (n 95) 283–85. See also Lauren Berlant, *The Queen of America Goes to Washington City: Essays on Sex and Citizenship* (Duke University Press 1997) 195–96 on the importance of immigrant women to conform and thus enforce the 'desirability' of the US.

[130] This general pattern was discovered by Jacobsen and Stenvoll (n 95) 283.

[131] *Dahlab* (n 4) 13.

[132] ibid.

[133] *Ebrahimian* (n 5) [62].

[134] ibid [69].

[135] *Sahin* (n 2) [115]–[116].

pluralism, which is vital to the survival of a democratic society'.[136] Notice the terminology: European values are 'at stake', meaning the hijab is capable of disturbing them and thus making restrictions 'necessary to protect the democratic system'.[137]

The Grand Chamber further embraced the previous judgment in which it linked the hijab with 'extremist political movements',[138] indicating that the ban was necessary to protect students from 'external pressure from extremist movements'.[139] The Court bluntly confirmed Goldberg's observation: 'The Muslim image in contemporary Europe ... foments conflict: violence, war, militancy, terrorism, cultural dissension.'[140] 'The Muslim, and as his continuation the veil, signals the death of European secularism, humanism, individualism, libertinism.'[141]

The White Man's obsession with penetrating the veil serves another function: the fantasy of uncovering hidden 'truths', truths guarded by the Muslim Woman. The White Man assumes her to be deceptive, ill-willed, and conspiratorial behind her veil.[142] Returning to Fanon, we recall splitting the past into multiple Histories: deep down, the White Man knows and fears that the oppressed 'native never ceases to dream of putting himself in the place of the settler'.[143] The nightmare involves a general mistrust of women, but also a specific anxiety of being outsmarted by the savage, propelling the White Man to showcase his power through violence, seeking to preserve a fantasized racial hierarchy.

Fanon argued that the colonizer enforced a system of oppression through continuous violence. As such, the colonized could only pursue liberation through violence as well. To avoid this outcome, the colonizer insists that the slave should not 'regress' to his natural self and instead upholds 'civilized' values (which never served to protect him).[144] European values that dehumanized the colonized, are also the same values that will liberate them. Yet, as Walter Rodney enquired: 'By what standard of morality can the violence used by the slave to break his chains be considered the same as the violence of a slave master?'[145] Stated otherwise, how can resistance against oppression and the struggle for liberation be understood in the same terms as oppressive violence? To the colonizer, the breaking of chains is an act of violence and an attack, verifying the danger the colonizer feared and justifying further repression. Bhabha states:

> By 'knowing' the native population in these terms, discriminatory and authoritarian forms of political control are considered appropriate. The colonized population is then deemed to be both the cause and the effect of the system, imprisoned in the circle of interpretation. What is visible is the *necessity* of such rule which is justified

[136] ibid [110].
[137] ibid [114].
[138] Ibid [115].
[139] ibid [111]; citation in [113].
[140] Goldberg (n 16) 346.
[141] ibid.
[142] Yeğenoğlu (n 20) 51–53.
[143] Fanon (n 25) 52–54; Yeğenoğlu (n 20) 45.
[144] Fanon (n 25) 42–44.
[145] Walter Rodney, *The Groundings with My Brothers* (Verso 2019) 16.

> by those moralistic and normative ideologies of amelioration recognized as the Civilizing Mission or the White Man's Burden.[146]

Resistance thus legitimizes the colonizer's right to use further violence to maintain his 'civilized' rule and superior position.[147]

When it comes to the hijab, the story of the oppressed challenging his master has its own version. Because European colonizers identified the removal of the hijab as a measure of successful domination, some Algerian women signalled their resistance to the French occupier by embracing it.[148] During the Algerian War of Independence, some women even smuggled explosives under it,[149] sparking further French repression as Muslim women were publicly stripped, humiliated, and tortured.[150] Algerians living in France were racially profiled, with the French state fearing possible sympathies towards the National Front and unleashing violence against individuals now reduced to 'terrorists'.[151]

These strategies are not unique to the French-Algerian colonial context, as the hijab evolved into a shared form of resistance in many Muslim countries protesting Western military, economic, and cultural imperialism.[152] Both the adoption and removal of veils have thus come to represent acts of resistance and dominance between colonizing states and colonized peoples. In the words of Leila Ahmed: '. . . it is a discourse on women and the veil in which another history is also inscribed, the history of colonial domination and the struggle against it and the class division around that struggle . . . a discourse in which that history, those struggles, still live'.[153] Additionally, and often forgotten in these discussions and in the Court's jurisprudence, is that many women, like the applicants, wear the hijab out of religious commitment.[154]

[146] Bhabha (n 61) 83.

[147] Fanon (n 25) 54.

[148] Fanon (n 98) 61–62;

[149] See Fanon (n 98) 35–63 on the use of the veils as political (and military) resistance. See also Alloula (n 20).

[150] Gordon (n 97) 55.

[151] Yasser Munif, 'French Postcolonial Nationalism and Afro-French Subjectivities (PhD Thesis, University of Massachusetts Amherst, 2011) 1–2; Cherifa Bouatta, 'Feminine Militancy: Moudjahidates During and After the Algerian War' in Valentine M Moghadam (ed), *Gender and National Identity: Women and Politics in Muslim Societies* (Zed Books 1994) 27.

[152] For the Yugoslavian context around the 1950s, see Tea Hadžiristić, 'Unveiling Muslim Women in Socialist Yugoslavia: the Body between Socialism, Secularism and Colonialism' (2017) 7(2) Religion and Gender 184; for Türkiye in the 1920s and onwards, see Alev Cinar, *Modernity, Islam, and Secularism in Türkiye: Bodies, Places and Time* (University of Minnesota Press 2005); Merve Kavakçı, *Headscarf politics in Türkiye: a Postcolonial Reading* (Palgrave Macmillan 2014); Hilal Elver, *The Headscarf Controversy: Secularism and Freedom of Religion* (Oxford University Press 2012). For a detailed work on Egypt and the Middle East from 1800 onwards, see Ahmed (n 116).

[153] Ahmed (n 116) 130. The history of how the hijab became a symbol of political success for colonizers, a symbol of resistance for the colonized, and a symbol for the modernization of new states has been discussed by various scholars in different contexts. See, eg, the pioneering work of Franz Fanon developing his much-used theories on race in the Algerian context (1970); in the Yugoslavian context around the 1950s, see Hadžiristić (n 152); for Türkiye in the 1920s and onwards, see Cinar (n 152), Kavakçı (n 152), and Elver (n 152); and for a detailed work on Egypt and the Middle East from 1800 onwards, see Ahmed (116).

[154] This was explicitly stated in *Sahin* (n 2) [101] and in *SAS* (n 6) [11]. Although not explicitly stated in other cases, the human rights claim would probably have fallen under Article 10 (freedom of expression) if the veil was not worn for religious reasons.

Again, to support the fantasy, epistemological gymnastics are needed. By disconnecting the hijab from the oppression of European empires that politicized the hijab in the first place, European states have managed to brand it as an inherent evil originating in 'Islamic culture' and thus symbolizing opposition to everything Europe stands for. The boogie man encapsulates the trauma of the White Man, chased away from the colonies before he could complete his mission and now, instead of recognizing the violence he inflicted on colonized peoples, he claims a position of victimhood.[155] The Muslim Woman must be policed, her loyalties and thoughts controlled through restrictions and punishments until she ceases to threaten his superiority.[156] The removal of her hijab reassures the paranoid colonizer that her resistance has been vanquished,[157] allowing the continuation of his fantasy about himself.

The Muslim Woman who claims her rights and demands to be treated equally in accordance with human right standards that European states claim to follow is often accused of 'abusing' the tolerance of European states,[158] of causing 'harm to those who encounter her, a symbolic violence', or of 'perverting relationships between citizens'.[159] This narrative was very prevalent in *SAS* and *Dakir*, in which social relations between citizens were perceived to be under the threat of the face veil. It is also seen in *Dahlab*, in which Ms Dahlab allegedly threatened multiple values as a teacher, potentially harming her pupils. In *Sahin* and *Köse*, the demonstrations of students and the local populations against the bans were connected with 'extremist political movements' and interpreted as evidence of the hijab's power to provoke and disturb societal peace and order, instead of being a normal form of political action within a democratic society.[160] Ms Ebrahimian was accused of 'infringing' the patients' freedom of conscience[161] and risking impartial treatment.[162]

Yet, across their complaints, the applicants underlined the importance of an open and plural society for democracy.[163] The teacher (Ms Dahlab) stated that she was committed to secular teaching, never received complaints from pupils or parents, and promoted principles of diversity and tolerance of different beliefs.[164] The social worker (Ms Ebrahimian) had been praised by her former colleagues for her professionalism, with no indication of her discriminating against patients.[165] Most of them argued that religious tolerance was essential for a democratic society[166] with Ms Dakir noting that

[155] On white victimhood, see Nicky Falkof, 'White Victimhood: Weaponising Identity and Resistance to Social Change' in Richard Ballard and Clive Barnett (eds), *The Routledge Handbook of Social Change* (Routledge 2022); Katrina Rebecca Bloch, Tiffany Taylor, and Karen Martinez, 'Playing the Race Card: White Injury, White Victimhood and the Paradox of Color Blind Ideology in Anti-Immigrant Discourse' (2020) 43(7) Ethnic and Racial Studies 1130.

[156] Fanon (n 98) 43.

[157] On how punishments and exclusion are used to create conformable and docile subjects, see Sara Ahmed, *Willful Subjects* (Duke University Press 2014).

[158] El-Tayeb (n 91) 163.

[159] Sherene Razack, 'A Site/Sight We Cannot Bear: The Racial/Spatial Politics of Banning the Muslim Woman's Niqab' (2018) 30(1) Canadian Journal of Women and the Law 169, 178.

[160] *Sahin* (n 2) [23], [44], [115]; Köse (n 1) 3, 9, 12.

[161] *Ebrahimian* (n 5) [61].

[162] ibid [63].

[163] *Sahin* (n 2) [100].

[164] *Dahlab* (n 4) 10–11.

[165] *Ebrahimian* (n 6) [39].

[166] *Dahlab* (n 4) 11; *Ebrahimian* (n 5) [39]; *Sahin* (n 2) [100].

allowing 'homogeneity' to prevail 'over the right to difference' created 'a total reversal' of democracy and individual liberties.[167] In other words, they all were committed to the democratic society that the Court accused them of destroying. Again, within the epistemology of the White Man, the Muslim Woman transgresses him and his rule when she seeks to liberate herself via the same mechanics the colonizer uses to control her.

The case law recreated the well-documented need of the White Man to uncover the Muslim Woman. Throughout, she is portrayed as ill-minded, hiding something dangerous under her veil; whether a bomb or her 'true' self.[168] Within the White Man's nightmare, the applicants are caricatured as the dangerous and gendered Muslim. Instead of believing the applicants' declared commitment to the democratic state and acknowledging Muslim women as individuals with nuanced value systems, their individuality is denied. For the White Man, the truth is not in her words, but in her veil.[169] Because she is a veiled Muslim, the Court already knows her.[170] 'When wearing the *hijab*, the veiled Muslim woman is excluded from human rights because she recalls the nomadic culture of Muslims and their loyalty to the global ummah over and above loyalty to the state.'[171] She is connected with 'extremist political movements' and seeks to disrupt civil peace, to proselytize, to disturb religious harmony, to discriminate against students and patients, and to destroy democracy. To safeguard itself from the Muslim Woman, the democratic society must evict her from public institutions, not to mention the streets of Europe.

6. Conclusion: destroying the White Man's fantasy

In this chapter, I have used the framework of fantasies to explore how the Court legitimizes ontologies based on whiteness and patriarchy and deploys epistemological tools to smooth out contradictions that stem from purported equal human rights protection. These contradictions can be summarized as: (i) European states 'saving' and 'liberating' Muslim women from Muslim men by excluding them from education and work, (ii) forcing Muslim women to undress and socialize in public against their will in the name of French/Belgian values, and (iii) classifying her as a threat to democratic society when she practises her rights usually guaranteed by a democratic society. As a gendered and racialized Muslim, she is denied agency and treated as little more than an uncivilized object who can only achieve full subjectivity when she embodies French/Belgian/secular/European values. Ultimately, the Court has continued the civilizing mission, demanding she adhere to secularism, gender equality, and democracy as articulated by the White Man.

Fanon wrote:

[167] *Dakir* (n 7) [28].

[168] For bombs, see Fanon (n 98) 58; for hiding her 'true' self, see Yeğenoğlu (n 20) 44.

[169] Yeğenoğlu (n 20) 48–49.

[170] Said criticizes the continual legitimation on Western academics to 'study' and 'know' the 'Islamic mind' or the 'Arab character': Said (n 17) 262.

[171] Aneira Edmunds, 'Precarious Bodies: The Securitization of the "Veiled" Woman in European Human Rights' (2021) 72(2) The British Journal of Sociology 315, 320.

> There is a fact: white men consider themselves superior to the black men.
> There is another fact: Black men want to prove to the white men, at all costs, the richness of their thought, the equal value of their intellectual.[172]

If equal value is to be proven on the standards of the White Man, this reinforces his superiority.[173] The White Man is thus superior only as long as the Other (willingly or under coercion) submits and embodies his principles[174] and complies with the 'obligation to forget' the violence he inflicts.

By wearing the hijab, the 'symbol of Islam', the Muslim Woman refuses to conform to the White Man's code, and thus rejects his superiority.[175] This creates a flux in his control over the Other.[176] The veiled Muslim Woman is not neatly tucked away in the colony or housing projects anymore. She takes up space in the streets in Paris and Brussels, she administers medical care, handles case files, and teaches children. She lives and takes action like the White Man does, but without conforming to his expectations and without confirming his fantasy about himself. In fact, she challenges the monopoly of whiteness in these spaces, a wish Fanon voiced in his book: 'We shall see that another solution is possible. It implies a restructuring of the world.' [177] To reconstruct human rights law, the White Man must meet the gaze of his Other. Fanon and Yeğenoğlu both underline the importance of controlling the gaze, but do not engage with the moment when the gazes meet. Recall the White Man fears *the veiled woman who can see without being seen.*

In his fantasy, he desires control, but Žižek reminds us that desire is deceptive[178] and thus it is not the loss of control that he fears. Such a loss is welcome as it allows him to appropriate the identity of the victim, once again further legitimizing his fantasy. The key lies in Žižek's following assertion: 'fantasy is the screen by means of which the subject avoids the radical opening of the enigma of the Other's desire'.[179] The fantasy 'sustains the subject's "sense of reality"'[180] and protects him from the History that is remembered by the Other. Again, what hinders Europe from acknowledging its violent past and the material effects they produce is the fantasy itself; by framing the Muslim Man as the savage and eternal opposite, the White Man imprints the Other with his vices. The dichotomy makes it possible for the White Man, European states, and the Court to extricate themselves from pathology, while silencing History and legitimating the undressing of Muslim women as acts of common good.

The White Man's greatest fear is being acknowledged for what he claims to fight. When subjected to the gaze of the Muslim Woman, when she tells her History and applies her epistemologies, she compels him to see who he is to the Other. Yet, the White Man is accustomed to self-righteousness and fear, and thus cannot bear the flash of

[172] Frantz Fanon, *Black Skins, White Masks* (Pluto Press 1986) 12.
[173] ibid 149.
[174] ibid 210–50.
[175] Fanon (n 98) 62–63.
[176] ibid 63.
[177] Fanon (n 172) 82.
[178] Žižek (n 25) 53.
[179] ibid 39.
[180] ibid 54.

the mirror image, of seeing himself in the eyes of the Muslim Woman, grinning as he strikes her. It is at this moment that the White Man's fantasy dissipates, shattering his reality and himself in the process. If the Other is not the savage, the White Man is not the civilizer, the Master, or her saviour. He is simply an oppressor, rapist, and murderer.[181] The ghost of the past and the monster of the present is revealed to be within himself, causing him to lose the legitimation of his actions and thus his *raison d'être.* It is in her gaze that Europe realizes that the European fantasy is her nightmare, and that her fantasy, being recognized as equal on her own terms, is Europe's nightmare. Europe would effectively be Othered out from its fantasy.

As I have argued in this chapter, the Court retreated into the White Man's fantasies and made them into its guiding ontology. It victimized the Muslim Woman because of her gendered and racialized identity, advocating for her involuntary stripping in public spaces. By embracing these colonial fantasies, the Court became the White Man, supervising the defence of 'European values' from the threats of Muslim femininity. The Court refused to meet the applicants' gaze or their ontologies, and thus avoided contemplating its position in the chain of colonial violence. This chapter attempted to displace the Court from the centre of its fantasy and the position of the White Man,[182] by paralleling its argumentation with counter-narratives. It is only by recognizing the role European institutions play in the History of the Other that the reconstruction of the world can begin.

[181] See Walter and Lewis (n 29) for the compulsory repetition of violence by Europe throughout its history.

[182] Yeğenoğlu (n 20) 8.

PART IV
ANTIRACISM IN THE PLURIVERSE

15

Indian Approaches to Racism and Related Forms of Subordination under International Law

A Question of Interest Convergence

Suraj Girijashanker

1. Introduction

> India is the land of Gandhi and Buddha. We have fought consistently against racial discrimination. Mahatma Gandhi himself championed the cause of fighting against this evil. We can never have a racist mindset.
> Sushma Swaraj, India's former Minister for External Affairs, May 2016[1]

Following a rise in violence against African students across major Indian cities between 2016 and 2017, Indian officials responded by firmly denying any racial motivation to the attacks. Officials were quick to invoke India's historic position of support for African antiracist and anti-imperial movements, suggesting ties between India and the continent were rooted in 'solidarity' and 'brotherhood'.[2]

Indeed, in the lead up to and following its independence in 1947, India played a critical role in challenging racism and white-minority rule in South Africa and beyond at the United Nations (UN). This role was most pronounced during the tenure of India's first Prime Minister Jawaharlal Nehru, where anti-imperialism and anti-racism were key tenets of Indian foreign policy. Indian-led initiatives included a series of resolutions at the UN General Assembly (UNGA) between 1946 and 1962 which placed the racist laws and policies of South Africa's white minority government under international scrutiny.

In this chapter, I revisit this period and trace India's engagement with international law and institutions in both combating racism transnationally and deflecting claims of racism and related forms of subordination in a domestic context.[3] By extending

[1] Deccan Chronicle, 'Killing of Congo youth not a racial crime: Sushma Swaraj' *Deccan Chronicle* (31 May 2016) <https://www.deccanchronicle.com/nation/current-affairs/310516/attack-on-congo-student-heinous-unacceptable-but-not-racial-sushma.html> accessed 2 February 2023.

[2] UN Web TV 'India Review—27th Session of Universal Periodic Review' (*UN Web TV*, 4 May 2017) <https://media.un.org/en/asset/k18/k18qwiv2c9?fbclid=IwAR1CWp7_IkgQWlovJiGzgHe9Wd2WPLKBkjavrO1z8EKm4fbpnoORpvQ4LKQ> accessed 31 March 2023.

[3] Throughout this chapter, I will use the term related forms of subordination primarily to refer to subordination on the basis of caste in addition to other grounds of discrimination identified and interpreted

Suraj Girijashanker, *Indian Approaches to Racism and Related Forms of Subordination under International Law*
In: *Emancipating International Law*. Edited by: Mohsen al Attar and Claire Smith, Oxford University Press.
© Suraj Girijashanker 2026. DOI: 10.1093/9780198935605.003.0020

Derrick Bell's theory of interest convergence to an Indian context, I argue that beyond genuine solidarity, India's historic antiracist stance aligned with its geopolitical interests and was premised on the maintenance of hierarchies with African movements and subordinated groups within India. Given the conditionality of its approach, when attention shifted to its domestic treatment of racialized and subordinated populations, I contend that India's default position has been a double-move: to invoke its history of antiracism and to challenge the applicability of relevant international instruments in an Indian context. Such arguments have been most evident in India's resistance to the discussion of caste-based subordination under the ambit of the International Convention on the Elimination of All Forms of Racial Discrimination (ICERD). However, as I seek to demonstrate, they are likely to be replicated as international attention shifts to the racialization of Muslims and other populations in India as part of the construction of a Hindu nationalist state.

This chapter is divided into five sections. In the second section, I provide overviews of Derrick Bell's theory of interest convergence and racialization, racism, and related forms of subordination in an Indian context. In the third section, I outline India's early antiracist diplomatic initiatives at the UN, highlighting their legacy and fault lines in India's historic approach. The fourth section examines the relationship between India's early antiracist position at the UN and recent attempts to deflect international attention from domestic concerns including caste-based subordination and anti-Black racism. Finally, I assess the implications of India's approach in relation to the state's Hindu majoritarian identity today, briefly identifying potential sites of resistance through international law and institutions.

2. Interest convergence and racialization, racism, and related forms of subordination in India

Writing in 1980, one of the founders of Critical Race Theory, Derrick Bell argued that in the United States 'the interest of blacks in achieving racial equality will be accommodated only when it converges with the interests of whites'.[4] White majority interests he noted were both political and economic as well as domestic and international. In an international context, he contended that the Supreme Court decision in *Brown v Board of Education*, which determined that racial segregation of public schools was unconstitutional, provided 'immediate credibility' to the United States' struggle against communist states and won the 'hearts and minds of emerging third world peoples'.[5] Due to interest convergence, Bell argued 'racial justice—*or its appearance*—may, from

under Article 1(1) of the International Convention on the Elimination of Racial Discrimination (adopted 21 December 1965, entered into force 4 January 1969) 660 UNTS 195 (ICERD). Article 1(1) of the ICERD defines prohibited racial discrimination as 'any distinction, exclusion, restriction or preference based on race, colour, descent, or national or ethnic origin which has the purpose or effect of nullifying or impairing the recognition, enjoyment or exercise, on an equal footing, of human rights and fundamental freedoms in the political, economic, social, cultural or any other field of public life'.

[4] Derrick A Bell, 'Brown v. Board of Education and the Interest-Convergence Dilemma' (1980) 93 Harvard Law Review 518, 523.

[5] ibid 524.

time to time, be counted among the interests deemed important by the courts and by society's policymakers'.[6]

When applied to an Indian context, Bell's argument highlights the geopolitical interests and reputational stakes India's early commitment to antiracism aligned with. I suggest in this chapter that the *appearance* of solidarity was key to India's early position. As such, its approach fractured once international attention shifted to the treatment of racialized and subordinated populations in a domestic context, and India's reputational interests were put to question. A comprehensive overview of racism, racialization, and related forms of subordination in India is beyond the scope of this chapter. However, to provide context to Indian approaches to international law and institutions, a brief discussion is necessary.

As Dipesh Chakrabarty notes, in India, 'racism' is thought of as something the white people do to us. What Indians do to one another are variously described as 'communalism', 'regionalism', and 'casteism', but never 'racism'.[7] Indian state approaches to race and racial discrimination under international law are arguably grounded in such logic. While there are valid concerns that importing racial concepts to India may flatten 'pre-existing categories of social difference specific to the sub-continent', there are also common threads in the racialization and subordination of distinct groups which should be recognized.[8]

As an example, this chapter pays particular attention to anti-Black racism and caste-based subordination in India.[9] While these may appear as disparate issues, by adopting the framework of 'racialized casteism', Sureshi M Jayawardene is amongst the scholars who highlight common ground. She recognizes that the subordination of Siddis, an African-descendant population in India, is rooted in 'the historical entanglements of race, caste, colourism within the broader colonial context and the globalisation of

[6] ibid 523.

[7] Dipesh Chakrabarty, 'Modernity and Ethnicity in India' (1994) 17 South Asia: Journal of South Asian Studies 143, 145.

[8] Jesús F Cháirez-Garza and others, 'Introduction to the Special Issue: Rethinking Difference in India through Racialization' (2022) 45 Ethnic and Racial Studies 193, 194.

[9] Caste-based subordination is said to affect an estimated 260 million people worldwide, the majority who live in South Asia. See International Dalit Solidarity Network, 'Caste Discrimination' <http://idsn.org/caste-discrimination> accessed 4 May 2023. A comprehensive discussion of the construction of caste and the effects of the caste system in India is beyond the scope of this chapter. Annapurna Waughray and David Keane provide a helpful outline of two concepts, *varna* and *jati*, which denote caste in a South Asian context, as well as the position of Dalits in relation to the system. This will provide background for discussions further in the chapter. They state: '*Varna*, a concept in ancient Sanskrit religious texts, refers to the textual division of Hindu society into four hierarchical and mutually exclusive categories or *varnas* related to occupation or social function and involving the notion of "innate characteristics": Brahmins (priests), Kshatriyas (warriors and rulers), Vaisyas (traders and artisans) and Shudras (labourers and servants). Outside the *varna* framework is a fifth category – the Dalits, formerly known as 'Untouchables'. Caste is also used to refer to *jati*. *Jatis* are the thousands of local or regional endogamous birth groups, linked to hereditary occupation and hierarchically ranked within a geographical locality. Unlike *varna*, the concept of jati is not exclusive to Hinduism but is found across religious communities. While there are only four *varnas* the number of *jatis* has always varied as existing groups merge and new groups emerge.' See Annapurna Waughray and David Keane, 'CERD and Caste-Based Discrimination' in David Keane and Annapurna Waughray (eds), *Fifty years of the International Convention on the Elimination of All Forms of Racial Discrimination* (Manchester University Press 2017) 127–28.

Western ideas'.[10] Similarly, while caste-based subordination is frequently associated in an international context with discrimination on the basis of descent and work, colourism, and the widely discredited Aryan race theory which was often upheld by colonial officials, has contributed to its entrenchment.[11] Commonalities in the racialization and subordination of various populations in India, including Dalits—people belonging to lower castes—and Muslims, is also clearer when attention shifts to the construction of the Hindu nationalist state.[12] Establishing a strong Hindu majoritarian identity coincides with the othering, exclusion, and repression of these populations.

3. Revisiting India's early antiracist initiatives at the UN

At the inaugural session of the UNGA in 1946 and just nine months after the UN Charter came into force, India—which had yet to attain independence from Britain—placed racial subordination in South Africa under international scrutiny. Resolution 44 (I) 'Treatment of people of Indian origin in the Union of South Africa' was initially proposed by India and passed by a two-thirds majority, setting the foundations for Third World solidarity and further challenging racism in South Africa and beyond at multilateral fora. The head of the Indian delegation, Vijaya Lakshmi Pandit, termed the resolution's adoption as an 'Asian victory',[13] while African National Congress President Albert Luthuli later reflected 'the way in which India at the UN has taken up the cudgels on behalf of the oppressed South African majority and dragged the whole scandal of apartheid into the open, has heartened us immeasurably'.[14]

India's decision to bring the treatment of Indians in South Africa to the UNGA's attention was triggered by the Asiatic Land Tenure and Indian Representation Act of 1946. What came to be known as the 'Ghetto Act' restricted Indians from freely voting and owning property in the South African provinces of Natal and Transvaal. Indians in South Africa feared the Act would confine them to ghettos, and a passive resistance campaign against the law resulted in the detention of 1,750 Indians.[15]

The UNGA resolution coincided with strong bilateral measures from India, including withdrawing the Indian High Commissioner in Pretoria and the termination of a trade agreement with South Africa.[16] Heated debates and staunch opposition

[10] Sureshi M Jayawardene, 'Racialized Casteism: Exposing the Relationship Between Race, Caste, and Colorism Through the Experiences of Africana People in India and Sri Lanka' (2016) 20 Journal of African American Studies 323, 341.

[11] Ibid. For a discussion of the Aryan race theory, including its relationship with caste and colonial governance, see Romila Thapar, 'The Theory of Aryan Race and India: History and Politics' (1996) 24 Social Scientist 3.

[12] Ratna Kapur, 'Race-Making, Religion and Rights in the Post-Colony: Unmasking the Pathogen in Assembling a Hindu Nation' (2022) 18 International Journal of Law in Context 499; Balmurli Natrajan, 'Racialization and Ethnicization: Hindutva Hegemony and Caste' (2022) 45 Ethnic and Racial Studies 298.

[13] Lorna Lloyd, '"A Most Auspicious Beginning": The 1946 United Nations General Assembly and the Question of the Treatment of Indians in South Africa' (1990) 16 Review of International Studies 131, 148.

[14] Enuga S Reddy, *The Struggle for International Liberation in South Africa and International Solidarity* (Sterling Publishers 1999) 43.

[15] Lloyd (n 13) 133.

[16] ibid.

from South Africa and its supporters, chiefly Britain, resulted in the dilution of the original resolution. It initially stated: 'the Union Government's discriminatory treatment of Asiatics in general and Indians in particular on the ground of their race constituted a denial of Human Rights and fundamental freedom is contrary to the Charter.'[17] In contrast, the resolution which ultimately passed, tabled by Mexico and France, recognized that relations between India and South Africa had been 'impaired', and that the 'treatment of Indians in the Union should be in conformity with the international obligations under the agreements concluded between the two Governments and the relevant provisions of the [UN] Charter'.[18]

Although the final resolution did not contain explicit reference to racial discrimination or human rights, its significance should not be understated given the historic context. While the language of human rights and non-discrimination feature in the UN Charter, Article 2(7) limits the ability of the UN to 'intervene in matters which are essentially within the domestic jurisdiction of any state'. This clause proved a major hurdle to India's efforts. At the UN Conference on International Organization in San Francisco where the Charter was finalized, fears from states including Britain, the United States, and Australia, that racial subordination and racially exclusionary immigration policies would garner international attention were allayed by the inclusion of the domestic jurisdiction clause.[19]

South Africa and its supporters contended that the resolution drew attention to an internal issue which was beyond the scope of the UN Charter. India, however, demonstrated a legal basis for its interest in the conditions of Indians in South Africa by referring to the 1927 Cape Town Agreement between the two governments, where South Africa had agreed to support the advancement of Indians who were willing to assimilate to 'western standards of life'.[20] As the resistance faced centred on domestic jurisdiction, a resolution which sought to address the impact of white-minority rule in South Africa on the Black majority and ColouredPopulations was unlikely to be adopted. Thus, as Vijaya Lakshmi Pandit argued, despite its limitations, the resolution served as an important 'test case', particularly in relation to the scope of the newly created institution to address racial subordination against arguments of non-interference and the protection of state sovereignty.[21]

Resolution 44 (I) and India's broader diplomatic initiatives were critical in creating an infrastructure for further action against racism in South Africa and beyond at the UN. India tabled the 'Treatment of Indians in the Union of South Africa' annually at the UNGA until it merged with Resolution 1761 in 1962, which condemned apartheid in South Africa, established the UN Special Committee against Apartheid, and called for economic and political sanctions.[22] Resolution 44 (I) also laid the groundwork

[17] Vineet Thakur, 'The "Hardy Annual": A History of India's First UN Resolution' (2017) 16 India Review 401, 406.

[18] UNGA, 'Treatment of Indians in the Union of South Africa' (8 December 1946) UN Doc A/RES/44(I), 8.

[19] Paul Gordon Lauren, 'First Principles of Racial Equality: History and the Politics and Diplomacy of Human Rights Provisions in the United Nations Charter' (1983) 5 Human Rights Quarterly 1, 19–20.

[20] Lloyd (n 13) 133.

[21] ibid 147.

[22] UNGA, 'The policies of apartheid of the Government of the Republic of South Africa' (6 November 1962) UN Doc A/RES/1761.

for the UNGA's determination in 1954 that 'apartheid constitutes a grave threat to the peaceful relations between ethnic groups in the world'.[23] Avenues to discuss racism under the auspices of the UN had not been clearly established given its primary objective was to maintain peace and security following the Second World War.

Through Resolution 44 (I) and its opposition to attempts by South Africa to annex South West Africa (Namibia), where it highlighted annexation would subject the territory's inhabitants to racist laws and policies,[24] India assumed a leadership role at the UN on causes sitting at the nexus of self-determination, decolonization, and anti-racism. The approach of the Indian delegation at the UN closely reflected key tenets of foreign policy under India's first Prime Minister, Jawaharlal Nehru. Nehru took particular interest in the conditions of Indians in South Africa. As he expressed in a 1949 speech, the treatment of Indians in South Africa was not just of concern to India or South Africa but as a 'continuous challenge to the self-respect of a vast number of people in the world', it was also a threat to peace and security worldwide.[25]

Nehru's positions also indicated commitment to opposing racial subordination in contexts beyond the treatment of the Indian diaspora. India attained independence while a significant proportion of states in Asia and Africa were under colonial rule. Thus, Nehru intended for India to take a leadership role supporting decolonization, to which he saw challenging racism as a key component. As RP Anand suggests, India 'acted more or less as a spokesperson of the newly independent countries'.[26] In 1946, Nehru articulated India's experience of colonialism and the racial ideology at its foundation which informed Indian foreign policy:

> [W]e in India have known racialism in all its forms ever since the commencement of British rule. The whole ideology of this rule was that of the herrenvolk and the master race, and the structure of government was based upon it; indeed the idea of a master race is inherent in imperialism. There was no subterfuge about it . . . More powerful than words was the practice that accompanied them.[27]

The leadership position Nehru assumed was premised on extending India's experience in challenging colonial rule, and its racial foundations, particularly in Africa.

At the 1955 Asian-African Conference in Bandung, where Nehru and Indonesia's Sukarno were primary organizers, Nehru commented that 'the tragedy of Africa is greater than that of any other continent, whether it is racial or political. It is up to Asia to help Africa to the best of her ability'.[28] Through numerous initiatives, Nehru's rhetoric was matched with action. In addition to India being the first state to recognize the African National Congress and halt trade with South Africa,

[23] UNGA, 'The question of race conflict in South Africa resulting from the policies of apartheid of the Government of the Union of South Africa' (14 December 1954) UN Doc A/RES/820.

[24] Allana O'Malley, 'India, Apartheid and the New World Order at the UN' (2020) 31 Journal of World History 195, 209–15.

[25] Jawaharlal Nehru, 'Our Objectives' in *Jawaharlal Nehru's Speeches: September 1946–May 1949* (Publications Division, Ministry of Information and Broadcasting, Government of India 1967) 265.

[26] Ram P Anand, 'Jawaharlal Nehru and International Law and Relations' in Ram P Anand (ed), *Studies in International Law and History: An Asian Perspective* (Martinus Nijhoff 2004) 21.

[27] Jawaharlal Nehru, *Discovery of India* (Oxford University Press 1981) 327–28.

[28] Indian Council for Africa, *Nehru and Africa* (New Delhi, 1964) 18–19.

domestically Nehru set up the Indian Council of Africa, which worked closely with the Ministry of External Affairs to support self-determination movements.[29] Additionally, where interests of the Indian diaspora in Africa, who continued to benefit from racial hierarchies entrenched through colonial rule, conflicted with those of national independence movements, Nehru's allegiance remained with the latter. As an example, in a speech before the Lok Sabha, the lower house of India's parliament, Nehru expressed that East African Indians 'could expect no help from us, no protection from us, if they seek any special rights in Africa which were not in the interests of Africa'.[30]

As I have sought to illustrate, the significance of Resolution 44 (I) and India's broader antiracist initiatives under Nehru are not in question. However, perhaps in light of the unprecedented nature of India's actions, and the stringent opposition it faced, a critical assessment of India's approach to challenging racism transnationally has been lacking, particularly in the context of global racial hierarchies and the prevalence of anti-Black racism in India. Indeed, the relationship between India's antiracist diplomacy and the treatment of racialized and subordinated groups within India remains understudied. As observed by scholars such as Alexander E Davis and Vineet Thakur, it is important to acknowledge that India's antiracist diplomacy cannot be reduced to the views and actions of Nehru.[31]

A starting point for assessing the conditionality of India's antiracist stance lies in recognizing its strategic interests at play. Such interests suggest India's antiracist initiatives cannot be reduced to pure altruism or the state acting as 'the conscience of the globe'.[32] As a newly independent state which had experienced imperial and racial subordination, it was in India's interests to take a leadership position in supporting movements which challenged colonial rule and racism abroad. The debates at the San Francisco Conference and surrounding Resolution 44(I) provide a glimpse into the alliances between colonial powers and settler colonies, particularly in relation to preserving imperial and racial hierarchies. At the UN, matters of concern to India, including shifting from a Eurocentric refugee law and protection framework to address the needs of Partition refugees,[33] and its efforts to liberate Goa from Portuguese rule,[34] were stifled by Western powers. Through supporting anticolonial and antiracist movements, India intended to win 'hearts and minds' and also contribute towards the gradual recomposition of UN membership.[35] It hoped this would lead to greater support for its issues of interest. However, in challenging racial and imperial hierarchies between the West and African states, India maintained hierarchical relationships of its own.

[29] Gerard McCann, 'From Diaspora to Third Worldism and the United Nations: India and the Politics of Decolonizing Africa' (2013) 218 Past and Present 258, 265.

[30] Indian Council for Africa (n 28) 34.

[31] Alexander E Davis and Vineet Thakur, 'Walking the Thin Line: India's Anti-Racist Diplomatic Practice in South Africa, Canada, and Australia, 1946–55' (2016) 38 The International History Review 880.

[32] Carol Anderson, *Bourgeois Radicals: The NAACP and the Struggle for Colonial Liberation, 1941–1960* (Cambridge University Press 2014) 100.

[33] Pia Oberoi, 'South Asia and the Creation of the International Refugee Regime' (2001) 19(5) Refuge 36.

[34] As Anand notes these aims did not actualize, as reflected through the lack of support it received from African and Asian states during the Sino-Indian war of 1962. See Anand (n 26) 5–8.

[35] ibid 22–23.

These hierarchies were most apparent in India's approach to racism in South Africa beyond the treatment of the Indian population. While including reference to the subordination of Black and Coloured populations in South Africa at the UNGA may not initially have been feasible in light of arguments relating to domestic jurisdiction, there is indication that India's support was not always forthcoming in later years. Davis and Thakur highlight the importance of Rajagopala Thiruvenkata Chari, who headed the Indian High Commission in Pretoria after India recalled its High Commissioner in 1946.[36] Chari was critical of India extending support primarily to members of the diaspora and advised the Indian government to consider the ideological roots of apartheid and show solidarity to Black people and specifically the African National Congress, including at multilateral fora. Thakur notes that India's Ministry of External Affairs' initial response was 'dismissive'.[37] While its Secretary General Girija Shankar Bajpai commented that the 'oppressed must unite if they are to get rid of oppression',[38] archival evidence also suggests he continued to view the African continent through the prism of a transnational racial hierarchy. Notably, Bajpai wrote on his copy of a letter from Chari, that '[t]he days when a handful of whites could hold down a continent, even a backward continent like Africa, are numbered'.[39]

Statements from Indian officials which entrenched racial hierarchies and alluded to Africa's civilizational inferiority from the 1940s onwards were rare, particularly in light of public-facing acts in support of Black African causes. However, Bajpai's views cannot be easily dismissed as an anomaly amongst Indian officials. SK Patil, an Indian National Congress politician who led a 1955 delegation to East Africa, serves as another example of an Indian official who privately viewed Africans as inferior to Indians. While he called for solidarity between Africans and Indians in public meetings, an internal report by British officials based on conversations with Patil shed light into his views on segregation in East Africa:

> Speaking candidly there was some justification for the desire of the more advanced communities in East Africa to have a measure of social segregation from the more primitive peoples.[40]

Taken with the pervasiveness of anti-Black sentiments among Indians and India's position as a newly independent state in relation to African movements under colonial and white-minority rule, Bajpai and Patil's views suggest that perceptions of Indian civilizational superiority were likely more common than has been acknowledged, even if such views were not openly stated. Further support for this contention is reflected in Bajpai's standing at the time as the senior most official in the Ministry of External Affairs as well as the tendency of Indian leaders and officials prior to and post Bajpai's tenure expressing support for Africans while failing to engage with anti-Black racism emanating from Indians. I will elaborate on this in Section 4 of this chapter.

[36] Davis and Thakur (n 31) 884–86.
[37] Thakur (n 17) 412.
[38] ibid.
[39] Davis and Thakur (n 31) fn 30.
[40] Kalathmika Natarajan, 'The Privilege of the Indian Passport (1947–1967): Caste, Class, and the Afterlives of Indenture in Indian Diplomacy' (2023) 57(2) Modern South Asian Studies 321, 335.

Perhaps the Indian leader whose anti-Black sentiments have received the most contemporary attention is Mahatma Gandhi.[41] Reflecting on Gandhi's initial years in South Africa prior to his 'awakening' in terms of race-consciousness, Indian diplomat and anti-apartheid campaigner ES Reddy argues that the caste and colour prejudices he inherited from India were reinforced by his interactions with merchants and white officials in South Africa, contributing to an anti-Black worldview.[42] Reddy notes that Gandhi sought to challenge the racial subordination of Indians by referring to Indian civilizational superiority in comparison to Black Africans.[43] Indeed, colonial and racial hierarchies when combined with caste and colour prejudices have also contributed to anti-Black racism both within India and amongst its diaspora. In a domestic context, Jayawardene argues that Indian ideologies interacted with imported structures to produce racialized outputs for Siddis, an African-descendant population.[44] Tayyab Mahmud also recognizes that amongst communities where Indian indentured labour was deployed by Britain—including parts of the Caribbean, South Africa, East Africa, and Fiji—unfavourable representation of Black labour by colonial administrators continues to strain ethnic relations today.[45]

Needless to say, the relationship between ethnic Indians and Siddis and the Indian diaspora and Black populations in former colonial territories cannot be equated to that between Indian officials and African movements challenging imperialism and racism. However, in drawing parallels regarding the implications of anti-Black sentiments, it is necessary to recognize as Davis has that the representation of empire by colonial administrators was not singular. He notes that India was portrayed as part of the 'liberal empire', in contrast to the majority of African colonies.[46] Thus, while 'India and Indians were narrated as civilised and teachable, Africans were not'.[47] While a cursory study of India's antiracist diplomacy may suggest genuine solidarity with African movements, in reality, India remained in an advantaged position post-independence when compared to peoples under white-minority and colonial rule.[48] The steep power differential taken with common anti-Black sentiments and India's strategic interests suggest expressions of support for African movements are unlikely to have been devoid of ideas of civilizational and therefore racial superiority.

India's practice at the UNGA of maintaining a separate agenda item for the treatment of Indians well after attention to the broader struggle against white-minority rule was established also raises questions regarding the nature of its commitment to antiracism. India's delegation to the UN eventually paid heed to Chari's advice in 1952

[41] '"Racist" Gandhi statue removed from University of Ghana' *BBC News* (14 December 2018) <https://www.bbc.com/news/world-africa-46552614> accessed 19 April 2024.

[42] Enuga S Reddy, 'Some of Gandhi's Early Views on Africans Were Racist. But That Was Before He Became Mahatma' (*The Wire*, 18 October 2016) <https://thewire.in/history/gandhi-and-africans> accessed 4 April 2023.

[43] ibid.

[44] Jayawardene (n 10) 341.

[45] Tayyab Mahmud, 'Cheaper Than a Slave: Indentured Labor, Colonialism and Capitalism' (2013) 34 Whittier Law Review 215, 231.

[46] Alexander E Davis, 'Solidarity or Hierarchy?: India's Identification with Africa and the Postcolonial Politics of Race' (2018) 17 India Review 242, 248–49.

[47] ibid.

[48] ibid.

when it supported an agenda item focusing on 'the question of race conflict in South Africa'.[49] However, it is important to note that India continued to maintain a separate resolution focusing on South African Indians until 1962. When the items were eventually merged, officials recognized 'India had shown that it was not asking for any special treatment for persons of Indian origin, and that both items were facets of the same problem'.[50] Yet, the remarks of Mr Jantuah, the delegate from Ghana during the said session are perhaps more telling: '[the separate discussion] had no doubt been a source of satisfaction to the South African Government as being a blow at African-Asian solidarity'.[51] The separate items, I would contend, is another reflection of India's antiracist position being premised on the maintenance of hierarchies.

Beyond some reluctance to support the broader movement against white-minority rule, archival evidence of India's antiracist diplomacy also provides an insight into its relationship with subordinated groups within India and the diaspora. While seeking to alleviate the conditions of Indians in South Africa, another senior Indian diplomat, Benegal Narsing Rau, India's Permanent Representative to the UN, proposed a 'casteist solution to a racist problem'.[52] A 'private and secret' memo at the South African diplomatic archives in Pretoria details an informal dinner meeting held in 1949 between India and South Africa's delegations to the UN, in which Rau was said to have spoken with an 'unexpected measure of frankness'.[53] Rau suggested 'Indians who went to South Africa did not belong to the best type and . . . they may have exploited the local population and given India a bad name',[54] adding that the way South Africa treated them 'might be fully justified and that in fact India would not mind discrimination against our local Indian community if only it was not based on racial lines'.[55] As a compromise, Rau was said to enquire whether a proposal of citizenship for 'a small number, say 10, of the cultured and best type of Indians' would be amenable to South Africa 'as a token to the world that the racial equality of Indians was recognised'.[56]

As Thakur explains, the 'best type of Indians' Rau referenced was proxy for upper-caste Indians, given he also said that measures to combat caste-based discrimination in India had contributed to discrimination against dominant castes, including the Brahmin caste to which he belonged.[57] Although the conversation was not reported in Indian archives, given that the memo was deemed 'private and secret', Thakur argues 'there is a strong case for believing that this conversation actually happened in this form'.[58] In addition to highlighting that India's antiracist initiatives were centred on *appearance* rather than advocating for substantive change, such a conversation would

[49] UNGA (n 23).
[50] O'Malley (n 24) 230.
[51] UNGA, 'Official Records—Special Political Committee', 17th Session, 327th meeting (8 October 1962) UN Doc A/SPC/SR.327.
[52] Vineet Thakur, 'When India Proposed a Casteist Solution to South Africa's Racist Problem' (*The Wire*, 4 April 2016) <https://thewire.in/diplomacy/exploring-casteism-in-indias-foreign-policy> accessed 4 April 2023.
[53] ibid.
[54] ibid.
[55] ibid.
[56] ibid.
[57] ibid.
[58] ibid.

also indicate that policies towards its diaspora influenced hierarchies on the basis of caste. Indeed, the memo raises questions of the extent it supported the interests of a specific segment of Indian society.

Prior to and following this reported conversation, the Indian government's commitment to challenging casteism was openly questioned by South Africa and its supporters at the UN in their stance against Resolution 44 (I). Britain's Attorney General Shawcross asked: 'What would happen . . . if the UN should enquire into the caste system in India?'[59] South African delegates also termed casteism as 'apartheid in India.' On one occasion, South African delegate Mr Louw referred to the writings of an Indian author in order to question India's moral credentials:

> Our case at the United Nations would have been stronger, if the high moral standards of human rights that Pandit Nehru demands for our people elsewhere, were available to them at home. The maxim which says that whoever comes to equity, must come with clean hands, operates adversely on us, in view of some of the shocking manifestations of caste which are still to be seen in our 'deep south.'[60]

In response to a reference to casteism in India by the South African Law Minister Mr Nichols in 1946, the head of India's delegation, Pandit argued the comment was aimed to 'humiliate India by accusations that were entirely irrelevant to the matter under discussion.'[61] Although statements from South Africa and its allies sought to deflect international attention from the impact of white-minority rule, India's own deflection from its treatment of racialized and subordinated groups in subsequent years has raised questions regarding the conditionality of its commitment to challenging racism and related forms of subordination. As will be clear, the arguments later adopted by India to avoid scrutiny, rooted in non-interference and the maintenance of state sovereignty, mirrored the response of South Africa and its supporters to Resolution 44 (I).

4. Preserving India's antiracist credentials: deflecting attention from caste-based subordination and anti-Black racism

Resolution 44 (I) and India's role in challenging white-minority rule in South Africa continues to be invoked by Indian officials as a sign of its commitment to the transnational fight against racism. In addition to contributing to the erasure of fault lines in India's early antiracist diplomacy, this history has been instrumentalized to divert international attention from the state's treatment of racialized and subordinated groups, particularly Dalits, who are officially referred to as Scheduled Castes, Adivasis, Indigenous and tribal populations who are officially known as Scheduled Tribes, and people belonging to lower castes. References to history overlap with arguments that

[59] Lloyd (n 13) 142.

[60] David Keane, 'India, the UN and Caste as a Form of Racial Discrimination: Resolving the Dispute' in Ulrike Davy and Antje Flüchter (eds), *Imagining Unequals, Imagining Equals: Concept of Equality in History and Law* (Bielefeld University Press 2022) 207.

[61] Vijaya Lakshmi Pandit, *The Scope of Happiness: A Personal Memoir* (Weidenfield and Nichlson 1979) 209.

racism and casteism are either alien in an Indian context or overstated. India's approach suggests the interests of its ruling elite lie in the preservation of its *appearance* as an antiracist leader rather than in seeking to improve conditions for subordinated groups domestically.

India's strategy of deflection has been most evident before the Committee on the Elimination of Racial Discrimination (CERD), the treaty body for ICERD. Notably, India played a prominent role in the drafting of ICERD, particularly the special measures outlined in Articles 1(4) and 2(2) for the advancement of racial and ethnic groups or other individuals requiring protection. During the drafting process, Indian delegates referred to the state's affirmative action policies, citing lower caste groups as examples of potential recipients of special measures.[62] India's position at the time implied that it envisioned caste-based discrimination fell under the ambit of ICERD. However, as systemic human rights violations based on caste garnered international attention, there was a marked shift in India's approach.

Prior to 1996, caste-based discrimination received limited attention at the UN, but this changed due to the efforts of transnational Dalit advocates and organizations. Indeed, India's early periodic reports to CERD included information on Scheduled Castes and Scheduled Tribes. Yet, in 1996, India began to dispute whether caste-based discrimination fell under the ambit of racial discrimination as defined under Article 1(1) of ICERD. Notably, ICERD's definition includes discrimination based on descent, which India claims does not encompass caste. Its 1996 report noted: '[t]he term "caste" denotes a "social" and "class" distinction and is not based on race. It has its origins in the functional division of Indian society during ancient times.'[63] While acknowledging that caste was based on descent, the report also asserted, '[i]t is obvious, however, that the use of the term "descent" in the Convention clearly refers to "race" '.[64] India's interpretation was disputed by CERD, which maintained caste-based discrimination fell under its mandate and was critical of the state's failure to report information about Scheduled Castes and Scheduled Tribes.[65]

While deflecting focus from caste-based discrimination, India's periodic report in 1996 celebrated its purported status as a post-racial society: '[c]ategorical distinctions of "race" or "national or ethnic origin" have ceased to exist and race itself as an issue does not impinge on the consciousness or outlook of Indian citizens in their social relations.'[66] To support this contention, five paragraphs of the report included reference to India's early antiracist diplomacy regarding South Africa. Paragraph 13 exemplifies India's efforts to accentuate its antiracist credentials:

> At the international level, India's commitment to the cause of elimination of racial discrimination in all its forms, including apartheid, has been reflected in the role it has played in this field. India was the first country to inscribe the issue of racism in South Africa on the agenda of the United Nations in 1946. Since independence, this

[62] Waughray and Keane (n 9) 131.
[63] CERD, 'State Party Report, India' (29 April 1996) UN Doc CERD/C/299/Add.3 [6].
[64] ibid [7].
[65] CERD, 'Concluding Observations, India' (17 September 1996) UN Doc CERD/C/304/Add.13 [4].
[66] CERD (n 63) [2].

> opposition to racial discrimination has been reflected in a policy that saw the imposition of comprehensive sanctions against apartheid South Africa, the severing of diplomatic ties with that country and India's accession to the International Convention on the Suppression and Punishment of the Crime of Apartheid in October 1977.[67]

India's strategy of deflection peaked during and in the lead up to the 2001 World Conference Against Racism (WCAR) in Durban, South Africa. Transnational Dalit advocates sought the inclusion of caste-based discrimination in the WCAR's Draft Program of Action, using the phrase 'hidden apartheid' to highlight systematic subordination and segregation on the basis of caste.[68] The Indian government strongly opposed their efforts. Clifford Bob notes, India 'blocked foreign activists from entering India to attend a WCAR organizational meeting' and also sponsored the participation of advocates at preparatory meetings 'who backed the government position and minimized India's problems of caste discrimination'.[69]

At the WCAR, India was ultimately successful in ensuring that reference to discrimination on the basis of descent and work, which would encompass caste-based discrimination, did not feature in the conference's final programme of action and declaration. While this is indicative of the diplomatic pressure India exerted, India's strategy also involved adopting arguments of non-interference and highlighting its antiracist credentials. In a statement at the WCAR, Minister of State for External Affairs Omar Abdullah argued:

> In the run up to the [W]orld Conference, there has been propaganda, highly exaggerated and misleading, often based on anecdotal evidence, regarding caste-based discrimination in India. . .It is neither legitimate nor feasible nor practical for this World Conference or, for that matter, even the UN to legislate, let alone police, individual behaviour in our societies. The battle has to be fought within our respective societies to change thoughts, processes and attitudes; indeed, the hearts and souls of our peoples.[70]

While noting that the WCAR should be 'forward looking' and not 'confined to recriminations for historic wrongs', Abdullah did not substantively address issues facing racialized and subordinated groups in India.[71] Instead, he invoked what was by now familiar rhetoric of Gandhi, Resolution 44 (I), and India's anti-apartheid advocacy. While referring to India's historic stance at the UN, he ironically adopted similar arguments relating to non-interference as South Africa did in their opposition to Resolution 44 (I).

[67] ibid [13].

[68] Clifford Bob, '"Dalit Rights Are Human Rights": Caste Discrimination, International Activism, and the Construction of a New Human Rights Issue' (2007) 29 Human Rights Quarterly 167, 184.

[69] ibid.

[70] Omar Abdullah, Minister of State for External Affairs (Statement at the World Conference against Racism, Durban, 2 September 2001) <https://www.un.org/WCAR/statements/indiaE.html> accessed 2 February 2023.

[71] ibid.

The year after the WCAR, CERD issued General Recommendation XXIX, where it reaffirmed that discrimination on the basis of descent covers 'members of communities based on forms of social stratification such as caste and analogous systems of inherited status'.[72] Since General Recommendation XXIX, India has completed one reporting cycle before CERD in 2006, where its position on the non-equivalence of caste and race in relation to Article 1(1) of ICERD remained the same. Perhaps more emphatically, the report noted that the 'contribution by the Government and people of India is more than an act of solidarity with people of Africa: It has deep roots in India's own struggle for freedom and dignity'.[73] The report also termed India's historic support for African liberation movements as being grounded in its 'national duty'.[74]

A meeting between India's delegation and CERD regarding the periodic reports submitted in 2006 provides greater clarity about India's views on the relationship between caste and race. While recognizing that both caste and race were socially constructed, Mr. Gupta of the Indian delegation stated 'there was phenotypical resemblance between members of different castes, whereas there was none between members of different races'.[75] Mr Gupta also went on to dispute the subordination of lower castes in India: '[t]he principle according to which the Brahmins were unassailable and unchallenged at the top of the hierarchy was wrong . . . it was not the case that one caste exploited all other castes; all castes—whether high or low—thought poorly of the others.'[76]

Mr Gupta's reasoning goes against the grain of bodies of scholarship on race and caste. Although scholars recognize the risks in conflating race and caste, they also note the distinction between the two cannot be reduced to phenotypical resemblance or difference. Writing in the context of India, Zaheer Babar argues 'for racialization to occur, it is sometimes irrelevant whether a group of people share certain uniform phenotypical characteristics or not'.[77] Furthermore, although the social construction of caste goes beyond phenotypical ascription, as Jayawardene highlights, colourism 'occupies a complex position within South Asian caste systems'.[78] Caste may be incorrectly inferred from skin tone and its association with notions of 'purity' and 'pollution' which are inherent to the caste system. Finally, Mr Gupta appears to dispute the hierarchy associated with *varnas* in the caste system—traditionally associated with occupation or social function. Contrary to his claims, Annapurna Waughray recognizes that *varna* rankings are largely fixed and immutable, with social status based on caste being 'hereditary (determined by birth) and not susceptible to alteration through personal effort'.[79]

[72] CERD, 'General Recommendation XXIX on Article 1, Paragraph 1, of the Convention (Descent) (1 November 2002) UN Doc HRI/GEN/1/Rev 6.

[73] CERD, 'Addendum to the Nineteenth Periodic Reports of States Parties Due in 2006—India' (29 March 2006) UN Doc CERD/C/IND/19 [55].

[74] ibid.

[75] CERD, 'Summary Record of the 179th meeting, Geneva, 23 February 2007' (2 March 2007) UN Doc CERD/C/SR.1796 [10].

[76] ibid [11].

[77] Zaheer Baber, 'Racism without Races: Reflections on Racialization and Racial Projects' (2010) 4 Sociology Compass 241, 243.

[78] Jayawardene (n 10) 336.

[79] Annapurna Waughray, 'Caste Discrimination and Minority Rights: The Case of India's Dalits' (2010) 17 International Journal on Minority and Group Rights 327, 328.

Notably, Mr Gupta's remarks came a year after Indian Prime Minister Dr Manmohan Singh stated at the Dalit-Minority International Conference in New Delhi that 'Dalits have faced a unique discrimination in our society that is fundamentally different from the problems of minority groups in general. The only parallel to the practice of "untouchability" was Apartheid in South Africa'.[80] Dr Singh's analogy is more in line with the 'hidden apartheid' phraseology Dalit activists adopted during the 2001 WCAR than Mr Gupta's reasoning and India's approach to caste-based discrimination before CERD. While Dr Singh's statements on minorities and subordinated groups set him apart from the broader establishment and members of the incumbent government in particular, the dissonance between his approach and that of India's delegation before CERD raises key questions.[81] Adding complexity to these questions is the fact that India's resistance to discussing caste-based discrimination before CERD is particularly pronounced in comparison to other treaty bodies, including the Committee on the Elimination of Discrimination against Women.[82]

One potential explanation for these inconsistencies may lie in the special status of the prohibition of racial discrimination and, specifically, apartheid under international law. With India's need to preserve its antiracist legacy, Indian officials may have sought to avoid acknowledgement of state sanctioned discrimination and segregation. Given the sheer number of references to Indo-African solidarity in India's periodic reports to CERD, ranging from Indian development initiatives in Africa to Africa Day celebrations in New Delhi, India arguably sees the *appearance* of an unblemished record in relation to racism and related forms of subordination as key to maintaining favourable relations.[83] The preservation of its reputation as an antiracist leader also allows for diversion of attention from its treatment of subordinated groups, including Dalits, Adivasis, and lower castes, whose interests are generally not a priority for India's ruling elite.

Beyond the sphere of caste-based subordination, India's need to guard its antiracist credentials was most apparent in 2016–2017 following a spike in violent attacks against African students, several of which ended fatally. It is estimated that there are over 25,000 Africans studying in India, many whose lives are marred by systemic racism. Notably, initiatives to attract African students date back to Nehru's tenure.[84]

[80] Maseeh Rahman, 'Indian leader likens caste system to apartheid regime' *The Guardian* (28 December 2006) <https://www.theguardian.com/world/2006/dec/28/india.mainsection#:~:text=%22Even%20after%2060%20years%20of,of%20minority%20groups%20in%20general> accessed 2 February 2023.

[81] See Times of India, 'Muslim must have first claim on resources: PM' (9 December 2006) <https://timesofindia.indiatimes.com/india/muslims-must-have-first-claim-on-resources-pm/articleshow/754937.cms> accessed 21 April 2023. Since leaving office, Dr Singh has also been critical of the current government's treatment of minorities and subordinated groups. In April 2018, he stated: 'I need not dwell long on the current deep concern that attempts are being made to divide the Indian people on the basis of religion and caste, language and culture. Atrocities against minorities and Dalits are increasing. If unchecked, these tendencies can only harm our democracy. As a people, we must strongly reject divisive policies and politics.' See 'Manmohan Singh Breaks Silence on Rising Atrocities against Minorities and Dalits' (*The Wire*, 11 April 2018), <https://thewire.in/caste/manmohan-singh-breaks-silence-on-rising-atrocities-against-minorities-and-dalits> accessed 21 April 2023.

[82] See, eg, CEDAW, 'Consideration of reports submitted by States parties under article 18 of the Convention, Combined fourth and fifth periodic reports of States parties: India' (23 October 2012) UN Doc CEDAW/C/IND/4–5.

[83] CERD (n 73) [162], [163], and [165].

[84] McCann (n 29) 265.

However, attacks against African students in India also have an extensive history, being cited by South African delegates in response to India's annual resolution at the UNGA as an indication of the hypocrisy in India's antiracist stance.[85]

The presence of Africans in South Asia more broadly has a long history dating back to the Delhi Sultanate in the thirteenth century, when Africans were brought in as slaves, domestic workers, fighters, and guards.[86] As Baber notes, this history has implications for the treatment of African students today:

> Some prominent exceptions from the past notwithstanding, the long history of domination and marginalisation plays a not insignificant role in the ideological scripting and marginality that many African students experience in contemporary India.[87]

Violent attacks against African students, which have continued to take place post their peak in 2016–2017, are at one end of the spectrum.[88] However, African nationals have also reported encountering verbal abuse on a day-to-day basis, being denied accommodation and employment opportunities, as well as access to businesses and services.[89] Violence and abuse against Africans often shows racial animus. Multiple incidents have stemmed from the perception that Africans are involved in the drug trade, sex work, and even cannibalism.[90] At a domestic level, authorities often fail to take cognizance of the racial character of attacks and discrimination, and in some cases are complicit in attacks and violence.

In 2014, Delhi's Law Minister, Somnath Bharti ordered a midnight raid on a residence in the city's Khirki Extension neighbourhood, which housed hundreds of African nationals, on the allegation that it operated as a brothel.[91] When police refused to conduct the raid, Bharti and members of the ruling Aam Aadmi Party took the initiative, entering the residence and allegedly participating in the physical attack and molestation of a group from Uganda and Nigeria.[92] Rather than facing censure, Bharti received support from Delhi's Chief Minister, Arvind Kejriwal who commented: 'We are not against any race or country. We are against anti-social elements.'[93] In a separate incident in 2013, Indian police alleged that the death of a Nigerian national was caused by rivalry between Nigerian drug gangs. In response, the Chief Minister of

[85] Thakur (n 17) 421.

[86] Zaheer Baber, ''Race Might be a Unicorn, but its Horn Could Draw Blood': Racialisation, Class and Racism in a Non-Western Context' 48(1) Critical Sociology 151, 160.

[87] ibid 161.

[88] See CTGN Africa, 'Nigeria summons Indian ambassador over attacks on it citizens' (*CTGN Africa*, 15 June 2023) <https://africa.cgtn.com/nigeria-summons-indian-ambassador-over-attacks-on-it-citizens/> accessed 21 March 2024.

[89] Palash Ghosh, 'Delhi Government Raid on African Immigrants Exposes Indians' Racial Animosity Toward Blacks' *International Business Times* (2 March 2014) <https://www.ibtimes.com/delhi-government-raid-african-immigrants-exposes-indians-racial-animosity-toward-blacks-1552901> accessed 21 March 2024.

[90] Baber (n 86) 160.

[91] Ghosh (n 89).

[92] Al Jazeera, 'Delhi law minister accused of leading attack' *Al Jazeera* (22 January 2024) <https://www.aljazeera.com/news/2014/1/22/delhi-law-minister-accused-of-leading-attack> accessed 21 March 2024.

[93] Ghosh (n 89).

Goa ordered a crackdown on unauthorized Africans, while state lawmakers referred to the African population as 'wild animals' and a 'cancer' to the state.[94]

At a diplomatic level, the difference in responses from African and Indian officials to the attacks throws further light on India's *appearance* level commitment to antiracism. Terming the attacks as 'xenophobic and racial in nature', a statement from the African Heads of Mission in New Delhi contended that 'no known, sufficient and deterring measures were taken by the government of India'.[95] In response, Minister for External Affairs, Sushma Swaraj termed the African envoys' statement as 'unfortunate, painful and surprising' and proceeded to refer to Gandhi and Buddha, while denying the possibility of Indians having a 'racist mindset'.[96] As a measure arguably designed to control damage to India's reputation, Swaraj appealed to Indians on Twitter: 'Next time you meet an African citizen, pl shake hand and say "India loves you"'.[97] Her tweet was widely criticized, as were remarks from Tarun Vijay, a former member of the Rajya Sabha from the ruling Bharatiya Janata Party (BJP). Vijay argued:

> If we (Indians) were racist, why would we have the entire south? Which is you know ... completely Tamil, you know Kerala, you know Karnataka and Andhra. Why do we live with them? We have Blacks, Black people all around us.[98]

As was the case with the private discussions between Indian and South African officials in 1949, Vijay's remarks allude to hierarchies within India, whereby South Indians are racialized as the 'other', including on the basis of skin colour.

In 2017, African envoys called for an independent investigation of the attacks before the UN Human Rights Council.[99] However, the urgency for such a call eventually subsided and there has been no such investigation before the UN since. In fact, African states have largely avoided drawing attention to anti-Black racism in India and specifically attacks against African students, although attacks have occurred before and after their peak. One potential reason may be economic ties between India and African states. As Ezeugo Lawrence, a member of the Association of African Students in India stated with regards to the response of African diplomatic missions in Delhi to attacks: 'The embassy's role is to maintain bilateral relations between the two countries. Such events are pushed on the backburner so that commerce and trade isn't hampered, till such an attack repeats itself.'[100]

[94] India Today, 'Nigerians are like 'wild animals' and 'cancer': Goa ministers' statements amid an escalating diplomatic row' *India Today* (14 November 2013) <https://www.indiatoday.in/india/story/nigerians-like-cancer-goa-minister-diplomatic-row-216637-2013-11-05> accessed 21 March 2024.

[95] The Wire, 'African Envoys Slam GOI Inaction, Want UN to Probe Racial Violence in India' (*The Wire*, 3 April 2017) <https://thewire.in/external-affairs/african-envoys-india-racism-un> accessed 2 March 2023.

[96] Deccan Chronicle (n 1).

[97] Sushma Swaraj (@SushmaSwaraj) 'I appeal to fellow Indians ...', Twitter, 2 June 2016 <https://twitter.com/SushmaSwaraj/status/738228679289896961> accessed 1 May 2023.

[98] The Hindu, 'Tarun Vijay lands in trouble with "black people" remarks, later apologises on Twitter' (*The Hindu*, 7 April 2017) <https://www.thehindu.com/news/national/if-we-were-racist-why-would-we-live-with-south-indians-tarun-vijay/article17866698.ece> accessed on 1 May 2023.

[99] The Wire (n 95).

[100] Rahul Nair, 'Racism is Rampant, But Africans in India Hate the 'Victim' Tag' (*The Quint*, 21 March 2018) <https://www.thequint.com/news/african-nationals-in-india-on-racist-attacks#:~:text=A%20Stagnant%20Court,in%20this%20country.%E2%80%9D> accessed 21 March 2024.

The reluctance of African states to raise the issue is also reflected through their engagement with the Universal Periodic Review (UPR) process. During India's last UPR cycle in 2022, Ghana made the only recommendation on the matter, calling for a national action plan for combating hate crimes, racism, and negative stereotypes against people of African descent.[101] A similar lone recommendation was made by Haiti during India's previous UPR cycle in 2017, closer to the time of the rise in attacks, which also called for a public awareness campaign to address racism and Afrophobia.[102] India noted both recommendations. Due to the lack of sustained pressure on India, it is arguable that its surface-level commitment to antiracism has remained unchallenged at the UN and through international law.

5. Conclusion: the Hindu nationalist State, racialized minorities, and challenging India's interests

The need for a concerted challenge to India's treatment of racialized and subordinated groups is now more pressing than at any point in its recent history. Since the BJP led government under Prime Minister Narendra Modi rose to power in 2014, there has been a rapid deterioration in conditions of populations who fall outside the margins of the party's popular support base. The BJP and Modi are ideologically influenced by the Hindu nationalist organization Rashtriya Swayamasewak Sangh (RSS) which, since the 1920s, has advocated for India to become a Hindu *rashtra* (state).

As Ratna Kapur notes, the Hindu right articulates Hindu religious identity partly as a racial identity, drawing from upper caste or Brahmanical racism and European ideas about race from the colonial and fascist periods.[103] To support her point, Kapur refers to the work of a key thinker from the RSS, Vir Damodar Savarkar, whose writings continue to influence the BJP leadership today:

> [His] ideas of blood and race were partly influenced by European fascism and included Hitler's view of Aryans as a master race that had conquered Europe. The link between blood and race is also implicit in his views on Blacks in America. He argued that Muslims in India, which was to be secured for Hindus, would be treated the same as 'negroes' in America.[104]

In addition to Muslims, who are racialized as 'perpetual outsider(s) and an existential and epistemic threat(s) to the Hindu nation',[105] other populations at risk include Dalits, Adivasis, and individuals belonging to lower castes. The construction of the

[101] UN Human Rights Council, 'Universal Periodic Review—India—Fourth cycle—41st Session—Thematic List of Recommendations' <https://www.ohchr.org/sites/default/files/documents/hrbodies/upr/sessions/session41/in/UPR41_India_Thematic_List_of_Recommendations.doc> accessed 2 March 2023.

[102] UN Human Rights Council, 'Universal Periodic Review—India—Third cycle—Matrix of Recommendations' <https://www.ohchr.org/sites/default/files/lib-docs/HRBodies/UPR/Documents/Session27/IN/UPR27_India_ThematicListofRecommendations_E.docx> accessed 2 March 2023.

[103] Kapur (n 12) 505.

[104] ibid 506.

[105] ibid 409.

Hindu *rashtra* has been evidenced through recent events, laws, and policies, including a series of violent attacks against minorities; the revocation of autonomous status of Muslim-majority Jammu and Kashmir;[106] allegations that up to 70 million Muslims and Dalits were removed from electoral rolls in the 2019 elections;[107] an amendment to India's Citizenship Act to grant citizenship to 'persecuted' religious minorities from neighbouring Muslim-majority states;[108] and 1.9 million people who have effectively been made stateless, the majority of whom are Muslim, through their exclusion from India's National Register for Citizens.[109]

What role can international law and institutions play in challenging the racial foundations of the Hindu *rashtra*? Domestic institutions appear reluctant to challenge the government's actions, including through consideration of arguments grounded in India's international legal obligations. This is reflected, for example, in the Indian Supreme Court's stance on the mass expulsion of Rohingya refugees in 2021. In refusing to order a stay on the deportations, 'serious objections' were raised to assessing arguments put forth by the UN Special Rapporteur on Racism, E Tendayi Achiume, in an *amicus curiae* that India's actions 'would amount to discrimination on the basis of race, ethnicity, national origin, or descent and would rely on distinctions that have racially disparate effects', in violation of its obligations under international law including ICERD.[110]

In light of this, UN treaty and charter-based mechanisms may be a more appropriate fora for such challenges, particularly as part of a multi-pronged strategy. Given the racial-religious basis for the Hindu *rashtra*, CERD and its inter-state communications mechanism may be particularly suited. Notably, communications brought by Palestine against Israel as well as Qatar against Saudi Arabia and the United Arab Emirates (UAE) were deemed admissible by CERD, making them the first inter-state cases under an international human rights treaty (although Qatar, Saudi Arabia, and the UAE ultimately decided to end proceedings).[111] However, given that India has been able to effectively deflect attempts to draw international attention to caste-based

[106] Al Jazeera, 'Kashmir special status explained: What are Articles 370 and 35A?' *Al Jazeera* (5 August 2019) <https://www.aljazeera.com/news/2019/8/5/kashmir-special-status-explained-what-are-articles-370-and-35a> accessed 4 February 2021.

[107] Soumya Shankar, 'Millions of Voters Are Missing in India' (*Foreign Policy*, 9 April 2019) <https://foreignpolicy.com/2019/04/09/millions-of-voters-are-missing-in-india/> accessed on 4 February 2023.

[108] Michelle Foster and Adil Hasan Khan, 'Briefing Note—Citizenship (Amendment) Act 2019 and International Law' (*Peter McMullin Centre on Statelessness, the Asian Law Centre, and the Institute for International Law and the Humanities*, 19 April 2021) <https://law.unimelb.edu.au/__data/assets/pdf_file/0005/3769484/Citizenship-Amendment-Act-and-International-Law.pdf> accessed 4 February 2023.

[109] Rebecca Ratcliffe and Kakoli Bhattacharya, 'India: almost 2m people left off Assam register of citizens' *The Guardian* (31 August 2019) <https://www.theguardian.com/global-development/2019/aug/31/india-almost-2m-people-left-off-assam-register-of-citizens>, accessed 4 February 2023.

[110] *Mohammad Salimullah and Anr v Union of India and Ors*, AIR 2021 SC 1789. See also UN Special Rapporteur on contemporary forms of racism, racial discrimination, xenophobia and related intolerance, 'Legal Opinion on India's obligations under International Law to not deport Rohingyas' (*OHCHR*, 12 July 2019) <https://www.ohchr.org/sites/default/files/AmicusBrieftoIndianSupremeCourt.pdf> accessed 4 February 2023, 4.

[111] CERD, 'Decision on the admissibility of the inter-State communication submitted by the State of Palestine against Israel' (20 May 2021) UN Doc CERD/C/103/R.6; David Keane, 'CERD Reaches Historic Decisions in Inter-State Communications' (*EJIL: Talk!* 6 September 2019) <https://www.ejiltalk.org/cerd-reaches-historic-decisions-in-inter-state-communications/> accessed 14 March 2023.

subordination and the anti-Black racism, a more concerted strategy beyond CERD is required. Such a strategy would need to sufficiently challenge India's geopolitical and reputational interests, including its antiracist credentials.

On occasion, India's interests have been challenged enough to trigger a response. In May 2022, BJP spokeswoman Nupur Sharma made derogatory remarks against Islam and the Prophet Muhammad, which generated strong diplomatic responses from a range of Muslim-majority states including Saudi Arabia, Indonesia, Afghanistan, Qatar, Kuwait, Iran, and the Organization of Islamic Cooperation (OIC), a body of fifty-seven primarily Muslim-majority states.[112] While India responded by suggesting such views and statements came from 'fringe elements', ultimately Sharma was suspended from the BJP and a fellow spokesperson who supported her, expelled.[113] Although India did act, it also showed unwillingness to acknowledge the systemic nature of attacks against Islam and Muslims. When the OIC stated that Sharma's remarks took place in the 'context of intensifying hatred and abuse toward Islam in India and systematic practices against Muslims', India argued that the OIC's response was 'unwarranted' and 'narrow-minded'.[114] Similarly, in April 2023 following attacks against Muslims during the Hindu festival of Ram Navami, a spokesperson for India's Ministry of External Affairs rebuked remarks from the OIC which highlighted the systemic nature of attacks, stating that: '[w]e strongly condemn the statement issued by OIC Secretariat today regarding India. This is another example of their communal mindset and anti-India agenda. OIC only does its reputation damage by being consistently manipulated by anti-India forces.'[115]

India's responses to diplomatic censure shows that, while its interests may be sufficiently disturbed to prompt action, it will seek to deflect from claims of systemic subordination and state complicity. As this chapter has sought to demonstrate, however, behind India's self-projection as a leader in the transnational fight against racism lies a deep history of systemic racism and related forms of subordination. Given the limited results Muslim-majority and African states have been able to yield from acting within their respective blocs, a coordinated diplomatic initiative which involves a range of states and highlights the common threads contributing to the subordination of various groups in India today is needed.

While Muslim-majority states have demonstrated greater willingness to put pressure on India, such a coalition would benefit from the participation of African states. A shift in approach from African states may require states such as Nigeria, which is also part of the OIC, to take a leadership role. Several attacks against African students have targeted Nigerian nationals and, in what Shobana Shankar calls an 'economic

[112] Gerry Shih, 'India scrambles to contain fallout over insulting comments about Islam' *The Washington Post* (7 June 2022) <https://www.washingtonpost.com/world/2022/06/07/india-prophet-muhammad-bjp-islam/> accessed 21 January 2023.

[113] ibid.

[114] Sheikh Saalik, 'Muslim nations slam India over insulting remarks about Islam' *AP News* (7 June 2022) https://apnews.com/article/afghanistan-middle-east-india-new-delhi-pakistan-364cd94bd3b9895be5a4857f68262a9d accessed 21 January 2023.

[115] Ministry of External Affairs, Government of India, 'Official Spokesperson's response to media queries on the statement issued by OIC Secretariat regarding India' (*Ministry of External Affairs*, 4 April 2023) <https://mea.gov.in/response-to-queries.htm?dtl/36452/Official_Spokespersons_response_to_media_queries_on_the_statement_issued_by_OIC_Secretariat_regarding_India> accessed 27 April 2023.

dependency', India 'needs Nigeria's oil'.[116] The economic ties between both states put to question hierarchies some Indians believe still exist with states in the continent. A starting point for a coordinated diplomatic initiative is recognition that India has much to lose if its antiracist credentials are put under scrutiny, particularly by states across blocs. Such a challenge to its geopolitical and reputational interests may serve as one lever to counter structural forms of Indian racism and related forms of subordination.

[116] Zachariah Mampilly, 'Africa holds up a mirror to India: An Interview with Shobana Shankar' (*Africa is a Country*, September 2022) <https://africasacountry.com/2022/09/africa-holds-up-a-mirror-to-india> accessed 1 April 2024.

16

Japan

International Law as the Outward Looking Weapon

Saul Takahashi

1. Introduction

On the morning of 8 July 1853, two US Navy warships sailed unannounced into the entrance of Edo (now Tokyo) Bay. With their large cannons pointed towards the port, the US government demanded Japan open itself to trade. Gunboat diplomacy eventually ushered in the Meiji era of Japanese modernization.

Context is essential. Around the mid-seventeenth century,[1] Japan had gone into relative isolation when the military government known as the Shogunate issued a series of military orders aimed at reducing and even prohibiting contact with other countries. Foreigners were expelled, the Japanese were barred from travelling abroad, and those Japanese who were overseas could no longer return. The government also restricted international trade, though did not prohibit it altogether, strictly managing cross-border commercial activities (the source of the United States's ire). European traders, for example, were only allowed entry to an isolated landfill, far from the capital, built specifically for that purpose.

The military diktats launched a 200-year era known as the *sakoku* era, the 'closing of the country'. This label was juxtaposed to the Meiji *kaikoku* or the 'opening of the country'. The main reason for the *sakoku* policy was the perceived threat from Christianity, which had been spreading since the mid-sixteenth century through the efforts of Spanish and Portuguese missionaries. During the *sakoku*, Japan chose the Netherlands as its main window into the West, welcoming that country's willingness to trade without proselytizing. Japanese officials initially allowed Chinese merchants relatively freer access than Europeans, though they too were subjected to parallel restrictions in the late 1680s when it became clear some were also Christians, and the religion could potentially spread in Japan through them.[2]

The *sakoku* era came to an abrupt end with the arrival of the American warships. After a brief period of upheaval, Japan embarked on a frenzied rush of modernization,

[1] In recent decades, some scholars have criticized the 'opening' terminology, arguing that it implies that the 'wider world' consists only of Europe. See, eg, Yasunori Arano, *Revisiting Sakoku* (Iwanami 2019); Akiko Ishii, 'Questioning Modernity: a Historiographical Sketch' in Timothy D Amos and Akiko Ishii (eds), *Revisiting Japan's Restoration: New Approaches to the Study of the Meiji Transformation* (Routledge 2022) 87–95. Regardless of the arguments of these scholars, the terms *sakoku* and *kaikoku* remain in Japanese textbooks, and are prevalent in popular discourse.

[2] See, eg, Issei Iwao, *Sakoku* (Chukou 2005).

Saul Takahashi, *Japan* In: *Emancipating International Law*. Edited by: Mohsen al Attar and Claire Smith, Oxford University Press. © Saul Takahashi 2026. DOI: 10.1093/9780198935605.003.0021

industrialization, and militarization. Laws and institutions were established along the lines of Western models, and Western philosophies and ideas spread throughout Japanese society.

Consistent with the themes of this collection, amongst those ideas imported from the West were structures of racial hierarchy, asserting the superiority of not only Western science and technology, but also of the white, Western man. In its rush to model itself on the *advanced* West, Japan absorbed chauvinistic ideas of white intellectual and moral superiority with zest, gradually forming its own racial ideology that situated Japanese on an equal footing with Europeans, and thus superior to other Asians. This ideology conveniently justified Japanese imperial expansion in Asia since the 'civilized' nations of Europe were doing the same.

In the minds of the political elite, another degree of legitimation was necessary. In addition to adhering to a Western developmental standard, Japan needed to prove its worth to the West; to be recognized as their equal. Military and economic might was key, but equally important was achieving mastery over international law. As the 'universal law of nations', international law was regarded as the language of diplomacy amongst civilized peoples. Japan's endeavour was partially successful but led to disillusionment once it became clear the West had little interest in admitting Japan to its exclusive, hegemonic club. Consequently, international law became an outward facing tool for Japan to boast of its advanced status, not a standard against which it would measure its domestic policies and practices.

Japan imported not only international legal norms and techniques, but also the racial hierarchies inherent in international law. Naturally, though, those hierarchies had to be adapted to the Japanese situation, especially as the Japanese elite felt the need to emphasize its racial superiority over other Asians, in particular Koreans. Western notions such as 'civilization' were used to justify Japanese supremacy in Asia, and the Japanese were presented as uniquely moral and law-abiding. Even after Japan's defeat in the Second World War and the subsequent adoption of the democratic Constitution, this mindset has not changed, as evidenced by the racial discrimination that characterizes Japanese laws and policies to this day.

2. Mastering Western racial hierarchies

From the outset, international law was a key tool in Western engagement with Japan. The country was strong-armed into signing a string of what Japanese schoolchildren learn as the 'unequal treaties'—international agreements that blatantly advantaged the Western powers. For example, the treaties prohibited Japan from imposing duties on imported products, leaving fledgling Japanese industries vulnerable before overwhelming Western manufacturing capacity. The political elite believed—rightly—that Western military power compelled compliance with the treaties.

Far more humiliating and more salient for the current study were the provisions on extraterritoriality. Western nationals accused of committing crimes on Japanese soil were to be tried by their consulate and not by Japanese courts, as the Japanese legal system was deemed too 'primitive' for the prosecution of civilized persons. This was in line with the standard assumption of the European elite of the time. Recall

James Lorimer's 1883 treatise on international law, a standard text for Japanese scholars during the Meiji era, which divided humanity into three groups: 'civilized humanity', 'barbarous humanity', and 'savage humanity'.[3] Japan was situated in the second group, together with other non-colonized Asian states, though Lorimer did note that Japan could potentially be promoted to 'plenary political recognition' if it continued developing.

In the case of Japan, the day-to-day means of ensuring Western superiority were legal agreements designed to provide a veneer of legitimacy to exploitative relations that were based on racist assumptions. Of course, this was a pattern repeated by the Western powers across the globe (and later on by Japan towards its neighbours in Asia). Fundamental to these Western techniques were the racial hierarchies inherent in European international law, and in Western thought in general. Antony Anghie, for example, asserts that:

> Sovereignty was the exclusive preserve of Europe . . . For the non-European world, sovereignty was the complete negation of power, authority and authenticity. This was not only because European sovereignty was used as a mechanism of suppression and management, but because the acquisition of sovereignty [meant] the acquisition of [European] civilization.[4]

White Europeans held themselves as superior to other races: more intelligent, more moral, and having attained a higher level of civilization. In this worldview, the notion that the advanced race could be tried according to barbaric norms of other races was ludicrous. Such discourses of white supremacy were imported and disseminated on a large scale in Japan during this period.

Racist ideas were popularized by leading intellectuals, most prominently Yukichi Fukuzawa, the founder of Keio University, the first private university in Japan and still one of the top educational institutions in the country.[5] In his influential book *An Outline of a Theory of Civilization*, Fukuzawa wrote: 'The nations of Europe and the United States of America are the most highly civilized, while the Asian countries, such as Turkey, China, and Japan, may be called semi-developed countries, and Africa and Australia are to be counted as still primitive lands. These designations are common currency all over the world.'[6] He goes on to suggest the responsibility for this stratification lies with the people of the 'semi-developed' and 'primitive' countries, since '[t]hey rest content with being branded semi-developed or primitive, and there is not one who would take pride in his own country or consider it on a par with nations of the West'.[7]

[3] James Loriner, *The Institutes of the Law of Nations: A Treatise of the Jural Relations of Separate Political Communities* (William Blackwood and Sons 1883) 101–03.

[4] Antony Anghie, *Imperialism, Sovereignty and the Making of International Law* (Cambridge University Press 2005) 104.

[5] Fukuzawa remains highly regarded in Japan as an important figure in the country's modernization, and he adorns the JPY 10,000 bill.

[6] Yukichi Fukuzawa, *An Outline of a Theory of Civilization* (David A Dilworth and Cameron G Hurst III tr, Keio University Press 2008) 17.

[7] ibid.

Similar to Western self-portrayal, Fukuzawa characterizes people of the 'enlightened, civilized' West as industrious and hard working: 'They cultivate their own virtue and refine their own knowledge. They neither yearn for the old nor become complacent about the present. Not resting with small gains, they plan great accomplishments for the future and commit themselves wholeheartedly to their realization'.[8] Fukuzawa elaborates in a popular 1879 publication, in which he calls the African continent 'a world of ignorance and chaos'.[9] According to him, Black Africans are of low morality, uneducated, incapable of empathy, and 'utterly dim-witted and the lowest of all humankind'.[10] Like Lorimer, Fukuzawa adopts a shallow classification of races, placing them into four categories, with Black Africans in the lowest group of 'chaos' and North Africans a slight rung above: the 'savage' group.[11]

Though perhaps the most influential, Fukuzawa was complemented by several Japanese intellectuals who propagated this Western—now Japanese—racial hierarchy. For example, Suzuki notes how publications of the time adopted Fukuzawa's system, portraying Arabs as lazy, uncultured, and savage. Some also branded the Prophet Mohammad as a charlatan, proclaiming that the Quran was 'full of lies'.[12] Japanese delegations who travelled through Egypt on their way to Europe also represented 'the natives' as untrustworthy, uncultured, and even 'too disgusting to look at'. These accounts stood in stark contrast to the praise heaped on the technological and material marvels of the British colonizers.[13] A Japanese delegation visiting a Portuguese encampment in Mozambique had similar comments, describing Africa as the 'lowest ranking' of all continents, containing wild people 'far from any human culture'.[14]

It is important to stress that Japan was already a highly literate society at the outset of Meiji, attaining universal literacy within a matter of years. The publications produced by these intellectuals were widely read, not only by the political elite but throughout the country. Some of them were used as textbooks in the newly created education system, and were instrumental in creating and solidifying racist notions amongst the populace.

Racist ideas imported from the West, therefore, had a significant impact in shaping the subsequent trajectory of the country, in particular how it viewed itself in relation to both the West and to the rest of Asia. Given Japan's position as an Asian country, this required some intellectual acrobatics.

3. Race and volk: the Japanese distinction

Western racial hierarchies presented a conundrum for Japan. In essence, they meant that Japanese were inferior and doomed to subjugation by the West like other Asians.

[8] ibid 19.

[9] Yukichi Fukuzawa, *Atlas of the Countries of the World, vol 2 Africa* (1879) 4.

[10] ibid 1.

[11] ibid 25–42.

[12] Hideaki Suzuki, *Japanese Discover the Middle East: Comparative Cultural History within an Opposing Perspective* (Tokyo University Press 1995) 97–98.

[13] ibid 103.

[14] Midori Fujita, *'Discovery' of Africa: the Changing Image of Africa in Japan* (Iwanami 2005) 18.

Japan needed new ideas with its intellectuals gradually developing a distinction between *jinshu*—the newly created word for the Western term 'race'—and *minzoku*.

Though translatable as 'ethnic group' or 'nation', *minzoku* is conceptually close to the German Volk, with blood, soil, and cultural identity stressed in accordance with the (political) requirements of any particular time.[15] Accordingly, while the Japanese may be part of the wider Asian race (*jinshu*), their membership of the Japanese Volk (*nippon minzoku* or *yamato minzoku*) gave them a leg up. The Japanese were more hard working and intelligent than their counterparts, traits, of course, associated with White Europeans. Because of these characteristics, the Japanese were presented as more able to adopt superior Western technology and institutions, elevating them to the status of the advanced nation in Asia. As noted by Kawai, '[t]he dominant self-representation was deployed to differentiate the Japanese from the Asians as well as to create a hierarchical relationship between them. Defining the Japanese as not a jinshu but a minzoku was supposed to draw clear boundaries between the Japanese and other groups lumped together as yellow.'[16]

For this to be consistent, the Japanese *minzoku* had to be conceptualized as a homogenous entity: racially and culturally pure, without contamination from the outside. Thus was born the notion of the *tan'itsu* (singular or unique) *minzoku*, the ethnically homogenous group—a notion that, to this day, dominates the domestic public discourse on the character of the country. Japan racialized the notion of *Japaneseness*, in accordance with newly imported Western thought.

The idea of the *tan'itsu minzoku* naturally did not exist prior to the modernization period. In his groundbreaking study on the subject, Oguma notes how such an idea would have been heresy during the Shogunate, as the society was organized according to a rigidly defined, feudal class system.[17] Prominent intellectuals of Meiji and afterwards advanced the idea that ethnic homogeneity was equal to national unity and, by extension, national strength. They cited the Roman Empire as a warning about what would happen to a country that allowed membership to other groups, thereby falling into multi-ethnicity and inevitable discord and national weakness.[18]

The process of racialization of Japaneseness during this period was, of course, complex, and often paradoxical. Oguma calls Japan the 'coloured empire',[19] as opposed to the white European imperialist powers, and notes that the political elite felt the need to counter Western racial hierarchies that would leave Japan at the bottom of the heap. Completely transcending those hierarchies was, of course, extremely difficult, if not conceptually impossible: for example, for a short period, some scholars even attempted to explain the supposed superiority of Japan with the somewhat farcical notion that Japanese were the offshoot of a white European race.[20] In any case, these

[15] Yuko Kawai, *A Transnational Critique of Japaneseness* (Lexington 2020) 5–12.

[16] ibid 11.

[17] Eiji Oguma, *The Origin of the Myth of the Homogenous Nation: the Genealogy of the 'Japanese' Self-Portrait* (Shinyoku-sha 1995) 50.

[18] ibid 53. Such remarks were not uncommon amongst Japanese commentators, and even politicians, in reference to the United States during the 1980s, when many expected the country to surpass the United States as the world's preeminent economic power.

[19] Eiji Oguma, *The Border of 'Japanese': Colonial Rule to the Return Movement in Okinawa, Ainu, Taiwan, Korea* (Shinyoku-sha 2002) 661.

[20] Oguma (n 17) 172–79.

intellectual debates took place in parallel to (and had a mutually influential relation with) the political developments on the ground.

4. International law as a tool for Japan's imperialist ambitions

Revoking the extraterritoriality clauses of the unequal treaties was one of the main policy objectives of the Meiji government. It was clearly impossible to achieve this by force, and it was believed the only way forward was to prove to the West that Japan had attained a level of civilization which would allow it to apply its legal system to foreign nationals. Japan needed to show, first, that it had a modern (European) legal system and, second, that it could master international legal standards, the means and language of international diplomacy. Japanese scholars and government officials feverishly studied what was called 'the public law of nations'—international law—to precipitate Western recognition of Japanese 'civilization'.[21]

The Maria Luz case was an important milestone in these efforts. In 1872, a Peruvian ship docked in Yokohama for urgent repairs. The ship carried Chinese labourers, one of whom escaped to the British mission and pleaded for help from ongoing abuse at the hands of the captain. Upon request from the British, the Japanese impounded the ship and demanded the labourers be released and repatriated to China. The dispute was eventually referred to international arbitration by the Russian Czar who, in 1875, found the Japanese measures complied with international law.[22] The Maria Luz case was a monumental achievement for the Japanese authorities, who had produced a huge mass of legal briefs and arguments based on treaty and general principles of international law. Japan had civilized in leaps and bounds in a remarkably short period, and this success was one of the factors that enabled it to negotiate the end of the extraterritoriality clauses.[23]

Successes notwithstanding, palpable amongst the writing of many Meiji academics was a strong sense of threat in the face of overwhelming Western military might. While that sense was justified, Japanese plans were not purely defensive. The Japanese political elite already had imperial designs for Asia, in particular in the Korean peninsula, and ideas of Japanese racial superiority provided a theoretical underpinning for military expansion. Much as Europeans were doing on a global stage, Japan portrayed itself as a civilizing force: an advanced country that was destined to spread civilization

[21] See, eg, Susumu Yamauchi, 'Civilization and International Law in Japan During the Meiji Era (1868-1912)' (1996) 24 Hitotsubashi Journal of Law and Politics 1.

[22] Giorgio Fabio Colombo, *Justice and International Law in Meiji Japan: the Maria Luz Incident and the Dawn of Modernity* (Routledge 2023); Ryuma Daigo, 'International Arbitration Tribunal in the Maria Luz Case' [2012] Machikane Legal and Political Journal Osaka University Law Society 1.

[23] The case had the added bonus of reinforcing Japan's self-image as a humanitarian country, though Howland argues convincingly that 'Justice for coolies . . . was secondary to the overall national goal of international parity'. Douglas Howland, 'The Maria Luz Incident: Personal Rights and International Justice for Chinese Coolies and Japanese Prostitutes' in Susan L Burns and Barbara J Brooks (eds), *Gender and Law in the Japanese Imperium* (University of Hawai'i Press 2014) 39. A 2012 policy paper on Japan's continuing efforts to obtain a permanent seat on the UN Security Council cites the Maria Luz case, arguing that it shows the 'traditions and values of Japanese society, including compassion, based on caring for the weak, and the notion of public interest'. Masatsune Katsuno, *Japan's Quest for a Permanent Seat on the United Nations Security Council* (Freidrich Ebirt Stiftung 2012) 3.

amongst the savages of Asia. Japan was, in essence, the European in Asia, the enlightened people surrounded by the uncivilized masses.

In 1894, Japan took advantage of mass unrest in the Korean peninsula to intervene militarily, resulting in the Sino-Japanese war (which Japan won handily). Japan sought to justify the war in accordance with international legal standards and commissioned high-ranking military lawyers to produce two long accounts—in English and French—of how Japanese military conduct aligned with international law, in contrast with the barbarism of the Chinese forces.[24] Though the accounts were glowing, France, Germany, and Russia pressured Japan after the war into giving up most of its hard won prizes, and then, hypocritically, divided the spoils amongst themselves, a humiliation that would not be forgotten.

It is not uncommon in Japan to assert that the elite of the time were naïve. Japanese leaders, so the argument goes, believed that international law set the ground rules for fair play. Japan was convinced that, if it used international law effectively, Western powers would accept the righteousness of its positions. However, unlike Japan, the West was never interested in playing fair, forcing Japan into a corner, the dire result being the devastation of the Second World War.[25] There is truth to the narrative, but international law was also a tool to forward Japanese aggression towards its neighbours. Underhanded European actions also contributed to the rising Japanese self-perception of being a uniquely moral people, one that did not stack the deck in its own favour the way the West did.

In any case, cynicism spread amongst the Japanese elite. The country still went to great lengths to argue the legal righteousness of its positions and actions, and was an active member at the League of Nations after the First World War. However, more and more international law was seen as a tool for Japan to justify its imperial endeavours, not a fair and objective standard by which it should measure itself. Racist attitudes also solidified: Japan and the Japanese *minzoku* must be pure and protected against outside contamination.[26]

Japan forcibly annexed Taiwan in 1895 and the Korean peninsula in 1910. Both Taiwanese and Koreans were given Japanese citizenship (more accurately, 'subjects of the Emperor'), theoretically putting them on an equal legal footing as the Japanese and enabling them to enjoy the same rights under the Japanese Constitution. Since that was not acceptable to the political leadership, they created various mechanisms to legalize a double-standard. While people from the 'outer territories' were Japanese subjects and owed loyalty to Japan, they were both *de facto* and *de jure* second class citizens.[27]

Koreans, in particular, were subjected to sustained and often brutal assimilation policies, especially after 1937 when Japan realized Korean manpower was necessary for the war effort. Koreans were forced to adopt Japanese names, learn Japanese in school, and to recite their undying allegiance to the Emperor.[28] These measures were

[24] Cited in Yamauchi (n 21).

[25] ibid 24. The narrative of Japan being pure and naïve, lacking eloquence yet just, underpins the discourse on a wide variety of policy issues. See David Leheny, *Think Global, Fear Local: Sex, Violence, and Anxiety in Contemporary Japan* (Cornell University Press 2006).

[26] See Oguma (n 17) 76–77.

[27] See Oguma (n 19) 110–51 for an exploration of the legalities of the time.

[28] See, eg, Kyeungdal Cyo, *Colonial Korea and Japan* (Iwanami 2013) 182–92.

justified in Japan because, according to some commentators, Koreans were of the same race as the Japanese, even the same *minzoku*. They argued that the Japanese and Koreans were, in fact, originally the same people, and had only been separated by historical circumstances. The annexation of Korea, therefore, was not an act of colonialism but the 'reunification of two brothers'.[29] In this regard, Japanese policies were advertised as being morally superior to Western colonialism, which was the imposition of foreign values and a foreign religion upon different races.[30]

Of course, Koreans were never looked upon as equal to the Japanese, the defining factor being 'civilization'. Leading intellectuals argued that Japan had the 'spirit of Confucianism but was wearing the clothes of new, Western civilization', whereas Koreans were lazy, childish, and lacking in hygiene.[31] Japan was on a civilizing mission of peace and humanitarianism—one that Koreans should be, and eventually would be, grateful for. Japanese racial hierarchies therefore justified oppressive measures by the Japanese occupation, which were framed as the paternal scolding of wayward children. The overall picture and the associated thought processes have not changed fundamentally since Japan's defeat in the Second World War.

5. After the empire: the more things change . . .

Post-Second World War, Japan is now firmly amongst the major powers, enjoying one of the world's leading economies and a recognized partnership with the Western military alliance. In diplomatic fora, Japan often stresses its commitment to liberal 'universal values' such as human rights, democracy, and the rule of law, mainly in an effort to contrast itself with China.[32] Japan frequently reiterates its commitment to the Western club, most recently by quickly joining Western sanctions against Russia following the invasion of Ukraine and even announcing the resettlement of (a small number) of Ukrainian refugees.[33]

Outwardly, Japan remains very legalistic: positions taken at multilateral fora and in bilateral negotiations are based on international rules and consensus, and international law plays a prominent part in Japanese positions regarding ongoing border disputes with Russia, China, and Korea.[34] That is not to say that the

[29] Oguma (n 19) 163.

[30] ibid 164.

[31] ibid.

[32] See, eg, Prime Minister's Office of Japan, 'Protecting the citizenry: diplomacy and security' (Prime Minister's Office of Japan) <https://www.kantei.go.jp/jp/headline/seisaku_kishida/diplomaticsecurity.html> accessed 9 March 2023.

[33] On the other hand, Japan has tended to distance itself from forceful positions on the military rule of Myanmar since the coup of February 2021.

[34] See, eg, Japan Foreign Ministry, 'Japan's consistent position on title of Takejima' (Japan Foreign Ministry) <(https://www.mofa.go.jp/mofaj/area/takeshima/index.html> accessed 9 March 2023; 'Regarding the Senkaku Islands' (Japan Foreign Ministry) <https://www.mofa.go.jp/mofaj/area/senkaku/pdfs/senkaku.pdf)> accessed 9 March 2023; 'Our Northern Territories 2020 edition' (Japan Foreign Ministry) <https://www.mofa.go.jp/mofaj/files/000035437.pdf> accessed 9 March 2023. Ravina notes that: 'The triumph of the Western international system is so thorough that Chinese, Japanese, and Korean officials discuss their own past in Western terms . . . [the Japanese] approach to sovereignty marks how thoroughly the Meiji state had adapted to European notions of law and territoriality.' Mark Ravina, *To Stand with the Nations of the World: Japan's Meiji Restoration in World History* (Oxford University Press 2017) 210.

arguments advanced by Japanese officials are sophisticated or convincing, but that efforts are made to ensure there are legal grounds for the country's positions.

Consistent with its overall position, the Japanese government also uses international law in its attempts to evade responsibility for wartime abuses. We have seen this with regard to the so-called 'comfort women', mostly Korean women who were exploited as sex slaves by the Japanese military. The Japanese government insists that the 1965 treaty establishing relations with South Korea, which states that 'no [subsequent] claims shall be made with respect to . . . the property, rights, and interests' of either country, absolves Japan from any and all further responsibility for the violations. This position has been accepted by the Japanese judiciary, which in all cases has ruled against Korean women who have sued for compensation in Japanese courts.[35] Right-wing Japanese publications express the same cynicism towards international law and institutions that prevailed from late Meiji, the narrative being that Japan is criticized unfairly because it plays by the rules: the country naïvely believes in making its case according to international norms, while the other sides play dirty and manipulate international opinion.[36]

International law remains outward looking, a tool to promote Japan and its interests on the international stage. That Japan also has to change domestic policies and practices to abide by international legal obligations—in particular international human rights obligations—is far less accepted. This is clear in a variety of serious human rights issues, including the pretrial detention of criminal suspects, restrictions on freedom of expression, and refugee recognition, to name a few. Japan is a state party to most of the core international human rights conventions (though the country refuses to become party to any individual petition procedures), and United Nations (UN) human rights bodies have made numerous recommendations to address those issues. However, Japan routinely ignores those recommendations, leading the chair of the UN Human Rights Committee to lament that 'the overwhelming impression was that, from one review to the next, the State party did not take account of the Committee's concerns and recommendations'.[37]

Somewhat paradoxically, the government has even used international human rights law domestically to justify restrictive measures that go against these very standards. In 2012, the (then and now) ruling Liberal Democratic Party (LDP) published its proposal for a new Constitution, which would enable the government to restrict any human right on the basis of a sweeping 'public interest and public order' provision.

[35] UN human rights bodies have argued that the 1965 agreement only refers to the right of the Korean state to compensation claims, whereas the right of the individual to seek redress still remains. Since the Japanese courts refuse to entertain those claims, the result is an ongoing violation of the right to an effective remedy. See UN Committee on the Elimination of Discrimination against Women, 'Concluding observations on the combined seventh and eighth periodic reports of Japan' (10 March 2016) UN Doc CEDAW/C/JPN/CO/7-8.

[36] See, eg, Kyoko Kuwahara, *Why Japan's 'Righteousness' Does Not Get Across to the World: the Image Wars of Japan, China, and Korea* (Wedge 2020); Japan Real Voice, *From the UN, the Global Anti-Japanese Era* (Mediasoft 2017).

[37] UN Human Rights Committee, '111th session, Summary record (partial)* of the 3082nd meeting' (20 August 2014) UN Doc CCPR/C/SR.3082, 3.

In a Q&A published together with the draft, the LDP misquotes international human rights treaty provisions, claiming they allow for this broad provision.[38]

Of course, Japan is hardly the only country to attempt to evade human rights obligations while presenting a façade of adherence to international law. What is notable in the case of Japan is how, despite the dramatic political and social changes of the post Second World War transition, narratives of Japanese supremacy have managed to survive, albeit in somewhat different forms.

6. Racial supremacy in current Japan

In recent years, there has been increased awareness of the need to avoid blatant statements such as the 1986 one by Prime Minister Nakasone, who said that 'Japan has become a highly educated, very intelligent society. Much more so than America, on average. In America there are black people, Puerto Ricans and Mexicans, people like that, so on average they are very low.'[39] Yet, racial hierarchies and essentialism imported during the Meiji era remain embedded in Japanese discourse. In 2020 for example, the public broadcaster NHK caused a storm after posting a video about the Black Lives Matter movement in the US. The video was full of gross caricatures of African-American men, depicted as unintelligent, rough, and hulking or as street musicians only. The video also failed to touch on issues of police brutality, mentioning only the disparity in wealth between white and Black Americans.[40]

Despite the facile manifestation of anti-Black racism in Japan, Chinese and Koreans bear the brunt of racist portrayals, and are painted in the right-wing media as uncivilized, unhygienic, generally barbaric, and outright criminal.[41] A best-selling 2017 book by Kent Gilbert, an American lawyer and popular right-wing television personality, called the Chinese 'lower than beasts'[42] and stated they 'think nothing of breaking the law . . . they lie like they breathe air, with not the slightest bit of guilt.'[43] Koreans were 'spoiled brats'[44] who were jealous of Japan's success, and had a 'chip on their shoulders . . . they are beyond ugly, just pathetic.'[45] Gilbert persists with a Meiji-like narrative,

[38] Liberal Democratic Party, 'Draft Revisions to the Japanese Constitution, Expanded Q&A' (Liberal Democratic Party, 2012) <https://www.jimin.jp/english/news/117099.html> accessed 11 July 2023. The revision to the Constitution has yet to be adopted.

[39] See, eg, Masaru Ikei, 'Slip of the Tongue Diplomacy: The Case of Nakasone and Fujio 1986' (1995) 65(11) Keio University Journal of Law, Politics and Sociology 29.

[40] Japan Today, 'NHK removes video on U.S. protests after online outrage about depiction of African Americans' *Japan Today* (9 June 2020) <https://japantoday.com/category/national/japan's-nhk-removes-video-about-us-protests-after-online-outrage> accessed 11 July 2024.

[41] ERD Net, 'Joint Civil Society Report on Racial Discrimination in Japan to the Committee on the Elimination of Racial Discrimination for its Consideration of the Tenth and Eleventh Periodic Report of Japan' (*International Movement against All Forms of Discrimination and Racism*, August 2018) <https://imadr.org/wordpress/wp-content/uploads/2018/07/Revised_ERD-Net_Joint-Civil-Society-Report_CERD96_2018.pdf> accessed 11 July 2024.

[42] Kent Gilbert, *The Tragedy of Chinese and Koreans, Controlled by Confucianism* (Kohdan-sha 2017) 26. See also Kawai (n 15) 71–99 for an in-depth discussion of Gilbert's publications.

[43] ibid 41.

[44] ibid 77.

[45] ibid 95–96.

stating that both Chinese and Koreans think nothing of breaking international law and bilateral agreements, in contrast to the honest, law-abiding Japanese.[46]

Though not as overt as Gilbert's work, since the early 2000s Japan has seen a veritable explosion of publications of the so-called *ken-kan han-chu* (hate Korea, against China) genre. The apparent boom of such publications cannot be viewed in isolation from the equally popular, and often overlapping, *nippon sugoi* (Japan is amazing) genre. Those books attempt to argue against the reality of Japanese economic and social decline, often through somewhat fantastical claims of Japanese moral and intellectual superiority.[47]

Also starting in the early 2000s, frequent hate speech rallies were held in Korean neighbourhoods and around Korean schools, calling Koreans 'roaches' and demanding they 'all go home'. The main organizer of the rallies was the *Zainichi Tokken wo Yurusanai Shimin no Kai* (generally abbreviated to *Zaitoku-kai*) or 'Association of Citizens against the Special Privileges of the Korean Residents'. This organization propagates the idea that, far from suffering from discrimination, ethnic Koreans enjoy special privileges and advantages over the Japanese population, a fanciful notion familiar to observers of racism in many other contexts.

Makoto Sakurai, the founder of *Zaitoku-kai*, later founded the Japan First Party, a nationalist political party. Though the rhetoric of the Japan First Party is toned down compared with the ultranationalist hate of the *Zaitoku-kai*, the party adopts a clearly xenophobic platform, for example calling for foreign nationals to be excluded from welfare benefits. Sakurai ran for the Tokyo governorship in 2021 and received almost 180,000 votes. Though failing to win any seats, the party also received roughly the same number of votes in the 2022 national upper house elections.

Indeed, anti-Korean racism is at the root of one of the most problematic restrictions on human rights in the country's Constitution. After Japan's defeat, the American occupying force (General Headquarters—GHQ) drafted a new Japanese Constitution, which highlighted democratic principles and advanced strong protection for human rights, including equal rights protection for foreign nationals. This was unacceptable to the Japanese government, which had no intention of granting equal rights to Korean residents, the portrayal of Koreans during the imperial era as 'reunited brothers' of the Japanese *minzoku* notwithstanding.

According to the records of the negotiations, the Japanese team argued that this provision would prevent Japan from recognizing extraterritorial privileges for foreign diplomats. Despite the flimsiness of this argument, GHQ withdrew the offending provision.[48] Though not readily apparent in the English translation, the human rights provisions of the Japanese Constitution came to differentiate between rights afforded to all persons, and rights afforded only to Japanese nationals: in particular, only Japanese enjoy the right to equality under the law and non-discrimination (Article 14), and

[46] ibid 25, 77.

[47] See, eg, Satoru Fukushima, *Book Stores and Democracy: For the Arena of Speech* (Jinbun Sho-in 2016); Tadanori Hayakawa, *The 'Japan is Amazing' Dystopia: Self Praise during the War* (Asahi Shimbun-sha 2019); Kawai (n 15).

[48] Takeru Ebashi, *The Constitution of the Government and the Constitution of the People: National Referenda and Citizenry Leadership* (Shinzan-sha 2006) 76–78.

respect as an individual (Article 13). The Japanese elite used general principles of international law (rights of foreign diplomats) as a weapon to prevent changes to the domestic status quo.

A day before the new Constitution was promulgated, the government issued a sweeping order stripping Koreans and other former imperial subjects of their Japanese citizenship. Many Koreans left Japan during the post-war years, but since around 1960 the population has stabilized at 600,000–700,000 (around 400,000 of which retain Korean citizenship[49]), making Koreans the largest ethnic minority in Japan. As foreign nationals, Koreans have suffered a wide range of restrictions on employment, welfare, overseas travel, and other activities, and until 1990 were even liable for deportation for having committed minor offences.[50] After the 2011 tsunami and nuclear disaster, as well as other natural disasters in recent decades, large numbers of postings appeared in social media claiming that 'foreigners' (a dog whistle for Koreans and Chinese) were taking advantage of the chaos to break into homes or even poison the water supply. This is a clear reference to the period after a large-scale earthquake in Tokyo in 1923 when Koreans were accused of poisoning water wells and subjected to mass pogroms with the acquiescence of the authorities.[51]

Japan does not have a comprehensive anti-discrimination law, or even a comprehensive antiracism law—a fact pointed to with concern in successive reviews by human rights treaty bodies.[52] The government has argued that the situation in Japan is not serious enough to warrant such legislation, even though the first (and so far only) government survey on racism suffered by foreign residents took place in 2016. This survey mainly focused on every day, low-level racism such as restaurants or other businesses refusing services to foreign customers (not illegal in Japan), or 'being made fun of' for being a foreigner.[53]

In response to mounting international and domestic criticism of the anti-Korean hate speech rallies, Japan adopted an anti-hate speech law in 2016. This law was widely derided as inadequate by human rights actors (including this author): it states that its purpose is to 'spread awareness among the general public and to promote their understanding and cooperation', and contains no penalties. In addition, the law explicitly defines hate speech as directed at legal residents of Japan, leaving outside its scope hate speech against undocumented foreign nationals. Criticism notwithstanding, the law has enabled local governments to bar hate speech rallies from public spaces, and the number of rallies has dropped significantly, though many observers believe that

[49] Japan does not allow dual citizenship, mainly because of this issue.

[50] See, eg, Korean Resident's Union in Japan, 'NGO Report Concerning the 10th and 11th Japanese Government Report Submitted Based on the International Convention on the Elimination of All Forms of Racial Discrimination' (Korean Resident's Union in Japan, 4 July 2018); Kiyoteru Tsutsui, *Rights Make Rights: Global Human Rights and Minority Social Movements in Japan* (Oxford University Press 2018) 82–149.

[51] ERD Net (n 41).

[52] See, eg, UN Committee on the Elimination of Racial Discrimination, 'Concluding observations on the combined tenth and eleventh periodic reports of Japan' (30 August 2018) UN Doc CERD/C/JPN/CO/10, 2.

[53] Human Rights Education Promotion Centre, 'Report on Survey of Foreign Residents' (Human Rights Promotion Centre, 2017) 7.

hate speech has simply migrated online.[54] There is no hate crime legislation in Japan, and no official effort to document crimes that are based on racism.

7. Not just Koreans: racism and migrant labourers

Particularly notable in any examination of racism in Japan are government policies towards low-wage migrant labour. In the late 1980s, the Japanese economy was booming, with a serious shortage of persons willing to work in low-wage professions. There were of course large numbers of undocumented migrant labourers from Asia and Africa, but there was never any serious debate about amnesty or regularization, as those foreigners were perceived as racially and culturally incompatible, as well as incapable of assimilating.

In 1990, the government launched an immigration programme for ethnic Japanese South Americans: the descendants of Japanese who had migrated to countries such as Brazil and Peru in the late 1800s and early 1900s. Such persons would be provided with residency in Japan with no work-related restrictions to take the place of undocumented labourers. Astounding as it may seem, it was simply assumed that their Japanese ethnicity meant they would assimilate with ease, despite the fact that almost none of them even spoke the language. Over 300,000 South Americans with Japanese ethnicity migrated under the programme, to work in predominantly low-wage occupations. Official support in most cases ranged from inadequate to non-existent, and many faced—and still face—abuse and discrimination in the workplace, schools, and other institutions.[55]

The next government measure to admit low wage migrant labour was the Technical Internship Trainee Programme (TITP), which was created in 1993 and continues to this day. Foreign nationals from participating developing countries admitted to Japan under the TITP are not labourers but 'trainees', who will learn advanced skills at a Japanese workplace for three years, and then return to their country to utilize those skills for their own country's development. As of the end of 2019, a total of over 730,000 trainees had been admitted to Japan.[56] Unlike the South American programme, which kept the door open to migrants staying in the country indefinitely, the TITP is, in theory at least, a foreign aid programme, and until 2019, there were no avenues for trainees to stay beyond the three-year period.

Naturally, development assistance was always a façade, and from the outset the TITP was widely recognized as a way for companies to procure cheap labour. Exploitation and abuse under the TITP are commonplace, with many cases of companies

[54] See Shinji Higaki and Yuji Nasu (eds), *Hate Speech in Japan: the Possibility of a Non-Regulatory Approach* (Cambridge University Press 2021) for an in-depth exploration of the Japanese approach.

[55] See Japan Federation of Bar Associations 'Report on Response to the tenth and eleventh Report of the Japanese Government of the International Convention on Elimination of All Forms of Racial Discrimination' (*Japan Federation of Bar Associations*, 15 March 2018) <https://www.nichibenren.or.jp/library/ja/kokusai/humanrights_library/treaty/data/Racial_discrimination_en_10.11.pdf> accessed 23 February 2023; Hitoshi Shiura and Yoshinori Oki, 'Japan's Policies on Foreign Residents in the Era of Declining Presence of Japanese Descent from Latin America' (2018)7(1) International Studies Research 65.

[56] Immigration Services Agency, *Immigration Control 2020* (Ministry of Justice, 2020) <https://www.moj.go.jp/isa/policies/policies/03_00003.html> accessed 23 February 2023, 41.

confiscating trainees' passports and not paying the minimum wage. Horrific cases of physical and sexual abuse frequently come to light, and those who dare to complain are often forcibly returned to their country.[57] Trainees are not allowed to change their employer, and 2017 data showed that 67 per cent of trainees who had absconded had been paid less than the minimum wage.[58] Domestic and international human rights organizations and UN human rights bodies have condemned the TITP for years, and the United States lists the TITP as one of the main reasons for Japan being categorized as tier two in its annual Human Trafficking Report.[59]

Indicative of the true nature of the TITP is the case of the International Business Research Co-operative (IBRC), one of the many QUANGOs (quasi-autonomous non-governmental organizations) established to place trainees in Japanese companies. In 2017, in response to the longstanding shortage of Japanese caregivers, the government expanded the TITP to allow Japanese care homes to hire trainees (there was no debate as to what 'advanced skills' in caregiving Japan could offer). In this context, the IBRC established a categorized scorecard, ranking the alleged suitability for caregiving of six nationalities participating in the TITP. To illustrate, Burmese score 18 out of a maximum 20 points in the category of 'sincere concern towards vulnerable people' and their 'inclination towards taking care of elders'. Thais, on the other hand, score only 14 points, Vietnamese 12, and Cambodians only 10. Burmese also score high (18) on their 'ability to learn Japanese', whereas Cambodians score a dismal 4. Cambodians fare relatively well in the 'religion' category (8 out of 10 points), whereas Muslim majority Indonesians come out at the bottom with only 5 points. Perhaps most importantly for potential employers, though, is whether they can expect 'serious, pure, and morally upright' candidates, a category in which Burmese excel once again (10 out of 10 points) and Cambodians are viewed as inferior (5 points). The scorecard was taken down in a matter of days, after being featured in the media and receiving widespread opprobrium, but the IBRC remained in operation, and, indeed, appears to have renewed its licence in 2018.

Despite all of this, the pretence of the TITP as development aid remains: an instrument of Japan's civilizing mission, as the advanced and culturally superior country in Asia. Much like Koreans, to whom Japan brought civilization, trainees admitted through the programme would (*should*) be grateful to the Japanese people for their magnanimity. As with Japanese colonization of Korea and others, the veneer is hardly matched by reality.[60]

[57] See, eg, Shoichi Ibusuki, *Disposable Foreigners: Japan, the Country of Immigrants with No Human Rights* (Gleam Books 2020).

[58] The Mainichi, '67 of missing foreign trainees worked below minimum wage: opposition parties' (The Mainichi, 4 December 2018) <https://mainichi.jp/english/articles/20181204/p2a/00m/0na/008000c> accessed 20 March 2023.

[59] United States Department of State, '2022 Trafficking in Persons Report: Japan' (US Department of State, 2022) <https://www.state.gov/reports/2022-trafficking-in-persons-report/japan/> accessed 20 March 2023.

[60] In February 2024, the government announced its plans to abolish the TITP and replace it with a system that could potentially lead to long-term residency. Legislation has yet to be adopted, though, and details of any reforms have yet to be decided. See, eg, Kathleen Benoza, 'Japan to end technical intern program and allow transfers to new jobs' *Japan Times* (9 February 2024) <https://www.japantimes.co.jp/news/2024/02/09/japan/society/technical-intern-program-scrapped/#:~:text=Japan%20to%20end%20technical%20intern%20program%20and%20allow%20transfers%20to%20new%20jobs,-This%20image%20can&text=

The fear of 'contamination' by foreigners became a literal one during the COVID-19 pandemic. At the onset of the virus, Japan immediately barred not only foreign visitors but also foreign residents from entering the country—a measure that, unusually, impacted-white skinned residents as well as other foreign nationals. The result was that foreign nationals who had, for example, lived in Japan for decades but needed to travel were unable to return, often losing their employment and housing in the country. At the same time, Japanese nationals who had lived abroad for decades could enter the country easily.[61] These measures were nonsensical and counterproductive from the point of view of preventing the spread of the virus, but there was no noticeable protest from the public. While measures targeting foreign residents were rescinded in September 2020 after multiple demarches from foreign governments, foreign nationals who had yet to take up residency (eg exchange students and workers) remained barred from entering Japan, resulting in sarcastic remarks from the World Health Organisation.[62]

Though the international pandemic was announced in March 2020, it took some months for the virus to spread in Japan, during which time the Japanese media was full of narratives about cultural and racial superiority. These ranged from arguments that the Japanese were more hygienic, to farcical notions that speaking Japanese emitted less spittle than English (and therefore resulted in less contamination).[63] In June 2020, Taro Aso, the Finance Minister, stated in parliament that Japan's low contamination rate was because the Japanese were 'superior in public morals' to other nationalities.[64] All these narratives disappeared quietly as the virus spread dramatically during the summer of 2020.

8. Conclusion

From an early stage in the modernization process, the Japanese political elite recognized the utility of international law. International law was understood as an effective tool to prove to the world that Japan had attained a standard of 'civilization' sufficient to be admitted to the club of imperial powers. Insofar as international law was based

The%20government%20on%20Friday%20formally,system%20enabling%20long%2Dterm%20residency> accessed 18 June 2024.

[61] See, eg, Magdalena Osumi, 'Japan's entry policies increase alienation and deepen division' *Japan Times* (27 August 2020) <https://www.japantimes.co.jp/news/2020/08/27/national/social-issues/japan-entry-policies-coronavirus/> accessed 18 June 2024.

[62] Reuters, 'Japan drops blanket ban on inbound flight bookings amid criticism' *Reuters* (2 December 2021) <https://www.reuters.com/world/china/japan-drops-blanket-ban-flight-reservations-after-confusion-2021-12-02/> accessed 20 March 2023. See also Saul Takahashi, 'Another Sakoku? Japan's Ongoing Stagnation Is Closing the Country' (*SETA Politics Today*, 3 January 2022) https://politicstoday.org/another-sakoku-japans-ongoing-stagnation-is-closing-the-country/> accessed 20 March 2023.

[63] Patrick St Michel, 'This is a pen?' Taking a Preposterous COVID-10 hypothesis to another level on social media' (*Japan Times,* 6 June 2020) <https://www.japantimes.co.jp/news/2020/06/06/national/media-national/pen-coronavirus-theories/> accessed 20 December 2024.

[64] The Asahi Shimbun, 'Mr Aso's "superior public morals": we should not shrug our shoulders at yet another gaffe' (*Asahi Shimbun,* 6 June 2020) <https://www.asahi.com/ajw/articles/13432875> accessed 20 March 2023.

on racist notions of the superiority of Western civilization in general, and European races in particular, this naturally meant that Japan had to conceptualize itself as racially superior to other Asians. These ideas were in turn used to bolster Japan's colonial expansion in the region and remain prevalent in the public discourse today.

This chapter has focused on the narratives presented by governmental actors and elite actors close to the government. There is of course a counter-narrative in modern day Japan led by antiracist scholars (some of whom have been cited) and non-governmental organizations (NGOs) that use international norms to advocate for change.[65] In addition, there is a chance—however small—that Japan's shrinking population will force it to accept large numbers of migrants, inevitably precipitating dramatic cultural shifts.

For now, the notion of the Japanese as a *tan'itsu minzoku* remains pervasive, and international law an outward facing weapon. At least after the initial stages of the Meiji modernization, international law has been seen as a tool to further Japan's interests on the international stage, not as a standard to bring about anything more than cosmetic changes in the country's domestic processes. This resistance to foreign 'contamination' continues to this day.

[65] The voices of such NGOs are generally marginalized, but, at times, they have been successful. See, eg, Tsutsui (n 50).

17
Decolonial Fissures
Looking from and Beyond Brazil's Colour Lines

Henrique Weil Afonso

1. Introduction

Within the confines of an apartment building, the rules dictate that housekeepers are forbidden from using the main elevator. Many of them reside in cramped quarters adjacent to the kitchen and service area, toiling from dawn till dusk, their routines stretching from 6 am to 10 pm. Meanwhile, an enterprising 18-year-old fights through the relentless traffic, risking his physical well-being as he zips through the streets on his rented bicycle, delivering lunches to associates at a prestigious law firm for a fee of one dollar. In a casual conversation among friends, one father asks another how he would feel if his daughter married a Black man, to which he replies: 'I'd rather she didn't. But, you know me, I'm not a racist and do have black friends.' During a police stop, a suspect is locked up in the police car where a smoke grenade is callously thrown, causing the man to suffocate to death. The Chief of Police of a major city issues directives for police squads to regain control of a prison uprising, resulting in the deaths of 111 prisoners. A former President jokes about a *quilombola*,[1] comparing the man's weight to an ox. And time and again, members of Congress resurrect a proposed Constitutional Amendment aimed at regulating mineral exploration in Indigenous lands.

In Brazil, the long continuum of racialized violence spreads across five centuries. European colonialism put in place an array of strategies, including the enslavement of local Indigenous peoples, international human trafficking, the systematic exclusion of women from socially recognized roles, and the outright use of legitimized violence to enforce formal and informal racial lines. Perhaps the most prominent converging point for this multitude of barbarities is the centrality of law throughout, a key component in the demarcation of lines of superiority/inferiority where racism cuts across ethnic, linguistic, religious, gender, and cultural identity.

As the familiar examples above demonstrate, whether perceived in its structural dimension[2] as authorization for the indiscriminate use of violence by state agents, as

[1] *Quilombos* were fortified communities composed of enslaved peoples who escaped captivity in colonial Brazil. Such communities represented places of development of cultural practices, communal bonds, and modes of organization that challenged standard modern preconceptions about society and its institutions. Their descendents, today's *quilombolas*, continue to resist.

[2] Silvio Almeida, *Racismo estrutural* (Pólen 2019) 46–58.

Henrique Weil Afonso, *Decolonial Fissures* In: *Emancipating International Law*. Edited by: Mohsen al Attar and Claire Smith, Oxford University Press. © Henrique Weil Afonso 2026. DOI: 10.1093/9780198935605.003.0022

putatively harmless acts of quotidian life, as intersectional violence of differentiated consequences committed against poor Black or Indigenous women,[3] or as continuation of colonial conquest by other means,[4] racism and racialization have continued to circulate throughout Brazil. How visible are racial lines in contemporary Brazil? Moreover, to what extent do legal experts—and their usual methods—contribute to our understanding of the problem or to the problem itself?

This chapter delves into the realm of decolonial thinking to strategically unveil the power dynamics that intertwine law and race in Brazil. It seeks to chart the conceptual space where ontology is not simply denied but, rather, serves as the breeding ground for hegemonic knowledge that dictates which deaths are worthy of mourning and which are not.[5] While the analysis may appear specific to Brazil, these underlying racialized logics are not confined to the domestic sphere but emanate from the broader international legal order's contribution to and sustaining of racial hierarchies through doctrines such as sovereignty, civilization, and development. My aim is to foreground Brazil's colonial inheritance and racial mythologies to help understand how international law reinforces national projects, supporting the disavowal of structural racism and thus sustaining global racial hierarchies.

Taking as its starting point the representation of racism in decolonial thinking, this chapter unfolds along three interconnected paths: (i) it discusses dominant visions about the racialized formation of the Brazilian *nation*,[6] setting both its modernizing spirit and unifying mythology in the larger international ambiance; (ii) it engages in an exercise of *decolonial thinking* to locate forms of racism rooted in official institutions and social practices in Latin America[7] in countries such as Bolivia, Ecuador, and Haiti; and (iii) it centres contemporary Brazil, first to disclose possible racial lines hidden in constitutional and legal reforms and then to recognize *other* life experiences of radically transformative *knowledges*[8] surfacing in *fissures* and *cracks* in the colonial matrix.[9]

[3] Natacha Borgeaud-Garciandía, Nadya Araujo Guimarães, and Helena Hirata, 'Introduction: care aux Suds. Quand les travail de care interroge les inégalités sociales' (2020) 242 Revue Internationale des Études du Développement 18; Silvana Mariano, 'Cidadania na perspectiva das mulheres pobres e papéis de gênero no acesso a políticas assistenciais' (2009) 2 Revista Brasileira de Ciência Política 151.

[4] Mario Rufer, 'La raza como efecto de conquista' (2020) 22 ArtCultura 35; Rita Laura Segato, *La nación y sus otros: raza, etnicidad y diversidad religiosa en tiempos de políticas de la identidad* (Prometeo 2007).

[5] Vladimir Safatle, 'Beyond the Necropolitics Principle: Suicidal State and Authoritarian Neoliberalism' (2020) 7 Crisis & Critique 362.

[6] The term *methodological nationalism* is usually employed to indicate how the nation-state is treated as the natural and necessary representation of modern society. Daniel Chernilo, 'The Critique of Methodological Nationalism: Theory and History' (2011) 106 Thesis Eleven 99.

[7] Boaventura de Sousa Santos, 'Beyond Abyssal Thinking: From Global Lines to Ecologies of Knowledges' (2007) Review 45.

[8] Catherine Walsh, '"Other" Knowledges, "Other" Critiques: Reflections on the Politics and Practices of Philosophy and Decoloniality in the "Other" America' (2012) 1 Transmodernity 11; Walter Mignolo and Catherine Walsh, *On Decoloniality: Concepts, Analytics, Praxis* (Duke University Press 2018) 88.

[9] More than half a century ago, Aimé Césaire and Franz Fanon spoke about the cracks in Western Christian Civilization where places and possibilities of emancipation could flourish. Aimé Césaire, *Discourse on colonialism* (Monthly Review Press 1972); Franz Fanon, *The Wretched of the Earth* (Grove Press 1963).

2. How to build a nation and keep the racial lines out of sight

In Latin America, the postcolonial misery Partha Chatterjee described as 'our surrender to the old forms of the modern state'[10] stands out in nationalized racial cartographies. Along these spaces, coloniality represented a *sine qua non* condition to the desires of local postcolonial elites to achieve the vaunted model of homogenic nation-state and to do so in hyperreal European standards.[11] As with many Third World elites, recognition of the postcolonial state as conveyed in European international customary law was both the starting point and end goal. What once constituted a multitude of temporalities or, in Anibal Quijano's terms, a world of *dualities* (instead of a world of *binaries*) was flattened by the colonial enterprise, with the modern nation acting as an implacable bulldozer driven by local ruling classes. The ideological enchantment of long-held and widely nurtured *topoi* about race relations in Brazil—produced by bourgeois academic elites particularly concerned with the confection of a positive national identity in the first half of the 1900s—embodies the guiding principle upon which race has come to be understood and racial issues deliberated.

Miscegenation is the single most powerful element of nation building in this country, the compass that steers mainstream understandings of race relations. To assume its full performative capacity, miscegenation is conventionally flanked by two other equally persuasive elements. First, there is widespread belief that Brazil, as a *racial democracy*, experiences no grave conflicts and that everyone, of all colours, backgrounds, and economic statuses enjoys a harmonic coexistence. Second, equally popular is the idea of the *Brazilian singularity*: the portrait of a unique trajectory of national formation that I explain in further detail below and throughout this chapter.[12]

Political and economic liberalism represented the driving forces of modern imperial constitutionalism,[13] sufficiently influential to drive constitutionalist agendas across the region. Its inner connection with the imaginary of the nation-state was

[10] Partha Chatterjee, *The Nation and Its Fragments: Colonial and Postcolonial Histories* (Princeton University Press 1993) 11.

[11] Chakrabarty refers to Europe as a concept that exists in no concrete location, and yet works as the reference to the construction of a racialized other; therefore its hyperreal dimension. Dipesh Chakrabarty, *Provincializing Europe: Postcolonial Thought and Historical Difference* (Princeton University Press 2000).

[12] Jessé Souza, *A construção social da subcidadania: por uma sociologia política da modernidade periférica* (Editora UFMG 2012); Jessé Souza, *A tolice da inteligência brasileira: ou como o país se deixa manipular pela elite* (Leya 2015).

[13] James Tully sharply pointed out that the imperial dimension of modern constitutionalism had been expressed, among other relevant aspects, by the right of European states and their companies to trade freely in non-European societies and the duty to civilize non-European peoples, and the correlative duty of non-European peoples to open themselves to trade and civilization. James Tully, 'The Imperialism of Modern Constitutional Democracy' in Martin Loughlin and Neil Walker (eds), *The Paradox of Constitutionalism: Constituent Power and Constitutional Form* (Oxford University Press 2008) 328. Likewise, the authoritative form in which European and American interests were brought together to create modern international law has been materialized in the project of the *standard of civilization*—by civilization, Tully acknowledges, sided by eminent international jurists, one should read Western constitutional democracy. Martti Koskenniemi, *The Gentle Civilizer of Nations: the Rise and Fall of International Law* (Cambridge University Press 2001); Antony Anghie, *Imperialism, sovereignty and the making of International Law* (Cambridge University Press 2005).

noticeable in the adoption of *legal monism*-based institutions by the *criolla* elites.[14] On the one hand, that meant the predominance of individual rights as the content of the specific subjectivity of the *citizen*. On the other, it established the monopoly of legitimate violence and law-making by state bureaucracies, irrespective of the origin or teleology of these bureaucracies. Altogether, these foundational pillars of Latin American constitutionalism produced the normative justification for the dispossession of original peoples from their lands, the perpetuation of slavery within the logics of property law, and the institutionalization of a patriarchal order that, in the Brazilian case, postponed women's civil rights acquisition until the following century.

To better understand these political and normative registers, it is necessary to consider one of the foundational pillars of Brazilian social thinking: *Casa Grande e Senzala* by Gilberto Freyre.[15] First published in 1933, over the decades Freyre's text has achieved a singular academic status. By recourse to Hegelian dialectics, he explains the intricate and, we learn, *conducive-to-mutual-emancipation* relations between slave owners and enslaved populations. Regarded as an authoritative depiction of the nation's singularity, Freyre has since received credit for nothing less than the Copernican revolution in the country's self-portrait: the shift from the colonial blueprint of a land of degenerated races to a land of unique, progressive, and inclusive cultural miscegenation or, to use a term mentioned earlier, Brazilian *singularity*.[16] Treated as *the* mandatory textbook for anyone concerned with a *critical* understanding of race relations in the early 1900s, the book's legacy has gradually translated into national common sense.[17]

Of analogous academic standing is Sergio Buarque de Holanda's *Raízes do Brazil* (1936).[18] Holanda, elaborating on a Weberian conception of modernization, produces a putatively neutral interpretation of the Brazilian predicament: a modernizing society unable to achieve either the desired model of citizenship or the institutional maturity of fully modern social formations. Modern societies, according to Weber, substitute models of social regulation based on communal traditions and leadership charisma for societal designs grounded upon a formal legal system and an impartial, technical bureaucratic apparatus. In Weber's view, the citizen is the bearer of positive traits conducive to rationalized and specialized relations.[19] The explanatory impetus

[14] Raquel Yrigoyen Fajardo, 'El horizonte del constitucionalismo pluralista: del multiculturalismo a la descolonización' in César Rodríguez Garavito (ed), *El derecho en América Latina: Un mapa para el pensamiento jurídico del siglo XXI* (Siglo Veinteuno Editores 2011) 139–59; Roberto Gargarella, *La sala de máquinas de la Constitución: dos siglos de constitucionalismo en América Latina* (1810–2010) (Katz 2010).

[15] Gilberto Freyre, *Casa-Grande e Senzala* (Global 2006).

[16] Lilia Moritz Schwarcz, *O espetáculo das raças: cientistas, instituições e questão racial no Brasil 1870-1930* (Companhia das Letras 1993) 25, 57.

[17] See, as an example of this, the manner Roberto DaMatta interprets Freyre's legacy: 'In Casa Grande e Senzala, therefore, miscegenation [mestiçagem] figures inside the logics of the ambiguous and paradoxical. Now, Brazil was not mestizo because it was subject to a real and biological 'mixture of races', but because it was a culturally mestiza Society; a system that manifested itself by 'mixing' social institutions that in other places and other times have been treated apart. As a result, the mestizo could be appreciated as a positive element: as social value. From this perspective, the contradictions the mestizo accentuates in other places becomes a central point of the value system of the Brazilian Society.' Roberto DaMatta, *A originalidade de Gilberto Freyre* (BIB 1987) 6.

[18] Sérgio Buarque de Holanda, *Raízes do Brasil* (Companhia das Letras 2014).

[19] Max Weber, *Economy and Society* (University of California Press 1978) 956.

of Weber's theory equipped Holanda's work with the credentials to establish itself as a dominant sociological reading of the Brazilian trajectory as a semi-modern State. In this sense, it is worth following Holanda's argument.

Initially, the author contraposes Weber's idealized modern citizen with its negative counterpart: the *friendly man*. A potentially corrupt and emotionally driven individual, this representation engages primarily on the basis of familiar relations—a mode of behaviour in which the characters of sociability are forged upon a distorted image of the social sphere, itself understood as an extension of familial-cum-patriarchal bonds.[20] Next, rather than an outcome of republican ideals and emancipatory political movements, the state represents the institutional aftermath of patrimonial relations. In effect, and in contrast with the expected modern divide between public and private domains, Holanda argues that Brazil faces the permanent juxtaposition of both.

In sum, the nucleus that unites both Freyre and Holanda's works is composed of (a) a belief in Brazil's incomplete social differentiation, reflected in the absence of a modern bureaucracy coupled with a politically fragile social body; (b) the conviction in Brazil's unfinished transition to post traditional modes of sociability, a symptom that can be traced to the ample presence of religion in the public and private realms; (c) a porosity of private and public realms; (d) a specific emotional economy that taunts individuals' psyches with the incapacity to domesticate their inner desires; and (e) an insufficient separation of society and nature that harkens to individual and social dynamics of a pre-modern world.[21]

The myth of *miscegenation* offers a compelling narrative for a postcolonial society in search of self-understanding. Its persuasiveness stems from its capacity to play out as both critical academic knowledge and common sense.[22] Racialization stands out inconspicuously in both approaches. In Freyre, its effects are turned upside down through the celebratory impetus of cultural diversity; in Holanda, the idealized citizen captures the imagination of a nation ashamed of its backwardness, and its key agent, the *friendly man*, personifies all there is to know about Brazilian social relations.

The racial imaginaries constructed by Freyre and Holanda, though unique in their analytical frameworks, converge around a representation of Brazil as a nation perpetually caught between modernity and tradition, universality and particularity. While shaping academic and popular understandings of race, these narratives also laid the groundwork for a legal and political order that naturalizes racial inequality under the guise of national cohesion. For example, the 1988 Federal Constitution, with its promises of universal citizenship, initially appeared to mark a rupture with this legacy, offering a framework for racial and social justice. Yet, as recent legal and economic transformations reveal, the Constitution has itself become a site of contestation, where the historical ambivalence towards race re-emerges in neoliberal form. The shift from overt exclusion to a depoliticized, market-driven notion of citizenship echoes the very

[20] Surinder S Jodhka, Boike Rehbein, and Jessé Souza, *Inequality in Capitalist Societies* (Routledge 2018) 82–107.

[21] Sergio BF Tavolaro, 'A Tese da Singularidade Brasileira Revisitada: Desafios Teóricos Contemporâneos' (2014) 57 DADOS—Revista de Ciências Sociais 641.

[22] Jodhka, Rehbein, and Souza (n 20).

myths that have long structured Brazilian racial discourse—miscegenation, Brazilian singularity, and the illusion of racial democracy. In this light, contemporary constitutional reforms can be read not as departures from Brazil's racial history, but as its most recent legal iteration, where racial inequalities are not erased but reconfigured through the logic of neoliberal legality.

Following the enactment of the 1988 Federal Constitution, nationalism underwent a transformative process, as it adopted the language of universal citizenship. By contrast, recent legal developments have turned the Constitution on its head, injecting layers of inequality into the document. For example, in 2016, the Brazilian National Congress passed Constitutional Amendment n 95. Concealed beneath the grandiose title of the New Fiscal Regime, its core provisions (Articles 107 and 110) established limits on state investment in health care and public education, binding both public services for an unfathomable period of two decades. This action constituted a direct attack on the fundamental principles and social rights enshrined in the Constitution.

By suppressing the bedrock of popular sovereignty, these reforms further subjugated an already battered democracy to the demands of the market economy, accomplishing this feat with a calculated precision that safeguards formal avenues of political engagement such as voting, the right to run for office, and a basic set of individual rights. Even though scholars have developed the term neoliberal legality to capture the nature of this phenomenon,[23] it is yet to absorb the full impact of racialization and its asymmetrical consequences throughout the architecture of the legal system.

In response to the economic crisis of 2015–2016, a reformist agenda reimagined social rights from entitlements to a regime of conditional citizenship. As informal work supersedes formal labour—labour relations that consolidate a new precarious workforce—the Labour Reform of 2017 brought about the flexibilization of former guarantees of formal labour. The law now favours individual bargaining while curtailing the realm of collective negotiations, introducing new legal identities such as the intermittent worker. Instead of simply erasing myths, modern law redefines and reshapes them, particularly when it comes to the concept of constitutional citizenship, imbuing it with a neoliberal tenor. As the example of the delivery young man in the opening paragraph highlights, a racialized workforce provides a number of services in cheap, rights-free legally binding contracts with digital platforms that now occupy every single economic niche.

The pattern is also visible in the institutional standing of original communities and nations. Despite the purportedly liberating nature of legal provisions in the 1988 Federal Constitution concerning the protection, recognition, and implementation of collective rights of original communities (via public policies carried out by the state),[24] there remains a subtext of racialized hierarchies cloaked by the universalist

[23] Honor Brabazon, 'Introduction: Understanding Neoliberal Legality' in Honor Brabazon (ed), *Neoliberal Legality: Understanding the Role of Law in the Neoliberal Project* (Routledge 2017).

[24] There has been an apparent shift of paradigms that contrasts the 1988 Federal Constitution with previous ones. Before the present constitutional framework, the recognition of rights to Indigenous groups—such as the right to a territory or the right of cultural recognition—was based upon an integrationist approach: public institutions would be responsible for promoting the grounds for the assimilation of these groups to the broader nation—the Brazilian nation. Such an approach coexisted with open-scale extermination of groups who imposed any kind of resistance to the expansion of agricultural and mineral extraction frontiers. Gersem Baniwa, 'A conquista da cidadania indígena e o fantasma da tutela no

aura of human rights whenever these groups dare to challenge it—their status often diminished or even equated to animals, as shown in the example of the quilombola man.[25] Segato has aptly employed the term *punishing state*,[26] originally used to describe the operational norms of criminal law and politics that target individuals who fall within stigmatized categories, to characterize the rationale behind federal legislation that criminalizes aspects of Indigenous cultures and practices. This new legislation appears as a re-enactment of the civilizing mission of colonial states, just within a nationalist framework.

On the horizon looms the dawn of a society where individuals find themselves in a permanent struggle for scarce public provisions. Against the backdrop of rampant economic inequality, the demands for public services will continue to rise. However, as market-oriented reforms take centre stage, they hollow out constitutional norms that sustain welfare services, ushering in an alternative neoliberal model of citizenship. In this framework, the state transforms the provision of public services from a societal imperative to a source of commodification and profit. Education, health care, labour, basic sanitation, and security are all subject to this redefinition. Whether understood as an aspirational ideal or a societal equivalent, citizenship undergoes a metamorphosis, conveying an elementary sense that 'we are all in it together', and no racial lines appear to be visible enough to undo the kind of equality stemming out of a neoliberal Constitution in the making.

In his analysis of the nineteenth-century Brazilian elite, Roberto Schwarz employs the phrase 'ideas out of place' to capture the contradictory ambitions of this privileged group. While eager to import a liberal framework of rights and institutions, they did so in a society deeply divided by a history of slavery. This historical continuum is reflected in recent constitutional reforms that reaffirm centuries of racial violence. These reforms reinforce legal mechanisms aligned with neoliberal demands, creating a seemingly incongruous situation where liberally inspired rights coexist with pervasive racial violence. Paradoxically, this juxtaposition becomes a normalized feature of modern state-building in Brazil, filling the gaps of cultural distinctiveness.

A brief examination of Brazil's constitutional framework reveals how legal mechanisms, rather than dismantling historical inequalities, often adapt them to new ideological paradigms, yet contribute to the further entrenchment of racial hierarchies. Neoliberal legality has not erased racial stratification but has instead restructured it through market-driven exclusions and depoliticized notions of citizenship. The next section examines how racial stratification has evolved in the Brazilian context, tracing the material consequences of the discourse and the associated legal reforms on racialized communities and social relations.

Brasil contemporâneo' in Alcida R Ramos (ed), *Constituições nacionais e povos indígenas* (Editora UFM 2012) 206–07.

[25] Rita L Segato, *Crítica da colonialidade em oito ensaios e uma antropologia por demanda* (Bazar do Tempo 2021) 165.

[26] The term has been originally employed by critical sociologists and criminologists to explain the operative standards of criminal law and politics of containment of specific individuals who fall within stigmatized categories, such as poverty, gender, and race. Loïc Wacquant, *Punishing the Poor—the Neoliberal Government of Social Insecurity* (Duke University Press 2009).

3. Cartographies of violence: locating racism in the colonial power matrix

The debate surrounding the coloniality of power precipitated a significant paradigm shift in the history of critical thinking in Latin America. Serving as a powerful analytic tool, it confronts the violent, yet unchallenged normative background of modernity/coloniality, including the reigning assumptions about how the world should be ordered and who counts as an equal. Current beliefs were wrenched from history and superimposed on the present, permeating the colonial matrix of power as ahistorical, logical, and uncontested epistemic truths about the world. The debate critiques these truths including the treatment of Cartesian logic as a primordial epistemic paradigm[27] and the deification of scientific-cum-rational knowledge over the transcendental or natural frames that historically ordered human and non-human interactions.[28]

Within the diverse approaches to decolonial thought, one path offers valuable insights into the perpetuation of racism in Brazil. This path posits that acts of colonial conquest contributed to the enduring presence of racism, which evolved and adapted to changing conditions over time. Racism is framed in a given region of the world; it does not presuppose or predetermine a universalist definition of racism, but helps to appreciate the contingency of practices of domination and oppression which, in the case of race, can be marked by colour, ethnicity, language, religion, and/or culture.[29] Rather than a moment with a specific birthdate, decolonial thinking proposes a more engaging perspective that links racism to structural processes of brutality. In the case of Brazil, these processes litter the subterrain of conquest.

Whether associated with a state of nature or justified by evolutionary theories,[30] the continuous subjugation of multiple forms of being, knowing, and living[31] provides the decisive frame within which to explore racialization from a decolonial standpoint. According to Mario Rufer:

> ... race, being an effect of conquest, has two key characteristics: if it does not cease to happen, then it is a structure. And, if it is not an event, being a structure it outwits the possibility of being embedded in modernity's hollow time, and above all, ruling out the logical production of probable evidence, the archive of History. Race plays out as sign and non-whiteness consists in the significant of an all encompassing subjugation code: and, if the final reference of such sign is the primary dispossession of conquest, it is imperative that such a reference constantly fails in language ...: it shall not be named.[32]

[27] Boaventura S Santos, 'A Discourse of the Sciences' (1992) XV Review 9.

[28] Segato (n 25).

[29] '... the problem with making a particular racist marker as the definition of racism, leads us to adopt the false conclusion that racism does not exist in other parts of the world if the form of marking racism in one particular region or country does not coincide with the "common sense" form of marking it in one's own country.' Ramon Grosfoguel, 'What is Racism?'(2006) 22 Journal of World-Systems Research 10.

[30] Intellectual and economic elites of nineteenth-century Brazil engaged in a wide campaign to build a viable nation. According to racial theories of the epoch, the status of a second-class subject made the *mestizo* inadequate to such an objective. It was up to ethnographic institutes, museums, medical and law schools to produce relevant racial knowledge that suited the novel nation's needs. Moritz Schwarcz (n 16).

[31] Mignolo and Walsh (n 8) 4.

[32] Rufer (n 4) 40.

Conquest, the seminal act of domination, stands for the ongoing historical category that sustains racialization. Modern coloniality imposed the parameters according to which history would be written, the measure of time against which it would be evaluated, and the agents whose acts and memories would survive in the temple of historicism. In this scheme, national culture, as shown in the previous section on the singularity of the Brazilian national condition, operates as an origin myth for the modern multicultural nation. The duality at play keeps cultures in close management by governmental apparatus so that an *average national culture* 'that works as the observant eye, the blind spot about which it is not possible to attain a measurable parameter, [that] does not need an explanation'.[33]

Miscegenation operates on two levels: it fabricates and consecrates a national myth that everyone comes to presume and which requires no further clarification. At the same time, this myth creates blind spots, obscuring the enduring legacies of slavery, colonial violence, and racialized predation. Because these forms of violence are not recognized as *proper* violence—after all, how can racial violence exist in a society supposedly defined by harmonious mixing?—they are rarely understood as the driving force behind institutional brutality. Yet, as incidents like the grenade thrown inside a police vehicle or police operations that have claimed over a hundred lives reveal, colonial conquest is far from a relic of the past; its logic remains embedded in the structures of contemporary state violence.

As a consequence, a contemporary expression of the colonial pattern of violence has to do with the attribution of different status depending on whether we talk about a *person*—someone recognized as a bearer of rights under the protection of the State—or a *thing*: subjects degraded to the condition of *object*.[34] The ideology of miscegenation serves as a cloak, concealing the persistence of colonial hierarchies that relegate certain groups to a precarious sociolegal existence, maintained and reproduced through the enduring logic of colonial conquest.

'Race', explains Rita Segato, 'is a sign, the trace of a history on the subject, marking a position and signalling a heritage of dispossession'.[35] Even though this definition does not imply a mark on a given people or ethnic group, what nests at the nucleus of race in a decolonial prism is its *trace of conquest*: a digital fingerprint of an *otherness* history that created race to establish Europe as an epistemic, economic, technological, and moral-legal centre that distributes value and meaning in our world. Non-whites are not only Black Africans or native populations of the Americas, but *others* who carry the mark of historical dispossession. In other words, race is the mark of those who were dispossessed of their territories, knowledges, bodies, cultures, and histories.[36]

[33] Mario Rufer, 'El perpetuo conjuro: tiempo, colonialidad y repetición en la escritura de la historia' (2020) Special Issue Historia y Memoria 291.

[34] Necropower theorists like Achille Mbembe locate a racialized hierarchy in the margins of present-day manifestations of sovereign power that surpasses the modern distinction between reason and unreason upon which ideas about the political, the community, or the subject converge to the ambience of autonomy to be replaced by the generalized instrumentalization of human existence and the material destruction of human bodies and populations of a political realm founded around the categories of life and death. Achille Mbembe, 'Necropolitics' (2003) 15 Public Culture 14.

[35] Segato (n 4) 23.

[36] ibid.

The dynamics of conquest extend their grasp into the very fabric of time up to the point where 'to think about the colonial is to labour upon temporality'.[37] The temporality of the modern nation, with its linear progression, stability, and homogeneity, is paralleled by the monism of modern law. It operates as a gatekeeper, allowing entry only to narratives that adhere to its predetermined criteria, dismissing those that do not fit its causal rationality devoid of meaning and experience. For narratives that fail to meet these criteria, the realm of culture, situated below the world of history, provides an adequate space. Culture grants access to subjects whose institutions, languages, and characters are themselves the blank slate of knowledge.

Racial divisions draw upon colonial dynamics deeply rooted in an *ontological distinction*, persisting and transforming even in the aftermath of formal colonialism's collapse.[38] Colonial territories in Latin America were the sites of the first experiments of a rather different stripe: coloniality of power created the very possibility of drawing the line where *nonexistence* is the standard mode of subjectivity, agency, and historical denial, colonial spaces of unlimited appropriation and violence.

The 1550–1551 Valladolid controversy between Las Casas and Sepúlveda is an enduring reminder of how certain dichotomies—legal/illegal, law/non law—work in tandem with the imposition of universalist distinctions[39] that come out inconspicuously in modern state law or in the vocabularies of private rights upon which imperial relations were grounded.[40] In the international realm, for example, the principle of *terra nullius* was applied indiscriminately on the other side of the line, meanwhile law making experiments combined private law precepts with the logic of 'appropriation/violence that only recognizes the law of things, of both human and nonhuman things'.[41]

In different yet convergent ways, decolonial thinking in Latin America has emphasized the need to register a historical constancy between *la conquista* colonial and modern legal systems. This is the locus of racialization, the canvas where the racial lines are drawn, yet in elusive chalk. As Segato affirms, 'the need to acknowledge the historical continuity between the conquest, the colonial ordering of the world and postcolonial republican formation that continues until today'.[42] The historical operation of racialization takes the form of permanent confrontation that keeps certain populations in check. As Rufer highlights, 'hidden continuities in productive synecdoche that managed the replacement—under powerful political fictions—cast for mestizaje, racialization for inequalities, differentiation for recognition'.[43] In the final section, I engage in a decolonial scrutiny of possible intersections of racism and law in contemporary Brazilian society.

[37] Valeria Añón and Mario Rufer, 'Lo colonial como silencio, la conquista como tabú: reflexiones en tiempo presente' (2018) 29 Tabula Rasa 117.
[38] Safatle (n 5); Santos (n 27).
[39] Enrique Dussel and Gary MacEoin, '1492: the Discovery of an Invasion' (1991) 41 CrossCurrents 437.
[40] Martti Koskenniemi, 'Empire and International Law: The Real Spanish Contribution' (2011) 61 University of Toronto Law Journal 1.
[41] Santos (n 27) 15.
[42] Segato (n 4) 158.
[43] Rufer (n 4) 35.

4. *An-other* way forward: tackling the present-past racism of Brazil's future

They say that the Creator asked thus:

> 'Are white people treating you well?'
> 'You can tell me what whites are doing to you'
> If they are mistreating you, tell me
> The Creator said:
> When I see this river dry where you are with the whites destroying all
> I don't know what to do . . .
> When there are no more signs of you,
> When only white people remain
> I will move apart the frogs that hold both edges of the sky
> The sky will fall and everything will be over.
> Sadea Yudja[44]

Building upon Rufers's notion of the continuous act of conquest, in the twenty-first century, racism represents the convergence point of two nefarious agendas. On the one hand, we observe, in broad daylight, the necropolitics of obscene violence committed against negatively racialized peoples; on the other, we are confronted by a reformist spirit that seeks to establish novel frontiers of expropriation by eroding constitutional welfare provisions which, again, disproportionately harm racialized communities. As Yudja's quote brings to the fore, colonial modernity's epistemological enchainment manifests itself in Brazil via a double axis:[45] racialized and socially approved state violence inhabits the same discursive universe as normative propositions about what the prevailing model of rights should be.

Since the country's political independence, social boundaries have been blurred by a modernizing *ethos* translated into a legal framework, itself guided by principles of liberal equality and economic freedom operating in a highly racialized social sphere. The citizen—albeit in a form divergent from European frameworks—encapsulates the much-coveted, mestizo-inspired vision of a harmonious society where grave conflicts are believed to be nonexistent.[46] As we have seen earlier, this notion is a core value behind the myth of Brazilian singularity.

However, as explained in the opening section, racial hierarchies remain ever present. What is more, they are dynamic and pernicious. Indeed, due to coloniality of power's inherent entwinement with racism and modernity, it constantly imposes new

[44] Pajé Sadea Yudja in 'Where did the swallows go? (Instituto Socioambiental and Instituto Catitu, 22 July 2017) <https://www.youtube.com/watch?v=JQS7DQSYy-U&ab_channel=Institutocatitu> accessed 8 February 2023). The documentary reveals how the Xingu Indigenous peoples in the Northern part of Brazil observe the devastating signs of climate collapse, once these signs affect the forms of life that constitute their cosmological references.

[45] The inspiration comes from Karl Polanyi. In another context we tested the application of Polanyi's postulations to Brazilian reality. See Henrique Weil Afonso, 'Labour, Social Reproduction and the Time of Law' (2020) 2 Human(ities) and Rights Global Network Journal 136.

[46] Safatle (n 5); Jessé Souza, *Como o racismo criou o Brasil* (Estação Brasil 2021); Almeida (n 2); Raj Patel and Jason W Moore, *A History of the World in Seven Cheap Things: A Guide to Capitalism, Nature, and the Future of the Planet* (University of California Press 2017).

racial demarcations whenever old ones prove unsatisfactory, ineffective, or are exhausted. A sense of continuity is enabled by the ability to stealthy reinvent its engines. As Rufer describes, 'it is not [about] the logic of extermination as a project settlement colonial, but the logic of conquest as a necessarily re-editable frontier (and, much like extermination, it remains unspoken)'.[47] The conquest has never been truly concluded, as Rita Segato poignantly articulates, 'in our landscapes . . . it is an ongoing process without end'.[48] Accordingly, identifying and dismantling the violent mechanisms they breed, though essential, falls short for the type of renewal envisioned in this collection.

Instead of universalist abstractions rooted in the white male European model of modern law or the all-encompassing colonial matrix of unifying nationalism, what if we were to explore the radically transformative constitutional content and practices of the Haitian Revolution or, perhaps, the resistance movements of the *quilombos* in colonial Brazil? Similarly, rather than violently silencing, what if we genuinely listened to the wisdom and warnings of Indigenous peoples, who have long proclaimed the impending collapse of our civilization?

Unsurprisingly, late eighteenth-century events of Santo Domingo remain fully unaccounted for in leading constitutional law texts.[49] Nonetheless, applying a decolonial lens, we observe epistemic moves towards an *antiracist legal system* pursued by the Haitian revolutionary movement. Examples are plentiful, including normative innovations such as universal rights of Black individuals, the materiality of slavery as a founding problem to constitutional law and state institutions, the conception of diasporic citizenship, the principle of free ground, and the exclusion of human property from the content of the right to private property. In the Haitian experience, the founding pillars of modern law—individual freedom and private property—were confronted in their racialized nature.

Revolutionary Haitian constitutionalism connected the narratives of those subjected to extreme racialization with legally emancipatory provisions that operated from the opposite perspective of the one imposed by colonial conquest. It embraced a narrative to counter the oppressive forces and uplift marginalized voices and communities. 'Haitian poetics', affirms Marcos Queiroz, 'employed constitutional discourse to imagine a territory of rights destined to those who have faced the abyss, who have lived the experience of the unprepared confrontation with the unknown, who have had deadly doubts in face of the disintegration of all things that mattered'.[50] Whereas its hegemonic counterpart, firmly grounded in the intellectual aftermath of French and American Revolutions, became the driving force of nation building, in Haiti, the *non-subjects* of Hegelian dialectics—those who were denied both historical agency and human belonging[51]—rewrote modern constitutionalism on a non-racialized

[47] Rufer (n 4) 42.

[48] Rita L Segato, *La guerra contra las mujeres* (Traficantes de sueños 2016) 99.

[49] An analysis of constitutional law courses syllabi in ten leading law schools in the country revealed a complete absence of any mention of the Haitian Revolution or its nineteenth-century constitutions. Marcos Queiroz and Lucas Jupy, 'O Haiti é aqui? A Revolução Haitiana no ensino do direito no Brasil' (2021) 8 Revista Culturas Jurídicas 99.

[50] Marcos Queiroz, 'Constitutionalismo Haitiano e a Invenção dos Direitos Humanos' (2022) 13 Revista Direito e Práxis 2794.

[51] Susan Buck-Morss, *Hegel, Haiti and Universal History* (University of Pittsburgh Press 2009) 40.

canvas. It ruled out the legal abstractions that enabled racism to be accommodated with enlightened ideals, by turning it into an ontological impossibility. It is in this precise sense that the Haitian Revolution destabilized the discursive field of modern constitutionalism: it brought to the surface the patterns of conquest cloaked in a misleading emancipatory language.

In Brazil, a notable instance of comparable epistemic innovations can be found in the institutionalized resistance to slavery pursued by the *quilombos*, particularly in the case of Quilombo dos Palmares. Despite numerous repressive military campaigns undertaken by colonial rulers since the last decades of the sixteenth century, for over a hundred years, Palmares endured as a living territory of anticolonial *Amefrican* freedom. Neither derived from natural law nor conceptualized through a Western ontological prism, in Palmares, freedom derived foremost from collective resistance. *Amefricanity*, a concept developed by Brazilian philosopher and feminist Lélia Gonzalez, stands for a political-cultural category upon and with which one may approach African diasporas to uproot the symbolic and material basis of processes of unequal distribution of power and violence in Latin America.[52]

An attempt to answer the first question lies in the experiences of Haiti and Palmares, both of which stand as living counterhegemonic forces. They dislodge lasting Western assumptions about constitutional identity and normative universalism—not only by confronting their racist legacies in today's society but, more boldly, by offering alternatives to the ongoing colonial conquest.

Turning to the second question about the wisdom and warnings of Indigenous peoples—a living testimony of contemporary means of conquest aimed at vulnerable original Indigenous communities—the epigraph that prefaces this section reflects the richness of Amerindian cosmologies that envision the end of the world. Despite their varying points of origin—from South American Andean cultures to Northern Brazil Xingu's, where Pajé Sadea Yudja denounced the destructive effects of predatory extractivism and soy monocultures of private properties surrounding Xingu's territory—these cosmologies converge in recognizing the arrival of white men as the pivotal historical event that would lead to their annihilation.[53] The continuity of their existence was violently interrupted by the operation of coloniality of power's machinery five centuries ago, with their cosmologies subjected to an additional dimension of conquest, this time, of the future.[54]

In Latin America, these epistemologies have inspired important social movements followed by significant steps towards institutionalization. The 2008 Bolivian and the 2009 Ecuadorian constitutions established promising grounds for a legal pluralist, multi-ethnic, and interculturalist constitutional system. As an aftermath of continued resistance in both countries, original groups actively shaped the works of constitutional assemblies which gave rise to a framework that cherishes the mutual recognition

[52] Lélia González, *Por um feminismo afro-latino-americano* (Zahar 2020); Thula Rafaela de Oliveira Pires and Ana Luiza Pinheiro Flauzina, 'Constitucionalismo da Inimizade' (2022) 13 Rev Direito e Práxis 2823.

[53] One the most compelling accounts of the continuous struggles of Indigenous groups in Brazil can be found in Davi Kopenawa and Bruce Albert, *A queda do céu: Palavras de um xamã yanomami* (Companhia das Letra 2015).

[54] Segato (n 25).

of each nation's right (original nations and campesinos) to exercise their own jurisdiction over their ancestral territories. Emerging from the fractures caused by the colonial enterprise and its lingering influence in present-day law, the conception of *plurinationality* came to life. It seeks to account for bottom-up, counterhegemonic processes that challenge constitutional law's colonial impetus including components of racialized conquest such as legal monism, the encryption of constituent power in modern constituent forms,[55] the commodification of both human and non-human life forms, and the neoliberal reformist agenda. Tellingly, the challenge has come in a radically democratic and pluralist lexicon.[56]

Finally, in Bolivia and Ecuador, original nations have emerged as political subjects with the power to shape their own futures. Unlike the monist credentials of Brazil's 1998 Federal Constitution, in these countries the plurinational state and plurinational constitutionalism represent institutional responses to the legacies of colonization. By shifting the paradigm of rights recognition, they move away from a nation-state that holds a monopoly on power to a plurinational state that recognizes the collective agency of diverse communities. This recognition is based on the principle of equal participation, acknowledging the aspects that colonial conquest has long denied. A significant part of these constitutions was devoted to the cosmovisions of original peoples: the philosophy of *buen vivir* and *sumak kawsay*, the recognition of rights of nature (Pachamama), the equivalence of original nations' jurisdictions with State ones. These innovations of plurinational constitutionalism have emerged from the *concrete humanism*—their struggles to preserve ancient ways of living and integrate representative institutions—of marginalized groups who have long resisted colonial exploitation.

5. Concluding with beginnings

Normative abstractions like equality or citizenship serve as veils that conceal the deep-rooted racial inequalities of modern coloniality in Brazil. The *silence of the colonial* turns out to be a necessary cog in the machinery of society today.[57] While in the nineteenth and twentieth centuries, it was primarily the project of the Brazilian nation that perpetuated these silences, I argue in this chapter that contemporary constitutionalism builds a mythological framework to enforce various degrees of silence, ranging from deliberate forgetfulness to the epistemic impossibility of acknowledging certain forms of racialization. The foundational silences of Brazilian history are just as important as the myths disguised either as common sense or as sophisticated modernisms such as equal citizenship.

Everyday forms of racism, such as those mentioned in the opening paragraph of the text, exemplify these colonial silences that hover between denial—the anything-but-racism doctrine—and downplaying: 'I can't be a racist because I have black friends'.[58]

[55] Ricardo Sanín Restrepo, 'La Constitución Encriptada: Nuevas formas de emancipación del poder global' (2012) 8 Revista de Derechos Humanos y Estudios Sociales 115.

[56] Raquel Yrigoyen-Fajardo (n 14) 149.

[57] Añón and Rufer (n 37).

[58] Michel-Rolph Trouillot, *Silencing the Past: Power and the Production of History* (Beacon Press 1995).

Even in cases of subjective manifestation, to treat racism as individual acts to which legal sanction are applicable fails to confront both its deeply entrenched social lines and its discursive conquest apparatus. From the attempts to erase racial lines by inserting the mythology into the ontology of the nation to the apparently incontestable vocabulary of universal constitutional rights, this chapter problematized the continued exercise of colonial conquest.

As observed by decolonial jurists,[59] sociocultural narratives substitute the generative generalizations of conventional constitutional theory for process-based conception of rights whose contents are mediated by the historicity of concrete conflicts. Through the examples of Haitian constitutionalism and Quilombo resistance, we observe concrete confrontations with the myth of a homogenic nation. In lieu of the unitary myth, they present a pluralist conception of the people forged in the concrete resistance of enslaved and Indigenous peoples coexisting in a territory of escape.

Instead of deforming, denying, or merely erasing pluralism, as modern nationalism and its unifying apparatus do, they locate the possibilities of inclusive normative horizons. The history of conquest is then countered by an unwavering commitment to other imaginaries, seeking to reclaim historical foundations and forge a more promising future. For those of us attempting to come to terms with present-day *dystopias*, the cosmologies of original peoples and the transformative experience of Palmares carry vibrant lessons, though we are yet to learn how to hear them.

[59] Alejandro Medici, 'Teoría constitucional y giro decolonial: narrativas y simbolismo de la Constitución—reflexiones a propósito de la experiencia de Bolivia y Ecuador' (2011) 48 Gaceta Constitucional 343.

18

Norm Entrepreneurship at the UN

Addressing Racial Equality Across Borders and the South–North Divide

Yang Han

1. Introduction

Racism is integral to international relations, with racist beliefs in various forms—such as scientific racism and the 'yellow peril'—often used to justify colonialism in the past and imperial practices in the present.[1] Abundant cases speak of transnational and interstate racism, whereas the concept of sovereignty helps safeguard domestic racism from external interference.[2] During the Korean War, for example, scholars documented racist conduct and race-based violence against civilians committed by the United States-led United Nations (UN) army.[3] Additionally, Black American soldiers experienced institutional racism during the Second World War wherever they were deployed including the Asian continent.[4] Even the history and theories of international relations have been scrutinized for their role in perpetuating racism through the practices of 'white powers' towards their non-white counterparts and official delegates, not only during colonial times but also during the Cold War.[5] For instance, when expressing dissatisfaction with Japan's limited military contribution in the Pacific Alliance, Kissinger referred to Japanese strategists as 'little Sony salesmen', while Nixon lamented the Japanese presence 'all over Asia, like a bunch of lice'.[6]

[1] Gayatri Chakravorty Spivak, 'Can the Subaltern Speak?' in Cary Nelson and Lawrence Grossberg (eds), *Marxism and the Interpretation of Culture* (Macmillan 1988); Lila Abu-Lughod, 'Do Muslim Women Really Need Saving? Anthropological Reflections on Cultural Relativism and Its Others' (2002) 104 American Anthropologist 783.

[2] Zoltán I Búzás, 'Racism and Antiracism in the Liberal International Order' (2021) 75 International Organization 440.

[3] Bruce Cumings, *The Korean War: A History* (Random House Publishing Group 2010).

[4] Nathan H Brandt, *Harlem At War: The Black Experience in WWII* (Syracuse University Press 1996); Christopher Paul Moore, *Fighting for America: Black Soldiers-the Unsung Heroes of World War II* (Random House Publishing Group 2007); Douglas A Blackmon, *Slavery by Another Name: The Re-Enslavement of Black Americans from the Civil War to World War II* (Knopf Doubleday Publishing Group 2009); Phillip McGuire, *Taps For A Jim Crow Army: Letters from Black Soldiers in World War II* (University Press of Kentucky 2014).

[5] Shogo Suzuki, 'Japan's Socialization into Janus-Faced European International Society' (2005) 11 European Journal of International Relations 137; Sergey Radchenko, 'The Sino-Soviet Split' in Melvyn P Leffler and Odd Arne Westad (eds), *The Cambridge History of the Cold War: Volume 2: Crises and Détente* (Cambridge University Press 2010) 371.

[6] Michael Schaller, 'Japan and the Cold War, 1960–1991' in Melvyn P Leffler and Odd Arne Westad (eds), *The Cambridge History of the Cold War: Volume 3: Endings* (Cambridge University Press 2010) 171.

Yang Han, *Norm Entrepreneurship at the UN* In: *Emancipating International Law*. Edited by: Mohsen al Attar and Claire Smith, Oxford University Press. © Yang Han 2026. DOI: 10.1093/9780198935605.003.0023

Why, then, is there no international norm on racial equality that serves as a code of conduct among states? The absence of such a norm reveals, first, a gap in legal regulation and, second, a deeper unwillingness to confront racism as a structural, transnational problem within the international legal order. Studying norms—how they emerge, how they are resisted, and whose interests they reflect—offers insight into the values states choose to codify in international law as well as the violences it opts to normalize.

Decades after the decolonization era began, there is still no definitive answer to this question, and relevant research in international law and international relations (IR) is scarce. Insightful historical research has been conducted to highlight past attempts of states to advocate for global racial equality in international venues, such as the Paris Peace Conference and the Bandung Conference, while recent developments following the World Conference Against Racism (WCAR) have received disproportionately less academic attention. Further, IR scholarship on racial equality has mostly focused on domestic issues and rarely considered interstate racial injustices.[7] This lack of attention is problematic because it creates significant discrepancies between the theoretical critique of intellectual racism and the practical conduct of IR.[8]

We may assert that an international consensus on anti-discrimination has emerged, prohibiting racial discrimination. For example, researchers have found that in the United States, the principle of antidiscrimination has been more widely recognized than the principle of gender equality.[9] However, antidiscrimination is not equivalent to racial equality, for two reasons. First, the positive connotations of racial equality extend beyond the negative prohibitive implications of antidiscrimination. Second, existing legal accomplishments in antidiscrimination focus on the protection of individual rights, while the codification of racial equality at the interstate level would stipulate the appropriate conduct of states in the international community.

In the absence of a global norm of racial equality, the only relevant principles are perhaps the norms of sovereign equality for interstate relations and human rights protection for state–individual relations. However, they are often indirect and insufficient for achieving racial justice in instances of interstate racism (and intra). The global human rights agenda has also been criticized for sidelining racial equality;[10] similarly, the agenda of racial equality is often confined to the prism of domestic racial (in)justice, with forms of interstate and transnational racism left intact.[11]

[7] Audie Klotz, 'Norms Reconstituting Interests: Global Racial Equality and U.S. Sanctions against South Africa' (1995) 49 International Organization 451; Bertrand G Ramcharan, 'Normative Human Rights Cascades, North and South' (2016) 37 Third World Quarterly 1234; Malia Lee Womack, 'The United States' International Valuing of Anti-Racism Norms Over Gender Equality Norms' in Vasilikie Demos and Marcia Texler Segal (eds), *Gender Panic, Gender Policy* (Emerald Publishing Limited 2017).

[8] John M Hobson, 'Is Critical Theory Always for the White West and for Western Imperialism? Beyond Westphilian towards a Post-Racist Critical IR' (2007) 33 Review of International Studies 91; Meera Sabaratnam, 'Is IR Theory White? Racialised Subject-Positioning in Three Canonical Texts' (2020) 49 Millennium 3; Alison Howell and Melanie Richter-Montpetit, 'Is Securitization Theory Racist? Civilizationism, Methodological Whiteness, and Antiblack Thought in the Copenhagen School' (2020) 51 Security Dialogue 3.

[9] Womack (n 7).

[10] E Tendayi Achiume, 'Putting Racial Equality onto the Global Human Rights Agenda Repositioning Race in the International Agenda: Essays' (2018) 15 Sur—International Journal on Human Rights 141.

[11] Darryl Li, 'Genres of Universalism: Reading Race Into International Law, With Help From Sylvia Wynter' (2021) 67 UCLA Law Review 1686; Búzás (n 2).

This chapter sheds light on the efforts of countries in the Global South to promote the norm of racial equality in the UN system, observing that the Global North contests the development of a Global Racial Equality norm (GREN), principally by circumscribing antiracism and racial equality agendas within the borders of sovereign states. Provoked by George Floyd's lynching as well as global uprisings in support of global race equality, communities across the Global South began to re-advocate for a GREN, even petitioning the UN Human Rights Council in this regard. This progressive initiative was not new, having begun with decolonization, but was always resisted by the Global North.[12] Indeed, various actors within the Global North assign sole responsibility for racial equality to governments and their respective domestic populations, thus sidelining interstate and transnational confrontation with racial hierarchies.

The Global South's norm entrepreneurship and the issue of interstate racial equality provide valuable insights into non-Eurocentric understandings of norm entrepreneurship, as well as critiques of the colour line embedded within international law. However, this has not received sufficient attention as an empirical case for academic study. Existing research assumes that norm diffusion occurs between the Global North, as the norm-setting entity, and the Global South, as the norm-adopting entity. It also overlooks the significant case of the GREN in their examination of the agency question.[13]

This chapter's central argument posits that, on racial equality, Global North countries act as norm contesters, while the Global South assumes the role of norm entrepreneurs. This argument reveals the centrality of power in norm diffusion—the purpose of norm contestation is to maintain existing power structures, while norm entrepreneurship aims to challenge and overthrow them. Thus, the success of norm entrepreneurship depends on the outcomes of power struggles. Challenging the existing literature on norm diffusion, this study relocates the agency of norm entrepreneurship in the Global South and shows how power as an analytical category should not be marginalized in norm studies. Normatively, it aims to expose what Charles Mills identifies as 'white ignorance', a collective denial of the role of race and racism in the subordination of people of colour, perpetuating the belief in Euro-American ethical supremacy.[14]

I will proceed in three parts. First, I provide an overview of existing literature on international relations and public international law. I argue that existing research on norms exhibits the problem of 'racial blindness', ignoring the central role of race in the loci of agency and power. In the second part, I draw upon international legal perspectives and use an empirical example to illustrate the main argument. Specifically, I examine how the Africa Group and China engaged in norm entrepreneurship on the

[12] E Tendayi Achiume and Gay McDougall, 'Anti-Racism at the United Nations' (2023) 117 AJIL Unbound 82.

[13] Congyan Cai, *The Rise of China and International Law: Taking Chinese Exceptionalism Seriously* (Oxford University Press 2019); Carmen Wunderlich, *Rogue States as Norm Entrepreneurs: Black Sheep or Sheep in Wolves' Clothing?* (Springer 2020); Cristina G Stefan, 'The Responsibility to Protect: Locating Norm Entrepreneurship' (2021) 35 Ethics & International Affairs 197.

[14] Charles W Mills, 'Chapter 1. "White Ignorance"' in Shannon Sullivan and Nancy Tuana, *Race and Epistemologies of Ignorance* (State University of New York Press 2012); Charles W Mills, *Black Rights/White Wrongs: The Critique of Racial Liberalism* (Oxford University Press 2017).

issue of racial equality, while the Global North countries prevented potential progressive developments in this area. Finally, I conclude by explaining how this case study proposes an alternative understanding of norm entrepreneurship.

Ultimately, I argue that racialized power is central to understanding the development of norm diffusion, which does not always happen from the West to the non-West or from the core to the periphery. Similarly, it does not follow a model of linear progression. The success or failure of norm entrepreneurship is contingent upon the outcome of a power struggle between norm contesters and those seeking to maintain existing hierarchies and norm entrepreneurs who strive to dismantle them. Norm entrepreneurs face considerable resistance when norm contesters dominate existing hierarchies.

2. Norm entrepreneurship: insights from public international law and international relations

Norm entrepreneurs are key agents of norm advocacy and successful diffusion. Cass R Sunstein first coined the term 'norm entrepreneur' to describe individuals who seek to change social norms.[15] Martha Finnemore and Kathryn Sikkink then adopted it in their seminal three-stage life-cycle model (norm emergence, cascade, and internalization), highlighting the central role of norm entrepreneurs throughout the process.[16] The boomerang model by Keck and Sikkink[17] and the five-phase spiral model by Thomase Risse-Kappen and others[18] are also influential frameworks for conceptualizing norm diffusion.

Whatever the pathway of norm diffusion, there appears to be general agreement that norm entrepreneurship involves a group of individuals motivated by their moral beliefs and advocating for a specific norm. An outstanding example of a norm entrepreneur is Henry Dunant, who successfully advocated for the norm that medical personnel and wounded soldiers should be treated as non-combatants and neutrals in battle.[19] Another prominent case is Raphael Lemkin, who first coined the term 'genocide' and devoted his life to advocating for its codification as an international crime.[20] Many scholars have proposed various agents as norm entrepreneurs, including states,[21]

[15] Cass R Sunstein, 'Social Norms and Social Roles' (1996) 96 Columbia Law Review 903, 909.

[16] Martha Finnemore and Kathryn Sikkink, 'International Norm Dynamics and Political Change' (1998) 52 International Organization 887.

[17] Margaret E Keck, *Activists Beyond Borders: Advocacy Networks in International Politics* (Cornell University Press 2014).

[18] Thomas Risse-Kappen, Steve C Ropp, and Kathryn Sikkink (eds), *The Power of Human Rights: International Norms and Domestic Change* (Cambridge University Press 1999).

[19] Finnemore and Sikkink (n 16) 896–97.

[20] Douglas Irvin-Erickson, *Raphael Lemkin and the Concept of Genocide* (University of Pennsylvania Press 2017).

[21] Annika Björkdahl, 'From Idea to Norm: Promoting Conflict Prevention' (PhD Thesis/docmono, Lund University 2002) <http://lup.lub.lu.se/record/20760> accessed 9 April 2023; Annika Björkdahl, 'Constructing a Swedish Conflict Prevention Policy Based on a Powerful Idea and Successful Practice' (2007) 42 Cooperation and Conflict 169; Annika Björkdahl, 'Swedish Norm Entrepreneurship in the UN' in Eli Stamnes (ed), *Peace Support Operations* (Routledge 2008); Sara E Davies and Jacqui True, 'Norm Entrepreneurship in Foreign Policy: William Hague and the Prevention of Sexual Violence in Conflict' (2017) 13 Foreign Policy Analysis 701.

individuals,[22] lawmakers,[23] epistemic communities,[24] international bureaucracies, and transnational advocacy groups.[25]

A seemingly paradoxical but justified challenge to the study of norm entrepreneurship is the downplaying of the agency question—*whose ideas matter* in the canons' theoretical framework. A similar observation can be made regarding the wider narrative of human rights and public international law. For example, scholars have teased out the racist components of freedom and liberty, the key pillars of the human rights agenda. White freedom, as Tyler Stovall explains, sheds light on the intricately linked history of freedom and racism in the United States and France, unveiling how American and French intellectuals conceptualized freedom and liberty in racial contexts and as white privileges.[26] Ian Clark documents the rejection of Japan's proposal by major white powers on the racial equality clause in the Treaty of Versailles, which advocated for the equal treatment of nationals of all member states of the League of Nations.[27]

These cases raise several questions. Who has the agency to conduct norm entrepreneurship? Whose norms are advocated and rejected? Where did the norm originate, and is it framed as universal or particular? Later studies held that norm diffusion models did not provide satisfactory answers to these questions. Their first critique is that existing models of norm diffusion offer almost 'mechanistic and automatized processes', which paradoxically work to erase the agency of norm entrepreneurs.[28] Another criticism questions the idea of a fixed, universal norm being internalized by 'local' actors, such as national governments and lawmakers, and whether norm diffusion should be simply conceived as a unidirectional process where norm learners pick up the new norms instructed by norm entrepreneurs.[29] For example, Amitav Acharya famously proposes that norms are not simply replicated and internalized but *localized*, emphasizing both the agency of local political elites and the role of power and strategic considerations underlying their norm compliance.[30] Similarly, drawing from the postcolonial tradition of provincializing Europe,[31] Seth challenges the universality of international laws, cautioning against any claims of universal principles or

[22] Wunderlich (n 13) 24.

[23] Emanuela Carbonara, Francesco Parisi, and Georg von Wangenheim, 'Lawmakers as Norm Entrepreneurs' (2008) 4 Review of Law & Economics 779.

[24] Anthony R Zito, 'Epistemic Communities, Collective Entrepreneurship and European Integration' (2001) 8 Journal of European Public Policy 585; Kamil Zwolski and Christian Kaunert, 'The EU and Climate Security: A Case of Successful Norm Entrepreneurship?' (2011) 20 European Security 21.

[25] Keck (n 17); Risse-Kappen, Ropp, and Sikkink (n 18); Klotz (n 7); Sanjeev Khagram, James V Riker, and Kathryn Sikkink (eds), *Restructuring World Politics: Transnational Social Movements, Networks, and Norms* (University of Minnesota Press 2002).

[26] Tyler Stovall, *White Freedom: The Racial History of an Idea* (Princeton University Press 2021).

[27] Ian Clark, '4 Versailles and Racial Equality, 1919', in Ian Clark (ed), *International Legitimacy and World Society* (Oxford University Press, 2007) 87.

[28] Bernd Bucher, 'Acting Abstractions: Metaphors, Narrative Structures, and the Eclipse of Agency' (2014) 20 European Journal of International Relations 742, 742; Davies and True (n 21).

[29] Rebecca Adler-Nissen, 'Stigma Management in International Relations: Transgressive Identities, Norms, and Order in International Society' (2014) 68 International Organization 143.

[30] Amitav Acharya, 'How Ideas Spread: Whose Norms Matter? Norm Localization and Institutional Change in Asian Regionalism' (2004) 58 International Organization 239.

[31] Dipesh Chakrabarty, *Provincializing Europe* (Princeton University Press 2009).

normative values that are not generated bottom-up from local texts.[32] Pu also argues that norm diffusion should not be seen as one-way traffic, arguing that the socialization process in which norm diffusion occurs is a mutually interactive process.[33]

Building on this, I argue that the above canonical models also create a de facto white/non-white and North/South dichotomy, in which only the former has been empirically perceived as norm entrepreneurs providing momentum for norm diffusion. I have observed Western centrism[34] in existing research on norm entrepreneurship, which can be seen in the empirical examples used and the Normative Power Europe research agenda.[35] For instance, the cases of norm entrepreneurs offered by Finnemore and Sikkink[36] include 'Elizabeth Cady Stanton and Susan B Anthony in the United States and Millicent Garrett Fawcett and Emmeline Pankhurst in England' and Western-originated non-governmental organizations (NGOs) such as Greenpeace, the Red Cross, and Transafrica, an advocacy organization based in Washington DC. Most explicitly showing Western centrism is perhaps Risse and Sikkink's quote:[37]

> [W]e argue that the diffusion of international norms in the human rights arena crucially depends on the establishment and the sustainability of networks among domestic and transnational actors who manage to link up with international regimes, to alert *Western* public opinion and *Western* governments (emphasis added).

Illustrating the purpose of advocacy networks, Risse and Sikkink[38] declare the following:

> [T]hey put *norm-violating states* on the international agenda in terms of moral consciousness-raising. In doing so, they also remind *liberal states of their own identity as promoters of human rights* (emphasis added)

These statements not only succumb to an analytically fuzzy and homogeneous Western agent, but they also create a dichotomy between the agentic and moral West as promoters of human rights and the immoral non-West as violators who must be supervised and civilized by alerted, conscientious Western norm tutors. Given the

[32] Sanjay Seth, 'Postcolonial Theory and the Critique of International Relations' (2011) 40 Millennium 167.

[33] Pu Xiaoyu, 'Socialisation as a Two-Way Process: Emerging Powers and the Diffusion of International Norms' (2012) 5 The Chinese Journal of International Politics 341.

[34] Amitav Acharya and Barry Buzan, 'Why Is There No Non-Western International Relations Theory? An Introduction' (2007) 7 International Relations of the Asia-Pacific 287.

[35] Ian Manners, 'Normative Power Europe: A Contradiction in Terms?' (2002) 40 Journal of Common Market Studies 235; R Whitman, *Normative Power Europe: Empirical and Theoretical Perspectives* (Springer 2011); Anne Jenichen, 'The Politics of Normative Power Europe: Norm Entrepreneurs and Contestation in the Making of EU External Human Rights Policy' (2022) 60 Journal of Common Market Studies 1299.

[36] Finnemore and Sikkink (n 16) 897, 899.

[37] Thomas Risse and Kathryn Sikkink, 'The Socialization of International Human Rights Norms into Domestic Practices: Introduction' in Kathryn Sikkink, Stephen C Ropp, and Thomas Risse (eds), *The Power of Human Rights: International Norms and Domestic Change* (Cambridge University Press 1999) 5.

[38] ibid.

dominance of the white race in the 'West' or the Global North, it is fair to say that the fault line also coincides with the white/non-white racial boundary.

An emerging research trend is to go beyond the tradition of taking Global South countries only as norm learners, to take their agency and identity *as norm entrepreneurs* seriously. Rebecca Adler-Nissen theorized that states who are 'named and shamed' can exercise their own agency to counter the stigmatization from international society as transgressive norm-violators.[39] Stefan demonstrated that Global South countries such as Brazil and Egypt were the crucial norm entrepreneurs regarding the Responsibility to Protect doctrine.[40] Perhaps the most innovative is Wunderlich's attempt to re-imagine *rogue states* (here, Iran) as norm entrepreneurs.[41] These studies rectify the long-assumed misconception in mainstream norm research that norm diffusion is a unidirectional *social* process occurring only from the centre to the periphery and from the white Global North to the non-white Global South. Somewhat neglected, however, is that norm entrepreneurship is not just a social process, but also a *political* one. This critical constructivist approach highlights the importance of political debates and arguments in shaping norms.[42] Likewise, insights from international law are crucial for understanding the role of power dynamics and advocacy in shaping normative hierarchies[43] and the agency of 'non-great powers' in bringing about progressive changes.[44]

Several parallels exist between the academic interpretations of international laws and international norms, which can be likened to the concept of norm entrepreneurship.[45] Laws, like norms, are co-constitutive of societies. The emergence of both can be understood from a constructivist perspective, following the formation of 'greater solidarity' beyond the narrow understanding of individual states' interests.[46] Both law-making and norm-making entail a constant contestation process.[47] Moreover, this diffusion results from the broadening and thickening of the international community.[48] Both laws and norms can claim the status of 'universality' during their

[39] ibid.

[40] Stefan (n 13).

[41] Wunderlich (n 13).

[42] Mona Lena Krook and Jacqui True, 'Rethinking the Life Cycles of International Norms: The United Nations and the Global Promotion of Gender Equality' (2012) 18 European Journal of International Relations 103; Wayne Sandholtz, *Prohibiting Plunder: How Norms Change* (Oxford University Press 2007); Kees Van Kersbergen and Bertjan Verbeek, 'The Politics of International Norms: Subsidiarity and the Imperfect Competence Regime of the European Union' (2007) 13 European Journal of International Relations 217.

[43] Janice Bially Mattern, 'Why "Soft Power" Isn't So Soft: Representational Force and the Sociolinguistic Construction of Attraction in World Politics' (2005) 33 Millennium 583; Ann E Towns, 'Norms and Social Hierarchies: Understanding International Policy Diffusion "From Below"' (2012) 66 International Organization 179; Ann E Towns and Bahar Rumelili, 'Taking the Pressure: Unpacking the Relation between Norms, Social Hierarchies, and Social Pressures on States' (2017) 23 European Journal of International Relations 756.

[44] Adam Bower, *Norms Without the Great Powers: International Law and Changing Social Standards in World Politics* (Oxford University Press 2016).

[45] Lassa Oppenheim, *The Collected Papers of John Westlake on Public International Law* (Cambridge University Press 2014) 3; Cai (n 13) 14.

[46] Bruno Simma, 'From Bilateralism to Community Interest in International Law (Volume 250)' *Collected Courses of the Hague Academy of International Law* (Brill 1994) 229.

[47] Jutta Brunnée and Stephen J Toope, 'Norm Robustness and Contestation in International Law: Self-Defense against Nonstate Actors' (2019) 4 Journal of Global Security Studies 73.

[48] Cai (n 13) 18.

diffusion,[49] while also facing resistance due to conflicting values from different actors.[50]

One of the most significant contrasts between studies on norm and law entrepreneurship is how the latter is explicit about its political nature, highlighting the significance of power in accounting for the outcomes and states' motivations to engage in entrepreneurship.[51] In international relations, norm entrepreneurship is often understood to follow moral reasoning and the logic of appropriateness, whereas in international law, the general consensus is that states leverage law-making to advance their positions within global hierarchies. Historically, great powers have used international law to further their interests, particularly in the context of colonialism.[52] Likewise, great powers often resist and challenge the implementation of international laws that are unfavourable to their interests.[53]

After the Second World War, powerful and ascendant states sought to promote legal entrepreneurship to enhance the legitimacy of both the international order and their own rise. Furthermore, scholars reject the notion that international law is politically neutral and objective or simply a tool for rhetorical legitimation.[54] Instead, Shirley Scott proposes the concept of International Law as Ideology (ILI), which argues that states have a vested interest in promoting the ideology of international law in power struggles,[55] with international law thus becoming 'the vehicle for inter-state competition'.[56] Similarly, Congyan Cai insightfully observes that China has not only been socialized into the international legal order but has also actively made international laws to justify its rise, and eventually, to benefit it.[57]

The nexus between international relations and international law helps to reveal power dynamics and agency questions at the core of norm entrepreneurship. States can participate in the creation of norms, just as they do in law creation, and they also have a vested interest in promoting norms that align with their own legitimacy while opposing those that do not. This is evident through the case of 'norm-law gap'.[58]

[49] Bruno Simma, 'Universality of International Law from the Perspective of a Practitioner' (2009) 20 European Journal of International Law 265.

[50] Seth (n 32); Hisashi Owada, 'Conflict of Values in International Law: Universality of International Law in a Globalizing World' (2013) 14 Austrian Review of International and European Law 7; Stefan Oeter, 'Conflicting Norms, Values, and Interests: A Perspective from Legal Academia' (2019) 33 Ethics and International Affairs 57.

[51] Oscar Schachter, *International Law in Theory and Practice* (M Nijhoff Publishers 1991) 5–9.

[52] Antony Anghie, *Imperialism, Sovereignty and the Making of International Law* (Cambridge University Press 2005); Nico Krisch, 'International Law in Times of Hegemony: Unequal Power and the Shaping of the International Legal Order' (2005) 16 European Journal of International Law 369; Gerry Simpson, *Great Powers and Outlaw States: Unequal Sovereigns in the International Legal Order* (Cambridge University Press 2004).

[53] Helen Keller and Daniela Thurnherr, *Taking International Law Seriously: A European Perspective on the U.S. Attitude towards International Law* (Staempfli Publishers 2005).

[54] Radhika Withana, *Power, Politics, Law: International Law and State Behaviour During International Crises* (Brill Nijhoff 2008) 1, 19.

[55] Shirley V Scott, 'International Law as Ideology: Theorizing the Relationship between International Law and International Politics' (1994) 5 European Journal of International Law 313.

[56] Withana (n 54) 237.

[57] Cai (n 13).

[58] Zoltan I Búzás, 'Is the Good News About Law Compliance Good News About Norm Compliance? The Case of Racial Equality' (2018) 72 International Organization 351; Zoltan I Búzás, *Evading International Norms: Race and Rights in the Shadow of Legality* (University of Pennsylvania Press 2021).

Zoltan Búzás observes domestic racism in France and the Czech Republic regarding their 'humanitarian returns' of Roma communities, captioning it as the 'awful but lawful' practice.[59] Búzás's conclusion suggests that states can resist unwanted human rights obligations by violating international norms while remaining technically legal because only selective reflection exists between norms and laws.[60] This example challenges the widely held belief that the legalization of certain practices strengthens human rights norms, as it exposes the ways in which states use legality to evade their normative obligations and prioritize their own interests.[61] It further underlines the importance of integrating IR and IL perspectives in the study of norm entrepreneurship, as it provides a more comprehensive understanding of the power dynamics and interest calculations involved in states' normative entrepreneurship and contestation behaviours.

To summarize, the perspectives of IR and IL shed light on the dynamics and incentives of norm entrepreneurship. While frameworks from IR are extensive and rigorous, they sometimes underdeliver on the agency question, creating an implicit 'subject–object' dichotomy of norm diffusion along the global colour line. It is most often norms originating from white, Western contexts that are *imagined as the source of universality*, and norm diffusion imagined as proliferated by principally minded, white normative agents. Despite the evident bias, empirical white-centrism often eludes existing critiques of norm entrepreneurship. In the following section, I track Global South states' norm entrepreneurship in support of the GREN and analyse China's presence in this endeavour.

3. Relocating agency in the Global South: the case of global racial equality

The momentum for norm entrepreneurship on global racial equality often gathers pace following significant sociopolitical events, such as the decolonization movement after the Second World War, the civil rights movement in the US, and the recent Black Lives Matter movement. Some initiatives have proven successful, as seen in the struggle against apartheid in South Africa, while others flounder.[62] For example, despite the civil rights movement leading the way towards a more equitable US society, certain public spaces remain predominantly white and both de facto segregation and institutional racism persist.[63] Ashley Quarcoo even declares that 'all western democracies have an enduring race problem'.[64] Although racial injustices within domestic

[59] Búzás, 'Is the Good News About Law Compliance Good News About Norm Compliance?' (n 58); Búzás, *Evading International Norms* (n 58).
[60] Búzás, *Evading International Norms* (n 58) 4.
[61] ibid.
[62] Klotz (n 7).
[63] Kathleen Fitzgerald, *Recognizing Race and Ethnicity: Power, Privilege, and Inequality* (2nd edn, Westview Press 2017); Paul A Jargowsky, 'The Persistence of Segregation in the 21st Century The Summit for Civil Rights - Nov. 9-10, 2017' (2018) 36 Law and Inequality: A Journal of Theory and Practice 207.
[64] Ashley Quarcoo, 'Three Takeaways on the Protests for Racial Equality' (*Carnegie Endowment for International Peace*, 9 June 2020) <https://carnegieendowment.org/2020/06/09/three-takeaways-on-protests-for-racial-equality-pub-82021> accessed 10 April 2023.

society are being addressed through research and activism, interstate and transnational forms of racism are frequently overlooked.

At the heart of the UN legal system on racial equality are the International Convention on the Elimination of All Forms of Racial Discrimination (ICERD) and the Durban Declaration and Programme of Action (DDPA). The ICERD specifies the implications and manifestations of racial discrimination, including provisions that forbid segregation and apartheid, prohibit hate speech that is racist in nature, and establish the rights of people from diverse ethnic backgrounds, skin colours, or countries of origin.[65] Although it is commendable that international relations are in a progressive stage of decolonization, the legal obligation is for states to ensure racial equality only within their borders, with no provision regulating the conduct of states in international affairs. Moreover, because of Westphalian sovereignty, the existing tenets remain unchallenged.

The World Conference against Racism was held in 2001. This event led to the creation of the DDPA, which called for concrete action by states and other actors to address the needs of people of African descent.[66] This marked a significant development, since only a year earlier Afro-descendants were first recognized as subjects of rights in international human rights law at the Regional Conference in Santiago.[67] Durban I achieved a negotiated outcome remembered because of the breadth of its political contestation. In 2009, the Durban Review Conference (Durban II) was held, followed by a high-level UN General Assembly meeting in 2011 to commemorate the tenth anniversary of the DDPA (Durban III) and another in 2021 to mark the twentieth anniversary (Durban IV).

Another milestone towards global racial equality is the recent urgent debate called by the Africa Group. In 2020, following the extrajudicial killing of George Floyd (and the subsequent antiracism protests that spread globally), a group of fifty-four African UN member states, UN experts on antiracism, and transnational civil society advocacy groups formed a coalition of norm entrepreneurs. Through the UN Human Rights Council Resolution 43/1, the network called for international investigations into systemic racism in law enforcement, not only in the US but globally.[68] As such, it was the 'first and only [HRC Special Session] explicitly framed as concerning systemic racial injustice and anti-Black racism in a First World nation-state'.[69] The Global

[65] International Convention on the Elimination of Racial Discrimination (adopted 21 December 1965, entered into force 4 January 1969) 660 UNTS 195 (ICERD); Patrick Thornberry (ed), *The International Convention on the Elimination of All Forms of Racial Discrimination: A Commentary* (Oxford University Press 2016).

[66] Mary Robinson, United Nations High Commissioner for Human Rights, 'Opening Statement of Durban Conference' (Opening Statement at World Conference against Racism, Racial Discrimination, Xenophobia and Related Intolerance, Durban, 31 August 2001) <https://www.ohchr.org/en/statements/2009/10/statement-opening-durban-conference-mary-robinson-united-nations-high> accessed 10 April 2024; United Nations, 'Durban Declaration and Programme of Action' (*United Nations*) <https://www.un.org/en/fight-racism/background/durban-declaration-and-programme-of-action> accessed 12 April 2023.

[67] Roberto Rojas Davila, 'Afro-Descendants as Subjects of Rights in International Human Rights Law Repositioning Race in the International Agenda: Essays' (2018) 15 Sur—International Journal on Human Rights 151.

[68] Achiume and McDougall (n 12) 84.

[69] E Tendayi Achiume, 'Transnational Racial (In)Justice in Liberal Democratic Empire Comments' (2020) 134 Harvard Law Review Forum 378, 378.

South, particularly the African Group, took the lead in creating norms through the DDPA. I use the term 'reversed agency dichotomy' to capture the dynamic where the Global North was 'named and shamed', held accountable by the Global South to adopt a progressive global norm.

Currently, China is actively participating in a global racial equality regime. China has collaborated with the Africa Group to establish and maintain a coalition against racism to continue advocating for the promotion of racial equality norms within the UN. This coalition has provided critical insights and timely interpretations of the GREN, consistently surpassing the conventional understanding of racial equality as a national issue for sovereign nations. China has consistently supported the Durban Conferences through its participation in joint statements with the Group of 77. For example, the 2006 Joint Statement expressed concern about the rise of intolerance following the 11 September 2001 events, noting that '[i]t is regrettable that the fight against terrorism has been equated with Islam, which has given rise to racial and religious intolerance'.[70] Thus, this statement incorporates interstate conduct into the official understanding of racism, thereby widening the range of corresponding policy solutions. Another innovation involves the push to treat racism in sports as a transnational issue; for example, by urging FIFA to work towards creating 'a world of sport free from racism and racial discrimination'.[71]

China issued a 2021 Joint Statement with the Group of 77 on Combating Racism, Racial Discrimination, Xenophobia, and Related Intolerance, which specifically mentioned antiracism relating to Asians and people of Asian descent.[72] Similarly, the statement by the Chinese Foreign Minister made during Durban IV emphasizes that 'African and Asian descent and indigenous peoples' are commonly viewed as victims of the slave trade and colonialism and thus are eligible for inclusion in the DDPA's victim-centred approach.[73] This acknowledgement represents a new development in the global fight against racism, as it places racism against Asians on par with that against Africans. This may be a response to the surge in anti-Asian racism during the COVID-19 pandemic,[74] while also marking the first step towards addressing the historical injustices faced by Asians.[75]

[70] The Group of 77 and China, 'Statement on Behalf of the Group of 77 and China by Ambassador Dumisani S. Kumalo Permanent Representative of the Republic of South Africa to The United Nations on Agenda Item 65: Comprehensive Implementation and Follow-Up To The Durban Declaration And Programme Of Action, In the Third Committee of the General Assembly' (*G77*, 6 November 2006) <https://www.g77.org/Speeches/110606.html> accessed 13 April 2023.

[71] ibid.

[72] Permanent Mission of the People's Republic of China to the UN, 'Joint Statement on Combating Racism, Racial Discrimination, Xenophobia and Related Intolerance' (Permanent Mission of the People's Republic of China to the UN, 30 September 2021) <http://un.china-mission.gov.cn/eng/hyyfy/202110/t20211001_9568895.htm> accessed 12 April 2023.

[73] HE Wang Yi, 'Eliminating Racism and Building a World of Equality for All' (*The People's Republic of China Ministry of Foreign Affairs*, 23 September 2021) <https://www.fmprc.gov.cn/mfa_eng/wjdt_665385/zyjh_665391/202109/t20210923_9580294.html> accessed 13 April 2023.

[74] Hannah Tessler, Meera Choi, and Grace Kao, 'The Anxiety of Being Asian American: Hate Crimes and Negative Biases During the COVID-19 Pandemic' (2020) 45 American Journal of Criminal Justice 636.

[75] Erika Lee, 'The "Yellow Peril" and Asian Exclusion in the Americas' (2007) 76 Pacific Historical Review 537; Joel Franks, 'Anti-Asian Exclusion in the United States during the Nineteenth and Twentieth Centuries: The History Leading to the Immigration Act of 1924' (2015) 34 Journal of American Ethnic History 121.

China further endorsed Resolution 43/1, issuing a statement in support of the Africa Group's initiative for this urgent debate:

> We urge the U.S . . . to eliminate racism, racial discrimination and other human rights violations and protect the legitimate rights of ethnic minorities; to stop using human rights as a political tool and abandon double standards. We call on the international community to intensify consensus by fully implementing [DDPA].[76]

China's active involvement suggests that it is using antiracism as a crucial aspect of its identity and a means of fostering cooperation among African states, as it seeks to challenge the US for global prestige. For example, in March 2023, China published 'The Report on Human Rights Violations in the United States in 2022', which highlighted the increasing racial discrimination and inequality faced by African Americans, Asian Americans, and Native Americans.[77]

Despite its support for a GREN, China has also been criticized for its human rights record, particularly regarding the treatment of ethnic minorities.[78] The Committee on the Elimination of Racism (CERD) has urged China to 'immediately investigate all allegations of human rights violations in the Xinjiang Uyghur Autonomous Region'.[79] If one considers the global racial equality regime to be intertwined with the human rights regime, then China's participation can be seen as a double move. On the one hand, China has supported the development of a GREN, actively participating in existing institutions that promote racial equality and uphold the legitimacy of this architecture within the UN system.[80] China has strongly embraced antiracism in its official discourse. On the other hand, in response to criticisms of human rights violations, China asserts that it prioritizes collective well-being in its approach to human rights.[81] To China, this amounts to a form of provincializing the universality of human rights narratives, generating counter-narratives from non-Western, local contexts, a claim some critics argue amounts to a deflection of the underlying issue.

[76] Permanent Mission of the People's Republic of China to the UN, 'Statement at the Urgent Debate at the 43rd Session of the Human Rights Council' (Permanent Mission of the People's Republic of China to the UN, 17 June 2020) <http://geneva.china-mission.gov.cn/eng/dbdt/202006/t20200618_8192531.htm> accessed 12 April 2023.

[77] The State Council Information Office of the People's Republic of China, 'The Report on Human Rights Violations in the United States in 2022' (*Embassy of the People's Republic of China in Georgia*, 28 March 2023) <http://ge.china-embassy.gov.cn/eng/xwdt/202303/t20230328_11050361.htm> accessed 13 April 2023.

[78] Michael Clarke, 'Widening the Net: China's Anti-Terror Laws and Human Rights in the Xinjiang Uyghur Autonomous Region' (2010) 14 International Journal of Human Rights 542.

[79] OHCHR, 'China: UN Committee on the Elimination of Racial Discrimination Calls for Probe into Xinjiang Rights Violations' (*OHCHR*, 24 November 2022) <https://www.ohchr.org/en/press-releases/2022/11/china-un-committee-elimination-racial-discrimination-calls-probe-xinjiang> accessed 12 April 2023.

[80] Yinghong Cheng, 'From Campus Racism to Cyber Racism: Discourse of Race and Chinese Nationalism' (2011) 207 The China Quarterly 561; Yinghong Cheng, *Discourses of Race and Rising China* (Palgrave Macmillan 2019); Frank Dikötter, *The Discourse of Race in Modern China* (Hurst 2015).

[81] The People's Republic of China Ministry of Foreign Affairs, 'Position Paper on China's Cooperation with the United Nations' (*The People's Republic of China Ministry of Foreign Affairs*, 22 October 2021) <https://www.fmprc.gov.cn/mfa_eng/wjdt_665385/wjzcs/202110/t20211022_9609380.html> accessed 12 April 2023.

Nonetheless, China remaining within the UN's human protection schemes may result in some progress in human rights globally. Recent studies have shown that, despite its initial opposition to UN humanitarian protection activities based on sovereign equality, China has now become a crucial contributing actor in these efforts, even engaging in norm entrepreneurship by interpreting and influencing the implementation of relevant norms.[82] Continuing to support the UN's framework for racial equality and human rights and standing with the Africa Group in their norm entrepreneurship may imply that China is open for the gradual internalization of norms.

Despite the Global South's norm entrepreneurship, the diffusion of the GREN has not progressed seamlessly due to self-benefiting norm contestation from the Global North. In Durban I, with support from the wider Global South, the Africa Group advocated for a strong resolution designating slavery as a crime against humanity and the implementation of substantial debt cancellation. The Global North, comprising Western European states and the US, resolutely opposed these measures.[83] Ultimately, the conference failed to hold former colonial states accountable for reparations, with the US eventually withdrawing from the talks because much of the Global South advocated for a consensus that Zionism is a form of racism.[84]

Several Western states boycotted Durban II, ostensibly because of the Zionism as racism movement yet again.[85] At Durban III, fourteen countries from the Western Europe and Other States Group (WEOG), including the US, boycotted the event, and at Durban IV, the number of boycotting countries grew to thirty-eight, along with the European Union.[86] According to Tendayi Achiume and Gay McDougall—legal scholars who have held professional UN capacities—norm contestation by Global North countries represents a 'twenty-year-long, unprincipled opposition of members of [WEOG] within the United Nations to [DDPA], which they have used to block progressive efforts to dismantle contemporary and historic racial injustice'.[87] It should come as no surprise that several of these countries are the greatest beneficiaries of colonialism, historic slavery, and racial hierarchies.[88]

Norm contestation from the Global North also occurs at a conceptual level. The Global North's conceptual contestation insists on treating race as a matter of internal

[82] Rosemary Foot, *China, the UN, and Human Protection: Beliefs, Power, Image* (Oxford University Press 2020).

[83] Suhas Chakma, *The Issue of Compensation for Colonialism and Slavery at the World Conference Against Racism: A Fine Balance Between Rhetoric and Legality* (Brill Nijhoff 2003).

[84] It is noteworthy that some African member states expressed opposition towards reparations. However, this was not based on a disagreement with the principle of reparations itself, but due to the belief that colonial suffering continues to impact the present and that the closure that could be achieved through monetary compensation alone was insufficient. See Rojas Davila (n 67).

[85] Laura MacInnis, 'Western Boycott Threatens U.N. Racism Forum' *Reuters* (19 April 2009) <https://www.reuters.com/article/us-racism-un-idUSLJ34980320090419> accessed 12 April 2023.

[86] World Jewish Congress, '38 Countries Boycott Antisemitic Durban IV Conference' (*World Jewish Congress*, 24 September 2021) <https://www.worldjewishcongress.org/en/news/38-countries-boycott-antisemitic-durban-iv-conference> accessed 12 April 2023.

[87] Achiume and McDougall (n 12) 82.

[88] The United Office at Geneva, 'UN Expert Criticises Boycott of Durban Process against Racism, Calls for Action' (*UN Office at Geneva*, 28 October 2021) <https://www.ungeneva.org/en/news-media/news/2021/10/un-expert-criticises-boycott-durban-process-against-racism-calls-action> accessed 12 April 2023.

affairs, stifling discussions on transnational racial injustice and interstate racism.[89] Conceptual norm contestation has a profound negative effect on norm diffusion. By limiting the understanding of antiracism and racial equality within sovereign states' borders, institutional efforts at the global level to address and rectify such racial harm remain inconceivable.

In the aftermath of the global racial equality uprisings, members of WEOG strongly objected to the Global South's norm entrepreneurship around a GREN, resorting to 'economic and political threats against weaker states'.[90] Consequently, the UN Human Rights Council Resolution 43/1 was passed, mandating a comprehensive report on systemic racism, but avoiding calling for an international commission to investigate racism in US law enforcement, which was also proposed at the beginning of the urgent debate.[91] In other words, a possible resolution to institutional establishment was thwarted, which could have helped advance the struggle against racial injustice in the Global North. WEOG members shielded themselves from future legal claims and avoided putting their own racial equality practices under examination by the international society.

We observed evident hypocrisy from the WEOG. While the Global North has been actively endorsing responsibility to protect (R2P) since 2001, a norm that cuts across state boundaries and in a way erodes the sovereignty principle, it has resisted loosening its own sovereign boundaries when it comes to racial equality. Endorsing R2P while resisting a racial equality norm exposes the WEOG's selective commitment to global justice—intervention is permitted when it aligns with geopolitical interests, but withheld when structural racism implicates members of the bloc. This double standard reveals the deeply racialized character of the universality claimed when pressing R2P, foregrounding the power struggles involved in norm contestation and entrepreneurship.

4. Conclusion: norm entrepreneurship revisited

This chapter discusses norm entrepreneurship surrounding the GREN by the Global South as well as the related norm contestation from the Global North. I treated power as a crucial analytical category in understanding norm diffusion, challenging the existing Eurocentric literature that arrogates to the Global North more moral fibre and greater normative agency.

Re-introducing the lens of power into norm entrepreneurship reveals that resistance and contestation emerge when the Global North is the object of a normative challenge. The sustained boycott by the Global North of DDPA is the main reason the GREN has not yet become an accepted global standard. Successful counter-advocacy in the DDPA has also deflected discussions on the issue of compensation. The Global

[89] Li (n 11); Achiume and McDougall (n 12) 82–83.

[90] Achiume and McDougall (n 12) 84.

[91] OHCHR, 'Seminal UN Report Offers an Agenda to Dismantle Systemic Racism' (*OHCHR*, 29 June 2021) <https://www.ohchr.org/en/stories/2021/06/seminal-un-report-offers-agenda-dismantle-systemic-racism> accessed 12 April 2023.

North's norm contestation manifests in a parochial understanding of the norm, confining racial equality within state boundaries and avoiding systemic discussion on interstate and transnational racial equality.

This chapter centres agency in the Global South through the issue of global racial equality. The Group of 77 and China—especially the Africa Group—have led advocacy around a GREN. Together with other norm entrepreneurs, including independent legal experts and transnational civil advocacy groups, the Global South has achieved progress towards this new norm, among which the Durban Declaration and Programme of Action is a major milestone. Their meaningful antiracism coalition adds weight to the power struggle of norm entrepreneurship against norm contestation, gradually tilting the balance towards the overturning of existing global structural racial inequality. Although there is still a long way to go, persistent norm advocacy by the Group of 77 and China speaks for their powerful agency in shaping the agenda of global norms, redefining the full scope of racial equality, and negotiating action plans. This case suggests that norm research should not presume the Global South as the norm diffusion target or the Global North as the entrepreneur.

Similarly, China has contributed its own interpretation of the central notion of racism by elevating racism against Asian people to the same ontological level as African people, although this is still conspicuously missing in the 2021 Joint Statement. China is observed to oppose the current approach to human rights, insisting that it be elevated to the same status as other human rights protections. There is debate over whether China is seeking legitimacy in the international order through its efforts to establish new norms, as it competes with the US on a global scale. In this sense, power also provides a critical lens for understanding norm entrepreneurship by rising states.

Of course, the Global South is not homogeneous. Countries can have varied interpretations of global racial equality, and may act differently based on a delicate balance between self-benefiting calculations and normative reasoning. Among the recent groups boycotting Durban IV are Global South countries that are members of the Group of 77, such as the Dominican Republic and Honduras, which may suggest a wide spectrum of international (pressures from Western countries) and domestic power dynamics (status quo of domestic racial hierarchy) in shaping the coalition of norm contestation. The evolving struggle over the GREN ultimately underscores a deeper contest over global moral authority—one in which the Global South is no longer merely a subject of norms but an active force in their creation and contestation.

PART V

TAKING THE STRUGGLE(S) FORWARD

19

From Captives to Enslaved

International Law and the Making of the (Non)Human

Darryl Li[*]

> We are going to have to struggle for an entirely new definition of what it is to be human.[1]
>
> Sylvia Wynter

1. Introduction

What would international law look like if theorized from the institution of slavery—specifically, the system of racialized chattel slavery that emerged in the Atlantic world and was a founding condition of capitalist modernity?[2] Slavery was, after all, a thoroughly legal enterprise—it was structured and enabled by legal mechanisms, and it shaped legal systems in countless ways.[3] In the Atlantic context, it was also a key site of racialization, unfolding on a scale that linked disparate continents and cut across

[*] This is an edited excerpt from Darryl Li, 'Genres of Universalism: Reading Race Into International Law, With Help From Sylvia Wynter' (2021) 67 UCLA Law Review 1686.

[1] Greg Thomas, 'PROUD FLESH Inter/Views: Sylvia Wynter' (2006) 4 ProudFlesh: A New Afrikan Journal of Culture, Politics & Consciousness 1, 13.

[2] This premise builds on a voluminous literature. See, eg, Paul Gilroy, *The Black Atlantic: Modernity and Double Consciousness* (Verso 1993); Cedric J Robinson, *Black Marxism: The Making of the Black Radical Tradition* (University of North Carolina Press 1983); Walter Rodney, *How Europe Underdeveloped Africa* (Bogle-L'Ouverture Publications and Tanzania Publishing House 1972); CLR James, *The Black Jacobins: Toussaint L'Ouverture and the San Domingo Revolution* (Vintage Books 1989); Eric Williams, *Capitalism & Slavery* (University of North Carolina Press 1944); WEB Du Bois, *Black Reconstruction: An Essay Toward a History of the Part Which Black Folk Played in the Attempt to Reconstruct Democracy in America, 1860–1880* (Harcourt, Brace and Co 1935).

[3] Much of the international law scholarship on slavery focuses on abolitionist efforts—whether as instances of early human rights projects or as justification for imperial expansion—rather than the legal architecture of the institution itself. See, eg, Lauren Benton, 'Abolition and Imperial Law, 1790–1820' (2011) 39(3) Journal of Imperial & Commonwealth History 355; Jenny S Martinez, *The Slave Trade and the Origins of International Human Rights Law* (Oxford University Press 2012); see also WEB Du Bois, *The Suppression of the African Slave-Trade to the United States of America 1638–1870* (Longman, Green and Co 1896) 92–105. For more recent work highlighting the role of race in the international repression of slavery and its place in histories of international criminal law, see Emily Haslam, *The Slave Trade, Abolition and the Long History of International Criminal Law: The Recaptive and the Victim* (Routledge 2020); Vasuki Nesiah, 'Crimes Against Humanity: Racialized Subjects and Deracialized Histories', in Immi Tallgren and Thomas Skouteris (eds), *The New Histories of International Criminal Law: Retrials* (Oxford University Press 2019).

Darryl Li, *From Captives to Enslaved* In: *Emancipating International Law*. Edited by: Mohsen al Attar and Claire Smith, Oxford University Press. © Darryl Li 2026. DOI: 10.1093/9780198935605.003.0025

manifold jurisdictions. Transnational anti-Black racism as produced by this world poses particular challenges for international legal theorizing. As pan-Africanists have long argued, the geographical dispersion of the Black diaspora among nation-states where they are nearly always captive minorities makes resorting to a state-based system such as international law particularly unavailing.[4] The UN Commission on Human Rights has recognized this challenge by establishing a Working Group of Experts on People of African Descent.[5] But the Working Group's utility at times seems to come despite, rather than through, international law; perhaps its boldest move, supporting reparations for slavery in the United States, references not international law but rather proposed domestic legislation.[6]

This chapter argues that as a doctrinal matter, contemporary international law treats race as a generic form of social differentiation to be managed by separate nation-states, nearly indistinguishable from ethnicity and national origin. If international law constructs race as a category both local and vague, this Article argues for the importance of theorizing racialization instead as a process, one that is both transregional (if not global) and specific. In order to identify new ways of theorizing race and international law together, I turn to Atlantic slavery as a conceptual starting point, inspired by the writings of the Jamaican thinker Sylvia Wynter (1928–).[7] The Atlantic slave trade as a legal assemblage cannot be understood in strictly national terms; it cannot be understood apart from the emergence of specifically anti-Black forms of racism in the contexts of settler colonialism; and it cannot be understood without reference to political economy. For these reasons, theorizing from the history of Atlantic slavery is useful for confronting the key weaknesses in international law's prevailing approaches to race and, by extension, its assumptions about the category of humanity.[8]

A major figure in Black feminist theory, Wynter's work has had a far-reaching influence in numerous fields.[9] In this chapter, I argue that her work also presents a useful

[4] See, eg, Marcus Garvey, 'The True Solution of the Negro Problem' (Teaching American History) <https://teachingamericanhistory.org/library/document/the-true-solution-of-the-negro-problem> accessed 13 November 2024 ('If the Negro were to live in this Western Hemisphere for another five hundred years he would still be outnumbered by other races who are prejudiced against him. He cannot resort to the government for protection for government will be in the hands of the majority of the people who are prejudiced against him . . . The future of the Negro therefore, outside of Africa, spells ruin and disaster.').

[5] UN Commission on Human Rights, Resolution 68 (2002) UN Doc E/CN.4/RES/2002/68, 8.

[6] See UN Human Rights Council, 'Report of the Working Group of Experts on People of African Descent on Its Mission to the U.S' (18 August 2016) UN Doc A/HRC/33/61/Add 2, paras 91–95.

[7] In attempting to theorize international order from the paradigm of slavery, the analysis in this chapter is indebted to Adom Getachew's reconstruction of the 'dual critique of empire as a form of enslavement and international racial hierarchy' as developed by WEB Du Bois and other Black radicals. Adom Getachew, *Worldmaking After Empire: The Rise and Fall of Self-Determination* (Princeton University Press 2019) 80.

[8] The marginalization and erasure of the Atlantic slave trade has contributed to a parallel fragmentation and methodological nationalism in international labour law. See Amin Parsa and Niklas Selberg, 'Decolonizing Labour Law: A Conversation with Professor Adelle Blackett' (*TWAILR: Dialogues*, 24 January 2021) <https://twailr.com/decolonizing-labour-law-a-conversation-with-professor-adelle-blackett> accessed 13 November 2024.

[9] For some of the more influential texts that have taken up Wynter's thought, see, eg, Kathryn Yusoff, *A Billion Black Anthropocenes or None* (University of Minnesota Press 2018); Alexander G Weheliye, *Habeas Viscus: Racializing Assemblages, Biopolitics, and Black Feminist Theories of the Human* (Duke University Press 2014); Katherine McKittrick, *Demonic Grounds: Black Women and the Cartographies of Struggle* (University of Minnesota Press 2006) 121–41; Paget Henry, *Caliban's Reason: Introducing Afro-Caribbean Philosophy* (Routledge 2000) 117–43. For a helpful collection of essays about Wynter that include extensive dialogues with her, see Katherine McKittrick (ed), *Sylvia Wynter: On Being Human as Praxis* (Duke

site of theoretical reflection about law, and I hope this discussion encourages other legal scholars to engage with her work.[10]

Wynter's life story is also relevant for situating this intervention. Wynter was born in Cuba to Jamaican parents who returned home when she was still a young child. This background influenced her decision to study Spanish literature in the United Kingdom, where she joined a Caribbean dance troupe that toured Europe. Wynter later achieved acclaim with her 1962 novel *The Hills of Hebron*. A brief and disillusioning stint working with anticolonial nationalists in British Guiana, coupled with her experience with racial politics in the United States after her relocation there in the 1970s, led Wynter to reconsider her intellectual and political origins in Caribbean Marxism to more explicitly address questions of race and gender.[11] Wynter's competencies and experiences—thinking across Blackness and Indigeneity in both Anglophone and Hispanic imperial contexts—make her a particularly helpful interlocutor for those working in the Third World Approaches to International Law (TWAIL) and Critical Race Theory (CRT) traditions.

Over the course of several decades, Wynter has developed a theoretical vocabulary for reconsidering questions of the human subject that bear directly on international law's longstanding preoccupation with questions of universalism. Critical interventions regarding international law—to say nothing of law more generally—have long been characterized by a dialectic of 'reform and resistance'.[12] On the one hand, there is the impulse to unmask law's universalist claims as a façade for white supremacy, empire, capitalism, patriarchy, or other structures of domination. On the other hand, the total rejection of all universalist claims seems politically regressive and raises serious questions of conceptual coherence, thus encouraging advocacy for a more inclusive and just form of universalism. The TWAIL tradition in particular has excelled at undermining international law's claims to universality as concealing or justifying all manner of abuses, including colonialism, while also effectively invoking non-Western legal traditions as alternative sources of inspiration for thought or action.[13]

University Press 2015); Anthony Bogues (ed), *After Man, Towards the Human: Critical Essays on Sylvia Wynter* (Ian Randle Publishers 2005). A collection of essays in the journal Small Axe also helpfully reconstructs the trajectory of Wynter's thought in dialogue with her 935-page unpublished manuscript. See generally Aaron Kamugisha (guest editor), 'Sylvia Wynter's "Black Metamorphosis": A Discussion' (2016) 49 Small Axe 38; see also 'Special Edition: Sylvia Wynter, A Transculturalist Rethinking Modernity' (2001) 10(1) Journal of West Indian Literature 1.

[10] In her youth, Wynter considered studying law, but various mentors told her that it would be intellectually stultifying, advice for which she would be 'very, very grateful' later in her life. David Scott, 'The Re-Enchantment of Humanism: An Interview with Sylvia Wynter' (2000) 8 Small Axe 119, 128.

[11] See Derrick White, 'Black Metamorphosis: A Prelude to Sylvia Wynter's Theory of the Human' (2010) 16(1) CLR James Journal 127. For more on Wynter's critiques of Marxism, see, eg, Sylvia Wynter and Katherine McKittrick, 'Unparalleled Catastrophe for Our Species? Or, to Give Humanness a Different Future: Conversations' in Katherine McKittrick (ed), *Sylvia Wynter: On Being Human as Praxis* (Duke University Press 2015) 38–41; Sylvia Wynter, 'Beyond the Categories of the Master Conception: The Counterdoctrine of the Jamesian Poiesis' in Paget Henry and Paul Buhle (eds), *C.L.R. James's Caribbean* (Duke University Press 1992) 63, 63–67.

[12] Luis Eslava and Sundhya Pahuja, 'Between Resistance and Reform: TWAIL and the Universality of International Law' (2011) 3(1) Trade, Law and Development 103, 103; see also Darryl Li, *The Universal Enemy: Jihad, Empire, and the Challenge of Solidarity* (Stanford University Press 2020) 15–16.

[13] See, eg, Makau Mutua, 'What Is TWAIL?' (2000) 94 Proceedings of the ASIL Annual Meeting 31, 37 ('While it is certainly true that a certain degree of universality is inevitable, and even desirable, TWAIL

Wynter's thought is useful for revisiting this dynamic. She distinguishes the human species from what she calls 'Man', a category that purports to represent the human species but is modelled on white, male, bourgeois, cisheterosexual modernity and thereby produces figures of excluded others. In the early centuries of European colonization, this process of othering was accomplished primarily in terms of religious categories, such as idolaters or pagans; later on, it occurred in the more biological register of race science.[14] Given its universalist aspirations but largely Western provenance, international law has long served as a key site for the articulation of the category of Man. In this respect, international law is no exception: it reproduces a notion of Man as a bearer of rights vis-à-vis the nation-state in its emphasis on non-discrimination[15] and recapitulates a biocentric notion of the human species as divided into 'racial groups',[16] even if insisting that such groups should not be targeted for adverse treatment.

For Wynter, however, Man is merely one variant of what she calls 'genres of the human',[17] ways of being that emerge in different material contexts with their own respective knowledge and value systems. The etymological link between *genre* and *gender* is key, as gender provides an example of how biological differences can be inscribed with social meaning.[18] Both gender and race are forms of differentiation produced by genre.[19] In other words, if critiques of international law's universalism may ultimately demand inclusion or consideration of categories such as race and gender, then Wynter's discussion of genre is a call to rethink the human altogether. Treating Man as one genre of the human among others serves to relativize dominant forms of universalism as historically contingent and to highlight the forms of exclusion and subjugation they produce. At the same time, Wynter also refers to other ways of life encountered by colonialism as genres of the human, in refusal of the particularizing or ghettoizing label of 'cultures'.[20] Wynter's goal is not to reject all forms of universalism but rather to 'relativize Man' in favour of a radically utopian 'emergent Human Project'.[21]

[Third World Approaches to International Law] frowns on attempts to confer universality on norms and practices that are European in origin, thought, and experience.')

[14] Wynter distinguishes between what she calls Man 1 (a partially secularized political subject in the post-Renaissance encounter with the New World) and Man 2 (a post-Enlightenment subject that understands humanity primarily in biocentric terms, giving rise to modern notions of economism). See Sylvia Wynter, 'On How We Mistook the Map for the Territory, and Re-Imprisoned Ourselves in Our Unbearable Wrongness of Being, of Désêtre: Black Studies Toward the Human Project' in Lewis R Gordon and Jane Anna Gordon (eds), *Not Only the Master's Tools: African-American Studies in Theory and Practice* (Routledge 2006) 117, 123–25; Sylvia Wynter, 'Unsettling the Coloniality of Being/Power/Truth/Freedom: Towards the Human, After Man, Its Overrepresentation—An Argument' (2003) 3(3) CR: New Centennial Review 257, 263–67.

[15] See, eg, International Convention on the Elimination of Racial Discrimination (adopted 21 December 1965, entered into force 4 January 1969) 660 UNTS 195, Article 5.

[16] ibid Article 1(4), 2(2).

[17] Wynter, 'On How We Mistook the Map for the Territory' (n 14) 129.

[18] ibid, 117.

[19] Wynter 'insist[s] that "race" is really a code-word for "genre". Our issue is not the issue of "race". Our issue is the issue of the genre of "Man".' Thomas (n 1) 20.

[20] Wynter (n 14) 129.

[21] ibid, 161, 163. For Wynter, this process continues not only aspects of the Enlightenment tradition, but also the legacy of 1960s racial justice movements, which 'were all, fundamentally, struggles against their respective subjects' discursively and institutionally classified Human Other status'.

Wynter's thought shows us how relativizing the universalism of international law can be a useful step towards rethinking its historical vistas and its conceptual blind spots—or, to echo her formulation, to treat international law as one genre of universalism among others. In an essay on debates over female genital cutting in Africa—perhaps the most iconic flashpoint for debates over universalism versus relativism in human rights—Wynter refers to circumcision as an elementary example of 'inscripting practices', whereby physiological differences (in this case, between sexes) can be used as anchors for encoding forms of social distinction (including and especially race).[22] For Wynter, genital cutting is neither to be defended in the name of culture nor condemned as a deviation from the universal: rather, it is a clue to how all genres of the human must encode difference, from particular African societies to universal human rights and feminist projects.[23] Following Wynter, we can think of international law as another inscripting practice, an instrument for instituting subjects as particular kinds of humans—including in regimes of racialization.

We can illuminate such processes by turning to Wynter's method, and specifically to her essays, which engage in a historical re-visioning of the colonization of the Americas. In the early 1980s, Wynter participated in research sponsored by the Jamaican government in preparation for the 500-year commemoration of Columbus's first voyage to the Americas. She conducted archival research in Seville and spent a sabbatical year in Jamaica reconstructing the century and a half of Spanish rule on the island prior to British colonialism.[24] This work produced a series of insights that would infuse her writings on categories of the human for the next several decades. For the purposes of this chapter, however, Wynter's reinterpretation of the events of 1492 is especially pertinent for theorizing race and international law, which has also used this date to ground much of its historiography and theorizing.

2. Slavery and international law: a new world view

In many mythologies[25] of international law that touch on themes of empire and race, 1492 is a pivotal moment representing an encounter between the West and the rest. This mythology works backwards from the past two decades of Euro-American global hegemony to reconstruct how other polities were subjected to various forms of exclusion or marginalization in international law. In this narrative, the Spanish colonization of the Americas inaugurated a series of debates as to the legal status of Indigenous peoples that last in one form or another to the present day. This mythology, however, is invested in a *telos* of national sovereignty that marginalizes slavery, thereby impairing the theorization of race and its relationship with international law.

[22] See Sylvia Wynter, 'Genital Mutilation' or 'Symbolic Birth?' Female Circumcision, Lost Origins, and the Aculturalism of Feminist/Western Thought' (1997) 47 Case Western Reserve Law Review 501, 516, 521.

[23] Wynter refers to circumcision, or 'writing on the flesh' as 'the first origins of the techniques of humanization'; Thomas (n 1) 27.

[24] Scott (n 10) 190–92 (Wynter describing the background of the project).

[25] Here I refer to 'mythologies' as useful narratives that structure categories and assumptions of legal scholarship. There are, to be sure, ample works of historical scholarship, including by legal academics, that challenge or otherwise do not conform to the narrative outlined here.

This mythology appeals to and appears in the work of two influential scholars with radically opposed commitments: Carl Schmitt's *The Nomos of the Earth* is a lamentation for the breakdown of the Eurocentric international order by a Nazi jurist, while Antony Anghie's *Imperialism, Sovereignty and the Making of International Law* is a powerful Third Worldist critique of the colonialist nature of international law. Despite their many differences, these two works share crucial aspects of 1492 mythology. They both note the 1493 edict by Pope Alexander VI, which deeded nearly all of the newly discovered western hemisphere to the Crown of Castile, as well as the 1494 Treaty of Tordesillas, which accorded lands to the west of a new demarcation line to the Spanish and those to the east to the Portuguese, treaties which inaugurated a proud Western tradition of giving away other people's land.[26] Both works locate Francisco Vitoria's sixteenth-century justifications for Spanish colonization in the Americas as an origin point for modern international law.[27] And both proceed to narrate—albeit in very different ways—an account of how non-Western societies were excluded from full participation in international law, in which they were subject to various forms of conquest and subjugation and unable to participate as equal belligerents in war.[28]

These works, and the others that adopted similar 1492 narratives, have been generative for critiquing how international law continues to perpetuate inequality and subjugation worldwide. At the same time, however, this fundamentally dyadic structure—the West versus the rest, the colonizer versus the colonized, sovereigns versus non-sovereigns—sets the stage for a narrative that subsumes race into empire: colonized societies are the sites of racial exclusion that give rise to today's postcolonial nation-states. Regimes of racialization that cut across these categories do not fit into this story. Particularly striking is the near-total absence of the Atlantic slave trade in this narrative; indeed, the African continent only enters the discussion in a significant manner with the 1885 Congress of Berlin.[29] Emerging from histories of abolition, Haiti and Liberia are exceptions that prove the rule: they are among the few recognized states in the nineteenth century that are not white-ruled, yet are largely ignored for not readily fitting into the narrative of colonialism as mere denial of national sovereignty. Even the Indigenous peoples of the Americas, who play a prominent role as international law's constitutive other in the discussion of Vitoria mentioned earlier, are largely left aside and treated as functionally extinct after the initial moment of conquest.[30]

In contrast to the conventional narrative, Wynter's writing takes the triadic nature of the societies created by the colonization of the Americas—settlers, slaves, natives—as a starting point. This presents two important clues for crafting a different mythos

[26] See Antony Anghie, *Imperialism, Sovereignty and the Making of International Law* (Cambridge University Press 2005) 17; Carl Schmitt, *The Nomos of the Earth in the International Law of the Jus Publicum Europaeum* (Telos Press Publishing 2006).

[27] See Anghie (n 26) 13–31; Schmitt (n 26) 101–25.

[28] Schmitt is primarily focused on the development of an intra-European legal order based on equality of states, whereby the exclusion of non-Europeans is more or less taken for granted. See Schmitt (n 28) 42, 131–38, 209. Anghie, in contrast, carefully reconstructs various legal doctrines and categories of exclusion and subjugation that now tend to be collectively labeled as 'colonialism'. See Anghie (n 26) 32–87.

[29] See Anghie (n 26) 90–92; Schmitt (n 26) 214–26.

[30] See Amar Bhatia, 'The South of the North: Building on Critical Approaches to International Law With Lessons From the Fourth World' (2012) 14(1) Oregon Review of International Law 131.

for international law, one that can make space for race and empire as distinct yet overlapping categories. First, in an essay entitled *1492: A New World View*, Wynter integrates Africa squarely into the narrative of the conquests of the Americas. 'The basis of this triadic model', Wynter reminds us, 'was itself established some half a century *before* the voyage of 1492'.[31] Portuguese expeditions around Cape Bojador on the west African coast in the mid-fifteenth century were the first achievements to puncture the older cartographies that confined the habitable parts of the planet primarily to Eurasia and north Africa.[32] As Tiffany Lethabo King notes, '[b]y starting on the shores of what is today's Senegal and extending the inaugural moments of conquest back half a century to 1441, Wynter . . . push[es] back the curtains and position[s] Blackness, which was previously positioned just offstage, directly under the spotlight of the epic drama of conquest'.[33]

Second, in a two-part essay on the colonist and Dominican friar Bartolomé de las Casas (1484–1566), well-known for his ardent critiques of Spanish oppression of native peoples, Wynter points out that his efforts helped lead to the very first licence for the importation of enslaved Africans into the Western hemisphere.[34] This licence 'was to be the charter, at one and the same time, of the transatlantic slave trade, and, at a terrible human cost, of the African presence as a constitutive unit of the post-Columbian civilization of the Caribbean and the Americas'.[35] This substitution is largely ignored in the mythology of international law, which has tended to canonize Las Casas as an early champion of human rights and even of anticolonialism.[36]

By bringing Africa and the Atlantic slave trade into the analysis, we can appreciate anew key elements of the mythology mentioned earlier. The attempts to demarcate territories to the west of Europe between Spain and Portugal did not just divide up what is now Latin America; they also solidified Portuguese territorial claims on the western coast of Africa and kept Spain out of that continent. This set the terms for the slave trade that would unfold over subsequent decades: Portuguese merchants tapped into, expanded, and invigorated existing markets of enslaved persons, sending many of them to the Spanish colonies. Yet because neither Spain nor Portugal formally held territory in the African interior, the destructive and world-changing effects of the slave trade there largely fall out of the dominant international law narrative, making it possible to act as if most of sub-Saharan Africa was untouched by colonialism until the late nineteenth century.

[31] Sylvia Wynter, '1492: A New World View' in Vera Lawrence Hyatt and Rex Nettleford (eds), *Race, Discourse, and the Origins of the Americas* (Smithsonian Institution Press 1995).

[32] Schmitt notes these voyages in a footnote to the 1493 papal edict only to dismiss their lack of a 'global' character. See Schmitt (n 26) 89.

[33] Tiffany Lethabo King, *The Black Shoals: Offshore Formations of Black and Native Studies* (Duke University Press 2019) 18.

[34] It is worth noting that small numbers of enslaved Africans also accompanied the conquistadors. See Andrea Weindl, 'The Asiento de Negros and International Law' (2008 10(2) Journal of the History of International Law 229, 231. Under discussion here are the first licences for the importation of enslaved persons specifically to work in the Americas.

[35] Sylvia Wynter, 'New Seville and the Conversion Experience of Bartolomé de Las Casas: Part One' (1984) 17(2) Jamaica Journal 25, 25.

[36] See, eg, José-Manuel Barreto, 'Imperialism and Decolonization as Scenarios of Human Rights History' in José-Manuel Barreto (ed), *Human Rights From a Third World Perspective: Critique, History and International Law* (Cambridge University Press 2013) 140, 151–55, 168.

In the following sections, this chapter engages with Wynter's work to craft a different mythology of international law with the Atlantic slave trade at its centre. It seeks to complement Wynter's theorization of genre with an attention to legal form as it appears in her work.[37] First, by serving to both connect yet keep separate distinct legal regimes and markets, the slave trade provides methods for theorizing legal connections across disparate geographies in ways that are occluded by the fragmentation of race in contemporary international law. Second, the legal form of the slave importation licence also provides clues for treating regimes of racialization as distinct, conjoined, and connected to concerns of political economy—all important dynamics lost in international law's flattening of race.

3. From captivity to commodity

Against the fragmentation of race in contemporary international law, theorizing from the Atlantic slave trade requires thinking about race as a transregional phenomenon connecting diverse jurisdictions. This spatial movement also maps onto a deeper transformation in the legal institution of slavery from a non-racial category based primarily in captivity to the racialized form of commodification that characterized chattel slavery across the Atlantic. As Walter Rodney put it in his classic, *How Europe Underdeveloped Africa*, '[s]trictly speaking, the African only became a slave when he reached a society where he worked as a slave. Before that, he was first a free man and then a captive.'[38] Here, I would like to springboard from Wynter's preoccupation with conversion as a religious metaphor to also think about convertibility as a legally structured foundation for commercial activity.

Wynter notes that Las Casas made several proposals between 1516 and 1518 to abolish the *encomienda* system while seeking to ensure that the labour demands of Spanish colonialism were nevertheless met. Such alternative labour sources included enslaved persons, both Black and white, brought from Castile as well as from Africa. Most of these suggestions were not taken up, except the one pertaining to the importation of Black Africans for sugar production.[39] Wynter makes clear that Las Casas's proposals were not based in any racial animus but rather on using people 'who [could] be categorized as "justly enslaved" within the system of classification legitimated by Catholic Christian doctrine.'[40] In Las Casas's context, slavery was 'creedally rather than racially defined.'[41] Indeed, throughout mediaeval and early modern Europe,

[37] In the spirit of Evgeny Pashukanis's Marxist theorization of law, the analysis treats legal form as an instrument for mediating exchange under specific relations of production. See Evgeny B Pashukanis, *The General Theory of Law and Marxism* (2nd edn, Transaction Publishers 2003). For a helpful engagement with Pashukanis's work in theorizing the relationship between race, law, and empire that also cites Wynter's essay on Las Casas, see Robert Knox, 'Valuing Race? Stretched Marxism and the Logic of Imperialism' (2016) 4(1) London Review International Law 81, 113–14. The reading proposed here presumes the validity of Knox's claim about the compatibility of TWAIL and Marxist perspectives and instead attempts to think through the diversity of forms of racialization, each with a distinctive relation to law and political economy.

[38] Rodney (n 2) 95.

[39] Wynter (n 35) 46, 47–49.

[40] ibid 47.

[41] ibid.

slavery was primarily understood as an extension of captivity resulting from war or raiding.[42] Church doctrine as described by Wynter was grounded in Roman law notions of slavery as essentially the victor exchanging the right under natural law to execute vanquished foes in favour of keeping them in bondage. The Mediterranean region in particular was bound together by complex ties of captivity and ransom running in both directions across the faith divide.[43] Slavery was a contingency (and often a temporary one that could be ended through ransom), and it affected Christians and Muslims alike of many different skin tones. Las Casas's recommendation for the use of enslaved Africans was based on the assumption that they had been 'justly captured in war'.[44] By 1546, however, the rise of the sugar economy based in racialized slavery brought Las Casas to the conclusion that such an assumption was no longer tenable, and he therefore repudiated his earlier position.[45]

For Wynter, Las Casas's evolving positions on the enslavement of Natives and then Africans were 'conversion experiences' in a religious sense.[46] They were both moments where he came to oppose actions whose morality was self-evident to many of his peers, thanks to his unusual ability to recognize the validity of other genres of the human. Yet, by framing his opposition to slavery narrowly in relation to certain groups rather than to slavery in itself, Las Casas remained nevertheless trapped in his particular worldview. In other words, conversion was transformative but did not portend a total rupture with all that came before. In this light, Wynter's essay also raises the question of conversion in a different sense: between two different regimes of slavery, from (non-racial) captivity to (racialized) commodity.

Taking seriously the origins of slavery in a legal regime of captivity places the history of international law, and specifically the laws of war, at the centre of the analysis. Traces of this history remain an operative part of contemporary international humanitarian law, which permits states to conscript the labour of prisoners of war as well as civilians under belligerent occupation.[47] The everyday use of enslaved labour for private purposes may at first glance seem very different from state compulsion of labour in wartime, but this apparent divergence is the result of histories of abolition. In various contexts, persons who escaped or were freed from slavery by force were nevertheless commodified as contraband—in other words, potentially free of their private owners but nevertheless at the disposal of the state.[48] In the nineteenth century,

[42] ibid 47, 52.

[43] The literature on this era is extensive. See, eg, Daniel Hershenzon, *The Captive Sea: Slavery, Communication, and Commerce in Early Modern Spain and the Mediterranean* (University of Pennsylvania Press 2018); Joshua M White, *Piracy and Law in the Ottoman Mediterranean* (Stanford University Press 2018); Gillian Weiss, *Captives and Corsairs: France and Slavery in the Early Modern Mediterranean* (Stanford University Press 2011); Linda Colley, *Captives: Britain, Empire, and the World, 1600–1850* (Pimlico 2002).

[44] Wynter (n 35) 51.

[45] ibid.

[46] ibid.

[47] See Geneva Convention Relative to the Treatment of Prisoners of War (adopted 12 August 1949, entered into force 2 November 1950) 75 UNTS 135 (Third Geneva Convention) Articles 49–57; Geneva Convention Relative to the Protection of Civilian Persons in Times of War (adopted 12 August 1949, entered into force 21 October 1950) 75 UNTS 287, Articles 51, 96,

[48] See Haslam (n 3) 36 ('The origins of international slave trade repression law lay in the law of prize, the law that regulated the capture and detention of enemy property in war.'); see also Katherine Franke,

thousands of the African 'recaptives' on slave ships seized by the British Royal Navy were in turn pressed into military service in West Africa and the West Indies.[49] In other contexts, too, such as the Ottoman and Russian empires, attempts to reform the treatment of enslaved captives required and justified the growth of centralized state authority to implement new international legal obligations.[50] This contestation between public and private also remains in the contemporary laws of war, which insist that '[p]risoners of war are in the hands of the enemy Power, but not of the individuals or military units who have captured them. Irrespective of the individual responsibilities that may exist, the Detaining Power is responsible for the treatment given them.'[51] Expanding on these historical connections between slavery and captivity in the laws of war presents opportunities to highlight parallels with racialized coerced labour in domestic prison contexts as well.[52]

Wynter's focus on conversion calls to mind the legal mechanisms through which this transformation took place, namely alienability and heritability. Regimes of enslavement have often carried the right to transfer ownership rights to other actors. Alienability, when conceived as market exchange, is also a process of converting captives into currency (sale) or goods (barter) and is connected to alienation, or cutting the enslaved person off from their previous social ties.[53] The transatlantic slave trade took alienability and alienation to new and unprecedented heights. After all, enslavement by Europeans on the African continent rarely fit the mould of captivity in the context of war (just or otherwise); instead, the overwhelming majority of individuals enslaved were seized by regional actors under a variety of circumstances and then sold to Europeans. Transfers of enslaved persons between private actors also crossed various borders, spanning and knitting together diverse jurisdictions. This system allowed the mass enslavement of individuals without conquest or direct rule over the areas from which captives were taken—areas that were nevertheless transformed by these external influences. Captives were transferred across an ocean to be part of new economies that overwhelmingly relied on the extraction of their labour and in situations where cultural ties with communities of origin were actively suppressed.

Having produced radical alienation through crossing oceanic thresholds, the racialization of slavery law in the Atlantic was complemented by rules of heritability.

Wedlocked: The Perils of Marriage Equality (New York University Press 2015) 124–28; John Fabian Witt, *Lincoln's Code: The Laws of War in American History* (Free Press 2012) 245–53.

49 See Haslam (n 3) 2 ('Slaves on ships captured by the [Royal] Navy became recaptives. But the transition to recaptivity did not necessarily represent an assertion of their humanity, nor guarantee their liberation.'); Padraic X Scanlan, *Freedom's Debtors: British Antislavery in Sierra Leone in the Age of Revolution* (Yale University Press 2017) 97–129. Needless to say, former captives asserted their own rights to pursue lives defined neither by slavery nor by wage labour. See Jake Christopher Richards, 'Anti-Slave-Trade Law: "Liberated Africans" and the State in the South Atlantic World, c. 1839–1852' (2018) 241(1) Past and Present 179.

50 See Will Smiley, *From Slaves to Prisoners of War: The Ottoman Empire, Russia, and International Law* (Oxford University Press 2018) 105–24.

51 Third Geneva Convention (n 47) Article 12.

52 See, eg, Adelle Blackett and Alice Duquesnoy, 'Slavery is Not a Metaphor: U.S. Prison Labour and Racial Subordination Through the Lens of the ILO's Abolition of Forced Labour Convention' (2021) 67 UCLA Law Review 1504.

53 For the most influential exposition of this idea, see Orlando Patterson, *Slavery and Social Death: A Comparative Study* (Harvard University Press 1982).

In the context of settler colonies without significant pre-existing Black populations, the phenotypical distinctiveness of enslaved Africans furnished a basis for the inscription of new social statuses through law as well as other means. The principle of *partus sequitur ventrum*—that the status of a child follows that of the mother (literally, 'offspring follows belly')—effectively turned the wombs of enslaved women into sites of racialized commodity production, converting kin into property.[54] The hereditary transmission of racialized slavery also disrupted the logic of conversion and convertibility: unlike in the captivity-based slavery in the Old World, here racialization functioned as the mark of slavery or—for those manumitted—the possibility of re-enslavement.

Together, alienability and heritability enabled moving captive Africans between continents, between markets, and ultimately between different types of slavery altogether. The Atlantic slave trade produced forms of racialization that bound together very different contexts. Hence, although the interior of the African continent would remain dark and unexplored in the eyes of Europeans well until the late nineteenth century, it was irrevocably shaped by the demands of the slave trade from Las Casas's time onward and effectively integrated into a world system of trade.[55] It is unsurprising that the transatlantic slave trade was a prime example of what Marx called primitive (or original) accumulation of capital.[56] Primitive accumulation is not, of course, a story of backwards areas being brought into capitalist modernity, but rather of radically different spaces and modes of social organization being forcibly and unequally tied together by relations of capitalist development. In all of this, the alienability of captives tied together disparate zones while the heritability of racialized status allowed one region to maintain the illusion that Black Africans existed in a different stage of historical development, isolated and unaffected by the other zones.

4. Black skin, red lands

Wynter's work also provides clues for theorizing alternatives to the flattening of race that takes place in international law. Instead, the international law of the slave trade can be studied as a regime that materially inscribed distinct yet conjoined forms of racialization as Black and Native. As mentioned above, Las Casas's efforts to abolish Indigenous forced labour led to the promulgation of the first licence from the Spanish

[54] See, eg, Jennifer L Morgan, 'Partus Sequitur Ventrem: Law, Race, and Reproduction in Colonial Slavery' (2018) 22(1) Small Axe 1, 15 (English Atlantic slave regimes 'defined hereditary racial slavery through the irony of a kinlessness born in a woman's womb'); Dorothy E Roberts, 'The Genetic Tie' (1995) 62 University of Chicago Law Review 209 225–27 (on the heritability of racial status and slavery in English colonial law).

[55] For one classic overview of this history and its long-term effects on global patterns of wealth and development, see, eg, Rodney (n 2) 95–113.

[56] See Karl Marx, *Capital: A Critique of Political Economy* (Ben Fowkes tr, Penguin Books 1976) 915 ('The discovery of gold and silver in America, the extirpation, enslavement and entombment in mines of the indigenous population of that continent, the beginnings of the conquest and plunder of India, and the conversion of Africa into a preserve for the commercial hunting of blackskins, are all things which characterise the dawn of the era of capitalist production. These idyllic proceedings are the chief moments of primitive accumulation.').

Crown for the importation of enslaved persons from Africa to the Americas.[57] Wynter notes this type of instrument was called an *asiento*—indeed, it came to be known as an *asiento de negros*, marking the process through which slavery came to be racialized by settler colonialism in the creation of a New World. *Asientos de negros*, a type of legal instrument that evolved through many different forms from 1518 to 1779, were key to the legal architecture of the political economy of Spanish colonialism and, as such, play an important role in the history of international law.

Asiento de negros generally gave their holders near exclusive rights to bring enslaved persons from Africa to Spanish colonies, fixing quotas as well as setting prices. Many of the agreements also specified ports from which slave traders could embark and disembark, and some also required the use of Spanish ships, Spanish crews, or both. The earliest *asientos* were granted to favourite courtiers of the crown who had no experience in procuring enslaved persons.[58] And thanks to the 1494 Treaty of Tordesillas, Spain was barred from establishing trading posts on the African continent.[59] As a result, *asiento* holders treated the licences as speculative property and sold them off to the highest bidder, often Genovese or Portuguese merchants with connections to the trade in African captives.[60] Eventually, the Spanish crown contracted directly with foreign merchants and trading houses, and even foreign governments, most notably Britain (1713–1750). In this respect, *asientos* were instances of public–private contracting as well as acts of treaty making in international law. They also spurred the development of mechanisms for the crown to resolve disputes with both private actors and foreign governments, making them a significant milestone in the development of international commercial arbitration.[61]

The *asiento* was important for several reasons. The revenue raised was significant for the crown. And, by setting forth a framework for the direct importation of enslaved persons from Africa to the Americas, *asientos* were perhaps the single most important exception to mercantilist policies of the early modern period, which generally sought to restrict trade between European powers and their respective colonial possessions. Not only did *asientos de negros* depart from this pattern by allowing the importation of enslaved persons directly from Africa rather than Spain, but they empowered foreign actors to act as primary agents of this trade and thereby to directly access markets in Spanish colonies. As Andrea Weindl has noted, '[f]or Dutch, English, French, Danish, Swedish and even Brandenburg merchants, the *asiento* trade was the only possibility to get access to Spanish America in a legal way and to purchase American commodities not only in Seville but directly in the New World'.[62] It is also worth noting that *asientos* were perhaps equally powerful for the illegalities they facilitated: scholars have noted that *asiento* holders never met the quotas allotted to them under the contracts, since

[57] See Wynter (n 35) 25.

[58] The 1518 asiento was granted by 17-year-old ruler Charles I to his majordomo and friend, a Flemish aristocrat. See Leslie B Rout Jr, *The African Experience in Spanish America: 1502 to the Present Day* (Cambridge University Press 1976) 37.

[59] See Treaty Between Spain and Portugal Concluded at Tordesillas (7 June 1494) (The Avalon Project at Yale Law School) <https://avalon.law.yale.edu/15th_century/mod001.asp> accessed 14 November 2024.

[60] See Weindl (n 34) 232; Wynter (n 35) 25.

[61] See Anne-Charlotte Martineau, 'A Forgotten Chapter in the History of International Commercial Arbitration: The Slave Trade's Dispute Settlement System' (2018) 31 Leiden Journal of international Law 219.

[62] Weindl (n 34) 236.

the prices set, in combination with the inherent risks of maritime shipping, made fulfilling the terms of the agreements unprofitable.[63] Instead, by facilitating non-Spanish access to Spanish colonies the *asientos* were most valuable in creating opportunities for illicit smuggling of contraband of all kinds. The ramifications of this framework went far beyond commerce: the 1713 *asiento*, which gave Britain the exclusive right to bring enslaved persons to Spanish colonies in the Americas as part of the Treaty of Utrecht, was both immensely lucrative and also ceded significant political leverage to a foreign power through control over a crucial supply of labour. As such, the right to hold the *asiento* was also an object of intense geopolitical competition.

In their very form, the *asientos de negros* bear the traces of the racialization of slavery in law. In early modern Spain, the term *asiento*, literally 'seat' or 'agreement', denoted an instrument that allowed the crown to raise revenue from private actors in exchange for monopoly rights to sell certain goods.[64] The *asientos de negros* were an especially important subset of such agreements and hence emerged as a genre whose very name connoted and instantiated an emergent regime of racialization. Moreover, the work of racialization was also marked by the fact that the contracts came to be denominated not in numbers of enslaved human beings, but rather in a curious unit of measurement: *piezas de Indias*, or 'pieces of the Indies'. A *pieza de India* was said to represent the labour power of a single healthy young man; how this was calculated in terms of women, children, elderly, and infirm individuals varied widely across circumstances.[65] Numerous commentators have remarked that this unit of measurement dehumanized enslaved Africans by reducing them to abstract quantities of commodified labour power (which was also gendered as male),[66] including Wynter herself.[67]

What has gone less remarked, however, is the substitution—or conversion—at work here: just as Las Casas proposed the substitution of enslaved Africans for Indians, this move gave rise to a legal instrument whose very form implies distinct regimes of racialization. In its very name, the *asiento* racializes captive Africans as Black chattel, but does so using units that refer to a place rather than to a people. Colonialism here produces Blackness as a commodity and conjures Indigenous peoples as a misnomer, an absence who leaves only names and traces upon territory. 'Thus', according to Patrick Wolfe, 'it is no accident that the most durable names that have been applied to the two colonised populations, Black (or Negro) and Indian, refer to a bodily characteristic and a territorial designation respectively'.[68] In the spirit of this reading, the best

[63] ibid ('[T]he trade with black labour in the framework of the *asiento* was always a losing deal. Prices were fixed beforehand and the trade to Africa entailed great expenses and risk.')

[64] ibid 230.

[65] The term piezas de India first appeared in the 1662 asiento, which was granted to Genovese merchants. See ibid 235.

[66] The non-equivalence of piezas to individuals has also confounded historians' attempts to measure the scale of the transatlantic slave trade. See, eg, Philip D Curtin, *The Atlantic Slave Trade: A Census* (University of Wisconsin Press 1969) 22–23.

[67] In an extended appreciation, Wynter characterizes the thought of the Trinidadian Marxist thinker CLR James as employing a 'pieza theoretic framework', which uses the transatlantic slave trade (and its denomination in piezas) as a model for theorizing networks of accumulation based on coercive identities (eg African slaves, the working class, and consumers) that underlie the modern world. See Sylvia Wynter, 'Beyond the Categories of the Master Conception: The Counterdoctrine of the Jamesian Poiesis' in Paget Henry and Paul Buhle (eds), *C.L.R. James's Caribbean* (Duke University Press 1992) 63, 80–82.

[68] Patrick Wolfe, *Traces of History: Elementary Structures of Race* (Verso 2016) 4.

work in the tradition of both CRT and TWAIL is attentive to how race is produced not simply as a generically invidious form of social differentiation, but also as a distinct set of regimes grounded in a distinctive logic related to political economy. For instance, Cheryl Harris's landmark *Whiteness as Property* essay similarly distinguished between these two forms of racialization, 'the former involving the seizure and appropriation of labour, the latter entailing the seizure and appropriation of land'.[69] In drawing attention to the proposed substitution of one form of slavery for another in Las Casas's interventions and Spanish colonialism more generally, Wynter's essay provides a useful touchstone for reflecting on how these distinct logics can be interrelated to a broader analysis.

5. Conclusion

This chapter reasoned from the presupposition that in this moment of fascist resurgence and antiracist insurrection, critical theorization of international law can only hope to flourish if tended with water drawn from wells hitherto untapped—including and especially work by thinkers involved in Black and Indigenous studies. Engaging with these fields is important insofar as they centre the experiences of populations that are constitutively marginalized in the global nation-state order, even after the advent of formal decolonization in the erstwhile Third World.

By focusing on the single example of Sylvia Wynter, this chapter attempted to model a form of engagement with questions of universalism and humanity that could bring the insights of such fields into conversation with both TWAIL and CRT traditions. Needless to say, there are many other possibilities for moving international legal theorizing away from territorial conceptions and towards thinking with mobility, specifically the racialized captive mobility of slavery or—perhaps even more pertinent for contemporary legal regimes—indentured servitude.

Beyond the overdue re-theorizing of international law with race at the centre, this moment highlights the need for scholars in the field to join broader re-orientations towards treating insurgent social movements as partners for generating ideas rather than as objects of study or, worse, of disciplining and marginalization.[70] Insofar as such movements challenge the very logic of statehood that undergirds international law, their alternative experiments and visions in recasting the category of the human provide glimpses into alternative futures. The task for international lawyers is to develop relationships grounded in frank dialogue with and rigorous accountability to such movements, with an eye to helping concretize shared commitments to solidarity across borders of all kinds.

[69] Cheryl I Harris, 'Whiteness as Property' (1993) 106 Harvard Law Review 1709, 1715. See also Vine DeLoria, Jr, *Custer Died for Your Sins: An Indian Manifesto* (Macmillan 1969) 15 ('Because the Negro labored, he was considered a draft animal. Because the Indian occupied large areas of land, he was considered a wild animal. Had we given up anything else, or had anything else to give up, it is certain that we would have been considered some other thing.')

[70] See Amna A Akbar, Sameer M Ashar, and Jocelyn Simonson, 'Movement Law' (2021) 73 Stanford Law Review 821, 825 ('[L]egal scholars should take seriously the epistemological universe of today's left social movements, and their experiments, tactics, and strategies for legal and social change.').

20

Bodies of Knowledge

Re-framing Emancipation in International Law through Dalit Praxis

*Kamya Vishwanath**

1. Beyond the margins

We cannot talk about race without addressing violence, just as we cannot talk about violent racialization without confronting caste.[1] This confrontation demands engagement with Dalits. As one of India's most oppressed social groups, engagement reveals much about the country's insidious racial hierarchies. The case of Dalits also raises a critical question for this collection: how is caste a problem for international law?

The caste system is a unique and defining feature of Indian society—one that some argue has no parallel in other cultures. 'Caste', in and of itself, is contested by anti-Brahminical activists and scholars alike but receives twice as much backlash from others—primarily the casteist majority that aspires to preserve the perverse stratification that serves their interests and feeds their biases. On the one hand, some might contend that caste-based discrimination—including cognizable policies and practices—falls within the scope of international human rights law (IHRL), demanding a more rigorous reading of international law by domestic courts. On the other hand, purist-nationalists and sceptics—afraid of deploying novel vocabulary to address age-old problems—have rejected a universalization of the issue, arguing that subsuming caste within race would be grossly reductive.[2] Their critique could be framed within a Third World Approaches to International Law (TWAIL) perspective,

* The author (she/her) is profoundly grateful for the enthusiastic engagement with initial iterations of this piece at the Asser Institute's Methods, Methodology & Critique in International Law Conference in December 2021, and Abo Akademi's Many Gazes of Law Conference in April 2024 (where this was finally offered wings). She is indebted to Professors Mohsen al Attar and Claire Smith, whose interventions, invitations, and unwavering support offered her solace through the writing process. One such provocation questioned her initial decision to let 'Dalit' and other caste identities remain in lowercase throughout the text (in keeping with Anand Teltumbde's practice in 'The Persistence of Caste'). With timely redirection towards Matiangai Sirleaf, 'Rendering Whiteness Visible' (2023) 3 American Journal of International Law 484, she changed her mind. In an attempt to render caste visible—particularly, the lowercas(t)e—she has opted to capitalize all caste-based identities. The views expressed in this chapter are solely the author's and do not represent the views of her employer either in part or in totality. All errors remain hers.

[1] Vasanthi Venkatesh, 'International Casteist Governance and the Dalit Radical Tradition' (2022) 3 TWAIL Review 171.

[2] See Curtis Bradley, 'What is Foreign Relations Law' in Curtis Bradley (ed), *The Oxford Handbook of Comparative Foreign Relations Law* (Oxford University Press 2019) 3.

Kamya Vishwanath, *Bodies of Knowledge* In: *Emancipating International Law*. Edited by: Mohsen al Attar and Claire Smith, Oxford University Press. © Kamya Vishwanath 2026. DOI: 10.1093/9780198935605.003.0026

couched in opposition to Western and liberal legal influence, though I opt to think of Dalit resistance through a Dalit lens.[3]

To think of discrimination against Dalits—whether in India or elsewhere—as a purely domestic issue ignores not only the Dalits' claims for emancipation but also international law's reach and potential more generally. In India, caste functions as a marker of social, political, and economic status. Much like Black communities in the United States,[4] Dalits have resisted casteism by asserting their identity as a political group and engaging in organized political activities.[5] Yet, despite the spirited efforts of activists, leaders, and anti-caste writers, caste-based discrimination perseveres (almost) unchallenged.[6] In fact, the very existence of caste as an accepted social category *is* discriminatory, a distinction international law has grappled with.

In this chapter, I do not dwell on explaining why violence against Dalits is an international law problem; this has already been convincingly argued by Srinivas Burra,[7] Vasanthi Venkatesh,[8] and Ahmed Memon,[9] whose work is a collective premise to my analysis. Instead, I argue that international law's limited mechanisms of knowledge production have marginalized Dalits by treating them as passive recipients rather than active producers of legal discourse. This has denied the discipline awareness of Dalit subjectivity and an entire epistemology rooted in their lived experiences—knowledge that is essential for envisioning more equitable futures for international law.

Additionally, Dalit epistemology—shaped by their endless struggles against violence—is produced from their bodies.[10] Yet, international law's engagement with bodies has traditionally revolved around efforts to control, restrict, or save them, while neglecting the myriad ways in which the law itself perpetuates harm to *some* bodies. This 'descriptive omission'[11] is deliberate, underscoring the erasure of bodies from IHRL discourse. Ultimately, my investigation is driven by another straightforward question: where is the body in international law? While this chapter may not

[3] Srinivas Burra, 'TWAIL's Others: A Caste Critique of Twailers and their Field of Analysis' (2016) 33(3) Windsor Yearbook of Access to Justice 111.

[4] Barbara Jeanne Fields, 'Slavery, Race, and Ideology in the United States of America' (1990) 181 (95) New Left Review 95; Alan Hyde, *Bodies of Law* (Princeton University Press 1997).

[5] Arpita Chattaraj Mukhopadhyay, 'Literatures of Suffering and Resistance: Dalit Women's Testimonies and Black Woman Slave Narratives—a Comparative Study' in Joshil K Abraham and Judith Misrahi-Barak (eds), *Dalit Literatures in India* (Routledge 2021).

[6] Elaine Scarry, *The Body in Pain: The Making & Unmaking of the World* (Oxford University Press 1985). Scarry writes how the elaboration of pain can be understood in terms of the impossibility of speech, and the difficulties of articulating some concerns. Compellingly, she writes how 'the relative ease or difficulty with which any given phenomenon can be verbally represented also influences the ease or difficulty with which that phenomenon comes to be politically represented'.

[7] Burra (n 3).

[8] Venkatesh (n 1).

[9] Ahmed Memon, '"English in Taste, Indian in Blood": Caste Hegemony in the Making of British International Legal Thought' (2024) 12(1) London Review of International Law 23.

[10] Mukhopadhyay (n 5).

[11] Anna Spain Bradley, 'Book Review' (2018) 112 American Journal of International l Law 330 (reviewing Oona A Hathaway and Scott J Shapiro, *The Internationalists: How a Radical Plan to Outlaw War Remade the World* (Simon & Schuster 2017); See also James Thuo Gathii, 'The Promise of International Law: A Third World View' (2021) 36(3) American University of International Law Review 377.

provide a satisfactory answer, the aim is to initiate a dialogue around the 'presence of the absence'[12] of the body in international legal discourse.[13]

This chapter proceeds in five sections. In Section 2, I explore the caste system's violent origins and continuities in contemporary India, highlighting the failures of its domestic legal system in addressing violence against Dalits. Section 3 identifies modes of Dalit praxis for emancipation, relying on how their ways of being inform Dalit subjectivity. Section 4 critiques the limitations of the existing IHRL regime, contrasting mainstream international legal epistemology with Dalit epistemes to reveal the discourse's blind spots. Drawing on TWAIL critiques of the liberal international human rights framework, I conclude in Section 5 by turning to Dalit literature and poetry to better capture the nature of the emancipation they seek.

2. Still, born: the violence of caste and Dalit non-existence

> My birth is my fatal accident . . . Do not shed tears for me. Know that I am more happy dead than being alive.
>
> Excerpt from Rohith Vemula's suicide letter[14]

In 2016, Rohith Vemula, a PhD scholar at the University of Hyderabad, committed suicide shortly after his fellowship was revoked for participating in protests against caste-based discrimination.[15] His death triggered waves of anti-caste protests and exposed the persistent discrimination across India's institutions.[16] Nearly a decade later, the Telangana state police concluded that Vemula had *falsified* his Dalit status and closed the inquiry.[17] This dismissal exemplifies the denial of Dalit realities. As Vemula tragically observed in his suicide letter, discrimination against Dalits happens by virtue of their existence—a practice rooted in millennia of hierarchical social ordering.

2.1 A brief history of caste

Traditional Hindu society was organized into four '*Varnas*'—Brahmins (the priestly clan), Kshatriyas (the warrior clan), Vaishyas (the merchant clan), and Shudras (the

[12] Jacques Derrida, *Of grammatology* (GC Spivak tr, Johns Hopkins University Press 2016).

[13] Margaret Davies, 'What's Hot in Jurisprudence' (2000) 31(1) Victoria University Wellington Law Review 149.

[14] The Wire Staff, 'My Birth is My Fatal Accident: Rohith Vemula's Searing Letter is an Indictment of Social Prejudices' (*The Wire*, 17 January 2019) <https://thewire.in/caste/rohith-vemula-letter-a-powerful-indictment-of-social-prejudices> accessed 16 September 2024.

[15] ibid.

[16] Hiranya Bhandarkar, 'What is NLU Delhi Doing in Response to Student Suicides?' (*Bar and Bench*, 30 September 2024) <https://www.barandbench.com/news/lawschools/what-is-nlu-delhi-doing-in-response-to-student-suicides> accessed 16 September 2024.

[17] Online Desk, 'Rohith Vemula was not a Dalit', claim Telangana cops in closure report; DGP orders further probe' *The Indian Express* (Telangana, 4 May 2024) <https://www.newindianexpress.com/states/telangana/2024/May/03/rohith-vemula-was-not-a-dalit-claim-telangana-cops-in-closure-report-dgp-orders-further-probe> accessed 16 September 2024.

working class, fisherfolk, etc).[18] This stratification followed from the Purushashukta in the Rigveda, the oldest of the four 'Samhitas', which comprises ancient hymns of praise to God.[19] Over time, this framework was sanctified through Hindu religious texts such as the Vedas and was later codified in the laws of *Manu* or the *Manusmriti*, a foundational text on caste in modern India.[20] The *Manusmriti* included explicit instructions to administer violence against the Shudras when they disrespected the Brahmins.

Consider, for instance, the following excerpts from Section XLI of the *Manusmriti*, which addresses instances of 'Verbal Assault' (Abuse and Defamation), presented here in Sanskrit with their English translations:

I.
शतं ब्राह्मणमाक्रुश्य क्षत्रियो दण्डमर्हति । वैश्योऽप्यर्धशतं द्वे वा शूद्रस्तु वधमर्हति ॥ २६७ ॥
śataṃ brāhmaṇamākruśya kṣatriyo daṇḍamarhati | vaiśyo'pyardhaśataṃ dve vā śūdrastu vadhamarhati || 267 ||
On abusing a Brāhmaṇa the Kṣatriya should be fined one hundred; and the Vaiśya one hundred and fifty; or two hundred; the Śūdra however deserves immolation.—(267)[21]
Verse 8.267

II.
धर्मोपदेशं दर्पेण विप्राणामस्य कुर्वतः । तप्तमासेचयेत् तैलं वक्त्रे श्रोत्रे च पार्थिवः ॥ २७२ ॥
dharmopadeśaṃ darpeṇa viprāṇāmasya kurvataḥ | taptamāsecayet tailaṃ vaktre śrotre ca pārthivaḥ || 272 ||
If through arrogance, he teaches brāhmaṇas their duty, the king shall pour heated oil into his mouth and ears.—(272)[22]
Verse 8.272

The *Manusmriti* expresses open contempt for the Shudras. The concept of 'immolation' mentioned in the text refers to acts of extreme violence, such as cutting off tongues or killing those who violate caste boundaries.[23]

While it is commonly known that 'caste' is derived from the Portuguese word 'casta' meaning 'purity of blood',[24] debates continue over when exactly caste became entrenched in Indian sociopolitical life. Notwithstanding this debate, it is essential to recognize that the caste system has always been intertwined with a project of conquest.[25]

[18] Anand Teltumbde, *Dalits: Past, Present and Future* (1st edn, Routledge 2017).

[19] Michael H Fisher, *A History of India: The Great Courses Course Guidebook* (The Great Courses 2016) 37.

[20] ibid 121.

[21] Ganganatha Jha, 'Verse 8.267' *Manusmriti with the Commentary of Medhatithi* (1920), https://www.wisdomlib.org/hinduism/book/manusmriti-with-the-commentary-of-medhatithi/d/doc201200.html accessed 21 November 2024.

[22] Ganganatha Jha, 'Verse 8.272' *Manusmriti with the Commentary of Medhatithi* (1920), https://www.wisdomlib.org/hinduism/book/manusmriti-with-the-commentary-of-medhatithi/d/doc201205.html accessed 21 November 2024.

[23] Jha (n 21).

[24] MN Srinivas, *Caste in Modern India and Other Essays* (Asia Publishing House 1970).

[25] Ebenezer Sunder Raj, 'The Origins of the Caste System' (1985) 2(2) Transformation 10.

Unlike the *chaturvarna* system, caste is a more recent phenomenon, evolving from the concept of *varna* but solidified as a sociopolitical structure under colonial administration.[26] There are over a thousand different caste categories in India today, while nearly 17 per cent of Indians belong to marginalized groups that fall outside these categories.[27] Legally termed 'scheduled castes', these groups continue to experience systemic discrimination—ranging from overt violence to insidious exclusion—at the hands of dominant caste groups. Apart from Indigenous populations (the *Adivasis*), these groups are the 'outcastes' or those we refer to as 'Dalits' today.[28]

The word 'Dalit' means 'to split' or 'rupture'.[29] Historically, Dalits were referred to as 'untouchables', with their touch considered polluting to all non-Dalits. Denied access to education and basic civic participation, Dalits were relegated to serving the upper castes through menial labour. Although often described as a form of social stratification, caste operates as a dominant ideology of Indian society.[30] The system lives on under the guise of occupational divisions of labour,[31] a convenient argument advanced by British colonial officers to rule over the subcontinent.[32]

2.2 Dalit resistance

Anand Teltumbde highlights how anti-caste resistance dates back to the inception of the caste system, circa 1500–1000 BCE, with the rise of the Shraman traditions of Buddhism and Jainism.[33] This resistance, later termed the 'non-Brahmin movement', gained momentum during the colonial period, led by figures such as Jyotirao Phule in Western India and EV Ramaswamy Periyar in Southern India, both from the Shudra community.[34] Ironically, while colonial rule entrenched the caste system through its administrative structures, it also paved the way for forms of emancipation.[35] Indian lower castes were inspired by 'radical and liberal ideals of democracy, popular sovereignty and rationalism' that 'set in process among a section of them a time of intense critical appraisal of India's socio-religious practices', fuelling collective action and reform movements against 'Indian culture's repressive elements'.[36] This dual dynamic explains why Dalits had a more complex relationship with the colonizers compared to the wider Indian population, complicating their position within international legal discourses.

[26] V Das, 'Caste' in Neil J Smelser and Paul B Baltes (ed), *International Encyclopedia of the Social & Behavioral Sciences* (Elsevier Ltd 2001) 1529.
[27] Anand Teltumbde, *The Persistence of Caste: The Khairlanji Murders and India's Hidden Apartheid* (Zed Books 2010) 13.
[28] ibid 13.
[29] Teltumbde (n 18).
[30] Das (n 26).
[31] ibid 11; See also Teltumbde (n 18).
[32] Memon (n 9).
[33] Teltumbde (n 27) 18.
[34] ibid 22.
[35] ibid 20.
[36] ibid 21.

Dr Bhim Rao Ambedkar, affectionately known as 'Babasaheb', was an indispensable figure who helped embed an anti-caste impetus within India's legal system. A social reformer, economist, and political leader, Babasaheb advocated for separate electorates for 'untouchables' and other minority communities as early as 1918.[37] His writings proved instrumental in driving forward some of the legal safeguards enshrined in the Constitution. Indeed, as India moved towards independence, the Constituent Assembly began its deliberations on 9 December 1946, resulting in constitutional guarantees of equality for all castes. Articles 14, 15, and 16 of the Constitution of India enshrine equality of access,[38] and Article 17 explicitly abolishes 'Untouchability'.[39] These constitutional rights were supported by subsequent legislation, including the Protection of Civil Rights Act (1955) and the Scheduled Castes and Scheduled Tribes (Prevention of Atrocities) Act (1989) ('the SC/ST Act'). Despite these measures, as Ambedkar himself feared, laws and political will alone prove insufficient to curb violence against Dalits.

Today, caste-based atrocities have escalated as Dalit movements have weakened.[40] Dalits routinely face humiliation, physical and sexual abuse, and insidious forms of systemic violence embedded in societal structures.[41] As Teltumbde notes, '[w]hen Dalits were not held to be worth treating as human, there was no question of "human rights" or their violation'.[42] Most caste-based atrocities are normalized and go unreported. In contrast to precolonial and colonial India, where violence often occurred through direct, traceable relationships, today's caste violence is more diffuse, usually involving groups targeting isolated individuals.[43] The system and its tediousness have ensured that these matters escape legal scrutiny.[44]

2.3 Universal human discrimination

In December 2023, the National Crime Record Bureau released a report documenting a surge in caste-based hate crimes against Dalits, with nearly 57,582 cases reported between 2018 and 2022. The data reveals pervasive discrimination against students in educational institutions, brutal attacks on elders, and the rape of minors. Honour killings, often triggered by inter-caste marriages, have multiplied, with the lower-caste partner murdered for 'dishonouring' the family.[45] Dalit women are triply discriminated

[37] Indian National Congress, 'B.R. Ambedkar' (*Indian National Congress*) <https://inc.in/our-inspiration/dr-b-r-ambedkar#:~:text=He%20was%20initially%20 elected%20to,ahead%20of%20Shri%20GV%20Mavalankar> accessed 15 November 2024.

[38] The Constitution of India 1950, Articles 14–16.

[39] The Constitution of India 1950, Article 17.

[40] Teltumbde (n 27) 29. Teltumbde referred to them as 'essentially human rights violations with the added association of unbridled cruelty, brutality and inhumanness'.

[41] ibid 30.

[42] ibid.

[43] ibid.

[44] ibid 29.

[45] See, eg, Harpreet Bajwa, 'Honour Killing claims couple in Punjab village' *The New Indian Express* (18 October 2021) <https://www.newindianexpress.com/nation/2021/oct/18/honour-killing-claims-couple-in-punjab-village-2372703.html> accessed 20 October 2021; Ilangovan Rajasekaran, 'My husband, a

against by virtue of their caste, class, and gender,[46] suffering dehumanization through underpaid labour and sexual violence.[47] Dalits continue to work in degrading professions such as manual scavenging, which involves physically cleaning human excreta. This practice, widely condemned as a universally abhorrent violation of basic human dignity,[48] is criminalized in India, yet persists.[49] Structural segregation and inequities, often invisible to the ordinary eye, perpetuate caste divisions.[50] Affirmative action policies have been introduced to address some of these injustices but are met with resistance and have, paradoxically, resulted in further violence against beneficiaries. Tragically, instances of brutal physical violence are the only stories that gain traction. As a result, the everydayness of caste as a violent category[51]—the psychological wounds of casteist slurs, the discomfort stemming from the segregation of space and occupation, and knowledge that this is inescapable—is obscured from view.[52]

The Indian judiciary has also proven unhelpful. While it has frequently addressed cases of discrimination against Scheduled Castes, it has done so with inconsistency and delay—undermining justice by mandating preliminary inquiries before arrest[53] and refusing to recognize these atrocities as caste-based.[54] In *Khuman Singh vs the State of Madhya Pradesh*,[55] the Supreme Court held that section 3(2)(v) of the SC/ST Act—which imposes enhanced punishment for caste-based crimes—applies to crimes committed 'only' on the ground that '*such person is a member of a Scheduled Caste or a Scheduled Tribe*' (emphasis added).[56] This qualification, which does not appear in the legislation, weakens the law's intent and grants impunity to perpetrators of violence

Vanniyar, was victim of honour killing, says his Dalit wife; police arrest his father and brother on abetment of suicide charge' *Frontline* (8 October 2021) <https://frontline.thehindu.com/dispatches/my-husband-a-vanniyar-was-victim-of-honour-killing-says-his-dalit-wife-police-arrest-his-father-and-brother-on-abetment-of-suicide-charge/article36894706.ece> accessed 20 October 2021; Nidhi Suresh and Amitoj Singh, 'A year on, India Dalit rape victim's family waits for justice' *Al Jazeera* (2 October 2021) <https://www.aljazeera.com/news/2021/10/2/india-a-year-later-the-rape-case-that-shook-a-nation-forgotten> accessed 20 October 2021.

46 Venkatesh (n 1).

47 See Press Trust of India, 'Dalit woman gang-raped in U.P.'s Jewar, one arrested' *The Hindu* (12 October 2021 <https://www.thehindu.com/news/national/other-states/dalit-woman-gang-raped-in-ups-jewar-one-arrested/article36955171.ece> accessed 20 October 2021.

48 Swapnil Tripathi, 'The Dignity and Rights of Manual Scavengers in India' (*Oxford Human Rights Hub*, 14 October 2017) <https://ohrh.law.ox.ac.uk/the-dignity-and-rights-of-manual-scavengers-in-india/> accessed 20 October 2021.

49 The Prohibition of Employment as Manual Scavengers and their Rehabilitation Act, 2013, Act No 25 of 2013.

50 See, eg, Kiran Parashar, 'Temple entry fines, segregation: In this north Karnataka district, untouchability an open secret' *The Indian Express* (4 October 2021) <https://indianexpress.com/article/cities/bangalore/temple-entry-fines-segregation-in-this-north-karnataka-district-untouchability-an-open-secret-7550283/> accessed 20 October 2021.

51 Ania Loomba, 'The Everyday Violence of Caste' (Winter 2016) 43(1) College Literature 220.

52 Anupama Rao, *The Caste Question: Dalits and the Politics of Modern India* (University of California Press 2009).

53 *Dr Subhash Kashinath Mahajan v the State of Maharashtra* AIR 2018 SC 1498.

54 Rao (n 52).

55 *Khuman Singh v the State of Madhya Pradesh* AIR 2019 SC 4030.

56 Aishwarya Singh and Meenakshi Ramkumar, 'Failure of the Indian Supreme Court to Protect the Rights of Dalits' (*Oxford Human Rights Hub*, 30 September 2019) <https://ohrh.law.ox.ac.uk/failure-of-the-indian-supreme-court-to-protect-the-rights-of-dalits/> accessed 20 October 2021.

against Dalits.[57] By narrowly interpreting the law, the judiciary has eroded its efficacy and failed to protect Dalits from systemic violence.

Worryingly, the Dalit identity has gradually transcended the confines of caste Hindus, reaching Indian Christians and Muslims who also occupy socially marginal positions.[58] Equally troubling is that the caste system has also evolved and spread to other parts of the world. Burra highlights how the category of Dalit has reached other regions of South Asia, and even parts of Europe and the United States.[59] Caste-based discrimination is no longer a uniquely Indian experience. Venkatesh similarly discusses the perpetuation of 'international casteist governance', which sustains caste hierarchies and constrains the discourse of rights within narrow frames.[60] She illustrates how Brahmanical hegemony continues through the international economic order, migration policies, and the cyclical loss of opportunities tied to caste status.[61] For instance, Venkatesh cites American court cases where immigration claims were based on being a 'high-caste Hindu of pure blood', arguing that they were 'white by law' and entitled to special privileges.[62] Additionally, occupational divisions and caste-based discrimination continue to affect Dalits in diaspora communities.[63]

Entrenched in caste hierarchies, the systemic oppression of Dalits continues through both overt violence and structural exclusion. Dalits, however, are not passive victims; their resistance has shaped unique modes of knowledge production and self-definition. As I explore in the following section, through lived experiences and dynamic forms of resistance, Dalits articulate a subjectivity that challenges caste oppression and reimagines possibilities for emancipation.

3. The creation of Dalit subjectivity

It is hardly surprising that centuries of oppression and subjugation have produced repeated calls for the abolition of the caste system, with Dalits demanding basic human dignity and respect. Inevitably, religious conversion out of Hinduism has become a common means of escaping the caste system. This act has offered solace to many, yet even after their departure, most Dalits continue to face the same challenges. Such escape is only temporary because the body is permanent. Instead, through distinct forms of praxis, Dalits have used their bodies as sites of resistance to produce novel forms of resistance.

[57] ibid. Singh and Ramkumar also note how an additional amendment thereafter substituted 'on the ground' to 'knowing that such . . .'. This dilution necessarily admits that there was no higher burden to prove for a conviction.

[58] Burra (n 3).

[59] ibid.

[60] Venkatesh (n 1).

[61] ibid 184.

[62] *United States v Akshay Kumar Mozumdar* 296 F 173 (SD Cal 1923).

[63] Venkatesh (n 1) 185–87.

3.1 A threefold Dalit praxis

Dalit praxis can be understood through three distinct yet interrelated forms—the 'Three Rs': resilience, resourcefulness, and resistance. These modes of engagement form the basis of a unique epistemological perspective rooted in their lived experiences.

The first form of praxis involves Dalits' engagement with the domestic legal framework. Notwithstanding the specific laws in place to safeguard their interests, the legal system assumes the indelibility of the caste system, directly contradicting Dalits' basic calls for abolition. Nonetheless, Dalits navigate domestic spaces, opposing the caste system through protests,[64] advocacy, lobbying, and political participation, including the contestation of elections.[65] I am reminded of Angela Davis who once delivered two seemingly contradictory speeches in a single day:[66] she first argued that the legal system was corrupt thus making justice elusive, while later asserting that, even if governments lie, law and justice can remain above those deceptions.[67] Dalits also work with this 'multiple consciousness' employing a dualist approach when advocating for their rights.[68] While their ultimate goal is to abolish the caste system, Dalits tactically use controversies—large and small—to advance their cause. Speaking out against the brutalities they face is a powerful form of legal dissent.

The second form of praxis involves turning to international law and shifting the site of struggle beyond Indian social and political life. This sensibility galvanized the Dalit Panthers Movement, finding inspiration from the Black Panthers Party.[69] Given their fraught and ambivalent relationship with domestic protections, Dalits have sought external frameworks such as international law to counter the deficiencies of the Indian legal system.[70] Building on Cedric Robinson's concept of the Black Radical Tradition, Venkatesh proposes the idea of a Dalit Radical Tradition (DRT).[71] Grounded in Ambedkar's vision of a 'counter-hegemonic legal order based on abolitionist principles', Venkatesh articulates two components of the DRT.[72] First, the use of law as an emancipatory tactic constitutes the ultimate act of subversion for Dalits, who remain marginalized within existing legal vocabularies. Second, the strategic 'use of Eurocentric liberal rights' shifts the axis of power to confront the epistemic sites where caste operates and pervades epistemology.[73] As I argue in the fourth section, through international law Dalits have flirted with a DRT, challenging the limits of Indian legal discourse.

[64] Raj Gautaman, 'Dalit Protest Culture: The First Stage' in Ravikumar Azhagarasan (ed), *The Oxford Anthology of Tamil Dalit Writing* (Oxford University Press 2012) 264–69.
[65] IP Desai, 'Caste and Politics' (1967) 2(17) Economic and Political Weekly 797.
[66] Mari J Matsuda, 'When the First Quail Calls: Multiple-Consciousness as Jurisprudential Method' (1992) 14 (2&3) Women's Rights Law Reporter 297.
[67] ibid.
[68] ibid.
[69] Venkatesh (n 1) 177.
[70] Burra (n 3) 125.
[71] Venkatesh (n 1) 188.
[72] ibid 189.
[73] ibid 199–200.

The third form of praxis is Dalits' turn to alternative registers beyond the law—most prominently through writing. Dalit literature, considered a morally repugnant act to those opposed to Dalit emancipation, is a form of resistance, particularly given the longstanding discrimination Dalits face within educational institutions. Writing has allowed Dalit authors and poets to articulate the violence inflicted on their bodies, families, and communities in forthright and earnest ways.

3.2 The Dalit body: a subject

For Dalits, the body exists as both a site of resistance and a repository of trauma, experiencing what Adrien Wing describes as a 'spirit injury'—the 'slow death of the psyche, the soul, and the personal'[74] exacerbated by centuries of systemic oppression. Dalits lie at the intersections of caste, class, sex, and religion, making their bodies the focal point of layered and multifaceted oppression. James Giles wrote: 'my body is a maze of centres of perception which constitute my phenomenological point of view on the world'.[75] Viewing the body as a site of knowledge production is not novel, but gained traction within international law through critical feminist approaches.[76] Ratna Kapur observes that feminist and queer scholarship engage with 'affect theory' exploring 'how freedom and unfreedom are experienced in everyday life, an aspect often ignored in epistemological critiques'.[77] In this way, such scholarship aims to 'write the body back into theory'.[78]

As a phenomenological site of knowledge production, the body not only bears witness but also creates meaning and life beyond immediate comprehension.[79] However, the discourse around IHRL tends to neglect this material and embodied aspect of human experience. Bodies are inseparable from law;[80] in legal geography, the flesh-and-blood body and its discursive constructions through language can be studied together. The feminist perspective of the embodied legal geography emphasizes the body as a site of resistance, challenging the longstanding notion of law as a *disembodied* framework.[81] Instead, 'fleshy, vital, and dynamic bodies' refute the idea of law as something detached from lived experience.[82]

[74] Adrien Katherine Wing, 'Healing Spirit Injuries: Human Rights in the Palestinian Basic Law' (2002) 54 Rutgers Law Review 1087, 1088–89.
[75] James Giles, 'Bodily Theory and Theory of the Body' (1991) 66 (257) Philosophy 342.
[76] Hillary Charlesworth, Christine Chinkin, and Shelley Wright, 'Feminist Approaches to International Law' (1991) 85(4) American Journal of International Law 613.
[77] Ratna Kapur, *Gender, Alterity and Human Rights: Freedom in a Fishbowl* (Edward Elgar 2018) 153.
[78] ibid.
[79] Debjani Ganguly, 'Pain, Personhood and the Collective: Dalit Life Narratives' (2009) 33(4) Asian Studies Review 429.
[80] Alex Jeffrey, 'Legal geography II: Bodies and law' (2020) 44(5) Progress in Human Geography 1004.
[81] ibid.
[82] ibid.

3.3 The Dalit body: a subject

> Never was a man treated as a mind. As a glorious thing made up of stardust. In very field [sic], in studies, in streets, in politics, and in dying and living.
>
> Excerpt from Rohit Vemula's suicide letter[83]

When it comes to race and caste, the body is the focal point of study.[84] Subjectivity is tied to the 'experience of the connection to one's racialised body'[85] as 'racism never loses sight of the body'.[86] This understanding aligns with Fanon's assertion that the 'white man (as knower) constructs the white man through the black man (he who is to be known and negated)'.[87] As both subject and object, the body is capable of first-person experiences (such as immediate somatosensory perceptions) and third-person experiences (such as seeing one's reflection, which compensates for the impossibility of directly perceiving oneself).[88] To fully experience itself, the body must, paradoxically, step beyond itself.

For Dalits, life is experienced simultaneously as an object and as a body. In the public spaces they occupy, the roles they perform, and the lifestyles they are forced to follow, the Dalit body is both hyper-visible and vanished. It is through their muted presence as darker bodies that 'disembodied whiteness'—or in this context, upper-caste identity—is affirmed.[89] As Dipesh Chakrabarty explains, the Dalit body, in the eyes of a Brahmin, is perpetually associated with death and waste matter, effectively linking it to the non-human and non-living.[90] By being the 'known' or 'seen' object, the Dalit body comes into being only through these imposed terms. Its visibility perpetuates its invisibility, further exacerbated by the disgust and ostracization Dalits face, denying them even the most basic human dignity, such as the act of being touched.[91] This argument should not be mistaken for an exoticization of Dalits' bodies, or a glorification of the ills they suffer; instead, as an object, the Dalit body gains a unique vantage point, offering a distinct standpoint from which to engage with the world.

Indeed, as Almeida notes, there is an 'advantage that racialised bodies have in positions of exclusion and inclusion, having viewpoints from the margins and the mainstream ... this position liminal; between two worlds or states of understanding ... is pivotal to the deconstruction and dismantling of the white, western knower'.[92] Seeing the body as an object is essential to uncovering the narrative of pain unique to Dalit

[83] The Wire Staff (n 14).
[84] Shana Almeida, 'Race-Based Epistemologies: The Role of Race and Dominance in Knowledge Production' (2015) 13 (Summer) Wagadu 80.
[85] ibid 96.
[86] ibid.
[87] ibid 90.
[88] ibid.
[89] ibid.
[90] Dipesh Chakrabarty, 'The Dalit Body: A Reading for the Anthropocene' in Zoya Hasan and others (eds), *The Empire of Disgust: Prejudice, Discrimination, and Policy in India and the US* (Oxford University Press 2018) 5.
[91] ibid 6.
[92] Almeida (n 85).

experiences. These narratives reveal the transformation of Dalits from being 'objects of self-pity to self-owning objects', reclaiming their agency even amidst structural violence and exclusion.[93]

Dalit subjectivity is shaped by the embodied experience of enduring and resisting systemic oppression. Through the threefold praxis—resilience, resourcefulness, and resistance—Dalits engage with legal frameworks, both domestic and international, while also using creative expressions to challenge caste hierarchies. The Dalit body functions as a site of lived experience, carrying the weight of historical and ongoing trauma but also generating knowledge and disrupting abstract legal conceptions. As an object, the Dalit body is rendered hyper-visible through its association with stigma and marginality, while being erased and dehumanized. This dual role grants Dalits a distinct standpoint to critique and subvert the systems that oppress them, offering insights into the intersections of caste, law, and resistance. In the following section, I turn to the liberal subject in IHRL, examining how abstract and universalist assumptions fail to account for the realities of Dalit oppression and resistance, while highlighting the limitations of the rights framework in addressing caste-based violence.

4. The (liberal) subject in human rights law

International law is built on the foundation of 'rational' notions of individual rights and freedoms. With modernity came the Enlightenment, which championed rationality while simultaneously setting off imperialist projects across the globe. Within this framework, whiteness became synonymous with the mind, and Blackness the body, disparaged as irrational, uncivilized, and incapable of rational action.[94] This binary positioned white Europeans as possessors of objective truths, while relegating non-whites to the realm of savagery. Critical and feminist scholars have since exposed the fallacy of this representation: 'this is a fiction which devalues and excludes the roles of belief, language, culture, material context, and other non-rational dimensions of our beings.'[95] Furthermore, while international law emphasizes individuals as its central subjects, this rationalist tradition isolates the individual from their communities, erasing the social dimensions of lived experience.[96] As Burra asks: 'What needs to be examined is whether this exclusion of lived experiences of the lower caste peoples is also endemic to the studies in law, particularly international law?'[97]

[93] Riad Azam, 'Imagining the Dalit Identity: An Analysis of Narrative Techniques in Select Dalit Writing' (2022) 7(5) The Creative Launcher 69; Davies (n 13).

[94] Almeida (n 85).

[95] ibid 5.

[96] Dalit testimonies, by their very nature, are not restricted to the 'self', but 'switch to the collective memory of the larger group'. See Alexandra de Heering, 'Dalit Writing, Dalit Speaking: On the Encounters between Dalit Autobiographies and Oral Histories' in Joshil K Abraham and Judith Misrahi-Barak (eds), *Dalit Literatures in India* (Routledge 2021).

[97] Burra (n 3).

4.1 The Dalit within IHRL

When caste-based discrimination was first raised before the Committee on the Elimination of Racial Discrimination in 1996, India firmly opposed merging race with caste.[98] The Committee clarified that 'descent' not only included race but also caste, while expressing concerns about the persistence of caste discrimination in India despite the existence of legal safeguards for caste minorities.[99] This intervention was significant, but momentum slowed until the issue was raised at the 2001 World Conference Against Racism. Once again, participants called for caste to be recognized as a form of descent-based discrimination akin to racial discrimination, with India continuing to oppose.[100]

The IHRL framework is limited in addressing caste-based discrimination. Existing treaties focus on affirming; acknowledging; and protecting civil, political, social, and economic rights, but they fail to engage with the scale and complexity of caste violence.[101] Efforts like the interventions in Durban, Universal Periodic Reviews, and other international mechanisms have done little to generate sustained action or detailed strategies to combat caste oppression.[102] The issue has seldom gained any traction in these fora, remaining superficial and failing to capture the pervasive and everyday violence experienced by Dalits.[103]

4.2 Unlimited rights, limited freedom(s): the limits of IHRL

Makau Mutua argues that IHRL operates with a predetermined savage-victim-saviour dynamic, informed by chauvinism and racialization.[104] The IHRL regime's ideological blueprint imposes universal solutions onto local problems, often disempowering the victims it seeks to rescue in the process.[105] In Mutua's terms, human rights present oppressed people as powerless and voiceless, dependent on virtuous external saviours to rescue them from savage states or cultures: '[t]he usual human rights narrative generally describes victims as hordes of nameless, despairing, and dispirited masses.'[106] From this perspective, IHRL relies on the continual disenfranchisement of those it wishes to protect.[107]

[98] Committee on the Elimination of Racial Discrimination, 'Fourteenth periodic reports of states parties due in 1996' (29 April 1996) CERD/C/299/Add.3, [7].

[99] ibid.

[100] Burra (n 3).

[101] Makau w Mutua, 'Savages, Victims, and Saviors: The Metaphor of Human Rights'(2001) 42(1) Harvard International Law Journal 201, 228.

[102] International Dalit Solidarity Network, 'Caste related recommendations and observations by states during the 3rd India's UPR' (*International Dalit Solidarity Network*, October 2017) <https://idsn.org/wp-content/uploads/2017/10/Caste-references-India-UPR-3rd-cycle.pdf> accessed 21 October 2021.

[103] Burra (n 3).

[104] Mutua (n 102).

[105] ibid 221.

[106] Mutua (n 102) 229.

[107] Frantz Fanon, *Black Skin, White Masks* (Charles Lam Markmann tr, Grove Press 1967)

Similarly, Kapur critiques the Western liberal conception of human rights by making three compelling claims. First, she argues that human rights are not inherently tied to freedom; instead, their main function is to mitigate cruelty and suffering. Second, she disputes the assumption that culture and tradition hinder human progress and that the oppressed can only be 'rescued through the universalist premise of human rights and liberal individualism'.[108] Third, she contends that human rights are based on the existence of a common universal subject. Victims are predominantly non-white, and within this framework, efforts to 'save' Dalits from the caste system often serve only to reaffirm what is already presumed about their victimhood, without addressing the structural roots of their oppression.

Another key limitation of the current IHRL regime is its inability to capture atrocities on their own terms. Instead, it responds by promising rights after their violation, ignoring the inherent deficiencies in this reactive approach. The limitations of the current IHRL regime highlight its inability to engage with caste-based oppression. Rooted in a Western liberal framework, the human rights-based approach almost always applies a universal framework without considering alternative rights and obligations rooted in local contexts.[109] By relying on universalization, the regime assumes that a problem must be globally understood to warrant attention.[110] For instance, by the logic of IHRL, caste must transcend Indian borders and become a sufficiently international problem before action is taken, if ever. Should the violence and dehumanization faced by Dalits not already shock the collective conscience of humanity, regardless of its geographic boundaries, rather than demanding that Dalits tease the regime's need for ubiquity? Moreover, IHRL operates through assumptions that prioritize abstract, rational individuals over the lived experiences of real communities.[111] By relying on liberal solutions and abstract subjects, IHRL often dismisses cultural and historical contexts thus reinforcing the same racialized hierarchies they lament. Dalits within this paradigm are yet another example of how local struggles are absorbed into narratives that reaffirm preconceived notions of victimhood.

As Mutua observed, 'the human rights movement must be moored in the cultures of all peoples'[112] if it is to support the emancipation of oppressed peoples the world over. In the following section, I explore an example of mooring via a race-based epistemology that challenges the dominance of a Western episteme in international law.[113] Dalit poetry offers a unique political and aesthetic lens to express their pain and ideas for emancipation that transcend the narrow frameworks of human rights. Writers like Dhasal and Halder challenge conventional notions of beauty, legality, and social order, creating an alternative epistemology that bypasses the limitations of rational, universalist frameworks. Ultimately, engaging with alternate epistemes is necessary

[108] Kapur (n 77) 14.
[109] Anne Peters and Tom Sparks, 'Introduction: The History and Theory of the Individual in International Law' in Anne Peters and Tom Sparks (eds), *The Individual in International Law* (Oxford University Press 2024) 11.
[110] Kapur (n 77) 36.
[111] Mutua (n 12).
[112] ibid 208.
[113] Almeida (n 85).

for 'unveiling the hidden dynamics of knowledge production' and 'can be a powerful antidote against international lawyers' resignation to the present order of things'.[114]

5. Beyond ...

Building on their resilience and resourcefulness, I now turn to the third 'R': resistance—the creative and alternative registers, such as poetry and literature, that Dalits employ to articulate their struggle and embody their vision of emancipation.

> ... Upstream, the water is for you all to take
> Downstream, the water is for us to get
> Bravo! Bravo!
> How even water is taught the caste system
> Namdeo Dhasal, 'Water'[115]

Re-imagining emancipation requires acknowledging that it takes diverse forms, shaped by the contexts of those seeking liberation. As Namdeo Dhasal's 'Water' exemplifies, Dalit consciousness expressed through writing is a powerful political tool, generating novel sensibilities that challenge and exceed conventional worldviews.[116] As Oishik Sircar writes:

> What is required, then, is a re-imagining of emancipation by searching for and archiving material practices of being that embody insurrectionary knowledge: knowledge that brings an understanding of rights as embodied practices of resistance that disturb the linear trajectories of constitutional narratives of emancipation; and knowledge that reproduces the magic of modernity and normalizes inequality.[117]

Sircar describes this process as a 'poetic detour', a glimpse into forms of epistemic emancipation through Dalit literature and poetry, where Dalits engage with the world on their own terms.[118] Encountering the narrative experience in the law is not uncommon, as with law and literature. Where the former is seen as rational and objective, literature captures the nuance of affect and experience otherwise neglected. Narratives are crucial for international law as well, as argued by Julia Otten, where it provides a lens through which movements gain transformative power.[119]

[114] Tommaso Soave, 'International Law's Invisible Frames: Social Cognition and Knowledge Production in International Legal Processes' (2023) 117(3) American Journal of International Law 548.

[115] Namdeo Dhasal, *A Current of Blood* (Navayana Publishing 2011).

[116] Ravi Shankar Kumar, 'The Politics of Dalit Literature' in Joshil K Abraham and Judith Misrahi-Barak (eds), *Dalit Literatures in India* (Routledge 2021).

[117] Oishik Sircar, 'Spectacles of Emancipation: Reading Rights Differently in India's Legal Discourse' (2012) 49 Osgoode Hall Law Journal 527, 570.

[118] ibid 569.

[119] Julia Otten, 'Narratives in International Law' (2016) 99(3) Critical Quarterly for Legislation and Law 187. Otten cites Richard Wiesberg who had noted that law is too proud to admit it is 'basically narrative nature'.

Dalit poetry is written from 'impure' spaces, eschewing *Soundarya* or aesthetics of beauty.[120] Instead, it offers a distinct political and embodied perspective.[121] Debjani Ganguly notes that 'Dalit personhood', as understood in the Indian public sphere, exceeds legal subjectivity and abstract citizenship.[122] She argues that Dalit pain is expressed through an aesthetic 'not wholly translatable into the lexicon of rights and justice'.[123] Dalit testimonials function 'less as a proxy for the legal witnessing and amelioration of Dalit pain than as a rich and expressive medium of Dalit personhood'.[124] Testimonial narratives are as personal as they are political; as much an expression of one voice as it is of a collective.[125] As Pramod Nayar noted, Dalit life-writing generates 'abject-types'—'figures of abjection occurring in literatures of trauma across the world'.[126]

For Dalits, literary and poetic spaces offer refuge: they can engage with the 'parts of the self that do not function in explicitly verbal ways . . . and . . . remains an experience that is by its nature inexpressible'.[127] As Muthukkaruppan explained, caste is not a static thing but a dynamic relationship continually reshaped through violence—a reality narrated in Dalit poetry and bodies.[128] They can speak to their experiences of violence, discrimination, and exclusion that often defy legal verbalization; 'traumatic realism' places the body at the forefront of the debate.[129]

Figures like Namdeo Dhasal—a taxi driver who wrote poetry in his free time and was a pivotal member of the Dalit Panthers Movement—shook conventional notions of poetry and aesthetics with his raw imagery and uninhibited use of expletives. His writing condemned the status quo, describing subordination and violence in terms that evoke an emotional response different from news reports or legal texts.[130] Likewise, Ambedkar's writings became foundational for understanding oppression in its own terms, detailing his experiences from childhood to adulthood that demonstrate the banality of caste-based discrimination.[131] In *Annihilation of Caste*,[132] he uses language to portray suffering, calling for the annihilation of the caste system.[133]

[120] Roughly translates to 'beauty'.
[121] Kumar (n 117).
[122] Ganguly (n 79).
[123] ibid. See also Pramod K Nayar, 'The Poetics of Postcolonial Atrocity: Dalit Life Writing, *Testimonio*, and Human Rights' (2011) 42 (3–4) Ariel-a Review of International English Literature 237. Nayar says: 'An atrocity narrative is, then, irreducibly "double voiced": it is located within a discursive structure specific to a time and place, thus ensuring that the atrocity is made recognizable, and the demand for rights is made part of a universal schema of values.'
[124] Jeffrey (n 80).
[125] Nayar (n 123) 239.
[126] ibid.
[127] Jeffrey (n 80).
[128] Parthasarathi Muthukkaruppan, 'Critique of Caste Violence' (2017) 45(1) Social Scientist 49.
[129] Nayar (n 124) 240.
[130] Venkatesh (n 1) 189.
[131] BR Ambedkar, 'Waiting for a Visa' in Vasant Moon (ed), *Dr. Babasaheb Ambedkar: Writings and Speeches, Vol. 12* (Education Department, Govt of Maharashtra 1998). Ambedkar writes of Dalits having to 'regard the village in every way as their home—and yet never touch or be touched by any one belonging to the village'.
[132] BR Ambedkar, 'Annihilation of Caste (1936)' (*Colombia Centre for Teaching and Learning*) <https://ccnmtl.columbia.edu/projects/mmt/ambedkar/web/readings/aoc_print_2004.pdf> accessed 10 October 2021.
[133] ibid.

Other Dalit writers, such as Baby Halder, have expanded the Dalit aesthetic. Halder, a domestic worker turned writer, narrates her story of abandonment, abuse, and survival, all explored vis-à-vis her body, a Dalit's pre-eminent site of politics. In *A Life Less Ordinary*, Halder,[134] the third child of four children, moved to Delhi to escape her abusive husband.[135] After finding work as a domestic in the home of Prabodh Kumar—the man she fondly calls Tatush—she narrated her life in the notebook he gifted her. Hailed as a radical act of resistance, Halder resists the trope of a triumphant 'American Dream', remaining, as she declares, 'a servant, whose talents as a writer are found wanting'.[136] In *Sangati*, Bama, another prominent Dalit writer, tells an anecdote of a Dalit woman publicly berating her husband and humiliating him by 'lifting up her sari'. Yet, humiliation takes on a different connotation when viewed through the lens of Dalit experiences. Dalit women like Bama do not need polemics:[137] for these women, 'the world only exists through the filter of personal experience'.[138] Language continues to remain the primary medium through which Dalit self-expression continues. Even language, with its inherent multiplicity of meaning, often fails to fully capture the complexity of such experiences. As a result, certain truths remain hidden even from the speaker's own consciousness, only to be realized by the body, translatable into this non-legal language thereafter.

While IHRL often claims to give voice to the voiceless or foster caste-consciousness, such efforts risk oversimplifying and misinterpreting Dalit poetry. Through their literature, Dalits document the slow, even banal violence they must contend with, demonstrating that normative understandings of justice are incomplete. Unlike the resolution-driven narratives of IHRL, Dalit literature embraces incompleteness. It offers fragmented, raw accounts that are 'made interpretable [and] become bearable'[139] by their very gaps, inviting the reader to confront 'unconscious prejudices, superstitions, sentiment, and weakness'.[140] These narratives resist erasure, offering a consciousness of pain and resistance that Dalits seek to share—not through abstract concepts but through unfiltered depictions of their reality.

6. Conclusion

The *dark side* of the supposedly virtuous IHRL project lies in its persistent lack of self-reflection and its failure to look beyond itself. Yet, despite its limitations, the promise

[134] Baby Halder, *A Life Less Ordinary* (Zubaan Classics 2013).

[135] ibid. Baby's mother leaves with the youngest child, leaving the other three with their father. They reunite several years later after Baby has had children of her own. Baby had been unable to move past her childhood when her mother left a ten *paisa* coin in her palm and deserted her, never to return.

[136] Martine van Woerkens, 'A Life Less Ordinary: The Female Subaltern and Dalit Literature in Contemporary India' in Joshil K Abraham and Judith Misrahi-Barak (eds), *Dalit Literatures in India* (Routledge 2021); Amelia Gentleman, 'In India, a Maid Becomes an Unlikely Literary Star' (*The New York Times*, 2 August 2006) <https://www.nytimes.com/2006/08/02/books/02maid.html> accessed 10 October 2021.

[137] van Woerkens (n 137).

[138] ibid 242.

[139] Otten (n 120) 198.

[140] ibid.

of redemption within the rights framework remains difficult to abandon entirely, even for Dalits, who continue to seek justice within existing structures while also imagining alternatives. As Mutua, Kapur, and other critical scholars have argued, the IHRL regime must grapple with its epistemic silences and explore not only non-Western frameworks, but also non-Brahmanical ones in order to expand its understanding of justice and freedom. Dalit praxis and subjectivity offer a way forward.

Dalit praxis conveys a multitude of possibilities towards rethinking emancipation and advancing epistemic justice. Through their resilience, resourcefulness, and resistance, Dalits engage with oppressive systems that disinherit them. They do so not out of desperation but as a deliberate act of defiance. Dalit activism has involved pursuing safeguards from caste-based discrimination within the law—both domestic and international—whilst simultaneously calling for the abolition of the caste system altogether. Dalit bodies, as sites of knowledge production, similarly hold multitudes: they bear the scars of systemic violence as well as espousals to freedom that escape ordinary legal language.

To address the violence that sustains caste oppression, the IHRL regime must move beyond its liberal promises and embrace non-liberal, non-Western, and non-Brahmanical frames of thinking and being. While emancipation from the caste system seems elusive, Dalits have achieved immediate forms of freedom—from their bodies and through their bodies—and, via their literature, ensuring that their vision of resistance remains ever-present. Human rights scholars and advocates should take notice.

21

Racism, (Neo)Colonialism, and International Law

A Field in Search of a Philosophy?

Radha D'Souza[*]

> There is a zone of nonbeing, an extraordinarily sterile and arid region, an utterly naked declivity where an authentic upheaval can be born . . . Man is not merely a possibility of recapture or of negation . . . Man is a *yes* that vibrates to cosmic harmonies . . . We shall go very slowly, for there are two camps: the white and the black. Stubbornly we shall investigate both metaphysics and we shall find that they are quite fluid.
>
> Frantz Fanon[1]

1. Beginnings

What is the relationship of international law to racism? This chapter addresses the central theme of this collection by questioning its epistemological assumptions. It argues that an answer must clarify the philosophical premises of capitalist-colonial modernity as a knowledge system. This chapter takes Antony Anghie's seminal text *Imperialism, Sovereignty and The Making of International Law*[2] as its point of departure, probing philosophical, theoretical, conceptual, and methodological problems that lurk beneath contemporary attempts to put racism and international law in conversation. Anghie's *Imperialism* is influential and feeds into the renewed race consciousness in scholarship and activism. It provides an origin story for international law, and is deeply historical.

About 500 years ago, a Spanish theologian and jurist, a Dominican priest and Thomist, named Francisco Vitoria, upon learning about *discoveries* of ancient lands and peoples, sought to clarify the status of the Indigenous peoples and Spain's authority over them. In so doing, Vitoria's lectures, delivered between 1537 and 1539, established the architecture of international law in relation to non-European peoples.

* I wish to thank Leuphana Institute of Advanced Studies at the Leuphana University of Lüneburg for their generous fellowship which provided the time and research support to write this chapter.

1 Frantz Fanon, *Black Skin White Masks* (Pluto Press 2008) 2.

2 Antony Anghie, *Imperialism, Sovereignty and the Making of International Law* (Cambridge University Press 2005).

Radha D'souza, *Racism, (Neo)Colonialism, and International Law* In: *Emancipating International Law*. Edited by: Mohsen al Attar and Claire Smith, Oxford University Press. © Radha D'souza 2026. DOI: 10.1093/9780198935605.003.0027

In *Imperialism*, contemporary international law is the teleological development of a jurisprudence that is founded on cultural difference as its *telos*, something like the Aristotelian acorn that grows into an oak tree but always containing within it more acorn-oak proliferations.[3] *Imperialism* inducts Critical Race Theory (CRT) into the heart of International Law.[4] It lures international law scholarship to follow in the footsteps of the 'cultural turn' that social sciences and humanities scholarship has taken.[5]

The so-called *Discoveries* since the late fifteenth century presented new questions for European societies that they could not answer within the pre-modern European systems of knowledge. As I argue later, this period from the Renaissance, Reformation, and Counter Reformation was a period of transition from land-centric feudal social orders of mediaeval Europe to commodity-centric social orders of modern Europe. The social, economic, military, and intellectual transformations during that critical period laid the foundations for capitalist-colonial modernity including the ideological preconditions and presuppositions for the new order, the transition to modern law, and ontological ideas about the place of human beings in the cosmos which inform ideas about cultural and racial difference. The critique of racism, (neo)colonialism and law (national and international) needs philosophical, theoretical, and methodological premises that are grounded in the unique historical and social experiences of colonialism and imperialism at ideological, historical, and material levels that can be tethered to a unified philosophical critique of capitalist-colonial modernity as a knowledge system.

First, we must disentangle the use of the terms racism and (neo)colonialism. Racism sometimes includes (neo)colonialism, they can be used interchangeably, or applied without conceptual differentiation. The opacity of the terms has ramifications when putting racism in conversation with law. Racism is about relations between a class of citizens who became 'minorities' or were made 'marginal' within capitalist nation-states through processes of settlement, slavery, and migrations. It entails class-relations between segments of working peoples within and raises questions about citizenship and the constitutional order. National oppression, in contrast, concerns domination and subjugation over multiple states, colonial and neocolonial, *as* nations by a small group of powerful imperial/capitalist states. (Neo)colonialism, to the contrary, presents questions about national oppression *qua* nations in international law and the international order. The former is endogenous to capitalist relations while the latter is exogenous to it and entails different apparatuses of governance and legal orders that nonetheless share common epistemological and historical premises.

Likewise, capitalism and colonialism need clarification. Capital is not a 'thing' like money, a commodity, or any other object. Capital is a web of social relations that organize society in ways that reproduce those relations. Racism is one form of social

[3] HS Thayer, 'Aristotle on Nature: A Study in the Relativity of Concepts and Procedures of Analysis' (1975) 28(4) *The Review of Metaphysics* 725.

[4] Anghie (n 2) 289–91.

[5] Chris Rojek and Bryan Turner, 'Decorative Sociology: Towards a Critique of the Cultural Turn' (2000) 48(4) *The Sociological Review* 629.

relation with its genesis as a form of labour. Colonialism is a generic term that includes many legal forms of governance. Under the British empire alone there were four main forms of colonialism: settlement, protectorate systems, agency states, and crown colonies. Neocolonialism is the subjugation of a nation *qua* nation by inducting historically constituted states and societies in their entirety, as a node of imperialism. Since the end of the Second World War international law established and governed neocolonial relations.[6]

With definitions in hand, we can now chart the chapter. In the next section, I use the paradox of law and race in everyday practices of policymakers in imperial states—such as the United States and the United Kingdom—to map Marxist and CRT approaches to racism and (neo)colonial law, arguing that these approaches remain tangled in methodological problems of constant conjunctions in liberal theory. History is the source for an account of racism and (neo)colonialism's relationship to law. Section 3 unpacks the methodological moves in CRT and Third World Approaches to International Law (TWAIL) in writing legal histories that include colonized and racialized peoples. I argue that inclusive history writing is confronted by what I call 'philosophical autism'. In Section 4, I expand on the philosophical critique of capitalist modernity as a knowledge system arguing that it is a distinctive semiotic structure of thought that is characterized by dualism. The formative period for the genesis of modernist thought lies in the historical transition in Europe from a triadic structure of thought to a dyadic structure. The *medium, code, and message* of modernist knowledge as a system lies in grasping what is entailed in that transition for human and non-human lives. Section 5 uses the debate about Vitoria's contributions to international law and colonialism to underscore the significance of temporalities in the more embedded debates about the relationship of historical social structures to human agency in the history of ideas. The temporalities in structure-agency relationships reveal the medium, code, and message of the continuities and changes in legal histories. Histories of ideas, however, must be anchored to the materiality of capitalism and colonialism.

Section 6 argues that the historical and philosophical premise for racial-colonial relations in capitalism lies in what I call the 'original sin of capitalism', which is the introduction of the land–labour dualism. In turn, the original sin produces the dualism of labour as commodity and humans as social being, or 'social bipolarity', and the paradox of law which advances equality and non-discrimination, self-determination, and sovereign equality in ways that reproduce unequal relations between people and nations. The brief concluding section recaps the need to liberate the question of the relationship of racism and (neo)colonialism to law by putting it on more solid philosophical foundations, a task that calls for radically transforming the epistemological and methodological moves in scholarship.

6 See Radha D'Souza, 'Transcending Disciplinary Fetishisms: Marxism, Neocolonialism, and International Law' in Paul O'Connell and Umut Özsu (eds), *Elgar Handbook on Law and Marxism* (Edward Elgar 2021).

2. Constant conjunctions, causal mechanisms, and liberalism

An elucidative discussion happened in the newspapers as I prepared this chapter. Financial dailies reported that wages in the United States had climbed to a historic high, which was good news for working people. However, the US Federal Reserve worried because wage growth fuelled inflationary pressures, and controlling inflation was a statutory responsibility of the US Federal Reserve. In other words, the Federal Reserve would have to raise interest rates to balance the increases in the price of labour to bring down inflation.[7] In the US Federal Reserve's thought-world, increasing interest rates would increase the cost of borrowing for manufacturers (ie the employers) and they, in turn, would cut wage-costs and increase the cost of consumption goods and services, that is, the cost of living. What employers gave with one hand, the commodity markets could take away with the other. Working families would continue to struggle but that is nothing new. Newspapers told similar stories about the Bank of England and wage increases in the United Kingdom.[8]

Political news told a different story. A former US Secretary of Labour praised the Biden presidency's economic policies, especially the Inflation Reduction Act 2022, now labelled 'Bidenomics', that gave subsidies to hi-tech manufacturing sectors including chip manufacturers so that 'American' workers got well-paid jobs.[9] The Inflation Reduction Act targeted imports, including hi-tech goods from China and the European Union (EU) in violation of World Trade Organization rules prohibiting subsidies. The Act would adversely impact manufacturing and job markets in China (an adversary) and the EU (an ally), but that is another state's problem. For their part, the UK's Chancellor reassured industries that the government had budgeted for incentives for hi-tech industries so that 'British' workers had better jobs.[10] Two months later, the Chancellor reported that while employment did fall, the fall in real wages was steeper, adding that to balance the government's books, they would cut back welfare spending which would in turn push people into work.[11] By this stage, even an attentive reader of newspapers loses track of the multiple rationalities at work in the regulation of labour markets.

[7] Ben Casselman, 'Wages Continue to Grow, Good for Workers but a Worry for the Fed', *The New York Times* (New York, 28 April 2023) <https://www.nytimes.com/2023/04/28/business/wage-inflation-march.html> accessed 5 September 2023.

[8] Andy Bruce, 'Surprise UK Wage Jump Raises Likelihood of Higher Interest Rates' *Reuters* (London, 13 June 2023) <https://www.reuters.com/world/uk/uk-annual-wage-growth-72-excluding-bonuses-three-months-april-ons-2023-06-13/> accessed 5 September 2023.

[9] Robert Reich, 'Opinion: 'Bidenomics' is Working—Which Means Biden and Democrats May Win Too' *The Guardian* (2 August 2023) <https://www.theguardian.com/commentisfree/2023/aug/02/bidenomics-is-working-which-means-biden-and-the-democrats-may-win-too> accessed 5 September 2023.

[10] Jeremy Hunt, 'Chancellor Jeremy Hunt's Speech at Bloomberg' (Speech at Bloomberg, London, 27 January 2023) <https://www.gov.uk/government/speeches/chancellor-jeremy-hunts-speech-at-bloomberg> accessed 5 September 2023; see also Phillip Inman, 'Jeremy Hunt Overdoses the Es: Why His Economic Plan is a Let Down' *The Guardian* (London, 27 January 2023) <https://www.theguardian.com/business/2023/jan/27/jeremy-hunt-economic-plan-brexit-uk> accessed 5 September 2023.

[11] Larry Elliott, 'Hunt's Budget Aims to Push People Back to Work Just as the Jobs Market Weakens' *The Guardian* (London, 14 March 2023) <https://www.theguardian.com/business/2023/mar/14/jeremy-hunt-budget-work-jobs-market-employment-wage-growth> accessed 5 September 2023.

It is well known that investments in hi-tech jobs go, largely, to White male workers; that job losses in low paid sectors of the economy impact Black, Brown and ethnic minority people, and women disproportionately.[12] Central banks and governments who argue that their economic policies aim at increasing jobs for workers speak as if 'American' and 'British' workers had no race, ethnicity, nationality, or gender. If anything, states and employers proclaim their commitment to equal opportunities for all.[13]

I note three points from the above account. The first is the disjuncture between the economic and political logics, rationalities, and debates even when institutions and policymakers speak about related issues. The second is that the reserve banks will not even cast a glance at the social impacts of their policies, and the governments will not challenge reserve banks' policies even when those policies frustrate their stated social goals. The third is that while the spokespersons for the economy and polity both rely on the law to fix problems, they invoke different statutory and governance tools. Central banks are legally tasked to control inflation to generate growth and jobs; equalities regulators pursue non-discrimination goals without any authority over economic policies; and international trade policies seek to increase investments and trade without regard for the social or economic impact on other states. The Inflation Reduction Act and the Civil Rights Act do not speak the same language, creating distinct boxes: 'economic regulation' pertains to economic actors while 'social regulation' concerns working peoples. Each follows different rationalities and logics that do not meet. However, they do converge in the lives of people, precipitating profound implications for racialized and (neo)colonized peoples.

The separation of economics and politics is a well-rehearsed theme, especially in Marxist critiques.[14] The nub of Marxist theories of capitalism is labour: the extraction of surplus value; the exploitation and super-exploitation of labour as the engine of capitalist modes of production; and the political, legal, and institutional arrangements supportive of the extraction of surplus value from working peoples. From the abstract categorical, conceptual, and methodological analysis of the separation of economy from polity, and theories of surplus value under capitalism, explanations of racism and (neo)colonialism, and difference more widely, is neither straightforward nor self-evident. Nor is imperialism a simple extension of capitalism on global planes. Yet,

[12] US Bureau of Labour Statistics, 'Labour Force Characteristics by Race and Ethnicity 2021' (*US Bureau of Labour*, January 2023) <https://www.bls.gov/opub/reports/race-and-ethnicity/2021/> accessed 5 September 2023; Sam Avanzo Windett and others, '*The Future of Work: Protected Characteristics in a Changing Workplace*' (United Kingdom Equality and Human Rights Commission, 2023) <https://view.officeapps.live.com/op/view.aspx?src=https%3A%2F%2Fwww.equalityhumanrights.com%2Fsites%2Fdefault%2Ffiles%2Ffuture_of_work_report_eng.docx&wdOrigin=BROWSELINK> accessed 5 September 2023.

[13] See Julie Coffman and Maria Gordian, 'Workplace Racial Equity Depends on Job Retention as Much as Job Hires to Achieve a Truly Diverse Workforce' (*The World Economic Forum*, 26 May 2021) <https://www.weforum.org/agenda/2021/05/this-is-how-to-achieve-racial-equity-at-work/> accessed 6 September 2023; Jody Heymann and others, 'Race, Ethnicity, and Discrimination at Work: A New Analysis of Legal Protections and Gaps in All 193 UN Countries' (2023) 42(9) *Equality, Diversity and Inclusion: An International Journal* 16.

[14] Jonathan Nitzan and Shimshon Bichler, 'Capital Accumulation: Breaking the Dualism of "Economics" and "Politics"' in Ronan Palan (ed), *Global Political Economy: Contemporary Theories* (Routledge 2000); Ellen Meiksins Wood, *Empire of Capital* (Verso 2003).

those categories, concepts, and methods are central for analyses of racism and (neo) colonialism.

In CRT scholarship, 'racial capitalism' emphasizes the tangled relationship of racism and capitalism from multiple perspectives.[15] The racial capitalism literature is thin on analysis of capitalism, however.[16] At its core, racial capitalism is a critique about the role of markets in fragmenting working peoples and assigning certain social groups—white, Black, Brown, and yellow nationally, and different Third World countries internationally (Bangladesh, Benin, or Brazil)—to specific segments of labour in different industries at particular times and locations.[17] The critique of law in racial capitalism practised in capitalist centres like the United States focuses on racialized class relations between labour and capital. It asks why, despite constitutional rights to equality and non-discrimination, the majority of racialized citizens remain at the bottom of the social ladder, while some racialized citizens—Barack Obama, Rishi Sunak, Oprah Winfrey, or Jacky Wright—make it to the top. The law in these studies is usually national.[18]

Imperialism, in contrast, is about imperial-(neo)colonial relations, about national oppression and the subjugation of nations *qua* nations. Recent critiques of imperialism and (neo)colonialism and the asymmetric relations of domination between nation-states in the peripheries of capitalist centres, has brought back themes like super-exploitation, value extraction in global supply chains, and national oppression in contemporary imperialism.[19] However, international law scholarship has focused more on the *impacts* of international economic law and resource extraction on peoples and communities in the Third World[20] and less on the legal and regulatory mechanisms that assign places to countries in the global labour markets. Impact analysis leaves open the theorization of the relationship of international law to the international imperialist order.

[15] Charisse Burden-Stelly, 'Modern U.S. Racial Capitalism: Some Theoretical Insights' (*Monthly Review*, 1 July 2020) <https://monthlyreview.org/2020/07/01/modern-u-s-racial-capitalism/> accessed 6 September 2023; Michael Fakhri, 'Markets, Sovereignty, and Racialization' (2022) 25(2) *Journal of International Economic Law* 242; Ruth Wilson Gilmore, 'Fatal Couplings of Power and Difference: Notes on Racism and Geography' (2002) 54(1) *The Professional Geographer* 15; Catherine Hall, "Racial Capitalism: What's in a Name?' (2022) 94 *History Workshop Journal* 5; Destin Jenkins and Justin Leroy (eds), *Histories of Racial Capitalism* (Columbia University Press 2021); Michael Ralph and Maya Singhal, 'Racial Capitalism' (2019) 48(6) *Theory and Society* 851; Cedric J Robinson *Black Marxism: The Making of the Black Radical Tradition* (University of North Carolina Press 2000).

[16] Julian Go, 'Three Tensions in the Theory of Racial Capitalism' (2021) 39(1) *Sociological Theory* 38.

[17] Karen Brodkin, 'Global Capitalism: What's Race Got to Do with It?' (2000) 27(2) *American Ethnologist* 237.

[18] eg Brenna Bhandar, 'Disassembling Legal Form: Ownership and the Racial Body' in Matthew Stone, Illan rua Wall, and Costas Douzinas (eds), *New Critical Legal Thinking: Law and the Political* (Taylor & Francis Group 2012); Angela P Harris, 'Equality Trouble: Sameness and Difference in Twentieth-Century Race Law' (2000) 88(6) *California Law Review* 1923; Natsu Taylor Saito, *Settler Colonialism, Race, and the Law: Why Structural Racism Persists* (New York University Press 2020).

[19] Christian Fuchs, 'Digital Labor and Imperialism' (*Monthly Review*, 1 January 2016) <https://monthlyreview.org/2016/01/01/digital-labor-and-imperialism/> accessed 6 September 2023; Andy Higginbottom, 'A Self-Enriching Pact: Imperialism and the Global South' (2018) 5(1–2) *Journal of Global Faultlines* 49; John Smith, *Imperialism in the Twenty-First Century: Globalization, Super-Exploitation, and Capitalism's Final Crisis* (Monthly Review Press, 2016).

[20] See articles in James Thuo Gathii and Ntina Tzouvala, 'Racial Capitalism and International Economic Law (Special Issue)' (2022) 25(2) *Journal of International Economic Law* 199.

Racial capitalism scholarship and Marxist legal studies alike focus on the co-emergence, co-evolution, and co-existence of racism and capitalism, (neo)colonialism and imperialism, historically and at present which, its interlocutors argue is embedded in and co-constitutes the relations of race and capitalism. Scholarship on racial capitalism is weak on questions about the causes of this co-existence and the underlying mechanisms that place the majority of racialized people and marginalized nations at the bottom of the global and social order. This same scholarship is rich in empirical and historical detail that can be seen as 'thick descriptions' in the Geertzian sense.[21] Thick or otherwise, they are nonetheless descriptions, and methodological victims of the old liberal problem of 'constant conjunctions' that is, the epistemic fallacy that because two events occur simultaneously, one is the cause of the other;[22] in this case racism is the cause of capitalism and imperialism[23] or the reverse, that capitalism is the cause of racism internally and (neo)colonialism externally.[24] Because the two processes appear simultaneously does not mean they are, *necessarily*, causally connected.

Amongst Marx's most significant contributions to methodology for understanding capitalism as a social system was to show that beneath the manifest appearances of events in capitalist social orders, there are deeper causal mechanisms at work. For example, in *Capital* (vol 1), Marx demonstrated that behind the manifest appearances of prices of commodities produced, exchanged, circulated, and consumed, causal mechanisms transform the human capacity to work into a commodity that can be bought and sold in labour markets. Furthermore, labour as a commodity is the pivot around which commodity-centred capitalist societies are organized. Divisions of labour at the micro-level of the factory, the meso-level of states, and the macro-levels of global political economy are keys that hold answers to the central paradox of race in liberal legal orders. Why do legal frameworks insist on equality and non-discrimination while the labour market is invariably stratified as racial and national (and gendered) hierarchies?

Divisions of labour produce competitiveness at the enterprise and sectoral levels and between industries in a nation-state; they also produce international divisions of labour between nation-states. Relentless competition within and between industrial sectors and nation-states makes the capitalist system dynamic and ever-changing. Together with the skilling and de-skilling of labour and the relocation of industries and occupations, divisions of labour make constant reorganization of production and distributions of commodities possible. This is necessary to remain competitive. Notice, for example, that with the onset of globalization, global labour markets underwent radical geographical as well as technological reorganization in capitalist core-states as well as the imperial peripheries.[25] These reorganizations do not occur in the

[21] Clifford Geertz, *The Interpretations of Cultures: Selected Essays* (Fontana Press 1993).

[22] Roy Bhaskar, 'Philosophy and Scientific Realism' in Margaret Archer and others (eds), *Critical Realism: Essential Readings* (Routledge 2013); Mervyn Hartwig, *Dictionary of Critical Realism* (Routledge 2007); David Hume, *A Treatise of Human Nature* (Oxford University Press 1978) 1, 6, 15.

[23] Robinson (n 15).

[24] Gilmore (n 15).

[25] Phillip Brown and Hugh Lauder, 'The Great Transformation in the Global Labour Market' (2012) 51 *Soundings* 41; Stephen Castles, 'Migration, Crisis, and the Global Labour Market' (2011) 8(3) *Globalizations* 311; David Martin and others, 'Turking in a Global Labour Market' (2016) 25(1) *Computer*

abstract. They are enacted through embodied working people who always come with racial, ethnic, religious, linguistic, gender, and national characteristics. Any explanatory critique must explain, *within the same analytical framework*, the continuities *and* changes in the paradox of liberal legal systems. Two are primordial: the racial hierarchies of labour in societies that co-exist with equality and non-discrimination laws and the continued stratification of states in the liberal international legal order founded on sovereign equality of all states.

Scholarship on the constant conjunction of racism and capitalism highlights an important problem about the co-presence of racism and capitalism, (neo)colonialism and imperialism. However, for emancipatory politics, it is more important to understand *why* that correlation exists, whether it is inevitable, and how continuities and changes are ordered and reordered by markets such that racialized peoples and marginalized nations always end up at the bottom rungs of stratified labour markets. The paradoxes suggest deeper unresolved theoretical problems.

As liberalism's preferred method, constant conjunction highlights the problem of racism under capitalism using rich empirical material and descriptions that appear to connect diverse aspects of reality but fall short of explanatory critique. For example, constant conjunction as a method in Critical International Law or TWAIL deconstructs at an empirical level the association of international law and imperialist/(neo) colonial relations but falls short of revealing the causal mechanisms that undergird those interconnections.

The place of law in racial capitalism and (neo)colonial imperialism studies fall back on essentialism, arguing for race in capitalism or culture in imperialism as explanatory categories.[26] These approaches argue that law is 'complicit' in racism and (neo)colonialism in capitalist/imperialist relations. Complicity suggests that law, a set of doctrines and dogmas, has 'intention' and acquires a 'will' independent of social actors; for example, the governor of the Federal Reserve or the Bank of England as described above. Alternatively, law is instrumentalized by those capable of doing so, meaning racism and national oppression exist because those in power lack 'political will' to end it or because they are wilfully racist and/or xenophobic. The question remains: why does commodified labour need to be racialized and colonized and why is a legal framework of equality and non-discrimination necessary to racialize and colonize working people? Something more than constant conjunctions is needed.

3. Legal memory, philosophical autism, and capitalist modernity

Typically, scholarship on racism, (neo)colonialism, and law refer to their constant conjunctions historically as evidence of law's 'complicity' in racism and (neo)colonialism. History, however, is the epistemological fault line for scholarship on racism and

Supported Cooperative Work (CSCW) 39; Juliet Webster and Keith Randle (eds) *Virtual Workers and the Global Labour Market, Dynamics of Virtual Work* (Palgrave Macmillian 2016).

[26] eg Robinson (n 15); Anghie (n 2).

(neo)colonialism generally and legal histories specifically. The place of legal memory in modern law confronts the Third World and racialized legal scholar as an impenetrable hard rock. Modern law is located within European social and intellectual histories and traditions going back to Greek and Roman civilizations. In the two main legal traditions of modern law—English common law and European civil law—legal memory plays a formative role in the development of its concepts, doctrines, principles, theories, methods and practices, debates, contestations, and critiques. The changes in law over time are adaptations, modifications, repurposing, and reification of historical inheritances passed down as legal memory. For example, legal memory in the English common law tradition is fixed by the Statute of Westminster I of 1275 dating it from Richard I's reign in 1189 CE. Prior to the reign of Richard I, law was 'immemorial'.[27] In the European Civil Law tradition, legal memory is traced back to Roman law as codified in the Justinian Codes around the sixth century AD, which continue to provide the conceptual and theoretical resources for contemporary law.[28] Legal memory continues to shape changes as well as continuities in each subsequent generation of Euro-American legal scholars.

Regardless of the stances or controversies among legal scholars and practitioners, we observe an epistemological continuum. James Brown Scott (1866–1943), for example, founded the American Society of International Law and the Carnegie Endowment for International Peace, and was close to the US administration when it arose as the new imperial power at the turn of the twentieth century. He repurposed sixteenth-century theological doctrines of the Salamanca School—of which Francisco Vitoria (1483–1546) was a prominent member—to establish the moral and intellectual foundations of international law for the imperial United States.[29] Scott repurposed the emerging international legal order to espouse free trade and commerce as well as human rights, and establish institutions after the First World War.[30] Vitoria, who was a Dominican priest, Thomist, and Scholastic theologian, repurposed the teachings of Thomas Aquinas (1225–1274) borrowing, along the way from Justinian (sixth century CE), for a rising Spanish empire and a Europe at war with itself.[31] Thomas Aquinas, also of the Dominican order, by far the most influential Scholastic teacher and scholar, repurposed Aristotle by synthesizing the centrality of reason with Christian theology and the authority of the Church in his philosophy. Aquinas was responding to the new conditions created by the expansion of European states, especially in France, England, and Spain that required centralized administration of law.[32] Equally, Aquinas restored the legitimacy of the Church's doctrines, which were under challenge from sections of intellectuals influenced by the Andalusian jurist and

[27] See, eg, how the idea is carried forward to the modern era in Matthew Hale, *History of the Common Law of England* (E and R Nutt and R Gosling, (assigns of E Sayer) for T Waller 1739).

[28] See Geoffrey Samuel, 'Roman Law and Modern Capitalism' (1984) 4(2) *Legal Studies* 185; Franz Wieacker, 'The Importance of Roman Law for Western Civilization and Western Legal Thought' (1981) 4(2) *Boston College International & Comparative Law Review* 257.

[29] Paolo Amorosa, *Rewriting the History of the Law of Nations: How James Brown Scott Made Francisco De Vitoria the Founder of International Law* (Oxford University Press 2019).

[30] ibid.

[31] James Brown Scott, *Spanish Origin of International Law* (Clarendon Press 1934).

[32] Alan Harding, 'The Reflection of Thirteenth-Century Legal Growth in Saint Thomas's Writings' in Mag G Verbeke and D Verhelst (eds), *Aquinas and the Problems of His Time* (Leuven University Press 1976).

philosopher Ibn Rushd (Averroes), whose writings introduced neo-Aristotelian rationalism to the Western Mediterranean.[33]

For its part, the Dominican order was established in 1200 CE to suppress the Albigensian heresy, a rebellion in Southern France by landowners and communities opposed to the Church on temporal as well as theological grounds.[34] The brutal suppression of the Albigensian resistance occurred in the context of centralizing Church authority under Pope Innocent III that introduced doctrinal justifications for torture, persecution, and mass killings but, more importantly, it advanced a form of legal argumentation in which the normative claims based on theoretical/theological interpretations of heresy were in reality underpinned by land conflicts.[35] The hiatus between normative claims, truth, and reality, were already institutionalized in the Inquisition[36] long before the so-called *Discoveries*. Under Pope Innocent IV, legal developments on corporate personality and governance laid the legal foundations for centralized forms of governance.[37] These principles and practices were trialled and refined in conflicts in Europe by the Church and feudatories on one side and between feudatory landowners on the other. The so-called Albigensian Crusades is a milestone in legal histories that later extended to the peoples of Africa and the Americas. There is thus a continuum in philosophical and legal thought from Aristotle, Justinian, Aquinas, Vitoria, and Scott in legal histories regardless of where the scholar locates herself in legal debates.[38] The continuum is sustained by shared cultural understandings and *intersubjective meanings*—the collectively held assumptions, concepts, and norms that frame how legal actors interpret the world and justify their claims.[39] Intersubjectivity

[33] Richard C Taylor, 'Averroes' Epistemology and Its Critique by Aquinas'(1999) *Philosophy Faculty Research and Publications* 293 <https://epublications.marquette.edu/phil_fac/293> accessed 6 September 2023. See also Dominique Urvoy, *Ibn Rushd (Averroes)* (Routledge 1991).

[34] Assessments of the suppression of the Albigensian heresy continue to be debated by scholars depending on whether their sympathies lie with the Roman Church or the rebels. See Christine Caldwell Ames, *Righteous Persecution: Inquisition, Dominicans, and Christianity in the Middle Ages* (University of Pennsylvania Press 2008); Mark Gregory Pegg, *A Most Holy War: The Albigensian Crusade and the Battle for Christendom* (Oxford University Press 2009); Donald S Prudlo, 'The Friars Preachers: The First Hundred Years of the Dominican Order' (2010) 8(11) *History Compass* 1275.

[35] See John C Moore (ed), *Pope Innocent III and His World* (Routledge 2016).

[36] Elphège Vacandard and Father Bertrand L Conway, *The Inquisition: A Critical and Historical Study of the Coercive Power of the Church* (Hauraki Publishing 2015).

[37] See Walter Ullman, 'The Delictual Responsibility of Medieval Corporations' (1948) 64(1) *Law Quarterly Review* 77; JP Canning, 'The Corporation in the Political Thought of the Italian Jurists of the Thirteenth and Fourteenth Centuries' (1980) 1(1) *History of Political Thought* 9.

[38] *Imperialism* has produced a renewed interest in Vitoria's contributions to international law from Third World perspectives and in methodological questions in legal history; see Martti Koskenniemi, 'Vitoria and Us: Thoughts on Critical Histories of International Law' (2014) 22 *Rechtsgeschichte* (Legal History) 119. for the relationship between international law and imperialism, see, eg Anne Orford, 'The Past as Law or History? The Relevance of Imperialism for Modern International Law' (2012) *Institute for International Law and Justice Working Papers* 2012/2 (History and Theory of International Law Series) <https://papers.ssrn.com/sol3/papers.cfm?abstract_id=2090434> accessed 6 September 2023. In the wake of so-called 'globalization', I have used the example of the past and present of Vitoria's work to exemplify the epistemological continuum from Aristotle to the present-day international order. These epistemological continuums can be traced in other fields of inquiry and disciplines. As the British philosopher Roy Bhaskar argues, the problems for Western philosophy have remained more or less the same going back to Plato. See Roy Bhaskar, *Plato Etc: The Problems of Philosophy and Their Resolution* (Verso 1994).

[39] See Maricela Correa-Chávez and Amy LD Roberts, 'A Cultural Analysis Is Necessary in Understanding Intersubjectivity' (2012) 18(1) *Culture & Psychology* 99; Kevin P Groark, 'Toward a Cultural

refers to the socially constructed nature of meaning: how legal ideas gain authority not because they are objectively true, but because they are recognized as valid within a given intellectual and cultural community. This, as Jurgen Habermas suggests, is part of the 'life-world' that conditions how reason functions within legal scholarship.[40]

For the colonized, in contrast, settler and non-settler colonialism provoked a rupture between *their* life-worlds—the world of *their* social cognition and historical consciousness—and the rational world. The latter came to include modern education together with the economic and political worlds of the colonizers, a world not of the makings of *their* ancestors. The Third World/racialized legal scholar has two options when confronted with a legal history they can never access intersubjectively, only rationally. First, they can accept that the rock of history is too sturdy to move and walk around it, an option that could either turn to atavistic and/or anachronistic accounts of history disconnected from the realities of racialized and colonized peoples *today*. Second, faced with the impossibility of moving the rock of history, they can pretend they *too* have access to the intersubjective life-worlds of their Euro-American colleagues, walking as equals with them. Either way, they becomes entangled in methodological and doctrinal inconsistencies that will devalue their scholarship.[41]

The rupture in legal history, standing as it does on epistemological fault lines, produces what Shaun Gallagher has called 'philosophical autism'.[42] Philosophical autism creates problems for intersubjectivity and meaning-making, precipitating repetitive patterns of conduct in academic, legal, and state practices. Modern knowledge was ruptured from Third World histories, just as legal histories were cleaved from non-European nations, manifesting now as cultural difference. However, cultural difference is only a manifestation of philosophical autism, not the cause. In the absence of causal explanations, cultural difference is at best an inference from thick descriptions or, at worst, a set of assumptions about actors in history.

Given the philosophical autism of our times, how are we as scholars to treat the relationship of racism, (neo)colonialism, and international law in ways that improve intersubjective exchanges between mainstream and Third World/racialized scholars? As I argue next, answers to this question lie not in mimicking the theories and methodologies of mainstream legal histories, in writing better or different histories from Third World/racialized standpoints, or in 'talking back' as it were. Rather, the way forward is to examine more closely the epistemological foundations of European/capitalist modernity, and the place of modern law within it, to develop a critique of law. Why and how do the epistemological foundations of modern law—and modernist knowledge more generally—produce and sustain not just racism and (neo)colonialism, but also an adversarial social order that reproduces hostile and competitive relations between people and between nature and people, for their survival, without possibilities of transcendence? A critique of this variety involves putting modern law

Phenomenology of Intersubjectivity: The Extended Relational Field of the Tzotzil Maya of Highland Chiapas, Mexico' (2013) 33(3) *Language & Communication* 278.

[40] Jurgen Habermas, *Moral Consciousness and Communicative Action* (Polity Press 1990).
[41] It would be fair to say something similar happened with Anghie's *Imperialism*.
[42] Shaun Gallagher, 'Two Problems of Intersubjectivity' (2009) 16(6–8) *Journal of Consciousness Studies* 289.

on more solid philosophical foundations. The next section examines elements of what such a philosophy might look like, setting up the philosophical premise to consider law's relationship to racism and (neo)colonialism.

4. No place for nature and humans in modern law?

Since Edward Said's *Orientalism*,[43] the epistemological critique of European Enlightenment has expanded across disciplines, rendering phrases like 'the gaze' and 'reversing the gaze' vital to the vocabulary of critical social sciences and humanities.[44] The critique focuses on European intellectual thought in the seventeenth and eighteenth centuries.[45] Identifying the colonial 'gaze' and representing a reversal of the gaze as critique, highlighted the problem of modernist knowledge as a system and method and its instrumental role in the colonial project. A reversed gaze, however, straddles the same dualist epistemology that the 'gaze' critiques: 'us and them' and 'West versus Rest', or ontological dualisms. Dualist modes of thought foreclose epistemological transcendence that is necessary for emancipatory knowledge. By the seventeenth and eighteenth centuries, the European Enlightenment and the capitalist modernity it spearheaded were underway and the 'Other' was born. How was it born, however, and who were its parents? How did history deliver the 'Other' as the stepchild of European modernity?

In pursuing this line of inquiry, we must interrogate the intellectual developments that *preceded* seventeenth- and eighteenth-century European intellectual histories—notably those of the fifteenth and sixteenth centuries, during the period of transition from mediaeval to modern European thought—which prepared the grounds for new concepts and ways of thinking and being. Together, the Renaissance, Reformation, and Counter Reformation fundamentally transformed the semiotic structure of European thought.[46] Cumulatively, the three overlapping movements buried old mediaeval European modes of thinking and being and prepared the conceptual grounds for the two great revolutions that ushered in European modernity: scientific and political. A key question, then, is which modes and structures of thought came to occupy the modern mind as a result.

The semiotic structure of the pre-modern European conceptual world was triadic. The world and knowledge about it rested on the triad of God, world (nature), and humans.[47] It was a top-down order descending from the transcendental to the temporal

[43] Edward W Said, *Orientalism* (Knopf Doubleday Publishing Group 2014).

[44] eg Dipesh Chakrabarty, *Provincializing Europe: Postcolonial Thought and Historical Difference* (Princeton University Press, 2000).

[45] See, eg, Gayatri Chakravorty Spivak, *A Critique of Postcolonial Reason toward a History of the Vanishing Present* (Harvard University Press 1999) on Kant, Hegel and Marx; for dissident trends within the European Enlightenment, see Jonathan I Israel, *Enlightenment Contested: Philosophy, Modernity, and the Emancipation of Man 1670-1752* (Oxford University Press 2006); Sankar Muthu, *Enlightenment against Empire* (Princeton University Press 2003).

[46] JPS Uberoi, *The European Modernity: Science, Truth and Method* (Oxford University Press 2002).

[47] Thomas D Barton, 'Law and Science in the Enlightenment and Beyond' (1999) 13(2) *Social Epistemology* 99; JPS Uberoi, 'Mind and the World in Modern European Sociology' in JPS Uberoi and K Tyabji (eds), *Mind and Society: From Indian Studies to General Sociology* (Oxford University Press 2019).

to the human. The relationship of the temporal and transcendental worlds was cemented by rituals that unified mortal and immortal, transient life with eternal life; for example, the symbolic transcendence enacted by rituals like the Eucharist and the Mass.[48] Modernity transformed a triadic structure of knowledge into a dyadic one, discarding the transcendental (including cosmological and metaphysical) aspects of life, making them optional, or in the language of modernity a matter of 'choice', to existence.[49] In essence, European modernity inverted the order of the transcendental and temporal. Sources of knowledge descended to the temporal world, exemplified by the scientific method and supported by empiricism, phenomenalism, and positivism.

The transition from a triadic to dyadic structure of thought unfolded as theological debates, initially within the Roman Church and later against it.[50] The debates centred on the relationship of the material and spiritual worlds, between mind and matter, body and soul.[51] The Reformation was as important in the transition as the Renaissance. What Marx remarked about Martin Luther may be said about the emerging knowledge system as a whole: '[H]e freed man from outer religiosity because he made religiosity the inner man. He freed the body from chains because he enchained the heart.'[52] Modernity brought forth a new European mind that liberated the body but shackled the heart.

If the Reformation was a rebellion against the mediaeval Church, the Counter Reformation was an adaptation of the old Church to new realities of diminished authority. Challenges to Church authority came from the Reformation, underpinned by struggles for control over land and peasants (especially in Germany[53]), incessant rivalries and wars between European powers, and the formulation of responses to the so-called *Discovery* of the 'New World'. The so-called *Discovery* turned the focus of knowledge away from the Ancient World to the New World and effectively ended the Renaissance because, as James Brown Scott explained:

> ... instead of contenting themselves with adventures to be found in books ... succeeding generations sought adventure in the New World.[54]

48 Uberoi (n 46).

49 See Robert Gahl, 'Natural Law Approaches to Comparative Law: Methodological Perspectives, Legal Tradition and Natural Law' (2013) 8(2) *Journal of Comparative Law* 179, 183.

50 For a fascinating and nuanced account of this transition in relation to the concept of sovereignty, see Jens Bartelson, *A Genealogy of Sovereignty* (Cambridge University Press 1995).

51 Uberoi (n 46).

52 Karl Marx, *Critique of Hegel's Philosophy of Right* (Oxford University Press 1970).

53 Marx remarked: 'And if the Protestant transformation of the German layman into priests emancipated the lay popes, the princes, with the whole of their priestly clique, the privileged and philistines, the philosophical transformation of priestly Germans into men will emancipate the people. But, *secularization will not stop at the confiscation of church estates set in motion mainly by hypocritical Prussia any more than emancipation stops at princes. The Peasant War, the most radical fact of German history, came to grief because of theology.* Today, when theology itself has come to grief, the most unfree fact of German history, our status quo, will be shattered against philosophy. On the eve of the Reformation, official Germany was the most unconditional slave of Rome. On the eve of its revolution, it is the unconditional slave of less than Rome, of Prussia and Austria, of country junkers and philistines.' ibid, 6 (italics added)

54 Scott (n 31) 18.

If, as Anthony Carty argues, '[r]enaissance knowledge became a knowledge of resemblances between entities whose unity had been shattered',[55] the Counter Reformation did not seek to restore that unity.[56] Instead, under the European Enlightenment, the new dyadic structure of thought and knowledge flourished. Nature and human life were organized around adversarial categories and oppositional movements as both had been detached from a wider cosmology.[57] This period of transition in European thought, the crucible within which European modernity was forged, is the source for modern law, a legal system that is adversarial by definition and detached from cosmological conceptions of nature and human life. Law, too, developed esoteric and exoteric dimensions as it descended from the metaphysical and transcendental worlds to the temporal one. The erasure of transcendental sources of knowledge had profound implications for law, ushering in the eventual demise of natural law and paving the way for the ascendancy of positive law.

Moreover, the relocation of law to earthly sources removed transcendental constraints on ethics and set in motion the divorce of ethics and law in the European Enlightenment.[58] Cosmological understandings of the place of humans in the Universe would no longer provide the philosophical basis for law.[59] As Robert Gahl notes with reference to Aquinas, natural law in mediaeval times had a metaphysical context made up of three dimensions: 'anthropic, epistemic, and theonomic', and emphasized 'the social and communitarian nature of the human being' whereas 'advanced modernity offers each individual the opportunity to choose his or her moral good, to determine for him or herself the meaning of life and the content of one's deepest aspirations'. Consequently, '[t]he modern, atomistic self finds himself alone before a great void, as he faces the choice of meaning in life'.[60]

Natural law fared badly once brought down to earth by European Enlightenment thinkers. Confronted with the pragmatism of positive law and guided by the 'invisible hand of the market' natural law traditions struggled, and as Carty notes, they eventually 'evaporated after 1945'.[61] If Francisco Vitoria, a mediaeval man of the Counter Reformation, witnessed natural law slip away amidst the great transformations that occurred around him, Scott's was the last attempt at resuscitation, in the wake of the First World War. The World Wars was another period of great transition when, not just natural law, but modernity itself died. After Hiroshima-Nagasaki and the Holocaust, events seen as the culmination of modernist modes of thinking and being, there was nothing redeeming left in modernist knowledge, if possibilities for redemption ever existed.[62]

[55] See Anthony Carty, *Philosophy of International Law* (Edinburgh University Press 2017) 5.

[56] See Uberoi (n 46).

[57] For an extensive analysis of dualist structures of thought in European modernity, see Uberoi (n 47); JPS Uberoi, *Science and Culture* (Oxford University Press 1978).

[58] See Barton (n 47); Samuel E Stumpf, 'Austin's Theory of the Separation of Law and Morals' (1960) 14(1) *Vanderbilt Law Review* 117. For more contemporary debates on the separation of ethics and law in relation to torture, see Bradley Wendel, 'Legal Ethics and the Separation of Law and Morals' (2005–2006) 91(1) *Cornell Law Review* 67.

[59] See Carty (n 55) 5.

[60] Gahl (n 49) 183–84.

[61] Carty (n 55) 9.

[62] Uberoi (n 47) ix.

In such a context, how do we understand the place of the Black, Brown, yellow, white human, of the Muslim, the Jew, the Hindu, the Christian, the atheist, the African, the Asian, the Indigenous person, and the European? Modern law, guided by pragmatism and positivism, can no longer offer any guidance. For legal theorists and historians, the challenge is not to understand European modernity as a set of historical events and chains of causality and consequence, or a qualitatively distinct society, or an organic evolution of certain structures, processes, and functions. Rather, following JPS Uberoi, the challenge is to explain:

> (a) . . . the language of European modernity, its *medium*, *code* and *message* of the modernity project, (b) [to] attempt to uncover its *conditions of existence* . . . its presuppositions and assumptions . . . the limits of its art of the possible, so as (c) to better understand their role, meaning and effect as what are in mathematical science termed 'constants'.[63]

Given the absence of a cosmological place for nature and humans and their relationships, how might putting modern law on a sturdier philosophical foundation help us understand its '*medium*, *code*, and *message*' within the modernity project, of which colonial modernity is an integral part?

5. Temporalities and structure-agency dialectic in the history of ideas

Third World legal scholars writing after 1945 moved legal history away from doctrines, concepts, and scholars, to situate it in *real* social histories of racialized and colonized peoples. Their debates centred around two types of questions, the first being: When did European international law become the Law of international society? For Anthony Anghie, that moment was the so-called *Discovery* and Vitoria was its theorist.[64] For Onuma Yasuaki, '[i]nternational law was not born either with Grotius, Vitoria, or Vattel. Nor was it created by the Treaties of Westphalia'.[65] Rather, the moment of birth was the forced integration of Afro-Asian states into European societies in the nineteenth century.[66] Both approaches differ on the meaning of the 'international' in law and the 'inside'/'outside' divide when speaking of the international as a domain.

The second type of question for Third World and mainstream scholars alike is the challenge of reading the universalism of law together with the specificities of societies to provide an inclusive account of the histories of law.[67] Onuma warns against projection of the dominant views onto the past 'by assuming that such a reality had already

[63] ibid xi (italics added).
[64] Anghie (n 2).
[65] Onuma Yasuaki, 'The Birth of International Law as the Law of International Society' (2000) 94 *Proceedings of the American Society of International Law* 44.
[66] ibid.
[67] For debates on universalism and particularism of international law in the Third World, see proceedings of a special session on the subject Antony Anghie and others, *The History of International Law: Universality and Particularity* (Cambridge University Press 2000).

existed before'.[68] For Anghie, racial and (neo)colonial injustice is in the very DNA so to speak of international law. These attempts to write the experiences of colonized peoples into legal histories reveal deeper methodological problems about the relationship of the past, present, and future in evaluating the history of ideas. The past and the future both live in the present and are shaped by actions of humans in response to past injustices.

Recalling Marx:

> Men make their own history, but they do not make it as they please; they do not make it under self-selected circumstances, but under circumstances existing already, given and transmitted from the past. The tradition of all dead generations weigh like a nightmare on the brains of the living.[69]

The relationship of the past to the future via the present is also the relationship of past social structures and present agency and the frame of reference for understanding continuities and changes in laws and societies.[70] The Critical Realist philosopher Roy Bhaskar argues that human beings are born into social structures including their institutions, ideologies, laws, technologies, traditions, and norms. Social structures therefore precede individual and group lives. At the same time, social structures depend on human agency for their reproduction and transformation. Social structures are not reducible to agency or vice versa. Social practices are concept dependent but, contrary to the hermeneutical tradition in social science, they are not exhausted by their conceptual aspect: they always have a material dimension.[71] These insights point us to a temporal dialectic that is intrinsic to the structure-agency relationship and is essential to tease out in the relationship of racism and (neo)colonialism to law.

Social agents intervene in concrete problems handed down by *their* histories. They address new problems using the conceptual and theoretical resources *at their disposal.* In the process, they modify, revise, reify, renew, and alter the concepts and theories. At any given historical moment, social agents are diverse, with contradictory interests which they articulate as different normative ideas about proper responses to the problems of their times. Some of those views are 'mainstreamed' and come to dominate

[68] Yasuaki (n 65) 44.

[69] Karl Marx, 'The Eighteenth Brumaire of Louis Bonaparte' in *Karl Marx and Friedrich Engels: Selected Works in Two Volumes* (Vol I, Foreign Languages Publishing House 1950).

[70] The structure–agency relationship in Western academia has been a walk through a maze without exit. At one end, the structure agency problem has become mired in controversies based on, dare I say, caricatured arguments founded on presumptions about Marx's writings. For an excellent discussion on Marx's engagement with structure and agency, see Dileep Edara, *Biography of a Blunder: Base and Superstructure in Marx and Later* (Cambridge Scholars Publishing 2016). At the other end, new materialist theories like the Actor Network Theory (ANT) deny social structures altogether, seeing them as 'assemblages'. See Bruno Latour, *Reassembling the Social: An Introduction to Actor-Network-Theory* (Oxford University Press 2005). The induction of ANT into legal studies points to a dissolution of the social order within which law typically functions. See, eg, Emilie Cloatre, 'Law and ANT (and its Kin): Possibilities, Challenges, and Ways Forward' (2018) 45(4) *Journal of Law and Society* 646. Perhaps this is one reason why legal scholars have not shown much enthusiasm for ANT. I wish to move away from the structure–agency debates on determinism and reductionism on the one hand and society as nothing more than assemblages of actors on the other.

[71] Roy Bhaskar, *Reclaiming Reality: A Critical Introduction to Contemporary Philosophy* (Verso 1989).

future social structures; others are marginalized. The *code*, *medium*, and *message* of modern law lies in uncovering conceptual and ideational dominance, and equally in the revival of marginalized ideas by future social agents. This uncovering always has both a material dimension and an ideological one. Taking up the ideological dimension, how do we discern the *code, medium, and message* of modern law in Vitoria's writings?[72]

Vitoria was a man of the Counter Reformation, which officially began with the Council of Trent (1545–1563).[73] His response to the debates following the so-called *Discovery* were located within the structural conditions *he* inherited from *his* past and the limits of *his own agency* during the transformative moment of Renaissance, Reformation, and Counter Reformation. At a time when the Renaissance and Reformation was moving to dismantle the triadic structure of thought, Vitoria sought to accommodate the emerging dualist modes within the triadic structure of the old Roman Church. In other words, as a man of the Counter Reformation, Vitoria attempted to square the circle. He was a conservative for his times but one who nevertheless responded to new problems presented by the so-called *Discovery* and ways that could mitigate the worst for the Church.

Vitoria addressed two questions: (i) the status of Indigenous peoples of the Americas and the nature of Spanish jurisdiction over them; and (ii) the doctrine of 'just wars' and their justifications when waged against Indigenous peoples.[74] Both questions were contentious matters of public debate within Spanish society coming at a time when the Roman Church faced serious crises of legitimacy. Conflicts included disagreements between the Dominican missionaries in the Americas and the conquistadors pushing ahead with the *encomienda* system in the 'New World' with devastating effects;[75] litigations between Columbus and his heirs over contractual agreements with the Spanish monarchy that continued for decades;[76] the influential Genovese merchants of Seville with close ties to Columbus (a fellow Genovese);[77] and the monarchs King Ferdinand and Queen Isabella who had commercial interests in the voyages which conflicted with the Chancery officials in charge of safeguarding the constitution.[78] These were some of the disputes Vitoria sought to address.

In the triadic system of mediaeval sovereignty, monarchs embodied the state as the temporal sovereign with mandate from God, the transcendental authority, communicated through the Pope. Vitoria distilled multiple claims and contestations by formulating the two central questions for his times. In retrospect, both questions appeared from time to time during crises of colonial governance. They re-emerged again in the early twentieth century when European powers went to war with each other, and anti-colonial struggles challenged European powers as well as Vitoria's formulations

[72] See Fernando Gómez, 'Francisco De Vitoria in 1934, before and After' (2002) 117(2) *Modern Language Notes* 365.

[73] Scott (n 31).

[74] ibid.

[75] See Lewis Hanke, *Aristotle and the American Indians: A Study in Race Prejudice in the Modern World* (Henry Regnery Company 1959).

[76] See Helen Nader (ed), *Repertorium Columbianum: The Book of Privileges Issued to Christopher Columbus by King Fernando and Queen Isabel 1492-1502* (Wipf & Stock Publishers 2004).

[77] ibid.

[78] ibid.

of sovereignty, self-determination, and the status of colonized people. They returned during the First World War when the United States emerged as the new imperial power, and again in the late twentieth and early twenty-first centuries.

What is important for contemporary racism and (neo)colonialism is not whether Vitoria was the *father* of international law as we know it today or whether his doctrines were motivated by cultural difference. Rather, it is his *modes* of argumentation that became pivotal to the 'bourgeois liberalism' of later years. In retrospect, the significance of his intervention lies in his de-linking of the temporal and transcendental worlds, consistent with the transformations underway during *his* times.[79] Vitoria thus set the theoretical (theological) premises for separating ethics implied in 'God's Will'—and therefore diminishing its status as an intrinsic component of collective human actions—from 'Human Will': actions in the temporal worlds of societies and economies. Unlike his contemporary Luther, however, Vitoria did not banish ethics to an altogether different realm. He salvaged a place for natural law anchored to transcendental ideas of the place of human beings in the wider cosmos as the source for ethics, even if tenuously. Luther, in contrast, made a clean break between the temporal and spiritual worlds and left ethics to individual conscience.[80]

Vitoria distinguished between civil authority and spiritual authority. Going against the Pope's Doctrine of Discovery which granted the 'New World' to the Spanish monarchs on theological grounds, Vitoria rejected transcendental sources arguing that the legality or illegality of Spanish titles to colonized lands had nothing to do with doing God's work.[81] He severed mediaeval links between the piety of the monarch and their mortal sin arguing that 'a king can be a sinner but there is no kingship without dominion'.[82] Vitoria cleared the way for secular law divorced from God and Church, allowing the individuation of states as distinct entities. He rejected the prevalent idea that 'temporal goods' (property) were God's grace, arguing that God gives temporal goods to the good and bad.[83] In so doing, Vitoria met the challenges to the Church from the Renaissance and Reformation by separating ethics from law, separating the person of the sovereign from the institution of the state, and liberating acquisition of private property from ethical constraints. By bringing the Counter Reformation in sync with the Renaissance and the Reformation, Vitoria removed the last roadblock for the European Enlightenment, facilitating diverse orientations and innovations within the new dyadic structures of modernist thought.

Even Vitoria's inconsistencies proved useful, providing ready-made defences against challenges of liberal legalism that would emerge during the march to capitalist modernity. Indeed, he transformed ethics from being intrinsic to human actions, as in dominant mediaeval thought, to extrinsic, grounded in the transcendental-temporal relationship. Yet, he retained a place for the transcendental without reducing ethics to pure voluntarism contingent on reason. Also, there is no denying that Vitoria crafted

[79] See Katherine Elliot von Liere, 'Vitoria, Cajetan, and the Conciliarists' (1997) 58(4) *Journal of the History of Ideas* 597.

[80] For Luther's views, see JM Porter, 'Luther and Political Millenarianism: The Case of the Peasants' War' (1981) 42(3) *Journal of the History of Ideas* 389.

[81] Scott (n 31) 108.

[82] ibid 110.

[83] ibid.

a convoluted argument to condemn wars against Indigenous peoples; still, under certain conditions those wars could be justified. Indigenous people were sovereign, but Spain could exercise jurisdiction over them and, for that matter, jurisdiction is distinct from title and ownership in ideas of sovereignty.[84]

This mode of argumentation is an archetype of liberal legalism, where rules are complemented by exceptions to the rule. It is remarkable how the distinction between title, ownership, and jurisdiction in the concept of sovereignty has played out in the history of colonialism. For example, under the protectorate system in the British empire, native rulers were sovereign because they had title and ownership, yet Britain had jurisdiction over them.[85] More recently, the US Supreme Court in *Rasul v Bush* affirmed Cuba's sovereignty over Guantanamo Bay but also affirmed US jurisdiction over it.[86] While capitalist/colonial modernity forged ahead mainstreaming Lutheran dualism of the temporal and spiritual worlds, when those dualisms clashed in the numerous crises of capitalist modernity, Vitoria's natural law thesis in the form of 'human rights', or 'humanitarian intervention' for example, was available, offering a way out of an impasse in the governance of capitalism and imperialism.

Legal systems provided governance with the capacity to 'switch gears', to use Uberoi's phrase. When conditions demanded repressive racism and (neo)colonialism, doctrines, principles, and modes of legal argumentation could be invoked from modern law to weaponize criminal justice, economic regulation, and systems of classifications to manage the crises of colonial governance. Ethics in colonial governance is, after all, made extrinsic to political action under modernist knowledge systems. When different outcomes were needed for governance, the state and its institutions could switch gears again, invoking 'human rights' of racialized and colonized people, equality and non-discrimination, and respect for self-determination to advance a conflicting position. Whatever the gear, law navigates colonial roads to capitalist/imperialist destinations. Liberalism's promises retain their lure, assuring racialized and colonized peoples that despite the bumpy ride, they will eventually arrive at the promised destination of justice. Debate about whether Vitoria was progressive or conservative for his time continues to this day, providing further evidence of the value of his ideas for steering the vehicle of colonialism. 300 hundred years later, Marx described the liberal legal system as the 'empty shell' into which different substances can be filled or emptied depending on needs of the 'market'.[87] Vitoria's thought was critical to establishing a theoretical substance that could fill the empty shell of liberal legalism.[88]

The separation of law and ethics was pivotal for the emergence of modern law. At the same time, retaining some place for natural law—or later-day sublations

[84] See the section on Vitoria's convoluted arguments in Bartelson (n 50) 127–33.

[85] Sir Charles Lewis Tuppe, *Our Indian Protectorate: An Introduction to the Study of the Relations between the British Government and Its Indian Feudatories* (Longmans, Green, and Co 1893); WS Holdsworth, 'The Indian States and India' (1930) 46(3) *Law Quarterly Review* 407. For comparable distinctions between title, ownership, and jurisdiction that were made about tribal leaders in Africa, see Mahmood Mamdani, *Citizen and Subject: Contemporary Africa and the Legacy of Late Colonialism* (Princeton University Press 1996).

[86] *Rasul and Others v Bush and Others* (2004) 16 BHRC 445 (US Supreme Court).

[87] Karl Marx, 'On the Jewish Question' in David Mclellan (ed), *Karl Marx Selected Writings* (Oxford University Press 1987).

[88] For expanded arguments on liberalism and rights, see Radha D'Souza, *What's Wrong with Rights?: Social Movements, Law and Liberal Imaginations* (Pluto Press 2018).

such as human rights, racial justice, and self-determination—provides the tools for manipulating social relations in a constantly moving world of global capital. For modernist epistemology, Vitoria's interventions, inconsistencies included, salvaged something from the changing mediaeval context. However, it was the changing material conditions of the capitalist-imperialist world that allowed those ideological inconsistencies to flourish. It is to those material conditions that I turn next.

6. The original sin of capitalism

As explained in the foregoing section, the transition from mediaeval to modern structures of thought in European societies between the Renaissance, Reformation, and Counter Reformation is anchored to materiality of the historical transitions in Western Europe. At the time of the so-called *Discovery*, feudal mediaeval European societies were disintegrating under the weight of their own internal and external contradictions. However, the capitalist economic order, modern nation-states, and interstate system were not yet instituted.[89] It would take one hundred years and the bloody Thirty-Years War ending in the Treaty of Westphalia in 1648 for the modern state and order to emerge in Europe.

In the first half of the fifteenth century, Europe was ravaged by wars, famines, and plague which decimated economies and depopulated towns and countryside.[90] Peasant rebellions were common in the prosperous and poor areas alike.[91] Wars between feudatory alliances and states convulsed the ruling elite.[92] Against this background, war financing and war production became a vital activity that catapulted to power closely knit and well-organized groups of financiers and bankers, notably in Italy, as a new and alternate node of power and influence in European societies.[93] The emergent node became the pivot around which sections of the landed aristocracy and intellectuals coalesced to lead the transformation from mediaeval to modern Europe.

Capitalist–(neo)colonial social relations are unique in human history.[94] In land-centric pre-modern social orders, peasants and serfs were exploited and their labours expropriated but they could not be evicted from nature as the political economy depended on generating social wealth from the land. Slavery existed but on the margins. The so-called *Discovery* produced unexpected and unique material conditions for capitalism, one in which 'the tradition of all dead generations' did not 'weigh like a

[89] For a broad overview of the historic transformations underway in Western Europe, see Giovanni Arrighi, *The Long Twentieth Century: Money, Power, and the Origins of Our Times* (Verso 2010) 37–48. For examples focusing on France and Spain, see Henry Kamen, *Spain, 1469-1714: A Society of Conflict* (Routledge 2006) xv; also see Andrew Villalon and Donald Kagay, *The Hundred Years War: A Wider Focus* (Brill 2005).

[90] See Jerah Johnson and William A Jr Percy, *The Age of Recovery: The Fifteenth Century* (Cornell University Press 1970).

[91] For a study on peasant rebellions in Spain, see William Brustein, 'Class Conflict and Class Collaboration in Regional Rebellions, 1500 to 1700' (1985) 14(4) *Theory and Society* 445; in Germany, see Fredrick Engels, *The Peasant War in Germany* (International Publishers 1926).

[92] Villalon and Kagay (n 89).

[93] Arrighi (n 89).

[94] See Radha D'Souza, 'Land, People and Places: Double Visions and Corporate Land Ownership' in Robyn Bartel and Jennifer Carter (eds), *Handbook on Space, Place and Law* (Edward Elgar 2021).

nightmare on the brains of the living'. The conquistadors had no history in or bonds to the land and people in the Americas and were free of the constraints that history and culture (including belief systems) impose upon communities. Whereas large-scale displacement of people off land in Europe took several centuries and required a variety of governance techniques, in the Americas, it happened violently and within a few decades.[95] These differences became crucial for shaping both racism and the legal system. The violent severance of people from nature established the preconditions for a modern commodity-centric capitalist social order, based on class as the endogenic social relation and colonialism as the exogenic social relation of capitalism.[96] The eviction of people from land transformed them into a 'labour force', and confiscated land (including everything beneath and above it) into *modern* 'private property', making both land and people alienable commodities. Elsewhere, I have called this violent severance of land and people 'the original sin of capitalism'.[97]

Following the original sin, something as rooted as land had to 'circulate' as alienable property as if it were bricks or mortar, and people uprooted from communities and places circulate through the 'labour markets' as wage workers like shirts and shoes. Modern law operates as the social mediator bringing land and labour together and mediating relations between people, not as natural entities as in pre-modern societies, but as commodities through the mechanisms of markets. Markets are complexes of laws established by the state led by the ruling elites. At the time of the so-called *Discovery*, the ruling elites were the European merchants, a section of the aristocracy and the anti-feudal intellectuals—in other words, the very same social forces that spearheaded modernity in the ideological, philosophical, social, and cultural spheres discussed earlier.

The philosophical premise for decoding the relationship of law to racism on the one hand and capitalism on the other *is* the 'original sin of capitalism'. The forcible separation of people from land introduced the dualism of land and labour, the founding dualism that distinguishes capitalist societies from pre-capitalist ones, and transformed a natural relationship into an adversarial one. The land/labour dualism is the source of the nature/culture dualism that, in turn, generated all sorts of other dualisms in societies, ideologies, and cultures that characterize modernist epistemology. The land/labour dualism transforms a cosmological relationship of land and people into an adversarial relationship, an ontological question into an epistemological one.[98]

Labour as commodity has no race, religion, culture, or tradition. It is simply the capacity to work which is purchased (or appropriated for free as in slavery) from the 'owner' of the body that labours. At the same time, there is no human person without some race, religion, language, culture, or tradition. I call this tension 'social bipolarity', and it is foundational to the commodity-centric capitalist political economy. On one

[95] See Alek A Rozental, 'The Enclosure Movement in France' (1956) 16(1) *The American Journal of Economics and Sociology* 55.

[96] Karl Marx, *Capital: A Critique of Political Economy Vol 1* (Penguin Books 1990): See also Radha D'Souza, 'Imperial Agendas, Global Solidarities and Socio-Legal Scholarship on the Third World: Methodological Reflections' (2012) 19(3) *Osgoode Hall Law Journal* 409.

[97] Radha D'Souza and Jonas Staal, 'Introduction to the Court for Intergenerational Climate Crimes (CICC): A Conversation' (2021) 2 *Errant Journal* 45.

[98] See D'Souza (n 94).

side, the labour force is abstracted from its social attributes, while on the other, human beings must necessarily embody social attributes. Abstract labour exists as universal labour; the body that embodies abstract labour is always particular. The much-debated 'universalism versus particularism' in Critical Legal Studies, TWAIL, and CRT is in fact grounded in the dualism of labour as commodity and the specificities of people as embodied beings.

Indeed, if land is to be used for the purposes of commodity production—setting up a factory or building a highway—it must be abstracted from people who inhabit it *and* from the ecological relationships that sustain it. Yet, no life can exist without land, and land becomes life-sustaining *only* within specific ecologies and communities. The tension between land as abstraction—such as property—and land as embedded, for example in ecologies, is at the root of national oppression. Liberal modern legal systems act as the mechanism for establishing the dualisms and putting them together in different ways at different times and places, but always to facilitate the circulation of land and labour.

Modern legal systems establish institutions— for example labour markets or international organizations—that regulate intra- and inter-national relations. They also establish social relationships between people, employers and employees, or different ethnic groups and nationalities. The modern legal system is secular, delinked from any transcendental sources of life: *a*historical and *a*ecological. Statutes redefine socio-historically produced concepts and ideas in new ways for the specific purposes of establishing new types of capitalist/colonial social relations to land and people in *a*historical ways. For example, labour laws define who is/is not a worker and classify the 'workforce' into different segments to determine what each is worth without regard to the needs of people as embodied beings.

The dualist structure of law is a necessary condition for competitive and adversarial social relations that undergirds capitalist social relations in which all commodities must circulate to exist. Constant circulation of labour as commodities perpetuates competition between people and for nature that now circulates as a 'resource'. As the universal labour *qua* commodity is 'non-negotiable' in capitalist/(neo)colonial social relations, people can only compete in the labour markets based on racial and national differences, provoking greater social enmity. Likewise, constant circulation of nature prevents bonding between communities and places.

Brutality and savagery were not wanting in mediaeval Europe before the so-called *Discovery*.[99] Rather, the so-called *Discovery* modernized the *structure* of brutality by erecting adversarial political economies on the violence of 'the original sin of capitalism'. The severance of people from land created permanent material conditions for what is understood as 'structural racism'—a mass of placeless working people dependent entirely on the whims of capital and admission to capitalist and colonial institutions for their existence. The so-called *Discovery* modernized the *structure* of expropriation of nature. The severance of land from its ecological relationships, including people, made it increasingly difficult for nature to reproduce the conditions of existence for human and non-human species. In turn, the inability of nature to

[99] See, eg, the cruelty of the Spanish inquisition in Rafael Sabatini, *Torquemada and the Spanish Inquisition: A History* (The Riverside Press 1930).

support life in all forms intensifies competition for places in the market for survival, a life and death competition in which any ground for competition—racism *and* anti-racism alike—assumes market significance.[100]

History does not vanish, because liberal law, ostrich-like, has buried its head in the present as the fiats of statutes demand. History returns as what dependency theorists have called 'unequal development',[101] as structural conditions of inequalities between nations that are formed by multiple layers of the so-called *Discoveries*—different temporalities of conquests, occupations, displacements, and mechanisms of (neo)colonial imperial governance that form layers of social stratification and sedimentation. Social sedimentation and politico-economic stratification, in turn, create specific types of social bipolarities that give some social groups 'competitive advantage' or disadvantage over others.[102] Unlike forcibly displaced Africans who were absorbed into chattel slavery for modern plantation economies, and Indigenous people who were exterminated or expelled into confined territorial spaces, the European peasants evicted from land were pivotal in establishing three institutions that form the bedrock of capitalist/imperialist social orders as well as structural racism and national oppression.

European peasants evicted from land provided the manpower for instituting permanent professional armed forces and police as one of two pillars of the modern state that differentiate modern states from pre-modern ones. The creation of professional armies, together with technological advances in warfare, enhanced and unleashed capacities for colonial expansions and land occupations around the world. Next, displaced European farmers provided the workforce to establish a professional bureaucracy, the second pillar that characterizes the modern state. Displaced European peasants were also absorbed in industries as wage-labourers.[103] Lastly, peasants evicted from land were instrumental in land colonization in the Americas and around the world.[104] Evicted European peasants gained a 'competitive advantage' over the Africans, native Americans, and other nationalities precisely because history worked in particular ways in the sedimentation and stratification of Europe's dispossessed in the formation of capitalist/(neo) colonial social relationships. While the processes of historical sedimentation and stratification are important themes for research by anthropologists, ethnographers, sociologists, and other social scientists, for the purposes of this chapter, their significance for legal studies needs elaboration.

The liberal legal system that Marx described as an empty shell is the social mediator, a mechanism that intervenes to sediment and/or disrupt the social relationships

[100] See Karen Brodkin, *How Jews Became White Folks and What That Says About Race in America* (Rutgers University Press 1998).

[101] Samir Amin, *Unequal Development: An Essay on the Social Formations of Peripheral Capitalism* (The Harvester Press 1976); Ruy Mauro Marini, *The Dialectics of Dependency* (Monthly Review Press 2022).

[102] For an excellent analysis of how labour markets assign and reassign places to different social groups, see Brodkin (n 100). For settler colonialism modelled on corporations, see Robert E Wright, *Corporation Nation* (University of Pennsylvania Press 2014). For the impact of slavery on African economic development, see Walter Rodney, *How Europe Underdeveloped Africa* (Tanzania Publishing House 1973); for processes of historical sedimentation in Uganda specifically, see Mahmood Mamdani, 'Nationality Question in a Neo-Colony: A Historical Perspective' (1984) 19(27) *Economic and Political Weekly* 1046.

[103] Karl Marx, *Capital: A Critique of Political Economy Vol 1* (Penguin Books 1990).

[104] See Alfred W Crosby, *Ecological Imperialism: The Biological Expansion of Europe, 900-1900* (Cambridge University Press 1986), prologue.

of colonialism (settler and non-settler).[105] The historical stratification of social relationships is mediated by law through its very denial of history. At the same time, the processes of sedimentation are disrupted by the constant impulses for change. The dualist structure of modern thought makes the *a*historicity of law as well as the dualism of labour as commodity and social being possible. By externalizing ethics and the adversarial legal forms, modern law gains the flexibility to change gears—and mediate racism and antiracism, national oppression and national self-determination, competition and collaboration—all within the same legal paradigm. *A*historicity and externalization makes liberal legalism enticing as it lures people to its fold again and again, seeking justice and freedom even when, over and over again, the reality of racism and national oppression tells a different story.

7. Conclusion

If the reader expected a definitive answer to the question that informs this collection, they will be understandably disappointed with this perplexing roundabout route. However, as Einstein famously said, solutions to problems cannot be found at the same level of consciousness that created the problem. Solutions to racism and national oppression cannot be found within the same legal system or the same epistemologies that created the problem. Neither atavistic return to an ideal past, if it existed at all, nor surrender to modernist epistemology can aid theories and practices of transcendence.

This chapter has argued for the need to stubbornly refuse to be trapped by the social bipolarity of capitalism and (neo)colonialism by resisting the cleaving of the economic self from the sociohistorical self of people; by developing sound philosophical lenses that help to understand the structure of modernist thought; by thereafter, insisting on seeing the economic and socio-historical aspects as two sides of the same life; by seeking to reveal the workings of modern law in the varying assemblages of multiple facets of existence; and, most of all, by refusing to de-link socio-historical questions from eco-historical ones. In short, following in the footsteps of Fanon, to 'stubbornly . . . investigate *both* metaphysics' of the black and white camps and, following Uberoi, decode '*medium*, *code* and *message*' of the modernity project.

[105] For extensive development of the argument, see D'Souza (n 88).

22
Conceptualizing Race and Resisting Racism in International Law

E Tendayi Achiume, Asli Ü Bâli, and S Priya Morley

1. Introduction

The racial justice uprising of summer 2020 and subsequent advocacy brought attention to the importance of transnational approaches to combating racial injustice. After protests in support of the movement for Black lives erupted in the United States in response to the police murder of George Floyd, protests condemning police violence and brutality against Black people and other people of colour broke out in countries around the world, often tied to national experiences of racial discrimination. Racial justice activists in the United States explicitly aligned their movement with the demands from other racially marginalized groups, including Palestinians.[1] Similarly, protesters in other countries connected their struggles with the US and global movements; for example, Black migrants waiting in Tijuana, Mexico, to seek asylum in the United States chanted '*No puedo respirar*' ('I can't breathe'), evoking language that had been used in US racial justice protests.[2]

Over the past few years, unprecedented global challenges such as the COVID-19 pandemic, forced migration, and greater awareness of the urgent harms resulting from climate change have underscored how structural racism and inequality are transnational issues. The 'racialized distributional consequences' of structural inequities shot through the international order were made manifest in the context of what one scholar has called 'vaccine apartheid',[3] but the same pattern informs the burdens of risk and cost borne by Black and Brown communities globally in the face of supply chain disruptions, spiralling global food costs, and climate-related catastrophic harms.

This chapter addresses the question of how best to conceptualize questions of race and racism in the context of international law. In particular, we begin from an

[1] Hansi Lo Wang, 'The Complicated History Behind BLM's Solidarity with the Pro-Palestinian Movement' *NPR* (12 June 2021) <https://www.npr.org/2021/06/07/1003872848/the-complicated-history-behind-blms-solidarity-with-the-pro-palestinian-movement> accessed 22 November 2024; Aziz Rana, 'Keynote Speech, UCLA Law Review Symposium 2020: Law and Empire in the American Century' (2021) 67 UCLA Law Review 1432, 1446.

[2] Paulina Olvera Cáñez, Ebony Bailey, and Leslie Meyer, 'Commentary: "No puedo respirar". The Black Lives Matter movement is growing in Tijuana' *San Diego Union-Tribune* (25 June 2020) <https://www.sandiegouniontribune.com/opinion/commentary/story/2020-06-25/commentary-no-puedo-respirar-the-black-lives-matter-movement-is-growing-in-tijuana> accessed 24 November 2024.

[3] Matiangai Sirleaf, 'We Charge Vaccine Apartheid?'(2022) 50(4) Journal of Law, Medicine and Ethics 726.

E Tendayi Achiume, Asli Ü Bâli, and S Priya Morley, *Conceptualizing Race and Resisting Racism in International Law*
In: *Emancipating International Law*. Edited by: Mohsen al Attar and Claire Smith, Oxford University Press.
© E Tendayi Achiume, Asli Ü Bâli, and S Priya Morley 2026. DOI: 10.1093/9780198935605.003.0028

understanding that international law and international organizations are deeply implicated in producing and embedding racial injustice even as norms and institutions have also been designed at the international level with the goal of pursuing racial justice. The tensions implicit in this dual reality permeate domestic legal systems as well, but pose specific challenges at the international level, particularly for those who work on questions of global racial justice using the international human rights framework. In what follows, we offer illustrative examples of the magnitude of the problem we describe before turning to a more sustained discussion of some of the initiatives we have undertaken in trying to fashion critical perspectives on human rights that enable advocacy and scholarship to resist racism in international law. As we detail, we have placed a premium on building a community of international law scholars and advocates committed to defining alternative and more emancipatory practical interventions and broader research agendas to tackle race and racism in international law. To be sure, the strategies we have developed build on prior work by mentors and colleagues in other settings encompass many overlapping networks of scholars and advocates, constitute only one of a constellation of contemporaneous initiatives pursuing similar goals, and remain limited in important ways. We do not offer this example to suggest it is either the most innovative or advanced amongst strategies for resisting racial injustice in international law, but rather to set forward an example of a collective project that strives to answer the urgent challenges we identify.

2. Transnational understandings of racial injustice

In the wake of the racial justice uprisings, there were multiple efforts to grapple with race and racism from within the United Nations (UN) system. In one prominent example, the United Nations Human Rights Council (the Council), responding to a request of the Africa Group and demands from civil society, held in 2020 its first ever special session on systemic racism. The urgent debate 'marked a significant shift in global attention to systemic racial subordination as a global phenomenon, with a particular emphasis on anti-Black racism rooted in persisting legacies of colonialism and the trans-Atlantic trade in enslaved Africans'.[4] The special session was unprecedented in its explicit focus on systemic racial injustice and anti-Black racism, and because it was the first triggered by a human rights situation in the United States or any other Western liberal democracy.[5]

Despite these strides forward, the Council's subsequent resolution stopped short of demanding transformative change. It condemned 'racially discriminatory and violent practices perpetrated by law enforcement' but declined to create 'an independent international commission of inquiry' to study the situation and bring perpetrators to justice, as many had advocated.[6] Instead, in Resolution 43/1 (2020), the Council

[4] E Tendayi Achiume and James Theo Gathii, 'Introduction to the Symposium on Race, Racism, and International Law' (2023) 117 AJIL Unbound 26, 26.

[5] E Tendayi Achiume, 'Transnational Racial In(Justice) in Liberal Democratic Empire' (2021) 134 Harvard Law Review 378.

[6] UN Human Rights Council, Resolution 43/1 (19 June 2020) UN Doc A/HRC/RES/43/1, Article 2. But see 'Burkina Faso, Iran (Islamic Republic of)** and State of Palestine**: draft resolution 43/ . . . The promotion and protection of the human rights and fundamental freedoms of Africans and of people of

tasked the High Commissioner for Human Rights with preparing a report on systemic racism by law enforcement agencies, calling on all states to cooperate with the preparation of the report rather than singling out the states where practices of systemic anti-Black racism by law enforcement had resulted in global protests.[7] As Tendayi Achiume has argued elsewhere, the potential of the urgent debate was circumscribed by 'liberal hegemons [who] can keep the lid on [attempts to address] anti-Black racism through transnational means ranging from naked geopolitical bullying to normative insistence on liberal democratic norms and institutions to obstructive bureaucratic techniques'.[8]

Critiques of how the urgent debate unfolded expose a more fundamental concern with the UN system and international human rights frame more generally—that it creates and embeds racial injustice and acts as a barrier to racial equality. Among those who have offered these insights are Achiume and Gay McDougall, both of whom held positions within the UN's antiracism architecture during the uprisings and special session. As Achiume has argued, the urgent debate[9] provided a diagnosis of the problem, namely that 'the international human rights frame not only is neglectful of racial justice, but also can suppress the most promising avenues for achieving this racial justice'.[10] She goes on to note that those responsible for this suppression are 'nations and regions forming the liberal democratic wing of the international order—the conventional purveyors of the international human rights system as a universal good'.[11] Identifying racial injustice as a 'systemic feature of the liberal imperial project, rather than a pathology or aberration' requires that advocates of international human rights law treat it as an 'institutionalized feature of these systems' rather than something outside of the human rights frame.[12] This fundamental critique of the international human rights system raises an even sharper question: how do we develop goals for achieving racial justice that take account of this reality in developing an emancipatory strategy?

The challenge is especially acute when combined with an acknowledgement that the United Nations is a flawed institutional setting in which the international struggle for racial justice has often been suppressed and, nonetheless, a principal focal point for coordinating global action against systemic racism. A transnational racial justice movement produced the historic Durban Declaration and Programme of Action (DDPA), for example, a powerful demand and roadmap for undoing systemic racism rooted in the legacies of slavery and colonialism. Yet, powerful nations within the UN have worked tirelessly to marginalize the DDPA and its demands.[13] At the levels of international law practice and scholarship, the challenge of conceptualizing the role of

African descent against police brutality and other violations of human rights' (17 June 2020) UN Doc A/HRC/43/L.50 (the draft version of the resolution clearly included a plan for such a commission of inquiry).

[7] UN Human Rights Council (n 6) Article 6.

[8] Achiume (n 5) 380.

[9] The 'Urgent Debate' is a relatively rarely used form of special session previously convened in the cases of Syria (three times between 2012 and 2018) and Israel (2010).

[10] Achiume (n 5) 380.

[11] ibid.

[12] ibid.

[13] E Tendayi Achiume and Gay McDougall, 'Anti-Racism at the United Nations' (2023) 117 AJIL Unbound 82, 84.

race and racism in international law while also drawing on international legal frameworks and institutions to fashion antiracist resistance is stark.

3. The invisibility of race in international law scholarship

Despite the urgency of the problem, most international law scholarship to date has not confronted the historical and ongoing relationship between race, racism, and international law. James Gathii recently published a study examining 'to what extent scholarship has addressed international law's historical and continuing complicity in producing racial inequality and hierarchy, including slavery, as well as the subjugation and domination of the peoples of the First Nations'.[14] He reviewed all of the scholarship published in the American Journal of International Law (AJIL) and AJIL Unbound before May 2021 and found that fewer than 2 per cent of the publications in either journal 'substantially engaged with race in the bodies of their texts'.[15]

There are different ways of understanding the exclusion of race from international law scholarship. A recent AJIL Unbound symposium on Race, Racism, and International Law, edited by Achiume and Gathii, explored these exclusions within the context of the ASIL (American Society of International Law) itself, as well as in the broader field of international legal scholarship. Henry J Richardson III, one of the authors of the 'Richardson Report', which investigates racism within ASIL, describes how African Americans were excluded from ASIL until the early 1960s, as well as being excluded from AJIL's board of editors until 2014.[16] As he notes, from the time ASIL was founded in 1906, the organization 'was bathed in the widespread narrative that Blacks are not and must not be seen as the social equals of whites'.[17]

Even after ASIL began admitting some African American members, many themes of importance to Africans and African Americans remained sidelined at ASIL Annual Meetings. Despite some engagement over the years—including reluctant involvement with the global South African anti-apartheid movement—it was not until 2011–2012 that 'a racial critique was beginning to gather steam in [ASIL], led by Blacks and other minorities, with white allies, building on the emergence of [the Blacks of the American Society of International Law (BASIL) Task Force], and additional minorities on the Executive Council'.[18] It was only in 2020, months prior to the global racial justice movement, that ASIL's Executive Council was presented with the Richardson Report, and only in November 2021 that the Executive Council adopted a 'Policy Resolution on Past Discrimination'. That resolution included an apology for 'past practices that had the effect of excluding people of color' and resolved that ASIL would 'do

[14] James Thuo Gathii, 'Studying Race in International Law Scholarship Using a Social Science Approach' (2021) 22 Chicago Journal of International Law 71.

[15] ibid.

[16] Henry J Richardson III, 'Reflections on Race and the American Society of International Law' (2023) 117 AJIL Unbound 32, 33–34 (Richardson was one of five authors on a committee convened by ASIL to address this question).

[17] ibid 32.

[18] ibid 34.

everything in its power to right those wrongs of exclusion'.[19] Whether and how this commitment will transform international law scholarship on race and racism remains to be seen, as Richardson himself noted.[20]

Similar concerns about the exclusion of race from international spaces of legal scholarship and academic exchange have been raised in the European context. For instance, Mohsen al Attar has vividly described the disproportionately white and male scholars featured at a recent European Society of International Law conference, even though the theme of the conference was inclusion in international law.[21] He noted in particular how Achiume, the sole woman of colour on a panel comprised of white male scholars, was the only one to speak about racial justice.[22]

4. Building a community of scholars working on race and racism in international law

When the lacuna is this large, it is necessary to build and sustain a community of scholars invested in addressing it. Over the years, there have been a range of efforts to bring together scholars thinking critically about race and international law. From our perspective, beyond conceptualizing and investigating the role of race and racism in international law, it is imperative to identify alternative, emancipatory strategies. Our approach has been to adopt a scholarly commitment to building community through convenings that help define and expand a shared research agenda for pursuing racial justice through international law practice and scholarship. In this section we describe our efforts to create space in legal scholarship for work of this nature. In the next section, we provide examples of initiatives led by others, while acknowledging that our account is far from exhaustive or representative.

In October 1999, Ruth Gordon convened a symposium at Villanova University School of Law that focused on 'Critical Race Theory and International Law: Convergence and Divergence', which explored how critical race theory (CRT) 'can assist in understanding, and possibly transforming, the international system, and ascertaining how an international dimension might enrich the Critical Race critique of race and rights'.[23] The scholarship arising from this symposium 'highlighted the work that critical race scholars have done to address racial discrimination in the structure

[19] American Society of International Law, 'Diversity, Equity, and Inclusion at ASIL' (ASIL) <https://www.asil.org/about/DEI> accessed 26 November 2023.

[20] Richardson (n 16) 35–36.

[21] Mohsen al Attar, 'Tackling White Ignorance in International Law—"How Much Time Do You Have? It's Not Enough"' *Opinio Juris* (30 September 2022) <https://opiniojuris.org/2022/09/30/tackling-white-ignorance-in-international-law-how-much-time-do-you-have-its-not-enough/> accessed 22 November 2024; See also Mohsen al Attar and Claire Smith, 'Racial Capitalism and the Dialectics of Development: Exposing the Limits and Lies of International Economic Law' (2020) 35 Law and Critique 149; Mohsen al Attar, 'Symposium on Systemic Racism and Sexism in Legal Academia: The Promise of Victory' *Opinio Juris* (16 May 2022) <https://opiniojuris.org/2022/05/16/confronting-race-and-gender-based-oppression-in-legal-academia-the-promise-of-victory/> accessed 22 November 2024.

[22] E Tendayi Achiume, 'The In- or Ex-clusiveness of International Law' (2023) 34(1) European Journal of International Law 225.

[23] Ruth Gordon, 'Critical Race Theory and International Law: Convergence and Divergence' (2000) 45(5) Villanova Law Review 827, 829.

and operation of the international human rights system, including through intersectional analyses that bring structures such as gender to bear'.[24] Similarly, in July 2018, Antony Anghie held a symposium on Third World Approaches to International Law's (TWAIL) past, present, and future at the National University of Singapore School of Law.[25] Subsequently, in August 2018, Achiume, Jim Anaya, and Justin Destautels-Stein led a workshop on 'International Law and Racial Justice' at the University of Colorado, Boulder, School of Law where scholars discussed 'the place of race-centric analysis in contemporary international legal scholarship'.[26]

Building on these earlier encounters, in March 2019, Bâli and Achiume hosted at UCLA Law a symposium on 'Critical Perspectives on Race and Human Rights: Transnational Re-Imaginings' which brought together CRT, TWAIL, and human rights scholars, including early career scholars across these areas, to engage in critical reflection about the role of human rights in achieving racial justice and equality.[27] This symposium was intended 'to foster a transnational conversation among domestic and international legal scholars, and incubate a network of multidisciplinary academics interested in advancing critical, reconstructive, and even radical engagements with the human rights frame broadly construed, but with a focus on racial justice'.[28] Some of the scholarship arising from the symposium was published in a special issue of UCLA Law's Journal of International Law and Foreign Affairs, which contributed to meeting the gap in scholarship that investigates race and racism in international law.[29]

Alongside this symposium, Aslı Bâli and Achiume organized two workshops at UCLA Law. In the first, senior scholars were paired with early career scholars to provide feedback and mentorship on their written work. The second workshop, which focused on 'Race, Empire and International Law', convened CRT and TWAIL scholars to reprise the conversation that began at the Villanova symposium. Participants 'interrogated the history of transnational legal analysis and political mobilisation challenging racial domination' and 'discussed the difficulties and the possibilities of subaltern knowledge production across different fields (such as law, sociology, history) and at different scales (domestic and international), and interrogated some of the very premises that had motivated the convening'.[30] Through this workshop, Bâli and Achiume sought to create space for participants to ask questions that were so often excluded, '[f]or example, can we meaningfully talk about race globally or transnationally or must race always be engaged locally? Can we meaningfully talk about empire, even

[24] E Tendayi Achiume and Aslı Bâli, 'Race and Empire: Legal Theory Within, Through, and Across National Borders' (2021) 67 UCLA Law Review 1386, 1393.

[25] Third World Approaches to International Law Conference (TWAIL Singapore) (National University of Singapore, Singapore, 2 February 2018) <https://law.nus.edu.sg/twail/index.html> accessed 22 November 2024.

[26] International Law and Racial Justice (University of Colorado Boulder Law School, Boulder, 3–4 August 2018) <https://www.colorado.edu/law/sites/default/files/attached-files/ilrj_workshop_themes.pdf> accessed 22 November 2024.

[27] See generally Achiume and Bâli (n 24).

[28] ibid 1395.

[29] (2020) 24 UCLA Journal of International Law and Foreign Affairs 2. This symposium issue features the following authors: Prince Zeid bin Ra'ad Zeid al-Hussein, Kristen Carpenter and Alexey Tsykarev, Catherine Powell, Janine Silga, Kai Ambos, and Mia Lattanzi.

[30] Achiume and Bâli (n 24) 1396.

European colonial empire, in global terms when important distinctions inhere, for example, between settler and non-settler colonial projects?'[31] Sustaining and extending the momentum of these convenings, Bâli and Achiume hosted another symposium in January 2020 at UCLA Law, this time focused on 'Transnational Legal Discourse on Race and Empire'. At this convening, and in the subsequent publications in the UCLA Law Review, participants explored 'the significant contributions that a TWAIL-CRT union stand to make to our legal understanding of racial injustice and inequality as transnationally constituted and sustained'.[32]

Since 2020, the authors have organized and participated in several projects endeavouring to strengthen the community of scholars engaged in questions of race and racism in international law, and to create space for early career and senior scholars alike to collaboratively think critically and develop work that will help to meet the gap in traditional international law scholarship.

On 11–12 March 2022, UCLA Law hosted a closed-door workshop on Critical Law & Security Studies (CLASS), the third convening of a group of scholars exploring questions of law and security from a critical perspective. Emerging out of concerns that predominant approaches in conventional scholarship fail to attend to the relationship between national security and counterterrorism framings on the one hand and struggles over race and colonialism on the other, CLASS has evolved into a collective project to reshape core research agendas spanning the fields of critical race theory, national security law, and international humanitarian law. The group first gathered around the work of the CLEAR (Creating Law Enforcement Accountability & Responsibility) program at CUNY Law—and its indomitable director, Ramzi Kassem—and a shared interest in developing critical scholarship that analyses the systemic racism at the heart of the so-called Global War on Terror (GWoT) domestically in the United States and transnationally by the coalition of states that embraced the GWoT framing. Inspired by Kassem's work exposing the New York police department's racialized surveillance of Muslim communities—and suing to force reforms[33]—the group workshopped research scrutinizing the racialized character of counterterrorism globally. Drafts produced by one convening resulted in a symposium in the *Boston Review*, titled 'Islam on Trial', investigating anti-Muslim racism as a governance strategy in the war on terror.[34] The goal of CLASS workshops has evolved over time but at the heart of the project remains the commitment to critical

[31] ibid.

[32] ibid. See also S Priya Morley, 'Promise Institute for Human Rights, Trans-National Re-Imaginings, UCLA School of Law's Inaugural Series of Convenings on Race, Empire and Human Rights' *UCLA Promise Institute for Human Rights* (April 2022) <https://promiseinstitute.law.ucla.edu/wp-content/uploads/2022/06/Trans-NationalRe-ImaginingsUCLASchoolofLawsInauguralSeriesofConveningsonRaceEmpireandHumanRights.pdf> accessed 22 November 2024; S Priya Morley, 'Connecting Race and Empire: What Critical Race Theory Offers Outside the U.S. Legal Context' (2022) 69 UCLA Law Review Discourse (Law Meets World) 100.

[33] NYCLU, 'Court Releases Report on NYPD Reforms After Landmark Muslim Surveillance Settlement' (*NYCLU*, 8 June 2018) <https://www.nyclu.org/en/press-releases/court-releases-report-nypd-reforms-after-landmark-muslim-surveillance-settlement> accessed 22 November 2024.

[34] Amna A Akbar and Jeanne Theoharis, 'Forum: Islam on Trial' (*Boston Review*, 27 February 2017) <https://www.bostonreview.net/forum/amna-akbar-jeanne-theoharis-muslims-and-constitution/> accessed 22 November 2024 (The 'Forum' on 'Islam on Trial' featured writing by many of the core CLASS participants including Amna Akbar, Jeanne Theoharis, Wadie Said, Sudha Setty, and others).

engagement with the field of 'national security law' and a collective project to fashion alternatives to the liberal imperium of the war on terror and its racial entailments. The opportunity to host a convening of CLASS allowed us to connect our critical perspectives on race and human rights to projects examining how two decades of American-led counterterrorism have legitimated both the sidelining of human rights and deep structures of racial and religious subordination across the Muslim-majority world and Muslim communities in the Global North.

On 19–20 May 2022, building on the initial convenings at UCLA Law in 2019 and 2020, UCLA Law hosted a closed workshop focused on Palestine and international law. This convening brought together TWAIL scholars and Palestinian scholars from different disciplines with the goal of discussing priorities for a shared research agenda on Palestine and international law. The occupation and subordination of Palestine was, alongside South African apartheid, one of the paradigmatic global issues that inspired scholars of the Global South, whose legacy is carried forward in TWAIL scholarship. Yet, while Palestinian colonial subordination persists, Palestine and Palestinians have not received sustained attention within TWAIL scholarship. This convening sought to foster greater TWAIL engagement with Palestine and the ongoing settler colonial subordination of Palestinians. Participants, who came from law and other disciplines, drew on different methodological approaches, including TWAIL, CRT, political economy, and subaltern theory in considering the question of Palestine in international law. Participants also engaged in comparative analysis, considering Palestine in relation to other settler-colonial, postcolonial, or neocolonial/imperialist contexts. This exchange of ideas illuminated the racial and colonial logics at the centre of the ongoing situation in Palestine and the (failure of) current international legal responses to it. Alongside this convening, the Promise Institute for Human Rights at UCLA Law held a public event on Palestine and Apartheid Under International Law.[35] Following this convening, participants are preparing scholarship for publication in different publications, including the Journal of Palestine Studies, the Third World Approaches to International Law Review (TWAILR), the Palestine Yearbook, and others. With the support of co-organizers Noura Erakat, Vasuki Nesiah, and John Reynolds, the authors organized a follow-up convening at NYU and Rutgers in June 2024.

In March 2023, Achiume and Gathii edited a symposium issue of AJIL Unbound, published on behalf of the AJIL which was focused on Race, Racism, and International Law.[36] As noted above, ASIL has recently grappled with its own history of excluding racially marginalized scholars and scholarship focused on race and racism.[37] The very fact of the symposium was itself an important achievement in explicitly tackling gatekeeper institutions in international law scholarship that have long excluded the topic of race from the pages of leading peer-reviewed journals in the field. But beyond its path-breaking character in forthrightly addressing race in a forum organized by the

[35] UCLA Promise Institute for Human Rights, 'Palestine and Apartheid Under International Law' (24 May 2022) <https://promiseinstitute.law.ucla.edu/event/palestine-and-apartheid-under-international-law/> accessed 27 November 2023.

[36] Achiume and Gathii (n 4).

[37] ibid 26.

American Journal of International Law, the symposium also highlighted new and provocative scholarship across a range of different substantive areas of international law while adopting a diversity of methodological approaches. From an article investigating the racial hierarchies shaping international migration and mobility,[38] to the application of Marxist methodologies to offer a 'materialist' conception of race and racism analysing the expansion of capitalism into the non-European world with attendant processes of racialization,[39] to a contribution examining calls for reparations for racial and ecological injustices advanced by the Caribbean Community's Reparations Commission,[40] the symposium charts a roadmap for the kinds of research agendas necessary to fill the gap produced by the erasure of race in a discipline studying systems, practices, and norms that are, in fact, shot through with racial hierarchies.

Moreover, aspects of the symposium build on themes addressed and developed in earlier convenings that brought together different subsets of the contributing scholars. Vasuki Nesiah builds on Adelle Blackett's work, which was featured in our 2019 symposium, to develop her argument about the legacies of slavery that inflect the racialized commodified labour that is a product of the contemporary international labour law regime.[41] Christopher Gevers continues to explore themes from work he showcased at UCLA in his exploration of the overwhelmingly white character of histories of international law. Highlighting the paradoxical marginalization of race in histories of slavery—which focus overwhelmingly on white abolitionists, judges, officials, and settlers—his call for excavating the still unwritten histories of slavery is both a reminder of the centrality of race in the evolution of the discipline and practices of international law and its methodological erasure.[42] The article by Noura Erakat, Darryl Li, and John Reynolds draws on and develops the conversations initiated by the 2022 workshop we convened on Palestine and international law.[43] Their argument that ending apartheid in Israel–Palestine is impossible without recognizing the right to self-determination of Palestinians through a process of decolonization and reparations echoes many of the themes developed by applying the lenses of CRT and TWAIL to reveal that 'race and colonialism are conjoined concepts'.

On 11 March 2023, the Promise Institute for Human Rights at UCLA Law held an expert convening on Setting Institutional Priorities on Climate Reparations and Racial Justice: Learning from Social Movements. The uneven allocation of the burdens of climate change maps on to systemic racial discrimination, inequality, and marginalization within and between countries, all of which are the persistent impacts of global histories of colonialism, enslavement, and extractivism.[44] This convening

[38] Natsu Taylor Saito, 'Race, Indigeneity, and Migration' (2023) 117 AJIL Unbound 43.

[39] Robert Knox, 'International Law, Race, and Capitalism: A Marxist Perspective' (2023) 117 AJIL Unbound 55.

[40] Sarah Riley Case, 'Looking to the Horizon: The Meanings of Reparations for Unbearable Crises' (2023) 117 AJIL Unbound 49.

[41] Vasuki Nesiah, 'Slavery's Afterlives: Humanitarian Imperialism and Free Contract' (2023) 117 AJIL Unbound 66.

[42] Christopher Gevers, 'Slavery and International Law' (2023) 117 AJIL Unbound 71.

[43] Noura Erakat, Darryl Li, and John Reynolds, 'Race, Palestine, and International Law' (2023) 117 AJIL Unbound 77.

[44] UNGA, 'Report of the Special Rapporteur on contemporary forms of racism, racial discrimination, xenophobia and related intolerance, E. Tendayi Achiume—Ecological crisis, climate justice and racial justice' (25 October 2022) UN Doc A/77/549.

brought together experts from the United Nations, Inter-American system, and social movements to discuss the disproportionate impacts of the global climate crisis on racially marginalized peoples in North America, Central America, and the Caribbean—particularly people of African and Indigenous descent. The convening built on the work of social movements, including those working at the intersections of racial, Indigenous, migrant, and climate justice. It also drew on a series of recent reports on the human rights impacts of climate change, including its intersection with racial injustice, by experts from the UN and Inter-American systems. In particular, the convening responded to growing claims for climate reparations arising from social movements and Global South nations. It explored whether and how international law, the international human rights frame, and the institutional mechanisms of the UN and Inter-American Commission on Human Rights may be reimagined and wielded to meet social movements' demands for climate justice and transformative social change.[45] This expert convening was organized as part of the Reimagining Rights in the Americas Conference held at UCLA in conjunction with the 186th period of session of the Inter-American Commission on Human Rights.

This brief survey of the efforts we have made over six years in a shared institutional setting is, as we have indicated, no more than illustrative of an approach we found generative. We are fortunate to have had the institutional support to host the convenings we describe above, and we have attempted to include references to any publications that resulted from them as a resource to other scholars working at the intersection of race and international law. We benefited greatly from the rich and deep intellectual tradition and atmosphere forged by our colleagues in the Critical Race Studies Program at UCLA Law.[46] Having a critical mass of colleagues committed to serious study of race as analytically significant in the field of law made it possible to strive for connections with international law scholars elsewhere with similar commitments. We also benefited greatly from the material support made possible through the funding that established the Promise Institute for Human Rights at UCLA Law. We highlight this support because we are aware that many law schools range from outrightly hostile to passively disinterested in supporting work on race and international law. In other contexts where there is institutional openness to this work, resources may not be available.

We should also note that our convenings were far from perfect. We were not always able to be as inclusive as we would have liked, due to the limitations of our own networks and funding constraints. For example, the participants in our convenings were predominantly from institutions in the Global North and these convenings were entirely in English. We concede that there is still a very long way to go in fostering a transnational, global intellectual community of legal scholars collaborating to deepen interrogation of race and racism in international law. With these many caveats in mind, we nonetheless offer the model of community building as one constructive

[45] International Human Rights Clinic at UCLA Law, 'Setting Institutional Priorities on Climate Reparations & Racial Justice: Learning From Social Movements' *UCLA Promise Institute for Human Rights* (September 2023) <https://promiseinstitute.law.ucla.edu/wp-content/uploads/2023/09/Setting-Institutional-Priorities-on-Climate-Reparations-and-Racial-Justice.pdf> accessed 22 November 2024.

[46] 'Critical Race Studies' (UCLA Law) <https://law.ucla.edu/academics/centers/critical-race-studies> accessed 27 November 2023.

strategy for analysing and reshaping the problematic approaches to race and racism that suffuse international law scholarship and practice. In the next section, we highlight a selection of related contemporaneous projects spearheaded by other colleagues seeking to build intellectual community and develop knowledge production to shift international legal scholarly attention towards the urgent and deeply understudied problems of race, racism, and international law.

5. Tracing engagement with race and racism through knowledge production in international law

There are, of course, others doing important work in community building and analysing the role of race and racism in international law. The renewed engagement from academics to reckon with racism and international law in recent years has contributed to knowledge production across different substantive subject areas. While this section does not reflect the totality of convenings that have seeded new research and the related publications, it illustrates how scholars are reacting to international law's silence on race by taking on illustrative explorations that show how racialization stems from the tools and technologies of international law. They are drawing on different theoretical approaches, including but not limited to CRT and TWAIL, and other scholarly traditions within and outside of law. They are focused on a wide array of substantive topics, including migration (including, inter alia, discussion of migration and development nexus, sovereignty, and climate change-induced migration), socioeconomic equality (including, inter alia, slave labour, mass incarceration, and public health), environment and climate change,[47] and counterterrorism.

In July 2020, Matiangai Sirleaf edited a symposium on Racing National Security in Just Security. This symposium had the dual goals of 'render[ing] race visible in national security' and 'highlight[ing] the importance of a racial justice framework over and above one focused on racial discrimination'.[48] The scholarship in this symposium 'elucidate[d] how race and the associated racial valuations attached to groups influence assessments of when it is in the interest of institutions, laws, and society to act on issues of national security'.[49] That symposium resulted in the publication of a manuscript that makes a canonical contribution to the national security literature, providing transnational, comparative, and international law perspectives on racial justice in that field.[50]

Another path-breaking contribution to knowledge production on race and racism in international law was brought together by James Gathii and Ntina Tzouvala as they organized and co-edited a special issue of the Journal of International Economic Law

[47] Sarah Mason-Case and Julia Dehm, 'Redressing Historical Responsibility for the Unjust Precarities of Climate Change in the Present' in Benoit Mayer and Alexander Zahar (eds), *Debating Climate Law* (Cambridge University Press 2021) 170.

[48] Matiangai Sirleaf, 'Racing National Security: Introduction to the Just Security Symposium' *Just Security* (13 July 2020) <https://www.justsecurity.org/71373/racing-national-security-introduction-to-the-just-security-symposium/> accessed 22 November 2024.

[49] ibid.

[50] Matiangai VS Sirleaf (ed), *Race and National Security* (Oxford University Press 2023).

on racial capitalism. As Gathii and Tzouvala note in their introduction, 'while race and racism are central to the constitution of IEL, race and racism have seldom been analytic categories for understanding IEL'.[51] The special issue also demonstrates the value of diverse methodological approaches to the question of race in international law, complementing emphases on CRT and TWAIL with, for example, Marxist approaches.[52] The issue as a whole features contributions by leading scholars on topics ranging from slavery and forced labour in the international economic order to the racially discriminatory policing enabled by international trade law and intellectual property law, to the relationship between international investment law, race, and state violence. The broad array of substantive areas of international law canvassed through the lens of racial capitalism represents an important step in addressing the staggering gap on questions of race and racism in the international economic law literature. In the same year, Carmen Gonzalez and Athena Mutua co-edited a special issue of the Journal of Law and Political Economy on 'Racial Capitalism and Law', adding to the nascent turn to racial capitalism in international and transnational law literatures. The co-editors analyse the intertwined character of profit-making and racemaking to reveal how racial stratification, segregation, and the creation of racialized 'sacrifice zones' are constitutive of capitalist growth.[53] Their theory of the relationship between racial capitalism and law, in turn, informs analyses by other authors, including Tzouvala's analysis of the racialized assumptions that inform arbitrators' judgments on property rights[54] and Gil Gott's critique of the racialized and neoliberal ground on which microfinance operates in the Global South.[55]

Several other convenings have been hosted by colleagues considering core international law challenges in ways that centre race and racism. While some of these symposia and conferences have not yet yielded publications, they showcase new research agendas and draft scholarship that maintains the momentum of knowledge production on race in international law. For instance, questions of race, justice, and international law were central to a symposium on 'International Law and Global Justice' organized by John Reynolds at Maynooth University in April 2023. In addition to a keynote address on the challenge of racial justice in international law, the three substantive panels of the symposium addressed questions of economic justice, transitional justice, and environmental justice respectively in ways that attended to the centrality of race in the exclusions and distributional inequalities that result from systemic racial discrimination in each of these domains.[56] In June 2023, Victor Kattan organized

[51] James Thuo Gathii and Ntina Tzouvala, 'Racial Capitalism and International Economic Law: An Introduction' (2022) 25(2) Journal of International Economic Law 199.

[52] Marxist approaches were also highlighted in the special issue of AJIL Unbound, including Robert Knox's important contribution: Knox (n 39).

[53] Carmen Gonzalez and Athena Mutua, 'Mapping Racial Capitalism: Implications for Law' (2022) 2(2) Journal of Law and Political Economy 127.

[54] Ntina Tzouvala, 'Invested in Whiteness: Zimbabwe, the von Pezold Arbitration, and the Question of Race in International Law' (2022) 2(2) Journal of Law and Political Economy 226.

[55] Gil Gott, 'Microcredit and the Financial Frontiers of Racial Neoliberalism' (2022) 2(2) Journal of Law and Political Economy 278.

[56] Maynooth University, 'Symposium: "International Law and Global Justice"' (Maynooth University School of Law and Criminology, Maynooth, 21 April 2023) <https://www.eventbrite.ie/e/symposium-international-law-and-global-justice-tickets-560502085827> accessed 22 November 2023 (click 'View details'; then click 'View all event details').

a conference at Nottingham University examining systematic practices of racial discrimination and apartheid globally, beyond the South African context.[57] Deepening and broadening the discussion of apartheid addressed at the convening at UCLA on Palestine and international law mentioned above, Kattan brought together a transnational and interdisciplinary collection of scholars to debate the histories, meanings, and forms of apartheid while interrogating the failure to enforce the international criminal prohibition on apartheid across a wide variety of cases encompassing the contexts of the United States and Israel–Palestine among others.

The ways in which convenings across institutions, from UCLA to Nottingham, have brought together overlapping but also increasingly diverse groups of scholars to build a sequence of conversations and new scholarship about the role of race and racism is striking. We believe that the project of building intellectual community around a shared, if trans-substantive, intellectual project has begun to bear fruit through the many new networks and concrete instances of knowledge production we describe here. These projects, still nascent, may not be sufficient to fill the lacunae that have grown out of the longstanding erasure of race from international law, but we believe they chart an alternative trajectory that may contribute to reshaping the discipline over time while informing our own scholarship and enabling generative new research agendas to form.

6. TWAIL and CRT in the global policy context: reparations for slavery and colonialism, the global extractivist economy, and ecological crisis

How might these research agendas concretely shape governing legal and policy frameworks? In our work, we have sought to prepare not only academic scholarship and policy reports but also more digested materials that can be deployed for advocacy purposes or to shore up the understanding of interested audiences who wish to have an overview of the kinds of work seeking to fill the voids in the literature we have identified. Under the title 'Race and Human Rights Reimagined', we have curated a sample of our work to make it publicly available in a variety of formats online. Of course, this initiative can only represent the most preliminary of first steps and we are aware of the need to build collaborative and long-term research networks that can grow these kinds of platforms.

In light of the enormity of the silences and erasures in international law, the task of conceptualizing the role of race and racism in the discipline and imagining new pathways towards racial justice remains formidable. In this section we provide further examples of how we might identify domains of international law that warrant attention as sites of racial subordination and embedded racism through the agenda developed by United Nations Special Procedures mandate holders in conversation

[57] University of Nottingham, 'The Crime of Apartheid in South Africa and Beyond' (University of Nottingham School of Law, Nottingham, 22–23 June 2023 <https://www.nottingham.ac.uk/conference/fac-socsci/crime-of-apartheid-in-south-africa-and-beyond/documents/apartheid-conf-22-23-june-programme.pdf> accessed 20 November 2023.

with transnational civil society actors at the forefront of social movements for racial justice. While this pathway for seeding new research agendas and future scholarship might be available to any number of thematic mandate holders and country rapporteurs appointed by the Human Rights Council, we highlight some of the ways Achiume, in her mandate as UN Special Rapporteur on contemporary forms of racism, racial discrimination, xenophobia, and related intolerance, drew on CRT and TWAIL to illuminate the operation of race and racism across different substantive areas of international law.

In Achiume's reports, racial equality analysis presents contemporary forms of racial discrimination, for which states may be held accountable, as the persisting impacts of historical injustice. Her approach enables a transnational and transhistorical understanding of international human rights obligations, and particularly the principles of non-discrimination and equality. In one 2019 report, Achiume focused on the global extractivism economy[58] and the racially discriminatory human rights violations it produces. One of the strengths of Achiume's analysis is the explicit framing of contemporary resource extraction, including by corporations in the Global North of resources in the Global South, as rooted in and shaped by colonialism. As she describes, since formal decolonization, states in the Global North and Global South have supposedly been able to participate equally in the global economy or in the international legal system (ie the principle of sovereign equality). In reality, the 'colonial-era' inequalities between states persist, and the contemporary models of extraction perpetuate the racial, ethnic, and Indigenous exploitation that occurred during colonialism. She describes how 'it is those people who, under the colonial extractivism economy, were socially constructed as non-white or non-European that today remain subordinate, excluded and marginal within the global extractivism economy'.[59]

In a second 2019 report, Achiume focused on states' obligations under international law to provide reparations for slavery and colonialism. At its core, slavery constituted the dehumanization of people on the basis of their race, a social construct that still shapes the ability to access fundamental human rights today.[60] Colonialism similarly allocated human rights on a racial basis and relied on both domestic and international law to further global structures of racial domination and discrimination.[61] Adopting a similar analysis as in the extractivism report, Achiume emphasized that reparations

> concern both our past and our present' and 'the urgent project of providing reparations for slavery and colonialism requires states not only to fulfil remedial obligations resulting from specific historical wrongful acts, but also to transform contemporary structures of racial injustice, inequality, discrimination and subordination

[58] The global extractivism economy 'refers to the industries, actors and financial flows, as well as to the economic, material and social processes and outputs, associated with the globalized extraction of natural resources'. UN Human Rights Council, 'Global extractivism and racial equality* Report of the Special Rapporteur on Contemporary Forms of Racism, Racial Discrimination, Xenophobia and Related Intolerance' (14 May 2019) UN Doc A/HRC/41/54, 6.

[59] ibid 42.

[60] ibid 16.

[61] ibid 18.

that are the product of the centuries of racial machinery built through slavery and colonialism.[62]

Importantly, she argues for a 'structural approach' to reparations that seek not only to compensate for harms but also to transform society.[63] This requires 'decolonizing' international law and the barriers it creates to reparations claims; this law emerged from the same structures of racialized subordination that fuelled slavery and colonialism and therefore cannot be used as a bar to justice now.

In her final report as UN Special Rapporteur, in 2022, Achiume built on these analyses to explore the urgent, related issue of ecological crisis, climate justice, and racial justice. As outlined in the report, 'the devastating effects of the ecological crisis are disproportionately borne by racially, ethnically and nationally marginalised groups'.[64] The climate crisis is the product of centuries of natural resource extraction, industrialization, and industrial processes, and the consumption of the outputs of these processes by racist colonial regimes.[65] Between 1850 and 2002, industrialized countries produced three times the carbon dioxide emitted by the entire Global South. Yet, it is the Global South that is currently most affected and least able to mitigate and survive the global ecological crisis due to the colonial processes that caused these historical emissions in the first place.[66] The report critiques how dominant international approaches to climate issues, as with international law more generally, can reinforce racial inequality and injustice. Since many climate-related initiatives are designed without the input or consideration of racially marginalized people, they tend to reinforce patterns of racial discrimination that are already present in national and international economies.[67] Further, the exclusion of impacted groups from leading climate change governance has undermined their demands for systemic change to truly solve the enduring climate crisis.[68] For instance, the way that climate change is framed in international fora ignores the historical responsibility that should be borne by some states and transnational corporations.[69] Drawing on her earlier reparations report, Achiume recommends that states provide reparations for historical environmental and climate harms as well as contemporary harms that are rooted in historic injustice.

In sum, these examples offer illustrations of how academic work at the intersection of TWAIL and CRT can have practical implications for advancing racial justice within the existing framework of the United Nations, notwithstanding its challenges and contradictions.

62 ibid 8.

63 UNGA, 'Contemporary forms of racism, racial discrimination, xenophobia and related intolerance: note / by the Secretary-General' (21 August 2019) UN Doc A/74/321, 7–8 ('[R]eparations for slavery and colonialism include not only justice and accountability for historic wrongs, but also the eradication of persisting structures of racial inequality, subordination and discrimination that were built under slavery and colonialism to deprive non-whites of their fundamental human rights.').

64 UNGA (n 44) 1.

65 ibid 12.

66 ibid ¶ 4.

67 ibid 63.

68 ibid.

69 ibid 71.

7. Conclusion: racial justice as a collective project in international law

In concluding this non-traditional chapter in which we survey and hope to model alternative pathways in international law scholarship and policy through community building, we now make explicit the kinds of partnerships within and beyond the academy modelled by some of the convenings we have canvassed.

First, going beyond interdisciplinary approaches to scholarship, we believe work like the convenings organized by Achiume in her role as Special Rapporteur is critical for building an intellectual community in ways that includes perspectives from, and knowledge produced outside, the academy.[70] This means bringing together scholars as well as movement leaders, community organizations and representatives, policymakers, and those working within international institutions. We also believe that developing emancipatory strategies on race and racism in international law requires creating spaces which, even if convenings take place in academic settings, are not elite centred. Fostering meaningful inclusion and participation from all is an imperative of a collective project that seeks not only to seed knowledge production but also make real change in the practices and institutions of international law.

Of course, a political commitment of this kind also means avoiding exploitation-cum-extraction, on the part of academics, of the knowledge and lived experience of communities for their own professional clout or success. Rather, scholars thinking critically about race, racism, and international law should strive to co-create 'just relationships' with movement actors. In the mainstream of international law scholarship, there has been a revolving door between those in international law practice and scholarship. By creating spaces of inquiry that include and centre the voices of movements, we hope that it will be possible to build a new circuit of knowledge production across practice and scholarship, and to facilitate the flow of ideas in ways that do not entrench empire.

Second, the community we build must also be focused on the next generation of scholars, advocates, and movement leaders that are among our students and in our networks. We have prioritized creating convenings and fora that welcome early career scholars and students to both join in collaborative efforts at knowledge production and to workshop their own ideas. Providing opportunities for mentorship and early career–senior scholar interaction enables emerging scholars to find community and receive constructive feedback in academic settings that welcome perspectives too often marginalized in more conventional international law meetings. In addition, cultivating cross-generational learning and writing enriches the work of

[70] Some convenings include the 'Reimagining Rights in the Americas Conference' with the theme of 'New Horizons at the Intersection of Race, Indigeneity, Migration, and the Environment'. UCLA School of Law 'Reimagining Rights in the Americas' (Promise Institute for Human Rights, Los Angeles, 1–10 March 2023 <https://promiseinstitute.law.ucla.edu/wp-content/uploads/2023/02/Official-Program-Reimagining-Rights-in-the-Americas.pdf> accessed 30 November 2023 as well as the expert convening to discuss 'Human Rights, Racial Equality and Emerging Digital Technologies: Mapping the Structural Threats'. UCLA Promise Institute for Human Rights and UCLA Centre for Critical internet Inquiry, 'Human Rights, Racial Equality and Emerging Digital Technologies: Mapping the Structural Threats' (June 2020) <https://law.ucla.edu/sites/default/files/PDFs/Publications/Promise_Institute/Human%20Rights,%20Racial%20Equality,%20&%20New%20IT%20Report%203.pdf> accessed 22 November 2024.

senior scholars and provides the possibility of co-authored work encompassing expertise in a range of subjects and methodologies that any individual scholar would have difficulty mastering alone. Creating opportunities for students and early career scholars not only expands the range of work showcasing the alternative approaches cultivated by our burgeoning network, but also produces pathways for different kinds of future leadership in international law among those who will develop professional careers as practitioners, activists, or scholars. Bringing students into our convenings means that those who may be more interested in careers practising international law will find their trajectories informed by analyses centring race, enabling them to notice and address erasures they might encounter as they begin to work with international law norms and institutions.

Understanding our project in community building to have a knowledge production agenda also means ensuring that new approaches in international law are reflected in the curricula we teach. We have sought both to develop new courses and to revise syllabi for existing courses in ways that mainstream questions of racial justice and critical approaches in traditional public international law courses, drawing directly on the work emerging from the convenings we and others have organized. The sidelining of these subjects and perspectives in conventional law school curricula and the treatment of analytic approaches focused on race as marginal or fringe contributes to the intergenerational erasures of race that have produced the lacunae in this discipline that we hope to counter. We have sought to crowd-source bibliographies at each of our convenings to develop a shared canon across the intellectual networks we are building. Such a canon, in turn, forms a resource for devising new curricula, revising courses, and ensuring that our research draws on and recognizes the work of colleagues seeking to bring race to the analytic centre of international law scholarship.

Given the marginalization of race and racism within international law scholarship, many racially marginalized scholars—ourselves included—have had to navigate studying and teaching in institutions and being part of intellectual communities that reflect neither our own lived experience nor our critical perspective on international law. The absence of critical pedagogy when we were students first encountering the study and practice of international law and the challenges that have followed us into our careers have been a motivator of the enterprise we describe in this chapter. As scholars of colour navigating legal institutions and trying to develop analytic frameworks that capture the challenges we have long grappled with in our own careers—both our embodied experiences and the experience of examining the operation of international law in the Global South—the urgency of finding emancipatory alternatives to reimagine pedagogies, doctrines, and institutions of international law is keenly felt.

In seeking to build community and new networks to support a broader rethinking of the field of international law we—together with the many colleagues whose work we touch upon in this chapter—have tried to bring into existence the forms of collaboration and pedagogy we missed in our own early careers. As we have described, we were particularly fortunate to be early career scholars at the UCLA School of Law, which nurtured our work and facilitated critical perspectives as our senior colleagues had institutionalized a Critical Race Studies programme that modelled exactly the kind of intellectual collective we hoped to foster in international law. In answering the question of how to grapple with race and racism in international law, we are grateful to be able to end where we began—recognizing the value of building cross-generational intellectual communities within and beyond the legal academy that consciously choose to create space for critical perspectives that centre race as an analytic lens in both interrogating and challenging, but also seeking to reconstruct the emancipatory potential of international law.

23

Unburdening White Women

Antiracist Feminist Praxis as Revolution

*Claire Smith**

1. Introduction

Mainstream international legal feminism, while exercising awareness of race as a category, has been less attendant to *thinking through* race as analytic. Feminist approaches to international law have assisted in offering solutions and managing patriarchy, ultimately advancing the cause of emancipation.[1] Yet, at the same time they have struggled with the reproduction of racialized and gendered tropes,[2] engaging in practices of circumscription and essentialization when implementing emancipatory visions.[3] Chiefly, these approaches have failed to examine the co-constitutive power relations through which race came into being with gender and vice versa,[4] and a resulting inability to understand gender as co-constitutive in local, regional, national, and global relations of race.[5] In effect, international law's mainstream feminism has ignored the exercise and justification of racialized colonial domination through patriarchy, racism, and heteronormativity in the making and unmaking of women,[6] thus remaining 'inside rather than outside of whiteness'.[7]

Having originated primarily from inside the white racial frame, attempts to degender international law have ignored the racial edifice international law is itself built upon. While white ignorance has been covered in the pages of this text, what piques my interest are the historically constituted formations of whiteness that continue to

* I am deeply indebted to the feminists and their communities that allowed me to soundboard, develop, and write this chapter. I owe a huge and insurmountable feminist debt as a middle-class, cis-gender, able-bodied, white women who was raised in a settler colony and operates in the elite spaces of international law.

[1] Laura Shepherd, 'White Feminism and the Governance of extremism' (2022) 15 Critical Studies on Terrorism 727.

[2] Ratna Kapur, *Erotic Justice: Law and the New Politics of Postcolonialism* (Routledge 2005).

[3] Angela Harris, 'Race and Essentialism in Feminist Legal Theory' (1990) 42(3) Stanford Law Review 581.

[4] See, eg, Vasuki Nesiah, 'Human Rights, Human Wrongs: A More Demanding Relationship to History' in Neha Jain and Sarah MH Nouwen, *Race and Transitional Justice* (Oxford University Press 2026).

[5] Sirleaf refers to whiteness as the 'unspoken baseline of international law'. Matiangai Sirleaf, 'Do You Have To Say You Are Black?' (*TWAILR*, 15 June 2022) <https://twailr.com/do-you-have-to-say-that-you-are-black/> accessed 5 November 2024.

[6] Adrien Katherine Wing, 'Introduction Global Critical Race Feminism for the Twenty First Century' in Adrien Katherine Wing (ed), *Global Critical Race Feminism An International Reader* (New York University Press 2000).

[7] Gina Heathcote and Lucia Kula, 'Abandoning the Idealised White Subject of Legal Feminism: A Manifesto for Silence in a Lusophone Register' (2023) 12(3) Global Constitutionalism 469.

Claire Smith, *Unburdening White Women* In: *Emancipating International Law*. Edited by: Mohsen al Attar and Claire Smith, Oxford University Press. © Claire Smith 2026. DOI: 10.1093/9780198935605.003.0029

occur within feminist orthodoxies, and reflected into international law through its intervention, praxis, and institutionalization. In particular, I reflect on the role of 'white womanhood in maintaining the whiteness that corals international legal feminism',[8] and demand recourse to—at best—white-centred feminism.[9] White-centred feminism is antithetical to all forms of feminist knowledge production. It fails to equip international law with effective gender awareness, rendering feminist interventions inadequate and susceptible to wilful misapprehension of its perceived successes.[10] To unpack this claim, I centre the racialized epistemology that pervades feminist interventions, conceptualizing whiteness as an axis which orders the relationship between feminist theorizing, practice, and epistemic politics in the 'international'.[11]

This chapter moves in three parts: firstly, I understand feminist whiteness as an epistemic position rooted in power relations, reflecting the utility of white womanhood within international law's feminism. Secondly, I historicize the subject positions produced within the white racial frame to examine how white womanhood maintains notions of white innocence and immanence, linking the enduring afterlives of these subject positions to international white supremacy through methodological whiteness.[12] Thirdly, I examine feminist attempts to counter its embedded racial hierarchy—namely inclusion—as a form of epistemic violence that reinforce rather than dismantle racialized power structures. Finally, I introduce the concept of feminist debt to call for active forms of subversion aimed at disrupting the epistemic boundaries of international law that constrain feminist praxis. This includes imagining feminist futures that work against and outside international law as it exists.

A few caveats before I begin. This chapter does not suggest that whiteness is constituted outside of historically and socially specific contexts. Like any racial category, whiteness is neither 'synchronically uniform or diachronically static'.[13] Instead, I argue

[8] Heathcote and Kula conclude that this is a consequence of the 'perpetuation of a double knowledge frame: the first the knowledge of the international order, its specific origins in the Anglo-European frames that produced and benefited from colonialism and slavery; the second the amenability of narrow frames of western waves of feminism emergent in legal discourses in the final few decades of the twentieth century'. ibid.

[9] Aziz defines white feminism as feminism that comes from a white perspective, and is universalizing, subsisting through the failure to consider the context of power in which feminist interactions and actions take place, and the corresponding ability of feminism to influence that context. Razia Aziz, 'Feminism and the Challenge of Racism: Deviance or Difference?' in Helen Crowley and Susan Himmelweit (eds), *Knowing Women: Feminism and Knowledge* (Polity Press 1992) 296. Heathcote and Kula (n 7) define white feminism as that which prioritizes gender at the exclusion of other vectors of power and, often, uses gender to reproduce other sites of privilege in a civilizing fashion.

[10] Palestinian Feminist Collective, 'A feminist praxis for academic freedom in the context of the genocide in Gaza' (*Monoweiss*, 11 April 2024) <https://mondoweiss.net/2024/04/a-feminist-praxis-for-academic-freedom-in-the-context-of-genocide-in-gaza/> accessed 12 April 2024.

[11] Anne Orford, 'Feminism, Imperialism and the Mission of International Law' (2002) 71(2) Nordic Journal of International Law 275.

[12] Gurminder Bhambra, 'Brexit, Trump and Methodological Whiteness: On the Misrecognition of Race and Class' (2017) 68(1) British Journal of Sociology 214.

[13] Charles Mills, 'Revisionist Ontologies: Theorising White Supremacy' in *Blackness Visible: Essays on Philosophy and Race* (Cornell University Press 2015). Crenshaw describes such formation in 'Race, Reform and Retrenchment: Transformation and Legitimation in Antidiscrimination Law' (1988) 101 Harvard Law Review 1331. Harris highlights law's production of race and racial categories through the unspoken and unacknowledged. Cheryl Harris, 'Critical Race Studies An Introduction' (2002) 49(5) UCLA Law Review 1215, 217.

that international law's colonial and imperial origins—and the co-constitutive role of gender and race—are sustained by ongoing forms of coloniality through international legality.[14] Next, the call to recognize, interrogate, and dismantle white feminism[15] has long been made by Black, brown and Indigenous feminisms. Racialized and Indigenous feminists have been integral from the 'beginning',[16] informing the pre-configurations of international law, just as they have continued to create, contest, and resist it. I recognize the danger of centring whiteness; in naming it, I reify it. However, my aim with whiteness and its structural forms is 'not to describe it, but to work for its abolition'.[17] This requires moving beyond performative acknowledgements of privilege which work to perpetuate antiracist whiteness. This includes gestures that centre the moral positioning of 'good' whiteness without taking steps to end racism.[18] Finally, and in keeping with feminist methodology and practice, this chapter operates as an invitation: it is not a closed-circuit argument where thinking ends, but a starting point for thinking with and in concert with others.

2. Feminist pasts, futures, and presents: whiteness and the international

Whiteness functions as a process of subjectivation. It confers identifiable and measurable benefits:[19] elevating, normalizing, and homogenizing whiteness while stigmatizing, devaluing, and rendering disposable Black, brown, Asian, and Indigenous peoples.[20] White supremacy, as a distinctly global project, materializes through international law's ontological and epistemological frameworks.[21] As Christopher Gevers argues, the 'international' is embedded within a specific epistemic space[22]—historically constructed and maintained as a distinctly racial imaginary, authenticated from within and designed to reinforce a white supremacy racialized structuring of global power.[23] Gevers's analysis aligns with what Feagin terms the 'white racial frame': an organized set of racialized ideas, stereotypes, emotions, and discriminatory

[14] Claire Midgely, 'Introduction Gender and Imperialism: Mapping the connections' in Claire Midgly (ed), *Gender and Imperialism* (Manchester University Press 1988) 8.

[15] See, eg, Aileen Moreton-Robinson, 'Talkin' Up to the White Woman: Indigenous Women and Feminism (Queensland University Press 2000). Hazel Carby, 'White Women Listen! Black Feminism and the Boundaries of Sisterhood' in Heidi Safia Mirza (ed), *Black British Feminism A Reader* (Routledge 1997).

[16] The notion of the (singular) beginning of international law is itself enmeshed in the relationship between white temporality, and its commitment to linearities. See, eg, Charles Mills, 'WHITE TIME: The Chronic Injustice of Ideal Theory' (2014) 11(1) Du Bois Review 24; PJ Brendese, *Segregated Time* (Oxford University Press 2023).

[17] Vron Ware and Les Black, *Out of Whiteness: Colour, Politics and Culture* (Chicago University Press 2002) 2.

[18] Sara Ahmed, 'The Non-Performativity of Anti-Racism' (2006) 7(1) Meridians 104.

[19] Cherryl Harris, 'Whiteness as Property' (1993) 106(8) Harvard Law Review 1710.

[20] Sean Elias and Joe Feagin, 'Systemic Racism and the White Racial Frame' in Sean Elias and Joe Feagin (eds), *Routledge Handbook of Contemporary Racisms* (Routledge 2020) 16.

[21] Charles Mills, *The Racial Contract* (Cornell University Press 1997).

[22] Samera Esmeir, 'On Becoming Less of the World' (2018) 8(1) History of the Present A Journal of Critical History 88.

[23] Christopher Gevers, '"Un-whitening the World": Rethinking Race and International Law' (2021) 67(1) UCLA Law Review 1652.

inclinations that shape how societies are colour-coded and stratified.[24] This frame, operating as a 'distinct' yet unnamed perspective,[25] permeates international law's epistemic politics, shaping its methodologies, doctrines—from sovereignty[26] to *jus cogens*[27]—and globalized understandings predicated on distorted understandings of sex, gender, and race.[28]

Feminism within international law has emerged from and 'is housed within its intellectual and political racially hierarchical landscape'.[29] It is bounded within the white racial frame, yet remains unencumbered—or seemingly unaffected—by the historio-racial schema of race that has shaped international law's foundational assumptions about self, subjectivity, and knowledge production.[30] A lack of attention to methodological whiteness manifests in feminism's failure to recognize or reflect on the structuring role of whiteness in the construction of gender within international law, including the 'corresponding solutions, and the means through which these solutions might be achieved'.[31] Feminist legal scholarship frequently overlooks how whiteness continues to shape not only the lived experiences of women globally but also continues to structure relationships between women and among feminists themselves. Within the international: 'Patriarchal whiteness operates possessively as a raced and gendered epistemological *a priori* within knowledge production as universals, dominant norms, values, and beliefs.'[32] By neglecting race as a co-analytic to gender—relational, co-constitutive, and fundamental to the construction of gender—orthodox feminism has contributed to the invisibility of whiteness and therefore white womanhood, rendering them either unthinkable or, perhaps more tellingly, irrelevant. While feminist scholarship occasionally acknowledges and appropriately laments the problematic racialization of women, it fails to name its counterpart: global white supremacy. As duCille notes, whiteness is treated as natural, neutral, and unproblematic, with racial identity constructed as the 'property of the non-white': '[u]nless the object of study happens to be Other, race is placed under erasure as something outside immediate consideration, at once extratextual and extraterrestrial.'[33] This luxury of disinterest in race within feminist discourse, to quote Ahmed, matters 'both in terms

[24] Joe Feagin, *Systemic Racism: A theory of oppression* (Routledge 2006).

[25] Annalise Riles, 'The View from the International Plane: Perspective and Scale in the Architecture of Colonial International Law' (1995) 6(1) Law and Critique 39.

[26] See Mbori, ch 4 in this volume.

[27] See Riley Case and Mégret, ch 5 in this volume, noting the need for an intersectional analysis of *jus cogens*.

[28] Karen Engle, *The Grip of Sexual Violence in Conflict* (Stanford University Press 2020).

[29] Jennifer Morgan, 'Archives and Histories of Racial Capitalism An Afterward' (2015) 125 Social Text 153, 156.

[30] Shannon Sullivan, *Revealing Whiteness The Unconscious Habits of Racial Privilege* (Indiana University Press 2006).

[31] E Tendayi Achiume, 'Empire, Borders and Refugee Responsibility Sharing' 110 California Law Review 1011, 1014.

[32] Aileen Morton Robinson, 'The White Man's Burden: Patriarchal White Epistemic Violence and Aboriginal Women's Knowledges within the Academy' (2011) 26(70) Australian Feminist Studies 413.

[33] Ann duCille, 'The Occult of True Black Womanhood: Critical Demeanour and Black Feminist Studies' in Elizabeth Abel, Barbara Christian, and Helene Moglen (eds), *Female Subjects in Black and White: Race, Psychoanalysis, Feminism* (University of California Press 1997) 35.

of its reflection, existence or experience, as well as in the denoting who may dictate ways in which this occurs'.[34]

Where race matters, it has been rendered meaningful in relation to racialized womanhood, primarily through reductive frameworks that treat gender as race-neutral while simultaneously perpetuating stereotypes including those embedded in ethnicity, religion, or location through the racialized 'third world women'.[35] By ignoring the co-constitutive relationship between race—and particularly whiteness—and gender construction, hegemonic feminism sustains the illusion that gender exists independently of racial hierarchies. This persists despite the fact that international legal regimes have long defined—and often excluded—women based on racialized constructions of gender.[36] Inside international law, racialized-gender subjectivities have always been co-constitutive, invoked differently depending on historical contexts and the shifting needs of white supremacy.[37] The erasure of Black women from the category of 'woman', effectively denying them personhood and humanity, laid the groundwork for chattel slavery.[38] Similarly, the attribution of sexual deviance and immorality to Indigenous women served to justify colonial violence, including land dispossession, forced sterilization, and systemic dehumanization. Modalities of gender and race operated through international law to legitimize colonial conquest,[39] facilitating the appropriation of land, the imposition of racially hierarchical governance structures,[40] and the exclusion of women from entitlement to land ownership, positions of authority, and divorce.[41] 'Colonisation was a twofold process of racial inferiorization and gender subordination.'[42] Through its gender-cum-race logics, international law has always and continues to render certain bodies exploitable, fungible, and ultimately disposable.[43]

Reading whiteness into the construction of gender—and particularly the formation of white womanhood—is integral to understanding its role in sustaining

[34] Frankenberg highlights the multidimensionality of whiteness: as a location of structural advantage, a standpoint, and a set of cultural practices that are usually unmarked and unnamed. Ruth Frankenberg, *The Social Construction of Whiteness: White Women, Race Matters* (University of Minnesota Press 1993) 1.

[35] Ratna Kapur, *Erotic Justice Law and the New Politics of Postcolonialism* (Routledge 2005).

[36] BS Chimni, *International Law and World Order: A Critique of Contemporary Approaches* (Cambridge University Press 2017).

[37] Vron Ware, *Beyond the Pale: White Women, Racism, History* (Verso 2016).

[38] Diana Patton, 'Gender History, Global History and Transatlantic Slavery Racial Capitalism and Social Reproduction' (2022) 127(2) The American Historical Review 726; Jennifer Morgan, *Reckoning with Slavery, Gender, Kinship and Capitalism in the Early Black Atlantic* (Duke University Press 2021).

[39] Kathleen Wilson, 'Empire, Gender, and Modernity in the Eighteenth Century' in Philippa Levine (ed), *Gender and Empire* (Oxford University Press 2007).

[40] Elizabeth Dillenberg, *Empire's Daughters: Girlhood, Whiteness and the Colonial Project* (Manchester University Press 2024).

[41] Aoife O'Donoghue, 'The Admixture of Feminine Weakness and Susceptibility: Gendered Personifications of the State in International Law' (2018) 19 Melbourne Journal of International law 227. See also Linda Tuhiwai Smith, *Decolonizing Methodologies Research and Indigenous Peoples* (Zed Books 2004) 8.

[42] Oyèrónkẹ́ Oyěwùmí, *The Invention of Women: Making an African Sense of Western Gender Discourses* (University of Minnesota Press 1997).

[43] Shirley Anne Tate and Encarnación Gutiérrez Rodríguez, 'Critical Race and Gender: Dialogues Between Decoloniality and Intersectionality' in Shirley Anne Tate and Encarnación Gutiérrez Rodríguez (eds), *The Palgrave Handbook of Critical Race and Gender* (Palgrave MacMillan 2023) 5.

heteronormative, patriarchal, and racially capitalist dialectics.[44] Whiteness has functioned as an invisible organizing axis, structuring the international legal system in ways that racialized *others* must continuously navigate and resist.[45] Far from accidental or resulting from individual prejudices, this dynamic is embedded within political, economic, and legal institutions.[46] Whiteness operates through the shaping of vulnerability and threat, serving as a vehicle for moral panic where racialized bodies are cast as dangers, threats of despoliation of white womanhood.[47] For example, the myth of white slavery led to the adoption of the International Agreement for the Suppression of the White Slave Traffic, ostensibly aimed at protecting white women but rooted in anxieties about threats to national identity, immigration, and colonial subjects.

Historically, white womanhood has played a critical role in shaping the archetype of the legal victim—white, female, blameless, and passive—and worthy of legal protection,[48] while constructing threats as racialized and male. Historically, it was instrumental in justifying military interventions, framed as necessary to save white women in colonized contexts.[49] This dynamic is embedded within feminist institutionalism, particularly in international humanitarian and international criminal law, which reflect and reproduce a 'racialised division of forms of violence'.[50] Here, 'violence associated with white masculinity' is rendered invisible or permissible, and positioned 'in opposition with the hyper aggression of racialised men', as well as the 'passivity and innate helplessness of women'.[51] Yet, this narrative of passivity and helplessness belies its operation, which despite the construction of victimhood within the international becoming synonymous with Black and brown women,[52] continues to amplify the perceived urgency of threats to white or proximate to white womanhood and attract disproportionate attention and action. In contemporary contexts, feminist-aligned bodies have become battlegrounds, where feminist norms are mobilized to seek to legitimize military intervention against racialized populations.[53] These same frameworks now reinforce carceral responses for gender-based and/or sexual violence rendering racialized populations triply vulnerable to lawfare, warfare, and criminalization. As Gevers, utilizing du Bois notes, this is not aberration nor insanity.

[44] Mohsen al Attar and Claire Smith, 'Racial Capitalism and the Dialectics of Development: Exposing the Limits and Lies of International Economic Law' (2022) 35(1) Law and Critique 149.

[45] Kimberlé Crenshaw, 'Close Encounters of Three Kinds: On Teaching Dominance, Feminism and Intersectionality' (2010) 46 Tulsa Law Review 151.

[46] Meera Sabaranam and Mark Laffey, 'Complex Indebtedness: Justice and the Crisis of the Liberal Order'(2023) 99(1) International Affairs 161.

[47] Nira Yuval Davis, *Gender and Nation* (Sage 1997).

[48] Sabrina Balgamwalla, 'Trafficking in Narratives' (2016) 94 Denver University Law Review 1.

[49] Ruby Hamad, *How White Feminism Betrays Women of Colour* (Hachette 2020).

[50] Robert Knox, 'Hypocrisy, Race and International Law' (2024) 12(2) London Review of International Law 217.

[51] Ntina Tzouvala and Kathrine Fallah, 'Deploying Race, Employing Force' (2021) 67 UCLA Law Review 1580, 1592.

[52] Makau W Matua, 'Savages, Victims, and Saviors: The Metaphor of Human Rights' (2001) 42(1) Harvard International Law Journal 20; Gargi Bhattacharyya, *Dangerous Brown Men Exploiting Sex, Violence and Feminism in the 'War on Terror'* (Bloomsbury 2008).

[53] Karen Engle and Fionnuala Ní Aoláin, 'Forum Shopping, Feminism, and Fights Over Defining a Conflict' (2024) 12(2) London Review of International Law 221.

White women benefited—and continue to benefit—from the structures of empire. A key dimension of this benefit has been their increased potential in shaping imperial ideologies and participating in their implementation, with white women exercising their 'duty to bring civilisation to the uncivilised'.[54] This racialized and gendered subject construction is coloured with 'notions of imperial destiny, class and racial superiority'. As some have described, white women became an 'invincible global civilising agent'. The 'white woman's burden', as Orford notes, 'ideally placed, indeed duty bound' to 'contribute to the ongoing project of "saving" the third world'.[55] This subject construction has played a central role in Western feminist thought since the eighteenth century, manifesting in international law through narratives of emancipating the oppressed 'other' and 'inferior women'.[56]

This pattern is evident in pre-figurations of feminist engagement with international law, which have highlighted that liberal feminist anti-slavery movements were deeply invested in the ideologies of white superiority, Eurocentrism, and imperialism.[57] Similarly, as Baetens notes, at the Hague Peace Conference, the international congress of women drafted a new international, strikingly robust and forward thinking global framework, while excluding women 'of the colonies'.[58] Discussions of peace, sovereignty, and self-determination co-existed with the need to *protect* locals on the basis of their inability for self-government. Even in the embryonic international architecture like the International Labour Organisation and the League of Nations, Siegal's work on the Women's International League for Peace and Freedom reveals how the white Western women in attendance prioritized their roles and expertise.[59] As Siegal argues, these women strategically positioned themselves as capable of speaking 'for' women 'of the east who needed to be saved', reinforcing the utility of gender as a unifying factor that served to uphold white, Western superiority.[60]

As Otto has highlighted, in both international human rights law and international criminal law female subject positions are produced in relation to binary male subjects. The 'victim' subject is framed in ways that affirm the need for a masculine 'saviour of good women from "bad" and often native men',[61] who need protection from racialized men as much as they do from their own cultures. Yet, as Otto further notes, these saviour troupes are embedded within the gendered and racialized histories of colonialism, where white women acted as civilizing agents, saving racialized women from racialized men.[62] The saviour figure—'the actual rescuers,

[54] Ware (n 37).

[55] Orford (n 11) 276.

[56] Midgely (n 14) 14.

[57] Ware (n 37) 33.

[58] Freya Baetens, 'International Congress of Women (1915)' in Rudiger Wolfrum (ed), *Max Planck Encyclopaedia of Public International Law* (Oxford University Press 2010).

[59] Mona Siegel, *Peace on Our Terms. The Global Battle for Women's Rights after the First World War* (Columbia University Press 2020).

[60] Melinda Plastas, A *Band of Noble Women: Racial Politics in the Women's Peace Movement* (Syracuse University Press 2011); Joyce Blackwell, *No Peace Without Freedom: Race and the Women's International League for Peace and Freedom, 1915–1975* (Southern Illinois University Press 2004) 7, 67.

[61] Dianne Otto, 'Disconcerting Masculinities: Reinventing the Subject of International Human Rights' in Doris Buss and Ambreena Manji (eds), *International Law: Modern Feminist Approaches* (Hart 2005).

[62] Ratna Kapur, 'The Tragedy of Victimization Rhetoric: Resurrecting the "Native" Subject in International/Post-colonial Feminist Legal Politics' (2003) 15 Harvard Journal of International Law 1.

redeemers of a benighted world'—reflects both the successes of an international feminism,[63] and the persistence of the white woman's burden. Their success, however, is inseparable from the racial hierarchy that places white women above their non-white counterparts. White women's advancement, of course, is intertwined with the maintenance of racial superiority and control including within the epistemic hierarchies of international law.[64]

The durability of these racial-gendered constructions is evident in contemporary international law, where they are reproduced and adapted to meet the demands of evolving subject positions.[65] These subjectivities are 'constantly shaped and mediated by multiple, overlapping modes of self-fashioning in which the past and present function relationally'.[66] Whiteness remains the invisible organizing axis of the international legal system, structuring the field in ways that racialized subjects must navigate, resist, and contest.[67] This dynamic is not the product of accidents or individual prejudices; it is systemic, embedded within the organizational logics of political, economic, and legal institutions.[68] Through its failure to acknowledge and interrogate race, as Jonsson argues, feminist knowledge reproduces racial hierarchies and sustains structural ignorance regarding the operation of whiteness,[69] allowing the historically sedimented attachments to persist, shaping feminist praxis in forms that cohere with racialized domination.[70]

Ultimately, international law's hegemonic feminism has failed to recognize it is not 'white simply because white women adopt it, but because its stake is built on and depends on the racialised division of the world'.[71] A refusal to excavate or engage whiteness within the legacy of feminist thought—or to examine the interlocking and co-constitutive relationship between gender and race—results in an impoverished rubric that hegemonic liberal feminism takes forward in international law. This failure further obfuscates contemporary forms of domination, while perpetuating the historical baggage that feminist interventions often claim to resist. In failing to acknowledge its feminist debt, hegemonic feminism remains inside of and committed to whiteness. As a result—and despite its best intentions—critical opportunities have been missed to understand 'the ways in which feminist legal theory is invited to participate in the project of constituting women and the international community'.[72] Or, more importantly, to work against the constraints of that invitation.

[63] Matua (n 52).

[64] Alice Miller, 'Sexuality, Violence Against Women, and Human Rights: Women Make Demands and Ladies Get Protection' (2004) 7(2) Health and Human Rights 17.

[65] Laura Ann Stoller, *Duress Imperial Relations in Our Times* (Duke University Press 2016).

[66] Achille Mbembe, *On the Postcolony* (University of California Press 2001) 229.

[67] Crenshaw (n 45) 151.

[68] Sabaranam and Laffey (n 46).

[69] Terese Jonsson, *Innocent Subjects Feminism and Whiteness* (Pluto Press 2022).

[70] Patricia Hill Collins, *Black Feminist Thought* (Routledge 2000) 21, 246; Sherene Razack, 'Looking White People in the Eye: Gender, Race and Culture in Courtrooms and Classrooms' (University of Toronto Press 1998); Sara Salem, 'Intersectionality and Its Discontents: Intersectionality as Traveling Theory'(2018) 25(4) European Journal of Women's Studies 403.

[71] Françoise Vergès *A Decolonial Feminism Taking Sides: Decolonial Feminism* (Pluto Press 2021) 18.

[72] Orford (n 11).

3. The epistemic violence of inclusion

Despite its articulated façade of benevolence, international law occurs within highly racialized logics of knowledge production. It has made no little meaningful effort to acknowledge, let alone dismantle, the ideological edifice it both creates and sustains through its epistemological predilections. Rather than recognizing racialization as a 'defining or systematic feature of the imperial project', international law treats it as an aberration—a pathology that can be resolved through reformist commitments to diversity and inclusion.[73] A de-whitening of feminist engagements with international law requires a self-reflexive interrogation of the frameworks of feminist knowledge production, as housed within patriarchal white supremacy. This demands attention to how feminists understand gender in un-racialized terms and how these framings limit feminist understandings of the very systems they seek to remedy.

Within feminist orthodoxy in international law, the dominant remedy has been the pursuit of inclusion and diversity, with the laudable aim of creating plurality. However, this focus on material *access*—who is allowed into the conversation—without addressing epistemic *justice*—how knowledge is accepted as such and in turn valued, produced, and legitimized—leaves the underlying racial hierarchies of feminist knowledge intact and untroubled. The persistent call to 'make space' for the voices of 'other' women, both within and beyond the academy, obscures the racial power structures that govern knowledge production. It reflects a superficial gesture that abdicates responsibility for attending to the undercurrents of epistemic reception of the 'other' in international law.[74] In what follows, I examine three forms of inclusion within feminist engagements with international law: (i) the reparative reading of women into international law's histories (ii) the 'add women and stir' approach to institutional inclusion, and (iii) the conceptual inclusion of gender or race within legal debate.

3.1 The reparative reading of women into international law's histories

A key manifestation of the epistemic violence of inclusion is evident in the recent trend to read more women into international law's histories—a project often marked by an uncritical reflex that reinforces white innocence and white immanence within international law's epistemology. Disproportionately, this focus has centred on white women, both as a collective and as individuals, while the contributions and experiences of racialized women are marginalized. For example, de la Rasilla's exploration of women's roles in international law confines its scope to the West, noting that 'the last part of the 19th century and early 20th century witnessed the slow emergence of Western women's activism and engagement with international law', as if feminist legal

[73] E Tendayi Achiume, 'Transnational Racial (In)Justice In Liberal Democratic Empire' (2021) 134 Harvard Law Review Forum 378, 381.

[74] As Charlesworth and Chinkin note: 'Greater diversity in the considerations to be taken into account': Hillary Charlesworth and Christine Chinkin, *The Boundaries of International Law A Feminist Analysis* (Manchester University Press 2000) 258.

history begins—and ends—within Euro-American borders.[75] In contrast, Tallgren's *Portraits of Women in International Law*[76] demonstrates a far more nuanced awareness of intersecting inequalities, yet highlights the difficulty of fighting against the white racial frame achieving a 1:5 ratio of negatively racialized women to white women. Both texts ultimately reveal the struggle of adopting a gender-centric approach that fails to grapple with the demands of international law's construction of subjectivity at the intersection of race, class, gender, and colonial power. Ultimately, in different ways and with differing levels of awareness and intention, they reproduce the beneficiaries of white supremacy as innocent or morally excused through strategic absences in the historical record.[77]

These reparative readings neglect the ideological and structural power relations that have shaped the 'international' as both a legal and epistemic project—relations that made the dominance and visibility of white women both possible and probable. By failing to trouble the white racial frame, these accounts leave the immanence of whiteness as a direct consequence of racial capitalism unexamined, thus missing how the acquisition of territory, resources, and markets depended heavily on racemaking, alongside the corresponding accumulation, extraction, and dispossession of the third and fourth worlds.[78] Likewise, they overlook the narrative of white innocence embedded within international law's liberal frameworks, which sanitizes the violent histories that underwrite its foundations. It remains an unsurprising yet rarely mentioned fact that the intellectual and institutional centres of international law's feminist thought are located within metropoles and settler-colonial states. The same sites that continue to benefit from the imperial legacies that feminist histories omit yet disproportionately operate far away—whether figuratively or literally from racialized women.[79]

As a result, histories rooted in feminist whiteness become the dominant narratives invoked to provide authority, background, and power to feminist intervention within international law. This stabilization of white feminist immanence and innocence is achieved by disconnecting the prevalence of whiteness from the dialectical conditions of colonialism and imperialism that reduce 'Black women and women of Colour only as decoration or examples of female victimisation'.[80] Such omissions reflect a failure to challenge the epistemological privilege of androcentric whiteness. Instead, rhetorical

[75] Ignacio de la Rasilla, *International Law and History Modern Interfaces* (Cambridge University Press 2021) 195–96. Of course, the 'adding' of women into history is not an inherently feminist act.

[76] Immi Tallgren, *Portraits of Women in International Law* (Oxford University Press 2023).

[77] Jane Haggis, 'Gendering Colonialism or Colonising Gender' (1990) 13(1/2) Women Studies International Forum 105.

[78] As Meera Sabaratnam notes: 'Collective mapping of belonging, responsibility and justice . . . which separates racially privileged people from their historical and contemporary production of privileges . . . make possible and manage these contradictions of racialised political governance in society.' Meera Sabartnam, 'Is IR Theory White? Racialised Subject- Positioning in Three Canonical Texts' (2020) 19(1) Millennium Journal of International Studies 3.

[79] Many thanks to Paulina Jimenez-Fregoso for raising this point, who notes that '. . . access to spaces such as the UN or other international mechanisms is limited by both education and money, which automatically eliminates women of colour because we rarely can access higher education, let alone in famous Universities. Poverty is, of course, disproportionately a woman phenomenon.' See also Angela Mudukuti, 'Decolonizing Human Rights Practice to Promote Racial Justice' (2023) ASIL Proceedings 184, 183–84.

[80] Audre Lorde, An Open Letter to Mary' in *Sister Outsider* (Penguin Books 2019) 69.

silences precede and shape feminist historical narratives, promoting the benevolence of white feminism while shielding its proponents from critically engaging with their own investment and complicity in systems of racial subordination.[81] White Western humanism continues unchallenged, leaving behind an unexamined and innocent white gendered inheritance to be taken forward, without accounting for the racial debts embedded within.[82]

3.2 Bringing more women into the fold: the limits of physical inclusion

The inclusion of more women—whether within 'international law's halls of power', international institutions, or legal processes—was thought to make law more responsive to gender issues. However, inclusion has been largely subsumed within liberal frameworks that render it susceptible to co-option into imperialist legal projects.[83] Rather than challenging the structural foundations of international law, inclusion has been undercut by the structural ordering of international institutions and their 'neo-colonial structural bias'.[84] As both Heathcote and Charlesworth have noted, there is little evidence to suggest that increasing the number of women has led to structural change.[85] While admirable, such efforts occlude the racialized foundations of international law by failing to acknowledge an episteme that privileges white, patriarchal forms of knowledge—those knowledges it finds recognizable, palatable, and easily assimilated into a disciplinary status quo.[86]

The call to add 'more women', and particularly to 'stir' in 'Third World women', has received considerable criticism.[87] Ramji-Nogales observes that feminist strategies of inclusion encourage women in international law-making to identify marginalized groups and provide platforms for them to speak and 'present themselves'. However, this approach relies on the assumption that those with privilege will both willingly and unproblematically cede power.[88] Moreover, the strategy conflates acts of resistance with genuine emancipation, failing to account for unintended effects such as legitimating and bolstering existing structures of heteropatriarchal racial capitalism that shape international law.[89] To be both heard and more importantly understood, racialized women must be first accepted, and then conform to an epistemic framework

[81] Jonsson (n 69) 19.

[82] Cora Chaplan, *Sea Changes Essays on Culture and Feminism* (Verso 1986).

[83] Gina Heathcote, *Feminist Dialogues on International Law Successes, Tensions, Futures* (Oxford University Press 2019) 60.

[84] Mudukuti (n 79)

[85] Hillary Charlesworth, 'Talking to Ourselves? Feminist Scholarship and International Law' in Sari Kouva and Zoe Pearson, *Feminist Perspectives on Contemporary International Law* (Hart 2011); Heathcote (n 83) 58.

[86] Moreton-Robinson (n 32) 413.

[87] Engle (n 28) 24.

[88] Jaya Ramji-Nogales, 'Revisiting the Category "Women"' in Susan Harris Rimmer and Kate Ogg (eds), *Research Handbook on Feminist Engagement with International Law* (Edward Elgar 2019).

[89] Grejte Baars, *The Corporation, Law and Capitalism* (Brill 2019) 370–71.

that prescribes racial hierarchy and their place within it.[90] Prandini Assis highlights that even where marginalized women are brought into the law and are able to speak for themselves, the 'violence of the frame' remains intact.[91] The legal structures that claim to amplify their voices reproduce racialized and gendered tropes, ultimately failing to trouble law's reductive logic. For example, Razack highlights that racialized women seeking asylum actually achieve more successful outcomes when they fulfil the racialized and gender subject positions international law demands of them. Baars notes the civilization-*esque* fallacy of 'bringing international law' to the people—or perhaps bringing people to law and the reproduction of white privilege. The bringing of law to people/people to law rarely reflects on the technologies of marginalization that produce and maintain legal exclusion in the first place, nor the centring of international law (and lawyers) and its violence. Instead, for a claim to be 'valid and recognized', it must join 'the system', to be articulated in a racialized legal vocabulary that recodes their grievances and desires into racialized and erasing norms.[92]

Within scholarly communities, as al Attar argues elsewhere in this collection, the integration of race and Third World critiques are easily absorbed into the epistemic frameworks that house their critiques. Often, the invitation to participate is conditional, predicated on a level of ornamentalism whereby the racialized scholar offers an 'alternative' or 'additional perspective' accepted only where they do not challenge the core foundations of the discipline. As Ahmed warns, inclusion becomes synonymous with diversity, reducing structural critique to the legibility, palatability, or forced translation of the intervention to the white racial frame.[93] This process of epistemic interpellation relies on the audibility of racialized knowledge within orthodox frameworks and naturalized positionings, further legitimizing the status quo by depoliticizing and neutralizing challenges to the tenets of the discipline. For instance, as both Heathcote and Stauffer argue, Indigenous epistemologies—predicated on alternative relationships with land, sovereignty, and distinct legal traditions—remain largely inaudible and untranslatable in the international context.[94] Even where gender operates as a specific epistemological anchor within these traditions, such frameworks are marginalized because they do not conform to the universalizing logics of international law. The result is a form of inclusion that preserves the structural whiteness of the discipline, legitimized through granting visibility to 'diverse' voices while rendering their critiques intelligible only when stripped of any radical potential.[95]

[90] Martina Ferrari, 'Questions of Silence: On the Emancipatory Limits of Voice and the Coloniality of Silence' (2020) 25 Hypatia 123, 126–27.

[91] Mariana Prandini Assis, 'Frames of Violence and Violence of Frames: Setting a Feminist Critical Agenda for Transnational Rituals of Speaking' in Susan Harris Rimmer and Kate Ogg (eds), *Research Handbook on Feminist Engagement with International Law* (Edward Elgar 2019) 469

[92] Baars (n 89) 371.

[93] Sara Ahmed, *On Being Included Racism and Diversity in Institutional Life* (Duke University Press 2012).

[94] Gina Heathcote, 'Gendered Security' in Robin Gleiss and Nils Meizer (eds), *The Oxford Handbook on the International Law of Global Security* (Oxford University Press 2021) 94–95; Jill Staufer, 'You People Talk Paper': Indigenous Law, Western Legalism and Cultural Variability of Laws Materials' (2019) 23 Law, Text, Culture 40. See also Sumi Madhok, 'Anti-Imperial Epistemic Justice and Re-making Rights and Justice "After Rights"' (2024) 28 International Journal of Human Rights 1478.

[95] Jill Staufer, *Ethical Loneliness The Injustice of Not Being Heard* (Columbia University Press 2015).

3.3 Reading the racialized other into the white frame: The limits of conceptual inclusion

The epistemic violence of inclusion extends beyond physical presence, where international law's knowledge production systems render racialized perspectives inaudible and untranslatable into the conceptual realm 'in most of thc world' as well.[96] As Eghbariah argues in his work on the Nakba, international law's architecture is insufficient, incapable of capturing historical experiences and forms of violence that do not fit within its predefined categories.[97] This conceptual exclusion reflects the entrenchment of epistemic racism within international law's frameworks, which systematically banish forms of knowledge rooted in alternative axiologies, ontologies, and epistemologies.[98] This failure is integral to the maintenance of international law's authority and exclusivity: by treating 'various modes of power' as discrete or parochial, international law preserves 'the distinctiveness and separation of these modes and effects as if they were isolated elements that could be easily enumerated' rather than interconnected structures of domination.[99]

The lifecycle of intersectionality within international law, for example, highlights how the Black feminist experience—or radical concepts more generally—are depoliticized when they are 'taken up' into the international.[100] While intersectionality was born from Black feminist thought as a tool to analyse the interlocking systems of race, gender, and class oppression, it has been stripped of its political roots as it has albeit very slowly 'travelled' and been mainstreamed into international law.[101] In international criminal law, intersectionality has been reduced to a doctrinal argument, decoupled from the antiracist praxis and critical traditions that originally bore it. Intersectionality is now read as—reduced to—'a doctrinal legal argument'[102] to be achieved 'through more progressive law interpretation' rather than a reflection of and challenge to the racial, gendered, and colonial logics embedded within the international.[103] This reorientation away from black feminism 'deteriorates its emancipatory possibilities'[104] and strengthens international criminal law's white,

[96] Sumi Madhok, 'A Critical Reflexive Politics of Location, Feminist Debt and Thinking in the Global South' (2020) 27(4) European Journal of Women's Studies 394.

[97] Rabea Eghbariah, 'Toward Nakba as a Legal Concept' (2024) 124 Columbia Law Review 4.

[98] With regard to the limits of overcoming privilege through silence, see Linda Alcoff, 'The Problem of Speaking for Others' (1991–1992) 20 Cultural Critique 2, 25.

[99] Saidiya Hartman, *Scenes of Subjection* (Oxford University Press 1997) 118.

[100] Sirma Bilge, 'Whitening Intersectionality: Evanescence of Race in Intersectionality' in WD Hund and A Lentin (eds), *Racism and Sociology* (LIT Verlag 2014)

[101] See Jimenez Fregoso, ch 13 in this volume.

[102] Jens T Theilen, 'Intersectionality's Travels to International Human Rights Law' (2024) 45(2) Michigan Journal of International Law 233, See also Lars van der Ent, 'Queering the Rome Statute: Searching for the International Criminal Court's Potential to Do Justice to Queer People' (2024) 50(2) Australian Feminist Law Journal 185.

[103] Gregor Maučec, 'The International Criminal Court and the Issue of Intersectionality—A Conceptual and Legal Framework for Analysis' (2021) 21 International Criminal Law 1. This is not to say that mitigating the way in which the law affects and maintains racial inequality is not a worthwhile antiracist project. See E Tendayi Achiume and Devon Cabardo, 'Critical Race Theory Meets Third World Approaches to International Law' (2021) 67 UCLA Law Review 1462, 1497.

[104] See Patricia Hill Collins, 'Intersectionality and Epistemic Injustice' in Ian James Kidd, José Medina, and Gaile Pohlaus, Jr (eds) *The Routledge Handbook of Epistemic Injustice* (Routledge 2017).

masculine, and colonial pathologies, co-opting it into international law's institutions and logics.[105] As Theilen notes, intersectionality now operates through forms of non-performativity, operating as 'ornamental intersectionality'—a symbolic commitment devoid of substantive impact. Rather than unsettling the epistemic boundaries of international law, intersectionality has been absorbed into its framework in ways that favour expressive commitment rather than real impact.[106]

Inclusion without disruption to the epistemic boundaries of international law facilitates both the historical and ongoing 'pillaging and silencing of communication and ways of being'.[107] Antiracist feminist praxis demands the inclusion of marginalized voices but also a critical interrogation of the terms of entry of feminist thought into global space. This includes reflection on the processes of translation, containment, and co-optation that occur. Failure to examine the power relations that shape feminist interventions in international law, and the dynamics between feminists and feminisms, allows epistemic violence to persist and amounts to methodological whiteness, which is evident in international law's failure to reflect on the structuring role of whiteness and its importance in shaping legal norms and mediating the lives of women and feminists across different contexts.

A recognition of one's whiteness rarely garners interrogation on the intersection of where this meets gender, on the sociohistorical hold of race in the present, or on breaking down white-supremacist-ablist-imperialist-hetero-patriarchy and the co-constitutive sociohistoric racially capitalist assemblage that allows and promotes a privileged subject position.[108] Hegemonic feminism has assumed the benefits of inclusion rather than its potential to damage those it includes, just as it has curtailed the disruptive potential of feminist critiques, strategically validating and reinforcing the status quo under the guise of diversity and progress. Crucially, these risks are not borne equally. Racialized feminists disproportionately face the burdens of navigating spaces where inclusion serves as both an invitation and a constraint. The failure to challenge the epistemic structures that bind international law and hegemonic feminism—particularly those that feminists are advised to uphold—[109] risks perpetuating the erasure through the discourse of inclusion itself. Mohanty argues that expanding the frame of international law to create a feminist ecosystem inclusive of difference is necessary but insufficient. Difference cannot be imagined as benign or pluralistic; instead, it exists within asymmetrical and incommensurate spheres situated within racial hierarchies of domination and resistance.[110]

[105] Randle DeFalco and Frédéric Mégret, 'The Invisibility of Race at the ICC: Lessons from the US Criminal Justice System' (2020) 7(1) London Review of International Law 55.

[106] Bilge (n 100) 84–85.

[107] Zainab Batul Naqvu and others, 'Back to the Kitchen Table: Reflections on Decolonization and Internationalizing the Global South Socio-Legal Writing Workshops' (2019) 27(2) Feminist Legal Studies 123.

[108] Grietje Baars, '#LesbiansAreHot: On Oil, Imperialism and What it Means to Queer International Law' (2017) 7(1) Feminists@Law.

[109] Anne Orford, 'Contesting Globalization: A Feminist Perspective on the Future of Human Rights' (1998) 8 Transnational Law and Contemporary Problems 171.

[110] Chandra Talpade Mohanty, 'Under Western Eyes: Feminist Scholarship and Colonial Discourses' (1984) 12(3) On Humanism and the University I: The Discourse on Humanism 333.

Inclusion alone, therefore, is an 'inadequate response to the race and racialisation within the field. The need to state, disrupt and perhaps overcome the whiteness baked into the epistemologically limiting logics themselves.'[111] As Ahmed reminds us, the convenient benevolence of white feminism, with a myopic focus on 'inclusion and diversity' often comes at the expense of an antiracist praxis committed to the eradication of white supremacy in all its forms.[112] Without this critical focus, inclusion risks becoming yet another mechanism through which international law sustains the very hierarchies it claims to dismantle.

4. White feminist debt as white woman's burden

Feminist histories of international law reveal the embeddedness of whiteness in its epistemic contours, as well as the role of gender in reproducing white supremacy. Bhandar and Ziadah observe: 'The institutionalised power of white feminism remains an obstacle for those who centre race in our work'.[113] Yet, looking beyond international law's narrow confines, we find feminist histories replete with revolutionary praxis—survival, resistance, and joy—despite international law's efforts to circumscribe them. Black, brown, and Indigenous feminisms repeatedly have shown that revolution is not an endpoint achieved via a manifesto, policy change, or law reform. Instead, it is a methodological upheaval central to feminist praxis, embedded in everyday acts of defiance and worldmaking.[114] The outcomes that international feminist lawyers seek are not linear; they unfold hand-in-hand with an ongoing critical process: international law's knowledge structures are not neutral and require active dismantling and repair.

The concept of feminist debt is a productive lens through which to understand this feminist responsibility. Madhok explains that feminist praxis is grounded in critical, reflexive ethics that require: (i) documenting the power relations underpinning knowledge production and the privileging of certain sites of knowledge; and (ii) fostering 'a dynamic, theorised and historicised relationship between self and the collective in specific locations and contexts of struggle'. Feminist debt is not transactional and cannot be repaid. Rather, it highlights the 'thinkability of particular knowledge and what counts as knowledge, acknowledges the responsibility and ethics that involve the call to be responsible to (re)produce conditions of thinkability and open up the possibilities for different knowledge'.[115] Just as particular forms of knowledge have been made possible through histories of exclusion, dispossession, and oppression, feminist debt calls for a commitment to creating conditions that make different forms of knowledge *thinkable* within, against, and beyond international law.

[111] Sabaratnam (n 78).
[112] Sara Ahmed, 'Embodying Diversity: Problems and Paradoxes for Black Feminists' (2009) (12)(1) Race, Ethnicity and Education 41.
[113] Brenna Bhandar and Rafeef Zaidar, 'Introduction' in *Revolutionary Feminisms: Conversations in Collective Action and Radical Thought* (Verso 2021)
[114] Ruth Houghton and Aoife O'Donoghue, '"Ourworld": A Feminist Approach to Global Constitutionalism' (2020) 9(1) Global Constitutionalism 403.
[115] Madhok (n 96) 396.

Reframing the *white woman's burden* as a form of *white feminist debt* shifts the focus from colonialist narratives of 'bringing about diversity and inclusion' into an acknowledgment of the structures that have enabled whiteness's privileged positions within international law's static frames.[116] This debt entails more than recognition: it demands action to disrupt feminist whiteness by tackling racism[117]—including in sedimented epistemic forms[118]—and sustained, antiracist praxis aimed at dismantling the epistemic foundations of white supremacy within international law. For example, while noting the coherence between peoples' tribunals and feminist standpoint theory, Otto highlights the lack of resonance between the lived experiences of survivors and interpellation of the 'international' as *universal* agendas of international experts, she also observes a palpable disconnect.[119] The politics of listening, she concludes, must not only include performative empathy but also challenge structural injustices by 're-visioning' fundamental forms of justice.[120]

Heathcote and Kula call for the strategic use of *active silence*—a deliberate practice of investigating the underpinnings of feminist spaces, relationships, and epistemologies. This includes actively learning from—and with—alternative knowledge practices that challenge dominant legal narratives and reframe feminist praxis as a dynamic, pluralist project: to 'generate a pluralist feminist whose knowledge frames need to be learnt—perhaps re- learnt—to understand the meaning of feminist praxis'.[121] Such praxis calls to move beyond the passivity of inclusion to the acknowledgement of hegemonic feminism's location inside whiteness. It necessitates subverting white supremacy and changing the way international law constructs both its knowledge and knowers. This involves challenging legal frameworks that present themselves as neutral, universal, or objective, and embracing feminist pluralism that acknowledges the partial, situated nature of all knowledge. Feminist debt is thus a call to action: to create epistemic spaces where multiple feminisms can at the very least co-exist equitably, and more hopefully disrupt, and reimagine the structures of international law or beyond.

Madhok notes feminist debt requires more than alternative theories of power; it demands the conceptual production of knowledge that captures different historically specific and contextually embedded forms of worldmaking.[122] International law's inability to accommodate such forms of knowledge speaks to its deep-seated epistemic racism. To be effective, feminist engagements with international law must grapple with the multidimensional forms of power in which the law is embedded, as well as the layered violences it perpetuates. Legal recognition—the classification of knowledge as legitimate—is not a neutral act. The process through which knowledge is translated, validated, and incorporated into international law involves reshaping it to

[116] Ahmed (n 112).

[117] Ramón Grosfoguel, 'The Structure of Knowledge in Westernized Universities Epistemic Racism/Sexism and the Four Genocides/Epistemicides of the Long 16th Century' (2013) IX(1) Human Architecture: Journal of the Sociology of Self Knowledge 73; Mills (n 22).

[118] See, eg, Assis (n 91).

[119] Dianne Otto, 'Beyond Legal Justice: Some Personal Reflections on People's Tribunals, Listening and Responsibility' (2000) 5(2) London Review of International Law 225.

[120] ibid.

[121] Heathcote and Kula (n 7) 493–94.

[122] Madhok (n 96).

fit 'dominant legal paradigms'.[123] 'Rejecting the provincialism of the universalist pretensions'[124] therefore requires feminists to acknowledge the parochial nature of the white racial frame and to challenge its totalizing claims. This means rejecting gender as a static and separate category in its construction and pushing ahead with the complexity and plurality of feminist experiences and thus of legal knowledge. It calls for lifting the veil on international law's epistemic violence and reimagining feminist praxis as a tool for worldmaking, embedded from within the communities it serves, and beyond the constraints of the status quo.

Epistemic communities are essential in this process of opening up. These communities are repositories of knowledge and sites of prefigurations of the world, where alternative futures are theorized, debated, and enacted. As Chadery, Abdelkarim, and Sen remind us, feminist praxis has long been rooted in relationality—centring care, community, and collective struggle in visions of freedom-making.[125] To them, community operates as both a radical vision and fugitive space where new possibilities for living and knowing can emerge. Implicit in antiracist feminist imaginations is a commitment to *epistemic justice*, grounded in the demands of epistemic equivalency. The demands of feminist debt thus extend beyond individual reflection to encompass community responsibility and ethics when pursuing impactful feminisms. This includes interactions between international legal feminists, and international legal feminists and those 'brought into' international law, and the reading into the field bodies of knowledge and the rejection of the technologies of white ignorance, including the depoliticization, and dehistoricization of race and racialization.[126] The goal is not simply to diversify international law's epistemic landscape but to dismantle the circuits of power through which feminist knowledge is co-opted, neutralized, and repeatedly called into service for whiteness.

This is not a call for superficial solidarity; rather, it is essential to engage with interlocking structural accounts to understand which feminist issues are taken up, which are left behind, and the epistemic processes through which this occurs.[127] Difference is shaped by asymmetrical power relations rooted in histories of racism, ableism, class, heteronormativity, and patriarchy. Genuine feminist solidarity requires confronting these hierarchies head-on, recognizing the violence that inclusion can enact, and resisting the re-inscription of white supremacy through the language of diversity. The challenge then is to imagine feminist praxis not as a project *within* international law, but as a dynamic and constant struggle *with*, *against*, and *beyond* it. This means rejecting the false equivalence of struggles, acknowledging the partiality of legal knowledge, and embracing the interconnectedness of feminist movements. This is not the same reductionist approach that suggests sameness or equivalency of

[123] Heathcote and Kula (n 7) 493.

[124] Dipesh Chakrabaty, *Provincialising Europe: Post Colonial Thought and Historical Difference* (Princeton University Press 2000).

[125] Farnush Ghadery, Shaimaa Abdelkrim and Rohini Sen, 'Collaborative Praxis: Unbinding Neoliberal Tethers of Academia' (*Feminista Journal*, 5 June 2021) <https://feministajournal.com/collaborative-praxis-unbinding-neoliberal-tethers-of-academia/> accessed 22 June 2024.

[126] Gevers (n 23) fn 22, 23, 24.

[127] Heathcote and Kula (n 7) 484.

struggle united through a singular experience of gender.[128] Rather, it is predicated on the understanding of the boundedness of liberation across matrices of domination through hegemonic regimes and their articulation.[129] Feminist debt is not a burden to be carried—it is a continuing reckoning with the histories that have shaped us, a commitment to dismantle them, and the responsibility to build alternative futures to them.

5. Conclusion

Feminist approaches to international law are heralded as 'progressive, even revolutionary',[130] yet its transformative potential is constrained by the very structures it seeks to challenge. Embedded within the white racial frame, hegemonic feminist approaches have often failed to confront the co-constitution of race and gender in shaping subjectivities and have neglected the racial power dynamics that structure relationships between feminists.[131] As Heathcote and Kila note, international law has routinely 'deployed feminist knowledge to shore up the legitimacy and persistence of international forms, while simultaneously reinscribing feminist forms of knowledge that continue to define and redefine *via* dominant white and mainstream feminist histories'.[132] The inclination of feminist approaches to focus on women rather than the structures which both produce and act in concert with gender—of which race is one—and the resulting thin feminist message has come to haunt international law.[133] Whiteness is not incidental—it is relational and systemic. Therefore while feminist approaches have a strong commitment to international law's potential for women,[134] concerns persist about the limits whiteness places on feminist success, form, and aspiration.[135]

Feminist debt reframes the white woman's burden as an obligation to dismantle the epistemic foundations of whiteness within international law. The histories of feminist intervention in 'the international' remind us that the appeasement mechanisms of whiteness—superficial commitments to diversity or inclusion—necessitate ongoing

[128] Matsuda's conceptualization of the 'other question' is illustrative here—the interconnection between violence, and the holistic understanding of the 'matrix of race'. Matsuda argues that challenges to emergent and existing forms of domination must be flexible enough to ask the other question—referring to the interconnection of all forms of subjugation. Mari Matsuda, 'Beside my Sister, Facing the Enemy: Legal Theory out of Coalition' (1991) 43 Stanford Law Review 1183. See also Stuart Hall on the construction of solidarity politics 'through and with difference which is able to build those forms of solidarity and identification which make common struggle and resistance possible'. Stuart Hall, 'New Ethnicities' in Kobena Mercer (ed), *Black Film, British Cinema* (Institute of Contemporary Arts 1989)

[129] On articulation, see Stuart Hall, 'Race, Articulation and Societies Structured in Dominance' in *Sociological Theories: Race and Colonialism* (UNESCO 1980).

[130] Ware (n 37).

[131] Verónica Gago, *A Feminist International: How to change everything* (Verso 2020) 3.

[132] Heathcote and Kula (n 7) 492.

[133] Emily Jones, Hilary Charlesworth, and Gina Heathcote, 'Scholarship in International Law in 1990s and today: A Conversation between Hilary Charlesworth, Gina Heathcote and Emily Jones' (2019) 27(1) Feminist Legal Studies 79.

[134] ibid.

[135] Dianne Otto, 'Beyond Stories of Victory and Danger: Resisting Feminism's Amenability to Serving Security Council Politics' in Gina Heathcote and others (eds), *Rethinking Peacekeeping, Gender Equality and Collective Security* (Palgrave Macmillan 2014).

vigilance to sustain antiracist struggle against the structures that reproduce white supremacy. These submerged histories are integral to recognizing the 'worlds that international law makes impossible'[136] and to affirming the need for utopian imagining based on the collective labour of feminist praxis.[137] The task is not simply to reform international law but to imagine and enact alternative futures—ones grounded in feminist plurality, collective struggle, and the refusal to be contained by the limits of the law.

[136] Christopher Gevers, 'Lands beyond the White World": (Re)imagining the International Through Fiction' (2024) 36 Law and Literature 241.
[137] Angela Y Davis and others, *Abolition. Feminism. Now* (Penguin Books 2022).

24

The Slow and Benevolent Violence of International Law

An Oceanian Perspective

Dylan Asafo

For racism is not only history and sociology, economics and politics. Racism is also the psychology of subjugation.

Haunani-Kay Trask[1]

1. Introduction

Across a range of contexts, critical international law scholars have explored and articulated the 'violence' of international law. For example, Balakrishnan Rajagopal argued that international law is implicated in the 'violence of development' in the 'so-called Third World', where 'international law has always been under the shadow of violence, and in fact under the danger of being overwhelmed by it'.[2] Similarly, Vanja Hamzic remarked in his analysis of the Security Council's invocations of LGBT rights that '[i]f all law is violence, then international law is perfectly suited for global violent pursuits. It is well entrenched and institutionalised and it provides multiple fora of engagement, each violent in its own right'.[3] In the context of climate change, In the context of climate change, Julia Dehm drew on Rob Nixon's concept of 'slow violence'[4] to expose international law's 'incremental violence' as demonstrated by the 'indefinite deferral of responsibility' for loss and damage under the United Nations Framework Convention on Climate Change (UNFCCC).[5]

[1] Haunani-Kay Trask, 'The Color of Violence' (2004) 31 Social Justice 8, 13.

[2] Balakrishnan Rajagopal, 'International Law and the Development Encounter: Violence and Resistance at the Margins' (1999) 93 Proceedings of the Annual Meeting (American Society of International Law) 16, 22.

[3] Vanja Hamzić, 'International Law as Violence: Competing Absences of the Other' in Diane Otto (ed), *Queering International Law* (Routledge 2017) 79.

[4] Rob Nixon, *Slow Violence and the Environmentalism of the Poor* (Harvard University Press 2011) 2 (explaining slow violence as 'a violence that occurs gradually and out of sight, a violence of delayed destruction that is dispersed across time and space, an attritional violence that is typically not viewed as violence at all').

[5] Julia Dehm, 'Climate Change, "Slow Violence" and the Indefinite Deferral of Responsibility for "Loss and Damage"' (2020) 29 Griffith Law Review 220, 220.

Dylan Asafo, *The Slow and Benevolent Violence of International Law* In: *Emancipating International Law*.
Edited by: Mohsen al Attar and Claire Smith, Oxford University Press. © Dylan Asafo 2026.
DOI: 10.1093/9780198935605.003.0030

While these and other crucial works have elucidated some of the systemic, structural, institutional, and physical dimensions of international law's violence, this chapter follows an intuition that articulating some of the more *psychological* dimensions of this violence may be helpful to Indigenous and racialized peoples'[6] ongoing efforts to resist against racist interlocked systems of oppression and imagine futures beyond them. Such attempts are important to make because, as Haunani-Kay Trask's enduring words remind us, racist oppression not only has historical, sociological, economic, and political dimensions, but psychological ones as well.

In this chapter, I examine some of the psychological dimensions of international law's violence from my perspective as an Oceanian[7] in relation to its responses to the impacts of climate change in Oceania. My main argument is that these responses show that international law inflicts slow[8] and benevolent[9] forms of violence that operate not just to inhibit climate justice[10] for Oceanians and other Indigenous and racialized peoples, but to prevent it altogether.

More specifically, I argue that international law's slow and benevolent violence is enacted by at least two interconnected myths that gaslight[11] these communities about international law's capacity to achieve climate justice. One of these myths is that Global North states are committed to—or even interested in—working towards climate justice. The other myth is that climate justice takes time and requires

[6] This chapter uses the phrasing of 'Indigenous and racialized peoples' not to suggest that people can only be either Indigenous or racialized, but to clearly encompass racialized peoples who may not identify as being Indigenous to the lands and waters they live on.

[7] This chapter uses the term 'Oceania' rather than the 'Pacific' or the 'Pacific Islands', and 'Oceanians' to refer to Indigenous peoples of Oceania rather than 'Pacific peoples' or 'Pacific Islanders'. As Epeli Hau'ofa explained: '"Pacific Islands", is the prevailing [term] used everywhere; it connotes small areas of land surfaces sitting atop submerged reefs or seamounts, whereas "Oceania" connotes a sea of islands with their inhabitants. The world of our ancestors was a large sea full of places to explore, to make their homes in, to breed generations of seafarers like themselves', Epeli Hau'ofa, 'Our Sea of Islands' in Eric Waddell, Vijay Naidu, and Epeli Hau'ofa (eds), *A New Oceania: Rediscovering Our Sea of Islands* (University of the South Pacific 1993) 8.

[8] By 'slow' violence, I refer not only to the violence of physical degradation as emphasized by Nixon and Dehm, but the violent degradation of individual and collective psychological well-being, spirituality, identity, and culture as well.

[9] By 'benevolent' violence, I draw on the concept of 'white benevolence' which is 'a form of paternalistic racism' that manifests when 'white settler professionals profess to support Indigenous peoples yet reproduce colonial narratives that uphold white supremacy.' See Amanda Gebhard, Sheelah McLean, and Verna St Denis (eds), *White Benevolence: Racism and Colonial Violence in the Helping Professions* (Fernwood Publishing 2022) 1.

[10] While there can no single authoritative definition or understanding of 'climate justice' for Oceanians and other Indigenous and racialized peoples, in this chapter, I use 'climate justice' to include, but not be limited to, the demands for climate justice advanced by the Pacific Islands Climate Action Network leading up to COP26. These demands include: 'ending the expansion of fossil fuel production', '[t]he urgent establishment of a Loss and Damage Finance Facility with new, additional, needs-based, and predictable finance' and acknowledgement of 'the links between climate action and self-determination struggles of our Pacific territories, including of West Papuan and Kanaky peoples', Pacific Islands Climate Action Network, 'Pacific COP26 Demands' (*350*) <www.350.org/pacificdemands/#one> accessed 2 June 2023.

[11] While there might be more appropriate terms to capture this pheneomenon, I cautiously adopt this term and the following broad dictionary definition of 'gaslighting' as referring to the 'psychological manipulation of a person usually over an extended period of time that causes the victim to question the validity of their own thoughts, perception of reality, or memories and typically leads to confusion, loss of confidence and self-esteem, uncertainty of one's emotional or mental stability, and a dependency on the perpetrator', see 'Gaslighting', *Merriam-Webster Dictionary* <https://www.merriam-webster.com/dictionary/gaslighting> accessed 2 June 2023.

incremental progress in international law. Naming these myths allows us to recognize that climate justice cannot be achieved via international law. Rather, it will only ever provide the fora and mechanisms for ruling classes to inflict multi-dimensional violence on vulnerable communities. Next, I consider the implications of this argument for Oceanians, specifically, the tricky question of whether Oceanians should now resist *against* international law rather than within it? Rather than provide any answers to this tricky question, I explore two somewhat more manageable questions it raises and offer some provisional reflections for further debate.

This chapter proceeds as follows. To illustrate the gaslighting myths, Sections 2 and 3 examine two case studies of international law's responses to the impacts of climate change in Oceania: first, the negotiations around securing liability and compensation for loss and damage at the annual Conference of the Parties (COP) of the UNFCCC,[12] and secondly, the UN Human Rights Committee's decision in *Ioane Teitiota v New Zealand*.[13] Section 4 then offers provisional reflections around how Oceanians should engage with international law moving forward, before Section 5 concludes.

2. The slow and benevolent violence of COP negotiations

To illustrate how international law's gaslighting myths enact their slow and benevolent violence on Oceanians and other Indigenous and racialized peoples seeking climate justice, this section provides a brief timeline of COP negotiations around loss and damage from 1991 to 2022.[14]

2.1 Early progress on loss and damage

In 1991, Robert Van Lierop, chair of the Alliance of Small Island States (AOSIS) and Vanuatu's ambassador to the UN, proposed to include an international fund and insurance pool in the UNFCCC to 'compensate the most vulnerable small island and low-lying coastal developing countries for loss and damage resulting from sea level rise'.[15] This proposal was 'anathema' to Global North states who promptly rejected it.[16]

Oceanians and other Indigenous and racialized peoples then waited fifteen years to have loss and damage mentioned in COP13's 2007 Bali Action Plan.[17] While there

[12] Margaretha Wewerinke-Singh and Diana Hinge Salili, 'Between Negotiations and Litigation: Vanuatu's Perspective on Loss and Damage from Climate Change' (2020) 20 Climate Policy 681, 682.

[13] *Ioane Teitiota v New Zealand*, Communication No 2728/2016, CCPR/C/127/D (23 September 2020).

[14] This timeline of negotiations around loss and damage owes a significant scholarly debt to the works of Wewerinke-Singh and Salili (n 12) and Dehm (n 5).

[15] Vanuatu on behalf of States participating in the Committee which are members of the Alliance of Small Island States, 'Draft Annex Relating to Article 23 (Insurance) for Inclusion in the Revised Single Text on Elements Relating to Mechanisms' (17 December 1991) UN Doc A/AC.237/WG.II/Misc 13.

[16] John W Ashe, Robert Van Lierop, and Anilla Cherian, 'The Role of the Alliance of Small Island States (AOSIS) in the Negotiation of the United Nations Framework Convention on Climate Change (UNFCCC)' (1999) 23 Natural Resources Forum 209, 218.

[17] UNFCCC, 'Decision 1/CP.13: Bali Action Plan' (14 March 2008) UN Doc FCCC/CP/2007/6/Add 1, para 1(c)(iii).

was some minor progress following the Plan, a significant milestone for loss and damage would not happen again until COP19 with the establishment of the Warsaw International Mechanism for Loss and Damage associated with Climate Change Impacts (WIM) in 2013. It was aimed at addressing 'loss and damage associated with impacts of climate change, including extreme events and slow onset events, in developing countries that are particularly vulnerable'.[18]

Against the efforts of Oceanian and other Global South states and advocates, no provisions were made at COP19 for loss and damage. Nevertheless, the optimistic rhetoric from the Global North continued, with the Polish president of COP19 remarking: 'Warsaw has set a pathway for governments to work on a draft text of a new universal climate agreement, so it appears on the table at the next UN Climate change conference in Peru. This is an essential step to reach a final agreement in Paris in 2015.'[19]

2.2 The 2015 Paris compromise

Despite the hype for COP21 in Paris (2015), loss and damage continued to be an uphill battle. At COP21, Oceanian leaders and advocates sought to anchor the WIM in the highly anticipated agreement and establish a mechanism to determine liability and compensation.[20] However, it was reported that US negotiators used bullying and bribery to inhibit progress.[21] The Global North's efforts almost succeeded[22] until Vanuatu's head of delegation arranged an emergency meeting with the COP21 presidency to make clear that Vanuatu would refuse to join the Paris Agreement if loss and damage obligations were left out.

Vanuatu's intervention was partially successful; loss and damage did feature in a standalone article,[23] but, once again, it failed to include mechanisms for determining liability and compensation. Despite this hard compromise by Oceanian and other Global South nations, the benevolent rhetoric from the Global North about the progressive nature of COPs continued, with the French president proclaiming: 'This is a major leap for mankind. The [Paris Agreement] will not be perfect for everyone if everyone reads it with only their own interests in mind.'[24]

[18] UNFCCC, 'Decision 2/CP.19: Warsaw International Mechanism for Loss and Damage Associated with Climate Change Impacts' (31 January 2014) UN Doc FCCC/CP/2013/10/Add 1.

[19] Fiona Harvey, 'Warsaw Climate Talks Set 2015 Target for Plans to Curb Emissions' *The Guardian* (24 November 2013) <https://www.theguardian.com/environment/2013/nov/24/warsaw-climate-talks-greenhouse-gas-emissions> accessed 22 May 2023.

[20] Mary Baines, 'Pacific Leaders Call for Climate Action' *RNZ* (1 December 2015) < https://www.rnz.co.nz/international/pacific-news/290986/pacific-leaders-call-for-climate-action> accessed 22 May 2023.

[21] Oscar Reyes, 'Seven Wrinkles in the Paris Climate Deal' (*Foreign Policy In Focus*, 14 December 2015) < https://www.fpif.org/seven-wrinkles-paris-climate-deal/> accessed 22 May 2023.

[22] UNFCCC, 'Draft Paris Outcome: Proposal by the President—Draft Text on COP21 agenda item 4(b), Durban Platform for Enhanced Action' (10 December 2015) UN Doc 1/CP.17.

[23] See Paris Agreement (adopted 12 December 2015, entered into force 4 November 2016) UN Doc FCCC/CP/2015/L.9/Rev/1, art 8; Wewerinke-Singh and Salili (n 12) 685.

[24] John Vidal and others, 'World Leaders Hail Paris Climate Deal as "Major Leap for Mankind"' *The Guardian* (13 December 2015) <https://www.theguardian.com/environment/2015/dec/13/world-leaders-hail-paris-climate-deal> accessed 22 May 2023.

2.3 The disappointment of Fiji's COP23

Subsequent COPs only delivered limited progress. This was even the case for COP23 when Fiji was the first Oceanian nation to preside over the negotiations. While Oceanian and other Global South nations hoped that COP23 would see strong progress for the WIM, it was reported that the US, Australia, Canada, and the EU 'aggressively blocked' any discussion around funding.[25] There were also reports that both the Fijian presidency and the Polish COP24 presidency kept the proposals of Oceanian and other Global South countries at bay.[26]

It was thus unsurprising that the COP23 decision did not mention liability and compensation for loss and damage.[27] As Aruna Chandrasekhar remarked: 'Having a Fijian presidency might have been good for the COP's image and for the many Pacific platitudes. But it's clear that older power dynamics continue to dominate and to avoid any damages for the losses they have inflicted over generations.'[28]

2.4 A 'historic' victory at Sharm El Sheikh

Following small moments of progress from COP24 to COP26,[29] COP27 in Sharm El Sheikh would finally reach a milestone. Over three decades since AOSIS's first proposal in 1991, a consensus was reached amongst the parties to establish 'funding arrangements' for 'assisting developing countries that are particularly vulnerable to the adverse effects of climate change, in responding to loss and damage, including . . . by providing and assisting in mobilising new and additional resources'.[30]

State leaders from Oceania celebrated this milestone as 'historic'[31] and 'a victory for the Pacific Island countries'.[32] However, as David South notes, 'a host of questions remain about how the [funding arrangements] will operate and whether it can act

[25] Aruna Chandrasekhar, 'No Support for Climate Change Victims as Fiji Sides with Historical Polluters' *The Wire* (17 November 2017) <https://www.thewire.in/politics/no-support-climate-change-victims-fiji-sides-historical-polluters> accessed 22 May 2023.

[26] Qimin Chai and Yue Qi, 'Reflections and Recommendations on China's Solutions to Climate Change in the Talanoa Dialogue' in Fuzan Xie and Yaming Liu (eds), *Annual Report on Actions to Address Climate Change (2018)* (Springer Nature Singapore 2022) 72.

[27] UNFCCC, 'Decision 5/CP.23: Warsaw International Mechanism for Loss and Damage Associated with Climate Change Impacts' (18 November 2017) UN Doc FCCC/CP/2017/11/Add 1.

[28] Chandrasekhar (n 25).

[29] See Dehm (n 5) 232–34.

[30] UNFCCC, 'Draft Decision -/CP.27 -/CMA.4: Funding Arrangements for Responding to Loss and Damage Associated with the Adverse Effects of Climate Change, including a Focus on Addressing Loss and Damage' (20 November 2022) Advance Unedited Version.

[31] Jon Letman, 'Pacific Leaders Celebrate Cop27 Victory on Loss and Damage Fund after Decades of Advocacy' *The Guardian* (21 November 2022) < https://www.theguardian.com/world/2022/nov/21/pacific-leaders-celebrate-cop27-victory-on-loss-and-damage-fund-after-decades-of-advocacy> accessed 22 May 2023.

[32] Lydia Lewis, 'Tuvalu Minister Hails Loss and Damage Fund but Fight for Action Continues' *RNZ* (22 November 2022) < https://www.rnz.co.nz/international/pacific-news/479242/tuvalu-minister-hails-loss-and-damage-fund-but-fight-for-action-continues> accessed 22 May 2023.

quickly to help countries most impacted by climate change'.[33] These questions include: whether the arrangements will account for the 'development deficits' vulnerable countries face,[34] how loss and damage will be identified and measured, and how they will address the Global North's enduring inability to deliver meaningful resource transfers to vulnerable states.[35] Further, Oceanians emphasized their deep disappointment at the Global North's ongoing refusal to agree to strong language to phase out fossil fuels and their lack of commitment to keeping the Paris Agreement's goal of limiting warming to 1.5 degrees Celsius alive.[36]

Still, Global North leaders shared hopeful and congratulatory messages, with Canada's Minister of Environment and Climate Change, Steven Guilbeault, remarking:[37]

> Over the last few days, Canada worked hard to achieve improvements in the final decision text, rallying together with developed and developing nations for a deal that all countries could get behind. We leave Egypt with an outcome that keeps the target of 1.5 alive.
>
> . . .
>
> COP27 has shown us that the world can achieve progress even during very challenging times. We will keep up the momentum . . . and rally for ambitious commitments to protect our natural world.

Notably, Guilbeault proudly espoused this benevolent rhetoric even after being criticized for including oil and gas corporations in Canada's delegation and ignoring Indigenous and racialized peoples' calls to phase out fossil fuels.[38]

2.5 Unpacking COPs' gaslighting myths

The above timeline of negotiations on loss and damage illustrates how COPs allow states and entities of the Global North to construct gaslighting myths about both themselves and international law. Many Indigenous and racialized peoples are aware of this gaslighting and have critiqued Global North leaders who espouse benevolent rhetoric while undermining negotiations and promoting climate destruction

[33] David W South, 'COP27 Loss and Damage Fund—Financial Band Aid or Effective Mechanism?' (2023) 39 Climate and Energy 29, 31.

[34] ibid 32.

[35] W Neil. Adger, 'Loss and Damage from Climate Change: Legacies from Glasgow and Sharm el-Sheikh' (2023) Scottish Geographical Journal 1, 4–6. As Adger notes: 'Developed countries have previously pledged $100 billion for mitigation and adaptation, but these pledges have not been upheld and the substantial majority have been allocated to decarbonisation rather than adapting to climate change impacts.'

[36] Lewis (n 32).

[37] Steven Guilbeault, 'Minister Guilbeault's statement on Canada's position and achievements on climate change at COP27' (2022) Government of Canada < https://www.canada.ca/en/environment-climate-change/news/2022/11/minister-guilbeaults-statement-on-canadas-position-and-achievements-on-climate-change-at-cop27.html> accessed 22 May 2023.

[38] Meghan Potkins, 'COP27 Goes into Overtime as Canada Continues to Face Criticism on Oil and Gas Stance' *Financial Post* (22 November 2022) <www.financialpost.com/commodities/energy/oil-gas/cop27-overtime-canada-face-criticism-oil-and-gas> accessed 22 May 2023.

outside of COPs. For example, in the lead-up to Fiji's COP23, climate advocate Samu Kuridrani stated:[39]

> It's a disgrace! The big polluters need to stop sugar-coating their climate destruction, step up and take responsibility for their actions . . . Nations signed up to the Paris Agreements continue to extract, export and burn coal, oil and gas. They think that we don't see the double game they're playing.

Still, there is a pressing need to explicitly name the two gaslighting myths that allow the multi-dimensional violence of international law to continue. The first myth is that Global North states are committed to, or even interested in, working towards climate justice. This myth is one of the core premises of COPs and the wider UN climate regime: that 'the global nature of climate change calls for the widest possible cooperation by all countries and their participation in an effective and appropriate international response, in accordance with their common but differentiated responsibilities and respective capabilities and their social and economic conditions'.[40]

However, these states and their ruling classes are not at all committed to climate justice. They have designed COPs, and international law more generally, to be structures where they can narrate this myth to secure the political, economic, and social benefits of claiming benevolence while simultaneously protecting their power and wealth against the demands of redistribution that are embedded in calls for climate justice. Climate justice for Indigenous and racialized peoples will thus always be out of reach at COPs, providing incremental goalposts that make true decolonial and anti-capitalist climate justice unobtainable. For those engaging in COPs in good faith, these goalposts create the illusion that climate justice is only x number of COPs away.

In this way, COPs intertwine the myth of the Global North's commitment to climate justice with the myth that climate justice takes time and incremental progress within international law. Specifically, COPs give space and structural force to this incrementalist myth—where Global North leaders can use the annual fora to actively prevent climate justice during the negotiations and then benevolently proclaim that more work is needed at the next COP. As such, COPs allow the ruling classes to extract the resource of time from Oceanians and other Indigenous and racialized peoples, depriving us of the sacred months, years, decades, centuries, and millennia we could have with each other, our oceans, lands, and all the living beings we hold dear.[41] In other words, our lifetimes, as well as our lands and waters, are 'racial sacrifice zones' for transnational corporations to 'funnel wealth towards the global North and privileged national and local elites globally'.[42]

[39] 'Pacific Islanders Crowdfunding to Call out Hypocrisy at UN Climate Meeting in Germany' *Greenpeace Australia Pacific* (13 October 2017) <www.greenpeace.org.au/stories/pacific-islanders-crowdfunding-call-hypocrisy-un-climate-meeting-germany/> accessed 26 May 2023.

[40] United Nations Framework Convention on Climate Change, 1771 UNTS 107 (9 May 1992) Article 2.

[41] Here, I briefly draw on intersectional theories of 'racial time' that encompass 'several ideas about how racial power dynamics shape group experiences and expectations of time' especially the reality of 'stolen time'; see Yuvraj Joshi, 'Racial Time' (2023) 90 University of Chicago Law Review 1625, 1635.

[42] UNGA 'Report of the Special Rapporteur on contemporary forms of racism, racial discrimination, xenophobia and related intolerance, E. Tendayi Achiume: Ecological crisis, climate justice and racial justice' (25 October 2022)) UN Doc A/77/549, para 2.

To draw on Toni Morrison,[43] the key function of these *racist* gaslighting myths is distraction. Instead of living in harmony with each other and our environment, many of us are made to spend time, resources, and energy fighting at COPs, and international law more broadly, to mitigate the violence of Global North states. Instead of pursuing alternative means of resistance against international law and its violence, these myths trap us into engaging with them on their own terms, despite mounting evidence that they have always sought to sacrifice us and our earth.

3. The slow and benevolent violence of *Ioane Teitiota v New Zealand*

To further illustrate the two gaslighting myths that perpetuate international law's slow and benevolent violence, this section critiques the *Teitiota* decision. In making this critique, I acknowledge that cross-border climate change-related displacement is a complex issue that often involves the imposition of 'impossible choices'.[44] This includes the 'choice' to either remain in one's ancestral home despite increasingly life-threatening circumstances or relocate in pursuit of safety. Therefore, rather than suggesting there are correct ways for displaced peoples to navigate these 'impossible choices' or arguing for a particular precedent in *Teitiota*, I focus on the reasoning of the Committee, which ignores the injustices embedded in these 'choices' and gaslights those forced to make them, most of whom are Indigenous and racialized peoples.

3.1 The *Teitiota* decision

Ioane Teitiota was deported from New Zealand to his Oceanian home nation of Kiribati following failed attempts to seek protection from climate change-related displacement in the domestic courts. Teitiota argued that climate change was causing sea-level rise, contaminating freshwater, eroding land, and provoking conflict amongst residents.[45] Therefore, Teitiota, his wife, and their young children—born in New Zealand—needed to remain in the country to live their lives safely and with dignity. Based on the testimony of a climate change researcher, Teitiota also argued that climate change would make his home in Kiribati uninhabitable in ten to fifteen years.[46]

New Zealand's highest appellate court rejected Teitiota's claims in 2015 and he was deported to Kiribati. He then filed a communication to the UN Human Rights Committee claiming that, by deporting him, New Zealand had violated his right to life

[43] Toni Morrison and others, 'Black Studies Center Public Dialogue, Part 2' (1975) 90 Special Collections: Oregon Public Speakers 1, 10 (remarking: 'The function, the very serious function of racism is distraction').

[44] See Lagipoiva Cherelle Jackson and others, 'An impossible choice: the Pacific's climate crisis' *The Guardian* (14 October 2021) <https://www.theguardian.com/world/series/an-impossible-choice-the-pacific-climate-crisis> accessed 28 September 2023; Karen E McNamara and others, 'The Complex Decision-Making of Climate-Induced Relocation: Adaptation and Loss and Damage' (2018) 18 Climate Policy 115.

[45] *Teitiota* (n 13) [2.1].

[46] ibid.

under Article 6 of the International Covenant on Civil and Political Rights (ICCPR). Specifically, Teitiota argued that (i) he faced threats to his life from overpopulation as well as intense flooding and breaches of sea walls, (ii) the courts erred in determining the time frame within which serious harm to Teitiota would occur in Kiribati, (iii) the courts did not give sufficient weight to the expert testimony of the climate change researcher, and (iv) Kiribati would become uninhabitable within ten to fifteen years.[47]

In January 2020, the Committee dismissed his claim by a 16:2 majority, upholding the original reasoning. Despite the negative outcome for Teitiota, the decision was celebrated as 'historic'[48] and 'landmark'[49] for people in the Pacific Islands and beyond facing the realities of climate change-related displacement. For the first time, an international quasi-judicial body affirmed that the impacts of climate change may expose people to life-threatening risks or cruel, inhuman, or degrading treatment, 'thereby triggering the non-refoulement obligations of sending states'.[50]

3.2 Unpacking the Committee majority's gaslighting myths

Importantly, the Committee majority's judgement propagated the same gaslighting myths that COPs propagate. It began by declaring that climate justice takes time and requires incremental progress at international law. While acknowledging that the decision was against Teitiota now, the Committee asserted that protection would surely be offered to him and other people facing climate change-related displacement in the future.

Its conclusions beg an essential question: if Kiribati is known to be at the frontline of climate change's destructive impacts, what threshold must life-threatening risks surpass to trigger states' non-refoulement obligations? Stated otherwise, how long must the people of Kiribati and other impacted areas wait before their circumstances are deemed sufficiently dire to warrant protection? Rather than answering this question, the majority opined that there is no need for Teitiota or anyone else in Kiribati to worry:[51]

> The timeframe of 10 to 15 years, as suggested by the author, could allow for intervening acts by the Republic of Kiribati, with the assistance of the international community, to take affirmative measures to protect and, where necessary, relocate its population.

These remarks raise another question: why does the majority believe that the international community *could* or *would* assist Kiribati in ten to fifteen years? As I have

[47] ibid [9.10].
[48] Melissa Godin, 'Climate Refugees Cannot Be Forced Home, U.N. Panel Says in Landmark Ruling' *Time* (20 January 2020) < https://www.time.com/5768347/climate-refugees-un-ioane-teitiota/>.
[49] Kate Lyons, 'Climate refugees can't be returned home, says landmark UN human rights ruling' *The Guardian* (London, 20 January 2020) <https://www.theguardian.com/world/2020/jan/20/climaterefugees-cant-be-returned-home-says-landmark-un-human-rights-ruling>.
[50] *Teitiota* (n 13) [9.11].
[51] ibid [9.12].

observed elsewhere, the majority did not substantiate this statement of faith in its judgement.[52] However, it is worth thinking about why the majority made this assertion, especially since considerations of the international community's ability or willingness to assist are irrelevant when determining Article 6 violations.[53] This leads to a third question: why did the majority even bring up the likelihood of assistance?

The majority's invocation of the international community was not just a passing acknowledgement that Kiribati, as a 'developing' nation, cannot protect its citizens against displacement without international support. Rather, it was a deliberate attempt to morally justify a judgement which condemned Teitiota and his family to the life-threatening conditions he was seeking protection from. In other words, to dismiss Teitiota's claim without seeming cruel and inhumane, the Committee relied on an unsubstantiated statement of faith in international law's benevolent façade. This is how the other gaslighting myth—that Global North states are committed to collective climate action—works in tandem with the gaslighting myth about time and incremental progress.

The violent impacts of these myths manifest at both proximate and distal levels. First, for Teitiota and other people facing climate change-related displacement, the gaslighting myth seeks to distort their views of their realities ('We know what's happening to you better than you do and, don't worry, your life isn't threatened yet') and about the Global North and its international law ('You can trust us to take care of you, even though we've never given you a reason to and we won't tell you when'). Second, these myths also distort perceptions about international law's capacity and willingness to achieve climate justice for the world at large. This distortion is facilitated by mainstream media, as evidenced by the headlines after the *Teitiota* case noted above, which presented Global North states not as perpetrators of violence but as saviours in waiting. But the violence here is not just that we are being gaslighted about international law, but also about ourselves, while being robbed of our ability to imagine and dream of a world beyond international law. This ongoing theft is particularly egregious for Indigenous and racialized peoples, who have already lost so much of our ways of being and the futures our ancestors dreamed for us. Ani Mikaere, Margaret Mutu, and Moana Jackson have articulated this point when discussing the impacts of colonization on Māori, the Indigenous peoples of Aotearoa: '[O]ne of the most devastating impacts colonisation has had upon us is that it has suppressed our ability to dream and imagine something different.'[54]

So, if we accept, or are willing to take seriously, the idea that we need to dream and imagine something beyond international law because it will always inflict multidimensional racist violence and never allow for the achievement of climate justice, a

[52] Dylan Asafo, 'The Racism in Climate Change Law: Critiquing the Law on Climate Change-Related Displacement with Critical Race Theory' (2021) 39 Berkeley Journal of International Law 249, 273–74.

[53] Michelle Foster and Jane McAdam, 'Analysis of "Imminence" in International Protection Claims: Teitiota v New Zealand and Beyond' (2022) 71 International & Comparative Law Quarterly 975, 981 (arguing that the only relevant legal assessment is the 'likelihood of harm in light of the likelihood of the home State offering protection against such harm').

[54] Margaret Mutu and others, 'Dreaming Together for Constitutional Transformation' (2021) 12 Counterfutures 37, 50.

key question arises: should Oceanians now resist *against* international law rather than within it?

This tricky question invites us—if not requires us—to grapple with a seemingly never-ending web of other tricky questions, all laden with their own assumptions and biases. The next section engages with two of these questions from my Oceanian perspective, though they may likely be relevant to other Indigenous and racialized peoples in similar and different ways.

4. Exploring some of the tricky questions

4.1. Questions regarding nation-states and regional organizations

Oceanians' engagements with international law are driven and made possible by the existence of nation-states and regional organizations in Oceania and beyond, where these forms are deeply dependent on international law and vice versa.[55] This raises the question: what roles, if any, can these forms can play in resisting international law's violence, or moreover, resisting *against* international law altogether?

Hau'ofa explained in 1987 that, in Oceania, formal decolonization in the form of nation-states and regional organizations did not facilitate 'real national sovereignty' but 'integration' into the West-led regional and global order which secures the power of 'ruling groups' in Oceania:[56]

> [W]e have seen that decolonisation has led to integration. Without self-reliance there can be no real national sovereignty in the South Pacific islands. It follows that what we call national sovereignty in the region is little more than a measure of local autonomy in the hands of competing national interests within the larger regional economy. These interests are represented by the ruling groups within each community... Many of the resources including aid moving from these centres to the regional communities go towards the support of elite groups...

This harmful 'integration' manifests in several ways that undermine climate justice and environmental justice more broadly, including in some Oceanian nation-states'

[55] For accounts of the interconnectedness between nation-states and international law in Oceania and beyond, see Cait Storr, *International Status in the Shadow of Empire: Nauru and the Histories of International Law* (Cambridge University Press 2020); Antony Anghie, 'Self-Determination and Beyond: Reflections on the Aftermath of the Nauru Case' in Kim Rubenstein (eds) *Traversing the Divide: Honouring Deborah Cass's Contributions to Public and International Law* (ANU Press 2021); Luis Eslava and Sundhya Pahuja, 'The State and International Law: A Reading from the Global South' (2020) 11 Humanity: An International Journal of Human Rights, Humanitarianism, and Development 118.

[56] Epeli Hau'ofa, 'The New Pacific Society: Integration and Independence' in Anthony Hooper (ed), *Class and Culture in the South Pacific* (Centre for Pacific Studies University of Auckland 1987). See also Tracey Banivanua Mar, *Decolonisation and the Pacific: Indigenous Globalisation and the Ends of Empire* (Cambridge University Press 2016) 218–19; Terence Wesley-Smith 'The Limits of Self-Determination in Oceania' (2007) 56 Social and Economic Studies 182, 203.

advocacy for deep seabed mining,[57] or in their supportive declarations for Japan's dumping of nuclear waste in the region.[58]

'Integration' is reinforced by regional organizations—including the Pacific Islands Forum— which functions to serve the interests of these nation-states, especially Australia and New Zealand, as its key funders.[59] This function has led the Forum to continuously stall in championing justice and liberation for West Papua, despite longstanding calls by West Papuan liberation movements for accountability for Indonesia's gross genocidal violence.[60] Australia and New Zealand also repeatedly inhibit 'effective' climate governance in the Forum and other regional organizations.[61]

The costs of 'integration' manifest in ways that undermine justice and liberation for other Indigenous and racialized peoples as well. For example, nation-states in Oceania have consistently voted in favour of Israel's genocidal settler-colonial regime in Palestine at the United Nations General Assembly (UNGA). This pattern not only reflects the strong presence of Christian Zionism in the region, but the imperialist violence of US-driven geopolitical pressure and Israel's efforts to secure support from state and Forum leaders through neocolonial development climate aid,[62] which the 'ruling groups' benefit from. Notably, support for Israel is being challenged by Oceanian feminist collectives and social movements who understand the deep interconnections between Oceanian and Palestinian struggles against empire.[63]

Therefore, if nation-states and regional organizations in Oceania are unable and unwilling to allow Oceanians to resist against the violence of international law and stand in solidarity with the other intertwined struggles of Indigenous and racialised peoples, we must imagine, dream, and work towards futures beyond them.

[57] See Viliame Kasanawaqa, Asinate Namuaira, and Solo Mara, 'Deep-Sea Mining in Pacific Small Island Developing States—The Role of Civil Society Organizations' in Lino Briguglio and others (eds), *Handbook of Civil Society and Social Movements in Small States* (Routledge 2023).

[58] See Joey Tau, 'Pacific leaders must hold Japan accountable at PALM10 for Fukushima nuclear waste' (*PANG—Pacific Network on Globalisation*, 10 March 2024)<https://pang.org.fj/fukushima/> accessed 20 December 2024.

[59] See Hau'ofa (n 55); Stephanie Lawson, '"The Pacific Way" as Postcolonial Discourse: Towards a Reassessment' (2010) 45 The Journal of Pacific History 297.

[60] See Free West Papua Campaign, 'A Historic Choice: ULMWP President Benny Wenda Pacific on the 2024 Pacific Islands Forum' (*Free West Papua Campaign*, 26 August 2024) <https://www.freewestpapua.org/2024/08/26/a-historic-choice-ulmwp-president-benny-wenda-pacific-on-the-2024-pacific-islands-forum/> accessed 20 December 2024.

[61] Marc Williams and Duncan McDuie-Ra, *Combating Climate Change in the Pacific: The Role of Regional Organizations* (Palgrave Macmillan 2018) 19, 32.

[62] Indira Stewart, 'Israel and the Pacific—a surprisingly close "friendship"' *1News* (10 March 2024) <https://www.1news.co.nz/2024/03/10/israel-and-the-pacific-a-surprisingly-close-friendship/> accessed 20 December 2024; Titilua Ikenasio, 'Six Pacific Islands Vote No on Israeli Ceasefire: Exploring the Factors at Play' *Feijoa Dispatch* (7 November 2023) < https://www.feijoadispatch.nz/p/six-pacific-islands-vote-no-on-israeli> accessed 20 December 2024.

[63] NGO Coalition on Human Rights in Fiji, 'Restrictions on solidarity marches for Palestine' (*Fiji Women's Crisis Centre*, 7 October 2024) <https://www.fijiwomen.com/news/media-release/restrictions-on-solidarity-marches-for-palestine/> accessed 20 December 2024; Hugo Hodge, 'Pro-Palestine views are a minority in the Pacific, but some activists are going against the status quo' *ABC* (15 January 2024) <https://www.abc.net.au/pacific/israel-palestine-pacific-islands/103307090> accessed 20 December 2024; Joanne Holden, 'Pacific Island leaders criticised for silence on Israel-Hamas conflict' *Cook Islands News* (11 November 2023) <https://www.cookislandsnews.com/internal/national/pacific-islands/52nd-pacific-islands-forum-2023/pacific-island-leaders-criticised-for-silence-on-israel-hamas-conflict/> accessed 20 December 2024.

4.2 Questions regarding counter-violence

Solidarity with interconnected liberation movements necessarily implores Oceanians to grapple with questions around *counter-violence*. For example, if we accept—or at least take seriously—the idea that international law inflicts multi-dimensional violence, is it time for us to pursue forms of counter-violence and, if so, which ones? As controversial as this question might be, it is unavoidable, as the connections between international law's support for imperialist violence and its role in facilitating the climate crisis are becoming increasingly clear and undeniable. Moreover, Oceanians, Palestinians, and other Indigenous and racialized peoples have long engaged in counter-violence[64] against the systems, structures, and institutions seeking to annihilate them .[65] Importantly, such counter-violence persists because the rules and mechanisms of international law are still 'failing' to disrupt the genocidal impunity of empire.[66]

In *The Wretched of the Earth,* Fanon made clear the necessity of counter-violence against empire as follows: 'Colonialism only loosens its hold when the knife is at its throat . . . Colonialism is not a machine capable of thinking, a body endowed with reason. It is naked violence and only gives in when confronted with greater violence.'[67] Unsurprisingly, Fanonian counter-violence has already been theorized in the context of climate change, where in light of ongoing ineffectiveness of UNFCCC negotiation processes and rising emissions, Andreas Malm posited that: '[t]here has been a time for a Gandhian climate movement; perhaps there might come a time for a Fanonian one. The breaking of fences may one day be seen as a very minor misdemeanour indeed.'[68]

While the case for counter-violence for climate justice may be compelling to some Oceanians, such theorizations are likely to be opposed by many others. For example, counter-violence is likely to be seen by some Oceanians as inappropriate and antithetical to the so-called 'Pacific Way', an institutionalized regional identity based on traditional Indigenous norms around collectivism and relationality that promotes

[64] See Simon Barber, 'Imagining beyond Decolonisation' (2020) 10 Counterfutures 156, 158–61 (outlining Māori armed resistance against the British Crown); Stewart Firth and Karin von Strokirch, 'A Nuclear Pacific' in Donald Denoon and Malama Meleisea (eds), *The Cambridge History of the Pacific Islanders* (Cambridge University Press 2008) 346 (outlining armed resistance in Ma'ohi Nui against French imperialism).

[65] See Te Aniwaniwa Paterson, '"We all have the same fight" says Kanak youth at solidarity fono' *Te Ao Māori News* (8 June 2024) <https://www.teaonews.co.nz/2024/06/08/we-all-have-the-same-fight-says-kanak-youth-at-solidarity-fono/> accessed 21 December 2024; Catherine Delahunty, 'West Papua: Whose lives matter?' *E-Tangata* (20 October 2024) <https://e-tangata.co.nz/reflections/west-papua-whose-lives-matter/> accessed 21 December 2024; Hamid Dabashi, 'War on Gaza: How critics are twisting Frantz Fanon's legacy' *Middle East Eye* (5 March 2024) <https://www.middleeasteye.net/opinion/war-gaza-how-critics-are-twisting-frantz-fanons-legacy> accessed 21 December 2024.

[66] Jadaliyya, 'Noura Erakat Nations, are meant . . . to ensure Discusses UN Security Council Failures on Al Jazeera' (12 December 2023) <https://www.youtube.com/watch?v=8xxYBJ3mKF0&t=202s> accessed 20 December 2024. Erakat remarked: '. . . In the aftermath of the second world war, the Genocide Convention, as well as the mechanisms with the United that [genocide] never happens again. So we see the incapacitation of these international legal mechanisms, and at this point . . . we need more people to demonstrate the failure of these International legal institutions . . .').

[67] Frantz Fanon, *The Wretched of the Earth* (Grove Press 1963) 61.

[68] Andreas Malm, *How To Blow Up a Pipeline* (Verso Books 2021) 161 citing Fanon (n 66) 94.

non-violent consensus building in regional fora and international law.[69] Counter-violence may also be deemed impractical and futile because Oceanians and other Indigenous and racialized peoples have the least resources and structural power to pursue this form of struggle but a lot to lose from its execution. [70] Other important concerns relate to the gendered dimensions of counter-violence.[71] As Michael Lujan Bevacqua posited in his reflections on the possibilities of Fanonian ideas for Oceanians, 'the Ocean is feminine' and intersectional Oceanian feminist analyses are required to truly reimagine decolonization in Oceania.[72] Last, counter-violence may be viewed as inappropriate for liberation in some contexts and spaces in Oceania, which cannot be flattened and homogonized. For instance, as Trask noted in 2004, the sovereignty movement required in Hawai'i is distinct from the revolutionary action Fanon called for in Algeria:[73]

> Fanon believed that revolutionary action was the only answer in Algeria and in Africa as a continent. Malcolm X believed that total separation of Black people from white people was the only answer in the United States. I believe that my own people need separation in Hawai'i. A separate land base, economy, educational system, language based, and so on. Sovereignty is what we call this in Hawai'i.

Still, despite all of these concerns and considerations, it is unwise for Oceanians to reject either the relevance or, in some cases, the necessity of counter-violence. Firstly, it is no coincidence that the imperialist and capitalist entities carrying out and facilitating genocides in Palestine, Oceania and around the world in apparent 'violation' of international law, are also simultaneously escalating the climate crisis and preventing climate justice at international law. This connection reveals the work international law does for empire and the material interconnectedness of all liberation struggles against it.[74] It also makes clear that armed resistance movements against empire in Palestine and beyond are actively dismantling the entities responsible for the climate crisis, and strongly suggests that such forms of resistance should be undertaken or at least supported by Oceanians as well. Indeed, it could be that all forms of counter-violence do not need to be physical or militarised, and that complementary psychological, slow and benevolent forms can be taken up as well. Secondly, and more fundamentally, various Oceanian laws and norms make clear that all peoples, living things, lands, and waters are deeply connected to each other. [75] These laws and norms follow that we

[69] UNGA, 'Speech by the Honourable Ratu Sir Kamisese Mara, K.B.E., Prime Minister of Fiji' (21 October 1970) UN Doc A/PV.1876 [205]-[206]; Williams and McDuie-Ra (n 61) 8–9.

[70] See Derrick Bell, 'Racism Is Here to Stay: Now What Thurgood Marshall Commemorative Issue' (1991) 35 Howard Law Journal 79, 91 (cautioning against the idea of a 'bloody revolution' for Black liberation in the US as '[w]e know who would suffer the most').

[71] Judith Butler, 'Violence, Nonviolence: Sartre on Fanon' in *Senses of the Subject* (Fordham University Press 2015) 197.

[72] Michael Lujan Bevacqua, 'Their-Our Sea of Islands: Epeli Hau'ofa and Frantz Fanon' (2010) 37 LiNQ (Literature in North Queensland) 80, 89.

[73] Trask (n 1) 14.

[74] 350 Australia, 'Palestine: A Climate Justice Issue' (*350*, 23 November 2023) <https://350.org.au/palestine-a-climate-justice-issue/> accessed 22 December 2024.

[75] For example, for Samoans, the concept of the vā underpins all relations. As Samoan scholar Albert Wendt explained: '[Vā] is the space between, the between-ness, not empty space, not space that separates

are obligated to honour and nurture our connections to Palestinians, Oceanians and all Indigenous and racialized peoples being forced to enact counter-violence against the entities seeking to annihilate them, and *act* in solidarity with them. Failing to do so would breach of our laws and norms, and therefore, who we may purport to be as Oceanians. In any case, while enacting or supporting counter-violence might appear to be inappropriate, unnecessary, and impossible to some Oceanians now, as Malm and others have suggested, refusing to do so will likely no longer be an option for more and more of us as the climate crisis and impunity of empire escalate largely uninterrupted.

5. Concluding thoughts

In writing this chapter, I sought to explore whether examining and articulating the psychological dimensions of international law's violence might be helpful to Oceanians and other Indigenous and racialized peoples' ongoing efforts to resist racist systems of oppression and imagine futures beyond them. I have found that these psychological dimensions not only contribute to rendering international law incapable of climate justice, but also function to distract us and inhibit our imaginings of other alternative tactics for resistance and alternative systems of relating to each other and to our earth.

However, as international law continues to enable escalating ecological collapse and concurrent genocides, the somewhat daunting challenge of confronting the tricky questions I raised above might be overcome by answering perhaps the biggest question of them all: will our *earth* survive another few decades of international law and its violence? To ask this question another way, invoking the words of Emmy Rākete on the need for prison abolition in Aotearoa: what if we have been reforming—or even transforming—international law this whole time and this is all a reformed or transformed international law will ever look like: a system that assures the destruction of our earth?[76]

Confronting this question may help all of us to dismantle international law's violence in the world and in our own minds. For us Oceanians, this dismantling can be further helped by continuously heeding the words of Hau'ofa, which remind us that it is not empire or its international law that binds us together, but our ocean that calls on us to liberate ourselves from the confines of our freedom:[77]

but space that relates, that holds separate entities and things together in the Unity-that-is-All, the space giving meaning to things . . . A well-known Samoan expression is . . . "teu le va" Cherish/nurse/care for the va, the relationships. This is crucial in . . . cultures that value group, unity, more than individualism[.]'; see Albert Wendt, 'Tatauing the post-colonial body' (1996) 42 Span 15, 17.

[76] The Spinoff, 'Who are prisons actually helping? | Alice Snedden's Bad News | The Spinoff' (27 September 2022) <http://www.youtube.com/watch?v=I6PvFDntjcc> accessed 20 December 2024.

[77] Hau'ofa (n 7) 16.

We are the sea, we are the ocean, we must wake up to this ancient truth and together use it to overturn all hegemonic views that aim ultimately to confine us again, physically and psychologically, in the tiny spaces which we have resisted accepting as our sole appointed place, and from which we have recently liberated ourselves.

...

We must not allow anyone to belittle us again, and take away our freedom.

Epilogue
The Abolition(s) of International Law

Christopher Gevers

1. This *is* international law

A little over a century ago, amidst a bloody war rooted in European colonial rivalry and in the aftermath of the first genocide of the twentieth century committed against the Nama and Herero peoples,[1] WEB Du Bois pre-emptively rejected the inevitable moves to exceptionalize the present—and ultimately redeem whiteness—declaring:

> As we see the dead dimly through rifts of battle smoke and hear faintly the cursing and accusations of blood brothers, we darker men say: This is not Europe gone mad; this is not aberration nor insanity; this *is* Europe; this seeming terrible is the real soul of white culture—back of all culture, stripped and visible today.[2]

Half a century later, European colonial empires were collapsing, precipitating more bloody wars fuelled by 'cursing and accusations of [white] blood brothers' and another European genocide, prompting Aimé Césaire to observe:[3]

> [T]he very distinguished, very humanistic, very Christian bourgeois of the twentieth century . . . without his being aware of it, . . . has a Hitler inside of him, that Hitler *inhabits* him, that Hitler is his *demon,* that if he rails against him, he is being inconsistent and that, at bottom, what he cannot forgive Hitler for is not *the crime* in itself, *the crime against man,* it is not *the humiliation of man as such,* it is the crime against the white man, the humiliation of the white man, and the fact that he applied to Europe colonialist procedures which until then had been reserved exclusively for the [racialized peoples] of Algeria, . . . India, and . . . Africa.

Today, amidst another genocide carried out in the name of 'Western civilization'[4] and another war amongst European blood brothers that threatens to engulf the world, the

1 See United Nations Human Rights Council, 'Report of the Working Group of Experts on People of African Descent on its mission to Germany' (15 August 2017) A/HRC/36/60/Add 2.

2 WEB Du Bois, 'Of the Culture of White Folk' (1917) 7(4) Journal of Race Development 434, 437. As Du Bois put it: 'This world war is primarily the jealous and avaricious struggle for the largest share in exploiting darker races.' ibid, 444.

3 Aimé Césaire, *Discourse on Colonialism* (Joan Pinkham tr, NYU Press 2000) 36.

4 In October 2023, Benjamin Netanyahu described Israel's military offensive in Gaza as the 'struggle between the children of light and the children of darkness, between humanity and the law of the jungle'. Sonam Sheth, 'Netanyahu deleted a post on X about a struggle against "children of darkness" around the time of a

words of Du Bois and Césaire ring true once more: this is not the 'Greater Europe'[5] gone mad, nor aberration or insanity, this *is* the White World.

This is also the White World's international law. The preceding pages are a timely reminder that, as international law's racialized violences are 'stripped and [made] visible today' in Gaza and elsewhere, we must resist the move to exceptionalize the present moment of naked violence and world-ordering, or to redeem 'the West'[6] and its international law and institutions. As this collection details, in chapter and verse, international law has been the engine and freight of the intersecting apocalypses that 'the West' has dragged the planet and its peoples through over the past five centuries, and that threaten to make this century its last. Like Du Bois and Césaire, *Emancipating International Law* insists that we resist these moves to immunize international law (let alone make it the victim!) and settle for 'the restoration of the velvet glove'.[7]

At the same time, this collection reminds us that emancipatory projects have arisen from the ashes of these apocalyptic events, some of which involved tactical engagements with international law and its institutions.[8] These include Du Bois's efforts in 1919 to internationalize the struggle against the colour line through the League of Nations,[9] as well as moves by Third World states and international lawyers to reimagine and then remake the global order in the aftermath of formal colonial rule.[10] Today, once more, amidst multiple ongoing catastrophes, the International Court of Justice (ICJ) has been positioned as a site of international law's redemption, perhaps. Even the International Criminal Court (ICC) seems to have provisionally—albeit reluctantly, belatedly, and in limited fashion—paused its longstanding commitment to looking past the crimes committed by the West (or in its name).

Herein lies the paradox at the heart of much critical international legal scholarship, a somewhat contradictory 'dynamic of resistance and reform'.[11] This paradox is registered in this volume's title: emancipation has a mixed record. Saidiya Hartman has detailed this ambiguous legacy in the United States, where 'emancipation appears less the grand event of liberation than a point of transition between modes of

tragic hospital explosion in Gaza' (*Business Insider*, 18 October 2023) <https://www.businessinsider.com/netanyahu-deleted-children-of-darkness-post-gaza-hospital-attack-2023-10> accessed 4 May 2025.

[5] As Blaut defines it, the term 'Greater Europe' refers to 'Europe and countries of European settlement overseas'. JM Blaut, *The Colonizer's Model of the World: Geographical Diffusionism and Eurocentric History* (Guilford Press 1993) 5.

[6] As Glissant put it, 'the West' is not a place, it's a *project*. Edouard Glissant, *Caribbean Discourse: Selected Essays* (University Press of Virginia 1989) 2.

[7] Sundhya Pahuja, 'Empire Comes Home?: The Continued Relevance of ISMIL today' (*CIL Dialogues: An International Law Blog, Verso*, November 2025) <https://cil.nus.edu.sg/blogs/empire-comes-home-the-continued-relevance-of-ismil-today-by-sundhya-pahuja/> accessed 28 January 2026.

[8] For an early articulation of the 'functional interpretation' of international law by newly independent states, see George M Abi-Saab, 'The Newly Independent States and the Scope of Domestic Jurisdiction' (1960) 54 Proceedings of the American Society of International Law at its Annual Meeting 88.

[9] WEB Du Bois, 'Memorandum on the Future of Africa', *W.E.B. Du Bois Papers*, Special Collections and University Archives, University of Massachusetts Amherst Libraries.

[10] See generally Luis Eslava, Michael Fakhri, and Vasuki Nesiah, *Bandung, Global History, and International Law* (Cambridge University Press 2017); Adom Getachew, *Worldmaking After Empire: The Rise and Fall of Self-Determination* (Princeton University Press 2019).

[11] Luis Eslava and Sundhya Pahuja, 'Between Resistance and Reform: TWAIL and the Universality of International Law' (2011) 3(1) Trade, Law and Development 110.

servitude and racial subjection'.[12] These 'entanglements of slavery and freedom' can be traced back to emancipation in the British colonies in the 1840s, and forward to international law's emancipation through the Slavery Convention and its colonial shadow the 'Native Labour Code'.[13] In all these instances, (international) law intervened to ensure that legal emancipation did not only fail to bring freedom, in many ways it consolidated and expanded white domination over Black land, labour, and lives. The question that this collection insists that we confront is: can international law be emancipated?

2. Whiteness as anti-intellectual property

International law is predicated on a racial imaginary—'the international'—and held together by racial contracts, including literal ones.[14] One of international law's 'Founding Fathers'—of whom, remarked another, 'every living [international] jurist is [a] pupil'[15]—made this plain, time and again. John Westlake defined international law as 'the rules which are internationally recognised between white men',[16] which governed *both* the 'international society of the white race'[17] (or states 'of European origin'[18])—and relations with 'other civilisations with which the white race is compelled to be in contact'.[19] Crucially, for Westlake this white 'international society' *preceded* and *exceeded* the international legal order that it produced—or, as he put it in 1904, the 'treaties by which the white world is bound together'.[20] In fact, modern international lawyers discovered that they were both white *and* 'international', 'and, by that token, wonderful' at the same time.[21] This begs the question: when did international law cease being white?

The epistemic *condition* (in both senses of the term) of this racial contract is 'global white ignorance', which Charles Mills describes as an 'epistemology of ignorance' that manifests as 'a particular pattern of localized and global cognitive dysfunctions (which are psychosocially and socially functional)'.[22] This 'agreement to misinterpret the world' amongst white people is necessary in order to preclude 'self-transparency

[12] Saidiya Hartman, *Scenes of Subjection: Terror, Slavery, and Self-Making in Nineteenth-Century America* (Oxford University Press 1997) 116

[13] See Christopher Gevers, 'Whiteness as Reparations' (2025) 119 AJIL Unbound 188; Christopher Gevers, 'Refiguring Slavery Through International Law: The 1926 *Slavery Convention*, the "Native Labour Code" and Racial Capitalism' (2022) 25 Journal of International Economic Law 1.

[14] Charles W Mills, *The Racial Contract* (Cornell University Press 1997) 20–21.

[15] Lassa Oppenheim, 'Editor's Introduction' in John Westlake, *Collected Papers of John Westlake* (Lassa Oppenheim ed, Cambridge University Press 1914) x.

[16] John Westlake, *Collected Papers of John Westlake* (Lassa Oppenheim ed, Cambridge University Press 1914) 146.

[17] John Westlake, *Chapters on the Principles of International Law* (Cambridge University Press 1894) 198, 134.

[18] John Westlake, *International Law* (Cambridge University Press 1904) 209, 1.

[19] Westlake (n 17) 198.

[20] Westlake (n 18) 208.

[21] See Christopher Gevers, '"Unwhitening the World": Rethinking Race and International Law' (2021) 67 UCLA Law Review 1652.

[22] Mills (n 14) 18.

and genuine understanding of social realities' and—most importantly—to provide the cognitive and moral justifications for conquest, colonization, and enslavement.[23] Mills provocatively described this 'invented delusional world' of global whiteness as follows:[24]

> There will be white mythologies, invented Orients, invented Africas, invented Americas, with a corresponding fabricated population, countries that never were, inhabited by people who never were – Calibans and Tontos, Man Fridays and Sambos – but who attain a virtual reality through their existence in travelers' tales, folk myth, popular and highbrow fiction, colonial reports, scholarly theory, Hollywood cinema, living in the white imagination and determinedly imposed on their alarmed real-life counterparts.

One could be forgiven for mistaking this for a definition of much of international law, past and present. As Anghie put it: 'the natives existed more vividly in Geneva . . . than they did in the mandate territories themselves'.[25]

Crucially, this 'epistemology of ignorance' is *socially functional*, enabling white people to 'learn to see the world wrongly . . . with the assurance that this set of mistaken perceptions will be validated by white epistemic authority'.[26] To paraphrase Cheryl Harris, whites have a 'property interest' in ignorance.[27] As international law is predicated on this racial contract and its 'epistemology of ignorance', whiteness is also *professionally* function: as a form of *anti*-intellectual property uniquely available to white international lawyers. Put differently, white international lawyers benefit from the racial contract *as whites* 'and' *as international lawyers* who professionally peddle white ignorance, delusions, and fantasies 'living in the white imagination', 'validated by white epistemic authority', and 'determinedly imposed' on the world. We are, at best, gentle *simplifiers*, committed to rule the world by misinterpreting it.

This raises the question of whether white international lawyers can ever be part of an 'emancipatory' vision for international law, for at least two reasons. First, 'white ignorance' is *structural*: like the racial contract,[28] it cannot be opted out of or overcome by 'heroic act[s] of confession' predicated on 'a supreme faith in the individual to discern and act upon the world, to be her or his own vehicle for effecting change'.[29] The fantasy that it can be is, in all respects, a white one (evident in some 'critical whiteness

[23] ibid 18–19.

[24] ibid. As Mills puts it: 'There is a pervasive racialization of the social world that means that one's race, in effect, puts on into a certain relationship with social reality, tendentially determining one's being and consciousness'. Charles W Mills, 'White Supremacy as a Sociopolitical System' in Ashley Doane and Eduardo Bonilla-Silva (eds), *White Out: The Continuing Significance of Racism* (Routledge 2003) 42.

[25] Antony Anghie, *Imperialism, Sovereignty, and the Making of International Law* (Cambridge University Press 2005) 184.

[26] Mills (n 14) 18.

[27] Cheryl Harris, 'Whiteness as Property'(1992–1993) 106 Harvard Law Review 1707, 1713.

[28] As Mills puts it, not all white people are signatories to the Racial Contract, but all white people are beneficiaries of it. Mills (n 14) 11.

[29] Cynthia Levine-Rasky, 'Framing Whiteness: Working Through the Tensions in Introducing Whiteness to Educators'(2000) 3(3) Race, Ethnicity and Educators 217, 277.

studies' scholarship).[30] The lesson of whiteness studies raises the second reason to question the place of white international lawyers in any emancipatory project: whiteness centres itself.[31] Ultimately, the answer to the question of whether 'we' should reform international law, or resist it altogether, might be: it depends on who's asking.

3. Unsettling white international law

The sight of the State of Palestine addressing the ICJ on the violation of Palestinian peoples' right to self-determination for over a century represents a (perhaps, *the*) high point of renewed optimism for the emancipatory potential of international law. Despite its limitations, the Court's vindication of that right in its Advisory Opinion of 19 July 2024 seemed to confirm it.[32] Yet, if one holds it to the light, blemishes appear.

While Palestine's address to the Court began by locating the violation of the right to self-determination of Palestinian peoples in Israel's colonialism and apartheid—as 'the gravest breaches of this right'[33]—it ended with Palestine's own counsel Philippe Sands reformulating the *legal* basis for this right as the general right of *all* peoples to self-determination, relocating its origins and evacuating its emancipatory potential. In doing so, Sands not only deracinated and de-radicalized the right, he erased seventy years of Third World thought and action about the right to self-determination of *colonized peoples* under international law. Sands did so by relocating the right to self-determination in Hersch Lauterpacht's *International Bill of Rights of Man* (1945)—which explicitly excluded certain peoples on the ground of race—and displacing the 1960 Declaration on the Granting of Independence to Colonial Countries and Peoples. Yet, that Declaration was 'prepared by forty-five Asian and African delegations whose countries [had] invariably passed through the colonial mill' as a deliberate and explicit effort to resist the co-option of the Third World's claim to self-determination into a Western frame.[34] It was a spectacular performance of white ignorance by Sands. For Palestinians, it was tragic.

There are at least eight problems with Sands's reformulation of Palestine's claim to self-determination. *First*, it is a lie. Lauterpacht did not say *all* peoples have a right to self-determination: he explicitly excluded Black South Africans—along with Black Americans and other 'Others'—from the 'the right of self-government' in his 1945 *International Bill of the Rights of Man*.[35] According to Lauterpacht, the situation in

[30] See Kehinde Andrews, *The Psychosis of Whiteness: Surviving the Insanity of a Racist World* (Penguin Books 2023).

[31] See Levine-Rasky (n 29) 276 (noting that 'the individual white is situated at the centre of a discourse on race and racism').

[32] *Legal Consequences arising from the Policies and Practices of Israel in the Occupied Palestinian Territory, including East Jerusalem* (Advisory Opinion) 2024 <https://www.icj-cij.org/sites/default/files/case-related/186/186-20240719-adv-01-00-en.pdf> accessed 4 May 2025.

[33] Verbatim Record (19 February 2024) *Legal Consequences arising from the Policies and Practices of Israel in the Occupied Palestinian Territory, including East Jerusalem* <https://www.icj-cij.org/sites/default/files/case-related/186/186-20240219-ora-01-00-bi.pdf> accessed 4 May 2025, 53.

[34] UN General Assembly, Official Records 15th Session, 927th Plenary Meeting (29 November 1960) [65] and [72].

[35] Hersch Lauterpacht, *An International Bill of the Rights of Man* (Oxford University Press 2013 [1945]) 138–43.

South Africa was '*sui generis*' because of what granting self-determination to Black people would mean for white South Africans: namely, 'a consummation which would signify the end of her Western civilization'.[36] Black self-determination in South Africa was an 'impossibility' for Lauterpacht, who insisted this was not 'a question of dignity, *but a question of existence*' (quoting none other than Jan Smuts, albeit not by name, for reasons only known to Lauterpacht but not hard to guess).[37] Three years later, Lauterpacht drafted another declaration denying racialized peoples the right to self-determination: a draft *Declaration of Independence of the State of Israel*, which Lauterpacht described as 'a great and beneficent act of international distributive justice'.[38]

Second, it is wrong. Palestine's legal right to self-determination is not of a general nature or one that belongs to *all* peoples. Rather it is the right of a *colonized* people subject to 'alien subjugation, domination, and exploitation' to 'freely determine their political status and freely pursue their economic, social and cultural development'.[39] A right recognized, first and foremost, in the 1960 *Declaration on the Granting of Independence to Colonial Countries and Peoples* (which, Sands only later cites, in number but not name).

Third, it is misleading. This reformulation has consequences for Palestinians' exercise of their legal right to self-determination, chief of which is to direct attention away from the 1960 *Declaration*'s requirement that '[a]ll armed action *or repressive measures of all kinds* directed against dependent peoples shall cease in order to enable them to exercise peacefully and freely their right to complete independence'.[40] In other words, more than simply an end to the unlawful occupation by Israel.

Fourth, this misdirection erases the corresponding rights that the prohibition on the forcible denial of self-determination grants Palestinians, rights codified by the efforts of Third World international lawyers and states in the 1970 *Declaration on Principles of International Law Concerning Friendly Relations*. The first of these is the legal recognition of Palestinians' 'right to resistance'.[41] As Abi-Saab argued in 1973: 'armed resistance to forcible denial of self-determination—by imposing or maintaining by force colonial and alien domination—is legitimate according to the [1970] Declaration', which grants 'liberation movements . . . a *jus ad bellum* under the Charter'.[42]

[36] ibid 140–41.

[37] ibid (referring to the 'Prime Minister of South Africa').

[38] Neil Rogachevsky and Dov Zigler, *Israel's Declaration of Independence: The History and Political Theory of the Nation's Founding Moment* (Cambridge University Press 2022), 118.

[39] Declaration on the Granting of Independence to Colonial Countries and Peoples, UNGA Res 1514 (XV) (14 Dec 1960) (adopted by 89 votes to none; 9 abstentions) [1] and [2]. Sands later cites para 2 as one of 'a multitude of instruments and General Assembly resolutions'. Verbatim Record (19 February 2024) *Legal Consequences arising from the Policies and Practices of Israel in the Occupied Palestinian Territory, including East Jerusalem* <https://www.icj-cij.org/sites/default/files/case-related/186/186-20240219-ora-01-00-bi.pdf> accessed 4 May 2025 [92].

[40] Declaration on the Granting of Independence to Colonial Countries and Peoples (n 39) [4].

[41] See Umo Umozurike, *International Law and Colonialism in Africa* (Nwamife Publishers 1979) 121; Umo Umozurike, 'The Geneva Conventions and Africa' (1971) 7 East African Law Journal 275, 282 (noting 'a war fought to remove colonialism, provided it involves the use or reasonable or commensurate force, is fundamentally backed by international law').

[42] Georges Abi-Saab, 'The Third World and the future of the international legal order'(1973) 29 Revue égyptienne de droit international 27, 47.

Fifth, Sands's reformulation directs attention away from the corresponding right of Palestinian peoples as colonized peoples fighting 'alien subjugation, domination and exploitation' to 'seek and to receive support' in their 'actions against, and resistance to, such forcible action in pursuit of the exercise of their right to self-determination', as explicitly stated in the 1970 *Declaration on Principles of International Law Concerning Friendly Relations.* A right, according to Umozurike, that also imposed a 'legal obligation [on Third States] to help colonized people defend themselves against colonial aggression.[43]

Sixth, by directing attention away from the colonial context of Israel's denial of Palestinians' right to self-determination, this reformulation erases its foundation in racial domination, and obscures its historical and theoretical connections to Global White Supremacy as a structure of domination (long insisted on by Third World States and international lawyers).[44] As Umozurike explained in 1971: a 'war waged to maintain colonial order is fundamentally condemned in international law' and as 'colonisation is imposed by an alien people on an indigenous population ... the conflict is ... invariably, a racial one as well'.[45]

Seventh, this erasure of racial domination disconnects Israel's denial of the right of Palestinians to self-determination from its ongoing genocidal project in Gaza, with which the Palestinian delegation had opened its address to the ICJ. Consider, in contrast, South Africa's opening address in the contemporaneous ICJ case concerning this genocide, which situating it within 'the ongoing Nakba of the Palestinian people through Israel's colonization since 1948, which has systematically and forcible displaced, and fragmented the Palestinian people, deliberately denying them their internationally recognized inalienable right to self-determination'.[46]

Eighth, the erasure of the racial and colonial context of the denial of Palestinians' right to self-determination had deleterious effects for the account of apartheid made by other representatives of Palestine. This includes its longer traditions of Third World praxis concerning the concatenations of slavery, colonialism, and apartheid.[47] The elision of race and colonialism shifted the framing of apartheid away from the 'anti-colonial reading that emphasize[s] the denial of a collective right to self-determination by an oppressive regime of racial domination'—that culminated in the International Convention on the Suppression and Publishment of the Crime of Apartheid (1973) —and towards the 'more liberal interpretation [of apartheid], as systemic discrimination within a state's legal system against individuals from a particular racial group', that is preferred by Western scholars and non-governmental

43 Umozurike, 'Geneva Conventions and Africa' (n 41) 282.

44 See Christopher Gevers, 'A "world problem": Apartheid, international law and the domestication of race' in Devon Carbado and others (eds), *Race, Racism and International Law* (Stanford University Press 2025).

45 Umozurike, 'Geneva Conventions and Africa' (n 41) 282. See also Umozurike, *International Law* (n 41) 121.

46 Application instituting proceedings and request for the indication of provisional measures, *Application of the Convention on the Prevention and Punishment of the Crime of Genocide in the Gaza Strip (South Africa v Israel)* <https://www.icj-cij.org/sites/default/files/case-related/192/192-20231228-app-01-00-en.pdf> accessed 4 May 2025 [17].

47 See Gevers (n 44).

organizations (NGOs).[48] Separating, once more, apartheid from colonialism and—at its most pernicious form—separating apartheid from *race*.[49]

In the end, tragedy became farce. When Sands cited 'commentators' as authority for the *jus cogens* nature of the right to self-determination, he referenced five white European men (one, twice), and one non-European woman, but not the generations of Third World scholars who have written on self-determination.[50] Nor did Sands mention the Black African ICJ judge and 'highly qualified publicist' seated before him, Judge Tladi, who wrote the ILC's Report on *jus cogens* and included self-determination,[51] and has recently written on the 'marginalization' of the Third World in 'international law-making' in the ICJ and International Law Commission.[52]

This is but one example—a telling one—of the limits and risks of the tactical deployment of white international law, especially through white international lawyers. There are many more examples one could reference. White international law, like race, is mercurial: deadly and slick.[53] If it is to be deployed, this must be done with due regard to the silences, elisions, evasions, and violences of international law's 'demographic and conceptual whiteness'.[54] And, at very least, with a healthy dose of suspicion of white men in well-pressed suits.

It is also a timely reminder that white international law, like international relations, is 'founded upon incomplete archives and/or dubious recollections of international events; contestable classifications of international reality; and less than transparent understandings of international morality' which reproduce 'disciplinary verities' that silence 'discourses or practices outside of the strictures of the Western political languages and imaginary'.[55] This is particularly true of international law's historical and theoretical account of 'race', which seeks to depoliticize and domesticate racial domination, and disconnect it from the West.[56] The tactical deployment of international law requires constantly contesting these 'incomplete archives' on the one hand, while opening up new ones and centring the political languages and imaginaries of Third World and Black Radical thought on the other.

[48] Noura Erakat, Darryl Li, and John Reynolds, 'Race, Palestine, and International Law' (2023) 117 AJIL Unbound 77, 79.

[49] See Yesh Din, *The Israeli Occupation of the West Bank and the Crime of Apartheid: Legal Opinion* (2020) (noting: '[I]t is important to pay attention to a common mistake: Despite its historical origin, the crime of apartheid can exist *without a racist ideology*'). See also John Reynolds, 'Apartheid without Race?' in Lana Tatour and Ronit Lentin (eds), *Race and the Question of Palestine* (Stanford University Press 2025).

[50] Verbatim Record (19 February 2024) *Legal Consequences arising from the Policies and Practices of Israel in the Occupied Palestinian Territory, including East Jerusalem* <https://www.icj-cij.org/sites/default/files/case-related/186/186-20240219-ora-01-00-bi.pdf> accessed 4 May 2025 [95].

[51] International Law Commission, *Draft conclusions on identification and legal consequences of peremptory norms of general international law (jus cogens)* (2022), <http://legal.un.org/ilc/texts/instruments/english/draft_articles/1_14_2022.pdf> accessed 4 May 2025.

[52] See Dire Tladi, 'Representation, Inequality, Marginalization, and International Law-making: The Case of the International Court of Justice and the International Law Commission'(2022) 70 UC Irvine Journal of International, Transnational, and Comparative Law.

[53] Cedric J Robinson, *Forgeries of Memory & Meaning: Blacks & the Regimes of Race in American Theatre & Film Before World War II* (University of North Carolina Press 2007) 4.

[54] Joel M Modiri, 'The Jurisprudence of Steve Biko: A Study in Race, Law and Power in the 'Afterlife" of Colonial-Apartheid' (PhD Thesis, University of Pretoria 2017) 4–5.

[55] Siba N Grovogui, *Beyond Eurocentrism and Anarchy: Memories of International Order and Institutions* (Palgrave Macmillan 2006) 6, 8–9.

[56] See Gevers (n 44).

This must begin with recovering and centring Third World international legal projects that speak to the present conjuncture, and Palestinian freedom in particular, such as those that culminated in the abovementioned Declarations and Conventions, as well as the Additional Protocol I to the Geneva Conventions, the Declaration for the Establishment of a New International Economic Order (1974), the UN Convention on the Law of the Sea (1982), and the Treaty on Principles Governing the Activities of States in the Exploration and Use of Outer Space, including the Moon and Other Celestial Bodies (1967).

4. Lands beyond the white world: the Black horizon

In 1921 WEB Du Bois reimagined the world in an unpublished essay titled 'News from Pan-Africa',[57] which set out the conditions of, and growing resistance to, white domination across the planet—in 'the United States, the West Indies, West, South and East Africa, Abyssinia, Haiti and Liberia', and all places in between—and imagined a 'land beyond the white world': Pan-Africa.[58] Like its antithesis 'the West', 'Pan-Africa' was less a place than a project[59]—a worldmaking *and unmaking* one in the broadest sense[60]—which aimed not only to liberate Africa, Africans, and Afro-descendent peoples from white domination, but sought to 'found . . . a New World'.[61] For Du Bois, 'Pan-Africa' lay 'so appropriately on the Black Sea', but he added:

> But the Black Sea of which I write lies much farther away from Russia. It lies even beyond Africa and is in the geographical third dimension of Fixed Ideas which makes it unusually difficult to approach; and despite our stream of travel, the cables of Yap and the swift flying trains and steamers, somehow, news and embassies from this land beyond the White World filter in even more slowly than before the war.
>
> The Africa of European expansion – of ivory, oil and rubber, of complicated labor systems, of economic empire – this Africa of the White World is but indirectly and negatively part of Pan-Africa – or better, it is its direct antithesis: Pan-Africa is the thought of the vast African World, not only on these but on other matters; not only of this African present, but of the past and future.

In 1935, Césaire gazed outside his window, not far from the Black Sea proper—onto an island off the coast of Croatia—and '[h]is vision, an alchemy of memory and magic, [was] struck by the haunting sense of seeing his own island home of Martinique'.[62] As

[57] WEB Du Bois, 'News from Pan-Africa' (1921) *W.E.B. Du Bois Papers*, Special Collections and University Archives, University of Massachusetts Amherst Libraries.
[58] ibid.
[59] Glissant (n 6) 2.
[60] See Christopher Gevers, '"Land[s] beyond the White World": (Re)imagining the International through Fiction' (2024) 36 Law & Literature 241.
[61] Du Bois (n 57) 1 and 25. In 1928 Du Bois wrote Pan-Africa into existence through fiction in WEB Du Bois, *Dark Princess: A Romance* (University Press of Mississippi 1995 [1928]). See generally Gevers (n 60).
[62] Vasuki Nesiah, 'The Non-Aligned Movement: "A Place for All at the Rendezvous with Victory"' (forthcoming). My thanks to Vasuki Nesiah for bringing this connection between the visions of Du Bois and Cesaire to my attention. See Alexandra Perisic, 'Aimé Césaire's Yugoslav Detour'(2023) 27 Small Axe 1.

Nesiah describes it, after discovering that the island in question was Martinska (the Croatian Martinique), '[h]aunted by the uncanny, driven by this dreamscape of home, [Cesaire] sits down at once and writes *Notebook of a Return to My Native Land*'.[63] Like Du Bois's speculative 'News from Pan-Africa', Césaire's poem is 'variously a lament, an indictment and a manifesto'.[64]

The 'freedom dreams' of Du Bois and Césaire were collective ones, shared by their contemporary Black Internationalists and threaded into the traditions of Third World thought more generally.[65] What is more, they were connected to concrete political (at at times legal) projects. From the turn of the century onwards—when the 1900 Pan-African Conference declared the 'problem of the twentieth century is the problem of the colour line'[66]—Black Internationalists had collectively mapped a 'world cut in two':[67] between the White World and the 'darker world' to which '[m]ost men belong'.[68] This was a world held together and apart by the *global* colour line written in blood, literal and figurative. It was also a world held together and apart by international law. It was this colour line that Cesaire would confront with Jane and Paulette Nardal of Martinique and others through 'Black Internationalism' ('*Internationalisme Noire*'),[69] and alongside Leopold Senghor and others under the banner of the *negritude* movement.[70]

In these freedom dreams, Du Bois and Césaire combined the political, the polemical, and the poetic to 'imagine and craft the world they could not live *without*, just as they worked to dismantle the world he could not live *within*'.[71] It was the disciples and descendants of these intersecting Black Internationalisms that dragged 'Pan-Africa' from the 'geographical third dimension of Fixed Ideas' into the real, albeit through the eye of the needle of 'self-determination' *as statehood*.[72] In the process, Du Bois's dream of a single, united 'Pan-Africa' as a continental political union was derailed by its 'Balkanization' into 'the forty-odd mini-states visited upon [Africa] by colonialism',[73] 'freedom' *within* the White World. This was partly the result of the Cold War's 'ideological wranglings'[74] that Third World states tried to avoid through the Non-Aligned Movement, the first meeting of which took place in Belgrade, somewhere between the

[63] Nesiah (n 62). See Aimé Césaire, *Notebook of a Return to My Native Land* (Mirielle Rosello and Annie Pritchard tr, Bloodaxe Books 1995).

[64] Nesiah (n 62).

[65] See Robin DG Kelley, *Freedom Dreams: The Black Radical Imagination* (Beacon Press 2002). On the Black Radical Tradition, see Cedric Robinson, *Black Marxism: The Making of the Black Radical Tradition* (University of North Carolina Press 2021 [1983]).

[66] Report of the Pan-African Conference, held on the 23, 24 and 25 July 1900 (on file), 10.

[67] See Frantz Fanon, *The Wretched of the Earth* (Constance Farrington tr, Grove Press, 1963) 38.

[68] Du Bois (n 2) 444.

[69] See Brent Hayes Edwards, *The Practice of Diaspora: Literature, Translation, and the Rise of Black Internationalism* (Harvard University Press 2003) 132.

[70] See Nesiah (n 62).

[71] Ruha Benjamin, 'Introduction' in Ruha Benjamin (ed), *Captivating Technology: Race, Carceral Technoscience, and Liberatory Imagination in Everyday Life* (Duke University Press 2019) 14.

[72] See Sundhya Pahuja, *Decolonising International Law: Development, Economic Growth and the Politics of Universality* (Cambridge University Press 2011).

[73] Walter Rodney, 'Aspects of the International Class Struggle in Africa, the Caribbean and America' in Horace Campbell (ed), *Pan-Africanism: Struggle against Neo-colonialism and Imperialism—Documents of the Sixth Pan-African Congress* (Afro-Carib Publications 1975).

[74] See UNGA 927 (n 34) [65] and [72].

Black Sea proper and Césaire's 'uncanny' island.[75] But it was also the result of newly 'decolonized' states placing too much faith in white international law.[76]

White international law cannot be emancipated; it must be *abolished*. But not the account of abolition given to us *by* the White World, as the 'outcome of the valiant battles waged by enlightened and humane European and Americans—usually white men—to liberate the slaves'.[77] Rather, the 'abolition' that international law needs today is of a different order, one that, as Ruth Wilson Gilmore explains, connects together disparate acts of resistance and 'way[s] of acting on problems in the political-economic geography that currently prevails', and seeks to create 'innovative social and spatial relationships and capacities for action—just as the "Third World" and "Pan-Africanism" did for earlier generations'.[78] In this respect Gilmore, drawing on Du Bois, warns of the 'the failure of imagination [that] rests in missing the fact that abolition isn't just absence; . . . abolition is a fleshly and material presence of social life lived differently'.[79]

This abolition of international law demands returning—historically, politically, poetically, methodologically—to these 'improbable islands of possibility', in order to 'seek out alternative horizons and imagine futures that are not predicted by the present conjuncture'.[80] To stretch to lands 'beyond the white world' and the 'archives . . . political languages and imaginaries' of its international law,[81] and towards the 'illimitable possibility' of what Nahum Dimitri Chandler calls the 'Black horizon'.[82] Leaving behind 'the carcasses of . . . prejudice and hatred . . . avarice . . . data banks and dead ideas . . . dead rivers and smoky skies',[83] and *perhaps* white international lawyers.

[75] Nesiah (n 62)

[76] See Christopher Gevers, '"A Season in the Color Line": International Law in Africa during the Cold War' in Matthew Craven, Sundhya Pahuja, and Gerry Simpson (eds), *Cambridge History of International Law: Vol XI* (forthcoming).

[77] Antony Anghie, 'Slavery and International Law: The Jurisprudence of Henry Richardson' (2017) 31(1) Temple International & Comparative Law Journal 11, 15.

[78] Ruth Wilson Gilmore, *Golden Gulag: Prisons, Surplus, Crisis, and Opposition in Globalizing California* (University of California Press 2007) 242.

[79] 'Prisons and Class Warfare: An Interview with Ruth Wilson Gilmore' (*Verso*, 2 August 2018) <https://www.versobooks.com/en-gb/blogs/news/3954-prisons-and-class-warfare-an-interview-with-ruth-wilson-gilmore> accessed 4 May 2025.

[80] Nesiah (n 62).

[81] Grovogui (n 55) 8–9.

[82] Nahum Dimitri Chander, *Toward an African Future—of the Limit of World* (Suny Press 2021) 56–57.

[83] Arundhati Roy, 'The Pandemic is a Portal (*rethinking schools*, 2020) <https://rethinkingschools.org/articles/the-pandemic-is-a-portal/> accessed 4 May 2025 (noting: 'Historically, pandemics have forced humans to break with the past and imagine their world anew. This one is no different. It is a portal, a gateway between one world and the next. We can choose to walk through it, dragging the carcasses of our prejudice and hatred, our avarice, our data banks and dead ideas, our dead rivers and smoky skies behind us. Or we can walk through lightly, with little luggage, ready to imagine another world. And ready to fight for it.')

Index

For the benefit of digital users, indexed terms that span two pages (e.g., 52–53) may, on occasion, appear on only one of those pages.